THE SOCIAL LIFE OF MONEY

To Dennis,

I hope you enjoy!

best wishes,

Nigel

THE SOCIAL LIFE OF MONEY

NIGEL DODD

PRINCETON UNIVERSITY PRESS
Princeton & Oxford

Copyright © 2014 by Princeton University Press
Published by Princeton University Press,
41 William Street, Princeton, New Jersey 08540
In the United Kingdom: Princeton University Press,
6 Oxford Street, Woodstock, Oxfordshire OX20 1TW

press.princeton.edu

All Rights Reserved

Jacket design by Chris Ferrante

Library of Congress Cataloging-in-Publication Data

Dodd, Nigel, 1965–
  The social life of money / Nigel Dodd.
    pages cm
  Includes bibliographical references and index.
  ISBN 978-0-691-14142-8 (hardcover : alk. paper) 1. Money—Social aspects. I. Title.
  HG221.D63 2014
  332.4—dc23   2014005411

British Library Cataloging-in-Publication Data is available

This book has been composed in Sabon Next LT Pro and Neutraface No. 2

Printed on acid-free paper. ∞

Printed in the United States of America

10 9 8 7 6 5 4 3 2

FOR GIO

CONTENTS

ACKNOWLEDGEMENTS IX

INTRODUCTION 1

1 ORIGINS
Barter 17
Tribute 23
Quantification 27
Mana 30
Language 34
Violence 43
Conclusion 46

2 CAPITAL
The Contradictions of Money 51
Credit Money 55
Finance Capital 59
Primitive Accumulation 63
When Credit Fails 66
Behind the Veil 72
Seeing Double 79
Conclusion 87

3 DEBT
Debt's Untold Story 94
Credit and Nothing but Credit 102
Neochartalism 106
Schumpeter's Banks 111
Minsky's Half-Century 117
Strange Money 121
Austerity Myths 126
Conclusion 132

4 GUILT
Übermensch and Eternal Return 136
Capitalism, Debt, and Religion 142
Filthy Lucre 149
Conclusion 158

5 WASTE
Money, Excretion, and Heterogeneous Matter 166
Derrida's Ghosts 179
Cool Money, Living Money 189
Conclusion 204

6 TERRITORY
Westfailure 216
Nomisma 222
Deterritorialization 226
Empire 237
Euroland 251
Conclusion 266

7 CULTURE
Money and Cultural Alienation 273
Polanyi and the Problem of Embeddedness 278
Relational Monies 286
Scales of Value 294
A Quality Theory of Money 298
Repersonalizing Impersonal Money 305
Conclusion 310

8 UTOPIA
Simmel's Perfect Money 316
Fromm's Humanistic Utopia 330
Giving Time for Time 342
Rotting Money 346
Proudhon's Bank 351
Vires in Numeris 362
Toward a Monetary Commons 372
Conclusion 381

CONCLUSION 385

BIBLIOGRAPHY 395

INDEX 421

ACKNOWLEDGMENTS

Numerous people have given me help, encouragement, and support while writing this book. At Princeton University Press, I have benefited greatly from the advice of Peter Dougherty and three outstanding referees—Keith Hart, Jocelyn Pixley, and Frederick Wherry. At the London School of Economics (LSE) over the years, I have enjoyed valuable conversations about the book with Bridget Hutter, Judy Wajcman, Paddy Rawlinson, Gwynne Hawkins, Matthias Benzer, Johannes Lenhard, and the late David Frisby—all superb colleagues, students, and friends. And at home, Isabella and Oscar Dodd would not forgive me if I failed to mention their advice about what to put on the cover. But my greatest debt is to my wife, Gio, who commented on multiple drafts of the book with tremendous insight and more than a little tact. Thank you all!

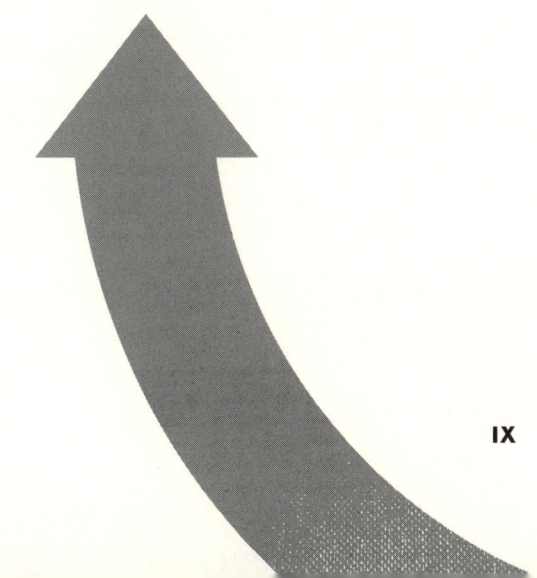

THE SOCIAL LIFE OF MONEY

INTRODUCTION

The people are never more fecund or more strong than on the morrow of a general bankruptcy.
PIERRE-JOSEPH PROUDHON

I know no creative person can thrive in this economy. *You will lose us.* I am the 99%.
OCCUPYWALLST.ORG

They have been freezing money in Greece. Between 2010 and 2012, approximately €72 billion was withdrawn from bank accounts and hidden in iceboxes, vacuum cleaners, bags of flour, pet food containers, mattresses, and under floors. The exodus of cash from bank to home, financial network to private sphere, prompted a significant rise in violent house burglary. While wealthier Greeks were investing heavily in London real estate, others were hoarding cash in more mundane domestic spaces because of what might happen to their bank accounts should Greece leave the Eurozone and launch its own independent currency. Fearful that their savings would be decimated overnight, Greeks were reversing the conventional wisdom that a bank is the most secure place to keep your money. What began as a crisis in the U.S. subprime mortgage market in 2007 was now manifesting itself as a slow-motion bank run. This problem was not confined to Greece but was happening throughout the Eurozone amid widespread doubt about the future of a project that had been launched with such optimism a little more than a decade before.

Since the collapse of Lehman Brothers in September 2008, the world's major central banks have been plowing vast quantities of money into the banking system. The U.S. Federal Reserve has made commitments totaling some $29 trillion, lending $7 trillion to banks during the course of one single fraught week. The Bank of England has spent around £325 billion on quantitative easing alone—a figure that could yet rise to £600 billion—while the U.K. government has committed a total of £1.162 trillion to bank rescues. The European Central Bank has made low-interest loans directly to banks worth at least €1.1 trillion. These measures are not addressing the crisis alone. In April 2013, the Bank of Japan embarked on a quantitative easing program worth some $1.3 trillion, designed to end more than a decade of deflation. The social costs of the crisis, too, have been devastating. These are the costs both of the crisis itself and importantly of the policies used by governments and central banks to alleviate its effects on those very institutions that caused it. Where governments have pursued austerity programs involving significant cuts in public spending, the effect has been greatest on the weakest members of society. In the United States and the United Kingdom and in countries on the periphery of the Eurozone, people on state pensions, working for low pay or relying on social welfare, alongside those in public sector jobs such as education and health, have been hardest hit, amid rising unemployment, creeping economic stagnation, and the threat of prolonged economic recession. It seems irrefutable that society's poorest are paying for the misjudgments of its wealthiest.

The underlying causes of the crisis are deeply entrenched in the history of modern capitalism, and its immediate catalyst was located in the U.S. subprime mortgage market. These were mortgages held by the poorest borrowers, those deemed most at risk of default and charged higher rates of interest as the price of that risk. The subprime market was demographically skewed: 47 percent of Hispanic homebuyers were issued subprime-mortgage loans in 2006, compared with 26 percent of white and 53 percent of African-American homebuyers (Leigh and Huff 2007: 5). Rising interest rates drove many of these borrowers into default in 2007, triggering a credit contagion that wove a red thread of insolvency from the poorest to the richest strata of society, spreading quickly across the global financial system throughout 2008. The outcome was multiple bank failures, an economic downturn in most Western economies that may go on for some years yet, and a protracted sovereign debt crisis in the Eurozone whose economic and political consequences are likely to be profound. Central banks were under political pressure to loosen their monetary policies, and sometimes to engage in competitive currency devaluation—so-called currency wars—as a means of boosting exports and kick-starting economic recovery. As what some experts believe is a further consequence of the crisis, by a circuitous but discernible route, several governments collapsed amid political uprising in the Middle East during the first half of 2011.[1] The broader ramifications of the crisis for the global economy, its effect on the emerging BRIC economies (Brazil, Russia, India, and China), for example, are yet to be fully discerned.

This is a crisis of *legitimacy* as much as *economics*, provoked by the contrast between the resources that governments have devoted to rescuing banks and on the other hand, their subsequent willingness to make dramatic and socially corrosive cuts in public expenditures. Many financial institutions have been saved from insolvency by a combination of public finds and creative accounting, but households and individuals tend to be granted no such leniency. The crisis has polarized every society that has been affected by it, giving birth to a meme—the 99 percent—that is inextricably tied to rising resentment and hostility toward Wall Street. Faced with these realities, it is little wonder that a war has been declared on the banking system through political protests that have embraced as wide a spectrum of society as the original crisis itself. The political rhetoric is not simply about unequal wealth and income distribution. At a more fundamental level, and in a more precise way, it attacks the financial system that is responsible for perpetuating it.

Of course, just calling this a banking crisis is too narrow a description. And to speak of banks as if they were all the same—to wit, part of an overarching Wall Street system—glosses over the complexity of financial institutions that do not operate in unison and are fragmented within themselves. Indeed, one could argue that divisions within banks, and their fragmented epistemic cultures, played a significant role in bringing the crisis about (MacKenzie 2011). Nevertheless, it is mainly the banks that have provided the conduit through which critique and protest have flowed since the crisis began. The Occupy movement is broad-based, its aims unclear, its progress uncertain. But its core thesis—that the financial system has grown absurdly disproportionate relative to the rest of the economy: distorting capitalism, widening inequality, damaging society, and exposing its key public institutions to unacceptable risks—has gained popular support across the political spectrum, on both left and right.

---

1   The crucial link is food prices, which rose sharply toward the end of 2007 and spiked during early 2008 in Egypt and throughout much of the Middle East and North Africa (MENA) region. According to some experts, this spike was a significant factor in provoking political unrest. Food prices were peaking worldwide, partly because speculators were turning to the commodities markets (instead of credit markets), such as food, in the immediate aftermath of the subprime crisis (Lagi, Bertrand, et al. 2011). See http://www.psmag.com/politics/why-the-middle-east-is-rioting-46792/.

This phenomenon raises a question that has been in the background of political discussion of events in the financial system since 2007 but remains largely unremarked upon by scholars: where did the crisis leave *money*? The way that governments and central banks have used their rights over money's production to provide liquidity and capital to the financial system is at the vortex of the crisis. The question of "who pays" goes to the very heart of issues about how society organizes its money. The right to create money raises profound questions about power, freedom, justice, and law. Simmel once described money as a "claim upon society" (Simmel 2004: 177). By doing so, he captured the sense in which the monetary system must be underpinned by *trust*, not merely between particular individuals, but also across society as a whole. The nexus of mutual obligation upon which money depends has been eroded by a system that allows immensely profitable banks to remain solvent at the public's expense. This erosion places the monetary system itself, configured around the state's special rights over the definition and production of money, under serious question.

My aim in this book is to stand back and reconsider the nature of money, particularly its social nature, not just in light of the specific events and political sentiments just described, but *in toto*. The book's purpose, in short, is to explore money's *social life* in all of its myriad complexity. Potentially, this moment could be a significant time of realignment in the way our money and credit systems are organized. To make the most of this moment, we need to return to some of the most fundamental questions there are about money, to refresh our thinking. These questions include those about the source of money's *value*, its relationship with *time* and *space*, its role in *society* and connections with *community*, its relationship with *power* and the *state*, its ancient links with *ritual* and *religion*, as well as its deep associations with the *unconscious* and with *culture, self,* and *identity*. These major issues have been addressed within correspondingly large scholarly literatures. My specific aim is to bring them to bear on the opportunities we have now, not simply to *rethink* money but also to *reframe* and *reorganize* it. The crisis and its aftermath have contributed to a sense that this could be a tipping point for money.

The financial crisis has provoked a widespread discussion about how the monetary system should legitimately be organized: about which institutions have the right to produce money and about the legitimate scope of banks' ability to create credit. Insofar as the crisis has given rise to a sense that the monetary system has become "tainted" through its close structural connections with a banking system that is dangerously inflated, the relationship between money and *society* about which Simmel had so much to say has been damaged, too. At the very least, the terms of that relationship need to be understood more thoroughly. Walter Benjamin—who as we see in Chapter 4, made some fascinating observations about capitalism and the history of debt—wrote of an "angel of history," surveying the past as a repetition of crisis and catastrophe. The angel wanted to "make whole what has been smashed" (Benjamin 2003b: 392) in order to redeem damaged history and thereby renew the present. This spirit resonates with my argument in this book. We have been living through a moment in monetary history in which we are confronted with not only the opportunity but also the *obligation* to revisit, and refresh, everything we thought we knew about the social life of money.

With rich possibilities for reforming money, however, conceptual difficulties arise. During the past two decades or so, there has been a growing interest in the changing nature of money. Researchers have been looking into the emergence of new monetary forms, for example, complementary currencies and Internet or electronic monies. Scholars have been predicting that the relationship between money and the *state* is coming under increasing threat from "alternative" monies. But for all the empirical richness that these recent contributions add to our understanding of money, there is no common view of what *counts* as money in a general sense. There never has been a consensus about this: the extant literature on money is replete with debates over competing definitions. Even our language is confused. Take the distinction between "money" and "currency." Most scholars accept that the second term is narrower than the first, but they are divided as to whether it should refer simply to legal tender, or whether currencies are monies that—literally—circulate in the sense of being passed from hand to hand.[2]

Definitional debates about what to *call* money run on, and theoretical disputes between the proponents of leading schools of monetary thought are as fiercely contested as ever. Even today, fundamental differences between economists about the need for austerity in monetary and economic policy are underpinned by doctrinal feuds (e.g., between Keynesians and "Austrians") about the nature of money. There are major differences here that are unlikely to be resolved. I am not seeking to resolve such differences in this book or to take sides in the debates they generate. Rather, my analysis seeks to encourage a sense of experimentation in the way that money is

---

2   The *Oxford English Dictionary* carries both definitions of currency: as "that which is current as a medium of exchange; the circulating medium (whether coins or notes); the money of a country in actual use," and on the other hand, as "the fact or quality of being current or passing from man to man as a medium of exchange; circulation."

conceived and organized—both to avoid the sense of estrangement and loss toward money that people often experience in the teeth of an economic crisis and to help realize that promise of fecundity about which Proudhon spoke. To *redeem* and *reinvent* money, we must also *rethink* it; indeed, these tasks are inseparable. To carry them out successfully, however, a clearer sense of order needs to be given to the vast scholarly literature on the nature of money.

There are three sets of questions in particular that I want to pursue in the book. The first set is *conceptual*. Is money a *process* or a *thing*? Is it a *commodity* or a *social relation*? What explains the *value* of money? What are money's key *functions*? Why are there so many competing (and contradictory) *definitions* of money? What were the *origins* of money, and how important are they for understanding how it works now? Money, I want to suggest, is essentially a fiction: a socially powerful—and socially *necessary*—illusion. Money's great, sweeping historical associations—with gold and with states, for example—are inessential. It can exist without them, as much as their structures linger. That is to say, money is not *necessarily* a creature of the state. Nor *must* it be a form of credit that is created, *ab initio*, by banks. Empirically, money is enormously complex, and the possibilities for organizing it are immensely varied. The monies we encounter in reality are not completely empty, not exactly fictional, and never absolutely fungible. But what do these apparently partial forms of money have in common that enables us to call them "money"? It is not possible to arrive at a satisfactory empirical answer to this question. Any answer that focuses on the functions of money, its material qualities or institutional affiliations, is bound to fall short: there are always exceptions and counterexamples. A more theoretically nuanced answer is required, one that embraces all of the various empirical forms of money without lapsing into an arbitrary nominalism.

This book, therefore, begins with the proposition that money is an extraordinarily powerful *idea*. My understanding of this proposition comes from Simmel, whose *Philosophy of Money* was published (complete) in 1907. Simmel's exploration of money had started more than fifteen years earlier, with an article about the social psychology of money. He was fascinated by the notion that—*as an idea*—money is a perfect means of exchange, able to convert qualitative differences between things into quantitative differences that enable them to be exchanged. His interest in money was psychological, philosophical, and sociological. It centered first on determining what the social, cultural, and economic preconditions are for such an intellectually remarkable tool of exchange to exist. He then set out to discover the effect of its widening circulation upon society. Since the book was published, most attention has been paid to Simmel's remarks on the negative consequences of money's expansion. According to this view, as our social relations are increasingly mediated by money, they become more abstract and featureless, and our inner lives are rendered ever more devoid of inner meaning and subjective value. Many sociologists and anthropologists disagree, arguing that money has not corroded social meaning in the way he suggested. One of the key concerns of this book is to examine the normative implications of this argument: to explore the possibilities for *improving* society through the way we organize its money. Simmel, too, had strong views about this prospect, which some readers may find surprising.

The diversity of notions of money within the literature provides us with ever-present opportunities for reinventing it. My aim in this book is to nurture this sense of diversity within monetary theory. We need to discover, clarify, and promote those qualities that make money such a potentially fruitful site for social, political, and economic reform. Galbraith once complained that scholarly discussions of money tend toward "priestly incantation" as those with expertise in the field deliberately cultivate the belief that they are in "privileged association with the occult" (Galbraith 1975: 4–5). The language is strikingly reminiscent of that in Adorno's withering critique of astrology, "Theses Against Occultism" (Adorno 2007). Against this language, I have sought to bring a narrow, specialist literature on money into contact with much broader debates in contemporary social thought. There is a rich seam of scholarly discussion of money by social and cultural theorists, philosophers, and literary critics that is rarely aired in discussions between monetary specialists. Many thinkers who are reasonably familiar to a wider readership—Agamben, Bataille, Baudrillard, Benjamin, Deleuze, Derrida, de Saussure, Negri, and Nietzsche, to name but a few—have made imaginative and potentially incisive contributions to our conception of the nature and significance of money. Their ideas on this subject are doubly intriguing when set against the arguments of scholars who are specialists within the field. In each of the chapters that follow, this is the kind of dialogue, and spirit of intellectual adventure, that I have sought to cultivate.

The second set of questions that I am exploring in the book is *sociological*, although I shall be seeking answers in a range of social science traditions besides the field of economic sociology, including anthropology, political science, social theory, and geography, as well as in heterodox (and especially Keynesian) branches of economics. In what sense is money—as Simmel describes—a *claim upon society*? What is this claim *based* on, and what *sustains* it? Does money require the backing of a *political authority* to be trusted by its users? What are the main social and political differences between fiat monetary systems, which are organized *vertically*, and *horizontal* systems, where there is no issuing authority? If money is a form of *debt*, to whom is the debt actually owed—and who owes it? How important are *banks* for the operation of money on a large scale? Once we start asking these more specific questions, we must also ask what exactly Simmel *meant* by "society" in this context. Was the term as he used it synonymous with *nation-state*, as it is often taken to be, or—as I intend to argue—did it have more in common with Simmel's own, much more fluid, notion of *sociation*? If so, much more needs to be said about Simmel's description of money, and above all, about its relevance to present-day debates about the way that our monetary systems are organized.

There are numerous ways of presenting the debate over the nature of money. Conventionally, economists define money according to its basic functions; or, following Keynes, they distinguish between money's abstract role as a *money of account* versus its properties as a *medium of exchange*. In this book, I focus more broadly upon money's features as a *social form*. It is, for example, the *universal commodity form* (Marx 1982: 162 and ch. 2), a *claim upon society* (Simmel 2004: 177), diffuse *social media* (Zelizer 1997: 21), a *social technology* (Ingham 2004b: 1; Smithin 2008: 36), an *instrument of collective memory* (Hart 2001: 243), a *generalized symbolic medium* (Parsons 1968), a *social process of commensuration* (Maurer 2007: 126), and a *communal illusion* (Karatani 2003: 203). Even if we agree with Simmel about the importance of trust in money, it is far from obvious that the "society" he had in mind when describing it was equivalent to a *nation-state*. As a sociologist, Simmel himself was not committed to the idea (*pace* Durkheim) of society as an entity that exists over and above the individual, as something both real and constraining. On the contrary, he defined sociology as the study of *sociation*, not society (Simmel 2009: 22–23; Pyyhtinen 2010). Keith Hart offers an alternative formulation to Simmel, which I take up later in the book. He accepts Simmel's underlying proposition that money is a "token of society" but opens up the idea of society by differentiating it into *state*, *nation*, and *community* (Hart 2001: 235). Each term offers its own distinct treatment of the sociological foundations of money. My argument is that these treatments are *alternatives*: they are not mutually exclusive and should not be run together. I have called this book *The Social Life of Money* to capture this flexibility and to escape from connotations of the term "society" that are all too easily associated with national borders. After all, the relationship between these borders and various kinds of money is increasingly open to question. By referring to the *social life* of money, I intend to draw attention to the sense in which money's value, indeed its very existence, rests on *social relations between its users*. These relations are shaped by a range of historical, cultural, political, and institutional factors. They are complex and dynamic, variable and contested. And crucially for my argument in this book, they are open to renewed—and urgent—critical questioning.

This notion leads into our third set of questions, which is *normative*. Is there an *ideal* monetary form, and if so, what are its social and political features? What is the purpose and scope of *monetary reform*—and why should it be attempted? Can money be a means for achieving social change, e.g., for addressing social inequality or extending social and economic inclusion? Should money be *neutral* in the way that classical thinkers suggested? Or is money inevitably a vehicle of *power*—and if so, how should its power be used or restrained?

Monetary reform has been on the agenda for a long time. Many of the new projects that we see today are variations on much older schemes and themes. Since the early 1990s, however—and especially since the crisis—there has been a genuine surge of interest in the changing nature of money, partly because of the emergence of new forms such as local currencies and digital monies. Whereas the financial crisis appears to have fueled the enthusiasm of wider publics for new forms of money and credit, it has also underlined the argument that the role of states and banks in money's social production may be undergoing a fundamental transformation. As the Cypriot banking crisis erupted during the early months of 2013, the value of Bitcoins (a currency that severs links with *both* the state *and* the banking system) rose sharply against both the euro and the U.S. dollar. There are many possible explanations for this, not least that we were simply witnessing a bubble. But the debates that have sprung up around the Bitcoin phenomenon are revealing because most of them are focused on the possibilities of developing a serious rival to state currency.

At a protest march in London during 2011, one cardboard banner, suspended from the entrance of NatWest bank in Paternoster Square, captured this view. It said, "We are the true currency."[3] The words strike an intriguing counterpoint in the war against banks because they imply that the system can be transformed, not completely overthrown, by being reconfigured on a more human scale. They suggest, moreover, that money's value is derived from *social life*. This idea would suggest that money is not simply a claim upon society, but—ideally—*is* social life, gaining its value not from the institutions that produce it but from the people who use it. The sentiment

---

3   See http://www.demotix.com/news/876663/occupy-london-st-pauls-cathedral#media-876391.

nurtures the idea that money *can* play a crucial and constructive role in imagining and shaping alternative economic and financial futures. Money, in other words, is as much a *solution* to the problems the banking crisis has exposed as it was ever a *cause*. Money, in short, is capable of achieving more for our societies than we have allowed it to.

Money, *all* money, contains a utopian strain. This strain is the quality that has fascinated and perplexed social thinkers of almost every possible outlook. Money rests on an extraordinarily powerful ideal, the ideal of complete fungibility. Money, Borges tells us in "El Zahir," "symbolizes man's free will" because it can be transformed into anything (Borges 1968). It derives its utopian quality from its sense of being absolutely unlike any other commodity or medium of exchange. In Borges's story, the holder of the Zahir (a 20-centavo coin) gradually finds himself unable to see anything else other than the coin, even after exchanging it for a drink. He eventually discovers that, according to Islamic folklore, the Zahir is an object that entraps anyone whose gaze falls upon it, erasing their capacity to see anything else. Money can be anything—everything—and derives its power from this fact.

In *Crack Capitalism* (Holloway 2010), John Holloway argues that changes to the global economy are most likely to occur on the level of the ordinary and mundane. The "method of the crack" means exploiting the myriad interstitial spaces in which small changes are possible. Holloway believes that money is integral to the system that needs to be cracked because the world is "ruled" by it. A similar tale is told by Gerald Davis in *Managed by the Markets* (2009), where he describes finance as "the new American state religion" (Davis 2009: vii), and by Greta Krippner, who argues that "we live in a world of finance" (Krippner 2005: 173). All three authors tend to portray money and finance—the terms are treated interchangeably—as immensely powerful and destructive forces, which by definition are almost impossible to resist, let alone reform. Krippner, whose superb *Capitalizing on Crisis* (2011) advances a subtle historical thesis that portrays financialization (she calls it the "turn to finance") as the unintended consequence of policy choices taken in the face of various social, fiscal, and legitimation crises of the 1960s and 1970s, suggests that the most likely outcome of this process is a return to those very problems. Financialization, in other words, has "now travelled its full arc," and any further movement in this direction will be self-defeating (Krippner 2011: 22). I want to advance a different thesis, namely, that money can be a *positive* force for change in its own right. Moreover, contrary to Holloway's thesis, it can be transformed—precisely—on the level of the *ordinary* and *mundane*. Instead of striving to rid ourselves of money, we should aim for different *kinds* of money. This is not just a question of "bringing down the banks." Rather, it is a matter of supplanting key ingredients of the present system (albeit in a piecemeal and localized fashion) by offering viable alternatives. There is no single solution and no magic pill. Proudhon said that human fecundity would be at its height when a general bankruptcy is imminent. It is open to debate how such a bankruptcy might be defined in today's world. But it is in the spirit of creative experimentation Proudhon identifies that this book has been written.

The book contains eight chapters, each devoted to a theme that presents opportunities for reinvigorating our theoretical understanding of and practical relationship with money. Chapter 1 is motivated by the observation that many of the debates about the predicament currently faced by governments, banks, and communities regarding the organization of the money and credit system are characterized by a tendency to invoke "myths of origin" to bolster their arguments about money's present and future. These myths operate in a similar way to what the philosopher Richard Rorty once termed a "final vocabulary": they are the places where doubt stops and circularity begins, where coherent and open-ended debate no longer seems possible (Rorty 1989: 73). Such beliefs underpin those expert voices that Galbraith associated with the occult. But I am calling these arguments myths to reflect the nature of their role in present-day monetary debates, not because I want to suggest that they are false. Their veracity, indeed, is beside the point.

Chapter 2 is prompted by the resurgence of interest in the work of Marx since the financial crisis began. Increasing sales of and references to his writings confirm my own experience as a teacher at the London School of Economics that Marx is back in intellectual vogue. Equally striking, however, is that despite this upsurge in interest in Marx, most of the talk concerns questions about social class and inequality, and not those of his writings that were surely most germane to the crisis, namely those on money and credit. This chapter therefore provides a systematized account of Marx's theory of money, paying particular attention to his thoughts on the credit system. My aim is to render Marx's theory as coherent as possible, not to highlight its weaknesses. Having characterized his theory in the strongest possible terms, the chapter then asks which (if any) of Marx's arguments about the contradictory nature of money and credit are most helpful as guides to our understanding of their role in capitalism today. As the discussion proceeds, we turn to the work of subsequent thinkers within the Marxist tradition—from Lenin and Luxemburg to Harvey and Marazzi—who have sought to "update" his core ideas in order to apply them beyond the empirical constraints imposed by the historical context in which they were conceived. The chapter concludes by discussing an unusual contribution to Marxist theory from the Japanese philosopher Kojin Karatani, whose smaller scale treatment of his ideas raises intriguing questions about how money might be reinvented from the standpoint of its users.

In Chapter 3, the discussion turns to the most widely discussed feature of contemporary capitalism, namely, debt. Although debt is much older than capitalism, capitalism has given it a negative, impersonal, and mass character. Current debates are focused on the vast scale of the financial obligations that have been accumulated in the modern era. But debt is a broader term whose moral economy is of crucial importance to its relationship with money. I focus on this wider significance of debt in this chapter. The discussion begins with the history of debt, which traces its development from being a fundamental (and wholly positive) feature of human society—a social lubricant—to its subsequent (and violent) appropriation by the state and financial capitalism. I then move on to examine the arguments of scholars (from Knapp and Mitchell-Innes to Schumpeter and Keynes) who argue that money itself is a form of debt; indeed, it is debt that makes money social. These conflicting sides of debt—its destructiveness *and* importance for the social life of money—are explored in the remainder of the chapter. Banks are crucial in both senses. Having played a pivotal role in the establishment of forms of credit money that are trusted and accepted throughout society, banks now lie at the heart of a potentially devastating spiral of debt and deflation.

Building on the discussion of debt in the previous chapter, Chapter 4 uses the arguments of Nietzsche as a lens to explore a moral economy of debt as *guilt*. Nietzsche offered important insights into such matters as the relationship between the money economy and the permanent decadence of modernity, money's effect on social hierarchy and individualism, and the moral economy of debt. His remarks on these themes are closely connected to two of his best known but controversial ideas: the eternal return and the *Übermensch*. I explore how some later thinkers have taken up Nietzsche's arguments, and these two concepts in particular. In particular, he informs Benjamin's examination of the "guilt history" of modern capitalism and Brown's psychoanalytic treatment of the roots and consequences of a neurotic money complex. Each of these thinkers provides a sharply critical perspective on the idea that money's expansion in the modern world reflects the individual's liberation from traditional social ties and ancient moral bonds.

In Chapter 5, I examine money from the perspective of *waste*. Throughout its history, money has been seen primarily as a means of managing scarcity; indeed, there is a tradition of monetary theory in which it is argued that money must itself *be* scarce to fulfill its primary functions as money. Money is not simply a tool for *managing* scarcity, however, but a means of *perpetuating* it. In this chapter, I explore a contrary vein of thought, wherein money is conceived as an expression of the way in which society manages *surplus*, *luxury*, and *waste*. This is money according to the theory of general economy. This perspective is most closely associated with Bataille, whose work on expenditure has some intriguing (but overlooked) implications for money. The chapter moves on to consider the monetary writings—scattered but invariably interesting and often illuminating—of Derrida and Baudrillard. These thinkers raise compelling questions about how key monetary problems such as inflation and debt can be understood once money is decoupled from the problem of scarcity and viewed, as it were, from the opposite direction.

Chapter 6 addresses the relationship of money and *territory* and in particular explores theoretical and substantive issues opened up by the argument that money has been *de*territorialized. The concept of Westphalian money, which has for many scholars framed the modern system of state currencies, has its roots in what Carl Schmitt described as the emergence of a territorial ordering of the globe that began with the discovery of the New World (Schmitt 2003). I suggest that what we now think of as state money is inextricably linked with territorial spaces that are *negative* or *indeterminate*, not simply those institutional forms that are purported to be at the center of territorial space, such as states and their agencies, i.e., central banks. So how should we think about monetary spaces and flows in the age of deterritorialization? And how does the decline of territorial money inform questions about money's connections with *society*? I tackle this issue by engaging with the arguments of thinkers—Deleuze and Guattari, and Hardt and Negri—whose work is most closely linked to the theory of deterritorialization.

Chapter 7 turns to the question of money's relationship with *culture*, focusing especially on its ongoing constitution in and through microsocial relations. These characterizations challenge conventional attempts to objectify money as a theoretically stable, homogeneous entity. Relational approaches to money emphasize its continual reproduction through the very transactions it mediates. Normatively, such arguments are particularly important for coming to grips with money's reinvention "from below" precisely in the sense captured by the declaration that "we are the true currency." The discussion first considers the conventional (and still influential) view—spelled out here via Marx, Nietzsche, Simmel, and Polanyi—that money's relationship with culture is overwhelmingly a threatening, destructive one.

I then explore the counterargument, which traces out the contours of a "quality" theory of money—advanced by scholars such as Zelizer, Guyer, and Hart—which holds that money is richly infused with the cultural conditions of its production and use. These analytical arguments raise significant and wide-ranging issues that speak directly to the normative inquiries being pursued throughout this book.

The prospect of money's active reinvention by its users is tackled at greater length in Chapter 8, which explores examples of *utopian* thinking in which there is a central role for the monetary system as both the site and vehicle of social, political, and economic reform. This type of thinking first appears in the work of Simmel as a notion of "perfect" money that sheds light on a largely unexplored aspect of his writings: his views on the relationship between money and socialism. The second instance is Erich Fromm's case for a human utopia in which money must be reconfigured in light of a distinction between "having" and "being" that framed Fromm's sociopsychological critique of advanced Western capitalism during its last major monetary and financial crises in the 1970s. These arguments resonate with a tradition within social, political, and economic thought in which the utopian spirit is defined not—*contra* More—by money's *abolition* but rather by its *transformation*. I explore several examples of this tradition here, as well as a number of actually existing alternative monetary systems, such as local and complementary currencies, mobile money, Bitcoin, and social lending. This discussion of monetary reform brings the book back to where it began, to the prospect that money is reconfigured from below, such that it lives up to Simmel's classic description of it as a claim upon society.

With states' role in the creation and governance of money being encroached upon from all sides, we seem to be facing a future in which money is more pluralistic than it has been throughout the modern era. This is not just a question of who *produces* money but also of who governs the infrastructure through which it flows. Our pluralistic monetary future raises fundamental theoretical issues for the analysis of money. In particular, it suggests that we need to develop a concept of money that can incorporate the full range of monetary forms in circulation, without treating them all as variants of currency or as having broadly similar features. Our monetary theories, in other words, need to match our monetary practices in being increasingly flexible and open-ended. What is needed, more than ever before, is an open, inclusive conversation about the nature of money and its role in society, about who has the right to create it, and why.

1 ORIGINS

At the beginning, there was no money.
BANCO CENTRO DO BRASIL[1]

Books on money, almost as a chorus, invariably begin with a discussion of its most simple, elementary forms, much as Durkheim began his investigation of religion. But whereas Durkheim suggested that "like any human institution, religion begins nowhere" (Durkheim 2001: 9), monetary scholars usually take the more bullish view that money must have started *somewhere*. They simply cannot agree on exactly where. Given the myriad forms that money has taken through history, and still takes today, one could be excused for thinking that there is no compelling reason to strive for a singular account of where it began. But many present-day debates about the future of money come down to differences of opinion about what money was originally, as if we can settle our arguments by regarding ancient history as lawyers treat precedent.[2] The problem with questions about where money *started*, of course, is that the answer usually depends on our assumptions about what money *is*, which, in turn, usually rest on arguments about where it *began*. Moreover, there is a crucial difference between the *history of particular monetary forms*, e.g., specie or coin, and the *history of money in general* (Grierson 1978: 6). We can be fairly confident about the identity of very early forms of *specie*, but it is open to debate whether these are also the most elementary forms of *money*. As we shall see, scholars who maintain that

---

1 http://www.bcb.gov.br/?ORIGINMONEY.
2 For example, Charles Goodhart once framed the question of monetary integration in Europe as a test of two competing theories about the origin of money (Goodhart 1997; see also Aglietta and Scialom 2003). His argument is now cited in connection with debates about why the project has run into difficulties, see http://www.economist.com/node/21560554. As for quantitative easing, its critics often cite Menger's theory that money originated as a widely sought after commodity.

money is not *essentially* metallic but fiduciary argue that to locate its origins, we should be exploring early forms of debt and tribute payment. These are less tangible than coins, and some experts dispute that they are money at all. There is, in short, an almost unavoidable circularity involved whenever academics try getting to grips with the origins of money. Schumpeter once said that "no theory of money can be refuted by demonstration of the falsity of any assertions of its author concerning the primitive history of money, and no theory can be proven to be correct by a demonstration of the correctness of such assertions by its author" (Schumpeter 1991: 526–27). Nevertheless, ancestor stories are powerful as tools of monetary polemics, not just monetary theory. Like all such stories, their significance lies in being told, not necessarily in being true.

So are these accounts of origin just myths? Several scholars have richly explored the role played by myth and narrative in the operation of money and markets. As Jeffrey Alexander notes, all economic actors—institutions, markets, states, and individuals—"engage in performances that project meanings" (Alexander 2011: 3). Economic actors need narratives insofar as they bolster confidence, justify pessimism, and shape expectations before being "transmogrified into monetary calculus and loss and gain" (Alexander 2011: 4). Jens Beckert takes up a similar refrain, exploring how narratives, myths, and stories—alongside conventional finance theory—underpin actors' expectations in financial markets. Indeed, it is inevitable that fiction should play an important role in economic situations because of their inherent uncertainty (Beckert 2013: 335). Beckert transports this analysis into the mechanism that works at the very core of the intersection between markets and money, namely, pricing. Although he does not agree with Durkheim's observation that prices reflect what a society deems to be just,[3] Beckert argues that "prices can only be understood with reference to social institutions, networks, and frameworks of meaning that structure the market field and individual decisions—and thereby influence prices" (Beckert 2011: 1). The formation of prices "from meaning" reflects the "cultural preconditions for the pricing of objects" (Beckert 2011: 16). For example, Viviana Zelizer's work on the development of life and children's insurance during the nineteenth century highlights how money's location within the complex relationship between the sacred and the profane had to be reconfigured in order for life itself to be given monetary value (Zelizer 1978, 1981, 1985). In a similar vein, Olav Velthuis has shown how the pricing de-

---

3 There is an underlying connection with *just price* theory here (see Kellermann 2008: 323), which is an approach to which I return in Chapter 8.

cisions of art gallery owners are made in conjunction with narrative practices that are "rich in symbolism [and] sharp moral judgments" (Velthuis 2005: 146). Arguing from the opposite direction but making what is essentially the same case, Zbaracki and Bergen have suggested that in some instances conventional price theory may itself "serve as a rational myth" used by actors to legitimize their decisions and to make sense of given situations: "Rational myths, like any myth, give meaning and order to a world," he concludes (Zbaracki and Bergen 2008: 49).

Nothing I have to say in this chapter contradicts these insights, but my argument operates on a different level. Myths are important not just in relation to the modus operandi of money, markets, and prices but, more fundamentally, in relation to our very *ideas* of money: specifically, to echo Galbraith (1975), our ideas of "whence it came and where it went." As I shall show, the academic literature is dominated by two major accounts of the origins of money. These accounts correspond to the two dominant mainstream theories of money in contemporary social science (i.e., the so-called Austrian and Keynesian viewpoints). The theories spotlight money's ancient connections with, on one hand, *barter exchange*, and on the other, special forms of payment such as *tribute* and *sacrifice*. They are discussed in the first two sections of this chapter. But there are other accounts, too, which emphasize cultural and psychological aspects of money, specifying its links with calculation, gift exchange, language, and violence. These add richly to our repertoire of myths and stories about the origins of money, and I explore them in the remaining four sections of the chapter.

BARTER

The classic (and—despite its controversial nature—best) presentation of the barter theory of money's origins is by Carl Menger, in his 1892 article, "On the Origin of Money." His question is why anyone would accept a commodity (money) that they do not need. Menger finds it curious that people should be ready to exchange their goods for useless metal disks, or worse, for documents merely representing such disks. Such practices are, he remarks, "opposed to the ordinary course of things" (Menger 1892: 239). Rejecting the old Aristotelian argument that money can be decided by law or convention, Menger's answer is that money emerges as a spontaneous solution to the problem of a double coincidence of wants in a barter exchange system. The theory continues to attract a sizable following, despite the weight of empirical evidence that has been used to refute it. Why?

Simply stated, the problem that Menger addresses is the difficulty of finding two parties where each wants what the other is offering in exchange. As long as this obstacle exists, trade is slowed down or prevented altogether. The most logical (and, indeed, natural) practical remedy, Menger suggests, lies in the same condition that gives rise to the problem, namely, that some commodities are more *salable* than others. Salability refers to the "facility" with which a commodity can be sold, at a reasonable price, and in a reasonable period of time (Menger 1892: 245).[4] When a person is in possession of a commodity that is difficult to sell, the rational thing to do is to acquire a more salable commodity, even if one does not need it. In this way, although one does not acquire what one ultimately wants immediately, one "draws nearer to that object" (Menger 1892: 248). Without legal compulsion or regard to vague notions such as "convention" or the "common interest," people have been led by their own self-interest to seek out the most salable goods, not because they need them directly but rather because these commodities can help them eventually to acquire what they do need. Certain commodities have emerged in particular places and times as objects of the demand for more salable commodities. These are the commodities that, through practice and habit, eventually become the most generally acceptable media of exchange: initially accepted by many, eventually by all. This, ultimately, is what we call money.[5]

Once a commodity is generally thought of as money, its salability inevitably rises until everyone has an interest in acquiring it. Money ensures its owner control over every commodity to be had on the market, and at prices that are appropriate to any given economic situation. As a consequence, the degree of differentiation between commodities that are more and less easy to sell (and, ultimately, between money and the rest) becomes increasingly more marked.[6] Political authorities may have played an important role in standardizing monetary weights and measures according to the needs of commerce,

[4] Several factors determine salability: the number of people who want it; the intensity and recurrence of their want; their purchasing power; the relationship between demand and supply; the commodity's divisibility (and other ways its supply can be adjusted to suit individual consumer needs); the nature of the market for the commodity, e.g., whether there is speculation; and social and political limitations on the commodity's production and sale. There are also spatial and temporal factors.

[5] Money, Menger says, is the "spontaneous outcome, the unpremeditated resultant, of particular, individual efforts of the members of a society, who have little by little worked their way to a discrimination of the different degrees of saleableness in commodities" (Menger 1892: 250).

[6] Precious metals have—above all—been in demand because they have their utility (and beauty) almost everywhere; they are naturally scarce but distributed evenly in geographical terms; they are divisible and so can be used in small as well as large quantities; they are homogeneous and therefore both fungible and easy to recognize; and their sale is subject to

as well as in ensuring that coinage can be trusted as to its content, but they have not determined what money is (Menger 1892: 255). Money's origins are therefore to be found in the *market*, not the polity.[7]

Menger's theory has been subjected to vehement criticism. According to Ingham, there is a logical fallacy at the heart of the evolutionary theory of money because it cannot explain why *all* agents choose a particular asset as "money." The problem, he argues, comes down to Menger's adherence to an untenable methodological individualism, with each agent trying to reduce transaction costs in isolation, both from each other and, more importantly, an overarching institutional authority: "To state the sociologically obvious: the advantages of money for the individual presuppose the existence of money as an *institution* in which its 'moneyness' is established" (Ingham 2004b: 23, original italics). Orléan sees the issue slightly differently, arguing that whereas the emphasis on reducing transactions costs is an *advantage* of Menger's model, "what the instrumentalist approach has never been able successfully to demonstrate is that money is an essential requirement for the existence of a market economy" (Orléan 2013: 51).

Other critics, most notably historians and anthropologists, argue that the image of barter Menger describes is simply false. Caroline Humphrey describes the theory as a logical deduction from an imaginary state—a fantasy. No example of a pure and simple barter economy has ever been described by ethnographic evidence, she says, let alone the emergence of money from it (Humphrey 1985: 48). There are further doubts about what Menger has to say about the nature of barter itself. Einzig argues that Menger's theory underplays barter's adaptability, as well as the adaptability of communities to its supposed disadvantages. Barter may look inconvenient to modern eyes, but the double coincidence of wants problem is unlikely to have caused much difficulty in a small community where people already know a great deal about everybody else's products and requirements (Einzig 1966: 343). Most of the difficulties that Menger and other economists come up with to explain money's evolution are merely projections backward toward an imaginary age when no money existed (Einzig 1966: 341–42). Historically, barter

---

few spatial and temporal restrictions (fewer, in fact, than almost every other commodity). For these reasons, their price tends to be both steady and reliable.

7   One intriguing by-product of the barter theory of money is what it tells us about the relationship between money and *private property*. In essence, a barter system is a private property system without money. This definition suggests that private ownership is *antecedent* to monetary exchange. According to Hart, this idea may explain the appeal of the barter myth to economists because apart from the absence of money, it portrays what they would think of as normal exchange relations. In particular, it "leaves the notion of the private property complex undisturbed" (Hart 2005a: 163).

usually took place between strangers and enemies: people rejected it because they preferred doing business with neighbors and friends, not because it was inefficient (Graeber 2011: 30). In its proper context, barter offered a number of distinct advantages relative to monetary exchange, such as the elaborate social and moral functions fulfilled by competitive gift exchange (Davies 1994: 9–10). In short, the argument that money emerged from barter relies on giving barter itself a bad name.

Nevertheless, Menger's thesis lives on. Many university economics degrees still teach that money evolved, much as he described, as a means of getting around the inherent inefficiencies of barter exchange. Countless books on money—including some rather good ones (Coggan 2011)—also begin here, and the orthodoxy is often repeated by governments and public agencies.[8] Menger's account of the evolution of money continues to thrive not only in economics textbooks, however, but also in the arena of monetary policy. According to Goodhart, for example, the Eurozone project was shaped by assumptions about the nature of money that were consistent with (and arguably, derived from) Menger's theory from the outset. By design, the euro entailed breaking up the relationship between money and political authority by assigning the task of monetary creation to a central bank that would be rigorously independent (Goodhart 1998: 425). This method is meant to treat money as if it were a commodity: a creature of the market, not of sovereignty, law, or society. According to Goodhart, the euro's design was informed by the theory of "optimal currency areas," in which it is assumed—consistent with Menger's theory—that money's spatial domain

---

8 · For example, the website of the Federal Reserve Bank of Minneapolis includes a presentation of Menger's theory which is given without question, despite the voluminous literature that has been devoted to its critique, see http://www.minneapolisfed.org/community_education/teacher/history.cfm?. Likewise, the Federal Reserve Bank of New York issues a teacher's guide for its financial literacy programme—"It's All About Your $"—which takes students through an exercise designed to demonstrate the inconveniences of the barter system, see http://www.newyorkfed.org/education/its_all_about_your_money.pdf. In a similar vein, the Banco Centro do Brasil includes a detailed account of the barter theory on its website, see http://www.bcb.gov.br/?ORIGINMONEY. Similar examples can be found in Europe. Peter Praet, a member of the European Central Bank's executive board, gave a speech in October 2012 that included an illustration of the evolution of money in the form of a "linear parable, which leads from a barter economy to a system with commodities as a medium of exchange; and from there to a fiat currency regime"; see http://www.ecb.int/press/key/date/2012/html/sp121010.en.html. There are exceptions, such as the Oesterreichische Nationalbank, whose website includes a page (see http://archive-at.com/page/2043297/2013-05-08/http://www.oenb.at/en/ueber_die_oenb/geldmuseum/allg_geldgeschichte/ursprung/the_origin_of_money.jsp) on the origins of money that references not only Menger but competing theories by Keynes, Knapp, and Laum. The text usefully states, "There are as many speculative accounts about the origin and beginnings of money as there are sound propositions."

can evolve on the basis of the progressive minimization of transaction costs (Goodhart 1998: 419).

If Menger's theory has been discredited by historical evidence that contradicts it, what explains its enduring appeal to economists? For one thing, the theory seems elegant and simple. As Goodhart notes, although the idea that money is a social or political artifact might be better supported by the empirical data, such a viewpoint "is somewhat woolly and socio-logical" (Goodhart 2008: 301), and does not lend itself easily to mathematical modeling. "So, economists have tended to ignore historical reality, to establish formal mathematical models of how private agents (with no government), transacting among themselves, might jointly adopt an equilibrium in which they all settle on a common monetary instrument" (Goodhart 2008: 301). The notion that money evolved as Menger described seems quite intuitive for noneconomists, too. It appears to capture all that is essential about money: its historic connections with trade and exchange, its apparent efficiency, as well as important features of objects that were initially used as money (like cowrie shells and precious metal), such as the ability to be counted and carried. The theory seems disarmingly modest in its claims. Nobody invented money; its origins are not mysterious, merely the outcome of practical common sense as societies and their trading systems have evolved. Students and readers of books about money may find it easy to sympathize with this account. Most of us have experienced a situation like the one described by economists as the problem of the double coincidence of wants: when we were children, for example, and wanted to swap unwanted toys. Few people disagree with the idea that a life without money, if it meant that we had to engage in barter, would be too complicated, even in the Internet age when information should be easier to come by.

Menger's theory is especially popular among libertarians, who believe that money is best organized by markets, not states. The argument that money began as an easily traded commodity offers persuasive support for the view that currencies should be linked to the value of a precious metal such as gold, which is naturally scarce. Menger's image of money often underwrites the arguments of those who promote "austerity" as the best available means of achieving economic recovery because—supposedly—it reduces the very dependence on debt that threatens to erode money's value. Advocates of the electronic currency, Bitcoin, also invoke Menger to promote the idea that through special software and advanced encryption, a virtual commodity can be created and used as a money that is even scarcer than gold (see Chapter 8). Bitcoin is immensely popular—its value often soars in relation to major currencies such as the U.S. dollar—but its price crashes frequently. Though the crashes do not refute Menger's theory per se, the rapidly rising prices may well do so. It was the finite supply of Bitcoins that rendered them especially attractive as a store of value, and therefore as an instrument of speculation. Left to markets, as Menger's theory suggests they ought to be, Bitcoins have not—or at least not *yet*—been an unmitigated success as money.

Exactly the same could be said of gold, arguably the ultimate salable commodity. Gold was worth less than $30 an ounce until the 1930s and less than $40 until 1970. Gold's price broke the $1,000 an ounce barrier in 2009, reaching a little more than $1,700 by early 2012. To sympathizers of Menger, this rise provides all the evidence necessary for the declining purchasing power of money once it is untethered from gold. Central banks would never have been able to pursue policies like quantitative easing, for example, if the supply of money was fixed to the supply of a reliable commodity, such as gold. Moreover, money would be worth considerably more as a result. To others, who sympathize with Keynes's famous description of gold as a "barbarous relic," linking the supply of money to a commodity with a finite supply spells disaster because it stifles the supply of investment that the economy needs. Gold, too, collapsed in value in 2013, falling by $200 per ounce between April 12 and 15, for example. The yellow metal still incites impassioned debate. In November 2011, Nouriel Roubini and James Rickards were engaged in a very public row on Twitter about gold.[9] Roubini's view, held in common with many major economists these days, is that it was countries that tried to stick to the gold standard that were a major cause of the Great Depression. Nations were forced into austerity policies that made economic recovery well nigh impossible. This is a view often repeated today as a warning to governments in the Eurozone, as once again we see cutbacks hurting the weakest members of society (pensioners and the growing army of unemployed). This suffering is all, apparently, for the sake of keeping a specific monetary standard alive by treating money, à la Menger, as a scarce commodity.

Rickards's response to Roubini was robust. It was not gold itself that was the problem, he said, but the high price of gold that governments were trying to defend. Had the price been lower, gold would have done its proper job, which is to ensure that governments cannot undermine the value of money through policies such as quantitative easing. For many people managing their household budgets, there is sound math, as well as good politics,

---

9   See http://www.businessinsider.com/roubini-rickards-twitter-war-2011-11.

in this argument. No matter how many times the major economists tell them that government finances simply do not work in this way, the arguments of Rickards (and the theory of Menger) continue to persuade. There is, it seems, something intuitively reasonable in seeing money as a commodity whose value rises and falls according to supply and demand. Equally reasonable is the logical corollary of this view: that no government (or bank) should be able to produce monetary tokens that have no intrinsic value and are not scarce and whose value may fall according to whim. Yet there is a powerful alternative view, which is that governments not only have the right to produce money but that at the beginning money was closely associated with such a right. This is our next origin myth.

TRIBUTE

If there is no evidence that a full-fledged barter economy actually existed, the argument that money evolved from such a system breaks down, and with it a major underpinning feature: the argument that commodity money is money's most elementary form. In its place, there is an alternative naturalizing discourse that is premised on the idea that other forms of payment besides barter were the original forms of monetary transaction. These were payments associated with religious and political functions and not with trade. For example, ancient rulers were collecting tribute long before the use of money as a means of exchange and markets emerged. Scholars writing histories of the Ottoman Empire, Europe, China, and Africa (Grierson 1978; Pamuk 2000: 1) tend to concur on this point. For the most part, large public institutions were crucial to the development of money, not spontaneous interactions among utility-maximizing individuals, even within the commercial economy (Hudson 2004: 114). If barter appears at all in this particular history of money, it is at its end, not its beginning, i.e., as "the final stage of debt-ridden economies" (Hudson 2004: 119). This is the view that is most often used to refute Menger, and it supports the theory that money is a form of debt in its own right (see Chapter 3).

The argument that money originated as a means of payment (i.e., forms of sacrificial payment, alongside various debts, fines, and tribute to religious and political authority) emerges from the view that its earliest forms were associated with violence and religious sacrifice. Examples include those found on the legal tablets of Babylonia and neighboring city-states: the Code of Ur-Nammu (2050 BC), the Laws of Eshunna (1930 BC), and the

CHAPTER 1

Code of Hammurabi (Babylon, around 1772 BC). In Eshunna, fines included 30 shekels of silver for destroying a person's tooth and ear, 60 for a nose and eye, and 40 shekels for severing a finger (Yaron 1988; Pamuk 2000: 1). According to Hudson, *Wergild* (literally: man money) is the example par excellence of such fines (Einzig 1966: 343; Hudson 2004: 101), operating during the fifth and sixth centuries among Germanic peoples (under Salic law) who were settled in and around the frontiers of the old Roman Empire. Evidence of it was also found in Irish, Welsh, Norwegian, and Russian law in the eleventh and twelfth centuries. Payments due were covered in detail: the loss of a specific limb or even a fingernail had a price, as well as the degrees of blows to the head. Price ratios were laid out and fixed in advance: a Russian's beard might cost four times more than one of his fingers, for example. As Simmel remarks, *Wergild* "not only makes money the measure of man, but it also makes man the measure of the value of money" (Simmel 2004: 356).[10] According to Grierson, the "conditions under which these laws were put together would appear to satisfy, much better than any market mechanism, the prerequisites for the establishment of a monetary system" (Grierson 1978: 13).[11]

Wergild laws were intended to prevent direct and violent retaliation: payment was essentially a pacifier.[12] There were broader functions, too. Ingham suggests two specifically. *Wergild* worked as a quantification of the functional contribution of social roles by levying a monetary cost for injury to individuals, but on the other hand, it codified the social values on which the social order itself depends (Ingham 2004b: 93). *Wergild* is an important case for monetary theorists who claim that money's origins are political and religious, not commercial. *Geld* derives from *gild*, meaning tax, and both words resonate with the old Icelandic *gjald* (recompense, punishment, payment) and the old English *gield* (substitute, indemnity, sacrifice) (Hudson 2004: 103–104). The etymology supports those who argue that money's roots lie not just in debt but in a particular *kind* of debt. This debt is payment to an authority: some scholars refer to it as "primordial" debt and

---

10 Moreover, the use money as a standard of value may also have originated in *Wergild*—using injuries as the common denominator for comparing distinct values.

11 The setting of price *ratios* is crucial to this point, underpinning the more general view that, historically, pricing systems such as *Wergild* were driven by administrative, not commercial factors, "although under normal conditions these public prices tended to provide a model for prices in the economy at large" (Hudson 2004: 101).

12 The English "to pay" comes through the French *payer* from the Latin *pacare*, to pacify (Grierson 1978: 13–14).

suggest that money's function as a debt between the *individual* and *society* originated here (Aglietta and Orléan 1998; Ingham 2004b: 90; cf. Graeber 2011: Chapter 3). The crucial point here (especially for those who oppose Menger's argument about the commercial origins of money) is that these were never payments between equals (Semenova 2011: 384). According to this view, money's roots are not in commercial life, as Menger argues, but in political and religious hierarchy.

Other monetary scholars reach back still further. In *Heiliges Geld* (1924), Bernhard Laum argues that money originated in sacrificial practices that can be traced to Greek antiquity, when precise rules were laid down governing the exact quality of animals deemed suitable as sacrificial payment to the gods: value was measured by the ox unit (Einzig 1966; Laum 2006: 40; Peacock 2011; Semenova 2011: 382). Early forms of money were associated with communal sacrifices of food and other commodities (including metal) that members of temple brotherhoods were obliged to make to religious guild organizations. Foucault makes a similar claim in his 1970–71 lectures, when he notes that, for the Greeks, money did "not emerge in the abstract sky of the commodity and its representation, but in the game of sacrifice and its simulacra" (Foucault 2013: 135).[13] Sacrifice was a means of bartering with the gods (Einzig 1966: 371), shaped by the logic of gift and countergift (Finley 1982). Laum's analysis is supported by Seaford in *Money and the Early Greek Mind* (2004). Seaford agrees that there were strong associations between early Greek coinage and various sacrificial objects. For example, it seems likely that iron spits "were the kind of objects that could function as money" (Seaford 2004: 102), whereas the Greek coin of low value, the *obol* (*obolos*) took its name from the spit (*obelos*), and "drachma" originally meant a handful of spits (Seaford 2004: 104).[14]

Why do these ancient associations matter for monetary theory? By sanctifying payments, religious connections rendered them *obligatory*. The empirical transition from religious payments to taxation may have happened as cities were conquered by overlords who turned the religious institutions

---

13   Foucault links money's appearance with the constitution of a new type of power whose sole raison d'être was to "intervene in the regime of property, in the interplay of debts and settlements" (Foucault 2013: 139).

14   Seaford concludes, "All this ... make[s] it extremely likely that iron spits did at some time, somewhere, perform one or more of the functions of money (means of payment and exchange, measure and store of value), even if they were never a general means of payment and exchange. They may have been prized simultaneously for their sacrificial use, as prestige objects, and for their monetary function or functions" (Seaford 2004: 107–108).

into collection agents (Hudson 2004: 104). In Mesopotamia around 3000–2000 BC, metallic money (mostly silver) was predominantly used to pay off debts to public institutions (i.e., royal palaces and religious temples) as rent and not for trade.[15] Intriguingly, Babylonian rulers periodically annulled all debt, ensuring that debtors were never in a position where they simply found their obligations impossible to meet (Hudson 2004: 115). So although debt caused problems, just as it does today, antiquity's economic balance was never irreparably upset. Rulers enjoyed the power to create and recreate society. Debt amnesties (analogous to the Mosaic[16] and later Christian idea of periodic debt forgiveness) were announced because excessive indebtedness poses a threat to social order: one bad harvest could reduce a large portion of the peasantry into debt peonage.

There are significant historical insights here, and it seems that the argument that the earliest recognizable forms of money were connected with tribute has better supporting evidence than does Menger's barter theory. But there is a normative angle to this approach, too, which is somewhat more questionable. Laum's argument that money originated as a cosmic debt is often used to naturalize the idea that the *state* is the immutable guardian of money. The "myth" of money as primordial debt is, as it were, a charter for chartalism. The chain of reasoning is simple. Money originated as a debt to the gods. This debt evolved as a debt to rulers and states, which are essentially surrogates for the idea of society. This would make a certain sense of Simmel's idea, for example, that money is a "claim upon society." But does it make sense to say that we are in debt to *society*, just as we once have believed ourselves to be in debt to *God* (see Chapter 4)? And why should "society" and "state" be run together in this way? Expressed in these terms, this looks like another origin myth, replacing one ancestor story (money began with aboriginal trade) with another (money is a primordial debt). Just as the first theory appeals to libertarians and gold bugs, the second theory appeals to those who believe that money must be controlled by the state because it is as "natural" as our most ancient religious obligations. If this latter view is correct, money is necessarily a creature of the state, and communities have no privileged rights of their own to produce it.

---

15   Even trade thrived on credit, bridging the gap between planning and harvesting, the consignment of goods to traders and their return on the sea or by caravan, and the advance of raw materials to craftsmen and the delivery of the finished products (Hudson 2004: 117).
16   Under Mosaic Law, the Jubilee, occurring every fiftieth year, was the occasion when all prisoners and slaves would be freed and all debts would be forgiven (see Leviticus 25:8–13). In Christianity, the Jubilee has been celebrated since around the fourteenth century.

QUANTIFICATION

At first glance, Simmel's theory of money sits oddly in the company of ancestor stories being recounted in this chapter. His *Philosophy of Money* (originally published in 1900, revised in 1907) deals not with the empirical origins of money but rather with its *conditions of possibility*. This is a philosophical investigation, inspired by Kant. "How is money possible?" is a characteristically Simmelian question, analogous to the question he famously asks at the beginning of *Soziologie* (originally published in 1908), "How is society possible?"[17] And yet Simmel belongs here, not least because his account of the social and philosophical preconditions for money's existence in the first "analytical" part of his book leads on to an analysis of the cultural and social effect of the mature money economy in the second, "synthetic" part. It is an important and influential theory, which we come back to a number of times in this book.

In his critical philosophy, Kant proposed that, to experience objects as part of a coherent world, we use a universal framework or lens (the categories of understanding) to synthesize raw sense impressions. Simmel applies a similar logic to economic value,[18] and this logic underpins his theory of money. Philosophically, he describes value as the "counterpart" to being (Simmel 2004: 60). For Kant, the natural world does not make itself known to us in a form that has been given in advance; we synthesize it in our minds. Likewise for Simmel, the economic world[19] does not lie in wait for us, discoverable and neatly ranked according to what is more or less valuable, so that we demand or desire things with appropriate degrees of intensity. Just like the appearance of a coherent world of being in Kant, the emergence of a coherent world of value in Simmel is the result of a synthesis: it takes place through exchange. We enter into exchanges because we want things. This desire is demand. "Just as the world of being is my representation, so the world of value is my demand" (Simmel 2004: 69). According to Simmel, however, demand does not precede exchange but happens within and through it in a process he describes as "mutual sacrifice." Crucially, then,

---

17   When describing Aristotle's theory of money, Schumpeter distinguished between *historical* and *logical* origins (Schumpeter 1986: 63–64). One could argue that Simmel is dealing with the latter. The same could be said about Menger, too.

18   In fact, Simmel wanted to construct a much more general theory of value, incorporating religious and aesthetic aspects, for example. This desire helps to explain why he takes sixty pages or so to get to the specific question of *economic* value and the value of *money* in the first chapter of *The Philosophy of Money*.

19   And, indeed, the social word as he discusses in "How is society possible?" (Simmel 2009: 40–52).

Simmel's synthesis—i.e., the synthesis that makes economic value (and ultimately money) possible—is not mental, but social.

As with his investigation of society, Simmel's account of the conditions of possibility of money begins with the dyad. This dyad is the relationship between two owners of objects, each of whom needs or wants what the other possesses. This mutual interest forms the basis of any exchange, which Simmel therefore describes as an act of reciprocal surrender or mutual sacrifice. Even a solitary act, such as taking a stroll, involves sacrifice insofar as something else, such as watching television, has to be given up in order to do it. This sacrifice is true of all kinds of value, religious and aesthetic as well as economic and monetary: to *gain* something, we must simultaneously *lose* (Simmel 2004: 82–90).[20] We make sacrifices to overcome the distance we experience in relation to the objects we want or need. This distance is not inherent in an object but emanates from our coveting of it. Objects are valuable to us because they resist our craving to possess them, not the other way around (Simmel 2004: 67). For this reason, value is not "ready made," but rather it accrues to the desired object by virtue of the sacrifice needed to acquire it in exchange (Simmel 2004: 84). Because exchange involves mutual sacrifice, value acquires a suprasubjective status.

Simmel argues that value is intrinsically connected to sociation (*Vergesellschaftung*). Just as society is made possible by the act of our being social, so is value. Value is not a property that "belongs" to an object like color, taste, or smell. It is a third category "which stands, so to speak, between us and the objects" (Simmel 2004: 68). Although both valuation (as described above) and exchange are intersubjective processes, they operate in such a way that value comes to appear as an objective property of things themselves. When two or more objects of desire are compared, the immediacy of our desire translates beyond the dualism of subject and object into something quantifiable (Simmel 2004: 66). This quantification enables objects to be measured against each other until value "appears in a very specific way as an objective, inherent quality" (Simmel 2004: 78). Once this quantification happens, objects stand before us as independent values whose resistance to our desire to possess them takes on an appearance of lawlike necessity (Simmel 2004: 74–75). Objects now confront us as independent powers, demanding sacrifices in order for us to acquire them.

It is this fluid interplay between subjects, subjects and objects, and objects themselves that makes money possible. Quantification is essential to

---

20 As long as the exchange takes place with each party willing to give something up to acquire something else, both parties gain, overall.

this possibility: only through a comparison of demands, as happens through exchange, can definite economic values be assigned to objects (Simmel 2004: 90). Value is a measure of the distance between a subject and the object he or she desires. That is to say, value is a measure of the extent to which we must overcome obstacles and difficulties to acquire that object (Simmel 2004: 62–64). Money measures this distance, and for this reason, value and price are almost identical: "Value is, so to speak, the epigone [i.e., undistinguished imitator] of price" (Simmel 2004: 94). The monetary price of an object is the external manifestation of the sacrifice that is offered in exchange for it: it is a quantitative objectification of that sacrifice (Simmel 2004: 100). Money represents this objectification in its most abstract form.

Simmel's emphasis on the importance of subjective desire in the formation of value has led a number of scholars to compare his approach with neoclassical economics and the theory of marginal utility. But Simmel's approach cuts more deeply than this. He was not simply asking how prices are formed through exchange. Rather, he sought to understand how money brings order to a world in which objects and values are in perpetual flux. This flux was perhaps the main source of Simmel's fascination with money and the reason he wrote a *philosophical* investigation of its nature. He suggested that as a tool of mutual valuation, money represents "the clearest embodiment of the formula of all being" (Simmel 2004: 128–29). This formula refers to the principle of relationism, which is the view that things receive their meaning only through each other and that their mutual relations determine their being. In this regard, money provides Simmel with a means to explore the epistemological implications of relationism. By "following the money" as it comes into contact with myriad people and things, he can explore the world just as he believes it is constituted.

For Simmel, then, money represents the generic *idea* of value. By virtue of its objective and abstract character, money is capable of standing in for *any* specific, concrete value in the process of exchange. This capability is why Simmel believes that money's increasingly widespread circulation fosters a distinctive outlook he describes as "intellectualism." It is the distance that money gives us in regarding things of value that allows us to compare them even though they are qualitatively different. Money allows us to measure their value against each other and ultimately to exchange them. In doing so, it encourages our increasing detachment from things. This detachment is why Simmel anticipated that money's widening circulation in modern society, and its use for exchanging an increasing range of objects (and even people), would have such an unsettling effect on modern life. In its more general sociological sense, Simmel sees the growth of the money economy as a manifestation of the increasing power of objective culture over subjective culture. Or in other words, money heralds the triumph of quantity over quality, a world in which something must be *measurable* against something else in order to be deemed to have value.[21] For this reason, money (alongside the city, in which monetized social relations thrive) is a vehicle for his critical reflections on the nature of modernity and its effect on the individual. I turn to this aspect of Simmel's work in Chapter 7.

Simmel's work, particularly its emphasis on historical connections between money and intellectualism, tends to be associated with (and criticized for) the view that money transforms social life by reducing *qualitative* relations to *quantitative* ones. Although I think it is questionable just how far Simmel goes in advancing such a view of money as a force for spreading a cold and calculating attitude throughout modern society, many scholars have offered considerable insights into the nature of money—and the social practices associated with its use—by setting out to challenge this viewpoint. Moreover, one of the most popular counterarguments ("money cannot buy everything") still plays well in the popular imagination, as numerous "postcrisis" books testify (Sandel 2012; Skidelsky and Skidelsky 2012). In this sense, it is arguably as a "contrarian" figure (someone to be argued against, albeit sometimes as a straw model) that Simmel's most immediate effect on contemporary monetary scholarship is most keenly felt. Later on, particularly when considering his (neglected) notion of "perfect money" and its relationship to the "perfect society" in Chapter 8, I hope to show that there is much more to Simmel's analysis of money than this.

MANA

In many Western cultures, monetary exchange and gift giving tend to be mutually exclusive.[22] Gifts are emotionally charged, morally loaded, and reciprocal. Monetary exchange, by contrast, seems to lack emotional significance, morality, and reciprocity. This contrast supports a more general (and

---

21   Money's expression of *relative* values is crucial to Simmel's approach; it is the ratio *between* quantities, not a direct or one-to-one correspondence with objects of value, that money enables us to objectify: "The proportion between the single commodity and the economically effective total quantity of commodities is, with certain qualifications, equal to the proportion between a certain amount of money and the economically effective total quantity of money" (Simmel 2004: 158). As we see in Chapter 8, this ratio is crucial to his notion of "conceptually correct" money.

22   There are exceptions, e.g., ritualized cash gifts at weddings such as the "money dance" in Greece.

supposedly Simmelian) view of money as a tool reducing every social relationship it touches to a pure and anonymous functionality. But as we see later in this book (Chapter 7), the notion that money is simply a colorless and anonymous tool for utilitarian economic behavior has been increasingly challenged by studies richly demonstrating that monetary transactions of many different kinds (from intimate domestic exchanges to major business deals) are socially and morally codified. This viewpoint gains support from the argument that originally, money *was* a gift. Though there is overlap between this particular account of money's origins and the argument about tribute that we looked at just now, there are important differences, which lead onto different pathways into the contemporary literature on money. It is prudent, therefore, to keep them distinct.

The gift exchange literature is dominated by Mauss's classic book, *The Gift* (1990, originally published in 1923). The book is very well known; there is no need for a detailed discussion of its main arguments here. The key example of gift exchange that Mauss discusses is the Kula ring of Papua New Guinea, as studied by Malinowski in *Argonauts of the Western Pacific* (1922). There is constant give and take within the Kula, marked by the continuous flow in all directions of goods and services. The system depends on *hau*, or *mana*, the spiritual power with which the gift is laden that underpins the obligation to reciprocate. Gifts must be passed on. For the receiver to retain what is given would be both morally and spiritually dangerous. *Hau* creates a tie between givers and receivers and pertains not just between people but also between souls, "because the thing itself possesses a soul" (Mauss 1990: 16). Its moral richness makes it comparable to a contract in Durkheim's sense, i.e., it is "only possible because of the regulation of contracts, which is social in origin" (Durkheim 1997: 162).[23] Gift exchange is a total social fact: it permeates economic, tribal, and moral life and has a broader social efficacy.[24]

---

23 According to Hart, ceremonial exchange and barter are merely "different means of securing the same ends, namely circulation of commodities between independent communities." The Kula is in this sense just a highly visible version of "that social glue that Durkheim insisted lies more invisibly behind the anonymity of market contracts" (Hart 1986: 648). The Kula valuables were "tokens of interpersonal relations, a sophisticated device for ranking political credit in an unstable environment of trade and war between communities" (Hart 1986: 649).

24 Likewise, Mauss writes of money itself as a social fact. It relies on confidence, like an idea, institution, or faith: "La monnaie n'est nullement un fait matériel et physique, c'est essentiellement un fait social; sa valeur est celle de sa force d'achat, et la mesure de la confiance qu'on a en elle. Et c'est de l'origine d'une notion, d'une institution, d'une foi, que nous parlons" ("Money is by no means a material and physical fact; it is essentially a social fact., and its value is that of its purchasing power and the extent of the confidence we have in it. And this is the origin of an idea, an institution, a faith about which we speak") (Mauss 1969).

The topic of money arises for Mauss during a discussion of the emblazoned copper objects of the American northwest and the mats of the Samoa. According to Malinowski (1921), these objects are not money because they have a magical nature as talismans or life givers, and their value tends to rise and fall along with the prestige of their owners.[25] They are too morally loaded to be money. Mauss disagrees. As magical as such objects might seem, they fulfill the same basic functions of money: that is, they have a *purchasing power* that *discharges debt*. The idea of number is often present whenever such objects are exchanged (for so many American copper objects, a payment of so many blankets is due) at rates that are *fixed* and *publicly recognized*. Such objects could even be exchanged with European money in a passage between one system of values and another that "took place without a hitch" (Mauss 1990: 128 n. 29). In claiming that they are *not* money, Malinowski reads these objects retrospectively. That is to say, he assumes that something is money only when it corresponds to modern conceptions of it as an entity that is inscribed, impersonalized, and detached from all relationships other than with an issuing state. This view of money is delimiting from the outset. If Mauss is right, important historical examples of money are overlooked simply because of the way that money has been defined in the present day.

For Mauss, money's purchasing power is primordial. It is an expression of social power that is rooted in the affective states generated by collective life. As André Orléan remarks, Mauss's argument "opens up entirely new paths to tackle the phenomenon of money, paths which rely greatly on sociological and anthropological conceptions" by virtue of the fact that value in general, and money in particular, express "this particular power that society exercises over its members" (Orléan 2013: 55). Mauss therefore offers a powerful counterpoint to overly narrow "modern" conception of money (see Simmel, above). Nonetheless, it is important to understand that he was advancing a positive account of the origins and development of money and not simply a negative case against Malinowski. Both in *The Gift* and in a 1914 lecture, "Les origines de la notion de monnaie" ("The Origins of the Notion of Money") (1969), Mauss insists that there were recognizable and distinct forms of money that preceded our own. These were particular

---

25   It was a view shared by François Simiand, economist and sociologist, and a contemporary of Mauss, and author of 'La monnaie, réalité sociale' (Simiand 1934). In the passages I cite here, Mauss appears to be referring to private discussions he had with Simiand on these questions.

objects whose value was *not destroyed by use*. Because of the durability of these objects, they were allocated a special purchasing power and used both to measure the worth of riches and to circulate those riches. Although these objects were eventually depersonalized, and thereby turned into a more stable measure of value, in the first instance they possessed a certain magical, religious, or spiritual character that in no way disqualifies them from being thought of as money. This concept is that of *mana*.

In Melanesia, the concept of *mana* is directly related to the idea of currency. Among the Kwakiutl, the brass objects used as "real currency" in potlatch ceremonies were talismans. Money's purchasing power is not natural, but a symbol of the strength of the clan. Little wonder, Mauss suggests, that money was often used for the acquisition of luxury things possessing great authority over men, not merely for the purchase of basic objects of consumption. It is here, moreover, that we can find vestiges of gift exchange in later forms of money. Through hoarding, for example, where money is amassed and often expended to no avail, we can discern that "the whole of this very rich economy is still filled with religious elements" (Mauss 1990: 92). Modern society as a whole is permeated by the atmosphere of gift exchange: in the mutualism of insurance and Friendly Societies, in our personal relations, and even in markets, "obligation and liberty intermingle" (Mauss 1990: 83). We return to the question of money's *religious* underpinnings in Chapter 4.

Mauss's arguments, particularly the conclusions he extrapolates regarding the presence of gift exchange in subsequent economic formations, have attracted a voluminous literature. There is no need to review the debate in depth here because much of it concerns the nature of giving, and not money itself. What seems certain, though, is that whereas Mauss was challenging binary conceptions of traditional versus modern economic formations, these self-same conceptions have had a profound effect on money's place in social, economic, and political thought. Mauss's argument that money was originally a total social fact embracing reciprocity and moral integration, prestige and authority, spiritualism and power is a question of interpretation as much as anything else. Just as he charges Malinowski and others of conceptualizing money anachronistically, Mauss inevitably leaves himself open to a similar charge. If remnants of giving can be found everywhere, they may as well be nowhere. The analytical tensions between money and the gift that animate his argument begin to dissipate as one reads that the morality of gift exchange still operates in our own societies—"in unchanging fashion and, so to speak, hidden, below the surface" (Mauss 1990: 5).

Mauss enlivens the critique of modern orthodoxies in which money is portrayed (positively *or* negatively) as a cold, colorless medium of calculation. If money did not erode the gift economy but grew as an intrinsic component of it, it has an integral part to play in the formation of a human economy that emphasizes practical, context-specific, and holistic, rather than theoretical, abstract, and reductionist, aspects of our economic existence (Hart 2001, 2005b, 2007; Hart, Laville, et al. 2010). Western social theory (as personified—allegedly—by Simmel, for example) tends to view relationships involving money as marked by alienation and detachment. Money itself is portrayed as inherently cold and lifeless. Mauss, on the contrary, suggests that relationships mediated by money are just as likely to be personal and familiar as those in which money plays no part. His theory that money was *originally* infused with social meaning is integral to the thinking behind recent attempts to "rehumanize" money through practical reform. Moreover, Mauss's work is of pivotal importance to the growing social science literature that demonstrates how even within the most calculating environments, money is by no means as detached from *mana* as our predominantly economic, utilitarian mode of theorizing it has led us to expect.

LANGUAGE

Outside of literary studies, the connection between money and language has largely been overlooked, and for this reason I want to spend a little more time exploring this issue here. In social theory, there are some notable examples of thinkers such as Talcott Parsons, who saw money (alongside power) as a symbolic medium of communication that fulfilled specific functions of language (Parsons 1991; Dodd 1994; Parsons and Smelser 2010). By and large, though, money has simply been *compared* to a system of signs. Kant, for example, called money "the greatest and most useable of all the Means of human intercommunication through Things" and likened it to books, "the greatest Means of carrying on the interchange of Thought" (Kant 1887: 124–25). Marx described money as the "language of commodities" (Marx 1982: 143–44), Simmel compared money to a "universally understood language" (Simmel 2004: 210), and Barthes called it "the Gold of the signifier" (Barthes 1977: 46). Money has also been seen as a sociological numismatics that illuminates society through its symbols (Shell 1978: 5–6). Not all scholars agree. Benjamin suggested that if money is a universal language, it is most like Esperanto: contrived, emaciated, and unerringly divisive.[26] Money could therefore be part of a new Babylonian project: a godless language of unity with money as its universal sign (Hörisch 2000: 206). For Baudelaire, too, money stood for nothing other than vacuous impermanence; it is an entanglement of signs that only a language of perfection, poetry, can penetrate and overcome (Buchan 1997: 206–207; Meltzer 2011). Or consider Paul Auster's moon people, whose money is poetry: "actual poems, written out on pieces of paper whose value is determined by the worth of the poem itself" (Auster 1989: 39). More recently, the expansion of the financial sector has generated some colorful and (usually) dystopian language metaphors. Jean Baudrillard wrote of an "economy of signs" flowing endlessly through a domain of circulation that he likened to the grotesquely bloated, vacuous belly of Alfred Jarry's absurd king, Ubu Roi (Jarry 1977). Brian Rotman devised the term *xenomoney* to describe a form of money that promises only an identical copy of itself as redemption (Rotman 1993: 5),[27] and Bill Maurer has compared derivatives to a form of theological divination whose underlying moral structures have been repressed (Maurer 2002). What these varied treatments have in common is the idea that money is not just a symbol. It is the symbol of symbols. *In extremis*, it is the symbol of nothing.[28]

Like language, money is inherently metaphorical.[29] Operating as a system of comparison, money connects what would otherwise be unrelated. It is therefore unsurprising when one finds money being compared to language, and, conversely, language to money. Increasingly, money has been compared not to language per se, but rather to code, wherein it is the rela-

26 Benjamin also associates money with Baroque allegory, which—unlike a symbol or a fetish as he conceives them (Benjamin 2009)—never allows a signifier to be completely unified with that which it signifies: "The key to the allegorical form in Baudelaire is bound up with the specific signification which the commodity acquires by virtue of its price. The singular debasement of things through their signification, something characteristic of seventeenth-century allegory, corresponds to the singular debasement of things through their price as commodities" (Benjamin 1999: 22).

27 For Rotman, money's "illusion of anteriority" collapsed as soon as the banknote became an instrument of creating money (Rotman 1993: 46). Xenomoney is a tautological void that is "without history, ownerless, and without traceable national origin" (Rotman 1993: 89–90).

28 It can thus be likened to a *simulacrum*, bringing to mind the faux quotation (supposedly from Ecclesiastes) that Baudrillard uses at the beginning of *Simulations*: "The simulacrum is never that which conceals the truth—it is the truth which conceals that there is none. The simulacrum is true" (Baudrillard 1983: 1).

29 Marc Shell remarked that "a metaphor about language and a metaphor about money are both metaphors about metaphorization" (Shell 1978: 5–6).

tionship between signs themselves, rather than their connection to an external reality, that is key. The significance of language for monetary theory also shifted its focus, away from concerns about money's intrinsic value, or its underlying reality, and toward new preoccupations with the information that it conveys and the speed at which it does so. These chains resembled units of language. Polanyi once described money as a "system of symbols similar to language" (Polanyi 1968: 175), and Helen Codere has argued that money functions as a sign whose symbolic power rests "upon its co-ordination with other symbols or systems of symbols" (Codere 1968: 559). From the opposite direction, language scholars have sometimes appealed to monetary theory to explore the "economy" of language and the complex interconnections between linguistic signs that sometimes resemble the workings of a monetary system; indeed, one could describe the relationship between the two fields of scholarship—the study of money and of language—as one of mutual borrowing or cross-fertilization.[30] Consequently, our notions of truth and fiction, value and authenticity, have shifted too. Today's digital monies can be viewed as forms of language—or, more specifically, *writing* or *code*—in their own right (Hörisch 2000). And the key analytical questions they pose are no longer principally about value and representation. They are about security and encryption. It is no accident that such concerns coincide with the era of financialization, in which money has become increasingly self-referential.

The comparison between language and money took on increasing importance once banknotes and coins no longer stood for a fixed quantity of metal (albeit the coins were often clipped), but rather interlinked chains of value. Money's history is punctuated by debates about what lies beneath monetary symbols, giving ontological ballast and moral weight to the play of floating signs that monetary exchange entails. One of the earliest and clearest examples of the comparison between money and language can be

---

30   Money is sometimes used as a metaphor for thought itself: Nietzsche, most notably, compared money to "thinking as such" (Nietzsche 1996b: 44). More elaborately, Schopenhauer said that "our intellect is like a bank of issue which, if it is to be sound, must have ready money in the safe in order to be able, on demand, to meet all the notes it has issued; the perceptions are the ready money, the concepts are the notes" (Schopenhauer 1966: 71). Ayer added the following gloss and extended the metaphor: "William James had a phrase in which he asked for the 'cash value' of statements. This is very important. The early Logical Positivists were wrong in thinking that you could still maintain the gold standard—that if you presented your notes you could get gold for them—which of course you can't. There isn't enough gold. And there are too many notes. But nevertheless there has to be some backing to the currency. If someone makes an assertion, well, all right, perhaps you can't translate it out into observational terms—but it still is important to ask how you would set about testing it. What observations are relevant? This, I think, still holds good" (Magee 1979: 132).

found in the work of Anne-Robert-Jacques Turgot (1727–81), an etymologist and economist, student of François Quesnay and part of the Physiocratic school, and an (early) advocate of economic liberalism. Turgot considered the correspondence between money and language in *Réflexions sur la formation et la distribution des richesses*,[31] published in 1769–70, and in an unfinished article, "Value and Money." Comparing money with human speech, he argued that money brings natural things under a common term or standard (Turgot 1999: 41). In the case of speech, this standard consists of natural things (or our ideas of those things), which are common to all nations. With money, the common standard is, of course, an underlying form of value. Both speech and money are forms of measurement: speech measures ideas, organizing them in such a way that their value can be weighed up, whereas money measures value (Shell 1978: 4). Significantly in light of what de Saussure would later say, Turgot suggested that money could only be evaluated against other money, just as speech could only be interpreted against other speech.

Whereas Turgot suggested that both words and money can be viewed as "social symbols of exchange" (Shell 1978: 120), Jean-Jacques Rousseau went further to examine money as a generalized system of representation in its own right. In *Emile* (1991, originally published in 1762), he argued there can be "no society without exchange, no exchange without a common standard of measurement, no common standard of measurement without equality" (Rousseau 1991: 164). It was, he continued, this conventional equality between things that led to the *invention* of money because a term of comparison between the values of different things was needed. In this sense, money was the "real bond of society" (Rousseau 1991: 164). For Rousseau, it does not actually matter what gets used as money: cattle, shells, iron, leather, gold, and silver are equally useful as tools of comparison (Rousseau 1991: 164). Even the "stupidest" person can perceive the use of money when it is explained in this way (Rousseau 1991: 164).

Money, for Rousseau, is not just *like* a language. It essentially *is* a language. In *On the Origin of Languages*, he likens the development of the monetary economy to the emergence of the alphabet. Unlike ideograms and hieroglyphic writing, which involve the direct representation of things, alphabetic writing represents only sounds; it therefore distances us from things. Alphabetic writing functions like money in this particular sense, rendering words commensurable, enabling them to be exchanged. Languages vary and change according to our needs, but once society has

---

31   *Reflections on the Formation and Distribution of Wealth.*

assumed its "final form" and political discussion is superseded by the language of "arms and cash," we are all impoverished and the social bond on which money depends is fractured (Rousseau and Herder 1966: 72).[32] Likewise, in *The Social Contract*, published the same year as *Emile*, Rousseau contemplated the complete breakdown of political discourse through money: "As soon as public service ceases to be the chief business of the citizens, and they would rather serve with their money than with their persons, the State is not far from its fall" (Rousseau 2004: 62).

After Turgot and Rousseau, it was de Saussure who took the next step by treating monetary exchange as a *system of semiotics* from which much could be learned about the basic structure of language itself. In the *Course in General Linguistics* (1915), he proposed that the synchronic study of language (static linguistics, or the science of linguistic states) could be compared to the study of economics (de Saussure 1915: 79). Specifically, he used the analogy between language and money to flesh out his argument about the arbitrary nature of the linguistic sign.[33] Just as the value of a coin is rarely derived from its metallic content alone but varies according to the amount stamped upon it and according to its use inside or outside a political boundary, so it is with the linguistic signifier, which derives its meaning from "the differences that separate its sound-image from all others" (de Saussure 1915: 118–19). This principle applies to all the material elements of language. Even phonemes are not characterized by their positive qualities but by the fact that they are "opposing, relative, and negative entities" (de Saussure 1915: 119).[34] This argument is essentially about value. All values, even outside of language, must be composed of, first, a dissimilar thing with which they can be exchanged, and second, a similar thing with which they can be compared. This is exactly how money works. To determine the value of a five-franc piece, we must know that it can be exchanged for a fixed quantity of a different thing, such as bread, and that it can be compared with a similar value of a similar thing, such as a one-franc piece. "In the same way a word can be exchanged for something dissimilar, an idea;

---

32   Rousseau continues: "And since there is nothing to say to people besides *give money*, it is said with placards on street corners or by soldiers in their homes. It is not necessary to assemble anyone for that. On the contrary, the subjects must be kept apart. That is the first maxim of modern politics" (Rousseau and Herder 1966: 72).

33   Likewise, de Saussure's argument is analogous to the view that market processes do not produce "objective" prices that represent the "true" value of things.

34   Significantly, de Saussure was formulating his theory at the same time as Walras's general equilibrium theory in economics was flourishing (Piaget 1971: 77; McCloskey 1998: 29). Both sets of ideas emphasize cross-sectional and comparative static analysis. As McCloskey puts it: "The motto of both was 'Everything touches everything else, today'" (McCloskey 1998: 29).

besides, it can be compared with something of the same nature, another word," he concludes (de Saussure 1915: 115).

The idea of money as a "play on differences" was taken up later on by Jean-François Lyotard, but the comparison with language was treated more cautiously. Language is the "whole social bond," Lyotard argued, whereas money is merely an *aspect* of language: "the accountable aspect, payment or credit, at any rate a play on differences of place and time" (Lyotard 1993: 27). What Lyotard discerned in postindustrial society resonates with the fears that Rousseau had been expressing two centuries earlier. Rousseau worried that the social bond would disintegrate if the exchange of money replaced language and the exchange of ideas. For Lyotard, the decisive feature of postindustrial society was the penetration of capitalism (and money) *into* language. Phrases were being turned into messages to be encoded, transmitted, and arranged; and their unit of measurement (the gauge of the optimization of language itself) was information.

After de Saussure, language theory sought to come to terms with an understanding of meaning as entirely relational: words mean something not because they name things but because they occupy a position within a system of differences. Likewise, in monetary theory the question of value in general, and monetary value in particular, has been progressively wrenched away from an underlying substance: money's value has increasingly been understood as relational, not intrinsic. The de Saussurian characterization of money comes into its own in the age of dematerialization, and this notion is demonstrated with particular clarity in the work of Goux.

Goux's work on money combines the de Saussurian, or structuralist, approach to language, as used in anthropology, psychoanalysis, and literary analysis,[35] with an idiosyncratic interpretation of Marxism, focusing especially on Marx's account of the genesis of the money form in *Capital*.[36] Goux's thesis is that, through money, we can understand society's dominant mode of symbolizing. He means this in a broad sense; the symbolic economy includes aesthetic and religious representations as well as linguistic

---

35   Goux describes his point of departure as the fertile intellectual moment when the language paradigm that prevailed since Aristotle, consisting of a hierarchical relationship between words, ideas, and things, was replaced by de Saussure's theory of the differential sign: "Signs refer to other signs; meaning is determined by their relations" (Goux 1990: 1).

36   Marx, it must be said, dismissed the analogy between money and language that Goux wants to pursue, arguing in *Grundrisse* that money, even credit money, does not simply mediate production and exchange (like a language) but fundamentally alters its character. Likewise, he insists that ideas do not exist separately from language; rather they need to be translated "out of their mother tongue and into a foreign language in order to circulate." Hence the correct analogy "lies not in language, but in the foreignness of language" (Marx 2005a: 163).

and economic ones. The notion involves a subtle theoretical shift from Marxist theory. Goux suggests that every kind of society (ancient, primitive, feudal, capitalist) has a dominant mode of symbolizing that emerges in conjunction with its dominant mode of production. One does not simply reflect the other. Rather, they constitute each other through the correspondence between "on the one hand, the forms of consciousness and, by extension, the forms of the unconscious and, on the other, the rest of the conditions of social existence" (Goux 1990: 86–87). Society's mode of symbolization (to which language belongs) does not simply reflect its mode of production. Rather, social consciousness *objectively* consists of all the complex processes of symbolization in every sphere of activity: economic, legal, signifying, and libidinal. The dominant mode of representation itself, i.e., the dominant form of social consciousness, depends on these processes of symbolization. Thus for Goux, it is not a question of whether the analogy between money and language is theoretically correct because it has been practiced unconsciously (Goux 1990: 110). There are deep, hidden affinities between our conception of language and of money.

Goux argues that the earliest forms of money emerged alongside the development of alphabetic writing and the discovery of "the powers and value of the concept" (Goux 1990: 111). This correspondence between money and conceptual thought is logico-historical. Goux tries to capture this correspondence through the notion that in any given society there exists a mode of symbolizing, which he calls its *symbology* (Goux 1990: 113). This symbology is the structure through which all processes of exchange and valuation are constituted.[37] Thus the connection between money and language is not simply a useful tool of theoretical comparison (as it is in de Saussure's work, for example) but a "real sociohistorical occurrence" (Goux 1990: 96).

On the face of it, this is conventional narrative of dematerialization. Goux describes three stages (from gold, through paper, to the era of credit money) until money emerges as a "pure" token with no connection to an underlying material substance (Goux 1994). What makes Goux's approach novel and intriguing, however, is its use of the categories of the *real*, *imaginary*, and *symbolic* (drawn from the work of the psychoanalyst, Jacques Lacan) to describe this sequence of stages: the real is the state of nature from which we have been severed because of our entry into language; the imaginary is the mirror stage,

---

[37] This symbology is not restricted to the economic domain but "also applies to the signifying processes in which are implicated the constitution of the subject, the use of language, the status of objects of desire—the various overlapping systems of the imaginary, the signifying, the real" (Goux 1990: 113).

in which the child misrecognizes itself; and the symbolic is the order of language, through which the rules and dictates of society are given. Goux describes the era of financial capitalism in terms of the third stage, whereby society is dominated by the logic of the token, or the purely symbolic (Goux 1994). According to him, the dematerialization of money therefore reflects deeper changes in the relationship between language and the world, or the symbolic order. It is no accident that money's dematerialization and the emergence of a "radically nominalist" conception of monetary media have coincided historically with a deepening preoccupation with language theory, a profound concern with the philosophical status of language, and "an unprecedented rupture in the mode of representation" (Goux 1999: 115). The present-day monetary economy has common cause with philosophical idealism: both belong to the same dominant societal mode of symbolizing.

Goux is not just concerned with money's relationship to language per se. He argues, further, that a new and distinctive form of monetary symbology has emerged whose significance cannot be grasped through semiotics alone (Goux 1990: 128). This is digital money. Capitalism has replaced linguistic signs with code, "a circuit arrangement and cerebral operations with the electronic play of these circuits" (Goux 1990: 129). This system uses new forms of inscription, "an operational writing that manipulates mindless, desemanticized signs." The elements making up these circuits are not signifiers but merely "potential props for semantic attribution" (Goux 1990: 129–30). Monetary signs in the electronic age are no longer hieroglyphic and unfathomable but rather machinelike. They have lost their depth and interiority (Goux 1990: 132). However, Goux does not view this loss in negative terms: as a loss of meaning or crisis of value, for example. In electronic form, money is no longer a thing that *possesses* value. It is not even something that *represents* value. In digital form, money no longer operates like speech, but rather like writing. It is caught up in an indefinite network of traces, displacements, and deferrals, such that "the clearing of all accounts would never be possible or even thinkable" (Goux 1999: 120). This is the age of grammatology (the science of writing). In place of a stable substratum of meaning, there are only writings about writings, "an indefinite play of referrals that forever postpones the possibility of an actual value that would be anything more than writing" (Goux 1999: 120).[38]

---

38   Others, too, associate money and finance with writing. Marieke de Goede, for example, characterizes money as "a system of writing that is firmly rooted in cultural history" (Goede 2005: xxv).

42 CHAPTER 1

Goux describes digital money as the culmination of a process of evolution whereby the whole social organism is arranged "under the general equivalent" (Goux 1990: 41). But one wonders whether he went too far. Walter Benjamin memorably described banknotes as the ornamentation of the "façade-architecture of Hell" (*Fassadenarchitektur der Hölle*) and seemed fascinated by the satirical force of their solemn earnestness (Benjamin 1996e). To Benjamin, these banknotes were indexical,[39] like the dialectical images he sought to construct in *The Arcades Project* (1999). His description of banknotes came as part of what Agamben describes as his underlying theory of signatures (Agamben 2009: 72).[40] Goux's suggestion is that we have left this era behind. Yet money has not completely lost its material features, or its properties as an indexical image, or its signature. All forms of money, not only currency, retain important features (their own iconography, for example) that bind them to particular spaces, places, and relations of power. Even electronic monies, those very monies emphasized by Goux, have symbolic values projected onto them (Gilbert 2005: 378; see also Gilbert 1998). Moreover, the neat threefold distinction (between gold, paper, and digital currency) on which Goux's argument depends is equally open to question. Digital gold currencies such as Pecunix are a case in point. Explored in Neal Stephenson's novel, *Cryptonomicon* (Stephenson 1999), digital gold currency is hybrid: though it *represents* gold, its security is *protected* by code, i.e., digital cryptography. Dematerialization as Goux defines it has displaced money's underlying roots in time and space only up to a point, never completely; indeed, it has brought new forms of symbolic meaning into money's compass.

Perhaps there is a deeper issue here, an argument that concerns the status of writing and speech as much as it does the development of money. Goux's focus on writing resonates with Derrida's arguments about the tendency of Western thought to prioritize speech as a more immediate form of communication, as if spoken words were closer than written words to the truth of the world and to the commitment and ability of human beings to capture and express that truth. This emphasis on speech is analogous to the barter account of the evolution of money, which suggests that the primary mode of economic exchange that gave rise to money in the first place was the spot exchange, the act of barter between two individuals: immediate

---

39 The prospect of a "comparison between the images of saints in different religions and the bank notes of different states" intrigued him, for example.

40 Agamben refers to the mark on a coin as a signature which "transforms a piece of metal into a coin, producing it as money" (Agamben 2009: 40).

and situated in time, just like speech—and cash.[41] In this sense, Goux is making a broader case about the development of monetary forms whose circulation has no agency beyond that of the system, or machine. We return to this prospect in Chapter 5.

VIOLENCE

Money's connections with violence, most especially its use as a surrogate for violence, is a theme one often finds reflected in discussions of "currency wars" (Rickards 2011), and it is implied by research on the role of finance in the "war against terror" (de Goede 2012). But money's relationship with violence has a longer history, wherein practices such as counterfeiting have been strategically incorporated into more traditional military conflicts (Cooley 2008). By and large, however, mainstream theories of money posit violence as *extrinsic* to money, that is to say, as contrary to its "natural" mode of operation. For this reason, violence usually features only on the periphery of monetary scholarship, for example, as a by-product of gold's historic dependency on slavery (Bernstein 2004: 115). The idea that violence is *intrinsic* to money was first proposed in a systematic way by two French economists, Michel Aglietta and André Orléan in *La violence de la monnaie* (1984) and successive works dealing with the relationship between money and sovereignty (Aglietta and Orléan 1984, 1985, 1998). I discuss their work here because it rests on the claim that violence is interwoven with money's most elementary forms.

Aglietta and Orléan argue that money developed in conjunction with violence; indeed, violence is never far from the surface of its operation, even today. Their work draws particularly on René Girard's theory of mimesis and violence, *La Violence et le Sacré* (1972), which explores ancient mechanisms by which groups achieve a delicate stability, such as through the exercise of violence toward a single sacrificial victim. Girard's theory is premised

---

41   Material monies—digital monies present a distinctive set of problems, as the recent history of Bitcoin testifies—need to be "read" quickly, validated by a glance. But the technology needed to make such a reading infallible (raised print, watermarks, holograms) is increasingly costly and complex, and difficult to read by sight alone. Finance is read differently, with its history of charts and graphs (Preda 2009), although it may have caught up with money in some respects. Credit ratings, too, are instantly legible, although those attached to collateralized debt obligations turned out to be tainted and their very legibility became a source of contagion (Carruthers 2010). Even here, a narrative is attached to the rating, which is unraveled whenever the rating shifts, or when various ratings agencies offer different grades for a particular financial product.

on the notion of the "inauthentic" human being who has no natural desires but the compulsion simply to imitate others. It is when mimesis becomes excessive and descends into rivalry that violence can ensue: "Rivalry does not arise because of the fortuitous convergence of two desires on a single object; rather, the subject desires the object because the rival desires it" (Girard 1972: 145). It is by virtue of imitation that violence is contagious and therefore liable to spread throughout society "like a raging fire" (Girard 1972: 31). Only a central institution can prevent such a contagion. This is the primary function of *religion*, which "instructs men as to what they must and must not do to prevent a recurrence of destructive violence" (Girard 1972: 259). Mainly through religious elaboration, such mechanisms gradually assume a more benign form, so that violence is diverted, if never entirely denied (Girard 1972: 4). Religion, not social contract, is the foundation of society.

According to Aglietta and Orléan, money originates in those very ritual sacrifices that are underpinned by violence. Money owes its existence not to the utility-maximizing *homo economicus*, but rather the Girardian individual (*homo mimeticus*), who copes with radical uncertainty through imitation (Dumouchel and Dupuy 1978). As a symbol of an authority that originates beyond the market and that can nevertheless enforce marketplace rules, money diverts mimetic desire and deflects violent struggle by channeling rivalry into contract. Thus there are two facets of money: it expresses the violence inherent in all social relations; on the other hand, it legitimizes power as the basis of its generalized acceptance. This is money's regulatory function. Money therefore has "two souls—as a channel of social violence and vector of sovereignty" (Guttmann 2003: 210). Money pacifies because it occupies a position outside everyday production and consumption. However, though money is a conduit for deflecting social violence, violence always lingers around money, for example, in financial speculation. And it is because money only deflects violence, and can never eliminate it, that crises periodically arise. These crises are caused by the inability of the monetary system to absorb changes in the production and distribution of wealth. What appear to be technical problems in money's management (e.g., inflation) are eruptions of the rivalries and potential for violence that underpin money's very existence.

Aglietta and Orléan distinguish between two models of the monetary system. The *système fractionné* consists of multiple, competing monetary forms and financial intermediaries. It is a fragmented regime that favors debtors and is prone to bubbles. The *système homogène*, on the other hand, consists of a single form of money and one central bank; it favors creditors and is prone to panic runs. The contrast between these models reflects Aglietta and Orléan's view of money's conflicting dynamics, between its status as a private object of desire and its role as a social bond and homogenizer. This is the tension between *fractionnement* and centralization, two contradictory tendencies that must be reconciled in any viable monetary system. Money is not simply a special commodity, as Menger would have it. Nor is it merely a specific kind of payment, as Laum and others have suggested. Rather, it is a *lien social*, a *binding institution*, through which social relations of *interdependence* and *conflict* (e.g., buyer versus seller, worker versus manager, creditor versus debtor) are resolved. For this reason, violence is never far from the surface of monetary relations, and it is the role of authority, through regulation, to keep violence at bay. Confidence is key to this work: not simply in money's underlying value but in the entire money economy. Confidence depends partly on the central bank but also on our relations with each other. Mimesis is crucial to these relations, but to recall what Keynes said about animal spirits, trust in others can easily spill over into rivalry and violence. The relationship between confidence and violence is therefore dialectical, and this relationship endows money with a permanently ambivalent nature. It is an agent, simultaneously, of division (*fractionnement*) and of homogenization (centralization).

The work of Aglietta and Orléan makes interesting reading during an era in which currency wars have once again become a leading theme in international relations. In *La fin des devises clés* ("The end of key currencies"), published in 1986, Aglietta imagined a future in which there would be no leading currency (Aglietta 1986). Writing in the wake of the Bretton Woods collapse, Aglietta suggested that gold—specifically—had been the monetary analogue to religion.[42] In this sense, Nixon's decision to decouple the dollar from gold could be seen as an act of *desacralization*. Without a religious analogue such as gold, the global monetary system could not operate well because it is built on sovereignty, and therefore the threat of violence. Once gold loses its key role and money is desacralized, the central bank's independence is judged in terms of its distance from private interests (creditors and debtors). Stable money depends on the central bank, whose role is

---

42   Bretton Woods refers to the international monetary system that was established in 1944, wherein countries agreed to adopt monetary policies aimed to ensure that their currencies maintained fixed rates of exchange against the U.S. dollar, which was in turn "pegged" to gold. After a series of difficulties during the 1960s, the system finally broke down in 1973, when a system of "floating" exchange rates was adopted. President Nixon's decision to suspend the dollar's convertibility into gold in 1971—known as the "Nixon shock"—was a major step toward this breakdown.

to conceal the arbitrary nature of the monetary sign (Grahl 2000). According to Carlo Tognato, money retained its quasisacred character even after the demise of gold. Drawing on Durkheim and Bourdieu,[43] Tognato assigns to money a pivotal role "in the consolidation of national space and in the production and reproduction of citizens within it" (Tognato 2012: 136). To this end, central banks (and central bankers) have played a central role in the *"re*sacralization" of money: for example, by dramatizing monetary politics as a "morality play about collective identity" (Tognato 2012: 136).

Aglietta has recently extended his theory of money as a pacifier in his analysis of the crisis within the Eurozone. The single currency, he argues, is akin to the gold standard: an external currency, beyond the reach of national governments. The euro is therefore incomplete because it has no overarching sovereign that can act as a guarantor (Aglietta 2012: 23)—or pacifier. *Fractionnement* has overruled centralization since the Eurozone crisis began, amid violent upheavals that pitch citizen against state, and citizen against citizen, within countries that are deemed to be on the "periphery" of a union of states. The single currency continues to bind its member societies together, but mainly through common problems, such as excessive public and private debt, failing banks, and economic stagnation, that are a driving force behind intensifying geopolitical divisions that make its eventual balkanization seem inevitable. In a book written to celebrate the euro's "success story" that was published in 2008, Otmar Issing[44] drew attention to the benefits that integration brought to Europe that go beyond the economic: "It cannot be denied that the Community has also helped to secure the peace," he said (Issing 2008: 233). If the theory of Aglietta and Orléan has any merit, we would have to conclude that to crystallize that project around a single currency was a singularly destructive act.

CONCLUSION

Each of the accounts of the origins of money that I have discussed here can be said to be a progenitor of the major contemporary approaches to money that I shall be using later in the book (Figure 1). This is sometimes obvious: nobody need be surprised to find Laum's arguments about money and

---

43   It was Bourdieu who accused Hans Tietmeyer, then President of the Bundesbank, of perpetuating a "monetarist religion" (see Tognato 2012: 135).
44   Issing was a key figure in the euro's design and a founding member of the executive board of the European Central Bank.

tribute reflected in modern-day chartalism, where it is argued that money is properly a creature of the state. In other instances, the connections between a contemporary theory of money and the origins myths I have been discussing here are less obvious, and debatable. For example, how far might violence feature in theoretical accounts of money as a form of credit and debt? Is there an implicit theory of language—or a conception of money *as* language—in most forms of digital money? As a form of debt, does money necessarily have quasisacred underpinnings? If money's roots can be found in gift exchange, what might this imply for the notion that, to be valuable, money must be scarce? And how comfortable are the hip new users of Bitcoin with the connections—which I take to be almost self-evident—between the *Wunderkind* of the world of alternative money and the account of money's origins that is increasingly taken to be the most "mythical" of them all, i.e., that of Menger? But all of the theories described here operate, after a fashion, as myths in today's monetary debates, furnishing our discourse with a historical resonance, and a depth of perspective, that seems necessary whenever money's operation is at its most perplexing, and the question, "What is to be done?" seems to be most intractable. I have devoted a chapter to discussing these six accounts—organized around the themes of barter, tribute, quantification, *mana*, language, and violence—because they also play a powerful role in monetary scholarship. One seldom finds a book about money that does not discuss its origins or invoke them as a means of validating claims about its nature today or a means of justifying prescriptive judgments about what needs to be done. I have followed that practice here, not least by pointing out instances where contemporary debates about money's future appear to hinge on our assumptions about its most distant past.

FIGURE 1: ORIGIN MYTHS AND MONETARY THEORY

Barter (Menger)	→	Metalism [Chapters 2, 3, 8]
Tribute (Laum)	→	Chartalism [Chapters 3, 6]
Quantification (Simmel)	→	Cultural alienation [Chapters 4, 7]
Mana (Mauss)	→	Human economy [Chapters 5, 7, 8]
Language (de Saussure)	→	Digital money [Chapters 5, 6, 7, 8]
Violence (Aglietta & Orléan)	→	Social power [Chapters 2, 3, 5, 6]

By introducing not one theory of money's origins but six, I want to open a line of argument about monetary diversity that runs through each of the chapters that follow. Throughout the discussion in this chapter, I have been referring to money, and to myths about money, in the plural. Money is a remarkably diverse phenomenon—not just in theory, but in practice, too. But its variance is an opportunity, not an impediment. In this chapter, we have considered some richly contrasting ways of describing the origins of money. After discussing them all, I see no compelling reason (on empirical or theoretical grounds) to opt for just one. It is not imperative that we settle—finally—upon an overarching definition of money; indeed, doing so would be a mistake. What is needed, rather, is a framework in which money can be understood as a field of variation: not as one entity, but as several. This framework requires a very specific conception of what is entailed in a *theory* of money, and we return to this concept a number of times. The varying features of our monetary forms—their fungibility, trustworthiness, ease of use, level of anonymity, and so on—should be explored without implying that some are superior, others inferior.

Simmel suggested that money in its purest form is infinitely fungible: it can be exchanged with anything and everything. Money thus serves as a universal means of quantifying value. When conceived in this way, no empirical form of money is pure or complete: in practice, all have only a limited fungibility. Nevertheless, all monetary forms—large and small currencies, digital monies, bus tokens, Ithaca hours, and so on—can be classified as "money" according to Simmel's definition. At the same time, none of them are *equivalent* to money in its purest form. If not all dollars are equal, to paraphrase Zelizer (Zelizer 1997: 5), then no dollar is perfect. Simmel's concept of money provides an ideal basis on which to treat money as a generic category. For the time being, I propose that we treat money in exactly this way: as an *idea*. This idea of money presents the conceptual limit against which all of the myriad forms of money can be understood, however diverse they might be. As such, it provides the malleable surface on which the complex contours of the contemporary monetary landscape, and the complex history of monetary scholarship, can be mapped out. This will be my task in the chapters that follow.

2 CAPITAL

> This boundless drive for enrichment, this passionate chase after value, is common to the capitalist and the miser; but while the miser is merely a capitalist gone mad, the capitalist is a rational miser.
> **MARX, CAPITAL**[1]

At the Stop the War demonstration in Manchester, United Kingdom, on September 20, 2008, an elderly woman carried a homemade placard consisting of four sheets of printer paper taped onto cardboard. In block capitals drawn in black felt tip pen were the words, "If Karl Marx was alive he would say 'I told you so.'"[2] Five days earlier, financial services firm Lehman Brothers had filed for Chapter 11 bankruptcy protection in a case that remains the biggest in U.S. history. The firm held more than $600 billion in assets. The *Financial Times* headline warned of a "Day of Reckoning on Wall Street"; the *Telegraph* called it "Meltdown Monday"; and Hong Kong's *South China Morning Post* simply said, "Wall Street Crumbles." One month after the collapse of Lehman Brothers, *The Times* (London) carried a feature on Marx under the headline, "Did he get it all right?"[3] And as sales of *Capital* increased threefold, a quotation from the book, suggesting that Marx had shown prescience worthy of Nostradamus, went viral on the Internet. It read, "Owners of capital will stimulate the working class to buy more and more of expensive goods ... until their debt becomes unbearable. The unpaid debt will lead to bankruptcy of banks, which will have to be nationalized, and the State will have to take the road which will eventually lead to communism." The passage appeared on countless blogs, while *Politika* (the Serbian newspaper of record) published an article exploring its wider implications. Marx's prediction was also given a leading role in a best-selling

---

1   Marx 1982: 254.
2   See http://www.flickr.com/photos/binaryape/2873634346/.
3   *The Times* (London), October 21, 2008.

account of the subprime crisis, *The Storm*, whose author (Vince Cable) subsequently became (as Business Secretary) a member of the Coalition Government in the United Kingdom (Cable 2009: 8). The quotation was a fake.[4]

Marx's presence in this crisis has been compelling.[5] Had he really told us so, as the placard proclaimed? Did his arguments capture the underlying causes of the credit crunch? Could a theory of money based on his work—formulated in the nineteenth century—really help to explain the global imbalances that fueled the subprime crisis, as well as the various other crises (e.g., the crisis in the Eurozone) that followed? Three and a half years after the Lehman bankruptcy, the *Financial Times* ran a series of articles under the heading "Capitalism in Crisis." The first article picked out "greedy bankers, overpaid executives, anaemic growth, stubbornly high unemployment" as key factors driving the Occupy protests and causing "the wider public in the developed world to become disgruntled about capitalism," which is "widely perceived to be failing to deliver" (Plender 2012). Here, though, were shades of Keynes's critique of the "decadent international but individualistic capitalism" that emerged after the First World War (Keynes 1933). It was capitalism's failure to deliver, not its underlying rationale, that was being questioned. This was crisis Lite, cast in the image of Schumpeter and Minsky, not Marx. It is a spirit that had been encapsulated by the *Financial Times*'s editorial published just two weeks before. "Capitalism will endure, by changing," it said.[6] Capitalism is dead; long live capitalism.

In this chapter, I argue that Marx's theory of capitalism in crisis contains important insights for understanding the global financial crisis. Of course, he would not be able to say "I told you *precisely* so." His arguments about money and credit are diverse and uneven, containing several significant gaps in the context of the present day. Banks, for example, scarcely figure as major players in capitalism as he described it. Nevertheless, his theory does point to a fundamental contradiction in the nature of money, which is as relevant now as it was in his own time. By exploring this contradiction, we can open up the analytical space in which banking properly belongs in

---

4   Misquotes are difficult to track down on the Internet. One theory is that this one started on NewsMutiny, a U.S. satirical website, see http://www.newsmutiny.com/pages/Communist_Reeducation.html.

5   The crisis has motivated a number of books discussing Marx's contemporary relevance (Choonara 2009; Harman 2009; Sitton 2010; Eagleton 2012; Musto 2012). By contrast, in his impressive biography of Marx, Sperber insists that we should be thinking of him as a thinker rooted within the economic and political circumstances of the nineteenth century, whose response to those circumstances was if anything looking backward to the eighteenth century, not forward to the twenty-first (Sperber 2013).

6   Editorial, "Capitalism is dead; long live capitalism," *Financial Times*, December 27, 2011.

Marx's framework. In addition, we can bring to the fore the spatial and geopolitical dynamics that characterized the emergence of the state (and state money) as key elements of modern financial capitalism. These are the spaces that latter-day Marxists—from Hilferding and Lenin, through Luxemburg to Harvey—have explored so productively. Only a fool would suggest that Marx could have predicted, *in toto*, the finance-driven crises that punctuated capitalism's history throughout the later twentieth and early twenty-first centuries. But it would take purposeful myopia to deny the enduring relevance of his theory.

THE CONTRADICTIONS OF MONEY

Marx writes most extensively about money in his great works on political economy, *Capital* and *Grundrisse*, as well as in earlier texts such as *The Poverty of Philosophy*.[7] Throughout these writings, Marx conceptualizes money in terms of a tension between the *particular* and the *universal*. Capitalism assigns a universal status to money, which is analogous to the role assigned to the state by Hegel in *Philosophy of Right* (Hegel 1991). Money is the abstract representation of economic, societal, and moral value. On the other hand, money is a definite object, a form of private property whose universal properties are transformed into particular powers for anyone who possesses it. Every owner of money "carries his social power, as well as his bond with society, in his pocket" (Marx 2005a: 157). These two aspects of money correspond to its two key functions. As the universal representative of commodities, it is a *measure of value*. And as a particular commodity, it is a *medium of*

---

7   There are important differences between these texts, especially between *Grundrisse* (which was not disseminated until the 1960s) and *Capital*, most especially in the priority Marx gives to commodity as opposed to credit money. These questions are highly debatable, but the most important thing to bear in mind is that, for Marx, money takes on a specific form within capitalism; that is to say, it includes credit money as well as other instruments that work as monetary substitutes. More abstractly, in the later works on political economy, most notably *Capital*, Marx's theory of money begins with its primary functions. Money is a measure of value, medium of circulation, and store of value. De Brunhoff proposes a threefold division within Marx's theory of money, between measure of value (or standard of price), medium of circulation (currency and minted coins), and instrument of hoarding (gold) (de Brunhoff 1973: 48). This division corresponds to the "conventional" three functions of money (measure of value, medium of circulation, and store of value). Marx adds other functions too, such as *means of payment* (whereby money is an "ideal" means of purchase, or a promise to pay), and *money of account* (whereby transactions are recorded on a ledger as commodities circulate "on tick"). There is much variation and inconsistency across the different texts, although this problem does need not to preoccupy us here.

circulation. There is a fundamental contradiction between these two functions, which emerges whenever money's "third function" (as a *store of value*) comes into play.[8] This is when money is acquired for its own sake and hoarded; in other words, it is valued as a particular commodity, not as the universal representative of commodities. As Marx writes in *Capital*, volume 1,

> When the circulation of commodities first develops, there also develops the necessity and the passionate desire to hold fast to the product of the first metamorphosis [between the commodity form and the money form]. This product is the transformed shape of the commodity, or its gold-chrysalis. Commodities are thus sold not in order to buy commodities, but in order to replace their commodity-form by their money-form. Instead of being merely a way of mediating the metabolic process [*Stoffwechsel*], this change of form becomes an end in itself. The form of the commodity in which it is divested of content is prevented from functioning as its absolutely alienable form, or even as its merely transient money-form. The money is petrified into a hoard, and the seller of commodities becomes a hoarder of money (Marx 1982: 227–28).

Money can only resume its role as a self-expanding value by reentering circulation. Hence money contains a contradiction. It is both pure abstraction (or pure fantasy of wealth) and real wealth that, in order to be real, must be thrown back into circulation.[9] During a credit crisis (the dynamics of which I am about to describe), these contradictions are laid bare because the instruments used to supplement and even replace money as a medium of circulation—i.e., credit money—are no longer acceptable. The value of these replacements collapses: "I can really posit its being for myself only by giving it up as mere being for others. If I want to cling to it, it evaporates in my hand to become a mere phantom of real wealth" (Marx 2005a: 234).

Marx disagrees with two explanations of the origins of money we discussed in Chapter 1. He dismisses the argument that money originated as

---

8   To these three monetary functions—*measure of value*, *medium of circulation*, and *store of value*—Marx adds others, specifically, *means of deferred payment* (i.e., credit), *interest-bearing capital*, and *means of international payment* (world money). A specific crisis dynamics corresponds to each function. For example, as a medium of circulation, money may be involved in a liquidity crisis, whereas as a means of deferred payment, money can be the expression of a more serious insolvency crisis (Callinicos 2010: 82). In the early stages of the global financial crisis, during 2008, these two crises were often confused, and sometimes deliberately, as banks sought to convey an insolvency crisis as a more minor problem of cash flow.

9   "Its very entry into circulation must be a moment of its staying at home [*Beisichbleiben*], and its staying at home must be an entry into circulation" (Marx 2005a: 234).

the means for paying tribute to authorities such as the king or God. In *The Poverty of Philosophy* (originally published in 1847), he takes Proudhon to task for suggesting that money "is born of sovereign consecration." On the contrary, Marx argues, it is not the sovereign who forced gold to be money by fixing his seal upon it, but rather commerce that *forced* him to do so. "Gold and silver are acceptable by law only because they are acceptable in practice; and they are acceptable in practice because the present organization of production needs a universal medium of exchange" (Marx 2005b: 63). Marx also disagrees with the argument that money evolved simply through barter. Exchanges mediated by money (commodity–money–commodity, or C–M–C) are different in kind from those involving barter (commodity–commodity, or C–C); indeed, this difference explains money's function as a store of value and also explains the destabilizing effect of hoarding. In other words, money is not *only*, and not *primarily*, a medium of exchange. It is by virtue of fundamental differences between barter exchange and money that the acquisition of money (as opposed to any other commodity) can become an end in itself. Money's contradictions originate here.

The idea of acquiring money for its own sake gives rise to the first crucial move in Marx's argument: the presence of money in the economy creates a gap between purchase and sale. This is where he takes issue with what is known in economics as Say's law.[10] This is the idea that products are paid for with other products: money just mediates what would otherwise be an economy consisting of so many acts of barter. Marx dismisses this view as a "childish dogma" that misses the fact that commodities are frequently brought to market *to obtain money*, not other products. "The purpose of commerce is not consumption, directly, but the gaining of money, of exchange values" (Marx 2005a: 149; Lapavitsas 2003: 64–67). As Marx sees it, money does not simply make direct exchange more convenient. Rather, it splits exchange up into two distinct segments, sale and purchase (Marx 1982: 209). The difference is not trivial. The separation of purchase from sale makes it possible for money to be immobilized in between (Marx 1982: 227). This is Marx's second key move. The gap between purchase and sale means that money is not simply used as a medium of exchange; it can be hoarded, too. Hoarding is made possible when money appears to have "an

---

10   Named after the French economist, Jean-Baptiste Say (1767–1832). Say argued that producers are always anxious to sell their products as quickly as possible, and equally anxious to get rid of the monetary proceeds from such a sale because "the value of money is ... perishable." For this reason, money only ever performs a momentary function in a double exchange: "when the transaction is finally closed, it will always be found, that one kind of commodity has been exchanged for another" (Say 2001: 134).

independent existence outside circulation; it has stepped outside it" (Marx 2005a: 216).

Hoards have an important, but potentially damaging, function within the capitalist economy that Marx describes. Rising and falling according to prices and the velocity of money, hoards ought to act as conduits for the supply of money to (and withdrawal from) circulation. Ideally, the movement of money in and out of the hoard is such that the quantity of money in circulation always meets economic necessity (Marx 2009: 183; de Brunhoff 1973: 21). The capitalist is a "rational miser" (Marx 1982: 254). In principle, the very existence of a hoard should ensure that money "never overflows its banks" (Marx 1982: 232).[11] In practice, however, hoarding creates blockages in the circulation of money. This phenomenon takes us to the third crucial step in Marx's argument: hoarding creates the need for credit money, alongside token money, as an alternative means of *circulation*.[12] This happens to prevent the system from seizing up, and it is the basis for understanding where exactly money features in Marx's account of capitalism in crisis. Marx argues that hoarding and circulation are in constant tension, expressing a contradiction within money that has no middle term. The contradiction is revealed whenever an ever-lengthening chain of credit payments contracts, and "money suddenly and immediately changes over from its merely nominal shape, money of account, into hard cash" (Marx 1982: 236). Here, money shifts from being a universal representative of value to a particular value. It changes from being an abstraction with no material form—credit money—into something "real."

Before moving on to discuss this scenario, it is important to note that, for Marx, credit money springs from, but is not identical to, token money, i.e., everyday banknotes. Potentially, this difference is a source of confusion,

---

11   A crucial distinction here is between a *hoard*, which consists of money taken out of circulation altogether as treasure, and a *reserve*, which is money kept on call for when payments become due. In Volume 2 of *Capital*, Marx discusses hoarding in terms of a distinction between latent money-capital (building up a surplus for reinvestment) and a "money accumulation fund" that serves as "a reserve fund to cope with disturbances in the circuit" (Marx 1978: 165). This coping mechanism is now performed by public institutions, such as central banks (Harvey 2010a: 81).

12   There are hints of functionalist explanation in Marx's argument at this stage, particularly when he says that credit money "takes root spontaneously in the function of money as the means of payment" (Marx 1982: 224)—as if the *need* for credit money was enough, historically, to bring about its *emergence*. As Harvey notes, the credit monies Marx refers to originated as private bills of exchange that had two key advantages: their supply adjusted quickly to changes in commodity production (unlike ordinary money, credit notes disappear from circulation once they are paid off), and they helped to reduce transaction costs (Harvey 2006: 245–46).

especially when we read Marx's work in the present day context. Token money is *state fiat money*. In Marx's time, fiat money represented a material base, i.e., the state's gold reserves.[13] Banknotes, not just credit money, stand in for the "real" money that has been withdrawn from circulation by hoarding. Now, of course, there is nothing behind banknotes, no material source of value such as gold. For Marx, by contrast, banknotes worked like shadows cast before the "real" money (gold) and enabled the commodity to move from seller to buyer. A banknote is a nominal means of purchase with no intrinsic value. "Gold, unlike Peter Schlemihl, has not sold its shadow, but buys with its shadow," Marx says (Marx 2009: 151).[14] This notion seems outdated today, more than forty years after the gold standard collapsed. But it is important to understand that, for Marx, token money and credit money are not the same thing. What we are really interested in, moreover, is what he has to say about credit money, not banknotes.

CREDIT MONEY

Credit money consists of debt loaned by private banks. Because it circulates *as if* it were regular money, credit money circumvents obstacles to money's circulation, clearing blockages created by the need to keep money in reserve. But crucially for Marx, credit money also becomes an instrument of accumulation in its own right, a means of making money through forms of lending that do not depend on production. Marx's theory of credit is premised on the view that as individual firms get larger, they lack the money that is necessary to keep things moving on their own. They need credit. Financial capitalists (or banks), who specialize in mediating between productive capitalists with idle money balances and those who need those balances, meet this demand. For these financial capitalists, money has a highly specific character that resonates with global capitalism today. They do not simply hoard money as if it were treasure, but they put it to work as interest-bearing capital. This step takes us to the fourth key point in Marx's analysis: credit money creates the illusion that capital is self-expanding and leads to the formation of what he calls "fictitious" capital.

13 Gold, in turn, was the main constituent of international means of payment, or world money. When gold functions in this way, Marx said, money reverts to its "primitive" form (Marx 2009: 202).

14 Peter Schlemihl is the main character in Adelbert von Chamisso's novel, *Peter Schlemihls wundersame Geschichte* (1814) (von Chamisso 2008), who sells his shadow to the devil in exchange for an endless supply of gold. I come back to this text in Chapter 4.

Interest-bearing capital is capital par excellence because it seems to increase in value all by itself, as if it had occult properties. This idea might seem like an exaggeration, but the point Marx is trying to make is that interest-bearing capital seems to expand automatically: "it has acquired the occult quality of being able to add value to itself. It brings forth living offspring, or, at the least, lays golden eggs" (Marx 1982: 255). This impression is heightened, Marx suggests, the more distance there appears to be between profit and actual production. Banking does precisely this because profit appears to emanate not from production but from money itself, i.e., the act of lending it. The banking system is "the most artificial and elaborate product brought into existence by the capitalist mode of production" (Marx 1894: 742). The greater the number of steps between the production of real commodities and the making of profit, the more that profit seems to come on its own, without the need for labor or production. Money begets money in the "bewitched, distorted and upside-down world haunted by Monsieur le Capital and Madame la Terre, who are at the same time social characters and mere things" (Marx 1894: 969). This notion is money as mystification, and is the fountainhead of greed.[15]

Marx's theory of credit is extended in Volume 3 of *Capital*, where he conveys the dynamics of credit inflation as a bubble. Specifically, he shows how capital must simultaneously assume various forms in order for capital accumulation, the "M–C–M" cycle, to continue. It must assume the form of money, the form of commodities, the form of means of production, and (back again) the form of money. This is where credit money and the financial system come into play. Now that we have all the key players of a credit crisis arranged on the stage, we can move on to the fifth key step in Marx's analysis: the existence of fictitious capital makes it inevitable that capitalism goes through a repeat cycle of bubbles and crashes. Marx argues that speculative lending inevitably increases whenever financiers become more confident. By speculative lending, he means lending that has *no direct relationship*

---

15   In *The Economic and Philosophic Manuscripts of 1844*, Marx invokes the idea of money's magical self-expansion in his analysis of its ability, as the "almighty being," to transform its possessor: "I, in my character as an individual, am *lame*, but money furnishes me with twenty-four feet" (Marx 2007: 138). At the beginning of this passage, Marx cites *Faust*: "Six stallions, say, I can afford, Is not their strength my property? I tear along, a sporting lord. As if their legs belonged to me" (Marx 2007: 137). According to Hans Christoph Binswanger, *Faust* can be read as an "alchemical drama"—just as Jung once suggested it was—precisely through its monetary themes: "He explains the economy as an alchemical process: the quest for artificial gold. Out of this quest develops an addiction that ensnares forever the individual who has 'sold his soul.' Whoever fails to understand this alchemy... cannot grasp the gigantic dimension of the modern economy" (Binswanger 1994: 1).

to production. In its fictitious form, all capital "seems to double itself" because of the various forms the same capital or claim upon debt can take, and the various hands through which it goes.[16] A complex chain of claims and counterclaims can build, and the appearance of a solvent business with a smooth flow of returns persists even after we see that those returns are illusory.[17] When loans go into default, the chain of payment obligations fragments. The ensuing confusion leads to acute crises and to sudden and forcible depreciations, which can result in prolonged disruption of the process of reproduction, and thus to economic stagnation (Marx 1894: ch. 15). This pattern exacerbates capitalism's already-unstable nature, its tendencies toward the cyclical overstocking of markets, depreciation of commodities, and interruption of production. This step takes us to the sixth and final stage in Marx's argument: credit always contracts as soon as a speculative bubble gets too large, creating a sudden demand for real money, or hard cash.

Marx once remarked that though the monetary system is essentially a Catholic institution, the credit system is Protestant.[18] Credit, he explained, cannot detach itself from money, "any more than Protestantism has emancipated itself from the foundations of Catholicism" (Marx 1894: 727). Marx insists, too, that there is nothing the state can do to avoid a sudden contraction of credit. The contraction arises because of fundamental contradictions in money's form: between its status as the universal representative of commodities on one side and as a particular commodity on the other. It is the process of accumulation, and the associated demand for credit, that leads to crisis. By themselves, tight or sound monetary policies cannot prevent overproduction. Only in a hypothetical system in which production is organized in such a way that credit is rendered unnecessary could a credit crisis be avoided. But this system would be tantamount to returning to barter. Capitalism needs a credit system just as much as it requires money. And it is impossible to abolish either without abolishing the capitalist system itself.

So, to summarize, there are six important steps in Marx's account for money and credit in the form I have presented it here. First, the presence of money in the economy creates a gap between purchase and sale (this is the

---

16 As I discuss in Chapter 7, Polanyi also uses the term "fictitious" in relation to money. But whereas Marx defines fictitious capital as money that *lacks any material basis in production*, Polanyi refers to *all* money (alongside land and labor) as a fictitious commodity because it *cannot legitimately be bought and sold*: money is a generalized promise to pay that *belongs to society as a whole* (Polanyi 1957b: 76).

17 "Business is always thoroughly sound and the campaign in fullest swing, until the sudden intervention of the collapse" (Marx 1894: 534).

18 "Credit is founded on the belief in a 'predestined order' of self-expanding value, whereby individuals are mere personifications of self-expanding capital" (Marx 1894: 727).

critique of Say's law). Second, the gap between purchase and sale means that money can (and will) be hoarded, not just used as a medium of exchange. Third, hoarding creates the need for credit money, as well as for fiat money, as alternative means of circulation to real money (or hard cash). Fourth, credit money creates the illusion that capital is self-expanding and leads to the formation of fictitious capital. Fifth, the existence of fictitious capital makes the cycle of speculative bubbles and crashes an inevitable feature of capitalism. Sixth, a credit crunch always follows from the formation of a speculative bubble, creating a sudden demand for real money, or hard cash.

When reading through these steps, it is not difficult to see how one could imagine Marx saying, "I told you so." In the 2007–8 crisis, we saw a sudden credit depreciation trigger a flight from risk, whereby investors sought to offload financial instruments in a rush for the safe haven of money, or at the very least, the higher rated sovereign bonds, such as U.S. Treasury bills. Foreshadowing Hyman Minsky's theory of Ponzi finance (see Chapter 3), Marx portrays the monetary and credit system as a pyramid with the riskiest and most speculative instruments (fictitious capital) at the top, credit money in the middle, and "real" money (or hard cash) at the bottom. The crucial point is that this hierarchy grows more top heavy with each credit inflation, as increasingly confident (and reckless) financial capitalists lend money purely though speculation, not as capital for production. When the credit bubble (inevitably) bursts, the owners of fictitious capital dump it in large quantities in order to transfer their assets lower down the pyramid. Protestants revert to Catholicism. To Marx, this "sudden reversion from a credit system to a system of hard cash heaps theoretical fright on top of the practical panic" (Marx 2009: 198). The dismay is *theoretical* because it reveals contradictory aspects of money that were hitherto concealed. Money no longer enters circulation as a transient circulating medium but suddenly becomes the "final resting form" of the universal equivalent (Marx 2009: 197).

But the question is begged: what exactly *is* real money, or hard cash, to Marx? On one level, the answer is obvious: gold. "While gold circulates because it has value, paper has value because it circulates," he argued (Marx 2009: 160). On another level, however, the argument is more complex. Marx suggested that there was certainly nothing "natural" about the monetary status of gold. As he once remarked, "Nature does not produce money, any more than it produces a rate of exchange or a banker" (Marx 2005a: 239). The distinction between token (fiat) money and credit money is important here because it adds complexity. Token money represents the "real" value of the monetary base, which in Marx's time consisted of gold. Credit money consists of a debt that has to be repaid in some instrument other than itself. This gap must be closed during a monetary crisis. Nevertheless, many notable scholars have dismissed Marx's arguments as too narrow. Schumpeter accused him of a simple-minded metalism, and Keynes saw him as a naive follower of Ricardo, who had argued in favor of the convertibility of paper money into gold (de Brunhoff 1973: 35).[19] As we see in the next chapter, there is a school of thought (to which Keynes belonged) that suggests that *all* money is credit money, i.e., a form or token of debt. From this perspective, Marx's insistence upon the distinction between credit money and real money (or hard cash) looks like dogma. But we must not run away with ourselves. Before investigating theories of money that are outwardly opposed to that of Marx, we need to examine the work of thinkers who have tried to extend his account of money and credit in order to apply it to other circumstances later.

FINANCE CAPITAL

The period between Marx's death in 1883 and the First World War was one in which several of his most significant empirical predictions, e.g., about falling profit rates, were not borne out. For example, although poverty levels and unemployment rose relentlessly until the 1880s, in the 1890s profit rates recovered in Britain while the U.S. and German economies expanded. Moreover, there were positive reforms for workers around the turn of the century in Germany and subsequently in Britain, with a shorter working day and the establishment of pension schemes (Harman 2009: 88–89). Marx's image of capitalism as an economic system also looked increasingly out of date. The economy he described (particularly its "internal" market, to borrow Rosa Luxemburg's idea, which is discussed later), based mainly on his observations in England, was laissez-faire: with small firms, fierce competition, and small government. By the time of the First World War, the system in Europe and the United States was dominated by large firms that were increasingly monopolistic, and the banking system had grown considerably in size, so much so that capitalism appeared to be increasingly driven by finance, not industry (Grossman 2010). Finally, and most importantly, finance appeared

---

19   Keynes may have been thinking of Ricardo's views about fictitious capital, which Schumpeter describes in scathing terms: "Ricardo . . . kept on repeating again and again—almost unintelligently—that 'fictitious' capital cannot stimulate industry, that capital can only be created by saving and not by banking operations, and so on, without ever facing the issue squarely" (Schumpeter 1986: 693). Schumpeter's explanation for this was that Ricardo "had pinned his colours to the mast of a rigid quantity theory" (Schumpeter 1986: 693). Marx is sometimes accused of exactly the same thing (Ingham 2004b: 61–63).

increasingly to be operating in conjunction with the state. In short, capital was more *centralized*, *organized*, and *imperialist* than it had been in Marx's time. The nature of such changes, and their broad effect on Marxism, has been widely debated (Arrighi 2005a, 2005ba; Harvey 2005b; Callinicos 2009), and there is no need to rehearse the arguments in detail here. Our primary interest is in their implications for Marx's theory of money and credit. The most significant contributions toward revising Marxist theory in light of the changes just mentioned came from Hilferding and Lenin.

In *Finance Capital* (originally published in 1910, 2007 cited here), Hilferding sought to capture the transition from a competitive and pluralistic "liberal" capitalism toward a monopolistic form of capitalism in which finance had a crucial role. In particular, he focused on the merger, which he saw taking place in Germany, between banking capital and industrial capital. Hilferding suggested that the ultimate outcome of such a merger would be the formation of a general cartel through which capitalist production would be regulated, as by a "single body which could determine the volume of production in all the branches of industry" (Hilferding 2007: 304). Whereas this phenomenon would mean a decline of competition within capitalist societies, it would increase it internationally and thereby put states under pressure to come to the aid of capital: protectionism rather than laissez-faire would increasingly be the model, which in turn "leads directly to a more active colonial policy," contributing ultimately to the greater likelihood of war (Hilferding 2007: 325, 366). War, characterized in terms of competition between states, was therefore part of the internal logic of capitalism. This logic encouraged imperialism. Nothing quite like this argument can be found in Marx.

Other scholars, too, were discussing the relationship between finance capital, monopoly, and imperialism at around the same time as Hilferding. In *Imperialism* (1902), John Hobson argued that finance capital was more likely than industrial capital to be attracted to imperialism as a source of profit (Hobson 1902). In *Imperialism: The Highest Stage of Capitalism* (originally published in 1916, 1999 cited here), Lenin argued that once capitalism had reached the stage in which the world's natural resources had been captured by just a few "gigantic monopolistic associations," it would be the "territorial division of the world ... the struggle for colonies," and the "struggle for spheres of influence"—not the dynamics of the market—that determines capitalism's future direction (Lenin 1999). Finally, in *Imperialism and World Economy* (originally published in 1918, 2003 cited here), Bukharin argued that capitalism had been militarized: "the state ceases to be a simple protector of the process of exploitation and becomes a direct, capitalist collective exploiter" (Bukharin 2003). For Bukharin, the logic of this system was not simply connected to investing abroad but also to wresting control of industry and raw materials overseas.

Hilferding's arguments raised important questions about the development of capitalism and the capacity of Marx's basic theory to deal with it. Significantly, he suggested that a credit crisis was less likely in the early twentieth century, when capitalism was less pluralistic and anarchic, than it had been in Marx's own time.[20] According to Lenin, however, Hilferding made a fundamental mistake about the theory of money; indeed, his emphasis on finance went too far (Lenin 1999: 33). In particular, Hilferding lost sight of the crucial argument in Marx about the contradictions *within* money that lead to the growth of credit in the first place. As we have just seen, Marx argued that there is an underlying tension between money's status as both the *universal representative of value* and as a *particular form of value*. Hence a credit crisis inevitably feeds through to money. Hilferding, by contrast, treats money merely as an organ of finance. He therefore misses the argument about a *credit contraction* leading to a full-scale *monetary crisis*.[21] This is a powerful moment of singularity, when the dual sides of money—as the universal representative of value and as a particular commodity—collapse into one, and money becomes an instrument of hoarding (de Brunhoff 1973: 116). It is an important moment precisely because money cannot be represented in this form; there is no substitute for it, and circulation freezes. It is a brutal reappearance of what Marx calls the law of value.

The question is whether this reappearance really matters. Do we still need a concept of money that is distinct from finance? Is such a concept even *viable* after thirty years of financialization[22] in which an increasingly wide array of

20   The "mass psychoses which speculation generated at the beginning of the capitalist era... seem gone forever," he said (Hilferding 2007: 289–90, 294).
21   De Brunhoff characterizes Marx's approach as a monetary theory of credit (de Brunhoff 1973: 86–99). In these terms, Hilferding merely provides a financial theory of monetary phenomena.
22   Financialization has a specific meaning within Marxism. For Hilferding and Lenin, finance capital is a distinctive phase of capitalism, perhaps even its latest and highest phase. For Braudel and Arrighi, by contrast, finance capital—characterized as *financial expansion*—is part of a recurrent cycle of overaccumulation, defined by Arrighi's "long centuries" (Arrighi 2009), and a precursor to a series of geopolitical shifts in hegemonic capitalist power. Braudel calls the phases of financialization "signs of autumn" that signal the maturity of a particular hegemonic regime (Orhangazi 2008: 45). Arrighi, who builds on the analysis of Braudel, is sometimes criticized for failing to explain the mechanisms involved, both in terms of financial expansion itself (what form it takes, what its sources are) and the transition (what the processes are) (Orhangazi 2008: 48). Harvey draws on Arrighi's work when describing financialization as a spatiotemporal fix that redirects global capital flows (Orhangazi 2008: 51). More recently, the notion of financialization has been used to depict the growing dependence of individuals and corporations on the financial system, both its monetary resources and its logic.

instruments, some of them privately produced, have served as low-risk monetary substitutes? In this respect, Hilferding seems more in tune with present-day scholarship than Marx. Even within Marxism, few researchers now accept the distinction that Marx drew between money and finance (or "hard cash" and "credit money").[23] Scholars have come to see complex financial instruments such as derivatives, which Marx would define as fictitious capital, as *money*, and thus as beyond the reach of a theory in which money has to consist of a commodity such as gold. LiPuma and Lee, for example, argue that Marx's theory of money applies only to a "labour- and production-centred capitalism," which is a perspective that "sidesteps rather than confronts the growing autonomy and authority of financial circulation" (LiPuma and Lee 2004: 16). Likewise, Bryan and Rafferty suggest that although financial derivatives appear to be consistent with Marx's prediction that capitalism will produce increasingly abstract media of circulation, his theory of money was constrained by the gold standard, and thus by the belief that only gold can provide the universal equivalent form of value (Bryan and Rafferty 2007: 160–61). Such remarks beg the question as to whether even the *concept* of money is a viable proposition in today's system of financial capitalism—let alone Marx's version of the concept, which seems to equate "real" money only with gold.

There is a defense of Marx, however, that deserves to be aired because it involves shifting attention away from the material properties of money and onto the social conditions of its production and exchange. Marx, as much as any thinker, drew attention to the crucial importance of the social life of money to any understanding of its nature, and in particular, its role in the dynamics of capitalism. Remember what he actually said: Monsieur le Capital and Madame la Terre are *social characters* as well as *mere things*. Likewise with money: "Capital is the means of production as transformed into capital, these being no more capital in themselves than gold or silver are money" (Marx 1894: 953). Hence Marx's theory of money only makes sense if we take both parts of the formulation (*social characters, mere things*) together. When Marx wrote *Capital*, most forms of money, especially fiat money, were related to gold. But his account of money did not end there. For Marx, money is *not* a thing; rather, it is a *fetishized social relation*. Moreover, he argues that money is not just a single social relation but also a complex and contradictory *ensemble of social relations*.[24] Likewise with gold: Marx always sought to empha-

---

23   Harvey, discussed later, is the notable exception.
24   As cultural sociologists have subsequently shown, even prices are not objective or neutral but are rather embedded in complex systems of social classification and meaning (Wherry 2008; Alexander 2011).

size the *social, economic, and political conditions* that gave it its particular role as money in capitalist society: as both the representative of money as the universal equivalent, and as a particular commodity in its own right. This, then, is the basic *social* contradiction within money that underwrites Marx's argument. To grasp its full ramifications, we need to take a step backward to consider an aspect of his argument right at the end of the first volume of *Capital* that tends to be overlooked, particularly its implications for the theory of money. This aspect is the account of primitive accumulation.

PRIMITIVE ACCUMULATION

Marx defines primitive (originary: *ursprünglich*) accumulation as "the historical process of divorcing the producer from the means of production" (Marx 1982: 875). This divorcing is the process whereby producers lose ownership and control over the fruits of their labor. Harvey calls it "accumulation by dispossession" (Harvey 2005b: ch. 4). Historically, it has occurred in various ways: for example, through the seizure of land and the expulsion of the resident population. As Harvey notes, whatever form it takes, primitive accumulation invariably involves "appropriation and co-optation of pre-existing cultural and social achievements as well as confrontation and supersession" (Harvey 2005b: 146). Marx was not the first to discuss this idea. Adam Smith did so when trying to describe the accumulation of stock that necessitated the development of the division of labor (Perelman 2000: 25). Marx dismissed Smith's argument (with its references to beehives and anthills) as mythical, likening it to the doctrine of original sin.[25] Instead, Marx argues that the division of labor Smith sought to explain originated with the violent dispossession from small-scale producers of their means of production, leaving producers with no choice but to submit to the "freedom" of wage labor. This submission, Marx states, was the "pre-historic stage of capital" (Marx 1982: 875). He describes examples of primitive accumulation spanning several centuries, including the discovery of gold and silver in the Americas; the enslavement of America's indigenous population in mining; the conquest and plunder of India; and Africa's conversion into "a preserve for the commercial hunting of blackskins" (Marx 1982: 915). These, Marx said, characterized the dawn of capitalist production. They were the "chief

---

25   Marx parodies Smith thus: "In times long gone-by there were two sorts of people; one, the diligent, intelligent, and, above all, frugal elite; the other, lazy rascals, spending their substance, and more, in riotous living" (Marx 1982: 873).

moments of primitive accumulation," and they support Marx's view that conquest, enslavement, robbery, and murder were the "midwife" of capitalism itself (Marx 1982: 915–16). This is a broad and controversial topic. Our interest in it is motivated by what Marx says about the connections among primitive accumulation, money, and financial capitalism.

Marx argues that it was primitive accumulation that first endowed money with the "magical" power of capital, i.e., the ability to expand by itself. Through colonialism, primitive accumulation was a "forcing-house for the credit system" (Marx 1982: 919). This argument lies behind his memorable remark that capital comes into the world "dripping from head to toe, from every pore, with blood and dirt" (Marx 1982: 926). Marx's treatment of this idea is brief and underdeveloped, but what makes the argument interesting from a monetary perspective is his suggestion that the state was the crucial agent of capitalism's violent prehistory. The system of national debt, starting in Genoa and Venice in the Middle Ages, served as a powerful lever of primitive accumulation, transforming unproductive money into capital as with "the stroke of an enchanter's wand" by using "easily negotiable" public bonds to ensure that private creditors were never exposed to the troubles and risks that should have been associated with capital's application in such usury (Marx 1982: 919). Public debt, which Marx describes as the "alienation by sale" [*Veräusserung*] of the state, along with the tax system, thereby acted as the concentrated and organized forces of society, hastening "as in a hothouse" the transition from feudalism to capitalism (Marx 1982: 915–16). Treasures captured from the colonies by looting, enslavement, and murder flowed back into Europe to be transformed into capital (Marx 1982: 918). Finance capital originated here. The great banks were decorated with national titles, but in reality they were associations of private speculators, a modern bankocracy (Marx 1982: 919). Moreover, they were the agents and beneficiaries of economic violence.

Marx used the idea of primitive accumulation exclusively to describe capitalism's prehistory. In *Grundrisse*, he lambasts the "bourgeois economists" who subsequently portray this prehistory in terms of thrift and hard work: "These attempts at apologetics demonstrate a guilty conscience," he snorts (Marx 2005a: 460). But although he leaves us in no doubt that violence was central to the momentous changes that were responsible for capitalism's *birth*, it was not, so it seemed, part of capitalism's subsequent *life*. Scholars have subsequently contested this assumption, arguing that primitive accumulation is a feature of *mature* capitalism (particularly the relationship between the global North and South), not just the transition from feudalism (Amin 1974; Perelman 2000; Glassman 2006; Brass 2011). But it was Rosa

Luxemburg, in *The Accumulation of Capital* (originally published in 1913, cited here in 2003), who made one of the earliest and most significant attempts to rehabilitate the notion of primitive accumulation within Marx's general theory, using the idea to elaborate and extend his more general thesis about capitalism's contradictory nature. This rehabilitation matters to a Marxist interpretation of money and credit in the context of the present day.

Luxemburg identified two forms of accumulation in Marx's theory: primitive accumulation and accumulation via the commodity market. This distinction was between capitalism's external and internal markets, respectively. It is the external market (which depends on primitive accumulation) that Marx neglects.[26] This market is important because it provides capital with an outlet in the face of falling profit rates and overaccumulation while offering a quick-fix solution to the temporal contradiction whereby goods produced in one period cannot be consumed in the next. According to Luxemburg, the more that capitalism matures in any single country, the greater this contradiction becomes. For this reason, capitalism *must* expand outward and seize control of other, precapitalist societies. External parties are needed, specifically, "consumers other than the immediate agents of capitalist production" (Luxemburg 2003: 350). Other theorists have disguised the presence of such parties in forms such as unproductive consumption by feudal landowners (Malthus), militarism (Vorontsov), the liberal professions (Struve), and foreign trade (Sismondi, Nicolayon) (Luxemburg 2003: 350–51). Luxemburg's theory suggests that the logic underpinning what Marx had called primitive accumulation is an inherent feature of capitalism per se, not just its prehistory. Moreover, as we see in the discussion of Harvey later, the *temporal* contradiction she identifies in capitalism has profound consequences for its *spatial* transformation: expansion in geopolitical space is an intrinsic, not extrinsic, feature of capitalist accumulation (Harman 2009: 100). This feature is the enlarged reproduction of capital (Luxemburg 2003: 358).

These remarks have an important bearing on our discussion in this chapter for a number of reasons. First, Marx's initial assertion that *public* debt played an important role in endowing capital with magical powers of self-expansion is a crucial addition to the account of credit money and fictitious capital that we looked at just now. This connection, between the state and finance capital, was subsequently developed in the work of Hilferding and

---

26   Luxemburg defines this external market as "the non-capitalist social environment that absorbs the products of capitalism and supplies producer goods and labour power for capitalist production" (Luxemburg 2003: 366).

Lenin. Second, Marx's remarks on the significance of primitive accumulation for gold suggest that the hard cash that underwrites money in his theory is endowed with is own sociopolitical history: even "real" money is *not a mere thing*. Moreover, the state played a crucial role in that history—just as it continues doing so today.[27] Third, Marx's analysis of the role of the "modern bankocracy" opens up an analytical space in which finance can be understood in relation to a particular kind of accumulation, more akin to mercantilism and rent seeking than more conventional forms of capitalist production.[28] Financial derivatives did not exist in Marx's day. Nor did hedge funds or sovereign wealth funds. Nonetheless, his analysis of primitive accumulation provides a powerfully suggestive means of framing these forms of financial capitalism (McNally 2009; Ekman 2012). Although Marx's arguments soon became outdated empirically, in theoretical terms his analysis of money and finance, and especially the distinction between them, are as resonant today as they ever were. Nowhere is this resonance more evident than in the work of David Harvey, whose work I examine next.

WHEN CREDIT FAILS

Harvey has written extensively on money, through systematic presentations of Marx's theory (Harvey 2006, 2010a), as well as in works on urban geography (Harvey 1996, 2000, 2012), postmodernity and globalization (Harvey 1991), and most recently, the global financial crisis itself (Harvey 2010b). While explicating and refining Marx's core theoretical framework, he adds some key ideas of his own, most significantly the "spatial fix." His development of Marx's theory of accumulation draws on Luxemburg, and his analysis of money and credit relies on the work of Keynes and Minsky. Of greatest interest to us here is Harvey's attempt to produce a full-fledged Marxist theory of money and credit that can be applied to the present day, taking account of developing connections between finance and the state, the near-disappearance of gold from the world's monetary system, and the recent

[27] Finance has played a crucial role throughout the modern era in funding states' escalating military costs. Major central banks (e.g., the Bank of England in 1694 and the Banque de France in 1800) were established, as private institutions, for this reason, and this connection was key to the origins of modern money. From the beginning, modern money was created by monetizing sovereign debt. This step was the transformation of credit into currency—a form of state financing that, as Ingham argues, "conferred a distinct competitive advantage in the geopolitical struggles of the time" (Ingham 2004b: 129).

[28] Rent seeking refers to the practice of using assets to increase one's share of existing wealth without creating new wealth.

huge expansion of financial services as a major force in the dynamics of contemporary capitalism. In light of our discussion so far, Harvey's approach is particularly interesting because he draws out the theme of primitive accumulation in Marx and applies it to key aspects of financial capitalism, such as rent seeking and debt.

Harvey's analysis is underpinned by the crucial assumption that capitalism needs to sustain an average compound growth rate of around 3 percent in order for most capitalists to make a reasonable profit (Harvey 2010b: 27). Anything less is problematic, and zero or negative growth defines a depression. The problem for capital is to find a way to achieve such growth in perpetuity. This achievement is becoming increasingly difficult. The consequences for capitalism's geography, and for the development of the monetary and credit system, are profound. Inspired by Luxemburg, Harvey distinguishes between two forms of capital accumulation: through the exploitation of labor and via primitive accumulation (Harvey 2006: xvii). The second category plays an important role in his adaptation of Marxist theory to the particular conditions of late advanced financial capitalism.

Harvey integrates the analysis of money and credit within a general theory of commodity production, arguing that Marx's analysis of falling profit rates in Volume 3 of *Capital* fails to incorporate insights about circulation, especially money and hoarding, that he provides in Volume 2 (Harvey 2006: 157, 171, 188). Most Marxist theories of crisis tend to focus on single factors, such as the falling rate of profit, the profit squeeze, or underconsumption (Harvey 2006: xxxiii, 77). Harvey, by contrast, takes account of "the multiple ways in which crises can form in different historical and geographical situations" (Harvey 2010b: 117). These ways include monetary and financial problems, crises of labor, sector disproportionalities, natural limits, and unbalanced technology. His account of money is defined by a tension between *fixity* and *flow*. This tension is at the core of Marx's theory of capitalist crisis, whereby fixed capital periodically acts as a fetter on the flow of variable capital, or what Harvey calls *capital in its pure monetary form*. This notion points to broader tensions within capital, such as those between concentration and dispersal, that strain the organizational capacities of capitalism and fuel the demand for credit (Harvey 2006: 194, 442). For example, capitalist infrastructure (e.g., roads and canals) requires an investment over time that only credit can meet, as do major purchases on houses and white goods (such as stoves and refrigerators) and public goods (such as parks and walkways). This credit gets integrated into the circulation of interest-bearing capital, on the basis of which lenders expect a return. Hence, a secondary circuit of capital is formed, whose rhythm conforms to that of fixed capital.

Surplus capital tends to be thrown into this secondary circuit, as a solution, albeit only ever a chimerical one, to the problem of overaccumulation (which is discussed later). A capitalist crisis often reflects the differences between the two circuits (Harvey 2006: 236–38).

Against Luxemburg, Harvey suggests that accumulation by dispossession is not only an internal but also a *permanent* feature of financial capitalism. It is not simply something that happens when capital comes into contact with noncapitalist markets. For example, during the past two decades in the major "neoliberal" economies of the global North, the logic of primitive accumulation has been internalized via the systematic "theft" (mainly by financial institutions) of rights in relation to land, education, and pensions, asset stripping, as well as through taking a number of other common assets (including various natural resources) into private ownership (Harvey 2010b: 310). This taking defines financial capitalism, wherein the logic of primitive accumulation connects to later theories of imperialism and finance capital (Harvey 2006: xvii). According to Harvey, it is the role of the state in this process (accumulation by dispossession) that presents the greatest analytical challenge for Marxism. The basic ingredients of such an analysis can be found in Marx's own treatment of the centralization of capital, as joint stock companies and monopolies and cartels develop to curtail capital's anarchic qualities. Engels provides further insight, arguing that the state eventually becomes the official representative of capitalist society. This notion is subsequently elaborated by Hilferding and Lenin as finance capital, i.e., a unification of banking and productive capital (Harvey 2006: 137).

Primitive accumulation (or accumulation by dispossession) is an alternative to Keynesian demand management (Harvey 2010b: 108). The need for this alternative arises because of surplus capital, or overaccumulation. According to Harvey, there are several manifestations—or "forms of appearance"—of overaccumulation: a commodities glut, surplus inventories, idle productive capacity, unemployment, falling rates of return, and a surfeit of money or credit (Harvey 2006: 195). The problem can be addressed *temporally*, by channelling capital between short- and long-term uses (Harvey 2006: xxiv), and *spatially*, by absorbing the surplus in new markets (Harvey 2000: 33). If these fixes fail, a crisis of devaluation is likely to ensue, as in the 1970s, which not only resulted in chronic stagflation, but furthermore set in place the preconditions for neoliberalism as political, financial, and military barriers to foreign trade were dismantled, often by violent means (Harvey 2006: xxv). Further surpluses, built up during the 1980s and early 1990s, were absorbed by financial speculation, resulting in a series of devaluation crises: Mexico (1994), Indonesia (1997), Russia (1998), South Korea (1997), and Argentina (1999), each foreshadowing the global crisis that erupted in 2007–8 (Harvey 2006: xxvi–xxvii). Finally, global imbalances were integral to the supply of cheap credit that underpinned the subprime crisis.

Harvey's account of the credit system is fundamentally in line with that of Marx. The financial system contributes to crisis formation in three ways: it exacerbates tendencies toward disequilibrium because it helps accelerate technological change and competition; it fuels factional struggles within the bourgeoisie by giving money capitalists independent power; and it encourages fictitious capital and speculation (Harvey 2006: 286–88). Through expanding, credit money does not just express deeper problems in capitalist accumulation. Rather, it widens their reach and increases their intensity (Harvey 2006: 264). When credit instruments are used as means of accumulation in their own right, credit is extended ahead of the production of value through labor, which produces fictitious capital. Many forms of such capital, such as share certificates and government bonds, are illusory: mere titles of ownership that express a claim to future earnings, which circulate at prices that have little to do with *actual* accumulation. When their value is undermined through debasement and inflation, steps must then be taken to preserve the value of money. Harvey describes this as a return to the "eternal verities of the monetary base" (Harvey 2006: 254).

As Harvey points out, the monetary basis in contemporary capitalism no longer consists of gold, but rather a panoply of structures designed to sustain the concept of an international monetary standard. Harvey redefines core money as state fiat money backed by a hierarchy of international and national public and private institutions: "as the banks do for the individual capitalists, as the central bank does for the private banks, as a de facto 'world banker' does for national central banks" (Harvey 2006: 249). At the top of the hierarchy, the question of the value of world money is posed, but never satisfactorily answered: the fundamental contradiction that Marx identified within money is never resolved (Harvey 2006: 251).

Institutions at the top of the hierarchy are able to exercise only a particular, negative form of power. This is the power of financial repression, whereby forms of discipline (such as austerity) are imposed upon those lower down. What these institutions cannot automatically do, however, is restore money's underlying value. In order for this to happen, capital must find some way to "re-establish its footing in the world of socially necessary labour" (Harvey 2006: 293). In Marx's account, capital can do this either by reattaching itself to gold, or by renewing its connections with commodity production. In

Harvey's version, myriad intermediary measures are involved, incorporating central banks and money creation. But the essential problem remains the same: capital's value must be restored.

During the Bretton Woods era, central banking was premised on the idea of trying to match the quality of money to a measure of social labor, such as the productivity of the economy as a whole. Painful devaluation was frequently the outcome, mainly because *national* monies cannot be managed in isolation from *world* money. Alternatively, central banks could "print" money to counter devaluation and thereby transpose the problem into inflation. Marx did not consider this outcome, although it is theoretically consistent with his account of how a credit crisis rebounds onto the monetary base. In theoretical terms, this is the contradiction between capital in its *money form* and capital in its *commodity form* (Harvey 2006: 296). This contradiction expresses the underlying antagonism between the concept of money as a measure of the value of social labor and the notion of money as an instrument of financial engineering and credit. Both the demand and supply for money as capital as well are shaped by a configuration of conditions that virtually guarantees that interest rates remain unstable. These rates are determined by a struggle of interests between financiers and industrialists that is comparable to that between capital and labor. Given the complexities, equilibrium is unlikely to be achieved, other than by accident.

In extremis, these dynamics of a monetary and financial crisis may provoke a brutal class realignment through what Harvey calls the "socialization" of the devaluation of capital: prominent examples include Roosevelt's New Deal in the 1930s, and more recently of course, the "austerity" programs pursued by governments in the global North. Marx once remarked: "No social order is ever destroyed before all the productive forces for which it is sufficient have been developed" (Marx 2009). For Harvey, capital's centralization through the credit system is integral to this idea because a credit crisis (the devaluation of capital) invariably leads to the destruction of money (inflation) (Harvey 2006: 328). In these terms, the policy whereby governments (via central banks) seek to stimulate effective demand by keeping interest rates low (or, recently, through quantitative easing) amounts to replacing *privately created* fictitious capital (such as collateralized debt obligations) with *state-backed* capital (or money). This additional money can be reinvested in production (leading to wage increases), channeled into speculative finance (leading to the creation of even more fictitious capital), or pumped into consumption (creating further upward pressure on wages). Either way, a crisis may be eased but cannot be averted; indeed, its symptoms are likely to be worse. In other words, the burden of devaluation shifts from private capital onto money, as private problems (money's *particularism*) are transposed into public ones (money's *universalism*) (Harvey 2006: 310).

It is at the top of the hierarchy of monetary institutions that the fundamental question of money's value must always be defended. It is on this level, moreover, that capitalist crises take on an international dimension through money. After the collapse of Bretton Woods, states with floating exchange rates were competing to determine which of them bear the brunt of devaluation. Alternatively, in the aftermath of the 2007–8 banking crisis, periodic "currency wars" have ensued as states seek to boost export-led growth by devaluing their currencies. For Harvey, the increasing involvement of the state in the economy since Marx's time is not a refutation of his basic law of value. Rather, it provides evidence that such a law is moving toward a kind of perfection. Insofar as the state participates in the circulation of capital through demand management, it is periodically held to account by stronger states and international organizations such as the International Monetary Fund (IMF). Therefore states, especially through their role in monetary governance, are increasingly subject to forms of capitalist "discipline" (e.g., competition and bankruptcy)—just like corporations (Harvey 2006: 153). Every state is a borrower in its own right, and it is precisely here that deeper theoretical puzzles arise in Marx's approach. Modern states are subjected to dual monetary and financial imperatives. Arguably, these imperatives correspond to the original contradiction within money, between the measure of value and the medium of circulation, that Marx identified. They clash, sometimes violently, whenever states are disciplined, not just by other states and transnational institutions but also by private creditors. States face difficulties as debtors (and by extension, as monetary authorities) whenever their policies stray from prevailing views of prudent finance.

Harvey's interpretation of Marx demonstrates the social dynamics that emerge from the contradiction within money. Money is a universal representative of value: a collective measure of wealth. At the same time, it is a particular commodity and a form of value in its own right. In Harvey's terms, this is the tension between mobility and fixity. When the tension unravels, money's expression of what Marx called our bond with society is undermined. It is a social affair with private and particular consequences (Harvey 2006: 311). Once the limit of the state's capacity to manage the economy creatively is reached, the increasingly authoritarian use of state power (potentially, over both capital and labor) is likely (Harvey 2006: 328). Such, then, is the richness of Marx's theory, uncovering the deep and far-reaching social, political, and economic consequences of the fact that the question of money's value refuses to die.

BEHIND THE VEIL

For Marx, money's broader role in capitalism is to conceal its most basic contradictions by making their effects seem both *natural* and *just*. Money, it should be emphasized, is not actually responsible for those contradictions. Marx dismisses the argument that capitalism's problems could be resolved through money's reform or abolition, as advocated by Proudhon, for example (Proudhon 1927; Marx 1987), as misleading. It is nonetheless a major strength of Marx's theory that it seeks to penetrate behind the veil of apparently objective, quasitechnical aspects of money to uncover the social relations that underpin its circulation and accumulation. This is what Marx meant when he said that, through money, a person carries his social power, as well as his bond with society, in his pocket. Money is never a "thing," for Marx, but a complex amalgam of social, economic, and political relations. If those relations—or money's social life—disappear behind money's thinglike appearance, this disappearance is a consequence of commodity fetishism, of which money itself is the quintessential form. As we have already discussed, when the underlying value of money is put in question, the ramifications extend from the top to the bottom of the monetary hierarchy: from the institutions responsible for the governance of world money, to the workers, consumers, and pensioners whose very livelihoods are put at stake by the dynamics of inflation and deflation. Harvey cites Roosevelt's New Deal as one major example of these forces at work. Two more recent instances that I want to discuss here are the aftermath of the collapse of the Bretton Woods regime, which saw major struggles between capital and labor being waged against the background of a new international regime of floating exchange rates, and the ongoing crisis within the Eurozone, whose devastating effect across classes and generations is still being played out.

One of the classic analyses of the Bretton Woods crisis from the perspective of Marx's theory of money and credit was advanced by Christian Marazzi in his 1976 paper, "Money in the World Crisis" (Marazzi 1995). Marazzi, an economist, is one of several Marxist thinkers who explored the theoretical implications of post-Fordism (Marazzi 2008, 2010). During the 1970s, his work—together with other notable theorists of the Left such as Antonio Negri, Paolo Virno, and Franco Berardi—was associated with the Italian extraparliamentary movement, *Autonomia Operaia* (Lotringer and Marazzi 2008).[29] Their philosophy was informed by autonomism, i.e., the belief that

---

[29] *Autonomia Operaia* was a decentralized movement containing Marxist–Leninist, anarchist, and libertarian strains, all focused on the idea of worker autonomy.

society's wealth is the product of collective work that goes unaccounted for; consequently, few of its proceeds are redistributed to workers themselves.

Marazzi's argument hinges on Marx's original distinction between *money* and *credit*. He defines a credit crisis as a situation where credit circulates more rapidly than core money, pushing the cycle of production beyond the limits of its valorization (i.e., capital's capacity to expand in value) and realization. This situation brings to mind Harvey's account of a credit crisis, where credit money expands to the extent that it becomes impossible to convert back into hard cash, or the monetary base (Harvey 2006: 324–29). Likewise, Marazzi suggests that during the gold standard era cyclical crises occurred because of the disproportionate expansion of credit money, relative to gold. Each crisis of overproduction marked a violent reappearance of the law of value. He formulates the argument in terms of the "monetary consumption" of gold, whose value had barely risen throughout both the sterling and dollar eras. Gold reserves would never have been sufficient to keep up with a steady increase in the supply of token and credit money. Hence currencies have *never* been truly convertible, and gold has always been more or less *nominal*. According to Marazzi, the importance of credit expansion is first and foremost its effect on wages. The primary obstacle that credit enables capitalists to overcome (albeit ultimately without success) is a direct confrontation with workers. Indeed, he suggests that each successive phase in the history of capitalism has involved using ever-greater amounts of means of payment in meeting workers' demands. There is, in short, a structural connection among money, credit, and class politics, which in the first instance is expressed through wage costs.[30]

Marazzi deals with the issue of how to define the monetary base in the absence of gold by focusing on power. He suggests that sterling, and subsequently the dollar, had already displaced gold as the "money of all monies" long before the Bretton Woods system collapsed. Increasingly the international power of states, not gold, determined the value of all currencies.[31]

---

[30] There are some fascinating parallels between Marazzi's arguments during this period and the "political economy of inflation" that was emerging in Britain at around the same time through the work of Fred Hirsch, John Goldthorpe, and others. The idea of the "political economy of inflation" was launched at a conference held at the University of Warwick in Coventry, U.K., in 1977. Sadly, although perhaps inevitably, the organizers excluded both "a full blown Marxist analysis as well as a hard line or purist monetarism" because their participation would not have been "consistent with effective communication" (Hirsch and Goldthorpe 1978: 2). I am grateful to Jocelyn Pixley for pointing out this connection.

[31] Or to put it another way, the gold standard was an extension of specific "imperialist" policies as pursued, first by Britain, and then by the United States. Both countries stood to benefit from the international reserve status of their currencies. The United States, having

Credit was increasingly being created *ex nihilo*, no longer based on accumulated surplus value but on no existing value whatsoever. The demise of Bretton Woods made it impossible for money to maintain even the *appearance* of being detached from basic struggles over wages. Money and credit now had to take sides in social struggle because their underlying value increasingly depended not on a relationship with gold, however tenuous that relationship might have been, but—directly and explicitly—on their capacity to command labor. In other words, if the underlying value of money was to be sustained, workers would have to pay the price through lower wages. This arrangement, Marazzi argues, was the key problem that states increasingly faced after Bretton Woods. Money became the site of an explicit assertion of state power against the working class. Money lost its mystical appearance. Its apparent independence from politics, and its quality as a *thing*, were exposed as illusory. Money's social life, in all of its depth and complexity, came brutally to the fore.

Given that the Bretton Woods system was international in scope, the international ramifications of its collapse must also be understood. The demonetarization of gold had had a direct negative effect on Italy, France, and Portugal, whose reserves were dependent on the gold price, and upon the Soviet Union, which used gold to settle its accounts with the outside world. But the most pressing concern for states focused on the new regime of floating exchange rates. The inconvertible dollar became the basis for a new international regime of discipline in which monetary governance was intensely politicized. On one level, this was another era of finance capital. For Marazzi, however, the "unproductive" class no longer consisted of rentiers (who live off the rent paid by others), but workers. States' use of the credit system to boost economic recovery was becoming increasingly mired in struggles over wages and productivity.[32] The money being pumped into the economy for investment was being subverted into higher wages.[33] States were becoming lenders of last resort to the capitalist economy *in toto*, forced to run a debt economy to support industry and the public sector. In a narrow sense, this was old-style Keynesianism: deficit spending, purchase of treasury bonds, and provision of guarantees for banking loans to industry. But the partnership between man-

---

accumulated around two-thirds of the world's gold reserves by the late 1930s, steadily built up a large foreign debt, which had exceeded IMF limits by 1957–58. We come back to this issue in the next chapter.

32   This was a logic Marazzi describes as "simple circulation" because the money created to feed wage increases was merely fueling inflation and further wage demands, and so on.

33   Marazzi criticizes Hilferding for "hypostatizing" finance capital by focusing only on banks and the financial services industry and failing to explore the relationship between credit and labor.

agement and workers—on which postwar Keynesianism had relied—now ceased to function. As wage demands proliferated, money's command over labor, crucial to the very notion of stimulating effective demand, was undermined: the task of transforming money into *capital* gave way to the task of transforming money into *income*. Inflation could no longer be controlled through the conversion of money into capital, and thence into growth. Money was effectively blocked from becoming capital altogether.[34]

The fiscal crisis in New York in 1975–76 was paradigmatic, as well as symptomatic, of this new monetary and financial regime (see also Harvey 2005a: 116, 129). In a condition of U.S. fiscal bankruptcy, and with central government refusing to lend, the city authorities turned to the city unions and their accumulated pension funds to finance their own bonds. In the era of floating exchange rates, entire nation-states were set to assume the status of New York on the international stage, subjecting their citizens to a downward spiral of devaluation and forced austerity in order to stave off bankruptcy. Labor movements and parties on the Left were increasingly being co-opted into this "monetary terrorism," subjected to lawlike financial forces that remained hidden behind the veil of money's objective value—its (illusory) properties as a "thing." Marazzi described this terrorism as a deflationary attack on the working class, but he was also skeptical about the potential benefits for capital. As Marx had predicted, states were coming up against the contradictions, and therefore the limits, of the money form itself. By seeking solutions in austerity, a vicious circle was being reproduced that could only lead back to the same underlying contradictions and ultimately to a "permanent state of international emergency," in which multinational banks would play the leading role. This state of emergency was a breakdown in the capacity of the state to use money and credit to mediate class relations and thereby maintain its own power.

In his recent analyses of post-Fordism and cognitive capitalism, Marazzi has subsequently reconfigured Marx's distinction between the real economy (where material and immaterial goods are produced and sold) and the monetary–financial economy (where investment and speculation take place).

---

34   Marazzi writes, "Given these parallel pressures in the factory and in the social factory, the time of transformation of money into capital has become the time of the working class transformation of money into income … When money is blocked from becoming capital, it can only remain at the level of simple circulation; instead of becoming capital, it becomes 'funny money.' It is in this sense that inflation is no longer 'controllable,' a solution for capital which is no longer a solution, for it has become 'runaway inflation' imposed by working class struggle for income" (Marazzi 1995). In other words, money is not put to "productive" use but is used directly to maintain the social wage and to service growing municipal debts.

Cognitive capitalism (or the cognitive–cultural economy) refers to the New Economy: high-technology industry, business and financial services, personal services, the media, and e-cultural industries. Digital technologies have a key role to play, and as a result, cognitive (or cultural) labor is in high demand. In essence, this fact means that work increasingly consists of the exercise of linguistic, interpersonal emotional and intellectual skills, using "raw materials" that are by their nature intangible and difficult to quantify. Both the "real" and the "financial" dimensions of contemporary capitalism are now characterized by a reliance on intellectual labor (Marazzi 2008: 93–94). Whereas the monetary and financial problems that shaped the immediate post-Bretton Woods era were based on the contradictory relationship between the real and financial economies, i.e., the ability of money to recuperate itself as capital, financialization has spread across the entire business cycle (Marazzi 2010: 27–29, 49). The new economy is driven by excessive levels of financial activity (lending and speculation), with no brake or threshold within the real economy to slow things down. This situation is financial saturation. Moreover, whereas Harvey continues to see the state as key to reestablishing money's underlying value in the aftermath of credit crisis, Marazzi brings the argument he began with Bretton Woods to its logical conclusion: this is a *post-Keynesian* system in which the old internal and external solutions for restoring capital's value—effective demand management and colonialism, respectively—have been exhausted. As others, such as Colin Crouch, have suggested (Crouch 2009), financialization enacted a form of privatized Keynesianism, whereby individual demand was stimulated through debt. The subprime crisis showed just how far the poor needed to be drawn into the nexus of finance in order to feed this form of capitalism (Marazzi 2010: 40).[35]

These arguments reveal what is distinctive in Marazzi's work compared with that of Harvey. Marazzi's earlier interpretation of the failure of Keynesian demand management and the inflationary crises of the 1970s focuses on their implications for workers' struggles in the face of forced austerity. The increasing difficulties faced by central banks in influencing economic behavior (e.g., through interest rates) are indicative of a profound shift, whereby monetary policy has been turned into a dependent variable of financial markets. In particular, this is a crisis of U.S. monetary governance, the contours of which were defined after the Asian crisis when central banks in

---

[35] Class from the very outset shaped the subprime phenomenon. The working class and urban poor, particularly nonwhites, were disproportionately represented among subprime borrowers.

emerging market countries began accumulating foreign reserves of currency as a means of insulating themselves from contagion in any subsequent financial crisis (Marazzi 2010: 68). In an analysis that resonates with Hardt and Negri's work on empire (Hardt and Negri 2001, 2005, 2009), Marazzi describes this system as "headless": in particular, there is neither a *state* nor a political *subject* (Marazzi 2008: 86). Germane to this view, the mimetic character of financial panics is indicative of the uneasy alliance of individualism and collectivism that financial capitalism demands: "everyone returns to his own property and, simultaneously, he finds himself closer to the others because of effects of mimesis, because of the contagion and the reactions it provokes" (Marazzi 2008: 129).[36] In place of a rational subject, Marazzi substitutes Spinoza's idea of the multitude as the collective nonsubject that resides in the new economy. The multitude is an effigy of money, the very form of its sovereignty: "After having killed the god Pan, the multitude has to learn to protect itself from those momentary gods who, like little gremlins, haunt accidental events" (Marazzi 2008: 135). Like the new economy itself, the post-Fordist panic is characterized not by atomism and alienation but by its opposite, what Paolo Virno called "the magnetic adherence of the individual to the *general intellect*" (Marazzi 2008: 130). Financial panic is a mass escape to a formless world, a world in which the referentiality of language itself has broken down. We come back to these themes in Chapter 6.

Viewed from a present-day perspective, the comparison Marazzi once drew between the near-bankruptcy of New York in 1976 and the fate of the nation-state could hardly have been more prescient. Besides the recent repeat performance of California (Harvey 2012: 32), there is an even stronger resonance in the Eurozone crisis, where citizens in several nation-states—Greece, Ireland, Italy, Portugal, and Spain—have been caught up in a situation that bears close comparison with what Marazzi described as the condition of forced austerity that earlier confronted the residents of New York. What Marazzi described as a crisis of financial circulation in which the city of New York was reduced to a form of "pension fund socialism," has in Europe taken the form of a crisis in which pensioners—alongside welfare claimants and public sector workers—have been brutally exposed to a

---

36 Marazzi draws attention to the etymology of the word "panic," from *panikon deima*, *Panikos*, "of Pan," the god of woods and fields who was the source of mysterious sounds that caused groundless fear in herds and crowds. The violence of a financial crisis reflects not the irrationality of raw nature but rather our "fear of the inadequacy of the conventions and the institutional powers in knowing how to manage the changed social conditions of economic development" (Marazzi 2008: 130).

broader struggle between creditors and debtors that incorporates states (within and outside the Eurozone) and private financial institutions.

The Eurozone crisis needs to be set in the context of the global banking crisis that immediately preceded it, which, in turn, has its own prehistory of global payment imbalances that fueled the supply of cheap credit in the United States. These imbalances played themselves out within the Eurozone, both in relation to the insolvency problems faced by banks after 2007 and in relation to structural imbalances that had been building up between member states before that crisis even began.[37] But it is the role of *money* in the crisis that stands out in the context of the discussion in this chapter. The Bretton Woods breakdown led to a flexible exchange rate regime whose effect on labor was devastating as states tried to secure their currencies by forcing down wages. Within the Eurozone, by contrast, it is the *absence* of a flexible exchange rate regime that has compelled those states most seriously in deficit to embark on socially corrosive austerity programs. In a regime of floating exchange rates, economic imbalances can be redressed via exchange rates (i.e., a weaker currency should make exported goods cheaper abroad). In the Eurozone, no such option exists, leaving the "peripheral" states with two unedifying choices: withdraw from the system altogether or embark on a policy of internal devaluation, which (theoretically) forces labor costs down sufficiently to increase competitiveness. Internal devaluation (e.g., wage cuts, public spending cuts, or an engineered recession) is a poor substitute for exchange-rate devaluation. The social costs of internal devaluation are severe and disproportionate because the burden of adjustment is placed almost entirely on deficit countries (O'Rourke 2011).[38]

The Eurozone crisis is especially interesting in the light of Marx's theory of money for two key reasons. First, the fault line along which the crisis has unfolded, i.e., between the euro as a single currency and multiple regimes of national debt, corresponds to Marx's distinction between the monetary base and credit money. There is a crucial difference, however. Whereas the monetary base has been shared across the different member states, the buildup of credit (both public and private) has remained fragmented into national

---

37   While the problems faced by these states are often put down to fiscal policy, Lapavitsas argues that the "true cause is cumulative loss of competitiveness by peripheral countries as unit labour costs kept rising relative to the core" (Lapavitsas 2012).

38   The efficacy and justice of internal devaluation has been widely questioned, on both the political left and right. The United Kingdom's *Daily Telegraph* carried an op-ed on June 18, 2012, in which the policy was described as fascist: raising unemployment levels so high that "it breaks the back of the labour movement sufficiently to clear the way for drastic pay cuts" (Evans Pritchard 2012).

segments. This difference breaks up the social bond upon which money relies because it removes the individual state completely from its role as the guarantor of the monetary base after a credit contraction. This similarity makes the parallel with New York in 1975 so telling. Member states within the Eurozone—nations with their own elected governments—have been reduced to the status of municipal authorities. Second, there are striking parallels between the euro itself, as a single currency and monetary standard to which all member states must adhere, and gold standard regimes in the past. The specific parallel that most observers reach for is with the 1920s, when their defense of the value of their currencies against the standard gold price led a number of countries into prolonged recession. The key point, for Marx, is less the technical issue of gold versus paper, or a regime of fixed versus floating rates. Rather it is the existence of "real" social, political, and economic relations that any monetary regime seeks to conceal once it becomes the sole focus of attention (of policy as well as commentary and analysis).

The Eurozone crisis offers a further example of how deeply a financial crisis can cut into the structure of society and of how monetary policies designed to secure the objective value of a currency are deeply implicated in the reproduction and exacerbation of social inequality. Conventionally, Marxism would lead us to expect an economic crisis to begin in the sphere of production and spread into the sphere of circulation through a breakdown in the credit system. As we have discussed already in this chapter, however, Marx's theory can be adapted quite easily in order to grasp the dynamics of a credit crisis *sui generis*. In this sense, the euro crisis (like the banking crisis that immediately preceded it) can be seen as a crisis that *began* in the sphere of circulation: it is the direct outcome of financialization. But in addition, the crisis needs to be understood as part of the much broader phenomenon of financial expropriation that has resulted from the steady decline of social welfare since the breakdown of Bretton Woods. Just as public provision of goods and services was breaking down, the financial industry profited by simply providing such funds itself, through debt (Lapavitsas 2009: 8). This situation raises broader questions about debt (and its importance as an inherent feature of money) that I return to in the next chapter.

SEEING DOUBLE

So far in this chapter, we have discussed Marx mainly in conjunction with macroeconomic issues such as imperialism and the international monetary regime. But his understanding of money's contradictory nature can also be used on a smaller scale. Kojin Karatani has proposed a novel interpretation of Marx's theory that focuses on the prospects for building alternative, non-capitalist monetary forms. Karatani is a literary theorist, teaching Japanese literature at Yale and writing major studies of modern Japanese literature and writers such as Sōseki, and a philosopher who has engaged with the work of Wittgenstein, Derrida, and (in *Transcritique*, which we focus on here) Kant and Marx. Besides being notable for its unusual treatment of the contradiction Marx finds at the heart of the money form, Karatani's argument warrants discussion because Marx himself was generally skeptical about the prospects and value of monetary reform. In *Grundrisse*, for example, he doubts whether "the different civilized forms of money—metallic, paper, credit money, labour money (the last-named as the socialist form)—can accomplish what is demanded of them without suspending the very relation of production which is expressed in the category money." We may make piecemeal reforms to money, he says, and "one form may remedy evils against which another is powerless," but no single solution is capable of "overcoming the contradictions inherent in the money relation, and can instead only hope to reproduce these contradictions in one or another form" (Marx 2005a: 123). This is an argument we reconsider in Chapter 8.

Karatani's interpretation of Marx focuses on the arguments from Volume 1 of *Capital* about the temporal gap between production and exchange, or money to commodity (M–C), whereby surplus value is created through production (M–C) but only realized in the circulation process, or commodity to money (C–M). We discussed this argument in Marx earlier, in which he criticizes Say's law: M–C–M is a synthesis between two discrete stages, M–C and C–M, which is only achieved temporarily by the fatal leap (*salto mortale*) that takes place whenever a commodity is sold. For Karatani, these are *two distinctive value systems*, and it is from the difference between them that surplus value is realized (Karatani 2003: 239). The M–C/C–M separation also points to a logical difference between merchant and industrial capitalism: in the former, the two value systems are organized spatially, whereas in industrial capitalism, capital sustains itself by continuing to produce different value systems that are separated in time (Karatani 2003: 239). Although in practice, capital uses both M–C and C–M, the key point for Karatani is that the difference between them *must be concealed*. Capital has to discover and create this difference continuously by presenting its profits as part of a seamless flow, or M–C–M (Karatani 2003: 11).

Seeing surplus value through the gap between M–C and C–M generates what Karatani calls a *parallax view* of capitalism (see also Žižek 2004, 2009). The parallax (from *parallexis*, or alteration) refers to the way an object can change its position according to our line of sight. This, Karatani says, is what happens during a financial crisis, when the chronic dependence of the system on credit is exposed (Karatani 2003: 8). As we have already seen, the separation between these crucial moments (M–C and C–M) plays an important role in capitalist crisis formation. But for Karatani, the separation is important also because it enables us to *see double*: to grasp a dualism *within* money that is otherwise concealed. This dualism is not the historical origin of value, but rather its *arche*. That is to say, it is a "form whose traces remain in the already complete capitalist economy" (Karatani 2003: 158). For Karatani, the parallax view means seeing value creation in capitalism from the perspective of consumption as well as production. After Marx, Marxists tended to present the momentary synthesis of capital (M–C–M) as permanent, treating circulation as a unity. Even after the so-called "cultural turn," when consumption was given priority, Marxism merely constructed the same unity, but from the opposite direction—theorizing capital from the perspective of *exchange* as opposed to *production*.

Treating the M–C–M cycle as a unity means viewing production and consumption as logically equivalent and regarding money as a secondary or incidental feature of the circulation of commodities and capital. From this perspective, money would merely be superimposed onto a system of production and exchange that operates, to all intents and purposes, according to the logic of barter. This, to reiterate, was the central point of Marx's rejection of Say's law. As we have already discussed, it was by opening up a gap *between* production and sale that Marx sought to give money a distinctive role in capitalism and to explain the role of credit money. Karatani wants to exploit the very same gap, not simply to show how money is contradictory but also to argue that it can be meaningfully reformed. His analysis focuses on the second stage of the M–C–M cycle, C–M, when commodities are turned back into money. This is the moment when workers become consumers. It is an important moment not only logically (for reasons Marx explored) but sociologically, too: consumers are more "active" (and thus more threatening, potentially) because the realization of surplus value now depends on them (Karatani 2003: 20). Hence workers have a greater capacity for resisting capital's power as consumers, not as workers.[39] Crucially for our discussion here, their opportunity for doing so lies within the nature of

---

[39] Hence, there "should be a movement of workers qua consumers, and consumers qua workers. The movement has to be a transnational association of consumers/workers" (Karatani 2003: 295).

money. This part of the argument relies upon a particular reading of Marx through Kant.

Karatani's interpretation of the interconnections between Kant and Marx hinges on the idea, which he considers central to both, that our experience of the empirical world is mediated by symbolic forms. This mediation is made possible through the category of understanding in Kant and through the value form in Marx. According to Kant's critical philosophy, our experience of the world is derived from categories we use to synthesize a world of objects that we can regard as objective. In Marx, we fetishize (or reify) value as an inevitable outcome of production and exchange. For both thinkers, there is a crucial (and ultimately unbridgeable) gap between the world of appearance (*phenomenon*) and the world as it is (*noumenon*). For Karatani, it is within this space that critical reflection resides, and thus the possibility of change. Money also comes into play here. As the general equivalent, it, too, is sustained by appearance—Karatani calls it an illusion—which enables it to function as the dominant value form in capitalism. This equivalence is important because it suggests that money is neither a thing-in-itself ("real" value) nor simply a representation (merely the "appearance" of value). Rather, money is the form through which the capitalist economic order is organized (and, crucially, *synthesized*) according to principles that can be deemed both necessary and inevitable.[40] Money is where *form* and *idea* coalesce. In this context, the "idea" is underpinned by the logic of capital accumulation. More specifically, the idea Karatani refers to is *capital's self-expansion*: money begets money.

As Marx never tires of reminding us in Volume 1 of *Capital*, money is not just a veil covering the production and exchange of goods, nor only a simple denominator of values whose absence would make no fundamental difference to how surplus values are created. In a similar vein, Karatani makes two key arguments. First, money exists as an organizer (or synthesizer) of the system of commodities. In Kantian terms, it is the "transcendental apperception X" of human exchange. In Kant, the transcendental apperception X refers to the spontaneous "I think" that accompanies our representations through the synthesis of structure. The transcendental apperception is what makes experience possible, where the self and the world come together, the former as the observer-in-motion whose synthesizing activities give the world its coherence. But there is a second aspect to Kant's

---

40 "The stance to see [money] in relation to its materiality is what Marx called fetishism. After all, money as substance is an illusion, but more correctly, it is a transcendental illusion in the sense that it is hardly possible to discard it" (Karatani 2003: 6).

argument, which Karatani also brings to money. Just as the world as experienced by Kant's observer-in-motion is experienced as the *necessary* world, so it is with money, whose fetishization as a substance with real value supports the illusion that *capital is self-expanding*. We discussed this idea earlier in relation to fictitious capital. It is what Karatani calls the appearance of the "auto-multiplication of money" (Karatani 2003: 22).

Marx maintained that money is an expression of deeper contradictions within capitalism; hence, to advocate its abolition as a means of overthrowing the system would be just as illusory as the belief that money begets money, all by itself. Karatani agrees but argues that in any future postcapitalist society, money must take a radically distinctive form. It is necessary to supersede (*aufheben*) money, not abolish it. Karatani accepts that, realistically, money cannot be abolished, so he insists that the market economy cannot simply be overthrown or abandoned: "It would result in total loss." Marx's analysis of money in Volume 1 of *Capital* suggests—simultaneously— that "money should exist, money should not exist" (Karatani 2003: 22). Karatani turns once more to Kant to uncover something within Marx's analysis that is not an *exit* from the capitalist system, but rather a means of achieving an ethically sustainable form of life from *inside* it. This is consistent with the idea of *transcritique*, which he describes as a reflexive engagement between perspectives.[41] *Transcritique* has several interrelated meanings: it is a reflexive engagement between two thinkers (Kant and Marx) that nevertheless does not aim to achieve a synthetic position; it refers to the methodology used by each thinker, creating perspectives that resist such a synthesis, and it represents a more general series of engagements between cultures, communities, and perspectives (e.g., East–West, Kant–Marx, commodity–money, or word–idea). Through practicing *transcritique*, Karatani is playing distinctive critical systems off against one another without reducing one to the other or simply trying to unify them, as a "cross-reading." In some respects, this is exactly what he believes that Kant and Marx themselves were doing, the former working between rationalism and empiricism, the latter between

---

41 Karatani uses the Japanese term *cho-shutsu* to describe this reflexive engagement. *Cho-shutsu* is a compound of *ex-scendent*, which means both *exiting* and *transcending* (Karatani 2003: 308, n. 14). This concept is rather intriguing to use in this context because it usually refers to a process of enlightenment or spiritual enhancement that occurs to an individual—not a social or economic system—by virtue of a switch of perspective. Curiously, Karatani does not use the term *cho-shutsu* in the Japanese version of *Transcritique*, which was published one year after the English version of the text. Though the meaning of the concept is difficult to render in English, presumably it would have been clearer to Japanese readers. I am grateful to Yu Katsumata for his advice on this matter.

Ricardo (emphasizing *production*) and Samuel Bailey (emphasizing *circulation*) (Ricardo 1821; Bailey 1825).

To theorize an internal reconfiguration of capitalism, Karatani replaces the base–superstructure dichotomy in Marx with a tripartite arrangement among *capital*, *state*, and *nation*, corresponding to the Trinity of the French Revolution: *liberty*, *equality*, and *fraternity*. Each term describes a distinctive form of *exchange*. *Capital* creates human relations through money, the *state* operates through plunder and redistribution, and the *nation* is grounded in the principle of gift and return. *Money* binds each of the three exchange forms together, and this notion explains why it was pivotal in the formation of the modern nation-state. Karatani then introduces a fourth form, alongside capital, state, and nation. This form is *association*, which he describes as an ethico-economic form in which different elements of the other forms are conjoined. Within the ethico-economic association, we engage with others not as an instrumental means for achieving our own ends but for the sake of mutuality. Association is "a form of mutual aid, yet neither exclusive nor coercive like community" (Karatani 2003: 13).[42] Proudhon was the first to theorize association, but Kant's ethics already contained it. However, there is a similar notion in Marx: the idea of workers' cooperatives, in which Marx saw the possibility of communism (Karatani 2003: 17). "The Critique of the Gotha Programme" (based on an 1875 letter from Karl Marx) was not an argument against cooperatives per se but rather against their subsumption by the state (Marx 1996). Likewise, Karatani finds in Marx's critique of Proudhon not a critique of the aim of devising alternatives to the capitalist money-form, but rather of the *specific* idea of labor money.[43]

According to Karatani, there is a set of monetary arrangements capable of unifying the three forms of human exchange (market, state, and nation) and therefore of realizing *cho-shutsu*. He finds them in the idea of the local exchange trading scheme, or LETS. A LETS is an organization in which people trade services among themselves, usually paying a small member-

---

[42] There are echoes of Simmel in Karatani's treatment of the notion of association, particularly in relation to money, although Karatani does not cite him. In constructing his Kantian interpretation of the concept of society in "How is society possible?" (in Simmel 2009: 40–52), Simmel's key term is *Vergesellschaftung*, variously translated as socialization, association, or associative relationship. In the translation of Simmel's *Soziologie* published in 2009 (Simmel 2009), the term is sometimes rendered as "creating society," which resonates with Karatani's arguments even more.

[43] "Labour money would tacitly rely on the existing monetary economy; even if it tried to challenge the existing system, it would just be exchanged with the existing money for the difference in price with the market value. What it could do at best would be to neutralize money" (Karatani 2003: 22).

ship fee to cover administration costs. Michael Linton founded the first such scheme in Canada in 1982. The organization mains a directory of services both offered and required, thereby helping to bring members together for exchanges. Members pay each other with printed notes, logging each transaction, or by writing checks that are subsequently cleared. When a member's account balance gets too high or too low, they are obliged to spend or earn accordingly to bring it back into line. This is not a system of direct barter. The currency takes the form of a credit that is earned through one's own labor and can be spent with anyone who is a member of the scheme.[44] The idea of a LETS falls between mutual aid (where prices for services are not high and there is no interest on loans) and a conventional market (where exchanges can take place at a distance).

Crucially for the notion of *cho-shutsu*, the LETS currency is issued anew on every occasion that an exchange takes place. The system is organized so that the sum of gains and losses of everyone is zero (Karatani 2003: 23). What this means is that LETS participants cannot buy labor power and then try to sell the commodities produced by somebody else. There is no separate sphere (i.e., the consumer market) in which surplus value is realized. The distinction between labor and consumption is eroded. M–C and C–M are no longer differentiated; hence, there is no need to create an illusion of unity in money's circulation (M–C–M). As a consequence, there is no transcendental apperception X of human exchange. Money no longer has an independent existence; it does not transcend labor and consumption; ergo, it cannot be hoarded.[45] Marx insisted that the contradiction within money has no third term; it cannot be resolved without a more general transformation of capitalism. Karatani argues that through LETS, "the antinomy—money should exist and should not exist—is deemed solved" (Karatani 2003: 299). Money still plays the role of the general equivalent just as Marx theorized. But all that it does now is connect various goods and services. Money is no longer capable of being "an autonomous, autotelic drive" (Karatani 2003: 299).

---

44   Karatani describes a LETS as a "multifaceted system of settlement where participants have their own accounts, register the wealth and service that they can offer in the inventory, conduct exchanges freely, and then the results are recorded in their accounts" (Karatani 2003: 23).

45   In Chapter 8, we look at a different scheme for preventing hoarding, namely, the practice of *demurrage*, as conceived by Silvio Gesell (Gesell 2007). We also examine Fromm's neglected analysis of the "social psychology" of hoarding, to which he counterposes his own "humanistic" utopia (Fromm 1976).

Karatani likens LETS to anticancer cells, counteracting the most negative aspects of capitalism from both within and without, by using money as an agent of simultaneous destruction and renewal (Karatani 2003: 25). In cooperatives, commodities must be produced and brought to market, so inevitably, such schemes often falter when competing with full-scale capitalist enterprises. By contrast, "LETS could nurture the free, autonomous subjectivity of consumers-as-workers" (Karatani 2003: 24). A LETS resembles the association as imagined by Proudhon but without the flawed system of money he envisaged at its heart. LETS tokens are money, but not as we have come to understand it in capitalist market exchange. With LETS, it is not possible for money to become capital. There is no sense in accumulating it and no need to worry about inflation—not because it has been allowed to deteriorate with time but because it has to be created anew within each exchange: "The fetish of money would not occur here" (Karatani 2003: 299). Currency is formed entirely within the circulation process, exactly where the status of workers is fused with their role as consumers. The LETS scheme abolishes the gap in which money-as-capital resides. This is a zero-sum system of exchange. The difference that remains between production and consumption within a LETS exists purely in time. Time literally *is* money in this context. But it is not monetary *gain*. There is no *profit*. Thus, there can be no *capital*.

So are LETS tokens really money, or are they merely a glorified form of barter exchange, as some critics have suggested? Although there are many practical issues with LETS—indeed, the schemes have declined over the past decade or so—Karatani is surely justified in calling this money. LETS currencies are credits: promises to pay that hold value over time and circulate between people who may be strangers. There is no direct bartering: value earned working can be spent buying services. In Marx's terms, a LETS appears to work first and foremost as an accounting system. If there are tokens involved, they correspond to what Marx calls the nominal means of purchase, or means of payment. If no tokens circulate, they are monies of account, whereby money is a means of keeping track of exchanges, recording credits and debts in a collective ledger. Karatani himself draws attention to the fact that within a LETS, money is by its very nature multiple. There is no central issuer. Unlike state currency, LETS currencies are pluralistic. Moreover, there are no restrictions on the right to create money. Each participant can issue his or her own currency, merely by registering. "If one aspect of the sovereignty of the state exists in its right to issue the currency, one can say that LETS actually offers sovereignties to the multitudes, going far beyond the specious motto 'Sovereignty rests with the people'" (Karatani 2003: 299–300).

The contrast Karatani draws between singular state (or national) money, and multiple LETS currencies, appears intuitively to be sound, but on closer inspection is slightly confused. If the basis for describing a currency as singular or multiple is a question of who issues it, then state currencies, which are effectively created by commercial banks through their lending, are as multiple as any other form of money.[46] Thus to oppose the singular sovereignty of "the state" to the multiple sovereignty of "the people" as Karatani does is not completely justified. Now these are not matters that would necessarily interest Marx. His main question would be how local monies such as LETS fit in with the monetary system in general, or more specifically, with the process by which capital is accumulated. Actually, existing LETS are too varied to allow such generalization, and many schemes have a limited life span. But such questions are for a later chapter. In the final analysis, Karatani's use of Marx to theorize LETS is intriguing because of the subtlety of his grasp of Marx's core argument, and for the way that he combines that perspective with the critical philosophy of Kant and applies it to local monetary practices, not just large-scale monetary systems. This blend yields the most enigmatic part of Karatani's conclusion, and the crux of his interpretation of Marx: that money, ideally, both *should* and *should not* exist. It is a sentiment that we revisit a number of times in this book.

CONCLUSION

The contradiction Marx identifies between money in *stasis* and money in *motion* is revealed whenever money is withdrawn from circulation. Token money was developed as a solution to this problem, bridging the time gap in the circulation of commodities and making up the shortfall whenever money as a medium of circulation is in short supply. Credit money, as we have seen, "springs" from this. But for Marx, credit money is not money; or rather, it answers only one requirement of money. Hence the proliferation of monies in modern capitalism—commodities, paper, coins, and various forms of credit, derivatives, collateralized debt obligations, and so on—has been driven by the attempt to reconcile the desire for a quality store of value with the requirement for a frictionless medium of exchange. Periodically, *fixity* inevitably comes into conflict with *flow*.

There are two important points to be taken out of this discussion of Marx's theory of money and credit. The first point concerns the connection

---

46   I examine these questions in more detail in the next chapter.

between money and the real economy. Marx insists that though money does not act as the sole *cause* of capitalism's major contradictions, it does play a unique role in their *reproduction*, serving initially to neutralize and disguise them by appearing to operate independently, and subsequently to exacerbate them during periodic episodes of overaccumulation. One important consequence of this role is that it compels us to investigate how seemingly autonomous circuits of credit, i.e., financial flows that appear to have no connection with the production and exchange of real goods, can collapse back onto households, public sector workers, welfare claimants, pensioners, students, and various public institutions. Marazzi's analysis of the demonetization of gold after the Bretton Woods crisis was one example of this phenomenon that we discussed. The Eurozone crisis was another.

The second crucial point to take from this discussion concerns the role played by money as the primary conduit through which the effect of a credit crisis resonates through society as a whole. Money socializes not only risk but, through inflation as well as austerity, the very destruction of capital itself. Marx suggests that the initial effect of a credit crisis is felt during the scramble to turn private debts (finance) into the safe haven of money, or hard cash. Harvey takes the argument further, suggesting that in a system of fiat money, the ultimate consequence of this scramble is inflation, fueled by the efforts of monetary authorities to prevent the credit system from collapsing altogether (quantitative easing is the most recent example of this situation). In this way, private risks and obligations originating in finance are made public, or collectivized, through money. This process, as Harvey sees it, inevitably leads to the destruction of money's value. The question of money's value never dies. But in this latest crisis, we see a different scenario being played out, involving not inflation but rather a vicious cycle of debt, default, and *de*flation. This cycle, as I argue in the next chapter, is even more deadly than that of inflation. Through its unfolding, we see once more that money is a process that is inextricably social, inherently dynamic, complex, and contradictory, a process whose meaning is contested and unstable, and whose value chronically depends on economic relationships that are all too real. Insofar as the crisis has demonstrated exactly this point, Marx would indeed be in a powerful position to say, "I told you so."

3 DEBT

All money, properly so called, is an acknowledgement of debt.
JOHN RUSKIN, UNTO THIS LAST[1]

The moral economy of debt embraces everything from friendship, through neighborliness, to revenge. Debt is part of the very business of everyday life (Nietzsche 1996b: 45), like a balance sheet that enters into every human relationship and interaction. Historically, notions of debt have played an important role in many of society's religious, ethical, and moral belief systems and are crucial to their systems of justice and law. More recently, however, debt has come to be viewed more narrowly as a financial relationship. In such terms, excessive debt is often regarded as symptomatic of a damaged life, as a form of peonage and a source of shame.[2] In the advanced economies of the global North, large swaths of the population are mired in financial debt.[3] Since the 2007–8 banking crisis, levels of central government debt

---

1 Ruskin 1997: 185.
2 In a series of surveys conducted since 1987, between 80 and 85 percent of respondents have consistently expressed broad agreement with the statement, "I don't like the idea of being in debt" (source: British Market Research Bureau, see http://www.marketresearchworld.net/content/view/643/77/).
3 Household debt has been increasing, particularly up until the 2007 financial crisis, when it rose from 113 percent (in 2000) to 175 percent (in 2007) of GDP in Britain, and from 100 to 135 percent in the United States during the same period. In Iceland, total (public and private) debt rose from 289 percent of GDP in 2003 to 1189 percent by 2008. It doubled in Ireland, reaching 700 percent of GDP in 2008 (Roxburgh, Lund, et al. 2010: 20). Debt was increasing in the BRICS economies, too. Before the banking crisis, total debt was growing at an annual compound rate of 15 percent in China and Brazil, 16 percent in India, and 32 percent in Russia (Roxburgh, Lund, et al. 2010: 21). There are roughly 191 million credit cards in Brazil, or one per member of the population: the number of cards doubled between 2004 and 2007 alone (Source: Euromonitor International, see http://www.euromonitor.com/financial-cards-and-payments-in-brazil/report). In the most indebted countries, Americans now owe around $775 billion on 686 million credit cards, and Britons owe more than £55 billion on about 54.5 million cards (Source: Euromonitor International, see http://uk.creditcards.com/credit-card-news/uk-britain-credit-debit-card-statistics-international.php). Student loan debt in the United States

have also risen inexorably. For reasons I discuss below, the public debt burden has *increased* in the aftermath of the financial crisis, and as a direct consequence of it. More recently, the relationship between debt and state bankruptcy has become a focal point of intense academic and political controversy (Reinhart and Rogoff 2009; Herndon, Ash, et al. 2013).[4] However unrealistic it might be, the ideal of a debt-free existence is used to give political and moral legitimacy to austerity programs pursued by governments in Europe, both voluntarily (Germany and the United Kingdom) and as a condition of continuing membership of the Eurozone (Ireland, Greece, Italy, and Portugal).[5] In the United States, the entry of terms such as "debt ceiling" and "fiscal cliff" into the mainstream political lexicon reflects a deeper sense that debt has become a byword for living irresponsibly, both as individuals and societies.[6]

The idea that debt is morally corrupting is not new. Excessive debt has long been portrayed, alongside drinking and gambling, as a form of self

---

now totals around $1 trillion, at an average of $28,000 per student (Federal Reserve Bank of New York; Consumer Finance Protection Bureau, see "Too big to fail: Student debt hits a trillion," March 21, 2012, http://www.consumerfinance.gov/blog/too-big-to-fail-student-debt-hits-a-trillion/).

4   Since 2000, government debt has risen from just under 50 percent of GDP to around 100 percent in Britain, from 42 percent to 82 percent in the United States, 104 to 172 percent in Japan, and 39 to 56 percent in Germany. (Source: OECD, StatExtracts, http://www.oecd.org/statistics/). Within the Eurozone, France has about US$5.275 trillion of foreign debt, or 182 percent of GDP, Spain has US$2.29 trillion (167 percent of GDP), Italy has US$2.46 trillion (108 percent of GDP), and Greece has US$0.583 trillion (174 percent of GDP). (Source: Bank for International Settlements, IMF, World Bank, UN Population Division. See https://www.cia.gov/library/publications/the-world-factbook/fields/2079.html#42). The total public debt in the world's 20 largest economies is more than $36 trillion, equivalent on average to more than 80 percent of their GDP.

5   In both the Eurozone and in the United States, real economic growth has been declining steadily throughout the past half century, making the prospect of reducing the debt burden through economic expansion look increasingly remote. In the United States, real GDP growth has fallen from 49.4 percent in the 1960s to 17.3 percent in the 2000s; in Britain, the fall is between 33.9 and 19.7 percent; in Germany, from 53.5 to 8.4 percent (OECD) (see "Growth Problem," *The Economist*, December 17, 2012).

6   In attitude surveys in the United States, national debt frequently emerges as a major area of concern, as troubling for many people as a major geopolitical crisis. Gallup's annual World Affairs Survey, conducted among Americans in early February 2012, placed political tensions in Iran below the amount of foreign-held U.S. debt as matters about which respondents were "very concerned" (the figures were 57% and 73%, respectively) (see http://www.gallup.com/poll/153179/Americans-Fear-Impact-Foreign-Held-Debt-Economy.aspx). In a 2012 study conducted by the Pew Research Center, the size of the national debt was cited as the second biggest major threat to well-being (behind unemployment) in Britain, France, Germany, Spain, and the United States, and as the biggest threat in Greece (see http://www.pewglobal.org/files/2012/05/Pew-Global-Attitudes-Project-European-Crisis-Report-FINAL-FOR-PRINT-May-29-2012.pdf).

harm (Manning 2000), whereas freedom from debt is aligned with a principled and contented existence. "What can be added to the happiness of a man who is in health, out of debt, and has a clear conscience?" Adam Smith once asked (Smith 2007: 41). As Janet Roitman suggests, within the social sciences debt is usually viewed as "something contracted, exterior to a primary, original situation," and thus as "a perversion of deviation in human relations—an abnormal situation that needs to be rectified" (Roitman 2003: 212). In behavioral economics, researchers have suggested that consumers tend to display an aversion to debt, preferring to enjoy consumption without thinking about the need to pay for it in the future (Prelec and Loewenstein 1998). Other forms of debtor behavior, such as patterns of paying off credit card debt, strongly suggest that consumers typically want to be debt free (Amar, Ariely, et al. 2011; Besharat 2012).

In any era, indebtedness exacerbates the major fault lines of inequality within society: in terms of class, race, and gender, and across generations (Yarrow 2008). But more than this, debt is often used to justify those inequalities morally. Creditworthiness lends moral authority and is deeply implicated not only in how money is used but in its very organization as a social institution (Polillo 2011). When debt is portrayed as a moral relationship, an assumption of "guilt" is often placed upon the debtor. Just as Walter Benjamin once said that history tends to be written by and for its victors (Benjamin 2003b), so the power asymmetries that characterize the relationship between debtors and creditors tend to be viewed—morally—from the perspective of creditors, and debtors are exposed to what Bourdieu (1992) called symbolic violence.[7] As Marion Fourcade notes, "nowhere is the entanglement between social position, economic worth and moral worth more obvious than in the case of debt, where the economic standing and character of borrowers are simultaneously constituted as the precondition for the economic relationship and as its essential stake" (Fourcade 2013: 22). Debt underwrites hierarchy and moral order among nations as well as individuals, as if the "price of a country's sovereign debt (the interest rates its bonds command on these markets) appears as an objectified measure of some sort of underlying moral worth in the eyes of investors" (Fourcade 2013: 22). According to Wolfgang Streeck, this attitude has been especially pronounced during the Eurozone crisis, with Greece cast as the morally

---

7   Intriguingly, however, Bourdieu himself characterizes debt as a means through which *overt* violence is exercised—"through the overtly economic obligations imposed by the usurer"—whereas the "generous gift" gives rise to the moral obligations and emotional attachments he associates with *symbolic* violence (Bourdieu 1990: 126). What he does not mention, however, is the symbolic violence that is invariably carried out *toward* debtors.

dubious debtor: "The moral discourse on Greek public finances focuses on 'the Greek citizens' and their presumed duty to pay off debt taken up by their past governments, supposedly to enable their voters to enjoy an easy life on unearned income" (Streeck 2013: 18).

Such evaluations of creditors and debtors are by no means universal, however (Gregory 2012). A moral case is often made against creditors, too. Connections between debt and evil are found throughout literature, a coupling from which creditors frequently come off worse (Atwood 2008). Goethe, Marlowe, and Irving all cast creditors as devils in the form of Mephistopheles. As we saw in Chapter 1, it was not uncommon for Babylonian kings to cancel debts en masse to alleviate the terrible social consequences that could ensue from a crescendo of unpaid financial obligations. In the advanced capitalist countries, the debt burden is such that for the first time in more than fifty years, those now reaching adulthood face a more impoverished future than their parents and grandparents.[8] In the Eurozone and the United Kingdom, debt—and the politics of austerity that have surrounded it since the crisis—is linked to rising health problems and, in particular, suicide (Economou, Madianos, et al. 2011; Stuckler, Basu, et al. 2011; Barr, Taylor-Robinson, et al. 2012; Fountoulakis, Grammatikopoulos, et al. 2012; Stuckler and Basu 2013). In Italy, an organization called *Vedove Bianche*—"White Widows"—was established in 2012 to highlight what its members, describing themselves as debt widows, believe is incontrovertible evidence of the capacity of financial obligations to kill. It is as if, through financial excess, debt has been transformed into a social levy whose price is life itself.

The idea of debt as morally damaging raises far-reaching questions for the theory of money. The image of debt-*free* money that often emerges from these discussions sits uneasily with a raft of monetary theory that sees *all* money as a form of debt. Debt's status in relation to money is ambiguous. Debt is arguably what makes money social, defining its capacity to be what Simmel called a claim upon society. Or to express this in another way, it is debt's fundamental sociability that makes it possible for money to exist.[9] The debt relation within money is social in a different way than private debts between two parties (irrespective of whether those parties are individuals, firms, or states). This relation, as we shall see, gives rise to a number of puzzles about how money works as a form of "collectivized" debt. On the

---

[8] "Generations see fortunes reversed," *Financial Times*, March 16, 2012.
[9] Kiyotaki and Moore reverse the argument, arguing that money exists because people could not be trusted to pay off their personal debts (Kiyotaki and Moore 2002).

other hand, excessive levels of debt can be the cause (and consequence) of significant problems in the monetary system. Monetary theorists are deeply divided, however, on the question of what exactly these problems are. Any conception of money that takes full account of debt must pay heed to both sides of the argument: to money's *dependence* on debt and to debt's capacity to *destroy* money.

My aim in this chapter is to explore the argument that, as Ruskin once put it, *all* money is an acknowledgement of debt (Ruskin 1997: 185). This is a well-established and increasingly widely accepted viewpoint; indeed, it seems close to becoming the mainstream view in monetary theory. Ruskin can therefore be aligned with a host of eminent thinkers who subscribe to the "credit" theory of money.[10] Indeed, the argument goes back at least as far as Aristotle, who in *The Nicomachean Ethics* insisted that money is not natural but a creature of law or convention whose value is subject to alteration.[11] It is important to clarify what is meant by debt in this context in order to avoid conflating debt with various forms of contractual relation. Although using money often entails obligations—and the notion of money as a form of debt surely implies exactly this—money itself is not usually a contract between two self-interested parties (Markowits 2004), but rather a generalized promise to pay, which, as I argue here, often takes the form of a collectivized debt. This phenomenon is what Simmel meant when he described money as a claim upon society. As he describes it, money entails a relationship that each of us has "with the economic community that accepts the money" (Simmel 2004: 177). As Simmel sees it, the obligation in question here is assumed by the community toward the holder of money, whom he describes as a creditor.

Besides discussing these aspects of the theory of money, I have a more specific set of questions to ask about how the debts that money consists of are connected with the public and private debts referred to just now. Insofar as the global financial crisis emanated from the way in which debts have been accrued and handled (by states, banks, firms, and households), where exactly does *money* feature in this crisis? If debt is a major problem in contemporary society, and money itself is a *form* of debt, how can we deal with

---

10 These latter arguments are often reinforced by the assumption, pursued by chartalists in particular, that money's material properties are increasingly irrelevant to our understanding of its most essential features.

11 Although Aristotle is sometimes described as a metalist, for example, by Schumpeter (1986: 60), he presents equally strong arguments in favor of the view that money's value can be altered through *collective will*, *convention*, or *law*. Hence Gordon suggests that Aristotle stands at the head of both traditions (Gordon 1961, 1964).

the debt problem without first tackling money? Debt is a two-sided relationship, and as we shall see, there is an intriguing bifurcation within the contemporary literature, between European (largely Franco-German) scholars, who tend to view all money as a token of *debt* (derived from one's debts *to* society), and Anglo-American scholars, who regard all money as a form of *credit*, i.e., an obligation *from* society to the individual. So if money is a form of debt—a claim upon society, perhaps—*to* whom and *by* whom is this debt payable? Is debt-free money, and even a debt-free monetary system, a worthwhile goal or simply a theoretical error?

DEBT'S UNTOLD STORY

In his magisterial history of the subject, *Debt: The First 5000 Years* (2011), David Graeber begins by positing a fundamental distinction between old-style credit and interest-bearing credit. Debt is a fundamental feature of all human relations; it is foundational to most of the obligations that social life ordinarily involves. This is old-style credit: in English, for example, "thank you" derives from a phrasal verb meaning "I will remember what you did for me." The key question for understanding the relationship between debt and *money* is how such moral obligations turned into *interest-bearing debts*. "The inexorable nature of interest-bearing debt, and the alternately savage and calculating behaviour of those enslaved to it, are typical above all of dealings between strangers ... The great untold story of our current age is how these ancient credit systems were ultimately destroyed" (Graeber 2011: 326–27). Graeber's "untold story" is about the transformation of an *economy of credit* into an *economy of interest*.

Although precise historical shifts are never easy to pin down, Graeber's analysis of the initial breakdown of the economy of credit focuses on ancient civilization (around 2700 BC), when groups were large enough to conquer and enslave their neighbors. The practice of lending out at interest may have started when material goods that were housed within temples (this is where surplus commodities were often held) were loaned out by temple administrators to traveling merchants for trade. They were charged a fixed rate—interest—as a share of the profits. Graeber's analysis focuses on how this practice of lending out at interest spread. He suggests that to hold the debtors to their debt, the creditor would need collateral against the debt. This collateral existed in the form of the debtor's property, but if the debtor fell on such difficult times that all of their property would still not be able to pay off the interest, the only option left would be to offer themselves (or their families) in the form of debt peons, "forced into perpetual service in the lender's household" (Graeber 2011: 65). The transition made possible here was hugely important: it was a shift from only treating war captives as slaves to treating anyone—any debtor—as a potential slave. All people were now reducible to mere matter.

As we discussed in Chapter 1, debt forgiveness was common in ancient societies. Rulers were all too aware of the catastrophic consequences of excessive amounts of unpayable debt, as might happen after a bad harvest, for example: "the world plunged into chaos, with the farmers defecting to swell the ranks of nomadic pastoralists, and ultimately, if the breakdown continued, returning to overrun the cities and destroy the existing economic order entirely" (Graeber 2011: 217). Debt forgiveness probably started in Mesopotamia, but it was common throughout the ancient world: Babylonian kings made it part of their New Year festival. They framed the practice in terms of justice, citing the rationale, as Hammurabi did in 1761 BC, that "the strong may not oppress the weak" (Graeber 2011: 217). A different system was used in the Mediterranean civilizations of Greece and Rome. Here, limitations were placed on debt peonage. Instead, supposedly "free" peasants and their children were used as soldiers in conquering neighboring lands, with the war captives used as slaves in metal mines, whose proceeds were used to pay the soldiers. Graeber—adapting Ingham (Ingham 2004b: 99–100)—calls this method the "military-coinage-slavery complex" (Graeber 2011: 229). This complex led to the next crucial step in transforming debt from a *human* into a *financial* relationship. The state's role was crucial here, for example, when rulers required their subjects to pay taxes in the selfsame metal coins they issued to their soldiers. Competitive markets probably came into being this way, with subjects vying with one another to produce things of value to the soldiers. Hence "there is every reason to believe that slavery, with its unique ability to rip human beings from their contexts, to turn them into abstractions, played a key role in the rise of markets" (Graeber 2011: 165).

Graeber tells the complex history of swings between a monetary system dominated by *coinage*, and one underpinned by *debt*. He also conveys various attempts to challenge debt peonage morally. Modern religions were especially important in regulating and sometimes outlawing usury, although loopholes were invariably found to evade such restrictions. Modern money—national currency—stands apart from much of this, being neither debt in its earlier forms nor bullion. Here again, however, debt did play a crucial role, as bankers developed the practice of fractional reserve lending while keeping their bullion safely locked up in vaults. Banks' debt—their banknotes—would eventually become national currency or legal tender. And

96 CHAPTER 3

most importantly for Graeber, war was crucial to the development of these modern national currencies because all of the major central banks were established to finance rulers' military adventures. Hence, modern money originates in the waging of foreign wars, with the value of national currencies reinforced by the state's decree that the banknotes issued by private banks—now central banks—should be used as legal tender. Essentially, then, the modern monetary system is rooted in state violence.

Graeber describes the capitalist era in terms of a "gradual transformation of moral networks by the intrusion of the impersonal—and often vindictive—power of the state" (Graeber 2011: 332). The state was responsible for legalizing interest. Hitherto, the ban on usury had helped to protect debtors for the simple reason that (illegal) creditors were reluctant to draw attention by chasing defaulters. Paradoxically, legalizing usury criminalized debt, drawing more and more families into debt litigation. By the eighteenth century, credit in general came to be seen as morally tainted, bordering on criminality, whereas cash came to be seen as intrinsically moral (Graeber 2011: 332). This is a world in which money was thought to have originated in barter (see Chapter 1) and in which debt could be associated with evil. Nowhere is this logic clearer than in Adam Smith, whom Graeber paints as a utopian who "wants to imagine a world in which everyone used cash" (Graeber 2011: 335). The entire history of capitalism from 1825 to 1975—the era of gold—could be described as a prolonged attempt to realize Smith's utopia: to build a world of cash in which coins are produced in sufficient quantities for trade, wages are paid on time, and debt is a sin (Graeber 2011: 352).

Graeber's sweeping historical analysis—one can scarcely do it justice here—raises some compelling theoretical questions. The first takes us back to one of the themes we explored in Chapter 1, concerning the relationship between money and *violence*. According to Graeber, the role of violence in economic and monetary affairs is inscribed in the very logic of our economic common sense: the economic institutions we take for granted could not exist outside of the monopoly and systematic threat of violence that is maintained by the contemporary state. This view is not Aglietta's, however, as we discussed it in Chapter 1. Violence does not explain the origins of money per se, in Graeber's account, but rather the development of specific *forms* of money. If there is a fundamental connection between money and violence, it does not begin with debt but with *coinage*. Graeber's history is characterized by long-wave cycles between periods in which the predominant form of money consisted of coinage, and periods in which credit money held sway. There is a pattern: "credit systems tend to dominate in periods of relative social peace" (Graeber 2011: 213). By contrast, in periods characterized by widespread war and plunder, money has consisted largely of precious metal. Why? First, bullion is easier to steal. Second, coinage was invariably the best medium with which to pay soldiers. Third, metal does not require trust in the way that debt does. "A debt is, by definition, a record, as well as a relation of trust" (Graeber 2011: 213). Bullion is cash, unmarked bills, useful for soldiers who are after all a poor credit risk, and simplifying transactions when there is a threat of violence everywhere. Credit systems, by contrast, require a certain degree of peace and networks of trust.

The second theoretical issue arising from Graeber's analysis concerns the distinction between the *commercial* as opposed to the *human* economy and the specific relationship that money has to each. In the human economy, money acts as a social lubricant. It is variously used as a social currency: "to arrange marriages, establish the paternity of children, head off feuds, console mourners at funerals, seek forgiveness in the case of crimes, negotiate treaties, acquire followers—almost anything but trade" (Graeber 2011: 130). In such an economy, "each person is unique, and of incomparable value, because each is a unique nexus of relations with others" (Graeber 2011: 158). The commercial economy, by contrast, emerged when it became possible to treat human beings as comparable values capable of being exchanged, i.e., as fungible. Graeber cites the example of the "honour price" in medieval Ireland, using *cumal* (slave-girls) as units of account in order to extract a price for breaches of honor and dignity: "Every free person had his or her 'honour price': the price that one had to pay for an insult to the person's dignity" (Graeber 2011: 173). Honor, of course, means not just integrity, but something that must be defended, if necessary, with violence. Some of the earliest forms of money were used "as measures of honour and degradation" (Graeber 2011: 171). The moral crisis came later, when money began to be used commercially to buy things. It was only now that the idea that there is an equivalence between such things and human life (and honor) came under strain: "Money . . . passed from a measure of honour to a measure of everything that honour was not. To suggest that a man's honour could be bought with money became a terrible insult" (Graeber 2011: 188). The shift to a commercial economy was based on the idea that humans can be measured and traded. It takes violence to achieve this (Graeber 2011: 211). Equivalence requires violence because it is possible only if people are ripped out of context, "so much so that they can be treated as identical to something else" (Graeber 2011: 386). Slavery "dislodges people from the webs of mutual commitment," making it possible to subject them to debt (Graeber 2011: 163). It is the logical end point and most extreme form of human decontextualization. Hence our commercial economic system, unlike the human economy, is based on the "logic of slavery" (Graeber 2011: 211).

The third set of theoretical questions Graeber throws up is about the relationship between the "monetary/financial" and "real" dimensions of the economy. We have become accustomed to thinking of the monetary and financial apparatus of capitalism as peripheral to its "real" business, which consists of factories and industrial production. According to Graeber, however, the development of capitalism was driven less by the need to manufacture things than by the need to maintain the "gigantic financial apparatus of credit and debt" that had developed since the Middle Ages, often in connection with *military*, not commercial, activity. Given debt's increasing burden, and its criminalization, this system was built on forcing people into work. This, says Graeber, is the "secret scandal" of capitalism: from African slaves to Chinese "contract laborers" working on the U.S. railroad to Indian "coolies" building South African mines, "at no point has it been organized primarily around free labour" (Graeber 2011: 350). It would therefore be quite wrong to believe that capitalism is founded on free labor: this would be to treat the "millions of slaves and serfs and coolies and debt peons ... as temporary bumps along the road [or] a stage that industrializing nations had to pass through" (Graeber 2011: 351). Graeber's argument here recalls the discussion of primitive accumulation in Chapter 2, except that for him—unlike for Marx—this logic is absolutely central to capitalism. Moreover, as Graeber himself notes, viewing primitive accumulation through the lens of debt criminalization—as opposed to land enclosure, for example—tells a "less familiar side" of the story that Marx sought to capture (Graeber 2011: 447, n. 66).

The discussion of primitive accumulation in the last chapter suggested that modern money is underpinned by the *national* debt, and Graeber's analysis is broadly consistent with this idea. According to his schema, the latest regime of credit (as opposed to bullion) money began when the Bretton Woods system broke down. Nixon's decision to leave the gold standard in 1971 initiated a "new phase of financial history" that "nobody completely understands" (Graeber 2011: 362). The post–Bretton Woods era has attracted its fair share of myths and conspiracy theories: specifically about gold, banks, and free markets. But of crucial importance to Graeber's analysis is that, quite unlike previous credit money regimes, the post-1971 period has been far from peaceful. The foundations of trust that credit money has hitherto relied upon have been replaced by an asymmetrical regime in which one country (the United States) enjoys a unique status. At the heart of this system is the dollar, which has been acting as the world's reserve currency since World War II. Even before Nixon abandoned the dollar–gold peg in 1971, the international monetary system rested on U.S. debt. The phrase "exorbitant privilege" was used by Valéry Giscard d'Estaing to describe the position of the United States under the gold standard, denoting the advantages that accrue to any country when others are bound (or merely inclined) to use its currency for their international trade. It was when its debt became too large to sustain the dollar's parity against gold, a consequence of costs incurred during the Vietnam War, that Nixon abandoned gold. But herein lies the paradox. The demise of Bretton Woods initiated a new phase of financial history in which U.S. debt has played an even *greater* role. The system allows the United States a unique status as the "risk-free" borrower, and at levels that would be unsustainable for any other nation.

Instead of a gold standard, the post–Bretton Woods system has relied on a "Treasury bill standard" whereby central banks no longer cash in their dollar inflows for gold but rather Treasury bills at rates of interest that are near zero. These flows have been fuelled by a U.S. balance of payment deficit that has been growing more or less constantly. This is the so-called "risk-free" rate, although it looks increasingly like an accounting fiction: the corresponding debt is perpetually rolled over. But the unique privilege that the United States appears to enjoy as a debtor cannot be explained by economics alone. It is underpinned by a political logic and reinforced by a military power:

> The essence of U.S. military predominance in the world is, ultimately, the fact that it can, at will, drop bombs, with only a few hours' notice, at absolutely any point on the surface of the planet. No government has ever had anything remotely like this sort of capability. In fact, a case could well be made that it is this very power that holds the entire world monetary system, organized around the dollar, together (Graeber 2011: 365–66).

In Graeber's terms, this latest era of credit money is therefore unusual. It relies on violence. We have not seen a return to trust and honor in economic relations after the gold standard. During credit money eras, history leads us to expect "the creation of some sort of overarching institutions, global in scale, to protect debtors" (Graeber 2011: 368). Precisely the opposite has happened. Global institutions such as the International Monetary Fund (IMF), the United Nations, and the World Trade Organization all "operate on the principle that (unless one is the United States Treasury) 'one has to pay one's debts'" (Graeber 2011: 368).

This situation takes us to the fourth and final series of theoretical questions generated by Graeber's study, which concerns the relationship between *debt* and *money*. Even if we can agree that *all money is debt* (of one kind or another), Graeber's own historical argument makes it clear that *not all debts are money*. Where should we draw the line? Graeber's account introduces state violence as the key historical factor underpinning the transformation of certain kinds of debt into money. (He also—rightly—complicates things by distinguishing between credit money and bullion money and by connecting the latter to state violence.) This is the greatest point of contrast between his position, which is fundamentally anarchist, and classical Marxism. His core thesis is that by focusing on debt rather than conventional categories such as feudalism and capitalism, we can grasp the crucial importance of violence, war, and slavery in shaping the basic institutions of what we now call the economy—and money, in particular. But what *is* a debt anyway? For Graeber, financial debt is a perversion of a promise: from a favor owed to a debt enforced by law, from something that cannot be calculated into something that can, and from something that has no equivalent to something that does. In these terms, "just as no one has the right to tell us our true value, no one has the right to tell us what we truly owe" (Graeber 2011: 391). To criminalize debt is therefore tantamount to "the criminalization of the very basis of human society" (Graeber 2011: 334).

Graeber's analysis therefore ends where we always suspected it might, with a call for a debt jubilee: "Nothing would be more important than to wipe the slate clean for everyone, mark a break with our accustomed morality, and start again" (Graeber 2011: 391). In *The Democracy Project* (2013), he argues that debt forgiveness should be part of a broader revolution in common sense:[12] "money is really just a human product, a set of promises, that by its nature can always be renegotiated" (Graeber 2013). This definition begs the question: a set of promises *to whom*? Morally, Graeber's argument is that for all the financial reforms we have discussed since the latest crisis, the underlying principle that all debt *must* be repaid has never been properly discussed, although the way that the subprime crisis was handled (through bailouts, for example) suggested that only *some* debtors have to honor their debts. But it is in conceptual terms that this argument warrants

---

12 Although Graeber is vague about the details of such a proposal, he argues that the "ridiculous" demand to provide a detailed program of proposals is merely a hangover from defunct Enlightenment ideas that social change can be managed from above. Challenging conventional wisdom—e.g., that debts must always be repaid—does not place one under the obligation to provide a detailed blueprint of a utopia (Graeber 2013: 282–83).

further discussion. Graeber's argument that money is a human product suggests that it is a set of promises to ourselves.

Graeber is adamant, however, that it is wrong to imagine that our monetary promises are made to, and can be renegotiated with, something called "society." There is no natural unit of human association that corresponds to a fixed or stable notion of society: "What is 'society' for me? Is it the city where I grew up, the society of international merchants (with its own elaborate codes of conduct) within which I conduct my daily affairs, other speakers of Armenian, Christendom (or maybe just Orthodox Christendom), or the inhabitants of the Mongol empire itself, which stretched from the Mediterranean to Korea?" (Graeber 2011: 66). According to Graeber, the idea that money corresponds to an obligation we have to a "society" is a variant of the notion that each of us is born with a primordial debt to *God*. This is the territory inhabited by Durkheim, who viewed religion as a projection of society (Graeber 2011: 70). In the long run, primordial debt theory is merely a species of the argument that each of us is born with a debt to the *state* or *nation*. And once the question is asked, "Who exactly has a right to speak for the cosmos, or humanity, to tell us how that debt must be repaid?" (Graeber 2011: 68), the notion of money as societal debt becomes difficult to separate from specific claims about money's relationship to certain authority, power, and—ultimately—violence.

> The problem is that for several hundred years now, it has simply been assumed that the guardian of that debt we owe for all of this, the legitimate representatives of that amorphous social totality that has allowed us to become individuals, must necessarily be the state. Almost all socialist or socialistic regimes end up appealing to some version of this argument (Graeber 2011: 71).

Graeber's alternative is to see debt in terms of a relationship among three moral principles on which all human economic relations are founded: *mutuality*, *exchange*, and *hierarchy* (Graeber 2011: 103). Mutuality describes the fundamentally moral basis not simply of all economic life but of all *social* life ("We are all communists with our closest friends"); it consists of shared expectations and responsibilities. It is quite unlike exchange, which is an interaction involving self-interest, and even more unlike hierarchy, in which no equality is involved but merely variations on a continuum that runs from charity to theft. These three modalities do not describe distinct and discrete societies, but rather "moral principles that always coexist everywhere" (Graeber 2011: 113). Debt is an exchange that has not been brought to completion. It is what happens when two parties cannot walk away from exchange. The debt relation is necessarily hierarchical, but it exists "in the shadow of eventual equality" because the debt is eventually repaid (Graeber 2011: 122). The theory and history of debt, Graeber argues, is about everything that happens in between the moment when this debt relation begins and the moment when it ends. Money belongs here.

This notion, for me, is in conceptual terms the most interestingly problematic feature of Graeber's position, and it poses far-reaching questions for the sociological theory of money. If *society* is nothing more than a stand-in for *power*, the idea of money as a debt to ourselves (rather than as a claim upon society) becomes difficult to pin down. Conceptually, the link that Graeber is keen to break is between the *society* with whom the individual has a debt relation and the *structures of authority* that are responsible for enforcing debt repayment. What he strives for is a more diffuse notion that places in question the idea that any one or any thing has the authority to define what (and how much) we owe. In the present day, the structures of authority that do just this are dual: they consist not only of political agencies but financial ones, too—states *and* banks, increasingly acting together. Viewed in this way, however, the notion of society is not just broken up. It is completely displaced. But if the financial crisis has demonstrated anything, it is the *separateness* of society from the political and financial elites at the heart of the Wall Street system. This separateness takes us into some deep and productive dilemmas within the theory of money as debt, which we can move on to investigate now.

CREDIT AND NOTHING BUT CREDIT

The first attempts to construct a full-fledged theory of money as debt emerged during the early twentieth century, in the work of George Frederich Knapp and Alfred Mitchell-Innes. Knapp, professor of political economy at the University of Strasbourg, and Mitchell-Innes, a British diplomat,[13] made path-breaking contributions to monetary scholarship within a decade of each other, each advancing the case that money is debt when metalism was in vogue. Knapp's work has figured regularly in the monetary literature as a leading exponent of the theory behind state fiat money, known

---

13   Mitchell-Innes was based in Washington, D.C.; he had previously served as the Undersecretary of State for Finance in Egypt.

as chartalism.[14] By contrast, Mitchell-Innes's work, despite being praised by Keynes, was somewhat overlooked until "new" chartalists such as Randall Wray revived interest toward the end of the twentieth century. Although their arguments are closely associated, there are some differences that I want to emphasize because they are important to our discussion of money's status as a "claim upon society."

Knapp defines money as a *system of tokens the state is willing to accept as payment of taxes*. The state's unique role as a creditor, specifically the tax collector, authorizes its power to define money. According to Knapp, the state fulfills two important roles: defining the unit of value for money and choosing the means of payment (Knapp 1924: 24). Though the state cannot simply declare what money is by law (Knapp 1924: 111),[15] taxes are the biggest and most frequently arising debt that most people have (Lerner 1947: 313). Thus if the state issues tokens and declares that it will accept them as payment of taxes, it is inevitable that these tokens become widely accepted as payment for other kinds of debt (Knapp 1924: 52). Even if other kinds of money circulate, there is always one, which he calls *valuta*, to which the others are accessory: the money in which taxes are paid (Knapp 1924: 158).

When *The State Theory of Money* was published, Knapp's theory provoked what Schumpeter later described as a "tempest in a teapot" in Germany. Weber, who praised Knapp's work as "absolutely correct" (Weber 1978: 169), argued that Knapp underestimated the importance of private and political interests in determining monetary policy. Weber argued that pure token money makes it possible to deliberately generate inflation, which can benefit the state by lowering its borrowing costs and also entrepreneurs, who can exploit rising prices (Weber 1978: 186–87). Knapp's own view was that the state's interest in a strong currency abroad would guard against inflation, but this viewpoint did not prevent his theory from being used to justify lax monetary policy in the aftermath of the First World War, which was probably the pretext of Weber's criticism (Schumpeter 1986: 1057). Schumpeter

14   Arguably, the first modern chartalist was actually Alexander Del Mar, who in *The Science of Money* (1885) defined money as a "measure whose limits can only be adjusted by the State" (Del Mar 1895: 52). But it was Knapp, in the *State Theory of Money* (originally published in 1905, cited here in 1924), who coined the term "charta" (ticket) to describe a form of money that is just a token, with no connection to an underlying commodity. Against the prevailing wisdom, he even said that token money was the most *advanced* form of money. So it is with Knapp's name, not Del Mar's, that chartalism is linked (Aschheima and Tavlas 2004; Mundell 2004; Goodhart 2005a).

15   Knapp did describe money as a "creature of law," but his argument is premised on *convenience*, not law.

was subsequently more damning in his treatment of Knapp's text, dismissing it for expressing the platitudinous truth that when the state declares that it will accept a certain token in payment of taxes, that token increases in value. This, he argued, said nothing about the *nature* of money: one might just as well say that *marriage* is a creature of law (Schumpeter 1986: 1056). Present-day chartalists insist that Schumpeter misrepresented Knapp's theory. Wray, in particular, argues that Schumpeter waters chartalism down by suggesting that government money is supposedly accepted because of legal tender laws (Wray 2004a). To be fair, Knapp explicitly dismissed such laws as "pious hope" (Knapp 1924: 242).

One major economist who was in broad agreement with Knapp, however, was John Maynard Keynes. In *A Treatise on Money* (originally published in 1930, 1976 edition cited here), Keynes argued that Knapp's theory is "fully realised" when the state assumes the right both to *name* money and to declare what *thing* must correspond to the name: "when, that is to say, it claims the right to re-edit the dictionary" (Keynes 1976: 4). For Keynes, as for Knapp, money is "anything which the State undertakes to accept at its pay-offices, whether or not it is declared legal-tender between citizens" (Keynes 1976: 6–7). Thus chartalism begins when the state designates which objective standard corresponds to the money of account (Keynes 1976: 11).

Less than a decade after Knapp's theory appeared, Mitchell-Innes published two articles in the *Banking Law Journal* (Mitchell-Innes 1913, 1914) that have come to be regarded as seminal statements of the credit theory of money.[16] He describes money as "credit and nothing but credit": it is an elaborate system of circulating transferable debt: "A's money is B's debt to him, and when B pays his debt, A's money disappears. This is the whole theory of money" (Mitchell-Innes 1913). Money, in other words, is not a promise to hand over a material thing such as gold, but the *opportunity to cancel a debt*. The most important characteristic of money is the right—recognized by every society—that it confers on its holder to liberate himself from debt by its means. This description of the monetary system as an arrangement in which debts and credits are perpetually trying to get into touch with one another, in order to be written off against each other, resonates with what Knapp says about the role of tax debts in defining *valuta*. Knapp and Mitchell-Innes shared an antipathy toward metalism: the latter described it as an "invented tradition." Credit is older than cash, he argued. For many centuries, the primary instrument of commerce was not the coin,

---

16 Mitchell-Innes described his credit theory of money as a Copernican revolution, which reversed common-sense perceptions of money.

but the tally: a transferable instrument, like a bill of exchange, organized through public fairs used for settling of accounts, like clearing houses.[17] Even where coins were used as money, they were never a uniform size or weight: it was the issuer's mark, not their material properties, which determined their value as money.

The arguments of Knapp and Mitchell-Innes are often treated in tandem, but their views differ on two critical points. First, Mitchell-Innes had no sympathy for the idea that the *state* has special naming rights over money; indeed, he rejected the idea that debts to the state (in the form of taxes) confer any special privilege over declaring what money should be. On this issue, his position has more in common with monetary reformers today who would *exclude* the state from money's production and regulation. As I discuss in Chapter 8, this is a broad and eclectic grouping, which includes libertarians who agree with Hayek's original call for money to be denationalized (Hayek 1976), designers of electronic peer-to-peer currencies such as Bitcoin, together with the advocates of local currency schemes in which money is issued by the community. The second important point of divergence between Mitchell-Innes and Knapp concerns the banking system. Knapp scarcely mentioned banks, whereas Mitchell-Innes described them as "wonderfully efficient machinery." For Mitchell-Innes, the debt relation within money is not between citizens (or taxpayers) and the state. Rather, it consists of a triadic relationship among lenders, borrowers, and *banks*. Banks are the mechanism by which debts are centralized and cleared. In this context, government money is no more important than bank money: "A government dollar is a promise to 'pay,' a promise to 'satisfy,' a promise to 'redeem,' *just as all other money is*" (Mitchell-Innes 1914: 54, italics added). Indeed, *banks* appear to play a role in Mitchell-Innes's theory that is analogous to the role the *state* plays in Knapp's theory, i.e., coordinating and underwriting the monetary system as a whole.[18]

For Mitchell-Innes, unlike for Knapp, a government coin confers a right to satisfaction that is no different from any other form of credit. Each taxpayer is responsible for redeeming his or her own portion of the debt the government has contracted through its issues of money, whether in the form

---

17   These fairs were often held outside churches, suggesting that they were not really commercial markets but were connected to religious festivals. This juxtaposition is often cited as a reason for further doubting Menger's theory, as discussed in Chapter 1, which suggests that the origins of money were commercial.

18   This idea further explains why Mitchell-Innes's arguments are sometimes linked with monetary circuit theory (or the theory of endogenous money), which views any monetary transaction as a tripartite relationship among a buyer, a seller, and a bank.

of coins, certificates, notes, or drafts on the treasury. All that matters is the creditworthiness of the issuer, and a banker's credit may be just as sound (if not moreso) than a government's. A dollar is a dollar, no matter where it comes from. In principle, *anyone* can issue money. "Everybody who incurs a debt issues his own dollar, which may or may not be identical with the dollar of any one else's money" (Mitchell-Innes 1914: 55). This notion raises the question: what guarantees the value of such a personalized form of money? We can all issue debt, of course, simply by writing out an IOU. But for the debt to be used as money, it has to be transferable (Ingham 2004b). Therefore, the debt relation within money presumably has to work differently than in the case of regular debt. Might it be the case that these promises require the backing of an identifiable collective body—a "society"—in order to function as money? If so, has the state—alongside the banking system—merely become an institutional proxy for "society"? To answer such questions, we need to turn to the present-day proponents of chartalism.

NEOCHARTALISM

In essence, the "new" chartalists seek to combine elements of the work of Knapp and Mitchell-Innes with a theory of credit that places greater emphasis on the banking system. The leading exponent is the American economist, Randall Wray, whose approach is usually referred to as "modern monetary theory." Wray's work is premised on the "post-Keynesian" argument that the effective quantity of money within the economy is determined by its *own internal dynamics*: specifically, it is driven by the demand for credit.[19] Wray's version of this theory is "chartalist" because he places an especially strong emphasis on the role of the state, which can be summarized by the idea that *taxes drive money*. Like Knapp, he argues that the monetary tokens issued by a government are always in demand because they are accepted at its own pay offices (Wray 2004a: 252).[20] The state creates a demand for its own currency simply by imposing a tax liability.[21]

---

19 Besides new chartalism, the economists most closely associated with the idea of endogenous money are proponents of monetary circuit theory, such as Nicholas Kaldor, and post-Keynesians such as Paul Davidson, Basil Moore, Victoria Chick, and Sheila Dow (Ponsot and Rossi 2009; Zazzaro 2002).
20 Wray defines money as TWINTOPT, i.e., that which is necessary to pay taxes.
21 The liability need not, however, be imposed on everyone: if only half of the population pays tax, the tokens used for that purpose are widely accepted even by nontaxpayers because they know that the tokens are in demand (Wray 2006: 169–70).

Wray's model incorporates government spending *and* borrowing as essential elements of what money is within the economy as a whole. The government spends by issuing checks drawn upon its treasury department. The recipient of the check then takes it to the bank and either uses it to withdraw currency (in which case the bank's reserves first increase and then decrease) or pays it into their account (in which case the bank's reserves are credited by the central bank). In addition to being used for buying goods and services, these government IOUs are also used to pay taxes and buy government bonds. According to Wray, the central bank does not play a pivotal role in any of this. The treasury's checks increase the supply of fiat money in the system. The central bank simply credits bank reserves: it cannot control the quantity of money or reserves because these quantities depend on the actions of the treasury or the private sector (Wray 2006: 98). Fiscal policy (government spending) determines the quantity of money. Monetary policy simply determines overnight interest rates (Wray 2006: 98). This explanation inverts conventional thinking about how government spending is financed. Crucially for Wray, the treasury spends *before* it collects taxes or sells bonds: treasury spending adds to reserves, and taxation drains them. Government bonds are sold, too, to drain reserves (Wray 2006: 81).

This part of Wray's argument is in three steps (Wray 2006: 169–70). First, whenever there is a government deficit, there are excess bank reserves, i.e., the amount of fiat money created exceeds the amount removed from bank reserves via tax payments. Second, wholesale markets only move funds around; they cannot eliminate them. Third, bonds are sold to drain the excess and avoid the overnight rate going to zero, which would cause serious market disruption. This system requires coordination between institutions: in the United States, between the Fed and the Treasury (the former uses repos, the latter organizes bond sales); in the United Kingdom, between the Bank of England and the Debt Management Office, which operates under the Treasury (Wray 2006: 86).[22]

---

22 According to Wray's theory, the Eurozone was *always* unlikely to succeed because it undermined the link between governments and their currency. The Eurozone has a central bank but no fiscal branch, the central treasury. In effect, each Eurozone member-state has to operate its fiscal policy in a foreign currency and to borrow from private markets to fund deficit spending (Wray 2006: 169–70). Should their borrowing costs become too high, these states have little option but to raise taxes and cut public expenditure. This system leaves them in an invidious position. On one side, they are unable to run large counter-cyclical deficits on their own. On the other side, bond buyers can switch from one country to another within the Eurozone without exposing themselves to currency risk. This situation renders the balance of power between states and their creditors asymmetrical and points to a fundamental difference between the United States and those Eurozone member-states that have been running current account deficits.

Wray's theory combines a *verticalist* approach to *fiat money creation*, which follows Knapp, with a *horizontalist* view of *bank money*, which is modeled on Mitchell-Innes and Minsky (we discuss Minsky below) (Wray 2006: 115–19). What Knapp called *valuta*, i.e., fiat or high-powered money, is legal tender because the government accepts it. This is the money into which all other monies must be convertible. It is used in clearing, it is the money that links public and private pay communities, and it is the most liquid money domestically (Wray 2006: 77). Most important of all (and this is where Mitchell-Innes and Minsky come in), *valuta* sits beneath the debt pyramid that makes up the monetary and financial system. Other forms of money (e.g., bank money, commercial paper, privately issued bonds, and various IOUs) are "a leveraging of the money things accepted by government" (Wray 2004a: 259).[23]

The leading sociological exponent of neochartalism is the Cambridge sociologist Geoffrey Ingham. Like Wray, Ingham's approach brings the state and credit theories of money together. In particular, he accepts Mitchell-Innes's argument that *all money is credit*, but Ingham also insists that *not all credit is money* (Ingham 2004b: 240). The argument is advanced through a sociological analysis of the historical emergence of what Ingham calls *capitalist credit money*.[24] He dates this emergence back to the seventeenth century, when tokens that were used to represent private debt evolved into more widely accepted (and, eventually, legally enforceable) means of payment. This acceptance was made possible by two developments within banking and trade in early modern Europe: first, the disconnection between merchants' bills of exchange and the commodities they referred to, and second, the separation of the bill from the identity of specific creditors and debtors. The crucial condition for the latter was the development of written contracts, enabling bilateral debts to settle a third-party debt. These were the paper bills that subsequently became money. Not until they began to circulate beyond the networks of bankers could these private debts be regarded as money. Although the transition to money relied on the state, paradoxically it was the institution of strong metallic standards for money that provided the financial infrastructure in which credit money could thrive. These standards were put in place in England, initially through reforms carried out under Elizabeth I by Thomas Gresham in 1560–61, but chiefly

---

23 This horizontal component of Wray's approach is the theory of endogenous money: the supply of bank money (deposits) is determined within the system by the demand for loans and the willingness of banks to lend. This approach is similar to monetary circuit theory.

24 Echoing Keynes, Ingham also calls this the *monetary production economy*.

through the creation of the Bank of England in 1694, and subsequently during Isaac Newton's governance of the Royal mint in 1699–1727. Such standards are crucial to providing the socially and politically secure monetary space, underpinned by a stable political system and a solid fiscal system, that provided an infrastructure for the emergence of capitalist credit money (Ingham 2004b: 124–31).

For Ingham, the monetary system does not simply consist of a specific set of institutional arrangements binding together the government treasury and central bank on one side and private banks on the other. Rather, the state is caught up in an *ongoing conflict of interests between creditors and debtors* that Ingham likens to a *struggle between two great social classes*. Max Weber saw prices as an expression of the conflict of interests between producers and consumers.[25] In similar vein, Ingham regards the interest rate as an index of the contest between creditors—seeking to preserve and store value in money, control its supply, and extract interest—and debtors (producers of commodities and consumers) attempting to monetize their market power through rising prices or by borrowing. This struggle determines the value of money (Ingham 2004a: 207–208). These two protagonists are distinct and relatively autonomous,[26] but the state, through its central bank and treasury, constitutes both a third corner within this triadic power struggle (Ingham 2001: 318) and the site on which the struggle takes place (Ingham 2004a: 150). Monetary disorder, e.g., inflation, arises whenever this struggle becomes unstable. Thus the production of money involves a "continuous rebalancing of the power relations between economic interests" (Ingham 1998: 14): monetary policy is in this sense a *"reinforcement* of any balance of power that has been forged" (Ingham 2004b: 150, italics in original).

Ingham argues that although money's *value* is determined by these competing interests, the definition of what *counts* as money is declared by a political authority that *transcends* such interests (Ingham 2001: 318). Although he underscores banks' role in money creation, Ingham insists that it is the *state* that imposes a hegemonic meaning of money by defining the money of account. This is how Keynes saw things, too (Keynes 1976: 3). Ingham argues that this unit of account is vital to our understanding of the nature of money: money "is always an abstract claim or credit whose 'moneyness' is conferred by a money of account" (Ingham 2004a: 198). His definition of

---

25 Prices, Weber once said, are "estimated quantifications of relative chances in this struggle of interests" (Weber 1978: 107–108).

26 Each side "imposes limitations on, and continually threatens to perturb or impede, the operation of the other" (Ingham 2004a: 151).

money is therefore twofold. First, he draws on Simmel's characterization of money as a "generic promise to pay": money is a *unique form of credit* because it expresses a relationship not between two individuals but between every individual and the entire "society." Second, Ingham argues that only those promises to pay that are denominated in the official money of account can be thought of as money. Only the state has the requisite authority to define a money of account. Money is therefore "a form of sovereignty, and as such it cannot be understood without reference to an authority" (Ingham 2004a: 12). What matters, however, is that in attempting to exercise its sovereignty the state is constantly embroiled in a struggle between creditors and debtors. Indeed, the ideal of stable money whose value is objective and above any such struggle is only ever a *working fiction* whose construction and maintenance is the outcome of a complex configuration of *institutional* and *epistemological* arrangements. Monetary policy and policy makers, central banks, and economists must appear to operate independently of political and class conflict. In other words, they must do everything in their power to obscure the social life of money: to wit, by acting as if the prevailing monetary standard were an objective thing.

So who exactly *are* the creditors and debtors involved in this struggle? Besides the state, Ingham refers to three groups: *producers, consumers* (who are both debtors), and *capitalists* (who are creditors) (Ingham 2004b: 45, 195, 202).[27] Empirically, of course, the constitution of these groupings is likely to be complex and fluid. Those Ingham calls capitalists are increasingly likely to be professionals managing huge pension funds, not just wealthy individuals and families. The creditor–debtor line can also be drawn in other ways, for example, between young and old (Goodhart 2005b: 821) or between regions of the global economy (Wolf 2010; Rajan 2011). Though such issues hardly deflect Ingham's analysis, indeed they potentially make it even more compelling, they do suggest that his approach is not as close to that of Wray as it initially appears to be. For example, whereas Wray denies that the monetary system is driven by borrowing at all (taxes and bonds are for *draining reserves*, not to *finance deficit spending*), Ingham states that high-powered money "is the result of the struggle between debtors' demand for money and creditors' belief that the state can service its debt" (Ingham 2004b: 150). In other words, Wray's theory focuses on the flow of money throughout the economic system and emphasizes the state's role in regulating that flow *from within*, and Ingham's approach focuses on

---

27   Ingham also refers to this third group as rentiers.

the role of debt, which in many cases reduces states to a condition of dependency on *external* forces.

There is a difference of emphasis between the approaches of Wray and Ingham, but the difference points to a much deeper tension within the relationship between the state and the financial system. On one side, the state appears to enjoy a *unique status* as a creditor, part of which is because of its *naming rights* over money. On the other side, the state acts as a *guarantor*, too, partly by virtue of its role in *monetary and financial governance*. The financial system still operates on the presumption that, in the event of failure, the major banks are covered by state guarantees. As several recent banking crises (not just in 2007–8) have shown, however, the question of *which* financial institutions should be subject to that guarantee has become increasingly complicated and difficult. The issue becomes more complex still when we take into account the fact that several of the very institutions those guarantees might apply to are connected, directly and indirectly, with the state's own debt. As I move on to discuss now, money is at the very core of this tension.

SCHUMPETER'S BANKS

Banks play a crucial role in money's actual creation. They do so through their actions as lenders; indeed, it is banks' capacity to create money *ab initio* simply by making a loan that prompted John K. Galbraith to complain that they "repel the mind" (Galbraith 1975: 18). He was referring to the fractional reserve system, whereby a bank can lend out considerably more money than the deposits it holds. This is the process of money creation, via the mere flick of a pen or, these days, a stroke on the computer keyboard. For a long time, economic theory portrayed banks mainly as intermediaries between depositors and borrowers. The microeconomic theory of banking was not developed until after the 1970s.[28] Schumpeter, however, made the earliest significant contribution to understanding the importance of banks and finance to economic development and the business cycle (Clark 2010: 209). In this respect, his arguments represent a major step forward from Mitchell-Innes. Mitchell-Innes mentioned banks but did not build them into the theory of money: like states, they are merely components of the circulation of credit and debt. For Schumpeter, by contrast, banks are a

---

28   The Arrow-Debreu general equilibrium model was the standard reference, and it offered no explanation for the role of banks in the economy (Zarlenga 2002).

major structural feature of capitalism, its *differentia specifica* (Schumpeter 2008: 69).

Schumpeter worked for a long time on a book dedicated to monetary theory.[29] He completed the manuscript in the late 1920s but went on to revise it, suffering a setback when Keynes's *Treatise on Money* was published in 1930 (Freixas and Rochet 2008: xvii, 2–10). One chapter of the book was called "The Sociology of Money," and its arguments moved in several different directions: toward Menger and the commodity theory of money for its analysis of money's role as a medium of exchange (Earley 1994; Messori 1997; Ingham 2003; Swedberg 2003); toward historical accounts, such as that of Laum (Schumpeter 1991: 534), which show a variety of reasons why a particular object is adopted as a measure of value (Laum 2006); and toward anthropological, sociological, and historical approaches for showing how money both shapes and is shaped by the "total social process" (Schumpeter 1991: 537). In practical terms, Schumpeter argued that by creating money through lending, banks are the key agents of capitalist entrepreneurship. He described the money market as the headquarters of the capitalist system where plans for its future development are decided (Schumpeter 2008: 33, 74, 126).

In his *History of Economic Analysis* (originally published in 1954), Schumpeter remarked that there were two rival views of banking (Schumpeter 1986: 303–304): the first saw banks simply as mediating between depositors and borrowers, and the second focused on their role in creating money through lending. He argued, furthermore, that because finance is a significant "complement" to capitalist production and trade, the development of the law and practice of negotiable paper and "created deposits" was of crucial importance for dating the rise of capitalism (Schumpeter 1986: 75, n. 1). Earlier in his career, Schumpeter maintained that the theory of money should begin with banking and bank credit. For example, in *The Theory of Economic Development* (originally published in 1911), he said that whereas money plays an essentially passive role in the circular flow of goods and services in the economy, credit creation is necessary for there to be economic development (Swedberg 1991: 81). Financing is described as a "spe-

---

29 Only the first two chapters have been translated into English, and a German edition, *Das Wesen des Geldes* ("The Nature of Money") came out in 1970 (Swedberg 1991; Messori 1997: 76, 80). In a letter to his colleague, René Roux, in 1949, Schumpeter wrote that "my views of money have been presented only incidentally in works of mine primarily devoted to other topics" (Messori 1997). Since then, his work on the topic has been taken up in post-Keynesian monetary theory, e.g., in the theory of endogenous money (Kaldor 1970, 1982), monetary circuit theory (Graziani 2009), and neochartalism (Wray 2012) (Schumpeter 1991: 500, n. 2).

cial act" (Schumpeter 2008: 70) that does not simply involve thrift but the *creation of new money*. Because the banker is a producer of money by generating new purchasing power out of nothing, he or she is "the capitalist par excellence . . . the *ephor* of the exchange economy" (Schumpeter 2008: 74). Even the wealthy capitalist needs credit to carry out a "new combination" that cannot simply be financed out of returns from previous production.

Banks have come a long way since Schumpeter. But arguably they resemble the *ephor* (overseer) of capitalism in the present day more than ever. And it is by virtue of this resemblance that their relationship with money creation begins to be problematic. The range of institutions involved in banking has broadened far beyond the fractional reserve system (the Bank of England now uses the phrase "complex financial institution," not bank), and the financial instruments banks use, such as derivatives and collateralized securities, are formidably complex and varied. Moreover, financial markets now perform many of the services previously performed by banks as financial intermediaries. But even today, fractional reserve banking features prominently in popular criticism of banking, as if this were the essence of what banks do. Fractional reserve banking is often presented not only as fraudulent, but also as inherently destabilizing. An example of the genre is the work of Paul Grignon, a Canadian artist and filmmaker, who made two films under the generic title, *Money as Debt*, in 2006 and 2009 (Grignon 2006, 2009).[30] Grignon argues that the system incentivizes banks to ensure that debts are not only perpetually renewed but also increased.[31] Another version of the argument is that because of their need to lend against collateral, the system gives private banks an incentive to allocate credit to property speculation rather than production and divests governments of control over the allocation of credit. According to this view, it is mistaken even to refer to the practice as fractional *reserve* banking because the link between banks' lending and reserves is extremely tenuous (Zazzaro 2002; Arena, Graziani, et al. 2004; Graziani 2009; Ponsot and Rossi 2009). A third version, as proposed by the American Monetary Institute—a monetary reform pressure group established in 1996—argues that the power of money creation should be placed in the hands of government, not private banks.[32] The argument hinges on making a clean separation between the business of banking on one side and money creation on the other (Ryan-Collins, Greenham, et al. 2012).

30   See https://www.youtube.com/watch?v=CB5M5nuTD9w and https://www.youtube.com/watch?v=6_lB3AJSMRg.
31   See http://paulgrignon.netfirms.com/MoneyasDebt/Analysis_of_Banking.html.
32   See http://www.monetary.org/intro-to-monetary-reform.

CHAPTER 3

What, then, is a bank? The examiner's report on the bankruptcy of Lehman Brothers ran to 2,200 pages. The bank had assets worth $600 billion when it collapsed, leaving a number of major institutional cash funds exposed, alongside 100 hedge funds that had used the bank as their prime broker, several Japanese banks, energy companies, real estate firms, and insurers. Although Lehman's was a U.S. bank, its global interests were such that its bankruptcy had major ramifications for financial systems in a number of countries. The breadth, severity, and complexity of the Lehman case reflected a series of structural changes within the global banking system that had been underway for some time. The major banks had been growing inexorably in size—Lehman was the fourth largest investment bank in the United States (behind Goldman Sachs, Morgan Stanley, and Merrill Lynch)—but the financial sector as a whole had been expanding relative to the real economy.

In Britain at the beginning of the twentieth century, the largest three banks had assets worth 7 percent of GDP; by mid-century, the figure reached 27 percent, and by 2007, 200 percent of GDP (Haldane 2011: 10; Haldane 2012: 14). These changes form part of a broad underlying trend whereby the financial sector has grown significantly in size relative to the real economy. In the United States, the contribution of the financial services industry (including insurance) to GDP in 1947 was 2.35 percent; by 1987, the figure had risen to 5.8 percent, and by 2009, 8.4 percent.[33] Market concentration has also been rising, reflecting an industry increasingly dominated by large, complex firms: the share of the top three largest U.S. banks in total commercial banking assets rose from 10 percent to 40 percent between 1990 and 2007,[34] and the share of the top five largest global banks in the assets of the largest 1,000 banks doubled from 8 percent in 1998 to 16 percent in 2009 (Haldane 2010). This growth is linked to financialization, a broad term that refers to increasing leverage, rapid innovation in structured finance, and growing volumes of trading in financial instruments. Leverage is a key indicator of increasing risk exposure. For the world's biggest fifty banks, the leverage ratio (assets as a multiple of equity) rose from 20 in 2000 to 32 in 2008, whereas in the United Kingdom, bank assets as a percentage of GDP have risen from 50 percent to more than 550 percent over the past four decades.[35]

---

33   U.S. Bureau of Economic Analysis, see http://www.bea.gov/scb/pdf/2011/07%20July/0711_brief_indy_tables.pdf.
34   Source: Federal Deposit Insurance Corporation, see http://www.fdic.gov/bank/statistical/.
35   Source: World Bank, see http://search.worldbank.org/quickview?name=%3Cem%3EBank%3C%2Fem%3E+capital+to+assets+ratio+%28%25%29&id=FB.BNK.CAPA.ZS&type=Indicators&cube_no=2&qterm=bank+debt+leverage.

In *Capitalism, Socialism and Democracy* (originally published in 1942), Schumpeter suggests that the entrepreneurial figure he had celebrated in his earlier work will be forced into the background by monopolistic firms with increasingly bureaucratically minded managers: "The perfectly bureaucratized giant industrial unit not only ousts the small or medium-sized firm and 'expropriates' its owners, but in the end it also ousts the entrepreneur" (Schumpeter 2003: 135). There is an intriguing sociological thesis at the heart of this argument. According to Schumpeter, as soon as the entrepreneur's economic function begins to wane, so does his or her social position, which in turn "affects the position of the entire bourgeois stratum" (Schumpeter 2003: 134). That bourgeois class—industrialists, merchants, financiers, and bankers—"depends on the entrepreneur and, as a class, lives and will die with him," Schumpeter suggests (Schumpeter 2003: 134). These remarks come in the part of the book that predicts the demise of capitalism because of fundamental changes in its institutional structure. Given what Schumpeter says about the decline of the entrepreneur, one can surmise that this demise would have a significant effect on banks, whose capacity to create money is crucial for the entrepreneur who needs capital.

His arguments here focus on the disappearance of "feudal" elements that helped to stabilize capitalist society and the emergence of huge corporations, but it is in the next part of the text—much less commented upon—when Schumpeter looks forward to the prospects for socialism, that his most interesting remarks about the future of banking and finance are made. Strikingly, these remarks resonate with recent debates about changes in the banking industry and the role of finance in society. Capitalism in decline, he suggests, would be unchanging: an economy consisting of a few giant corporations, with interest rates converging toward zero (Swedberg 1991: 159). Under a socialist system, however, banks would be transformed into "branch offices of the central institution" (Schumpeter 2003: 222). As such, they would not only retain many of their previous functions—which he calls "social bookkeeping"—but they may actually take on new functions, such as the power to grant or refuse credits, in which case "the central bank might be left independent of the ministry of production itself and become a sort of general supervisor" (Schumpeter 2003: 223). Once banks were combined with the treasury, there would need to be inflation: partly to counter the economic paralysis that a socialist revolution would inevitably bring about and also because inflation is "an excellent means of smoothing certain transitional difficulties and of effecting partial expropriation" (Schumpeter 2003: 226). As for the Bank of England, Schumpeter suggests that it is already "ripe" for socialization; indeed, if anything it is *less* independent from

CHAPTER 3

government "than a well-ordered socialist community may well wish its financial organ to be" (Schumpeter 2003: 230). And in a remark that ought to have intrigued those who compared the bank bailouts of 2008–9 to socialism (Blackburn 2010), Schumpeter suggests that in commercial banking, "concentration and bureaucratization seem to have done full work" (Schumpeter 2003: 230).

These remarks suggest that Schumpeter would not have been surprised by the growth of the financial system that took place in the last quarter of the twentieth century. Nor would he have been especially fazed by the return of troubled global banks to the apparently secure sovereign spaces provided by governments wielding "asset relief" funds in the immediate aftermath of the crisis. But whereas Schumpeter clearly did envisage that the link between banking and entrepreneurialism would be eroded, he did not really foresee the changes that took place in terms of what *banks actually do*. Lehman Brothers was a wholesale bank. It was not part of the fractional reserve system that repelled Galbraith's mind. Likewise, the financial system that Schumpeter described had deposit-taking banks at its heart. Alongside these were specialist institutions, such as merchant banks. Universal banks now dominate the system, offering a full range of retail, commercial, and investment banking services, as well as trading on their own behalf. Moreover, a massive shadow (or parallel) banking system has developed, which includes finance companies, asset-backed commercial paper conduits, structured investment vehicles, credit hedge funds, money market mutual funds, securities lenders, limited-purpose finance companies, and various government-sponsored enterprises. These organizations perform similar functions to traditional banks (i.e., credit, maturity, and liquidity transformation) but are not regulated in the same way and are not covered by public sources of liquidity, such as the central bank overnight lending or government deposit insurance.

Even after the 2007–8 crisis, the shadow banking system is still highly leveraged. Net liabilities peaked at around $22 trillion in 2007 (compared to around $14 trillion of traditional banking liabilities). Although the gap has closed since then, with the 2011 figures at around $15 trillion and $14 trillion, respectively, there are still substantial institutional "cash pools" outside the banking system (Pozsar, Adrian, et al. 2012). Whereas the traditional image of a bank is as a crucial intermediary between lenders and borrowers, banks today operate not simply as *issuers of debt* but also as *repositories of risk*. To grasp the significance of this difference for money, I want to turn to the arguments of Hyman Minsky and Susan Strange.

MINSKY'S HALF-CENTURY

Hyman Minsky was a doctoral student of Joseph Schumpeter and Wassily Leontief at Harvard during the 1940s. Whereas Schumpeter had drawn attention to banks' importance in the business cycle, Minsky's main focus was on the effect of financial markets on the wider economy (Minsky 1993a, 1993b). During the 1970s, Minsky developed the *financial instability hypothesis*, in which he argued that speculative bubbles and spells of financial market instability are part of the normal life cycle of the economy (Minsky 1992). It is a fundamental characteristic of capitalism, he said, that the economy swings between episodes of robustness and fragility. It befalls to governments to try to alleviate the worst effects of such swings, but it would be naive and mistaken to believe that they can be eradicated. The relevance of Minsky's hypothesis to our discussion in this chapter stems from the central role he gives to the relationship between financial assets and what he calls "cash."

Minsky's hypothesis describes a buildup of unsustainable credit inflation, and the subsequent collapse of confidence and rapid credit deflation, as part of the routine operation of an economy that is increasingly dominated by financial markets. Although Minsky was broadly Keynesian in his sympathies, he argued that Keynes underestimated the potential effect of the growth of financial markets on the rest of the economy. According to Minsky, there are four stages in the development of capitalism: commercial capitalism, finance capitalism, managerial capitalism, and money manager capitalism. It is the final stage, consisting of the buildup of debt financing, that is absent in Keynes's theory: "he did not make the final step to an analysis of the capitalist process that is fully rooted in 'the City' and 'Wall Street'" (Minsky 1975: 126–27). Scholars who followed Keynes were slow to pick up on the significance of this absence because, until the mid-1960s, banks' reserves were laden with government debt.

Minsky portrays the monetary system as a pyramid of interbank liabilities: the public uses bank deposits as money, and banks use central bank deposits as money (Minsky 1986: 231). The key to his theory, however, is the relationship between three forms of finance: *hedge*, *speculative*, and *Ponzi*.[36]

---

36 The latter is a reference to Charles Ponzi, origin (but not originator) of the term "Ponzi scheme." A Ponzi scheme is a fraudulent investment scheme that pays returns to its investors not from earned profits but from the monies paid into the scheme from new investors. Ponzi operated such a scheme, via his Securities Exchange Company based in Boston, which collapsed in 1920. He spent the next fourteen years in and out of prison (Zuckoff 2006).

These terms refer to the capacity of firms or units to meet their contractual obligations. Units with *hedge financing* units can fulfill all of their contractual payment obligations by their income cash flows. Those with *speculative finance* can meet their interest payments out of their income cash flows, but not the principal of their loans. They will therefore need to issue new debt to meet commitments on maturing debt. Units with *Ponzi finance*, finally, lack the income cash flow even to pay interest on their debt (let alone the principal); they need either to sell assets or borrow to do so.

Minsky uses the three terms (hedge, speculative, and Ponzi finance) to describe successive stages in the buildup of credit in the economy. It is inevitable, he said, that economic activity veers increasingly toward Ponzi finance as confidence grows. Much of the originality of his argument lay in this claim because it suggests that the system is *bound to crash* from time to time: not necessarily because it is badly governed or because banks are poorly managed, but simply because of the intrinsic nature of finance as a profitable business. For Minsky, finance does not simply mediate the relationship between depositors and borrowers. Nor does it just sustain enterprise, as Schumpeter argued. By its very nature, *finance fuels speculation*. Bankers, he argued, are speculators, just like all businesspeople, "always speculating on their ability to refinance their positions in assets as withdrawals of deposits take place" (Minsky 1975: 119). They are bound to speculate on the composition of their assets, selling out positions in marketable securities to finance additional loans during periods of optimism. During booms, bankers inevitably buy back lending ability, selling their investment portfolios and rewarding those prepared to part with cash with higher interest rates (Minsky 1975: 120). This speculation is simply what banks *rationally* do: substituting time deposits for demand deposits, replacing lines of credit with actual credit, varying the efficiency with which reserves are used through interbank transactions in reserves, and selling debt as commercial paper in the open market, further activating short-term cash balances.[37]

According to Minsky, trouble always starts for Ponzi finance as inflation builds and the authorities try to exorcise it through monetary restraint. Rising interest rates lead to rising debt costs, whereupon "the net worth of previous Ponzi units will quickly evaporate" (Minsky 1992: 8). This situation leads to debt deflation, as units short of cash try to sell out their positions, and asset values rapidly fall. From this point onward, the very

---

[37] The sophistication increases when nonbank financial institutions use bank debt, open-market debt, and long-term bonds to acquire debts and a "layering" of debt occurs (Minsky 1975: 121).

financing techniques that had been used to fuel the credit expansion now exaggerate the speed and severity of the contraction. In the later stages of the boom, loan terms would have risen sharply and would increasingly have been financed with short-term borrowings. Those high financing charges would now feed back upon and adversely affect the value of earlier deals as they come up for refinancing (Minsky 1975: 121). For Minsky, in finance the present always rules: particularly during periods of radical optimism or pessimism, there is a built-in tendency for loans to be made on the assumption that, to use Keynes's expression, "the existing state of affairs will continue indefinitely" (Keynes 2008: 136). Keynes described this assumption as a tendency to fall back on convention. It is caused not by an underlying belief that nothing ever changes. Rather, it is an expectation that *nothing will change in the near future*.[38] Just as investors feel relatively secure during a boom, during the subsequent debt deflation, the guiding wisdom is that all debts lead to disaster: "Each state nurtures forces that lead to its own destruction" (Minsky 1975: 126).

In April 2006, the IMF's "Global Financial Stability Report" noted a "growing recognition that the dispersion of credit risk by banks to a broader and more diverse group of investors, rather than warehousing such risks on their balance sheets, has helped to make the banking and overall financial system more resilient" (IMF 2006: 51). By 2008, the phrase "Minsky moment"[39]—when overindebted investors are forced to sell even their good assets to pay off their debt—had become as much a part of the lexicon surrounding the crisis as "too big to fail."[40] According to Paul Krugman, Minsky had previously been quite a marginalized figure who "was warning—to a largely indifferent economics profession—not just that something like that crisis could happen but that it *would* happen" (Krugman 2012: 42). Minsky's big idea was to focus on the problem that excessive leverage poses, not just to indebted households and firms but also to the *economy as a whole*.

---

38   "Thus investment becomes 'safe' for the individual investor over short periods." Keynes's point was that each investor expects to be able to revise their expectations "before there has been time for much to happen." Investments that are "fixed" for the community "are thus made 'liquid' for the individual" (Keynes 2008: 137).

39   This was not Minsky's phrase. It was first used by Paul McCulley (of the California-based investment management company, Pimco) to describe the 1998 Russian crisis. "Yesterday's 50 basis-point Fed funds rate cut was a very positive signal that Fed policy makers grasp that we're facing a debt-deflation Minsky Moment," he warned in January 2001 (McCulley 2001a: 4). Three months later, he wrote, "Macroeconomic life after bubbles is not a self-correcting process of renewal, but a self-feeding process of debt deflation—to wit, it's a Minsky Moment" (McCulley 2001b: 4).

40   This expression was first used in relation to the bailout of Continental Illinois in 1984.

High debt levels leave the economy vulnerable to a "death spiral" in which the efforts of debtors to rid themselves of debt (by selling off assets) make the debt problem worse (Krugman 2012: 44). What sets Minsky's theory apart, then, is not so much the *psychological* argument he makes about the conventions that inform the behavior of investors—Keynes made it too[41]—but rather his analysis of the *structural* properties of an economy once it becomes too heavily dependent on a certain mode of finance. Once the Ponzi stage is reached, not just individuals but also the economy as a whole, is excessively leveraged. Minsky's message, which Krugman says economists failed to heed until 2008, was that once an economy is *deeply* in debt, virtually *any* event (however small) can trigger a catastrophic collapse.

Although many economists, commentators, and analysts were discussing the emergence (both in theory and in fact) of the Minsky *moment* during 2008, what they were in fact witnessing was arguably the culmination of a Minsky *half century*. This era would have spanned the entire post–World War II period, during which the Wall Street system was transforming capitalism, leading to a succession of Minsky moments, as well as a financial system in which fraudulent activity was increasingly being seen as part of "normal" business practice. This was a period culminating not just in the subprime crisis, but also in the LIBOR affair (a series of fraudulent actions connected to the LIBOR, London Interbank Offered Rate, and also the resulting investigation and reaction). For some time, Minsky had been warning of the growth of "megabanks" that were predatory and inefficient, and more generally, of the emergence of "money manager capitalism" (Minsky 1993a), arguing that this emergence was fueling the development of an excessively leveraged economy.[42] As part of this analysis, Minsky specifically addressed the practice of securitization in a memo written in 1987 that he used for teaching monetary theory. He argued that securitization emerged as a "lagged response to monetarism," starting with the thrifts[43] but becoming more widespread as financial institutions sought to supplement fund income with fee income. More generally, this change was a result of the globalization of finance and the declining importance of banks in favor of

---

41   Irving Fisher also captured the dynamics of debt deflation in "The Debt-Deflation Theory of Great Depressions" (Fisher 1933).

42   Money manager capitalism refers to an economy dominated by fund managers as opposed to banks. For example, the bank share of all financial assets fell from around 50 percent in the 1950s to around 25 percent by the 1990s. Until then, capitalism had gone through three stages: commercial, finance, and managerial capitalism (Wray 2010).

43   I.e., savings and loans associations in the United States, which specialized in accepting savings and making mortgage loans.

managed money. One significant implication of securitization, Minsky argued, was that there was in principle *no limit to banks' capacity to create credit*: they needed no recourse to bank capital, and the credit thereby created did not absorb high-powered money. Securitization therefore shed new light on the nature of money as debt: we could, he suggested, soon be using $100 interest-bearing short-term securities as currency. For Minsky, this currency would essentially be *private credit money* (Minsky 2008: 3). It was, one suspects, a world in which Mitchell-Innes—but not Knapp—would have felt quite at home.

STRANGE MONEY

Minsky's arguments resonate with a thesis developed by a political economist writing at around the same time, Susan Strange. Her analysis in *Casino Capitalism* (1986) and *Mad Money* (1998a) focused on the decline of banks' role in intermediation (between savers and depositors) and their inducement by deregulation to take bigger risks. This is the backdrop for her distinction between the global *financial* system (i.e., the system of creating, buying, and selling credit money that in recent decades has "developed somewhat independently of governments") and the international *monetary* system (i.e., the relationship between national currencies) (Strange 1994a: 49).[44] Strange's core thesis was that the emergence of money substitutes such as derivatives—Minsky's private money—were taking finance increasingly beyond the control of national governments (Strange 1994a: 49). These money substitutes—"strange money"—undermine monetary policy. Central banks have long been grappling with the implications of financial innovation for measuring and controlling the aggregate money supply, seeking rather to influence the demand for money through "channels" such as interest rates and capital reserve requirements. Monetarism lapsed for this reason. In the United States, the 1982 Banking Act, allowing banks to pay interest on basic deposit accounts was a key moment in the Federal Reserve's move away from seeking to control M3 directly because it broadened the funds available for

---

[44] In drawing this distinction, Strange was criticizing peers in the international relations field for paying too much attention to *money* and too little to *finance*. She argued that deregulation and the emergence of money market mutual funds had enhanced the power of financial markets over the state in the world economy. She also identified a fundamental tension between the international financial structure and the power and wealth of states. International relations scholars had overlooked this, she said, because their key problem was the prevalence of violent conflict and war between states (Strange 1998a: 41).

transaction purposes. More recently, securitization exacerbated the problem (Estrella 2002). The Bank of England changed its M4 reporting rules in January 2010 (Owladi 2010), and the European Central Bank (ECB), through bulletins and published papers, has warned that securitization directly undermines the bank lending channel of monetary policy transmission (ECB 2008, 2010; Altunbas, Gambacorta, et al. 2009).[45] The underlying problem in all such instances is how to identify money. Strange, like Minsky, suggests that this problem has deepened the more the financial system has grown.

Strange argues that the development of money substitutes encourages *overbanking*, i.e., "the imprudent expansion of credit with increased profits to the banks but increased risk to the system of financial panic and collapse" (Strange 1994b: 96). A new language had to be invented to describe these devices, she argued, incorporating "money market mutual funds, swaps, options, NOW accounts, zero coupon bonds, off balance-sheet financing, and so on" (Strange 1994b: 110). Overbanking, Strange argued, can lead to the *death of money*, which, "whether it comes about by inflation or by a political revolution sweeping away the government, inevitably brings trade, investment and economic life generally to a standstill" (Strange 1994b: 95, 99). Finance, by generating a volatile international environment through overbanking, is dangerous for *society* insofar as it is a threat to its *money*.

For Strange, casino capitalism had its roots in attempts to *manage* risk, which unwittingly *increased* it. These were the monetary risks associated with globalization and floating exchange rates: of doing business in different currencies, for example, and in different regions of the world with various economic and monetary conditions. Modern financial derivatives, for example, were developed in the midst of the riskier exchange rate regime that followed the demise of Bretton Woods. Their role was to *hedge* risk. Financial markets do not want to gamble, Strange argued (Strange 1986: 106). A speculative market requires both uncertainty and risk aversion on the part of others, a speculative fund "and a supply of young men eager to work hard for above-normal gain" (Strange 1998b: 10). But this speculation led to a vicious circle of

---

45 The terms "M3" and "M4" refer to measures of an economy's money supply and are used by central banks for the purpose of directing monetary policy and trying to control inflation. There are five categories in all: M0 and M1 (also called narrow money) include coins and notes in circulation and other money equivalents that can be converted into cash with ease; M2 includes M1 and short-term time deposits (i.e., bank deposits that can only be withdrawn with notice or, if immediately, with a penalty) in banks and 24-hour money market funds; M3 includes M2 plus longer term time deposits and money market funds with more than 24-hour maturity. M4 includes M3 plus other deposits. The exact definitions of the measures depend on local conditions (McLealy et al. 2014: 23). See http://lexicon.ft.com/Term?term=m0,-m1,-m2, -m3,-m4.

uncertainty, whereby systems devised for managing global risks generate the very uncertainties on which speculators thrive, thus making risk avoidance even more necessary (generating further uncertainty, etc.) (Strange 1986: 111).

Securitization, too, was devised to reduce risk, breaking it down and distributing it across the banking system (Minsky 2008). Instruments such as collateralized debt obligations (CDOs) were integral to techniques developed to deal with the riskier loans made by the U.S.government-sponsored mortgage companies, Fannie Mae and Freddie Mac, during the 1960s. The large investment banks did not enter the market for these securities until the 1990s, when they provided unwelcome competition for the government-sponsored lenders. The technique expanded as a form of outsourcing, and securities were structured according to different tiers of risk. This system was significant because it enabled risk to be handled via the market rather than within banks themselves. As a consequence, the debt relation became increasingly *fragmented* and *diffused*. Theoretically, risks were spread out, first, through fragmentation, and second, by being sold. High-risk debt became increasingly attractive in this system, satisfying investors' search for yield while interest rates were historically low (and had been low since 2001) while seemingly presenting a minimal risk to banks that could either sell them or move them offshore as special investment vehicles (SIVs). But although it had been used successfully in commercial lending, securitization did not work well for domestic mortgages, for example, because default correlations were unknown (MacKenzie 2011).

Subprime lending did not expand in a vacuum but was fueled by surplus funds from outside the United States, using the very architecture of global finance that preoccupied Minsky and Strange. In 2005, as the CDO market was nearing its peak, the U.S. current account deficit approached 6.25 percent of GDP, or the equivalent of 1.5 percent of world GDP. China's current account surplus reached $371.8 billion by 2007,[46] against a U.S. current account deficit of $738.6 billion that year (BEA).[47] To finance this debt, the United States needed to attract 70 percent of the world's capital flows (Rajan 2005, 2011). Surplus countries (Asian governments and households, and oil-rich countries) were providing the shadow banking system with the speculative funds it needed (Nsouli 2006). By 2007, the market for CDO issuance totaled $485.726 billion, up from $157.419 billion in 2004.[48] This combina-

---

46   Source: Chinese Foreign State Administration of Foreign Exchange, see http://www.safe.gov.cn/wps/portal/english/Data/Payments.
47   Source: Bureau of Economic Analysis, see http://www.bea.gov/iTable/index_ita.cfm.
48   Source: Securities Industry and Financial Markets Association, see http://www.sifma.org/research/statistics.aspx.

tion of global financial imbalances and a specific orientation toward risk would doubtless strike a chord with Strange. Investors from surplus countries were looking for low-risk securities, ideally U.S. Treasury bills, which were in short supply. This is where securitization was key, enabling surplus countries to invest their funds in deficit countries without taking on two crucial forms of risk: credit risk and liquidity risk. SIVs and hedge funds assumed the former, and investment banks (as prime brokers) took on the liquidity risk (Brender and Pisani 2010: 6). Credit ratings helped to sustain an illusion of safety about mortgage-backed securities, reassuring many economic actors (both sophisticated investors and those at the other end of the securitization chain) that they were not being reckless.

This analysis suggests that banks were playing a nontraditional intermediary role by taking assets and, with the help of financial engineering and credit rating agencies, effectively "de-risking" them. The risk attached to subprime loans was borne by risk takers as links within the shadow banking chain (Brender and Pisani 2010: 120–21). Just as Minsky's hypothesis would predict, when this chain broke down, governments stepped in, taking on both liquidity and credit risks (Brender and Pisani 2010: 162–63). The key point here is that securitization did not so much involve diversifying risk as its wholesale *transfer*: first to counterparties, many of whom misunderstood what they were buying because the technology was opaque; and second, the transfer of "toxic" risks, through government, to *society*. These "private" risks, in other words, were ultimately socialized. It was, in Strange's terms, a classic case of overbanking, with society bearing the costs.

Although she rarely examines the concept theoretically, there are deeper sociological assumptions about the nature of money underpinning Strange's analysis. These take us back, once again, to Simmel's description of money as a claim upon society. In *Casino Capitalism*, Strange steps back to consider "the more philosophical side of money ... that has rather been lost sight of and overlooked in recent decades" (Strange 1986: 103). This is the question of "what the use of money does to human relations, and to human behaviour in society" (Strange 1986: 103). She specifically suggests that money's social foundations are being eroded by finance. To make this argument, Strange draws on Simmel to highlight the attributes of trust and confidence that money relies on to fulfill its basic functions. The following remarks, prescient in 1986, are striking now: "At a time when the most secure jobs are apt suddenly to vanish and still more people are made redundant, the capacity of the monetary system to offer—as it should—a secure store of value that people can use to cushion themselves against such misfortunes or against illness or old age, seems less than it ever was" (Strange 1986: 103).

Strange's remarks about money being a "secure store of value" resonate further with Keynes's description of money as *risk free*. Keynes once asked: "Why should anyone outside a lunatic asylum wish to use money as a store of wealth?" (Keynes 1937: 216). Strange's answer, like Keynes's own, would surely be this: because the future is chronically uncertain. Keynes described money as a "subtle device for linking the present to the future" (Keynes 2008: 269). Money "lulls our disquietude" (Keynes 1937: 216), and our desire to hold it "is a barometer of the degree of our distrust of our own calculations and conventions" (Keynes 1973: 116). This desire is the source of money's high liquidity premium. So did Keynes influence Strange's understanding of money? There is no direct evidence of this influence, although she attributes to Keynes "the only coherent, rigorous and influential theory concerning the conduct of financial markets," approvingly describing his work as "more of a *sociological* theory than a purely *economic* one" (Strange 1998b: 10, italics added). In fact, most of her interest is in so-called Keynesianism, i.e., the belief that states can use monetary policy to stimulate demand. Nevertheless, her remarks on money and uncertainty are consistent with those of Keynes, and this direction is one in which they might productively be developed to deepen the distinction she draws between (national) *money* and (international) *finance*.

As far as *money* is concerned, trust is crucial to Strange's position. Citing Simmel's description of money as a claim upon society, she argues that trust in money can only be established by faith and experience, not fiat (Strange 1986: 106).[49] These arguments bring the discussion back to the distinctiveness of the debt relation that resides *within* money. When Simmel describes money as a claim upon society, he likens it to "a bill of exchange from which the name of the drawee is lacking" (Simmel 2004: 177).[50] This definition suggests that the debt money involves (this is the bill of exchange metaphor) is between the individual and a wider payment community (the nameless drawee), not between two parties. In other words, money is a form of *socialized debt*, a relationship between the *individual* and *society*. This notion explains why, through her reading of Simmel, Strange could regard money as a secure store of value that people use to cushion themselves

---

49   She subsequently criticized Fukuyama's *Trust* (Fukuyama 1995) because, even in distinguishing between high- and low-trust societies, he failed to address the problem of trust in the value and stability of *money*, which, she argued, "causes most conflict at every level of social interaction" (Strange 1998b: 7).

50   *Drawee*: The person who is requested to pay, e.g., the drawee could be the bank, ordered by one of its depositors, the drawer, to pay a sum of money to a third party. Simmel adds, "The liquidation of every private obligation by money means that the community now assumes this obligation towards the creditor" (Simmel 2004: 177).

against an uncertain future. As Simmel suggests, we *expect* money to settle a transaction because its value seems to be *guaranteed* by the wider payment community. If money is a debt, it is a debt that society owes to itself. Strange's complaint, essentially, is that banks have gone too far in their mediation of this relationship. And this situation, in the end, is what overbanking means.

AUSTERITY MYTHS

Modern public finance emerged in northern Italy around the Renaissance. For the first time, states were run by merchants, not soldiers, and their finances were bolstered by the idea of repayable taxes, i.e., levies upon which interest would be paid if the government's finances were healthy enough. To be a citizen was to be a creditor of the state (Macdonald 2003: 4). The model was improved in rigor and reliability by other city-states in northern Europe, particularly in the Netherlands. After revolutions in 1688 and 1776, the British and the Americans adopted Dutch-style finance, funding wars by selling bonds to citizen creditors rather than resorting to excessive taxation or inflation. The contrast between France and England in the eighteenth century is especially illuminating: in both countries there were serious economic problems, triggered by the Mississippi and South Sea bubbles, respectively. The French devalued their currency, regulated finance tightly, and confiscated wealth gained from speculation, seriously damaging its creditor class. The English did exactly the opposite, canceling the South Sea Company's debt to the government. The English approach led to an accommodation whereby two separate classes (merchants handling financial affairs, landholders dealing in politics) eventually merged until the system operated in a unified fashion, much as the Dutch system had done. As trust in English government increased, the cost of borrowing was reduced. The French, despite the fact that its economy was healthier in many respects, usually had to borrow at higher rates. Hence, public debt does not necessarily threaten democracy but can, on the contrary, reinforce it (Macdonald 2003).

Today, this mutually supportive relationship between public debt and democracy has been fundamentally weakened. The spectacle of pensioners, public sector workers, schoolchildren, and students bearing the brunt of a public debt burden that grew dramatically since the banking crisis began sheds a new and disconcerting light on the ideals of public finance, its dependence upon the financial sector, and the relationship of both to the social production of money. The problem, in part, is that the bond markets no longer have the ideological underpinnings that reinforce this connection.

Institutions, many from abroad, now dominate the rentiers that Keynes once railed against. There is a crucial monetary dimension to this situation. States (and society) are most exposed when their sovereign debt is denominated in foreign currency (Wolf 2010: 171). Private borrowing is affected too: Krugman envisages a crisis emerging specifically because firms have a high proportion of their debt in foreign currency (Krugman 2002), and Robert Wade's analysis of the Icelandic crisis suggests that large borrowings by households and firms in foreign currency were crucial (Wade 2009). It is simply less risky for a government to borrow in its own currency.

In the aftermath of the 2007–8 banking crisis, many states ran into debt problems, not just because of the costs of bailout but also (and mainly) because of the recession that was triggered by the credit squeeze the banking crisis caused. States fund their debt through taxation (but revenues are in decline) and bonds (which have been downgraded in many cases), and central banks (especially in the United States and the United Kingdom) have been purchasing bonds to sustain the market. For countries borrowing in their own currency (irrespective of whether their creditors are domestic or foreign), there are two options for dealing with rising borrowing costs. One is to create money, not only accepting that this option may weaken the currency but welcoming the boost that new money gives to exports. The other option is to embark on a program of spending cuts and various other austerity measures: in short, to deflate. In practice, borrowing in one's own currency means that countries must—unavoidably—take sides in the "struggle" between creditors and debtors that Ingham identifies as the sociological basis of money. Overwhelmingly, governments have been pursuing the second option, citing the dangers of inflation and rising borrowing costs as the underlying rationale. Bluntly put, they have acted in the interests of their creditors.

The *direct* costs of the financial crisis have been considerable. In the United Kingdom, the cost to the taxpayer of various measures to support banks has been estimated at £124 billion,[51] although the government's total exposure to the banking system has sometimes reached a figure ten times higher. Those costs include the purchase of preference shares, making the U.K. taxpayer a major shareholder in a number of these banks. In the United States, loans were advanced to banks worth $45 billion, a bridge loan to AIG worth $44 billion, asset purchases valued at $39 billion, mortgage debt purchases totaling $930 billion, loan programs worth $450 billion, and a liquidity guarantee

---

51   Source: National Audit Office, see http://www.nao.org.uk/highlights/taxpayer-support-for-uk-banks-faqs/.

program worth around $300 billion. Some of this outlay will be recouped as loans are repaid, shares gain in value, and assets are sold. Although the remaining, and arguably greater, indirect costs of the crisis are ongoing and difficult to estimate, it seems likely that the monetary system, primarily through its connections with debt, will play a central role in their unraveling.

The *indirect* costs of the crisis are arguably far greater, longer lasting, and ultimately more damaging than the costs associated with bailouts. According to Jack Rasmus, the vicious spiral of debt, default, and deflation that developed since 2008 is constitutive of an *epic recession* (Rasmus 2010). Whereas a recession normally lasts for around three consecutive quarters of one year, great depressions (e.g., in the 1830s, 1890s, and 1929–33 in the United States) have lasted for around three years. An epic recession falls between the two, and in some cases develops into a great depression. The dynamics of an epic recession pivot around a combination of bad debt, default, and deflation. The danger inherent in bad debt and distressed selling is that falling asset prices spill over into the mainstream economy, generalizing deflationary expectations. Once this spillover occurs, the cycle of distressed debt and default intensifies as ordinary (nonbank) businesses, consumers, and households find themselves unable to meet their financial obligations, or turn over their debts as the credit market freezes up. One crucial characteristic of the epic recession, according to Rasmus, is that monetary policy proves to be an increasingly ineffective tool of crisis management; indeed, it may even become counterproductive. With short-term interest rates approaching (or actually reaching) zero, banks end up hoarding cash rather than lending it out, while price deflation merely increases the burden of debt.

In the Eurozone, exactly such a scenario has been unfolding since late 2009. The crisis has focused on the large deficits of specific member states, which reflect complex linkages among money, public finances, private debt, and the global banking system. These are combining to enact different aspects of what Strange called overbanking. The complex nexus of public and private debt that defines the parameters of the crisis has torn the democratic integrity of its constituent member states apart. According to Wolfgang Streeck (Streeck 2011), the form of democratic capitalism found in the Eurozone operates according to two conflicting regimes of resource allocation, one based on marginal productivity and determined by market forces, the other based on need or entitlement and determined by democratic politics. These principles almost never align; one usually holds sway until there is a reaction, and such a reaction, e.g., of democracy against the market, was described through Polanyi's notion of double movement (Polanyi 1957b).

Part of the reason for this reaction is that governments do not have the choices that would normally be open to them if they had their own central banks and their own currencies. The Eurozone crisis is a crisis of democratic capitalism, wherein governments have been facing conflicting demands from their citizens and their creditors[52] in their attempts to manage rising and increasingly unmanageable levels of sovereign debt during a period (since 2008) when unemployment has been rising to equally unsustainable levels:[53] "street riots and popular insurrection may be the last remaining mode of political expression for those devoid of market power" (Streeck 2011: 24). Having their own currencies would not have resolved these difficulties and dilemmas, although governments throughout the Eurozone would certainly have had greater room to maneuver. "Having your own currency makes all the difference," Krugman once remarked, playing down the prospect that the United Kingdom and the United States might encounter bond crises of their own.[54] However, the euro is not completely different from other modern state-based monetary systems: *all* are subject to underlying tensions with the financial sector, to the threat (real or imagined) of rising borrowing costs. "Having your own currency" may help manage these tensions, perhaps even displacing them via inflationary fiscal policies. But it does not resolve them.

The private debts built up within the banking system constitute a claim upon society by the financial sector. According to Michael Hudson, the 2007–8 global crisis came as the culmination of a transformation in the balance of power among *government*, *society*, and *finance* (Hudson 2011, 2012). The last emerged victorious, holding the bottom 99 percent of society in debt and using economic theory deceptively to persuade them to vote for policies that benefit the 1 percent at the expense of labor, industry, and

---

52   Even when the citizens *are* the creditors, as in Greece, where Greek pension funds with state bonds worth 21 billion euros took a 53 percent "haircut" in spring 2012.

53   Between January 2008 and December 2012, the unemployment rate rose from 6.5 to 11 percent in Italy (ISTAT); from just under 5 to almost 15 percent in Ireland (Central Statistics Office Ireland); 7.6 to 15.8 percent in Portugal (Instituto Nacional de Estatística); 9.63 to 25.02 percent in Spain (INE); and 8.2 to 26 percent in Greece (Hellenic Statistical Authority).

54   "Rashomon in the OECD," *New York Times*, June 3, 2010. Krugman subsequently went on to revise what he meant by "having your own currency," suggesting that member states within the Eurozone could be distinguished between those that had the backing of the European Central Bank because they could not be allowed to fail, such as France, and those that did not because they could be allowed to fail, such as Greece. In effect, Eurozone countries falling within the former group "have their own currencies and therefore can't run out of money—a club all of whose members have very low borrowing costs, more or less independent of their debts and deficits"; see "France has its own currency again," April 8, 2013, http://krugman.blogs.nytimes.com/2013/04/08/france-has-its-own-currency-again/, accessed May 10, 2013.

democratic government.[55] This transformation has relied upon a myth—he describes it as "Orwellian doublethink"—that systematically misrepresents the relationship between money and public debt. The myth is that governments should not run deficits because this leads to *excessive money creation*, which in turn leads to *hyperinflation*. The outcome of this myth, and the transformation its perpetuation has supported, is that most of the advanced capitalist economies have become overloaded with debt, forcing governments to sell off land, natural resources, public enterprises, and other assets to service their financial obligations. The problem is not simply that the public debt has grown. Rather, it is that its growth has enabled a process Hudson describes as "privatization by credit," whereby significant public assets have become a major source of rent extraction for the financial sector. These are the financial mechanisms behind the increasing enrichment of the 1 percent and the growing indebtedness of the 99 percent. The austerity doctrine, attacked by Keynes during the 1920s and 1930s, has been used by the IMF against Third World countries since the 1960s, and by European neoliberals against the most indebted member states in the present Eurozone crisis.

At the heart of Hudson's analysis is the "austerity myth" that relies on a bogus argument about excessive money creation by government as the *inevitable* path to hyperinflation.[56] Historically, banks have tried to block governments from creating money under normal peacetime conditions—for exactly the reasons that Keynes identified in his critique of the rentier class. Government bonds were their safest investment, as the financial sector monopolized public finance for its own ends. Only during the exceptional political circumstances of wartime were they *unable* to oppose government money creation. More recently, however, the bankers did not oppose the significant levels of money creation ($13 trillion of debt to rescue bad loans and other obligations) that went into the bailout and the quantitative easing (QE) program. QE began in March 2009, when the U.S. Federal Reserve bought $1,750 billion of government bonds and mortgage-related and agency securities, and the Bank of England purchased £200 billion ($308 billion) of (mostly) government debt. Despite this, and several subsequent

---

55   Hudson is invoking a meme of the Occupy movement, which is designed to capture the concentration of wealth in the richest 1 percent of Americans, whose incomes rose by 275 percent between 1979 and 2007, compared to a rise of 40–60 percent for the remaining 99 percent.
56   The precise nature of the myth is that excessive *government* spending leads to hyperinflation. In reality, Hudson argues, every hyperinflation has been caused by international payment deficits.

episodes of QE, *deflation*, not inflation, still appears to be the prevailing concern. Technically, quantitative easing consists of temporary bond purchases, but there is a view, increasingly predominant, that these purchases will turn out to be forever.[57] This would be helicopter money,[58] or what is otherwise known as direct (or overt) monetary financing.[59]

Monetary theory is at the heart of this idea. Unlike households and firms, sovereign governments are in a unique position to resist pressure to settle debts by selling assets because they can create the money to do so. According to Hudson, the austerity myth is working directly against this capacity, resting on the (false) belief that government budgets are like family budgets. There is a significant double standard in operation here because whereas the bailouts were urged as being "good" for the economy because they supported asset prices, other forms of expenditure requiring money creation, such as for policies designed to raise employment, are dismissed as reckless. The truth about budget deficits, Hudson suggests, is the reverse. He cites seven periods during which the U.S. government has achieved a budget surplus.[60] Six of these were quickly followed by a depression.[61] The seventh (1998–2001) was not, but this difference was caused by the dot.com bubble. The major financial problem now faced in the United States concerns corporate, state, and local pension plans. These need to grow at 8 percent, despite being underfunded. The only "plan" for achieving this growth appears to be for the government to provide the banks with almost-interest-free credit so that they can lend while exploiting huge margins. This policy has nothing to do with growing the economy; it is a "financial rake-off." Meanwhile, the Fed faces an interest rate quandary: if it keeps rates

---

57 See "Helicopter QE will never be reversed," *The Telegraph* (London), April 3, 2013; "Helicopter money and supply-siders," *Financial Times* (London), February 6, 2013; "Helicopters can be dangerous," *Financial Times* (London), February 17, 2013. The argument rests on the distinction between (a) QE for liquidity purposes (this is money "loaned" to the system and hauled back into the system once it has served its purpose, and (b) direct monetary financing (or monetizing debt, or printing money), which can even bypass the financial system and go straight into public works. Historical analogues to the second of these options include Weimar Germany (widely held to have been a disaster) and 1930s Japan (largely viewed as a success). Under Shinzo Abe, Japan is alleged now to be undertaking a significant program of direct monetary financing (see "Bank of Japan unveils aggressive easing," *Financial Times* (London), April 4, 2013).

58 The term comes from Friedman's tongue-in-cheek suggestion that price deflation could be countered by "dropping money out of a helicopter" (Friedman 1969: 4).

59 Simply put, direct monetary financing results in a permanent increase in the monetary base.

60 1817–21, 1823–36, 1852–57, 1867–73, 1880–93, 1920–30, and 1998–2001.

61 Starting in 1819, 1837, 1857, 1873, 1893, and 1929.

low, the financial sector will be forced to gamble to achieve the growth in asset values it needs; if rates rise, real estate values will fall and the banks and pension funds will be forced even further into negative equity.

If Hudson is right, we ought to be witnessing the end of *two* myths. The first is about free markets. We cannot continue to believe that they are free when they support rent seeking rather than real GDP, reward banks for pushing junk mortgages, and use credit rating agencies to make predatory finance look like sound wealth creation. Free markets need to be protected from fraud and rent seeking. The second myth is that central banks cause inflation by monetizing public spending. They do not cause inflation if the spending in question goes toward new production and employment. Instead, such spending is being diverted to support inflated asset prices and continued financial speculation.

CONCLUSION

This chapter has traveled across a broad terrain: from the argument that it is debt that renders money social, to the prospect that, *through* money, today's brutally one-sided debt relations pose a major threat to democracy. The problem lies, at least in part, along the fault line uncovered by Strange, between money and society on one side and banks and the rentier system on the other. Strange made powerful use of the casino metaphor. Whether or not we choose to enter the casino, she said, "all of us are involuntarily engaged in the day's play . . . The financial casino has everyone playing the game of Snakes and Ladders" (Strange 1986: 106). Few may gain. Everyone can lose. Bad luck tends to be unevenly distributed: not just the tables, she implies, but the entire casino, and the system of debt that sustains it, is rigged, affecting households, firms, and as I have suggested here, entire countries unevenly. The global financial system links various forms of economic instability: inflation, the price of credit, and energy costs. It is, Strange says, the rootstock of disorder in international political economy, "just as blight, disease or mildew attack the different branches of a plant" (Strange 1986: 4). This is "mad money," and "the prospects for reform, for cooling the casino, for making money sane again are slim" (Strange 1998a: 3). This is a pathological stage of capitalism, characterized by volatility and excess, seemingly driven by a financial distension that overwhelms the real economy and threatens the integrity of money as a secure store of value. In her final book, anticipating a major crisis, Strange said that the most radical proposals for financial reform (such as narrow banking[62]) would require trauma: "a period of such economic pain that people would accept drastic remedies" (Strange 1998a: 187). We have the pain. The remedies are open to debate.

Strange warned that the exponential growth of the global financial system could lead to the death of money. By contrast, Marx suggested that whenever capitalism's credit pyramid collapsed, the question of money's ultimate value would be the one thing that would never die. The arguments that we have been discussing in this chapter suggest how they may have been both right and both wrong. Debt's implosion in the Eurozone did not lead directly to the death of the currency, the euro itself, but rather to vigorous political efforts to ensure its survival, at least in *some* form. There is an argument to be made, however, that through these efforts, money has been turned into a mute force of destruction. Money's own collapse, or what Strange described as the death of money, is conventionally seen as the dramatic loss of its value, a hyperinflation. But deflation, too, can be destructive, affecting not just money's value in a narrow sense but also the social bonds that underwrite its status as a claim upon society. Keynes described deflation as "the oppression of the taxpayer for the enrichment of the rentier" (Keynes 1972: 189). However, the effect of austerity measures aimed at preserving the underlying value of money is experienced *throughout* society, not just by taxpayers. Economic statistics focus on inflation, growth, and unemployment, but death statistics are usually associated with pestilence and war, not money. Death statistics, however, are just as relevant to grasping the cruel social dynamics of debt, default, and deflation.

Galbraith once said that because everyone expects money's value to depreciate, we inevitably feel the need for a strategy for offsetting its deterioration (Galbraith 1975: 2). Finance (public and private) can be understood along similar lines: as a means of compensating for the fact that money's

---

62 Narrow (or safe) banks take deposits but do not offer loans and must stay highly "liquid" by holding only short-term, secure assets, e.g., government bonds (Kay 2009, 2010). Strange, too, discusses Henry Simons's narrow banking proposals (Simons 1948), published two years after his death in 1946 (Strange 1998a: 162–63). In Strange's terms, narrow banking aims to insulate the national monetary system from the riskier parts of the global financial system. A less restrictive distinction, between utility (or retail and commercial) and investment banking, was used by the United Kingdom's Financial Services Authority in its financial crisis report, although the report concludes that even this use would be "impractical" (Turner 2009). James Robertson has made similar proposals. He argues that private banks in Britain create around forty times more money (by issuing debt) than the government. If the government simply issued the money by "spending into circulation," the role of banks could be stripped back to a narrower credit-brokering role (Robertson 2012).

value tends to deteriorate. Stable money, or low inflation, tends to be viewed as an absolute good.[63] It is invariably held up as such whenever governments implore their citizens to accept the "sacrifices" that are necessary—on behalf of *society*—to aid economic recovery and to rebuild money after the latest episode of violent credit contraction. But when money's value is ultimately underpinned by debt, its value is no longer neutral, and it is not self-evidently a public good. Debt-induced austerity expresses not the force of a collective political will, but the interest of the creditor. When that creditor includes members of the very society that is in debt, there is a perverse and destructive logic at play. Characterized in these terms, the "debt problem" today seems especially serious, not simply in scale but in the fact that, perhaps for the first time in history, debtors and states, as well as individuals, are facing a financial climate in which the notion of debt forgiveness is absent. As Graeber points out, this is arguably the first era in which the most powerful institutions (the IMF and the World Bank, financial regulators, national and international law) are geared up to protect creditors, not debtors. A monetary system that is defined by an overarching orientation toward the interests of creditors is inimical to democracy. The exponential buildup of debt in the Eurozone has been absorbing all potential for growth, not to mention the very capacity for social expenditure in those countries that are now being deemed "peripheral." As a consequence, democracy, or society, now appears to be in open conflict with the needs of finance. Debt is no longer facilitating capitalism. It is driving it.

63   Susan Strange's description of money as a "secure store of value" implies this, too.

4 GUILT

> ... all at once we find ourselves standing in front of the horrific and paradoxical expedient in which tortured humanity has found a temporary relief, that stroke of genius on the part of *Christianity*: God sacrificing himself for the guilt of man, God paying himself off, God as the sole figure who can redeem on man's behalf that which has become irredeemable for man himself—the creditor sacrificing himself for his debtor, out of *love* (are we supposed to believe this?—), out of love for his debtor!
>
> **NIETZSCHE, ON THE GENEALOGY OF MORALS**[1]

In *Daybreak* (originally published in 1881), Nietzsche said that our sentiments toward money were taking the place of our religious feelings: "What one formerly did 'for the sake of God' one now does for the sake of money, that is to say, for the sake of that which now gives the highest feeling of power and good conscience" (Nietzsche 1997a: 123). Though his proclamations of the death of God have been widely discussed, few have dwelled on Nietzsche's remarks about their implications for money, particularly in the wake of a crisis—our own—that is closely associated with debt and financial excess. Nietzsche had strong ideas about money. As with most aspects of modernity, he regarded the spread of the cash nexus as a bleak prospect; indeed, almost everything he said on the subject was negative. "The educated classes are being swept along by a hugely contemptible money economy," he observed in *Untimely Meditations* (originally published in 1878, 1997b cited here). "The world has never been more worldly, never poorer in love and goodness" (Nietzsche 1997b: 148). In *Thus Spoke Zarathustra* (originally published 1883–85, 2003b cited here), he railed against the "superfluous people" who "acquire wealth and make themselves poorer with it" (Nietzsche 2003b: 77), while in *On the Genealogy of Morals* (originally published in 1887, 1996b

---

1   Source: Nietzsche 1996b: 72.

cited here) he mocked modern morality, with its notions of guilt and punishment rooted in archaic forms of "buying, selling, exchange, wheeling and dealing" (Nietzsche 1996b: 45).

In the previous chapter, I pointed out that debt both supports and is reinforced by a moral economy that is often used to justify the social, economic, and political asymmetries of power that exist between creditors and debtors. Debt often (although not always) carries a stigma of shame and is associated with self-harm and an abnormal, damaged existence. The discussion in this chapter takes its cue from Nietzsche's observation about the dual meaning of *Schuld*—as both *debt* and *guilt*—in order to delve more deeply into these associations by exploring the theme of guilt and its connections with money more broadly. Nietzsche was no monetary theorist, of course. He had nothing to say on technical matters such as the theory of value, the development of paper money, or the growth of commercial banking. But his philosophy did influence the reflections of several important thinkers on money and related phenomena, such as credit and debt. I consider three such thinkers in this chapter. The first is Simmel, whose *The Philosophy of Money* (originally published in 1907, 2004 edition cited here) contains a relativistic interpretation of value and an analysis of the negative effect of money on the individual in which Nietzsche's imprint can clearly be found. The second is Benjamin, whose enigmatic fragment on debt, "Capitalism as Religion" (originally published in 1920–21, 1996a edition cited here), can be read through its key Nietzschean figure, the *Übermensch*. The third is Brown, who in *Life Against Death* (1959) brings Nietzsche's juxtaposition between Apollonian and Dionysian concepts to bear on a Freudian account of money. There is, I want to suggest, sufficient resonance between these different arguments to justify asking what a "Nietzschean" concept of money might consist of and to weigh Nietzsche's potential contribution to the social theory and philosophy of money. What emerges from the analysis is a notion of money that is inextricably linked with broader, quasisacred ideals about human existence and morality: about our relationship to ourselves, to time, and to God.

ÜBERMENSCH AND ETERNAL RETURN

Nietzsche once described *Beyond Good and Evil* as "in all essentials a critique of modernity" (Nietzsche 1979: 112). David Frisby thought that the description might just as well apply to all of Nietzsche's published works, and it makes sense to approach his effect on Simmel's sociology in such terms

(Frisby 1985: 30). Simmel cites Nietzsche, for example, when writing about the "secret restlessness" of the modern age that results from overreliance on technology. He might have been referring to *Writings from the Late Notebooks*, where Nietzsche uses the metaphor of feeding and digestion to capture modernity's excitability: "the impressions efface each other; one instinctively resists taking something in, taking something deeply, 'digesting' something" (Nietzsche 2003c: 178). Nietzsche uses the same metaphor in *Daybreak* (originally published in 1881, 1997a cited here) to describe the "bad diet" of the modern age and wittily compares scholars to bankers: both load their table "on the principle of 'much too much' and 'lots of different things' ... To the devil with the dissoluteness and over-excitability which must generally follow from this!" The sense of agitation Nietzsche finds in the modern age is closely linked to money. The problem with modern attitudes toward money, he says, is not simply that we want to accumulate money for its own sake. It is our drive to do so quickly. Fraud—counterfeit coins, for example—is driven not by need, but by impatience (Nietzsche 1997a: 122–300). There are Nietzschean echoes, too, in Simmel's assertion that the confidence in the community ("society") that underpins our acceptance of money contains an "element of social-psychological quasi-religious faith" (Simmel 2004: 179).

Although Simmel cites Nietzsche directly just four times in *The Philosophy of Money* (Simmel 2004: 274, 278, 446, 484), Nietzschean themes are in evidence throughout the book. They include the transformation of all valuation, the leveling of values, the pathos of distance, the ideal of excellence (*Vornehmheit*), the growing role of mediation and mediators in modernity, the aesthetic value sensibility, the indifference to value, and the relativistic worldview (Frisby, in Simmel 2004: lix). These themes fall into two main groups, which are interconnected: the first deals with the theory of value, and the second with the plight of the individual in the mature money economy.

Simmel tackles the problem of value extensively in the first chapter of *The Philosophy of Money* (2004). In relation to economic theory, he tries to establish what Frisby describes as a "critical position that is, as it were, neither that of Carl Menger nor of Karl Marx" (Frisby 1992: 140, n. 23). He is concerned with value in a much broader sense, however; indeed, his aim was to develop a general theory of value incorporating its religious and aesthetic aspects, before developing an account of economic and monetary value as more specific forms (Canto-Mila 2005). Simmel is especially concerned with the conflict between these different registers of value. Money diminishes our capacity to appreciate qualitative aspects of value because of its unremitting orientation to *quantity*. This orientation emaciates both our *aesthetic sensibility* and our *moral life*. This point is where Nietzsche comes into play, especially his argument that the true measure of a culture are its "highest specimens" and rarest achievements, not its average and most common ones (Nietzsche 1980: 53). As Simmel puts it, "the quality of an artistic period is not the result of the height and quantity of good average achievements but only of the height of the very best achievement" (Simmel 2004: 274; 1991b: 154). Set against this quality, money stifles individual excellence: its very existence encourages us to emphasize the many, the most common, the average: to erase individual distinction. Money is the great leveler.

Nietzsche's argument appeals to Simmel on analytical, as well as substantive, grounds. In *Schopenhauer and Nietzsche* (originally published in 1907, 1991b cited here), Simmel remarks that Nietzsche "views the life of a humanity to which he is passionately devoted as exhibited only in individuals" (Simmel 1991b: 145), and commends Nietzsche for his image of society, which "does not dissolve the individual into social relations and into the functions of giving and receiving within a group: 'Man follows a single line to oneself'" (Simmel 1991b: 146). Simmel describes Nietzsche's image as "an aristocratic organization of society" that is informed neither by simple egoism nor outright altruism but is realized through "objective perfections, beauties, and deepenings of the human life" (Simmel 1902: 183). It is a characterization that resonates with Simmel's argument in *The Philosophy of Money*, where he describes society as "the universal which, at the same time, is concretely alive" (Simmel 2004: 101).

The meaning of "aristocratic" here is connected to Nietzsche's concept of "nobility of mind," in which he sees qualities such as good-naturedness and absence of distrust that "successful and money-hungry people are so fond of looking down on and laughing at" (Nietzsche 1996a: 180). Whoever possesses nobility of mind is indifferent to price, living in a style that is "diametrically opposed to that of the money economy where the value of things tends increasingly to be so identified" (Simmel 1991b: 166). Nobility, Simmel states, represents "the high-water mark of his personal being from which he floats into the empire of human desire" (Simmel 1991b: 180). Simmel includes Nietzsche (alongside Goethe and Carlyle) in a group of thinkers who are "fundamentally anti-intellectual [and] completely reject that mathematically exact interpretation of nature which we recognized as the theoretical counterpart to the institution of money" (Simmel 2004: 446).

Nietzsche once described himself as "a man of over forty-four" who never craved after money (Nietzsche 1979: 350). His apparent contempt for money stems from the belief that it flattens everything it touches. This is a theme that Simmel picks up on when he remarks that if money's tendency to level out social relations was carried through to its logical extreme, it would encourage a form of life that has "a profound affinity to socialism, at least to an extreme state socialism" (Simmel 2004: 296). Like the money economy itself, socialism encourages the widest possible diffusion of desirable conditions and values in society. Nietzsche's presence in Simmel's thinking on this point seems clear:

> What separates Nietzsche from all socialist evaluations is most distinctly characterized by the fact that, for him, only the quality of mankind has any significance, so that a single highest example determines the value of an era, whereas for socialism only the degree of diffusion of desirable conditions and values is relevant. (Simmel 2004: 278)

In his 1896 essay, "The Women's Congress and Social Democracy," Simmel disparages socialism for "wishing to solve all riddles and difficulties of things with a single formula or a single stroke" (Simmel 1997: 271). Although his position on socialism softened over time (Dodd 2012), in this early essay it is unmistakably Nietzschean: "worker protection and worker insurance, general and unrestricted education, gradual work towards a standard working day and a minimum wage" all add up to a "levelling of social distinctions" (Simmel 1997: 271–72). In "The Metropolis and Mental Life" (originally published in 1903, 2002 cited here), Simmel writes that "Nietzsche may have seen the relentless struggle of the individual as the prerequisite for his full development, while socialism found the same thing in the suppression of all competition" (Simmel 2002: 11). As he explains in *Schopenhauer and Nietzsche*, to respect such qualities within the individual puts one in direct conflict with money:

> Nietzsche's deep aversion to all the specific phenomena of the money economy must be traced to his fundamental value commitment to nobility: in the money economy one weighs benefits and sacrifices, and regards something as a value when it is not purchased at great expense; where, for Nietzsche, one dissolves the relation between value and price by remaining indifferent to expense. (Simmel 1991b: 166)

In *Human, All Too Human*, Nietzsche states that a shilling in the hand of a laborer should be given a different value than a shilling in the hand of a rich heir: "according to whether he did almost nothing or a great deal to get it, each ought to receive little or a great deal in exchange for it." He adds, "In the great world of money the shilling of the laziest rich man is more lucrative than that of the poor and industrious" (Nietzsche 1996a: 314). The argument reflects his broader commitment to individual distinction and has an ethical shading that may surprise those who insist on taking Nietzsche's remarks about nobility too literally. When he points to the misleading nature of the "equality" involved when we pay the "same" price, Nietzsche's concern is with the effort involved in earning the money in the first place. Such remarks are linked to two of his most important philosophical doctrines, *Übermensch* and eternal return. Though the meaning of both ideas is open to debate, it is striking that Simmel's interpretation stresses the strong *moral* imperatives they suggest for the individual in modern society (Frisby 1985: 35). For Simmel, both *Übermensch* and eternal return are "norms of and challenges to our conduct" (Simmel 1991b: 174). The *Übermensch*—literally, overman or superman—represents an ideal human form, which in philosophical terms is characterized as the reconciliation of "being" with "becoming," terms which have been in opposition since the dispute between Heraclitus and the Eleatics. Such a form is not transcendent, but earthly, a product of "breeding."

Some see in *Übermensch* an unrealized future ideal, or a being from another world. Kaufman, for example, says that *Übermensch* cannot be disassociated from *Überwindung*, or overcoming: "'Man is something that should be overcome'—and the man who has overcome himself has become an overman" (Kaufmann 1975: 309). Others wonder whether Nietzsche was advocating hedonism (Richardson 2002: 19–20). Simmel disagrees with both points of view. In *Schopenhauer and Nietzsche*, we find him arguing against those who see in *Übermensch* merely rampant egoism. On the contrary, says Simmel, the idea reveals Nietzsche's underlying commitment to "the absolute and indisputable value of life" (Simmel 1991b: 180); indeed, his declared victory over Schopenhauer was based on the argument that the pessimism of the latter simply *destroys* life. Perhaps this explains his remark, in *The Philosophy of Money*, about the "vague" tension and longing, the "hidden" sense of urgency just below the threshold of consciousness "that drives modern man from socialism to Nietzsche, from Böcklin to impressionism, from Hegel to Schopenhauer and back again" (Simmel 2004: 484).

The idea of eternal return, or the "eternal recurrence of the ever-same," appeared late in Nietzsche's writings. He is said to have regarded it as "the most important thought that ever came to him" (Young 2010: 318). As with the concept of *Übermensch*, there are negative and positive interpretations of the concept. Both figure prominently in "Nietzschean" treatments of money. Seen in a negative light, eternal recurrence is associated with nihilism and Nietzsche's proclamations about the death of God, which, as we saw before, he associates with the love of money. This particular sense of eternal return is captured in Nietzsche's description of permanent duration:

> the belief in the absolute immortality of nature, in aim- and meaninglessness, is the psychologically necessary affect once the belief in God and an essentially moral order becomes untenable ... Duration "in vain," without end or aim, is the most paralyzing idea, particularly when one understands that one is being fooled and yet lacks the power not to be fooled. Let us think this thought in its most terrible form: existence as it is, without meaning or aim, yet recurring inevitably without any finale of nothingness: "the eternal recurrence." (Nietzsche 1973: 35)

Frisby called this time the "nihilistic moment of modernity" (Frisby 1985: 34). It surfaces in Nietzsche's general portrayal of modernity as an era of permanent decadence and is linked to his account of the transvaluation of all values (*Umwertung aller Werte*). The idea is also implied by Walter Benjamin's portrayal, drawing on Baudelaire as well as Nietzsche, of capitalism's relentless, always the same production of newness in commodities: "Fashion is the eternal recurrence of the new" (Benjamin 2003a: 29). For Benjamin, Baudelaire's "experience of the universe is in exact accord with the experience comprehended by Nietzsche in the phrase "God is dead" (Benjamin 2003a: 27). We come back to this in a moment.

On the other hand, eternal recurrence also contains a positive possibility: as an affirmation of existence, of life lived independently of Christian morality. Nietzsche himself described the doctrine he developed through *Thus Spoke Zarathustra* as "the highest formula of affirmation that can possibly be attained" (Nietzsche 2003b: 99). In *Beyond Good and Evil*, this idea is expressed by the man who calls out "*Da capo!*"—repeat! from the beginning!—to his own life,

> the most exuberant, most living and most world-affirming man, who has not only learned to get on and treat with all that was and is but who wants to have it again *as it was and is* to all eternity, insatiably calling out *da capo* not only to himself but to the whole piece and play, and not only to a play but fundamentally to him who need precisely this play—and who makes it necessary: because he needs himself again and again—and makes himself necessary—What? And would this not be—*circulus vitiosus deus*? (Nietzsche 2003a: 82, italics in original)

It is this interpretation of eternal recurrence, crystallized in the idea that "eternity" exists within each separate moment of time, which Simmel preferred.

Frisby described it as "modernity's affirmation of each moment of existence" (Frisby 1985: 34). The idea occurs in *Thus Spoke Zarathustra*, for example, when two roads meet, each pointing—one forward, one backward—to eternity: "and must we not return and run down that other lane out before us, down that long, terrible lane—must we not return eternally?" (Nietzsche 2003b: 179). The idea that each moment in time contains all of eternity was a *leitmotif* in discussions of aesthetics at the turn of the century. It was also, as we shall see, crucial to the Dionysian conception of the ego that emerges in Norman Brown's treatment of money.

For Simmel, the concepts of *Übermensch* and eternal return are linked: the man who shouts "Da capo!" declares his willingness to relive his life, *again* and *again*. This is the man who possesses nobility of mind—and significantly for us here, an aversion toward money. In *Ecce Homo*, Nietzsche makes clear that *Übermensch* should not be understood as "an 'idealistic' type of higher species of man, half 'saint', half 'genius.'" Nor is it Darwinian. Rather, it is a "very thoughtful" word in Zarathustra's mouth, "a type that has turned out supremely well, in antithesis to 'modern' men, to 'good' men, to Christians and other nihilists" (Nietzsche 1979: 71). As Simmel reads him, Nietzsche's position is that life becomes "more disciplined and severe the more it ascends." *Übermensch* is not antisocial. He is merely social in a different way. His responsibility is not to others or to an external law. Rather, it is a form of self-responsibility that "springs from the depth of one's own being" (Simmel 1991b: 169). This is an appropriate moment to turn to Benjamin, because he also invokes the *Übermensch* to make sense of an economic condition in which our very capacity for exercising self-responsibility has been threatened, or even suspended, namely, debt.

CAPITALISM, DEBT, AND RELIGION

In "One-Way Street" (originally published 1923–1926, 1996e cited here), Walter Benjamin acts as our guide on "A Tour Through the German Inflation." He was referring to the Weimar hyperinflation of 1921–24. Money, he observes, "stands ruinously at the centre of every vital interest" (Benjamin 1996e: 451–52).[2] "Money and rain belong together," he continues in "Tax Advice," imagining a "cloudless realm of perfect goods, on which no money

---

2 Among the interests that were ruined by the hyperinflation were Benjamin's own plans to launch a journal, *Angelus Novus* (Brodersen 1996: 123).

falls" (Benjamin 1996e: 481). In the same text, we find a striking description of banknotes: "The innocent cupids frolicking about numbers, the goddesses holding tablets of the law, the stalwart heroes sheathing their swords before the monetary units, are a world of their own: ornamenting the façade of hell" (Benjamin 1996e: 481). In *The Arcades Project*, he asks: "Isn't there a certain structure of money that can be recognized only in fate, and a certain structure of fate that can be recognized only in money?" (Benjamin 1999: O3, 3; O7, 1; O13a, 3). This is the unique combination of concerns that Benjamin brings to bear on money: the ruinous condition of modernity, the centrality of law in the modern secular state, and the question of history as fate. They are most powerfully brought together in the fragment he wrote in 1921, which remained unpublished in his lifetime, "Capitalism as Religion" (1996a). Even Benjamin scholars rarely discuss the text in depth. The key figure in the piece is Nietzsche's *Übermensch*, whom Benjamin paints as an allegory of modern capitalism, a "superman" whose incessant growth leads to an apocalyptic "breaking open of the heavens" (1996a: 289). The growth Benjamin has in mind, however, is not a generalized expansion of the economy, as measured by increasing GDP or a healthy balance of payments. It is the burden of debt.

"A religion may be discerned in capitalism," Benjamin says at the beginning of the piece, but what is the nature of the relationship between capitalism and religion? There are causal connections: Weber argued that capitalism was "conditioned" by religion. There are psychological parallels, too: like religion, capitalism promises to allay our "anxieties, torments, and disturbances." For Benjamin, however, neither characterization gets to the fact that capitalism is an "*essentially* religious phenomenon" (Benjamin 1996a: 288, italics added). "The paradigm of capitalist religious thought is magnificently formulated in Nietzsche's philosophy," he writes (Benjamin 1996a: 288). This affinity is structural: capitalism and religion occupy the *same space of articulation*. There is, Benjamin suggests, a fundamental equivalence between the *Christian guilt economy* and the *deterministic debt religion* on which modern capitalism depends (Hamacher 2002: 85). This emphasis on the profound importance of debt to capitalism makes his argument both distinctive and prescient.

Benjamin likens capitalism not simply to religion per se but more specifically, to a cult: capitalism is a "purely cultic religion," he says, "perhaps the most extreme that ever existed" (Benjamin 1996a: 288). A cult is an emaciated religion: it lacks a proper theology, cannot answer questions of ultimate value, and offers only superficial comforts. A true theology would promise redemption: forgiveness, an encounter with God, or resolution of life's underlying tensions. A cult offers only distractions: it is closed and inward looking, and everything is drawn back into its nexus of value—"things have a meaning only in their relationship to the cult" (Benjamin 1996a: 288)—and every action and every deed is assigned a rating in its shallow moral economy (Hamacher 2002: 87). A cult offers ritual but not transcendence. Capitalism is such a cult.

Benjamin's argument focuses on two aspects of capitalism in particular, which are related. The first is its *peculiar temporal structure*. Capitalism is similar to a cult in its *permanence*: "There is no day that is not a feast day, in the terrible sense that all its sacred pomp is unfolded before us; each day commands the utter fealty of each worshipper" (Benjamin 1996a: 288). The remark recalls Nietzsche's idea of the eternal return: capitalism's permanence resides in the drudgery of its labor, the sameness of its products, the relentlessness of its pursuit of profit. Capitalism is specifically like a cult because such things are not simply practiced but must be celebrated constantly. Every day is a Sunday: "There are no 'weekdays'" (Benjamin 1996a: 288). On another level, however, Benjamin views capitalism's permanence in terms of a specific understanding of *guilt*. Crucial here is the connection between *debt* and *guilt*: as Nietzsche said in *On the Genealogy of Morals*, which Benjamin cites, both are conveyed by the word *Schuld* (Nietzsche 1996b: 44). Benjamin calls this a "demonic ambiguity" (Benjamin 1996a: 289).[3] His analysis echoes Nietzsche's argument that Christian ideas about punishment began as forms of violent revenge against defaulting debtors. By portraying capitalism as an economic system defined not by a system of production or exchange but by its moral economy of debt, he is comparing it to religion and its moral economy of guilt. Quite predictably, power is crucial to Nietzsche's portrayal of debt. When Sarthou-Lajus suggests that debt is "at the origin of a fundamentally asymmetrical social relation, which breaks with the logic of parity in exchange" (Sarthou-Lajus 1997: 37), Roitman understandably calls this a *Nietzschean* as opposed to a *Maussian* conception of debt (Roitman 2003: 213).

History plays an important role in the connection between capitalism (debt) and religion (guilt) that Benjamin wants to make; indeed the argument recalls the distinction between "conventional history" and "guilt history" that Benjamin draws in two contemporaneous pieces, "Fate and Character" (originally published in 1921, 1996c cited here) and "The Meaning of

3   In German, *Schuld* means both *debt* and *guilt*.

Time in the Moral Universe" (originally published in 1921, 1996d cited here). In *conventional history*, successive moments in time are linked by cause and effect. In *guilt history*, moments in time are joined not through cause and effect but through the *perpetual incurring of debts*. Each moment is not *caused* by what went before. Rather, it is *indebted* to what has gone before. History is guilty: each moment is in debt to its predecessor. A similar idea comes up in Nietzsche's *Philosophy in the Tragic Age of the Greeks* (from around 1873, unpublished), in which the following passage, from Anaximander, is translated: "Where the source of things is, to that place they must also pass away, according to necessity, for they must pay penance and be judged for their injustices, in accordance with the ordinance of time" (Nietzsche 1996c: 45). In his insightful commentary on "Capitalism as Religion," Werner Hamacher suggests that this "tragic" notion conveys time as an incessant oscillation between guilt and punishment. This is an image of history "in which the unavoidable incurring of guilt is atoned in an equivalent penance that is just as unavoidable" (Hamacher 2002: 81). Likewise, capitalism as Benjamin portrays it here functions within a temporal structure that is defined by the rhythm of debt. Time is crucial, too, in Benjamin's conception of money itself. In "One-Way Street," he suggests that a "secret connection" exists between the "measure of goods" and the "measure of life." This is the relationship between money and time:

> The more trivial the content of a lifetime, the more fragmented, multifarious, and disparate are its moments, while the grand period characterizes a superior existence. Very aptly, Lichtenberg suggests that time whiled away should be seen as smaller, rather than shorter, and he also observes: "a few million minutes make up the life of forty-five years and something more." When a currency is in use a few million of which are insignificant, life will have to be counted in seconds, rather than in years, if it is to appear a respectable sum. And it will be frittered away like a bundle of bank notes: Austria cannot break the habit of thinking in florins. (Benjamin 1996e: 481)

These remarks help clarify another feature of capitalism that comes to the surface when it is viewed as a cult: it offers no redemption. "Capitalism is probably the first instance of a cult that creates guilt, not atonement," Benjamin states (Benjamin 1996a: 288). "Guilt" has a dual meaning of course. This is not just guilt history but *debt* history: eternal return consists of the relentless accumulation of debt. However, Benjamin's argument goes further than this point. Just as the cult offers no atonement for guilt, capitalism offers no redemption from, nor any forgiveness of, debt. As a cult, capitalism offers no liberation from debt. The cult may not redeem guilt, but it does thrive on it, turning economic debt into moral guilt: like a deficit within the soul that becomes guilt's cause, both justifying the existence of debt while ensuring its perpetuation (Hamacher 2002: 86–87). Benjamin's metaphor is more than just a colorful way of portraying the moral economy of financial capitalism, however. It performs a crucial analytical function. Capitalism does not simply make debtors of us all; it also makes a debtor of the very *God* to whom all of our debts are payable: "A vast sense of guilt that is unable to find relief seizes on the cult, not to atone for this guilt but to make it universal, to hammer it into the conscious mind, so as once and for all to include God in the system of guilt and thereby awaken in Him an interest in the process of atonement" (Benjamin 1996a: 288–89).

We can read this passage in terms of the doctrine of predestination, as touched on by Benjamin himself in *The Origin of German Tragic Drama* (Benjamin 2009; see also Hamacher 2002). Predestination is especially pertinent here because, under this doctrine, guilt is borne without hope of redemption. *Not even God has the power to redeem* because He is bound by His own previous decisions, as if by law itself. He is, moreover, bound to behave with indifference to whatever humankind does, and thus to history. He is, in effect, indebted to His own decision. And He is therefore, in a sense, guilty. This, at least, is what Benjamin appears to have had in mind when he said that God himself is included in the system of guilt.

Benjamin makes the additional, and surely crucial, claim that once God "finally takes on the entire burden of guilt" the outcome is complete destruction, as "despair becomes a religious state of the world." This idea brings Marx to mind. But whereas Marx had envisaged capitalism's destruction and the emergence of socialism as the logically inevitable outcome of capitalism's recurrent crises of production, Benjamin foresees only the further development of capitalism's debt history. This difference suggests a different understanding of history than one finds in Marx. Benjamin makes this quite explicit when he argues that a "capitalism that refuses to change course becomes socialism by means of the simple and compound interest that are functions of *Schuld*" (Benjamin 1996a: 289). The implication of the argument becomes clearer once we unpack its economic content, specifically its reference to compound interest. The crucial thing about compound interest is that the interest charged on a debt is added to the original loan, the principal. When Benjamin emphasizes debt's relentless expansion, he is referring not to our appetite for it, as if we were continually taking out new loans, but to the fact that interest is always added to the original debt. Debt grows automatically, purely as a function of time's passing.[4]

Benjamin does not just read modern capitalism through religion but interprets religion itself through capitalism. In particular, he applies the logic of *financial* debt to Christianity's moral economy of guilt. In *On the Genealogy of Morals*, Nietzsche remarked that "setting prices, estimating values, devising equivalents, making exchanges ... preoccupied the very earliest thinking of man to such an extent that it, in a certain sense, constitutes *thinking as such*" (Nietzsche 1996b: 44). Benjamin's argument is that the very same logic, insofar as it defines the debt relation, governs the very passing of *time* under capitalism. This is guilt history.

The concept of the guilty God, the God who "takes on the entire burden of guilt," opens up a further, critical, question: What, who, is God according to Benjamin's metaphor? To answer this question, it is worth considering what Marx once said about public debt. As we saw in Chapter 2, this statement comes toward the end of the first volume of *Capital*, in a discussion of primitive accumulation. The language that Marx uses here, and to an extent, the meaning of the passage itself, bears a striking resemblance to Benjamin's later fragment:

> Public credit becomes the *credo* of capital. And with the rise of national debt-making, lack of faith in the national debt takes the place of sin against the Holy Ghost, for which there is no forgiveness. The public debt becomes one of the most powerful levers of primitive accumulation. As with the stroke of an enchanter's wand, it endows unproductive money with the power of creation and thus turns it into capital, without forcing it to expose itself to the troubles and risks inseparable from its employment in industry or even in usury. (Marx 1982: 919)

If Marx's use of a theological metaphor to describe debt is intriguing, even more striking is his use of such language to describe the *national* debt. National debt—crucially—is the debt that enchants *money*, underpinning its capacity to expand as capital. The magic is a delusion, of course. Historically,

---

4 In *Capital* volume 3, Marx refers to the "miracle" of compound interest: "Money bearing compound interest increases at first slowly. But, the rate of increase being continually accelerated, it becomes in some time so rapid, as to mock all the powers of the imagination. One penny, put out at our Saviour's birth at 5 percent compound interest, would, before this time, have increased to a greater sum than would be obtained in a 150 millions of Earths, all solid gold. But if put out to simple interest, it would, in the same time, have amounted to no more than 7 shillings 4½ d" (Marx 1894: 519).

as Marx himself describes, public debt renders money productive through funding primitive accumulation: capital ventured overseas to profit from colonization, slavery, theft, and murder. Hence, he makes his remark in the chapter's conclusion that capital comes into the world dripping with blood and dirt (Marx 1982: 926). But it is when Marx refers to the "modern doctrine that a nation becomes richer the more deeply it is in debt" that the resonance with Benjamin comes through most clearly. In particular, we can see its affinity with Benjamin's description of the "steady, though in the final analysis explosive and discontinuous intensification" of guilt, and, therefore, debt. Benjamin does not, however, return to Marx to analyze this expansion dialectically. He turns instead to Nietzsche: "The superman is the man who has arrived where he is without changing his ways," he writes, "he is historical man who has grown up right through the sky." The superman that appears here is the *universal debtor*, whose journey will end in synthesis with the guilty God.

Benjamin himself remarked about God: "he is not dead; he has been incorporated into human existence" (Benjamin 1996a: 289). The implication is that the *Übermensch* is both God and man. He is society, perhaps. Marx said, after all, that "a nation becomes the richer the more deeply it is in debt." A God who is nothing but debt, "historical man who has grown up right through the sky,"[5] a God who is utterly guilty, is a bankrupt God. Thus the *Übermensch*, "the man who has arrived where he is without changing his ways," seems to be none other than the bankrupt society: the Germany in which Benjamin was living when he wrote this fragment, or a latter-day Argentina, or a Greece.

As I pointed out in Chapter 3, any account of money's relationship with debt needs to come to terms with debt's dual status: it both *underwrites* money and is capable of *damaging* it. One way of describing money, after all, is that it is society's debt to itself. As such, it is money's potential for being destroyed by debt that comes through most clearly in Benjamin's image of the *Übermensch* growing up through the sky. In almost every historical instance, the single most significant expression of a nation's bankruptcy has been the eventual destruction of its money. It was Nietzsche, in *Daybreak*, who suggested an analogy between the death of God and the love of money (1997a). In the money economy he derides, what one can no longer do for

---

5   The image of inexorable progress-as-decay resonates with Benjamin's Angel of History: "The storm drives him irresistibly into the future, to which his back is turned, while the pile of debris before him grows towards the sky. What we call progress is *this* storm" (Benjamin 2003b: 392, original emphasis).

the love of God, one does for the love of money. Hence, by the force of Benjamin's own logic, not just capital, but *money* lies ruined as *Übermensch* grows up "right through the sky." It is public debt, essentially, that underpins the state's capacity to create money. Benjamin finds it here, in a state of seemingly irreversible decay: "where God, too, finally takes on the entire burden of guilt, the point where the universe has been taken over by that despair which is actually its secret *hope*" (Benjamin 1996a: 289).

FILTHY LUCRE

To the contrasting interpretations, by Simmel and Benjamin, of Nietzsche's concepts of *Übermensch* and the eternal return, we can now add a third, as put forward by Norman Brown in *Life Against Death* (1959). The book, which sets out a psychoanalytical theory of history combining arguments from Marx, Freud, and Nietzsche, was widely read and discussed during the 1960s. Brown's text is often compared with Marcuse's *Eros and Civilization* (1955), which contains a similar interweaving of philosophy and psychoanalytic theory (Marcuse 1955; Greenham 2001). Brown once described himself as a Marxist whose outlook changed after Henry Wallace's defeat in the 1948 presidential election, initiating his "passage to a post-Marxist world" (Neu 2005: 34). According to a *New York Times* obituary, Brown was "a victim of theories" (Neu 2005: 91). But he reads as an experimenter, not a victim. Brown was an extraordinarily versatile scholar, writing on myth, art, literature, and the theory of history, besides giving lectures on Islam. Contemporary claims about Islamic finance as an ethically superior alternative to Western finance (Maurer 2005) would surely have engaged him, especially in light of the brilliant chapter on money, "Filthy Lucre," in *Life Against Death*.

Brown's central thesis is that history has an underlying structure that can only be understood in terms of the theory of neurosis. At the book's heart is a figure, a collective individual, whose neuroses determine the way in which history unfolds. Brown characterizes this history as the "law of the increasing return of the repressed," in which humankind "has projected more and more of the Oedipus complex into the external world" (Brown 1959: 155). Capitalism, specifically capitalist money, stands at the apex of such a history, wherein repression reaches its most acute and, for the subject, most dangerous form. Brown's treatment of such themes bears comparison with Benjamin's thesis about the religious structure of capitalism, in two specific ways: first, in the connections he makes between *guilt* and *debt* in order to understand psychological and quasisacred structures within money; and, second, in his use of Nietzsche's *Übermensch* in order to examine the *intensification* and eventual *collapse* of those structures.

Brown argues that money *originates* in neurosis. His concept of neurosis is drawn from Freud's later work, where repression originates outside the individual (via the father in the castration complex) but is the result of "anxiety and instinctual ambivalence inside the child himself" (Brown 1959: 121). Crucially for Brown, this repression is *self*-repression and operates through the reality principle, i.e., the circumstantial reality that compels a man or a woman to defer instant gratification. Human beings make their reality "through the medium of culture or society" (Brown 1959: 9). Culture constantly produces new projections of the repressed unconscious. It is where infantile fantasies are apprehended or mastered, where human beings are liberated from their parental gods only so that they can form new attachments to "the paternalistic state and the patriarchal God" (Brown 1959: 155). The inner psychic conflicts that Brown explores are expressed through Christianity as well as capitalism. Indeed, his most important concepts—repression, guilt, debt, and redemption—are filtered through a theological lens.

Brown states that neurosis is not an occasional aberration but "is in us all the time." It is the "psychoanalytical analogue of the theological doctrine of original sin" (Brown 1959: 6). Guilt is central to his thesis. It explains both the source of our self-repression and its primary manifestations, above all, its connections with money. In psychoanalytic terms, guilt stems from a failure to deal with maternal separation. The mother's absence is experienced as her death, and the Oedipal complex is shaped by a longing to be reunited with her. Self-repression originates here. The subject cannot bear the mother's absence; therefore he or she cannot accept his or her own individuality. Such a subject is unable to live an independent life. Equally, the subject cannot face an independent death: humanity is "that species of animal that cannot die" (Brown 1959: 284). The death instinct—the drive toward death, self-destruction, and a return to the inorganic—originates here. One of its most important manifestations is the tendency to "eroticize death" (Brown 1959: 115).

What makes Brown's argument distinctive, and controversial, is the way in which he applies the theory of neurosis to the entire history of civilization, and especially to economics. It is the tendency toward guilt-induced self-repression, he argues, that gives rise to all forms of economic organization: from gift exchange, to the modern division of labor, to money. The psychology of economics is a psychology of guilt: "Giving is self-sacrificial;

self-sacrifice is self-punishment ... the derivation of work from Adam's sin expresses the psychological truth" (Brown 1959: 266). Capitalism molds these guilt structures into the production of surplus. For Brown, even the drive to accumulate, no less than the nonenjoyment that characterizes work, is ultimately a form of *self-sacrifice*: it is underpinned not by the desire for gain but rather by the impulse to produce beyond the bounds of utility. This desire to overproduce is our need to *squander*, to *waste* (Brown 1959: 264), and it is a theme we will return to in more detail in the next chapter.

Money, for Brown, is an expression of the impulse to lose. In and of themselves, most forms of money are inherently useless (Brown 1959: 254). Even precious metals serve no useful purpose *qua* money. Marx described gold and silver as "social expressions for superfluity" (Marx 1982: 228), and Arendt called gold "the most ancient symbol of mere wealth" (Arendt 1951: 379). Locke, too, said that money was shaped by the "desire of having more than men needed" (Locke 1696; in Brown 1959: 255). Thoreau criticized the "seemingly wealthy, but most terribly impoverished class of all, who have accumulated dross, but know not how to use it, or get rid of it, and thus have forged their own golden or silver fetters" (Thoreau 1995: 10; Brown 1959: 255), and Veblen's leisure class displayed a "reputable degree of wasteful expenditure" (Veblen 2009: 80; Brown 1959: 255). The Egyptian pyramids, regarded by Bataille as the quintessential expression of squander (Bataille 1991: 25), express "both the hope of immortality and the fruit of compound interest" (Brown 1959: 286). For Brown, these are the driving forces behind the modern division of labor, and ultimately, the development of capitalism itself. This thinking reverses the orthodoxy inherited from Adam Smith, namely, that the division of labor has its roots in economic necessity. According to Brown, by contrast, it was surplus—and, more fundamentally, loss, squander, and waste—that drove economic expansion forward.

Such connections among money, guilt, and loss are most clearly expressed by money's symbolic association with bodily waste. "In the last analysis," Brown said, "the peculiar human fascination with excrement is the peculiar human fascination with death" (Brown 1959: 295). Freud argued that feces are the child's first independent production; their retention is a form of "saving" often associated with sexual pleasure. The original erotic interest in defecation is extinguished at the very moment when the adult interest in money emerges (Brown 1959: 138; Freud 1908). Guilt, too, is unclean, and money's association with excrement is a form of sublimation, "the path whereby extraneous things acquire significance for the human body, and hence value" (Brown 1959: 293). This guilt and this money are filthy lucre.

This specific connection between money and excrement is made in all of the major psychoanalytical essays on money. Ferenczi traces the prehistory of the association through a series of monetary sublimations, including mud, sand, and pebbles (Ferenczi 1916; Trachtman 1999). Money can stand for almost anything that can be given or received, e.g., babies, breast milk, sperm, and power (Fenichel 1938). It can also represent freedom, prestige, wealth, and control (Turkel 1988). Later theorists made connections between anal eroticism and private property and the desire for possessions (Coriat 1924), miserliness (Ferenczi 1916), the habit of reading or even studying while on the toilet (Abraham 1917), debt (Harnik 1919), as well as in examples such as the image of the scarab (dung beetle) on Egyptian coinage (Desmonde 1976). There is a rich case history, too, from the patient who suffered from a monthly attack of diarrhea that coincided with lump-sum payments to her parents (Ferenczi 1916), through the banker who insisted that his children retain the contents of their intestines for as long as possible to maximize the nourishment they were receiving from expensive food (Abraham 1917), to the patient whose only apparent act of miserliness was an insistence that there should be no light in the toilet (Amar 1956).

Nietzsche enters Brown's text as a counterpoint to Freud. *On the Genealogy of Morals* was "the first attempt to grasp world history as the history of an ever increasing neurosis" (Brown 1959: 15). Brown compares Nietzsche's remark about "the disease called man"—"The earth has been a madhouse for too long already!" (Nietzsche 1996b: 73)—with that of Freud in *Civilization and Its Discontents*, where he tracks an "intensification of the sense of guilt . . . to a degree that the individual finds hard to endure" (Freud 2005: 125). A Freudian "solution" to this problem, as sketched out by a thinker such as Habermas, for example (Habermas 1986), would typically be derived from therapy. Brown takes a different route. His argument hinges on a conception of the relationship among guilt, debt, and time that he finds in Nietzsche's philosophy of eternal return.

According to Nietzsche, guilt feeds on a particular relationship with the past. In the second essay of *On the Genealogy of Morals*, he says that to turn himself into an animal that can promise, and therefore honor a contract, humans had to *learn how to remember*. Responsibility and conscience therefore began with the *loss of active forgetfulness*. Following Nietzsche, Brown describes this loss as the onset of a neurotic "constipation" with the past. The anal character of history is the man who "can 'get rid' of nothing" (Brown 1959: 267). The man who must always "vouch for himself as future" (Nietzsche 1996b: 73) cannot freely proclaim "Da capo!"—"that indebtedness to ancestors which is the guilty conscience, and which makes man constipated with the past and capable of promising, is formed in childhood by the incorporation of the parents and the wish to be father of oneself" (Brown 1959: 275–76).

Brown wants us to grasp the broader significance of this "neurotic constipation with the past" for the development of capitalism. He argues, for example, that the institution of private property on which capitalism depends is merely the economic expression of guilt and its close associate, the fear of death. Even *inheritance* comes into play here. Citing Zarathustra's "intoxicated song," Brown is drawn to Nietzsche's suggestion that the *desire for an heir* is a *refusal of one's own life* (Brown 1959: 107):

> But everything unripe wants to live: alas! Woe says: "Fade! Be gone, woe!" But everything that suffers wants to live, that it may grow ripe and merry and passionate, passionate for remoter, higher, brighter things. "I want heirs," thus speaks everything that suffers, "I want children, I do not want *myself*." (Nietzsche 2003b: 331)

Brown finds similar sentiments in Keynes's "Economic Possibilities for Our Grandchildren," which describes the "purposive" man who seeks a "spurious and delusive immortality for his acts by pushing his interest in them forward into time . . . For him, jam is not jam unless it is a case of jam to-morrow and never jam to-day" (Keynes 1972: 370). There are shades of Benjamin in Keynes's observation—which Brown cites (Brown 1959: 286)—that the financial corollary of the *promise of immortality* is the *principle of compound interest* (Keynes 1972: 371). To Brown, the ideal of immortality represents the repression of life. As such, it is an expression of neurotic anxiety about death. In economic terms (and this is the point of citing Keynes), "austerity" is the clearest manifestation of this psychological structure. This, then, would be the deeper myth—besides the more "technical" fallacies identified by Hudson that we discussed in Chapter 3—underpinning the politics of austerity.

According to Brown, our loss of the power of forgetting underwrites the very ideal of capital itself. Money figures centrally here, both feeding, and feeding off, self-repression. The "triumph over death" made possible through becoming father to oneself would be achieved if what is produced by the body, excrement, could also nourish it, as aliment (Brown 1959: 257). This would be *productive* money (Brown 1959: 293). It would also be *sacred* money: Midas, turning the worthless into the priceless, could be an allegory of man's acquisition of a soul—"he becomes the animal which does not live by bread alone, the animal which sublimates" (Brown 1959: 258). Marx,

Brown says, is at his profoundest when he addresses "the alchemical mystery of money and of the 'mystical,' 'fetishistic' character of commodities" (Brown 1959: 258). Interest-bearing capital is the ultimate expression of this logic, whereby "barren" capital appears transformed into self-expanding value. According to Marx, this is how money "surrounds itself with the qualities of the occult" as commodities are "thrown into the alchemistical retort of circulation" in order "to come out again in the shape of money" (Brown 1959: 258–59). As we saw before, it was its power to enchant money by rendering it productive that prompted Marx to describe public debt as the *credo* of capital.

In a lecture delivered in Santa Cruz in 1990, Brown looked back on *Life Against Death* and confessed that his Marxist background had given him "a healthy prejudice against money-making" (Brown 1992: 179). He cited Ferenczi's statement that money is "nothing other than deodorized, dehydrated shit that has been made to shine" (cited in Brown 1992: 179). Such statements are "the cornerstone of a Dionysian epistemology," he said (Brown 1992: 179), and the idea that "madness is not an individual but a social phenomenon in which we all participate collectively: we are all in one and the same boat or body" (Brown 1992: 180). In *The Birth of Tragedy*, Nietzsche casts Apollo and Dionysus as the two gods representing stylistic opposites within art "which exist side by side and in almost perpetual conflict with one another" (Nietzsche 1999: 119). The Apollonian tendency exists in the *dream*, whereas the Dionysian (which is more "real") exists in *intoxication*. Apollonian art emphasizes appearance, and its finest achieves extraordinary *clarity*. Apollo is "the luminous one . . . a god of the sun and light who reveals himself in brilliance," whose eye must be "'sun-like' and calm" (Nietzsche 1999: 120). This is the principle of individuation. Dionysian art, fueled by "the drive of spring and narcotic drink," disrupts the principle of individuation because "subjectivity disappears entirely before the erupting force of the general element in human life, indeed of the general element in nature" (Nietzsche 1999: 120). Intoxication and clarity coexist here, and their coexistence is the high point of Hellenic culture.

Brown invokes Nietzsche's *The Birth of Tragedy* (Nietzsche 1999) to understand the choice faced by repressed man—and bearer of the money complex—between sublimation and some alternative to it. This dichotomy has its roots in the Apollonian and Dionysian tendencies in art. We were taught how to sublimate by those who worshipped Apollo, "the god of form—of plastic form in art, of rational form in thought, of civilized form in life" (Brown 1959: 174). But Apollonian form is a negation of instinct, for as Nietzsche says, this art form must not overstep the dream "if its effect is not to become pathological" (Nietzsche 1999: 120). It is this limit, the requirement that in dreams we must never go beyond the line into pathology, that separates dreams from instincts: it is "the boundary of repression separating the dream from instinctual reality" (Brown 1959: 174). The Dionysian impulse is not for "life kept at a distance and seen through a veil but *life complete and immediate*" (Brown 1959: 175, italics added). It is, says Brown, the image of the instinctual reality that can be found on the other side of that veil. The human being who confronts this reality faces "a great work of self-transformation," a destruction of the self-consciousness which Apollonian art preserves. If sublimation (the Apollonian tendency) underlies the cumulative abstractness and deadening of civilization, in Dionysian art we are dealing with bodily realities, not abstract intellectual principles (Brown 1959: 175–76).

Brown finds a Dionysian "witches' brew" in the eroticism of de Sade and the politics of Hitler, but he also discerns it in the Romantic reaction to both; indeed, he finds here "the entry of Dionysus into consciousness" (Brown 1959: 176). So where might its entry into *economy* be? Brown attributes to Keynes the correct diagnosis of the "crisis of our time." The text he uses is Keynes's "Economic Possibilities for Our Grandchildren," published in the same year (1930) as *"Auri Sacra Fames."* Keynes deplores the fact that "we have been expressly evolved by nature" for the sole purpose of solving the economic problem, that is to say, with tackling scarcity. He asks rhetorically what would happen to us were that problem to be solved: "There is no country and no people who can look forward to the age of leisure and abundance without a dread" (Keynes 1972). For Brown, what Keynes viewed with dread, every Freudian should relish, for "every ordinary man has tasted the paradise of play in his own childhood" (Brown 1959: 36). This is the immortal instinct for play, and it already exists, merely repressed by habits of work: "The foundation on which the man of the future will be built is already there"; it does not need to be created out of nothing (Brown 1959: 36). Brown finds this impulse in primitive economics, "in potlatch contests of prestige, in the merry-go-round circuits of gift-exchange" (Brown 1959: 37), and wonders whether a correspondence can be found between these two sides of the psychoanalytical understanding of life as work and play, and fundamental sociological categories such as *Gesellschaft* (society) and *Gemeinschaft* (community), respectively.

Brown questions social theories—that of Weber, for example—which suggest that modern capitalism has secularized ancient logics of religious guilt: "sociology has not connected money with the irrational and the sacred," he complains (Brown 1959: 240). Unlike Benjamin, Brown refuses to accept that the moral economy of debt is a mere shadow of formerly religious obligations. Banks are not analogues of temples; they *are* great temples. Money retains "at its very heart, the structure of the archaic sacred" (Brown 1959: 246, 248). Our illusion is not that money is sacred, but rather that it is not. The belief that the modern economy is secular has a powerful function. By divesting us of the fallacy that work leads to salvation, it actually intensifies our compulsion to work, and for no other end than work itself. Marx's theory of value, with labor at its core, is an expression of this compulsion: "The result is an economy driven by the pure sense of guilt, unmitigated by any sense of redemption; as Luther said, the Devil (guilt) is lord of this world" (Brown 1959: 272).

This is why Brown calls it the money complex. *All* money is essentially neurotic: it is created, defined, and shaped by neurosis. According to Brown, it is the modern capitalist economy that aggravates this neurosis, pushing it to its farthest and most damaging extremes. It is by doing so, in fact, that the money complex reveals itself most clearly. What separates capitalism from earlier economic formations in this respect is guilt's manifestation as *financial* debt. In the archaic economy, all debts were considered to be payable because they could be redeemed with the gods. From Luther onward, this prospect was denied. Brown reads Weber's *Protestant Ethic and the Spirit of Capitalism* (Weber 2001) as charting the rise of an economic system that thrives not simply on guilt but on the belief that *redemption is impossible*. After Luther, the modern subject remains burdened by the belief that Adam fell and yet is deprived of the illusion that Christ redeems. Our debts are unredeemable. "Man is bankrupt" (Brown 1959: 271) and yet deprived of the respite that such a condition should bring. Debt becomes a compulsion as we strive to pay that which, *ab initio,* cannot be paid.

One can but wonder why Brown never cites Benjamin, whom, as we saw above, envisaged capitalism's guilt history as the relentless piling up of debt, driven by the logic of compound interest. But guilt works differently in Brown's treatment of Nietzsche when compared to that of Benjamin. For Benjamin, as we saw, guilt has a decisive *systemic* role to play in financial capitalism because it helps to sustain a debt economy that depends on the belief that all debts must be repaid, even if the logic of capitalism itself—whose temporal order Benjamin defines as guilt history—mitigates against this idea. In an argument that has strong parallels with Benjamin's theory of history, the only "solution" to this predicament, if it can be seen as a solution at all, would be the ultimate ruination of the system of financial capitalism that renders debt and guilt—simultaneously—necessary. In Brown's hands, by contrast, guilt is a primary (or even primal) *psychological* condition that is inherent within *all* individuals. Crucially, capitalism (alongside other economic forms such as gift exchange) takes its form from this. Brown's solution (he calls it a "way out") to the subject's entrapment within guilt—an entrapment that takes its fullest economic expression through money—is first and foremost a psychological one, and it borders on mysticism.[6] Inevitably, then, his analysis of the fate of the modern, indebted subject takes a different (but no less surprising) turn from that of Benjamin, although Nietzsche's *Übermensch* once again plays the pivotal role. Where Benjamin views capitalism's permanence as cult through the living hell of grinding debt, Brown looks to Nietzsche's remark that the *Übermensch* seeks no heir, but wants "everything eternally the same" (Nietzsche 2003b: 331). This goal is not simply a desire for immortality, Brown says. It is an expression of the capacity to *die an independent death*:

> Nietzsche's perfection, which is unrepressed life (joy), wants eternity, but it also wants to die. Eternity is therefore a way of envisaging mankind's liberation from the neurotic obsession with the past and the future; it is a way of living in the present, but also a way of dying. (Brown 1959: 108)

Brown considers the doctrine of eternal return, if only we could bring ourselves to follow it, as essentially life-*affirming*. Even the prospect of death emerges as something joyful: "In contrast with Schopenhauer, Nietzsche, because he envisages the possibility of Superman, can affirm life and therefore death: 'What has become perfect, all that is ripe—wants to die'" (Brown 1959: 107; Nietzsche 2003b: 331). And so, by a wide arc, we return to where this discussion began: with the *Übermensch*. Brown does not, however, find in the *Übermensch* the synthesis of human and God, both riven by guilt, that Benjamin saw. Rather, he discovers the human who has the strength to refuse his or her debt: or in Nietzschean terms, the will to forget. According to Brown, "full psychoanalytical consciousness" can be attained only once one's debts are suspended. The power of suspension, however, no longer lies with the creditor. It lies with the debtor. Brown's unrepressed subject is the subject whose illusions fall away once he or she realizes that the debt cannot be paid off. This realization would be the achievement of a Dionysian consciousness: of Zarathustra's intoxicated singer, perhaps. Full psychoanalytical

---

6   As he writes in the final chapter of *Life Against Death*, "psychoanalysis has not psychoanalyzed itself until it places itself alongside the history of Western thought—inside the general neurosis of mankind. So seen, psychoanalysis is the heir to a mystical tradition which it must affirm" (Brown 1959: 310).

consciousness is the consciousness not only of the subject who is strong enough to die but also the subject who has renounced his or her debt (Brown 1959: 108). Such a subject has no money complex:

> the path to that ultimate reunification of ego and body is not a dissolution but a strengthening of the human ego. The human ego would have to become strong enough to die; and strong enough to set aside guilt. Archaic consciousness was strong enough to recognize a debt of guilt; Christian consciousness was strong enough to recognize that the debt is so great that only God can redeem it; modern secular Faustian man is strong enough to live with irredeemable damnation; full psychoanalytical consciousness would be strong enough to cancel the debt by deriving it from infantile fantasy. (Brown 1959: 292)

Nietzsche's God sacrificed himself for his debt—"out of *love*," he mocks (Nietzsche 1996b: 72). In a sweeping, typically Messianic reversal, Benjamin's God is transformed into a universal debtor. In his madness, Brown's debtor is perpetually on bankruptcy's brink but eventually gathers the presence of mind, and sufficient courage, to default. However, Benjamin's God merges with society; the gods that Brown imagines "retreat into invisibility (*Deus absconditus*)" (Brown 1959: 271). If there is a Nietzschean money in Brown's work, it lies here: not in ruins, but within a currency whose neuroses have been ripped out. The image on this coinage is of the unrepressed life, of "a man strong enough to live and therefore strong enough to die"—or an image of resurrection, perhaps.

CONCLUSION

If Simmel's image of money's relationship with the separateness and distinctiveness of the individual is closer to that of Nietzsche than one might have imagined, the arguments of Benjamin and Brown, especially their incorporation of ideas from Nietzsche, are strikingly close to each other. The money we encounter in the work of these thinkers has lost its old sacred and neurotic structures. Nietzsche declared the death of God and urged the *Übermensch* to forge a new morality. Benjamin and Brown predict that the psycho-religious guilt on which the moral economy of debt depends will eventually crumble. It remains open to question whether their vision of a life lived without neurosis, without guilt, and without debt might be reconfigured in the context of the present day. The image of a "debt-free" money that emerges from these analyses sits uneasily with the raft of theory we discussed in Chapter 3, which agrees with Ruskin's remark that "all money, properly so called, is an acknowledgement of debt" (Ruskin 1997: 185; see Wray 2004b). Debt, as I suggested there, is essentially part of what makes us social, not just a function of religious guilt or self-repression. And it is deeply implicated in the social life of money.

However, neither Benjamin nor Brown includes *all* forms of debt in their analysis. Their concerns were oriented specifically to the system of financial debt that grew up under modern capitalism. This is the debt that builds relentlessly through compound interest; or as Benjamin describes it, with the very passing of time. For both thinkers, such debt cannot be paid because it is monstrously large, but economic life goes on as if it will and must be paid. With extraordinary prescience, Benjamin saw debt that was not only unredeemed but also *unredeemable* as an inherent feature of capitalism's character as a cult, demanding all of the rituals of theology—or, one might just as well say, the rituals of financial accounting—but lacking its promise of redemption. Brown saw it in psychological terms, as compulsion. It is, perhaps, the logic more than the substance of their arguments that appeals. Benjamin and Brown offer contrapuntal images of a guilt-infused money that highlight the combination of moral and economic obligation that still color debates about the topic in the present day. In describing capitalism as a "religion" whose belief system is organized around a moral economy of debt, Benjamin—more than any other thinker of his era—portrays modern capitalism as a system that is driven by the logic of relentless debt accumulation. Brown offers a contrasting but complementary image of a debtor whose inner sense of moral guilt is driven by repression: this, as Brown himself suggests, is a psychic projection of all that is to be feared in the economics of austerity. Despite these differences, both thinkers point to the futility and unsustainability of a financial system that insists on treating as payable those debts that essentially cannot be paid. Such debts—especially when they are beyond redemption—retain their "archaic" structures of moral and religious guilt. Debt's connections with money are at the heart of this guilt and are therefore vitally important for untangling the question of where exactly money features in the debt crisis we are witnessing today. Both thinkers thereby expose the vacuous nature of the moral economy—the religion of debt or guilt-induced neurotic compulsion—on which our own financial system depends. These are insights that place both thinkers deeply in our time, not just their own.

"Great obligations do not make a man grateful, they make him resentful," Nietzsche once said (Nietzsche 2003b). He was talking about kindness, but the argument also applies to the obligations—and the repressive logic of guilt—that we impose upon debtors: especially when, as Benjamin and Brown depict, the debt is essentially irredeemable. Nietzsche argued that *ressentiment* is a force for the creation of new values. Entire belief systems—Christianity, socialism, and liberalism—are rooted in the outwardly hostile sentiments of a collective that always crush the strong individual. The process of valuation within the marketplace—pitting buyer against seller, with "man" designating himself as "the 'measuring animal'" (Nietzsche 1996b: 44)—predated those moral codes whose growth *ressentiment* subsequently encouraged (see Aspers 2007: 483). Curiously enough, the money economy as Nietzsche describes it would have emerged as a concrete manifestation of this process.

For all three thinkers discussed here, Nietzsche's thought seems to be appealing for its exposure of the morality that lies just beneath money's surface. More than anything else, his ideas offer a distinctive set of critical possibilities for exploring the nature of contemporary capitalism. At the heart of it all is that richly enigmatic figure, the *Übermensch*, who has renounced the metaphysics of morality. When pronouncing God's death in *The Gay Science*, Nietzsche conveys the parable of the madman who, asking his fellow murderers what they should do to console themselves, found that his time had not come: "This tremendous event is still on its way, wandering; it has not yet reached the ears of men" (Nietzsche 2001: 120).[7] After Buddha was dead "they still showed his shadow for centuries" (Nietzsche 2001: 109). Much the same might happen with the shadow of God. This shadow, one might well say, is the ominous shadow of God that we discover looming over Benjamin's treatment of capitalism as religion.

"Gay science," Nietzsche said, is all that is left once we have killed God: "no one until now has examined the value of that most famous of all medicines called morality; and for that, one must begin by *questioning* it for once" (Nietzsche 2001: 203, italics in original). Describing atheism as a "kind of *second innocence*" that might "release humanity entirely from this feeling of indebtedness to its origins, its *causa prima*" (Nietzsche 1996b: 71, italics in original),[8] the eventuality that Nietzsche seems most to have

---

[7] "Lightning and thunder need time; the light of the stars needs time; deeds need time, even after they are done, in order to be seen and heard" (Nietzsche 2001: 120).

[8] Seizing on this idea, Maurizio Lazzarato imagines an analogous second innocence in which mundane debts, not divine debts, are involved. Quite rightly, I think, he suggests that such "innocence" would not simply entail the annulment of debt, or acts of default, but more importantly, the "leaving behind [of] debt morality and the discourse in which it holds us hostage." Lazzarato concludes, "We must recapture this second innocence, rid ourselves of guilt, of everything owed, of all bad conscience, and not repay a cent" (Lazzarato 2011: 164).

feared is that everything once valued for the sake of *God* is now valued for the sake of its *price*. "The most industrious age—our own—doesn't know how to make anything of all its industriousness and money except still more money and still more industriousness," he suggests, "for more genius is required to spend than to acquire!" (Nietzsche 2001: 45). In *Untimely Meditations*, Nietzsche remarks how it was once quite natural to look down "with honest nobility" upon "people who dealt in money as a business." It is not that such people are unnecessary, he adds, "every society had to have intestines" (Nietzsche 1997b: 219). What irks him is the "vulgarity" of the modern age, whose great "theories of the state, of the nation; of the economy, trade, justice" are caught up either in "propelling the great economy- and power-machine"—or in "the defence and exculpation of the present" (Nietzsche 1997b: 220). This is the context in which Nietzsche's arguments about money, debt, and guilt should be read. His disdain for money and for capitalism, and his refusal of debt, are all too readily dismissed as expressions of naiveté and romanticism (Ansell-Pearson 2005). But by following Simmel, Benjamin, and Brown, one can read in Nietzsche a series of allegorical reflections on the nature of money and on the hypocrisy of the moral obligations—and the elaborate architecture of guilt—that underwrite our contemporary debt economy.

5 WASTE

> Sexual activity, whether perverted or not; the behaviour of one sex before the other; defecation; urination; death and the cult of cadavers (above all, insofar as it involves the stinking decomposition of bodies); the different taboos; ritual cannibalism; the sacrifice of animal-gods; omophagia; the laughter of exclusion; sobbing (which in general has death as its object); religious ecstasy; the identical attitude towards shit, gods, and cadavers; the terror that so often accompanies involuntary defecation; the custom of making women both brilliant and lubricious with makeup, gems, and gleaming jewels; gambling; heedless expenditure and certain fanciful uses of money, etc. together present a common character in that the object of the activity (excrement, shameful parts, cadavers, etc.) is found each time treated as a foreign body (*daz ganz Anderes* [sic]); in other words, it can just as well be expelled following a brutal rupture as reabsorbed through expulsion (or projection). The notion of the (heterogeneous) *foreign body* permits one to note the elementary *subjective* identity between types of excrement (sperm, menstrual blood, urine, fecal matter) and everything that can be seen as sacred, divine, or marvellous: a half-decomposed cadaver fleeing through the night in a luminous shroud can be seen as characteristic of this unity.
> **BATAILLE, "THE USE VALUE OF D.A.F. DE SADE"**[1]

Having looked at money's relationship to *capital* in Chapter 2, its configuration as a form of *debt* in Chapter 3, and its underlying structures of *guilt* in Chapter 4, we now turn to a fourth conceptual framework for exploring the theory of money, namely, notions that connect it to *waste*. This conception of money emerges with particular clarity when it is viewed through the

---

1   Bataille 1985b: 94.

perspective of *general economy*. The central thinker here is Georges Bataille, who although he remains largely a peripheral figure in anthropology and sociology, is best known for his theory of *expenditure* and the *accursed share*. Bataille's work has particularly strong connections with—although it must also be distinguished from—the arguments of Mauss on sacrifice, primitive classification, and gift exchange, which we considered in Chapter 1. Following a discussion of Bataille in which we consider his notion of money against the background of his philosophy of base materialism, his conception of unproductive expenditure and his theory of general economy, I want to look at two thinkers whose arguments resonate with his, although both move in quite different directions. These are Derrida and Baudrillard. I am not giving general introductions to these figures but focusing specifically on what they had to say about (and how they used) notions of waste and general economy, and more narrowly, what they said about the nature of money in relation to these notions.

By addressing money from the perspective of *waste*, I am inverting its more customary textbook treatment as a function of *utility*. This is a familiar theme in the study of consumption: luxury objects express the capacity of their owners to waste what they have, and the "Veblen good" is more coveted the higher its price goes. As Veblen describes it in *The Theory of the Leisure Class* (1899), the capacity to indulge in wasteful expenditure—and to make others use up their productive time catering to one's luxurious tastes—is a key marker of distinction (Veblen 2009). Waste is a *cultural symbol*, in Veblen's theory; indeed, one might refer to *wasteful* rather than *conspicuous* consumption (Varul 2006: 104–105). Waste is sociologically loaded as well as culturally rich.[2] Alongside gambling, conspicuous or wasteful consumption belongs to the group of "fanciful uses of money" that Bataille associates with expenditure. Having said this, I will focus specifically on theories that view money itself as a *form* of waste—or what Bataille calls *heterogeneous matter*.

Bataille's ideas are more likely to be found in scholarly discussions of surrealism and eroticism than economic sociology. When he is cited in the political economy field, it tends to be under the umbrella of work that has been influenced by Mauss's theory of gift exchange, but this theory reflects

---

2 According to Frederick Wherry, the prices paid by consumers for wasteful items "provide the seemingly 'unbiased,' quantitative evidence of their foolishness," while "some market fools calculate how people in mainstream society will judge their apparently noncalculating behaviors and conspicuously purchase high-priced goods in order to criticize the society they inhabit" (Wherry 2008: 368).

his arguments only partially. He initially pursued (and then rejected) a career as a Catholic priest, choosing instead to work at the Bibliothèque Nationale, where he was based in medallion collections and wrote several articles on numismatics, or the study of dead currency (Hutnyk 2003: 266; Hollier 1989: 124; 1995: 133). He wrote on a diverse range of topics: besides political economy, he explored poetry, philosophy, the arts, eroticism, violence, and myth, as well as writing on subjects situated on the borderline between literature and history, such as in *The Trial of Gilles de Rais*, which explores the case of the Breton knight and companion-in-arms of Joan of Arc who was hanged in Nantes in 1440 as a serial killer of children (Bataille 1996). A London exhibition catalogue from 2006 describes Bataille without much exaggeration as "numismatist, scholar, pornographer, social critic and idiosyncratic philosopher" (Ades, Baker, et al. 2006: 11).

Before moving on with my analysis of Bataille's work and its significance for our understanding of money, there are some intellectual linkages that may help to explain the rationale behind my argument in this chapter. Bataille cites Mauss extensively and is, in turn, cited (alongside Mauss) frequently by Baudrillard. Bataille—who was, incidentally, a friend of Walter Benjamin, who attended some of the seminars held by Bataille and his associates known as the "college of sociology" in Paris during the 1930s—developed a notion of the "sacred" in which group practices such as sacrifice are compared with the unnecessary or antiutilitarian expenditure of money as expressions of collective life (Bataille 1988a: 339). Derrida's book, *Given Time* (1994), explores a short story by Baudelaire, whose prose poems on prostitution and gambling can be regarded (as they were by Benjamin) as important allegories of modern life: money links them because the story Derrida is interested in is about the gift of a counterfeit coin. Derrida's book reads as an intense critical engagement with Mauss's theory of gift exchange, which has important ramifications for political writings that he (Derrida) was developing elsewhere on hospitality, forgiveness, and sovereignty. Finally, Baudrillard—a contemporary of Derrida but one whose work is rarely considered alongside his—drew extensively on Mauss and Bataille to develop his own critique of contemporary global capitalism in which they key trope is not—*contra* Derrida—the counterfeit, but rather the clone. Baudrillard's distinctive treatment of waste focuses not on the trivial or antiutilitarian expenditure of money but rather on its "inflation" within a financial system in which its conventional structures of signification and value have collapsed. These connections and resonances become clearer as our discussion in this chapter proceeds.

MONEY, EXCRETION, AND HETEROGENEOUS MATTER

In *The Enigma of Capital and the Crises of Capitalism* (2010), David Harvey proposes an intriguing variation of the problem he regards as crucial to the destructive dynamics of global capitalism. This is the problem of overaccumulation. According to Harvey, money renders this problem especially acute because in principle there are no material or practical limits to its accumulation. The huge salaries enjoyed by top hedge fund managers, for example, would be inconceivable—and probably unwanted—if they had to be paid in a material item such as shoes. Money, in other words, is inherently linked to capitalism's propensity to *hoard*. Harvey goes on to suggest that capitalism lacks what other social systems have had, namely, a mechanism for ensuring that wealth accumulation (and the power it confers) never gets out of hand: "What anthropologists refer to as the 'potlatch' in non-capitalist societies, for example, confers prestige on those who give away, renounce or in some instances even outright destroy, through elaborate ceremonies, the material possessions they have accumulated" (Harvey 2010b: 44). Although financial capitalism enables (and indeed encourages) the limitless accumulation of wealth, mechanisms do actually exist for its disposal: for instance, philanthropic generosity has a long tradition even within capitalism, as exemplified by the Carnegie, Ford, Rockefeller, Gates, Lerverhulme, and Soros foundations. There are other noncapitalist institutions, such as the Vatican, that also "soak up personal wealth" (Harvey 2010b: 44). Nevertheless, overaccumulation remains the core problem that renders capitalism so prone to crisis. This is the capital absorption problem, and it creates "a perpetual need to find new fields of activity to absorb the reinvested capital" (Harvey 2010b: 45).

Whereas Harvey suggests that the modern capitalist economy lacks the capacity to deal with overaccumulation, according to Bataille this failure is rooted in its untenably narrow conception of the "economic problem" with which all societies have to deal. This problem is widely taken (even by Marxists) to be the problem of scarcity. Bataille set out a bold alternative to it in the theory of "general economy" that he developed in *The Accursed Share* (originally published in 1949, 1991 cited here). It is an unusual work, drawing extensively on historical data to illustrate the principles of general economy, mainly drawn from human sacrifice among the Aztecs, the monastic institutions of Tibetan Lamaism, and toward the end of the book, the Marshall Plan. Of his own proposals regarding the latter, Bataille said, "It will be said that only a madman could perceive such things in the Marshall and Truman plans. I am that madman" (Bataille 1991: 197 n. 22). To understand how Bataille framed these proposals in terms of his theory of general economy, we first need to step back and consider three sets of ideas that play a crucial role in supporting that theory: first, his notion of *heterogeneous matter* and the philosophy of *base materialism* that sustains it; second, the distinctive conception of *unproductive expenditure* (and other "fanciful uses of money") that flows from the idea of heterogeneous matter; and third, the unusual understanding of the *sacred* that supports Bataille's "anti-utilitarian" approach to political economy.

In some respects, Bataille's work belongs alongside Mauss, especially his arguments on sacrifice and gift exchange. But there is a crucial difference between their arguments that can be illustrated by what they say about sacrifice. For Mauss, sacrifice is the means used by a group to establish both the *separation* and a *form of communication* between the *sacred* and the *profane*. Mauss looks at sacrifice extensively in the essay he wrote with Henri Hubert, *Sacrifice: Its Nature and Function* (1981), published almost twenty-five years before *The Gift* (1990). The earlier study, drawing mainly on Sanskrit and Hebrew documents as well as texts from classical antiquity and early Christianity, focuses on religious aspects of sacrifice and on its importance for mediating the exchange between society and the individual. The argument made in the earlier study is consistent with Durkheim's view that the notion of the sacred is social in origin and can be explained only sociologically, and it is notable that Durkheim himself chose to underline this connection by publishing his own essay on the definition of religious phenomena in the same volume of *Année Sociologique* (Durkheim 1899) in which the essay by Hubert and Mauss appeared (Fournier 1989: 71–72).[3] The unifying argument of the book is that, through sacrifice, the individual finds strength and protection in the social group as well as a means (through sacrificial rites) to put right what has gone wrong and reenter the community. The social order is sustained through sacrifice insofar as its rhythms are reproduced by it (Hubert and Mauss 1981: 102–103). As Mauss wrote to Durkheim at the time, "the religious act's aim is to place the individual at the centre of the collectivity" (Fournier 1989: 76).

The book might appear to be unpromising terrain for scholars of money. It contains only one direct reference to money, when economic aspects of certain forms of sacrifice (monetary profit) are discussed (Hubert and Mauss 1981: 37). However, when read in conjunction with various references to

---

3   In the conclusion to their study, Hubert and Mauss write, "Religious ideas, because they are believed, exist; they exist objectively, as social facts ... And this is enough to explain sacrifice" (Hubert and Mauss 1981: 101).

sacrifice in *The Gift*, the earlier study deepens our appreciation of money's importance as a material and visible sign through which wealth can be put into circulation and debts are settled. In *The Gift*, sacrifice is the additional, fourth obligation entailed in gift exchange besides giving, receiving, and reciprocation. Sacrifice is "the gift made to men in the sight of the gods and nature" (Mauss 1990: 18). In the earlier study, Hubert and Mauss define sacrifice as "a religious act which, through the consecration of a victim, modifies the condition of the moral person who accomplishes it or that of certain objects with which he is concerned" (Hubert and Mauss 1981: 13). It is worth comparing this description to the characterization of sacrifice that Durkheim had offered to the authors in his regular correspondence with them. Whereas the definition that Hubert and Mauss settled on emphasizes sacrifice as a *consecration* of its victim (Hubert and Mauss 1981: 11), Durkheim gives primacy to *destruction* when he defines sacrifice as a system of religious rites whose result is to destroy (through means such as manducation (mastication), punishment, and sacrifice by fire) or put out of common use (offering) one or several animate or inanimate objects (Fournier 1989: 75).

Curiously, Bataille's interpretation of sacrifice is closer to that of Durkheim than that of Mauss. According to Bataille, Mauss's approach misses the crucial element of *transgression* in sacrifice. This element applies to cases in which the roles of the object (e.g., animal) being sacrificed and that of the sacrificer are confused: to the extent that it is sometimes the god who *sacrifices himself* by uniting with his or her victim (Marcel 2003: 144).[4] This potential for *self*-destruction in sacrifice leads Bataille to suggest that the sacred world is connected less to the veneration of the social but rather to elements of hatred and disgust. Underlying this basic discrepancy in their interpretation of sacrifice and the significance of the sacred is a broader set of differences between Mauss and Bataille. The former, like Durkheim to a degree, was committed to pursuing a *rationalist* approach to sociology in which scientific method is combined with a normative commitment to the ideal of a society that acts as a moral force able to coerce individuals against their own irrational drives and impulses. Bataille's position is starkly different. For Bataille, those elements of subjectivity that Mauss distrusts are a crucial precondition for constituting a form of sacred life that is not religious but has a profound political potential. This element, in contradistinction to Mauss, underpins Bataille's specific understanding of *antiutilitarianism*, which we find in his theory of general economy.

---

[4] Note the echoes here of Walter Benjamin's image of the *guilty* god, as discussed in Chapter 4.

Despite their apparent variation, Bataille's writings display a striking unity of purpose. Underlying the many varied subjects he writes on is the "anti-theory" known as *base materialism*. Unlike more conventional forms of materialist thought, including historical materialism, base materialism derives its core analytical framework from an appreciation of the radicalizing potential of everything that could be described as repulsive and antithetical to reason. Bataille developed the notion through the review journal, *Documents*, in the fifteen issues he edited between 1929 and 1931. Bataille's version of materialism is not an ontological theory, a philosophy of matter. He never defined exactly what he meant by it, other than to suggest that base materialism is not a theory at all in the sense that it cannot be subsumed by reason. Michel Leiris (Leiris 1963) described the journal's mission as a "war machine against received ideas" (Ades and Bradley 2006: 11). One such set of received ideas against which Bataille and his collaborators on the journal (including Miró, Desnos, and Masson) were at odds was surrealism as it was being defined by Breton and the large group of artists around him (Breton 1969; Miró 1992; Desnos 2008; Poling 2008). According to Bataille, although the surrealists ostensibly sought to achieve immediacy of expression using techniques such as automatic writing, what they were in fact doing was practicing a form of *sublimation*, rendering the raw and violent realities of human thought and experience in an idealized form which, said Bataille, "placed the work before being" (Ades, Baker, et al. 2006: 11). Base materialism was developed as an expression of an antipathy toward surrealism as it was being understood by Breton, whose vehement response in the *Second Manifesto of Surrealism* included a description of Bataille as a "staid librarian" in contrast to de Sade, "who has spent twenty-seven years of his life in prison *for his beliefs*" (Ades, Baker, et al. 2006: 11).

Bataille derived the notion of base materialism mainly through his reading of Giordano Bruno and the Marquis de Sade (Stoekl 2007). Both thinkers sought to transform our understanding of the role of matter in creation. Bruno, the sixteenth century mathematician and philosopher, did so by formulating a conception of a god who animates matter. He was trying to draw out the theological implications of the Copernican revolution by "decentering" our understanding of cosmology and leaving us with an infinity of matter. De Sade removed god from the picture altogether, leaving only the energy contained in bodies that must be liberated through violence. This theory yields an image of matter as "constant movement, constant disruption, an endless burn-off of energy; it is also the momentary forms that this energy establishes, maintains, then destroys" (Stoekl 2007: 13). Bataille described his work as *heterology*, i.e., the study of *heterogeneous matter*. This is the matter whose "unjustifiable, a priori exclusion makes possible the coherence of rigorous, hierarchical systems of classification of thought" (Stoekl 2007: 21). Heterogeneous matter usually consists of objects that are charged with a taboo, such as orgiastic sexuality, mindless spending, and death. These are typically objects that the bourgeoisie abjure; indeed, Bataille dismissed the surrealists as "decadent aesthetes" because they lacked contact with the "lower social strata," which he characterized as society's "waste product." Energy is important here, too, and in addition to base materialism, Bataille's conception of it rests on a reading of Durkheim and Mauss, for whom the energy of *matter* is an expression of the energy of the *group*. There is a crucial difference, of course. For Bataille, unlike Durkheim and Mauss, such energy is neither rational nor "societal." That is to say, waste for Bataille is not a total social fact that is contained by society—and which sustains society in turn—but rather it is heterogeneous matter that *evades* society.

Heterogeneous matter also escapes *science*, and indeed any philosophical system—such as economics—that rests on a "homogeneous representation of the world" (Bataille 1985b: 97). Science (or economics) and heterology express two opposing impulses: respectively, *appropriation* and *excretion*. Science seeks to bring everything into its compass, to leave no problems unsolved. Its aim is to establish the homogeneity of phenomena (Bataille 1985a: 141). Its economic corollary is accumulation or hoarding: not only of food, but clothes, furniture, dwellings, instruments of production, and land: "Such appropriations take place by means of a more or less conventional homogeneity (identity) established between the possessor and the object possessed" (Bataille 1985b: 95). Heterogeneous elements, by contrast, are those we *excrete*. The economic corollary of excretion is a particular form of *expenditure*, which Bataille calls unproductive. He makes this particular connection in "The Use Value of D. A. F. de Sade" (1929–30), listing sexual activity, taboos, ritual cannibalism, the sacrifice of animal-gods, and gambling alongside "heedless expenditure and *certain fanciful uses of money*" as examples of the excretion of foreign bodies or heterogeneous elements (Bataille 1985b: 94, italics added). Here, then, we begin to see the important differences between the notions of *money* implied by the social theories advanced by Mauss and Bataille. For Mauss, money is coveted and valued, and even rendered sacred, by virtue of social relations that are inherently rational. Not so for Bataille. In his hands, money is often situated *beyond* the rational, in relation to that which *cannot be appropriated*, and is thus *excluded*. These are the expenditures he characterizes as wasteful, or unproductive.

Simmel once remarked that the only type of squanderer in the money economy who matters philosophically "is not a person who senselessly gives away money *in natura*, but rather one who uses it for nonsensical purchases that are unsuited to his circumstances" (Simmel 2004: 248). Martin Amis, too, captures this idea in the novel, *Money: A Suicide Note* (originally published in 1984, 2011 cited here), in which he parodies wild consumerism after a day spent shopping while drunk:

> For the next hour I took delivery of many additional purchases, the vast majority of which I couldn't remember purchasing. I just lay on the bed there, drinking. After a while I felt like Lady Diana would no doubt feel on her wedding day, as the presents from the Commonwealth contingent started arriving in their wagon trains. A squat kit of chunky glassware, an orange rug of Iranian provenance and recent manufacture, a Spanish guitar and a pair of maracas, two oil paintings (the first showing puppies and kittens asnooze, the second a nude, ideally rendered), an elephant's foot, something that looked like a microphone stand but turned out to be a Canadian sculpture, a Bengali chess set, a first edition of *Little Women*, and various other cultural treasures from all over the world. When it seemed to be over, I went to the bathroom and was explosively sick. Stress, it's expensive. There is great personal cost. But out it came, the lunch, the champagne, the money, all the green and folding stuff. (Amis 2011: 191)

In "The Notion of Expenditure" (1933), Bataille distinguishes between two forms of consumption. The first is the consumption of *useful* goods, that is to say, "the minimum necessary for the conservation of life and the continuation of individuals' productive activity in a given society." The second is what Bataille calls unproductive expenditure, that is to say, "luxury, mourning, war, cults, the construction of sumptuary monuments, games, spectacles, arts, perverse sexual activity (i.e., deflected from genital finality)— all these represent activities which, at least in primitive circumstances, have no end beyond themselves" (Bataille 1933: 118). Whereas Amis's depiction of mindless spending serves as an expression of *individual* alienation, for Bataille, squander is powerful when it is *collective* because it is tied to social rank, which is gained through deliberate and ostentatious loss.

He gives several examples of the principle of loss in operation. Jewels, acquired through the sacrifice of wealth, have a symbolic value that in psychoanalysis is connected with excrement. Within the unconscious, both jewels and excrement "are cursed matter that flows from a wound: they are part of oneself destined for open sacrifice," gifts that are "charged with sexual love." It is therefore imperative that jewels have immense material value. Fakes, however beautiful, are useless if they lack value. Religious sacrifice, too, involves the principle of loss: in Christianity, this principle reflects the idea of the crucifixion, which "carries human dread to a representation of loss and limitless degradation." Similarly, both competitive games and various forms of artistic production are examples of unproductive expenditure, of the principle that losses must be maximized (Bataille 1933: 119–20). In psychoanalytical terms, loss is connected to excretion and to death, eroticism, and sadism.

One of the best examples of socially powerful unproductive expenditure is the potlatch ceremony. Potlatch reverses the principle of conservation; value derives from what is *lost*, not gained: "There would be no potlatch if, in a general sense, the ultimate problem concerned the acquisition and not the dissipation of useful wealth" (Bataille 1933: 68). Crucially, potlatch relies upon *agonistic* social relations. It resembles a game of poker from which the players can never retire: "At no time does a fortune serve to shelter its owner from need. On the contrary, it functionally remains—as does its possessor—at the mercy of a need for limitless loss" (Bataille 1933: 123).

Besides heterogeneous matter and unproductive expenditure, the other key ideas that help to connect money to general economy in Bataille's writing relate to his distinctive notion of the sacred. In the late 1930s, Bataille was involved in two groups of thinkers with distinct but overlapping concerns. One was a group of renegade surrealists who lined up next to him, all critical of the work of Breton and his associates for practicing not immediacy of expression (as they claimed) but what Bataille dismissed as a bourgeois mode of expression that lacked the fundamental energy that is crucial to base materialism. The other group, whose ideas I want to discuss in more detail here, was the group of thinkers who formed the Collège de Sociologie.[5] Intellectually, their concerns ranged across subjects such as power, myth, animal societies, sexuality, public execution, shamanism, ritual, and festival. Although the group's core principles were subject to disagreements that eventually led to its fragmentation, the overarching concern was with the nature of the sacred and its implications for sociology's critical engagements with modernity.

Several members of the Collège had come into contact through their mutual association with Mauss. There were significant differences, however, in

5   This group, which met a handful of times between 1937 and 1939, included Georges Duthuit, Denis de Rougement, Anatole Lewitzky, Hans Mayer, Jean Paulhan, and Jean Wahl. Other, more occasional, visitors to the group included Georges Ambrosino, Jules Monnerot, Patrick Waldberg, Jacques Lacan, Georges Dumézil, Jean-Paul Sartre, Claude Lévi-Strauss, Max Horkheimer, Theodor Adorno, Walter Benjamin, Paul-Louis Landsberg, Henri Dubief, Julien Benda, Drieu La Rochelle, Jacques Chavy, Pierre Prévost, Pierre Mabile, and Bertrand d'Astorg. Talks were presented to this extraordinary collection of figures by Bataille, Roger Caillois, George Duthuit, Pierre Klossowski, Alexandre Kojève, René Guastella, Michel Leiris, Anatole Lewitzky, Hans Mayer, and Jean Paulhan.

the conception of the sacred put forward by Bataille and his associates when compared to the notion that had been developed by Durkheim and Mauss. For Durkheim, the sacred and profane constitute two distinct and autonomous realms: each is homogeneous and coherent in its own terms. This is not the case for Bataille, for whom the sacred is *heterogeneous, unstable*, and *violent*. For Bataille, the sacred is characterized by "the cruelty of sacrificing others and with the subsumption of individuals within totalizing group processes when they fearlessly confront death and are willing to sacrifice themselves" (Pearce 2003: 3). The members of the Collège saw the decline (and even disappearance) of the sacred from modern society as a "mutilation" (Hollier 1988: xxix). Their aim was not merely to diagnose this condition, to perform an autopsy on the corpse of the sacred, but to *reactivate* it. A society without a sacred dimension lacks something fundamental to its nature *qua* society. It is here that we begin to see more clearly the contours of a notion of *money* that stems from Bataille's arguments about the sacred, sacrifice, and waste.

It was in contrast to the sacred that Bataille, in "The Sorcerer's Apprentice" (originally published in 1938, 1988b cited here), portrayed modern existence as *dissociated*. Emaciated, lacking in energy and virility, life had "ceased to be existence," he argued (Bataille 1988b: 17). As slaves to the production of useful goods, we have been reduced to a condition of mere haplessness, "at liberty to love nothing" because "the man who is frightened by human destiny ... is unable to be virile" (Bataille 1988b: 14). Bataille directed his scorn especially against the belief that human destiny resides within reductive, overspecialized forms of knowledge: "Totality of existence has little to do with a collection of abilities and knowledge" (Bataille 1988b: 18). By contrast, existence in its totality is composed of a unity of elements and "has the simplicity of an axe stroke" (Bataille 1988b: 18). Such an existence, simple and intense and "not yet destroyed by a slavishness to function," can be found in the "fervent life" that is still possible only between lovers:

> When a man meets a woman and when it becomes obvious to him that here is destiny itself, the things that overcome him then like a silent tragedy are incomparable with this woman's necessary comings and goings. The image in which destiny has come alive for an instant finds itself thus projected in a world that is foreign to everyday fuss and bother. (Bataille 1988b: 18–19)

Crucially for us here, the space in which life, or existence in its totality, is able to thrive is the *space that money does not have at its disposal*. A similar notion of money features in Bataille's piece on fascism, written in 1935:

> The common denominator, the foundation of social *homogeneity* and of the activity arising from it, is money, namely, the calculable equivalent of the different products of collective activity. Money serves to measure all work and makes man a function of all measurable products. According to the judgment of *homogeneous* society, each man is worth what he produces; in other words, he stops being an existence *for itself*: he is no more than a function, arranged within measurable limits, of collective production (which makes him an existence *for something other than itself*). (Bataille 1985a: 138)

The existence Bataille emphasizes here relates to a particular *kind* of being, of course, not being per se. The being we find in rationalist philosophy is *immutable*, *unchanging*, and *abstract*: it is the corollary of social homogeneity. The form of being Bataille sets in opposition to this, he says three years later in "The Sorcerer's Apprentice," is "the double being who loses itself in endless embraces"—but also a *collective* being, "who tortures, beheads and makes war" (Bataille 1988b: 22). This being resides in an "aleatory" world, a world characterized not by the will to decide but rather—quite simply—to be (Bataille 1988b: 20). This world is crucial to "life" as Bataille understands it:

> In the fight for life against the teleological tendency, against the ordering of means and ends, luck, chance, divinely, ardently, suddenly makes its appearance and comes away victorious in the same way. Intelligence long ago ceased sensing the universe through reason that reckons. Existence itself recognizes that it is at the disposal of chance when it takes its measure by the starry sky or by death. It recognizes itself in all its own magnificence, created in the image of a universe untouched by the defilement of merit or intention. (Bataille 1988b: 21)

On the face of it, Bataille seems to be reproducing a familiar distinction between a monetary world that is rationalistic and coldly homogenizing, and on the other hand, a world that is more amenable to the nonrational and to qualitative judgment. But he does, in fact, find space for money in this latter, heterogeneous world. What makes this finding worthy of comment is that it depends on a particular (and unusual) conception of the social life of money. This is not money that is characterized by systems of measurement and a balancing of accounts but rather money that is gratuitously *wasted*. Bataille states, "Only actions committed to the pursuit of the seductive images of chance correspond to the need to live by the example of a flame" (Bataille 1988b: 21). This is a life in *decay*, a life that *burns*, and that

Bataille celebrates in the "holiness of the romanticism of gambling." This life is diametrically opposed to asceticism, which "makes monks and abstainers tepid" (Bataille 1992: 84). Here, then, Bataille is describing a "Dionysian" relationship with money, wherein money enriches life as waste. Such wasteful *uses* of money are connected, therefore, to a broader understanding of wealth as a *form* of waste in its own right.

Bataille confronts similar themes in *On Nietzsche* (originally published in 1945, 1992 cited here). To take risks "is to touch life's limit, go as far as you can, live on the edge of gaping nothingness!" (Bataille 1992: 84). And again: "'Money burns a hole in my pocket' when I gamble. Excited by the betting, I dedicate myself to gambling" (Bataille 1992: 84). Or, as he remarks in the same text: "*Morality has value only when advising us to risk ourselves*" (Bataille 1992: 28, original emphasis). Bataille's gambler presents a striking inversion of Weber's early capitalist, plowing gains back into the very activity that led to them. Just as sexual possession can prolong desire, so it is with gambling ("From now on I'll get no rest!"). Where Weber's Calvinists were rational, painstakingly methodical, and driven by a moral higher purpose (Wuthnow 1996: ch. 3), Bataille's gamblers are reckless, immoral, and intoxicated: "To play from formula or mathematical speculations is the opposite of gambling as a calculus of chance probabilities," he writes (Bataille 1992: 84). To resist the temptation to gamble, to lose everything, belongs to the morality of decline: "When we feel our strength ebbing and we decline, we condemn excesses of expenditure in the name of some higher good" (Bataille 1992: 34). This, Bataille concludes, is nothing other than the withered, bourgeois morality of restricted economy.

Religion plays a significant role in Bataille's analysis; indeed, one might as well say that the theory of general economy operates as a thinly veiled critique of what Weber once called the spirit of capitalism. Bataille argues that sacrifice restores to the sacred world that which *servile use has degraded*, that is to say, "rendered profane" (Bataille 1991: 55). If sacrifice is the "best means of negating a utilitarian relation between man and the animal or plant" (Bataille 1991: 56), religion is "the satisfaction that a society gives to the use of excess resources, or rather to their destruction (at least insofar as they are useful)" (Bataille 1991: 120). This is what gives religions their rich material aspect. For Bataille, as for Weber, Luther's significance was that he did not object to wealth per se so much as to its utilitarian use for religious ends, i.e., its use as a means of gaining access to heaven through the buying of indulgences. Luther insisted on a strict separation between God and "everything that was not the deep inner life of faith, everything that we can do and really carry into effect" (Bataille 1991: 121). In this way, wealth is deprived of all meaning, even charity. Calvin carried Luther's doctrine to its extreme, but with one crucial difference. He argued that any means used for man's glorification of God would be a negation of his own glory: "The sanctification of God was thus linked to the desacrilization of human life" (Bataille 1991: 124). It was this condition that was so favorable to the rise of industry.

In Calvin, the infinite wealth of the universe belongs to God, whereas the role of humans involves labor, wealth allocation, and the development of the apparatus of production. For Weber, Calvinism was crucial in exorcising emotions from the lives of the early capitalists (Barbalet 2008). For Bataille, the consequence was to associate *abundance* with God and *scarcity* with man. Calvinism crushed the sacred principle of nonproductive expenditure: "one can even say that by accepting the extreme consequences of a demand for religious purity it destroyed the sacred world, the world of nonproductive consumption, and handed the earth over to the men of production, the bourgeois" (Bataille 1991: 127). In the Middle Ages, churches had dominated our horizon, erecting steeples "wherever men were grouped together for common works." The higher purpose of even the basest works was "clear and visible from afar" (Bataille 1991: 132). When Benjamin Franklin said that time is money ("He that kills a breeding-sow, destroys all her offspring to the thousandth generation"), nothing was more opposed to the spirit of religious sacrifice (Bataille 1991: 126).[6] Bataille's crucial point is that the history of modern capitalism is a history of the church's defeat. God has become the distant expression of humans.

These, then, are the terms of the analysis Bataille finally takes up in *The Accursed Share*. His leading contention in the book is that gift exchange conforms to a model of *general* economy that contrasts with the modern Western model of *restricted* economy. According to the restricted view, scarcity is the fundamental economic problem: "Economic activity, considered as a whole, is conceived in terms of particular operations with limited ends" (Bataille 1991: 22). In advancing a theory of general economy, Bataille presents the opposite point of view: *excess* (overaccumulation) is the fundamental economic problem. This is the accursed share—*la part maudite*—of the work's title. The accursed share is the excessive, nonrecuperable part of an economy, which must be either consumed gloriously (in festivals), or catastrophically (through wars). Moreover, this is the consumption of *versions of ourselves*: our

6   "Of course, Franklin's principle—seldom formulated—continues to guide the economy (toward an impasse no doubt). But in Luther's time it could not be stated in overt opposition to that of the Church" (Bataille 1991: 120).

wasteful expenditures are inexorably bound up with rituals involving death and sex: "Beyond our immediate ends, man's activity in fact pursues the useless and infinite fulfilment of the universe" (Bataille 1991: 21).

"As a rule," Bataille writes, "particular existence always risks succumbing for a lack of resources. It contrasts with general existence whose resources are in excess and for which death has no meaning" (Bataille 1991: 39). The underlying argument in the theory of general economy is that living organisms *always* produce more than they need:

> I will begin with a basic fact: The living organism, in a situation determined by the play of energy on the surface of the globe, ordinarily receives more energy than is necessary for maintaining life; the excess energy (wealth) can be used for the growth of a system (e.g., an organism); if the system can no longer grow, or if the excess cannot be completely absorbed in its growth, it must necessarily be lost without profit; it must be spent, willingly or not, gloriously or catastrophically. (Bataille 1991: 21)

Expenditure as Bataille describes it is universal, whatever different forms it takes: "A certain excitation, whose sum total is maintained at a noticeably constant level, animates collectivities and individuals" (Bataille 1933: 128). These states of excitation are like toxic states, "the illogical and irresistible impulse to reject material or moral goods that it would have been possible to utilize rationally (in conformity with the balancing of accounts)" (Bataille 1933: 128). In nonmarket societies, the products of human activity flow to rich people to pay for spectacular acts of collective expenditure, such as through festivals, spectacles, and games.

These practices were diluted by the decline of paganism and through the individualization of property brought about by Christianity. Although such things still go on in market societies, they are no longer linked to loss; indeed, the onus is often placed on their organizers—of every Olympic Games, for example—to demonstrate that their expenditures have *not* been wasteful. The social obligation to lose in order to achieve rank has not completely disappeared from market societies; it merely takes a nonagonistic form. All that is generous, orgiastic, and excessive has disappeared, along with rivalry: "wealth is now displayed behind closed doors, in accordance with depressing and boring conventions," and the bourgeoisie with their minor fortunes debase and divide their ostentatious expenditure, putting on "petty displays" around banks and shops. Such is the "augmented splendour of a sinister industrialist and his even more sinister old wife," while beneath them stand the grocer and his wife with their "gilded clocks, dining room buffets, and artificial flowers" (Bataille 1933: 124). This is "bourgeois" economics, or the economics of restricted economy. Hatred of expenditure is the "raison d'être of and the justification for the bourgeoisie," which spends only *for* and *within* itself: "by hiding its expenditures as much as possible from the eyes of the other classes" (Bataille 1933: 124). Bourgeois rationality, driven toward an obsessive balancing of accounts, is economic in the vulgar sense, with its "humiliating conceptions of restrained expenditure" (Bataille 1933: 124). There are echoes of Nietzsche in Bataille's description of the bourgeoisie, with its "sordid face, a face so rapacious and lacking in nobility, so frighteningly small, that all human life, upon seeing it, seems degraded" (Bataille 1933: 124–25). Like Nietzsche, Bataille insists that human life cannot be contained by closed systems; indeed, it can thrive only when it forces itself out of those systems: "It is only by such insubordination—even if it is impoverished—that the human race ceases to be isolated in the unconditional splendour of material things" (Bataille 1933: 128).

The closest affinity Bataille has with conventional economics would surely be with Keynes, for example, when he states that he wanted to "give, in general, the reasons that account for the mystery of Keynes's bottles, tracing the exhausting detours of exuberance through eating, death and sexual reproduction" (Bataille 1991: 13). This is the passage in question, from *The General Theory*:

> If the Treasury were to fill old bottles with banknotes, bury them at suitable depths in disused coalmines which are then filled up to the surface with town rubbish, and leave it to private enterprise on well-tried principles of laissez-faire to dig the notes up again (the right to do so being obtained, of course, by tendering for leases of the note-bearing territory), there need be no more unemployment and, with the help of the repercussions, the real income of the community, and its capital wealth also, would probably become a good deal greater than it actually is. It would, indeed, be more sensible to build houses and the like; but if there are political and practical difficulties in the way of this, the above would be better than nothing. (Keynes 2008: 116)

Keynes made this argument in the teeth of a recession: the purpose of gratuitous expenditure as he defined it was to *stimulate demand*. The underlying premise of economics as he conceived it was *still* the problem of scarcity, although Keynes did believe that this scarcity would eventually cease to be of paramount concern.[7] By contrast, as we have seen, Bataille's theory begins with the problem of *too much*, not too little: "a human society can have ... an interest in considerable losses, in catastrophes that, while conforming to well-defined needs, provoke tumultuous depressions, crises of dread, and, in the final analysis, a certain, orgiastic state" (Bataille 1933: 117). Some commentators have linked such remarks to the period of economic upheaval (the 1929 Wall Street crash and subsequent depression) that Bataille would have been witnessing when he wrote the expenditure essay (Noys 2000: 105). For Bataille, however, expenditure is not *functional* in the way that it is in Keynes: the "point" of expenditure is not as a means of stimulating growth. Its point, simply, is waste.

DERRIDA'S GHOSTS

We now take what looks like a detour from general economy into the realm of language, to which scholars have compared money with ever-greater frequency during the past 100 years or so. But as we shall see, the ongoing conversation between the theory of money and the theory of language and semiotics is germane to the arguments about money's connections with general economy that I have been discussing so far in this chapter. The key connection is *exchange*. The *cyclical* logic underpinning gift exchange and potlatch is at odds with the *binary* exchanges that appear to prevail whenever money is involved. This is not just a difference in *form*. According to Baudrillard, there are some profound social, cultural, and political differences between monetary exchanges as they occur in late capitalist society, and the principles of general economy—he calls it *symbolic exchange*—as described by Bataille. We come to these differences in the next section. First, though, I turn to Derrida, for whom a particular and unusual comparison between money and language is suggested by what he believes is *impossible* in the nature of the gift exchange. Importantly for us, this comparison yields a distinctive approach to money.

Derrida's philosophy of language (and the argument about the nature of money that flows from it) incorporates a fundamental critique of the

---

7   "I look forward ... in days not so very remote, to the greatest change which has ever occurred in the material environment of life for human beings in the aggregate. But, of course, it will all happen gradually, not as a catastrophe. Indeed, it has already begun. The course of affairs will simply be that there will be ever larger and larger classes and groups of people from whom problems of economic necessity have been practically removed" (Keynes 1972: 331; Chernomas 1984).

conventional understanding of the sign as a two-sided unity consisting of a phonetic signifier and its signified meaning. Like de Saussure, Derrida views language and meaning in relational, rather than absolute, terms. Just as *money* is viewed not as a system for representing (and then comparing) an underlying set of values, but rather as a system of differences from which value emerges as the product of relations, so *language* is thought of not as a stable system of signs corresponding to an underlying reality, but rather as a complex interplay of signifying relations from which meaning emerges in a state of chronic uncertainty. Derrida, moreover, introduces a third term into the argument about language and meaning, namely, *time*. In his analysis, meaning is not only relational, but also *perpetually deferred*. This idea has an important bearing on his conception of money. Moreover, it takes his argument forward into a set of engagements with law, justice, and democracy that shed some powerful light on the wider significance of that conception.

Derrida's critique of the conventional philosophy of language hinges on two main arguments. The first concerns the concept of *différance*. As is well known, the term is untranslatable: a play on the French word *différer*, meaning both to differ and to defer. The first, spatial (or *synchronic*) aspect of this definition, to *differ*, reflects Derrida's broad agreement with de Saussure's argument that meaning derives from a system of differences and the idea that such differences cannot simply be heard or seen in the mind's eye but also consist of relations between signs. The second, temporal (or *diachronic*) aspect of the definition, to *defer*, comes from Derrida's argument that the meaning of any word is never immediately given but always depends on relationships with additional words: there is an unfolding chain of signification so that meaning is never exhausted but is continually put off, or deferred. This deferment is important because it implies that meaning is not a property of a static structure of relations between signs but is dynamic. The crucial role played by *time* in this conception is significant when it comes to grasping Derrida's interpretation of money.

The second key aspect of Derrida's critique of traditional language philosophy relates to his argument about the priority that has normally been given to *speech* (as opposed to writing) as the primary mode of linguistic communication. The classical view of such matters is that, historically, writing emerged as a powerful tool for communicating with those who are present but out of range. Although Derrida does not dispute the notion that writing developed later than speech, he criticizes the conclusion that language philosophy normally draws from this history, specifically about the *superiority* of speech. This question is partly about immediacy, and hence about time. According to Derrida, for reasons discussed just now in relation to the notion of *différance*, there is never an "immediate" meaning that can be discerned from language. Whether in speech or in writing, both the sender and the receiver of meaning are absent in the fundamental sense that for *neither* is meaning apparent *immediately and in full*. In linguistic terms, this absence challenges the image of writing as a debased form of communication (e.g., as secondary to speech). In philosophical terms, Derrida is challenging the idea of pure *logos*, which is potentially present to the *mind* or *spirit*. There are analogies with Nietzsche's proclamation of the death of God, especially his critique of the view of morality and humankind that Christian theology sustains.

Derrida's engagement with money echoes these broader arguments about language, writing, and speech. In *Specters of Marx* (originally published in 1993, cited here as 2006), he picks up on Marx's fascination with Shakespeare's *Timon of Athens*,[8] where money is celebrated for its power to convert everything into its opposite.[9] Money surfaces here as a power that distorts both the individual and society, rendering them no longer entities in themselves but sites of paradoxical inversion: fidelity is transformed into infidelity and back again, love becomes hate and hate becomes love, virtue changes places with vice, servant with master, idiocy with intelligence. Money *conjures*, it *brings forth what is not there* (Derrida 2006: 50). Money is not only specterlike, in Marx's treatment; it is a *remainder* or *shadow*—a *ghost*, an *illusion*, a *simulacrum*, and an *apparition*, recalling Marx's own remark about the state's endowment of money with the power of breeding through a stroke of the enchanter's wand (Derrida 2006: 56; Marx 1982: 919). This is a *funerary* space, too, where hoarders speculate on the use of money after death; capitalists relentlessly bring forth their own gravediggers; and at times of social crisis, treasures are buried and turned back into lifeless metal. Money here is betwixt and between: an apparition that is neither life nor death, a specter "like the conspirators [*conjurés*] of old Europe on whom the *Manifesto* declares war" (Derrida 2006).[10] Capitalism's

---

8   Marx discusses the play in *The Economic and Philosophic Manuscripts of 1844* (2007), as well as in *Capital* volume 1 (1982).

9   "This yellow slave / Will knit and break religions, bless the accursed; / Make the hoar leprosy adored, place thieves / And give them title, knee and approbation / With senators on the bench: this is it / That makes the wappen'd widow wed again; / She, whom the spitalhouse and ulcerous sores / Would cast the gorge at, this embalms and spices / To the April day again. Come, damned earth, / Thou common whore of mankind, that put'st odds / Among the rout of nations" (Act IV, Scene 3).

10   Marx also states that money "speaks different languages and wears different national uniforms" (Marx 2009: 139), which Derrida interprets as meaning that as circulating currency "money bears local and political character" (Derrida 2006: 129).

secret, too, is betwixt and between: opaque and transparent, and all the more secret because there is no substantial essence behind it. Simultaneously profound and superficial, money binds us together both as living humans and as half-dead apparitions of the commodity form (Derrida 2006: 193). This process of "spectralization"[11] within modern capitalism is most clearly manifested by its "anthill-city" (Derrida 2006: 193), and Baudelaire understood this better than most, portraying it in his writings through ghosts, the crowd, prostitution, and of course, money itself. There is an apocalyptic passage in *Intimate Journals* (Baudelaire 2006), in which Baudelaire says that when the end of the world arrives, when supreme evil wins out, everything ("even *crimes of the senses*") will be condemned—*except for money*: "Then, any shadow of virtue, everything indeed which is not worship of Plutus, will be brought into utter ridicule" (Baudelaire 2006: 57–58). Here is a striking image of money's dual character: its *power to destroy without destroying itself*. The world may have sunk into perdition, but its credit is still good.

Yet there is another, arguably more nuanced, view of money in Baudelaire's work, and this is the subject of Derrida's discussion of the prose poem, "La Fausse Monnaie" ("Counterfeit Money"), published posthumously in 1869 as part of *Le Spleen de Paris* (Baudelaire 1970). Derrida's examination of the poem focuses on the difficulty and complexity of the distinction between *true* and *counterfeit* money. On Derrida's reading, the poem provides a richly disturbing account of money as an empty signifier, symbol of nothing, and expression of decay. However, money's emptiness as Derrida understands it does not come at the apex of a process of unrelenting abstraction in the way that Goux (Goux 1990, 1994) describes (see Chapter 1). For Derrida, money is *essentially* empty, in the sense of being indefinable *ab initio*.

The poem recounts the story of two friends who meet a beggar. Both give something, but it turns out that what seemed to be the larger donation made by the narrator's companion was—he claims—a counterfeit coin. The narrator is irritated by the apparent pleasure his friend takes when anticipating the beggar's surprise on discovering that the coin is fake. Moreover, he is mystified by his friend's belief that he performed a charitable act, despite giving the beggar a false coin. It seems that he had wanted *both* to give *and* to make a good deal, "to gain forty sous and the heart of God" (Derrida 1994: 59). Derrida uses this dualism to reflect more broadly on the nature of the "true" gift as opposed to "false" money.

---

11   I.e., the multiplication of specters: "there is always more than one commodity, more than one spirit, and even more spectres' (Derrida 2006: 193).

Indisputably, the coin *was* a gift, irrespective of whether it was real or counterfeit. For Derrida, the crucial question is whether such a gift—*any* gift—can ever be true. What does it mean to say that a gift is genuine? For Derrida, the true gift must be a gift *without intention or motive*. Contrary to what Mauss said, a genuine gift is never given to receive a gift in return. That would simply be a loan. With true giving, there can be no reciprocity, no return, no exchange, and no debt. If the recipient *owes* the giver a gift in return, this is not a gift (Derrida 1994: 12). And for this reason, the true gift must never *reveal* itself as a gift; its recipient must be unaware that something has been given. "If the other perceives or receives it, if he or she keeps it as a gift, the gift is annulled" (Derrida 1994: 14). The true gift must hide itself: not as something false or counterfeit, but rather as something that is defined by its own impossibility. True giving (like true forgiving and true hospitality) is elusive not because it is too morally demanding but because it rests on a logical contradiction: it cannot be seen for what it is, even by the giver. This is therefore closer to what Bataille describes. Energy from the sun is a gift without return, for example. Likewise, absolute loss is loss without return. Unproductive expenditure as Bataille describes it involves *prodigality*: from *prodigere*, to drive away or squander.

Derrida suggests that counterfeit money bears an uncanny, unstable resemblance to the true gift. It, too, must hide itself *qua* counterfeit. And if people are fooled, the counterfeit coin can circulate and function as if it were good and true money. But this raises the question: what *is* good and true money? For Derrida, *both* genuine *and* counterfeit money rely on identical surface effects in order to be counted as true. Money functions, "as long as one can count with and on cash money to produce effects"—whether of alms, purchase, or speculation. Genuine and counterfeit money are both capable of expressing this truth. Given enough *faith*, they can both generate wealth. As Baudelaire's narrator remarks, the counterfeit coin is bound to produce events in the life of its recipient: it could be converted into real coins; or lead him into prison; or create the seed for several days' wealth, should the beggar decide to speculate.[12] Such is the unlimited potential of money. If even a *fake* coin can be used to generate wealth, the distinction between true and counterfeit money begins to break down. Derrida's analysis echoes what he said about spectralization in Marx. In Baudelaire's story, there is no means of ascertaining even whether the coin was a genuine counterfeit, that is to say, whether the friend's confession was itself true.

---

12   "And so my fancy went its course, lending wings to my friend's mind and drawing all possible deductions from all possible hypotheses" (Derrida 1994: unnumbered insert).

There are different possibilities for reading his claim: perhaps the friend really gave less, after all; perhaps it is cynical boastfulness; perhaps he is simply withdrawing from the gift cycle ("the poor man owes him nothing"); or perhaps he is lying (he gave real money, and the confession is counterfeit). We have only his word and our own faith. Like their money, even Baudelaire's characters are simulacra. The secret they carry—was it a genuine coin?—depends on a series of surface appearances and effects.

This interplay of value, appearance, and effect resonates with Baudelaire's own difficult relationship with money and his ill-disguised disdain for it. In *The Painter of Modern Life* (originally published in 1863, 1995 cited here), he contrasts the wealthy man ("the man who is rich and idle ... and whose solitary profession is elegance") with the dandy. Whereas money is indispensable to those who make a "cult" of their emotions, the dandy "does not aspire to money as something essential; this crude passion he leaves to vulgar mortals; he would be perfectly content with a limitless credit at the bank" (Baudelaire 1995: 27). Something of a dandy himself, Baudelaire was mired in debt. These debts invade his texts until debt and text are inseparable. "His journals are filled with lists of works to be published, or promised to editors. Alongside such lists are debts owed or payments promised to creditors" (Meltzer 2011: 155). What does this tell us about his understanding of money? Meltzer suggests that Baudelaire failed to understand the *symbolic* aspects of money. Despite all those lists of promises, works to be completed, and debts to be paid, all that Baudelaire really saw ahead of him were the *material things* he desired, not the mechanics of a money economy. His debts were premised on an underlying notion of money "as some sort of necessary abstraction needed to attain an object" (Meltzer 2011: 151). He failed to grasp "the allegorical aspect of a money economy" (Meltzer 2011: 155). He "will never see money as an exchange, a code, a system of signs" (Meltzer 2011: 153). But a different interpretation of Baudelaire is possible, in which money's inherent connections with *waste* and *decay* come to the fore. Here, money's allegorical significance lies in its expression of a much deeper crisis in the moral economy of representation and truth.

Baudelaire surely understood that money had severed its underlying connections with the "things" of value. Even the *money* object in his story—the coin—is apparently (but not definitely) a fake. If his own finances suggest a crisis of faith in money, his many references to expenditure are a testimony to it, too. In "The Double Room," also from *Le Spleen de Paris*, Baudelaire counterposes a "spiritual" world in which time stands still ("there are no more minutes, there are no more seconds!") and "the soul takes a bath of indolence," with a second room in which time returns in the form of a bailiff who has "come to torture me in the name of law." Money is the protagonist in this second room. The bailiff has come to collect a debt. Adding to Baudelaire's misery, he is accompanied by an unhappy lover who has arrived to declare her poverty, and a messenger boy from a magazine who has come to collect an article that Baudelaire had promised. By contrast, Baudelaire's various references to the expenditure of money have no obvious financial connection: gambling, prostitution, alcohol, and (in "La Fausse Monnaie") tobacco. These are expenditures in which money is not just wasted, but oddly absent, just as it was in that first room (Meltzer 2011: 167). They are expenditures through which one has escaped from the rigors of time that—as we saw in Chapter 4—underwrite the moral economy of debt.[13] Derrida even wonders whether smoking has some essential relationship to the sovereignty of self: "If there is some gift—and especially if one gives oneself something, some affect or some pleasure—it may then have an essential relation, at least a symbolic or emblematic one, with the authorization one gives oneself to smoke" (Derrida 1994: 107).

Similar themes can be found elsewhere in literature, most notably in Edgar Allen Poe's "The Gold-Bug" (1843), Mark Twain's "The Million Pound Bank Note" (1893), and André Gide's novel, *The Counterfeiters* (1925) (Twain 1957; Gide 1990; Poe 1991). Poe's "The Gold-Bug" deals with the transition from gold to paper money (or parchment), which was taking place in the United States at the time the story was written. In "The Philosophy of Furniture" (1840), Poe remarked that by virtue of its having no aristocracy of blood, the United States had fashioned for itself an aristocracy of dollars. Twain's story, too, could be read as a whimsical reflection on the powerful interplay of appearances made possible by the banknote in question, as its temporary owner, Henry Adams, becomes the subject of a bet that merely by possessing such a symbol of wealth, we can have almost anything we want—at least for a while. In a more serious vein, Gide's novel uses the metaphor of counterfeit money to explore the "faux" in human relations as they unfold behind the facades of Parisian mansions. The book attacks both language and money, and on identical grounds. Each is undergoing a crisis of realism—for the genuine gold coin, read naive semanticism—which as Goux points out, has a broader resonance: "Values, law, exchange, nature, sign, representation: all these notions are enlisted in the parallel between language and money" (Goux 1994: 8).

---

[13] Baudelaire writes in "Get Drunk," "One should always be drunk. That's the great thing; the only question. Not to feel the horrible burden of Time weighing on your shoulders and bowing you to the earth, you should be drunk without respite" (Baudelaire 1970: 74).

An allegorical warning of a different kind was offered by Adelbert von Chamisso, in *Peter Schlemihls wundersame Geschichte*,[14] written in 1814. Schlemihl was the man who exchanged his shadow for a purse that could produce endless quantities of gold coin, only to find out how much his shadowless appearance estranges him from others. Schlemihl's infinite wealth gives rise to an existence that is incorporeal, asocial, and atemporal. As his world falls apart, all he can do is put the gold to increasingly desperate, wasteful use: scattering it, squandering it, piling it up. But he has lost the very shadow which signifies that he is mortal, made of flesh, and will decay.[15] "Learn above all things first to reverence your shadow, and next your money," he concludes (von Chamisso 2008: 124). Bereft of his shadow, he is deprived of time. Each in its own way, these disparate works testify to the combination of fascination and fear that money attracts when its status as a mere sign (and thus as fiction) is suggested.

Money, for Baudelaire, has those spectral qualities that Derrida found in Marx. For him, its most significant features are those that according to "restricted" economics should be regarded negatively: its lack of value, truth, and substance. For Derrida, likewise, if counterfeit money is as *true* as genuine money, then genuine money is as much a *fiction* as counterfeit money (Derrida 1994: 124). "There is in any case no possible sense, no possible space, no possible mark for this difference, at least when the situation is framed thus, that is, in the contextual frame of this convention or of this institution" (Derrida 1994: 153). The counterfeit and genuine coins are indistinguishable. In this sense, the pure gift and the counterfeit coin are analogous. Each encounters a logical reversal as soon as we try to pin it down. The pure gift, like the counterfeit coin, depends on the *form of its impossibility*. The impossible—"aneconomic," *truly* wasteful—gift requires its own immediate self-effacement, just like the counterfeit coin when it enters into circulation. The *impossible* gift event is the *genuine* gift event, but in order to be so, it must be instantly forgotten (Derrida 1994: 16). It must be waste. And here, as waste, we find what one might call the secret—necessarily social—life of money.

---

14   *Peter Schlemihl's Miraculous Story*.
15   Shakespeare, too, makes an association between bodily and monetary decay. In *The Merchant of Venice*, Portia warns that should the pound of flesh leak blood, the debt in whose settlement it is offered will be forfeit: "Tarry a little; there is something else. / This bond doth give thee here no jot of blood. / The words expressly are 'a pound of flesh.' / Take then thy bond, take thou thy pound of flesh, / But in the cutting it, if thou dost shed / One drop of Christian blood, thy lands and goods / Are, by the laws of Venice, confiscate / Unto the state of Venice" (Act IV, Scene 1).

In logical terms, Derrida calls these problems possible–impossible *aporias*, as in the proposition: "The truth of the gift is equivalent to the non-gift or to the non-truth of the gift" (Derrida 1994: 27). Likewise, pure forgiveness—an act of unconditional forgiveness, or the forgiveness of that which cannot be forgiven—is impossible. To forgive unconditionally is difficult to distinguish from an act calculated to generate repentance, or an apology (Derrida 2001: 34–35). "Ought not a true forgiveness (a forgiveness in authentic money) absolve the fault or the crime even as the fault and the crime remain what they are?" (Derrida 1994: 163). Derrida's argument about the pure gift is directed against the "Christianization" of forgiveness that occurs by (for example) coupling it with reconciliation: to forgive *in order to* achieve reconciliation is forgiveness with a purpose or intention, and when there is calculation, forgiveness cannot be pure.[16] The logical impossibility of both the pure gift and pure forgiveness comes from the fact that their recognition (of forgiveness, of the gift) by the recipient turns them into a calculative, interested act.

These are broader themes in Derrida's reading of the story, reaching out to what he says elsewhere about forgiveness, hospitality, and justice. The beggar is not only defenseless and destitute but also mute. He does not *ask* for money, but rather *demands* it by way of his mute gaze. But he has nothing to give in return. He can only look implacably at those who happen by and at what is happening (Derrida 1994: 142). The beggar is like a beaten dog, "the fraternal allegory of social poverty, of the excluded, the marginal, the 'homeless'" (Derrida 1994: 143). But in this sense he represents *justice*, which for Derrida is an order that operates *beyond* money. He is a figure of the law, before which the two friends are destitute. But he is also a specter. In Mauss, the poor represent the gods or the dead, the return of the ghost: they are an "always imminent threat" (Derrida 1994: 138). In such conditions, the gift "obeys a regulating, distributive, compensatory principle" (Derrida 1994: 139). Likewise, "La Fausse Monnaie" can be restaged as a phantasmal trial. The two friends walk the story's length before the law. They are indebted—and guilty—as soon as the beggar looks at them. They are summoned to pay, to acquit themselves "by sacrificing, by offering or by offering themselves" (Derrida 1994: 145). At the story's conclusion, the narrator declares that he cannot forgive his friend. This judgment without appeal is based simply on looking into his friend's eyes ("I gazed into the whites of

---

16 Derrida also calls this "therapeutic" forgiveness. He says that though, politically, he might approve of it, as a philosopher he seeks to be rigorous and precise with words, and in these terms therapeutic forgiveness cannot be pure forgiveness.

188 CHAPTER 5

his eyes, and I was appalled to see that his eyes were shining with an incontestable candour"). The companion's crime, however, is not moral deficiency but lack of intelligence: the narrator finds him culpable for the ineptness of his calculation. He could be excused for knowingly being evil; indeed, there may even be some merit in knowing that one is. But to do evil through stupidity is a failure to use the faculty of understanding that nature itself has given: "He has failed to honour the contract binding him naturally to nature; he has not acquitted himself of his debt—of a natural debt, thus a debt without debt or an infinite debt" (Derrida 1994: 169).

Derrida makes the connection between money and giving via the counterfeit coin that was itself offered as an impure gift, but what is the logic at work here? Conventionally one might say: where there is calculation, where the gift is impure, monetary reasoning must be involved. Therefore, a direct exchange takes place that is logically incompatible with the purity implied by Derrida's own rigorous concept of the gift. Such rigor is absent in Mauss, for whom the "madness" of the gift[17] "is first of all the madness of the dissemination of the meaning 'gift'" (Derrida 1994: 55).[18] The question becomes "what does it mean to countersign and counterfeit? And especially, what does it mean to betray?" (Derrida 2004: 8). Counterfeit money is not simply fake money but "illegal money that *passes for* genuine" (Derrida 2005: 68, italics added). Hence with money, too, recognition is key: "true money or counterfeit money . . . can only be what it is, false or counterfeit, to the extent that no one knows it is false, that is, to the extent to which it circulates, appears, functions as good and true money" (Derrida 1994: 59). We might therefore want to say that, by Derrida's own standards of rigor, it is impossible to distinguish between true and counterfeit money: that is to say, the possibility of one (e.g., true money) rests on the fact its other (e.g., counterfeit money) is "always already" part of its existence.

The coin given to the beggar was a simulacrum: "money without value—devalued or counterfeit—that is, without gold reserves or without the corresponding accrediting value" (Derrida 1994: 61). Note Derrida's formulation. Counterfeit *or devalued* money: these are run together, just as they have been in countless discussions of paper money in which the dubiousness of money that consists of an "empty" token is a function of the possi-

---

[17] "Mauss will begin to proliferate signs . . . as if his language were about to go a little mad one page after it had insisted so strenuously on keeping the meaning of the gift for the gift" (Derrida 1994: 46).

[18] "To look for a unity of this meaning would be, to quote the narrator of 'Counterfeit Money,' to 'look for noon at two o'clock'" (Derrida 1994: 55).

bility of the counterfeit. For Derrida, *all* money is a simulacrum, just as—for Baudelaire—*all* money is in an irreversible state of decay:

> The "thing" in question, the thematized thing, the object of narration defined as counterfeit money, is not a thing like any other, precisely, in the strictly determined sense of thing; it is "something" like a sign, and even a false sign, or rather a true sign with a false sign, a sign whose signified seems (but that is the whole story) finally not to correspond or be equivalent to anything, a fictive sign without secure signification, a simulacrum, the double of a sign or a signifier. (Derrida 1994: 93)

Baudelaire's coin was loose change, left over from a transaction that took place just before the story began. It was an expenditure on tobacco, on a form of pleasure that is inextricably tied to wastefulness and decay: it leaves no trace, other than smoke and ash. Burned cigarettes have that ghostlike, spectral quality that Derrida associates with money. And so perhaps, in the end, only counterfeit money could be given as a pure gift, because such a gift must be incalculable, without any discernible outcome (Derrida 1994: 157). Had Baudelaire's coin been genuine, the gift of it could not have been pure.

COOL MONEY, LIVING MONEY

Baudrillard's understanding of money rests on a distinctive approach to capitalism and its prevailing notions of *value* and *reality*. He argues that there are four distinctive systems of value, operating as distinct but overlapping historical stages, which frame our conception of reality (Baudrillard 1981, 1993, 2009). The first is the *natural* law of value, whereby value is deduced from the grace of God and the beneficence of nature. The second consists of the *commodity* law, according to which value is governed by the logic of general equivalence, and derived from labor expended to produce useful commodities. The third law is *structural*, whereby value is organized by codes and models and derived purely from relations between signs.[19] Fourth is the *fractal* stage of value, in which value is derived from the haphazard proliferation and dispersal of signs. These are not signs *referring* to other signs, as in the third stage, but signs that simply *come into contact* with other signs: contact that may be arbitrary and chaotic. Value is propagated through contiguity alone, a process Baudrillard likens to the cancerous

---

19   This stage corresponds to de Saussure's theory of the sign.

proliferation of cells, a "return of the infinitely small" (Baudrillard 2001, 2002). Extending the metaphor, he argues that all systems within this fourth stage of value (e.g., systems for handling data, communication systems, and of course the financial system) are characterized by bloatedness, or to borrow from Susan Sontag's description of cancer, "demonic pregnancy" (Sontag 2009). In such a condition, these systems have become lethargic: not in the sense that they fail to produce anything but rather because they produce *too much*: "So many things have been produced and accumulated that they can never possibly all be put to use ... So many messages and signals are produced and disseminated that they can never possibly all be read" (Baudrillard 2009: 32).

For Baudrillard, reality (he often calls it "the real") is not a positivist category. It is not "out there"; it does not refer to an external reality about which we make statements of fact. Moreover, it is not an ahistorical category. Rather, it is a principle, or a mode of verification, which corresponds to the prevailing system (or law) of value. Baudrillard's analysis hinges on an argument about money and language that draws directly on de Saussure's theory of the sign. Baudrillard argues that just as linguistic signs lost their referential status after de Saussure, so the categories of political economy have mutated and become self-referential (Baudrillard 1993: 20). One of the most important categories is money. On Baudrillard's reading, de Saussure's conception of money rests on two distinct but interdependent dimensions of language. First, the *structural* dimension, whereby every signifier designates a signified: analogously, money must be exchangeable against a real good of some value. Second, the *functional* dimension, whereby each term is related to every other term within the whole system.[20] These structural and functional dimensions are separate but linked; they "mesh and cohere" as part of the same basic configuration that underwrites the classical configuration of the linguistic sign, where language ultimately points to that which it designates.

Baudrillard's argument rests on a parallel he draws between de Saussure's conception of the sign and Marx's theory of value. Use value corresponds to the first (structural) dimension of de Saussure's theory of the sign, whereas exchange value corresponds to the second (functional) dimension.[21] According to Baudrillard, de Saussure was expressing the "annihilation" of referen-

20   Analogously, each monetary unit has value simply by virtue of its relationship to all other elements within the monetary system.
21   In other words, "use-value plays the role of the horizon and finality of the system of exchange-values" (Baudrillard 1993: 6).

tial value, which gave rise to an order in which value operates autonomously through the interplay of signs, without reference to any underlying thing. The relationship between signs and the real was not simply mutating, but collapsing: "Determinacy is dead, indeterminacy holds sway. There has been an extermination (in the literal sense of the word) of the real of production and the real of signification" (Baudrillard 1993: 7). What emerges from this analysis is not simply another stage in the evolution of political economy toward ever-greater levels of abstraction (Goux 1990, 1994, 1999) but the end of political economy itself (Baudrillard 1993: 8, 186, 187).

Baudrillard's approach to money centers on the claim that capitalism has entered a phase in which conventional ideas about signification have broken down. He describes the belief that signs refer to an underlying reality as a "referential illusion" that fundamentally misconstrues the transformation that was wrought upon the world during the era of monopoly capitalism, during which consumption (not production) was the pivotal focus of capital accumulation. According to Baudrillard, this was an era in which not only commodities proliferated but also, mainly through advertising, the signs and spectacles that were used to promote them. As a consequence, he argued, all notions of "fundamental" value (such as use value) came under increasing strain as a new form of value—sign value—emerged. Crucially, with sign values, the relationship between the sign and what it signifies (its underlying "reality") has broken down. *In extremis*, all that remain are signs. This breakdown has significant ramifications for money.

When values no longer correspond to real underlying content, money floats free.[22] It is liberated from the obligation to refer to something real that has been produced. Alongside it, other political economic categories are "emancipated," too, such as value, labor, and utility. This is a system in which every term is commutable. Capital has liberated every sign from the "naiveté" that there is an underlying reality to which they must refer "in order to deliver them into pure circulation" (Baudrillard 1993: 7). The dialectic between the sign and the real, crucial to Marx as well as to de Saussure, is "in shreds," and the real has "died of the shock of value acquiring this fantastic autonomy" (Baudrillard 1993: 7). The crucial element in Baudrillard's analysis, underpinning what he says about utility and need, is *reality*: "The systems of reference for production, signification, the affect, substance and

22 As soon as they are liberated, things begin to float and they take both an uncertain and an exponential turn, leading to a critical threshold beyond which their effects go into reverse, "slipping abysally [*en abyme*] towards a reality that cannot be found. This is where we are today: undecidability, the era of floating theories, as much as floating money" (Baudrillard 1993: 44 n. 3; see also Baudrillard 2001: 53).

history, all this equivalence to a 'real' content, loading the sign with the burden of 'utility', with gravity—its form of representative equivalence—all this is over with" (Baudrillard 1993: 6–7). The dialectical relationship between use value and exchange value has also come to an end, and alongside it, all illusions that pertain to the idea that capitalism is a linear system of social production in which values are accumulated. This situation yields a different account of the problem of overaccumulation than we find in Marxism. Baudrillard's money is linked with *excess* but not overaccumulation.

Baudrillard's approach entails a fundamental inversion of classical Marxism. For terms such as *labor*, *production*, the *sign*, and *political economy*, Baudrillard substitutes notions such as *simulation*, *seduction*, the *code*, and *symbolic exchange*. Moreover, he broadens the analysis to incorporate (besides language and political economy) fashion, art, politics, morality, and sexuality. Indeed, he suggests that the loss of determinacy was underway in these fields ("the superstructure") long before it took place in the economy ("the infrastructure"). In the monetary realm, this "collapse" of signification has given rise to "speculation and a limitless inflation" (Baudrillard 1993: 7). The reference to *inflation* here is intriguing. On the face of it, Baudrillard is simply echoing prevailing economic opinion. *Symbolic Exchange and Death* was written in the early 1970s (1993 edition cited here), just after the gold standard had been formally abandoned, when many capitalist countries were encountering stagflation. It was a period in which Keynesian policies were seen to be failing and monetarism (with its emphasis on controlling the quantity of money in the economy to keep inflation down) was beginning to gain ground as the new orthodoxy for Western governments and central banks, paving the way for neoliberalism (Harvey 2005a). On closer scrutiny, however, Baudrillard's image of money does not echo these concerns. Rather, it parodies them.

This analysis resonates with the idea of overaccumulation, with which this chapter began, but points in a different direction. For Bataille, the problem of "too much" is a problem of *energy* that is displaced—*excreted*—through collective practices and rituals. For Harvey, it is *capital* that has been piled too high and must be dealt with through crisis management strategies he describes in terms of the spatial and temporal fix. For Baudrillard, by contrast, it is *reality* that has been accumulated to excess. But there is no fix. Money is the quintessential expression of this condition: not as capital, however, but as a *particular mode of simulating the reality of capitalist political economy*. It is against this background that we can make sense of Baudrillard's description of the post–Bretton Woods era as an era of "speculation and limitless inflation." The inflation he has in mind is not *price* inflation, but rather the cancerous distension of monetary instruments, and thus of the terms in which we perceive the prevailing "reality" of capitalism. Money has been proliferating as *simulacra*. The point is crucial. In conventional terms, inflation means that as a sign, money is *diminished* in relation to the underlying "reality" it depicts, and it therefore *loses value*. In Baudrillard's terms, this viewpoint is nonsensical: there is no underlying reality against which money can be compared, no underpinning substratum of value in relation to which money's own value has diminished. In both kinds of inflation, money is overproduced. But whereas inflation traditionally means that each monetary unit is worth less by virtue of that proliferation, in Baudrillard's terms, it simply means that money has entered a cancerous state. Baudrillard's understanding of inflation is impossible to convey in the conventional language of representation because the distinction between money (signs) and commodities (reality) has collapsed. For Baudrillard, it is not that money's connections with the underlying reality of commodities have been weakened or severed. Nor is it just a question of self-reference, i.e., of money referring to itself. Baudrillard's monetary signs do not *refer* to anything, not even themselves. In the fractal stage of value that he describes, signs are arranged in haphazard and arbitrary fashion, and they mutate through contact. In Baudrillard's terms, inflation does not make money less valuable and therefore less "real." Rather, it makes money *more* real; that is to say, money is *hyperreal*.

Couched in these terms, it is intriguing to consider Baudrillard's argument in light of the notion of capitalist "realism" recently advanced by Mark Fisher. According to Fisher, neoliberalism produced a form of reality closure in which its major actors and institutions articulate a single version of capitalism's reality and a definite, inexorable, vision of its future. There is, Fisher suggests, "a pervasive atmosphere, conditioning not only the production of culture but also the regulation of work and education, and acting as a kind of invisible barrier constraining thought and action" (Fisher 2009: 18). Any resistance to or protest against this singular version of reality is rendered impotent, excluded from discussion, ruled out as nonparadigmatic. For Baudrillard, by contrast, the problem is not that a single version of capitalism's reality predominates but rather that many—and, indeed, *any*—version of reality can be conjured by the system *as and when required*. Capitalism as Baudrillard sees it is capable of producing, sustaining, and verifying multiple and contradictory versions of its own reality. Where Fisher portrays a kind of information scarcity, Baudrillard describes saturation and excess, the infinite capacity of simulacra—and reality itself—to mutate.

This, then, is the era of cool money, characterized by the proliferation of monetary instruments, and resting on the capacity of these instruments (arbitrarily) to comingle and multiply. Besides money, Baudrillard also describes diaries, events, and memories as "cool." The term is taken from Marshall McLuhan's classic distinction between hot and cool media. In Baudrillard's rendition, cool phenomena lack semantic depth. They are emptied of the tension that comes from the ability to meaning something else and the capacity for contestation. The cool event, for example, is oververified; it lacks uncertainty and emotional charge and is played out as if history has "gone cold." The televised event is the cool event par excellence: innocuous because it conveys nothing imaginary; mesmerizing because it is essentially flat. Baudrillard likens the effect to a cold seduction, made possible by "the 'narcissistic' spell of electronic and information systems, the cold attraction of the terminals and mediums that we have become, surrounded as we are by consoles, isolated and seduced by their manipulation" (Baudrillard 1990: 162). A similar process has been underway with money. After having first escaped from use value, and then from exchange value, money is no longer the general equivalent that Marx described: "Money circulates at a greater rate than everything else, and has no common measure with anything else" (Baudrillard 1993: 22). Money has become "the *universal equivalent of nothing*" (Baudrillard 2001: 128, italics added). It is the disembodied sign: the antithesis of Klossowski's living coin (Klossowski 1997; see Baudrillard 2001: 122–31).

Baudrillard's arguments resonate with the era of financialization in which they were made. His description of money's "inflation" captures the expansion of monetary instruments that substitute for money. Susan Strange once remarked that "a whole new language had to be invented to describe these devices" (Strange 1994a: 110). Although she surely did not have Baudrillard's terminology in mind, her analyses in *Casino Capitalism* and *Mad Money* (Strange 1986, 1998a) echo his view that, in the post–Bretton Woods era, conventional descriptors such as "credit money" and "fictitious capital" fail to capture the new monetary forms that have proliferated. Financial derivatives are perhaps the closest empirical manifestation of Baudrillard's description of money as "the realised form of the system in its twisting abstraction" (Baudrillard 1993: 22). Derivatives can derive their value from almost anything. For example, they have been based on the weather, music sales ("Bowie bonds"), and the social effect of policies designed to reduce antisocial behavior. Their growth has bordered on the grotesque: the total notional value of the market in over-the-counter derivatives grew from around $10 trillion in 1990 to more than $700 trillion during the most recent peak in mid-2011 (Bank of International Settlements)—or ten times higher than the *world's* GDP. This is Baudrillard's money. It is circulation itself: empty of content, bloated in form. In this respect, an analogy can be drawn between monetary circulation and the reproduction of signs. As Baudrillard states, "Benjamin and McLuhan ... saw that the real message ... *lay in reproduction itself*" (Baudrillard 1993: 56, original emphasis). Just as the message is nothing but reproduction, so money is *nothing but circulation*.

In making such claims, Baudrillard has moved a long way from Marxism, and we can gauge just how far by considering what he has to say about the notion of money as a fetish. Marx wrote of commodity fetishism in first-order terms, as arising from "the peculiar social character of the labour which produces them" (Marx 1982: 165). According to Baudrillard, this language is outmoded and referential; it justifies the system it purports to criticize by framing it in terms of underlying utility and need. In promising access to a mysterious level of reality of underlying causes, Marxist political economy therefore acts like a *model of simulation*—concealing the catastrophic, unreal, state that capitalism has reached. By contrast, Baudrillard's treatment of the money fetish dispenses with reference altogether. As a fetish in Baudrillard's terms, money is "a pure, unrepresentable, unexchangeable object—yet a nondescript one" (Baudrillard 2001: 129). Fetish money operates *above and beyond the reproduction of capital*. It has no connection with wealth, labor, utility, or need. Rather, it expresses a deeper, universal breakdown, which Baudrillard describes in terms of the impossibility of "exchanging" the world for its meaning. Money is the most extreme form of simulacrum: "the sign which will best express the meaninglessness of the world" (Baudrillard 2001: 217).

Baudrillard's interpretation of cool money can be set against the theories he uses to frame his critique of political economy, specifically the analyses of gift exchange and potlatch put forward by Mauss and Bataille. Gift exchange sustains not just the material but also the moral economy. In referring to this type of exchange as symbolic exchange, Baudrillard draws attention to five key features of this moral economy, particularly as described by Mauss in *The Gift* (1990), and by Bataille in *The Accursed Share* (1991). First, gift exchange embraces the life of society *in its entirety*. Because these relations cannot be reduced either to the agents who enter into the exchange or to the objects that are being exchanged, Mauss refers to gift exchange as a *total social fact*, and it is from this broader context that the *mana* of the gift gains its obligatory power. Second, symbolic exchange is *cyclical*, a ritual involving not a binary relationship between two parties but rather the ongoing (and, in principle, never-ending) circulation of gifts as they are passed from hand to hand, accepted only so that they are subsequently moved along. Third, symbolic exchange is *inclusive*: gift relations incorporate not only the living, but also the gods, and the dead. Fourth, these exchanges are not based on a logic of *equivalence* (as is the case in commodity exchanges mediated by money), but are *asymmetrical* in the sense of being driven by a continual need to give something of greater value than one received, to *raise the stakes*. Finally, and for this reason, there is a profound *ambivalence* in symbolic exchange, insofar as meanings are never fixed but ever capable of being rendered uncertain, or reversed. What appears to be a gift might easily become an aggressive act, for example, if it is too large. There is in this sense a depth and opacity of meaning within symbolic exchanges that is essential to their operation and is a condition of their possibility.

Though drawing on Bataille's theory of general economy, Baudrillard's analysis also contains a significant critique of it. Echoing Bataille, and citing Sahlins's notion of the "original affluent society" (Sahlins 1972), Baudrillard suggests that the market is "the social form that *produces* scarcity" (Baudrillard 1993: 147, original emphasis). Baudrillard argues that Bataille commits the error of assuming that the desire to minimize expenditures is part of what makes us human, whereas nature is "boundlessly prodigious" (Bataille 1986: 60). On the contrary, Baudrillard protests, "Luxury is no more 'natural' than economics. Sacrifice and sacrificial expenditure are not part of the order of things" (Baudrillard 1993: 157). In another passage that recalls the arguments of Brown, Baudrillard associates accumulation with the fear of death that underwrites the political economy of capitalism. This association has important consequences for the idea that time itself is scarce (Baudrillard 1993: 147). Like Brown's debtor, capitalism as Baudrillard describes it "sees itself as immortal" (Baudrillard 1993: 186).

Baudrillard argues that there is a fundamental difference between symbolic exchange and monetary exchange. In "conventional" political economy, value is a homogeneous domain that consists of mutually convertible relations. Money makes these conversions possible, acting as a universal sign. Symbolic exchange works in a different way. The objects exchanged within the symbolic economy are not *commensurable*, but *singular* and *concrete*. In this sense, they do not have a use value but embody a much richer ensemble of social relations. Hence, there is no *equivalence* in symbolic exchange: objects do not cancel themselves out but depend upon (and sustain) broader social, political, and economic relationships. Strictly speaking, symbolic exchange is not actually "exchange" in the way that it has come to be understood in modern society. In the symbolic economy, there is no market: gifts have an *obligatory* character and are inexorably tied up with *power*.

Throughout his writings, Baudrillard uses symbolic exchange as a framework against which to mount a critical interrogation of the contemporary global landscape, whether he is writing about consumerism and advertising, movies, America, terrorism, the Gulf War, or debt. In "Hypotheses on Terrorism" (2002), he argues that global capitalism functions through controlling reality's production (Baudrillard 2003: 82). This control is achieved by "mirroring" every sign that it produces, thereby creating the "referential illusion" that those signs refer to something—a signified—and hence are not mere simulacra (Baudrillard 2003: 71). This method satisfies a creeping "negationism," i.e., an underlying suspicion that nothing is real.[23] The twin towers of the World Trade Center embodied this doubling:

> Paradoxically, if there were only one, the WTC would not embody the monopoly, since we have seen that it becomes stable only in a dual form. For the sign to remain pure it must become its own double: this doubling of the sign really put an end to what it designated. (Baudrillard 1993: 69)[24]

The World Trade Center was the epitome of the global financial system: "Shaped in the pure computer image of banking and finance, (ac)countable and digital, they were in a sense its brain" (Baudrillard 2003: 41). His remarks on the relationship between the towers' symmetry, their perfection of form, and the "power of power" (Baudrillard 2003: 7) of monopoly capitalism recall some of Simmel's remarks on the interconnection between architectural symmetry and monopoly power. In *The Philosophy of Money*, Simmel suggests that both socialism and despotism possess "particularly strong inclinations towards symmetrical constructions of society ... because they imply a strong centralization of society that requires the reduction of the individuality of its elements and of the irregularity of its forms and relationships to a symmetrical form" (Simmel 2004: 489). There is, Simmel suggests, an intellectual affinity between symmetry and autocracy, and this affinity resonates in his interpretation of the connections between socialism and money as a perfect form (Dodd 2012). For Baudrillard, the crucial link is not between perfect money and autocracy but rather between money's *purity of form* (as a simulacrum and its own double), and *global monopoly capitalism*. This "neoliberal" order he describes as "police-state globalization," which has produced a "maximum

---

[23] The terrorist model brings about "an excess of reality" (Baudrillard 2003: 18).
[24] In his later analysis, Baudrillard makes the additional point that the towers were an "architectural graphism" embodying capitalism in its digital phase, "a system that is no longer competitive, but digital and countable, and from which competition has disappeared in favour of networks and monopoly" (Baudrillard 2003: 38–39).

of constraints and contradictions, akin to those of a fundamentalist society" (Baudrillard 2003: 32). This power of power rendered the World Trade Center such a singular and symbolic target for terrorism.

Baudrillard's analysis of the attack on the World Trade Center is underpinned by his broader distinction between *monetary* and *symbolic* exchange. In an analysis that resonates with Derrida's interpretation of Mauss, Baudrillard suggests that the basis of absolute power is the absence of reciprocation: the *unilateral gift* (Baudrillard 2003: 101). Terrorism is an *impossible exchange* (Baudrillard 2003: 52): a nonreciprocal act, or a gift that cannot be returned. Such a gift is inevitable, Baudrillard suggests, when set against an economic system that has triumphed by "seizing all the cards for itself," forcing "the Other to change the rules" (Baudrillard 2003: 9). In this instance, changing the rules meant engaging in a "definitive act" that was "not susceptible of exchange" (Baudrillard 2003: 9). It was an act that was beyond economic or moral calculation, for which there is no adequate reply within the language of political economy. This was nevertheless a "terrorism of the rich" (Baudrillard 2003: 23), the effect of which was all the greater insofar as it appeared to have been instigated by those who have considerable resources and are able to use the weapons of the dominant power: "Money and stock market speculation, computer technology and aeronautics, spectacle and the media networks" (Baudrillard 2003: 19). A terrorism of the rich: "If life is only a need to survive *at any cost*, then annihilation is a *priceless* luxury" (Baudrillard 1993: 152, original emphasis). This, then, is terrorism as squander. It cannot be understood in utilitarian terms because there is a qualitative distinction between a *contract* undertaken by *individuals* and a *suicide pact* that is *collective* (Baudrillard 2003: 24–25). It is Bataille's logic of general economy that Baudrillard is reaching for here, as opposed to the narrow "realism" of restricted economy.

Understood in Baudrillard's terms, the aftermath of the global financial crisis was epitomized by a reversion—in public debate, at least—to a form of "monetary realism." This was a return to underlying notions of "fundamental value," both *economically*, in relation to what underpins the value of financial assets (Bryan and Rafferty 2013), and *ethically*, in relation to questions of greed and the moral obligations of the debtor. These issues resonate particularly with Derrida's distinction between real and counterfeit money. The financial practices that contributed to the 2007–8 crisis—such as securitization—have variously been likened to a *scam* (Coggan 2011: 178), a *protection racket* (Taibbi 2010: 81), and *white-collar crime*. Realism—which seeks to capture value's *truth*, as it were—plays an important part in such a critique. Paul Krugman described the system that made the crisis possible as "a world gone

Madoff," in which fraud is rife and bankers' salaries are based merely on the *illusion* of profit. According to Krugman, "the vast riches being earned ... in our bloated financial industry undermined our sense of reality."[25] In a similar vein, Slavoj Žižek called the Bernard Madoff case "an extreme but therefore pure example of what caused the financial breakdown itself" (Žižek 2009: 36). Madoff's crime (his wealth management business operated as a Ponzi scheme for many years before its collapse in 2008, costing investors around $18 billion) was merely a manifestation of a form of reasoning that is inscribed into the very system of capitalist relations, namely, that the sphere of circulation must be expanded—using "fraudulent" monetary instruments, if necessary—to keep the machinery running: "the temptation to 'morph' legitimate business into a pyramid scheme is part of the very nature of the capitalist circulation process" (Žižek 2009: 36). Peter Warburton, a member of the libertarian shadow monetary policy committee in Britain, once likened finance *tout court* to counterfeit money, arguing that reckless credit creation posed a profound threat to the rule of law: "anarchy in the global financial markets is masquerading as an agent of national prosperity and personal freedom," he argued (Warburton 1999).[26]

Baudrillard said that the age of the counterfeit began as soon as signs of prestige could be transmitted from one social class to another.[27] During the Renaissance, forgery ranged from "the deceptive finery on people's backs to the prosthetic fork, from the stucco interiors to Baroque theatrical scenery" (Baudrillard 1993: 51). For Baudrillard, however, there is a crucial distinction between the *forgery* and the *clone*, which he draws in relation to *a person*. The *automaton* is a forgery. Mechanical and theatrical, he is the analogon of *a person*. The *robot* is a clone. Striving to appropriate itself to *a person* as a functional unity, the robot is the equivalent of a person (Baudrillard 1993: 53). Forgeries are artful, relying on *effect*. Clones, by contrast, are mechanistic and rely on *function*. Expressed in these terms, Baudelaire's coin was a forgery, opening out to a theatrical realm of rich ambiguity and manifold possibilities. By contrast, Baudrillard's arguments about money belong to the robotic age: the era of the clone—or the digital copy.[28] The term "simulacrum" was

25 "The Bernard Madoff story tells us a lot about the nation's financial mess," *Seattle Times*, December 19, 2008.
26 Michael Rowbotham takes a similar line, but in much narrower terms, describing fractional reserve banking per se as a form of legalized counterfeiting (Rowbotham 1998).
27 "Stucco is the triumphant democracy of all artificial signs," he writes (Baudrillard 1993: 51).
28 As we see in Chapter 8, the idea behind Bitcoin is that no such copies are possible: each Bitcoin is unique.

used by Plato to mean a *bad* copy. The simulacrum is no longer a copy (there is no original). Baudrillard gives the (Borges-inspired) example of the map that merges with the territory it is supposed to represent until they are no longer separable: the map is the simulation that becomes real: "the territory no longer precedes the map, nor does it survive it" (Baudrillard 1983: 1). With old-style forgery, where there is an original and a copy, artifice rather than mathematics is key. In these terms, counterfeit coins and fake banknotes are *first-order simulacra*. By contrast, complex financial instruments are *second-order simulacra*: there is no tension, no theater, just mechanical efficiency (Baudrillard 1993: 53). In this sense, the critique alleging that banking has become an institutionalized form of counterfeiting belongs to another age, an outdated system of representation that—as Baudrillard said of Marxism—simply mirrors the system it is designed to critique.

Donald MacKenzie's analysis of the crisis as a "sociology of knowledge" problem contains a fascinating grace note in this discussion. Having observed some of his interviewees' *moral* dismay at the ease with which household mortgagees were defaulting on their loans, MacKenzie wonders whether these debts belonged to an "order of worth" (Boltanski and Thevenot 2006) that entailed much stronger moral associations than other debt forms:

> One interviewee told me how, as mortgage defaults mounted, traders in his bank started to exclaim, "No respect for the obligation!" I confess that I was so unused to hearing moralism of this sort from City of London or Wall Street traders that I asked him whether they were being ironic and was told they were not: they were genuinely affronted by what they took to be violations of moral obligation ... This may be an indication that—even among Wall Street traders—personal debts, especially home mortgages, with all their entanglement in the world of domesticity, implicitly enjoyed a special status, perhaps even that this special status in some way underpinned the pervasive sense that mortgage-backed securities were uniquely safe. (MacKenzie 2011: 1833–34)

In Baudrillard's terms, one might wonder whether these debts were regarded not only as *safe*, but as uniquely *real*. By contrast, Baudrillard suggests that, whereas debts in the exchanges described by Mauss and Bataille were perpetually repaid and recycled, those that define the financial economy are organized according to a logical expectation that they will and must be repaid, even if any "realistic" examination of the magnitude of such debts would suggest that, by and large, they cannot be (they are simulacra). It is hardly surprising that Baudrillard's arguments about money's collapse into pure self-referentiality are often applied to financial speculation.[29] It is an interpretation that he encourages by returning often to the idea, even using it to capture changes elsewhere in society such as in the art market, which, he suggests, "resembles nothing so much as floating and uncontrollable capital in the financial market" (Baudrillard 2009: 19).[30] And yet in the context of the present day, it is arguably in relation to debt that his arguments have their greatest potential critical purchase.

In "Global Debt and Parallel Universe" (Baudrillard 1997), Baudrillard compares debt to the experience of vanishing time during the countdown to the millennium: "As long as it hangs like that over our heads with no reference whatsoever, it also serves as our only guarantee against time" (1997: 38). The etymology of finance, *final* payment, is starkly at odds with this notion. If major debtor nations are unable to pay, "there will be no judgment day for this virtual bankruptcy" (1997: 38). Just as capital's acceleration exonerates money of all previous involvements with production, so the mutation of money into a cancerous state severs all connections with a universe in which debts can be cleared. This situation—recall Walter Benjamin here—is a *universal* bankruptcy, binding us all together "just as accomplices are tied by their crime" (Baudrillard 1997: 39). It is a common destiny served on credit. Baudrillard frames it using the national debt clock on 42nd Street in New York. The total on the debt clock rises inexorably; indeed, it ran out of digits in 2008 when the U.S. national debt exceeded $10 trillion for the first time. It is a curious inversion of Benjamin's logic because for Baudrillard, the notion that it could ever be repaid is mocked, not reinforced, by the passing of time. Debt is an inexorable swelling that Baudrillard associates with the distended belly of Jarry's surreal king, Ubu Roi (Jarry 1977).[31]

One wonders what Baudrillard would have made of the Rolling Jubilee project, launched in late 2012 as part of Occupy Wall Street. Ostensibly, the

29   Circulating at speed, speculative currencies are the epitome of an uncontrollable drifting of signs: "a simple play of flotation can ruin any national economy" (Baudrillard 1993: 23). Indeed, money's loss of referentiality mirrors the predicament in which subjects find themselves, disinvested and robbed of their fixed relations, drifting "into an incessant mode of transferential fluctuations: flows, connections, disconnections, transference/counter-transference" (Baudrillard 1993: 23).

30   He continues: "it is pure speculation, movement for movement's sake, with no apparent purpose other than to defy the law of value" (Baudrillard 2009: 19).

31   Another figure who appears repeatedly in Baudrillard's work is Peter Schlemihl, who—significantly—he describes as a man who sold his shadow and subsequently became a "rich and powerful *capitalist*," suggesting that von Chamisso's story demonstrates that "the pact with the Devil is only ever a political–economic pact" (Baudrillard 1993: 130–31).

campaigners are seeking donations toward a fund that can be used to buy debt in what it describes as a "bailout of the people by the people." The scheme involves a reversal of the practice (used by hedge funds, for example) of buying distressed debt for a fraction of its face value and then using aggressive legal means to collect the debt, as well as profiting from the high service charges associated with it.[32] The intention behind the Rolling Jubilee is to buy debt in a similar way. This is not in order to *collect* it, however, but rather to *abolish* it. On the campaign website, the total of monies raised is exhibited at the center of the page, a row of numbers reminiscent of the millennial clock but now rising inexorably.[33]

Baudrillard's work portrays an economic system that has entirely lost its grip on the representational functions of money: not, however, because the reality of money itself has collapsed but rather because of a profound reconfiguration of the world in which it circulates. *Reality* has collapsed, and money's various transformations—its changes of form—are merely symptoms of this collapse. There are some passages, however, in which—echoing Bataille—Baudrillard suggests that money's role as the general equivalent breaks down within particular kinds of exchange. For example, in *For a Critique of the Political Economy of the Sign* (1972; the 1981 edition is cited here), he portrays the art auction as a moment when the relationship between the work of art and the money that is paid for it collapses. Once the work of art has neither a use value nor an exchange value, money is nullified as the general equivalent and emerges as an indivisible form. Here, money becomes the homology of the unique painting, whereby there is no longer equivalence but rather "aristocratic *parity*" between money and canvas (Baudrillard 1981: 117). At auction, money paid for an artwork is "no longer a price but a wager (*enjeu*)" (Baudrillard 1981: 117 n. 4). This money is (and must continue to be) *wasted* in the specific sense characterized by Bataille. Likewise, money that is won through wager cannot be spent on useful things but must be put back into the game, "poured back into it, 'burned'—in a way, it is the *part maudite* [accursed share] of Bataille" (Baudrillard 1981: 117 n. 4). In *Seduction* (1979), Baudrillard suggests that money *gambled* is money *seduced*, and thereby "deflected from its truth" (Baudrillard 1990: 139). Money burns here, too, because it is cut off from the law of equivalences and the logic of representation. In gambling, money is not a *sign* but rather a *stake*—no longer invested, but set down as a challenge: "Placing a

---

32   The term "vulture fund" is often used in association with this practice.
33   See http://rollingjubilee.org/.

bet has as little to do with placing an investment, as libidinal investment with the stakes of seduction" (Baudrillard 1990: 139).

This is money as waste—or as *part maudite*—that nonrecuperable "accused share" that is destined for social expenditure. In this form, money is no longer money in its conventional, restricted, or capitalistic sense. This is money that no longer functions as a sign and does not obey the law of representation. It is *symbolic* money, after a fashion, insofar as "all the stuff of money, language, sex and affect undergo a complete change of meaning depending on whether they are mobilized as an investment or transposed into a stake. The two moments are irreducible" (Baudrillard 1990: 139–40). A man who placed a newspaper ad ("Send me a dollar!") received thousands of dollars in return not because the advertisement was couched in terms of need, exchange, or investment but because he had issued a challenge.[34] In the movie, *Indecent Proposal*, a basic economic exchange (sex for one million dollars) leads to seduction that is both romantic and symbolic: the protagonists (played by Demi Moore and Robert Redford) are "deflected from their own principle to enter into a dual relation" and an impossible exchange (Baudrillard 2001: 122). This is the "paradoxical utopia" of *living money*, in which "the economic becomes the place where singularity [*part maudite*] is embodied" (Baudrillard 2001: 122).

Baudrillard derives the idea of living money from Klossowski, who was a member (alongside Bataille) of the Collège de Sociologie. In *La Monnaie Vivante*, or *Living Currency* (Klossowski 1997), Klossowski sets out the concept of an economy that deals in libidinal *pulsions*, whose living currency is the human body. In a book that is partly an economic analysis and partly a photographic illustration, Klossowski argues that the "conventional"— restricted?—economy of commodity exchange that predominates in modern Western capitalism is inextricably linked to a very different—general?— economic system, which deals not with equivalent commodities but rather with emotional *pulsions*. Whereas standardized *money* (e.g., notes and coins) is the currency in the former system, the *body* is used as currency in the latter. This is *living currency*. Crucially for Klossowski, the system of commodity exchange has historically relied upon the system of bodily exchange to function at all. The industrial economy tries to silence this idea

---

34 For those who actually sent dollars, the outcome was ambivalent. They themselves might receive thousands of dollars in return, "in which case, one has received a sign of the Gods' favour (which Gods? those who had printed the ad?)." On the other hand, if nothing was received in return, the challenge had been accepted but not returned: "So much the better. Psychologically I have beaten the Gods" (Baudrillard 1990: 141).

with its rhetoric of standardized money but nonetheless persists in its dependence:

> ...all of modern industry rests on an exchange mediated by the sign of inert currency, neutralizing the nature of the objects exchanged; rests, that is, on a simulacrum of exchange—a simulacrum which lies in the form of manpower resources, thus a living currency, not affirmed as such, already extant. (Klossowski 1997: 88; cited in Kaufman 2001: 113–14)

For Klossowski, traffic in human bodies is a *driving force* of the market economy, not just an *epiphenomenon* or contingent outcome. Moreover, the "industrial slave" has a dual function, being both a *sign of wealth*, which is therefore capable of being exchanged, and *wealth itself*, which is necessarily singular and nonexchangeable. We do not own our bodies in this economy. Rather, the body is merely a point of intersection between various pulsional forces. This is where Baudrillard's idea of "living money" comes from: it belongs to an order in which seemingly vital distinctions between two systems of value—belonging to the realms of *monetary* and *symbolic* exchange—are collapsed. By positing singularity—*part maudite*—at the heart of the market economy, Klossowski's system opens up a negative, radical space for its *absolute polar opposite*. This system would necessarily be a perversion of the prevailing monetary order and a "misappropriation of the abstraction of money for impulsional ends" (Baudrillard 2001: 122). We revisit these themes in Chapter 6.

CONCLUSION

Geraldine Juárez, a Mexican artist based in Sweden, launched a performance art show in Berlin during early 2014 called "Hello Bitcoin."[35] Playing to growing public fascination with the digital currency that was launched in 2009—we look at the Bitcoin story in more detail in Chapter 8—Juárez's performance involves burning Bitcoins, "post-digital style." On the face of it, this seems to ironicize the question that skeptics often ask about digital currencies, namely, what can they be worth if they are not real? To the question, "What makes a currency real?," Juárez answers: "When we are able to *burn* them for real." What is surely in question here, however, is not the materiality of Bitcoin but the possibility that it can be *wasted*. "The

---

35   See http://www.transmediale.de/festival/programme.

real aspect making it into a currency is not when it is spent, but when it is burnt," Juárez suggests.[36] What defines the "reality" of money, in other words, is not how we spend it, but how we *waste* it. This, precisely, is the aspect of money that I have been exploring in this chapter.

Norman Brown once described Bataille as a "fellow traveller on the Dionysian path" (Brown 1992: 181). Bataille, said Brown, had embarked on the "transvaluation of economic value," which connected Marx's notion of surplus with "the Dionysian notion of life as the manifestation of a universal principle of excess" (Brown 1992: 185). This notion is where our journey began in this chapter. Moving forward from a Marxian conception of overaccumulation, I argued that general economy introduces an important *shift of perspective* in our understanding of money, similar in function to what Karatani called a *parallax view* (see Chapter 2). Moreover, the switch from restricted to general locates money within an even broader set of social practices than those we have already associated with the moral economy of debt. General economy highlights monetary practices that, although widespread, are usually treated as *deviant* or *perverse*. (These are the unproductive expenditures that might be described as "Dionysian"). In addition, as I suggested in Chapter 1, it throws open a different but complementary view of money's earliest forms. Although scholars are now familiar with the argument that money was "originally" a means of sacrificial or tribute payment, the emphasis on surplus draws attention to the sense in which these payments were not just debts (whether "primordial" or otherwise) but also "nonproductive" *expenditures*. They were, for example, items of personal adornment, such as beads, that had little use beyond being pleasant to look at, suggesting to Graeber that "for the most part, ['primitive'] money consists of things that otherwise exist only to be seen" (Graeber 2001: 92). Simmel made a similar connection between money and adornment, but contrary to the perspective that I have been discussing in this chapter, he suggested that the connection existed only when precious metal was *scarce*: "when there [was] a limited supply of precious metals, the value of money may have been determined by its alternative use for adornment, [but] this condition disappears as production is increased" (Simmel 2004: 143).

Furthermore, practical implications follow from viewing money through the lens of general economy. For example, Bataille's approach frees us from having to take *demand* as the "ultimate and unquestionable indicator of human needs" (Brown 1992: 185). Moreover, Bataille underlines just how far—and how *unquestioningly*—conventional economics views *growth* as

---

36 See http://fffff.at/hello-bitcoin/ for a video of burning Bitcoins.

the "self-evident destiny of all economic activity" (Brown 1992: 185). Once "the economic problem" is viewed in a different way and is seen in terms of how a society deals with its *surplus*, such conventional habits of thought become difficult to justify: accumulation now becomes a "problem" that has to be dealt with in economic policy. The immediate political ramifications of this problem are potentially far-reaching. Take, for example, the relationship between "surplus" and "deficit" nations within the Eurozone. Since the crisis began, this relationship has been framed overwhelmingly in terms of the failure of the latter nations to "live within their means." Not only have these nations borrowed excessively, but also their continuing membership in the Eurozone presents a danger for surplus nations of cross-subsidy: a "transfer union" in which money flows from strong to weak states, lending moral validity to the deficit nations' prolonged financial profligacy, their lack of fiscal self-control, and their poor work ethic. "Transfer union" became part of the Eurozone's lexicon only in the teeth of its crisis.[37] Jörg Krämer, chief economist at Commerzbank, claimed that the Eurozone "has moved away from a monetary union and towards a transfer union" (*New York Times*, May 11, 2010), and Columbia University economics professor Jagdish Bhagwati remarked in an interview that monetary union will turn into a transfer union "if the weak countries have problems."[38] The notion of a transfer union is generally used in such instances to describe redistributive functions that (so critics argue) were never intended for the euro.[39] This is the language of restricted economy.

The idea of a transfer union has been expressed, for the most part, in negative terms, and almost entirely from the perspective of the wealthier, so-called core member states. A contrary view, however, is consistent with Bataille's interpretation of the Marshall and Truman plans, which he addresses in the final chapter of *The Accursed Share* (Bataille 1991: 197 n. 22). Formally known as the European Recovery Program (ERP), the Marshall Plan (named after George Marshall, the U.S. Secretary of State) was put into operation in 1947 to 1951 to support the postwar reconstruction of the

---

37   The word "transfer" came up four times in the original Maastricht Treaty (the Treaty on European Union, see Articles 73h and 205) but never in line with the usage discussed here.
38   *Frankfurter Allgemeine Zeitung*, June 20, 2010.
39   As Ralph Atkins claimed in the *Financial Times* (London), "the ECB's critics believe buying government bonds even on a small scale blurs monetary and fiscal policies, favours the fiscally irresponsible and risks turning the Eurozone into a 'transfer union' in which richer nations support poorer rivals—all of which are against the terms on which Germans thought they had joined the euro in 1999" (July 7, 2010).

European economy. Some US$13 billion worth of economic and technical assistance (compared to a U.S. GDP of $258 billion in 1948) were given via the Economic Cooperation Administration (ECA) to those European countries joining the Organisation for Economic Co-operation and Development (OECD). Strictly speaking, transfers made under the plan were loans, not gifts: American suppliers were paid in U.S. dollars credited against ERP funds. The European recipients had to repay the monies in local currency, which was then deposited by the local government in a counterpart fund. The Marshall Plan was significant for the development of the international monetary system. It was instrumental in the establishment of the European Payments Union (EPU) in 1950, lifting the majority of capital controls in Europe while encouraging a system of fixed exchange rates and a degree of trade liberalization. Moreover, drawing rights connected to the EPU were supported by ECA funds and facilitated the process of establishing full convertibility under the Bretton Woods Agreement.

Describing it as "an investment in the world's interest," Bataille saw the Marshall Plan as an answer to the fundamental problem of general economy, namely, excess. He characterized its payments as "condemned wealth" (Bataille 1991: 182) that had been generated by an economy "so developed that the needs of growth are having a hard time absorbing its excess resources" (Bataille 1991: 179). In making this argument, Bataille drew on François Perroux's 1948 text, *Le Plan Marshall: Ou l'Europe nécessaire au monde* (Perroux 1948). Perroux, a professor at the Collège de France, drew a distinction between "classical" and "general" economy, which maps onto Bataille's own framework. According to Perroux, in "classical" economics we make calculations according to isolated interests, as opposed to the general interest, in which the "national point of view" was "irrelevant" (cited in Bataille 1991: 189). The differences between the postwar reconstruction of the European economy and the present-day plight of the Eurozone are, of course, significant: the Marshall Plan consisted of funds from outside Europe, and for all Perroux's talk of the general interest, the motivation to resist Soviet interests in Europe was an important part of the rationale behind the plan as it was eventually put into operation. Nevertheless, Bataille's framework can be used to place the idea of a "transfer union" in a rather more positive light because it suggests that the notion of a transfer union is not as problematic as it currently appears. Indeed, elements of such a union have arguably been a crucial feature of the Eurozone from its inception. The euro project has always been driven by a complex interplay of individual and general interests. According to Dumas, for example, those countries in the Eurozone that are now in account surplus have been benefiting directly from the deficits that have been accumulating elsewhere: "In effect, these economies have been taking a free ride, generating income and building up assets by selling into the domestic demand of the deficit economies, fuelled by borrowing that should not have taken place" (Dumas 2010: 160). Dumas applies this analysis to Italy (where real consumption rose by 3.5 percent between 2001 and 2009, as opposed to 0.5 percent in Germany) as well as Greece: "without those Italians spending away," he claims, "German output, jobs, incomes and consumption would have been even worse. The folly of the miser indeed" (Dumas 2010: 169–70).

Significantly, a "Keynesian" solution to the crisis in the Eurozone (using expenditure to stimulate aggregate demand) tends to be viewed as contrary to the interest of those states deemed to be strongest because it would mean surplus countries saving less and spending more. Saving may seem "virtuous" when considered in isolation—as may a balanced budget, which is the principle underpinning Germany's economic policy (Dumas 2010: 168)—but under the circumstances that prevail in the Eurozone, where there are significant current account imbalances between core and peripheral states, there is a classic paradox of thrift. In these terms, the Eurozone faces a dilemma between the interests of individual member states and what is in the collective interest, which relates to the problem of maintaining the integrity of the system as a whole. This paradox mirrors Bataille's perspective of general versus restricted economy. Once economic imbalances are viewed as a problem for the Eurozone as a whole, the problem is not one of expenditure per se but rather of *collective* expenditure. What seem like rational economic strategies when viewed in isolation—i.e., austerity (the denial of expenditure)—appear quite differently when seen in this way. This statement is not to suggest that the problem is any more straightforward to resolve, merely that when viewed through the lens of general economy, "rational" economic behavior emerges with a different complexion.

Although this brief discussion suggests that Bataille's "general" theory is relevant to the problem of economic imbalances within the Eurozone, just as he argued that it was relevant to the global inequities of wealth that were addressed by the Marshall and Truman plans, it would be a mistake to view his approach simply as an unusual (and even eccentric) variant of Keynesianism. Bataille does cite Keynes (Bataille 1991: 13), but he does not seek to justify seemingly irrational expenditure (e.g., burying bottles) as a growth stimulant. For Bataille, there is no need to rationalize such expenditure, above all as a means of encouraging economic expansion. There are other (deeper, darker) forces at work. These forces are connected to a society's—or a monetary union's—treatment of its heterogeneous elements.

This image of money as seen through society's heterogeneous elements is what makes the contributions of Derrida and Baudrillard intriguing. For Baudrillard, monetary "inflation" is a consequence of the attempt by society (or, rather, monopoly capitalism) to exclude its foreign bodies—or heterogeneous matter—entirely. This attempt, he argues, depends upon endlessly producing a reality principle that is underpinned by notions of limitless productivity by means of the "illusion" of financial growth. This idea is the metaphor of the demonic pregnancy, which is the affliction of a society that is unable to process its waste. In Derrida's hands, the counterfeit coin—left over after (wasteful) expenditure on tobacco—gives rise to a series of elaborate reflections of the paradoxical nature of giving as an act of "generosity," above all to a stranger who has nothing to give in exchange. The political implications of this imbalance are suggested when Derrida restages the narrative as a trial, with the outsider calling his donor to judgment. Heterogeneity matters not only to *justice* and *law* but also to *sovereignty*, rendering Derrida's treatment of Baudelaire's story pertinent to the discussion of money's connections with citizenship and marginality (see Chapter 6). In *Rogues* (2002), Derrida puts the counterfeit coin alongside the "dubious" characters who are of "suspicious" or "mixed" origin and are thus defined as rogues or outlaws. These are the foreign bodies, he suggests, that define sovereignty itself (Derrida 2005: 68). In his treatment of Baudelaire's story, two such elements (the *beggar* and the *coin*) are used to pose pressing questions about money's truth, which cannot be asked from any other location—or at least not in the same way.

> Well, it happens that Baudelaire, in a prophetic or apocalyptic passage from *Fusées* . . . reserves the status of absolute exception not for the gift but for money. At the end of the world, which is near, when "supreme evil" will win out, a "pitiless good sense" "will condemn everything, except for money." The only good thing that will be saved from perdition in this sinking world, the only thing that, since it is not a thing, will keep some credit in the eyes of this implacable good sense of tomorrow, in a mechanized and "Americanized" world, says Baudelaire's anger in what he himself calls an "hors d'oeuvre," is money. What has to be condemned in the advent of industrial capitalist society is democracy and "progress." Baudelaire does not differentiate between "universal progress" and "universal ruin." And he condemns them in the name of the spirit, but of the spirit of evil which he opposes here to the evil of progressivism or to the

triumph of historical optimism in industrial (capitalist and democratic) society. (Derrida 1994: 130)[40]

Derrida's own conception of the future resonates with Baudrillard's condemnation of progressivism. His notion of a "democracy to come" involves us in a complex and tense relationship with time: a continual anticipation but also resistance to anything conclusive that cannot be stabilized by categories such as intentionality (Glendinning 2011: 41). Democracy, *like money*, is irreducibly divided within itself, always falling short of its own definition. This is not simply a question of failing to realize today what might be realized in the future. It is an open wound.

40   The passage Derrida refers to is from Baudelaire's *Fusées*: "Then, the wanderers, the outcasts, those who have had several lovers, and who were once called angels, in recognition of the heedlessness which shines, light of luck, in their existence logical as evil—then these, I say, will be no more than a pitiless wisdom, a wisdom that will condemn all, lacking money, *even the faults of the senses!* Then, that which will resemble virtue, what do I say?—all that is not ardour toward Plutus will be considered enormously ridiculous" (Smith 1919: 211–12).

6 TERRITORY

Above the nations is humanity.
GOETHE[1]

Marx once said that money "wears different national uniforms" (Marx 2009: 139). The belief that money naturally divides itself into national units reinforces the argument that *states* are best equipped to look after money: to manage its production, regulate its supply, and guarantee its value. Indeed, many of the theories of money discussed so far in this book approach the subject almost unthinkingly as a territorially bounded entity, understood from the standpoint of a *society* or *nation-state*—which, mistakenly, are often run together. But the interconnections among money, nation-state, and society are far from natural. Until the nineteenth century, a mixture of domestic and foreign currencies was in use throughout Europe, and in the United States, silver coins from Mexico and Spain dominated the domestic money supply. Likewise in Canada, Latin America, East Asia, and the Middle East, foreign currency circulated freely until well into the nineteenth century. The monies used in these largely cosmopolitan monetary systems were usually coins with *some* kind of inherent value, although paper money issued by states and banks also circulated across state borders. Historically, as Carruthers and Babb have shown, debates about the precise nature of the

---

1   This quotation—in the original German, "Über den Nationen steht die Menschheit"—is usually attributed to Goethe (e.g., Stephens 1915: 229; Fromm 1976: 115), but to the best of my knowledge there is no evidence of the phrase being used by Goethe himself. He did, however, express a very similar sentiment in one of his Conversations with Eckermann, dated March 14, 1830: "national hatred is something peculiar. You will always find it strongest and most violent where there is the lowest degree of culture. But there is a degree where it vanishes altogether, and where one stands to a certain extent above nations, and feels the weal or woe of a neighbouring people, as if it had happened to one's own. This degree of culture was conformable to my nature, and I had become strengthened in it long before I had reached my sixtieth year," see http://archive.org/stream/conversationsofg02goetuoft/conversationsofg02goetuoft_djvu.txt. I am grateful to Philipp Degens for his help in this matter.

connection between money and government—such as that which took place between "bullionists" and "greenbackers" in post–Civil War America—were often bound up with disputes about the quality of the monetary medium itself, as well as the social consequences of alternative systems of monetary governance (Carruthers and Babb 1996).[2] These histories have been richly told (and theorized) elsewhere (Helleiner 2003; Ingham 2004b; Graeber 2011). I draw attention to them now mainly to declare, from the outset, that the "golden age" of state (and, especially, territorial) money was extremely short-lived—if, indeed, it ever really existed. If the systems that make up the world's monetary landscape today are increasingly heterogeneous, this is in one sense merely money's return to its pre-nineteenth century state of multiplicity, which was much longer lasting.

Broadly speaking, the relationship between money and geopolitical space has been understood by scholars in three ways: *ideologically*, in terms of the *mental image* we have of money; *geopolitically*, as a component of the *infrastructural power of the state*; and *historically*, as a product of the formation of the *trading and financial networks* in conjunction with which the *modern state* emerged. The modern era—its history, its statecraft, its technological and economic developments, and its political ideologies—would have been rather different had it not been for state currency. Likewise, the modern nation-state provides a crucial infrastructure for modern territorial currency: through its policing powers, its importance in the domestic economy, its centralized authority, and its capacity to garner trust (Helleiner 2003: 7). Equally, money is an important infrastructural resource for the modern state (Ingham 2004b). Strictly speaking, though, the world of pure territorial currencies never actually existed: state currencies have intermingled with other monetary forms for as long as they have been in circulation.[3]

It nonetheless does appear that the era in which states sought to *monopolize* the right to license the production and administration of money within

---

2   The case examined by Carruthers and Babb is especially interesting as it explores how several issues were intertwined in the discussion of money's future after the American Civil War, issues that were not just *technical* (i.e., relating to the relative merits of different monetary media, such as gold versus paper), but also *political* (i.e., addressed to the prospects for money's democratic control), and *social* (i.e., concerning the distributional consequences of different modes of monetary organization: "More was at stake than just money, for both sides perceived the monetary system to be a kind of condensed distillation of social relations" (Carruthers and Babb 1996: 1579).

3   Strictly speaking, what Cohen calls "pure territorial money" is not the same as "currency." "Pure territorial money" refers to a currency that circulates exclusively within the legal jurisdiction of its issuing authority. Cohen argues that this kind of currency is in decline. This—and *only* this—is what he captures with the concept of "de-territorialization" (Cohen 1998: 6). We examine other interpretations of this notion in due course.

their borders[4]—an era during which, moreover, such a monopoly has been widely perceived as "natural" or "inevitable"—is drawing to a close. Thus although Marx's statement was never entirely accurate, it is even *less* accurate today than it has been throughout the modern era: money is shedding its national uniform and adopting a broad variety of other guises, from euros to Bitcoins. Notes and coins bearing national symbols now constitute a tiny fraction—less than 10 percent[5]—of the total flow of money around the global economy.[6] Even taking a slightly broader definition and focusing on the proportion of money in circulation that states are able to *control*, the monetary base[7] adds up to just 15 percent of the total. As ever, though, such matters are as complex as they are controversial. Though the complications thrown up by such numbers are about measurement,[8] the controversies are mainly concerned with whether states *should* control money, and separately, whether they actually *can* in the face of the economic and financial conditions that we discussed in Chapters 2 and 3. There is, in short, a widening gap between our mental mapping of money, i.e., the spatial images we associate it with, which still tends to be state-centered, and the reality of its political governance, whereby states are increasingly unable to monopolize the issue and management of money.

Increasingly, then, money appears to be detaching itself from geopolitical space. A number of empirical trends are pertinent to this separation. First, there is the liberalization and expansion of international money and financial markets and the development of private monies, such as derivatives and

---

4   Chick and Dow refer to this arrangement as a *franchise*, which is an apt description. They characterize the 2008 crisis in the following terms: "government has given a franchise to the banks to produce our money, and . . . , for quite a time, it took some care to monitor the quality of the product. But in the run-up to the crisis, while the franchise was (and is) still in place, it gave its franchisees the freedom to do whatever they liked, while subsidising their borrowing costs through deposit insurance and the lender-of-last-resort facility" (Chick and Dow 2013: 108).

5   In Britain, the estimated figure is as low as 3 percent.

6   It has become commonplace to say that the use of cash appears to have been declining in the global North—for example, major Swedish banks (SEB AB, Swedbank AB (SWEDA), and Nordea Bank AB (NDA)) have stopped handling cash in many of their branches. But in fact, reports of the death of cash are somewhat exaggerated. In the United Kingdom, for example, cash was used in 58 percent of all retail transactions in 2011 (up from 55 percent in 2010), and credit payments fell by 11 percent (British Retail Consortium).

7   I.e., notes and coins as well as sight deposits (i.e., bank deposits that can be withdrawn immediately without notice or penalty) held by commercial banks at the central bank.

8   The terminology alone is convoluted. Terms that describe important components (but not equivalents) of total currency include the monetary base, the adjusted monetary base, base money, money base, high-powered money, reserve money, and narrow money. Then there are the distinct measures of money, such as M0, M1, M2, M3, and MZM.

collateralized securities (Bryan and Rafferty 2007). Second, there is the increasing use of major currencies beyond the legal jurisdiction of their respective authorities, whatever the preferences of governments, together with dollarization (where a government chooses to adopt a foreign currency in place of its own) (Cohen 2004). There is also widespread use of major currencies (especially U.S. dollars and euros) within the global informal economy, wherein currencies (normally in the form of cash) are used for transactions that take place in the interstitial spaces of the international system (Staudt 1998; Neuwirth 2011). Third, there is a transnational monetary union: although the Eurozone has been in crisis, it is by no means clear that the project will be abandoned altogether; indeed, with the inclusion of Latvia on January 1, 2014, the Eurozone has now expanded to a membership of eighteen states. Meanwhile, other major unions, such as one among Gulf states, are being discussed (Rutledge 2009). Monetary union seems desirable for such states because of the scale of the threat posed by unrestricted capital flows to most existing national currencies when their exchange rates are not fixed (Eichengreen 2008).[9] Fourth, there is the decline of the U.S. dollar as the world's reserve currency, and relatedly, the "currency wars" and the strengthening of the Chinese renminbi, along with other BRIC (Brazil, Russia, India, and China) currencies (Cohen 2011; Fratzscher and Mehl 2011; Rickards 2011). Fifth, in the wake of that decline, there is the prospect of a global currency such as the special drawing rights (SDRs) issued by the IMF (Cohen 2011; Mundell 2012). Sixth, and finally, there is the growth of monetary forms that are not issued by states, such as digital monies. Although these forms are by no means new, their development has accelerated since the 1990s, and there are now several thousand complementary currencies in operation worldwide (North 1999, 2005, 2007). This development constitutes a trend toward increasing *heterogeneity* and is characterized by the development of local currencies (e.g., time dollars, which are exchanged for person-hours of work), reputation-based currencies (e.g., Whuffie), and digital money (e.g., Bitcoin). Taken together, these six major trends can be viewed as indicative of a decline in the influence of states over the world's money flows (see Cohen 1998, 2004). So although it would be rash to deny states' continuing importance as sites of money's definition and administration, it does appear that their power and control over money are being increasingly eroded.

[9] The recent signal from the International Monetary Fund (IMF) of a softening of its position on capital controls suggests that this factor is changing after two decades of liberalization ("IMF drops opposition to capital controls," *Financial Times* (London), December 3, 2012).

To get to grips with such developments, we need to think imaginatively about money's complex and multifaceted relationship with space. In *Justice, Nature and the Geography of Difference* (1996), David Harvey explores money as a dynamic configuration of space, value, and time. He draws specifically on Nancy Munn's argument, in *The Fame of Gawa* (1986), that space, time, and value form the heart of a relational nexus that serves as a "*template* or a *generative schema*... for constructing intersubjective relations in which value is both *created* and *signified*" (Munn 1992: 121; cited in Harvey 1996: 215). For Harvey, Munn's analysis shows how value is constituted not simply *in*, but *through*, a particular construction of space and time. For example, Marx's idea of commodity fetishism demonstrates how things appear to take on a "life of their own" and acquire the status of independent or autonomous *values* precisely by virtue of their extension in *space* and *time*. Money is the example par excellence of this process; indeed, it stands as its highest point: "different social practices of valuation (varying from family-based valuations of self, to local trading systems to positionality in the world market), occur in different spatio-temporal domains (varying from the household to locality to global financial markets) but are built into a singular system under the relational umbrella of the money form" (Harvey 1996: 238). It is the increased stretching of these space–time relations through globalization, and their embodiment in the singular form of money, that explains money's extraordinary power:

> If things seem to have a life of their own, then it is only because these things which are handled in the realm of material practices are considered to internalize discursive effects of political economic power and spatio-temporal relations. Only in such terms can we unpack the composite problem of how it is that things become imbued with social relations and operate with such full force as to appear to govern us (as, for example, money typically does) more ruthlessly than any political dictator could ever hope to do. This in turn may explain why the one singular power dictators lack is the power to change the fundamentals of language. (Harvey 1996: 222)

Although he acknowledges that "each concrete money use defines a particular spatio-temporality" (Harvey 1996: 238), Harvey tries to connect these vast differences in scale by arguing that all of these instances of monetary transaction—i.e., all enactments, through money, of a specific and concrete set of spatial and temporal conditions—are connected to "abstract qualities of money on the world markets" (Harvey 1996: 238). We can presumably take these qualities as being universal. Harvey describes the connection between the universal and the particular in this context as a "riddle" and suggests that it can be solved by examining the dialectic "between use (often local and particular) and exchange value (simultaneously local and global)" (Harvey 1996: 238).

One important upshot of Harvey's argument is that we cannot talk simplistically about the "globalization of money." The idea that the nation-state is diminishing has become banal since the explosion of academic interest in globalization that began during the 1980s. In relation to money, the conventional way of understanding globalization follows the logic of Susan Strange, who set the forces of international financial *markets* (e.g., banks and hedge funds) against those of the *state*, which is where currencies have their locus: while *finance* erodes state boundaries, *money* (specifically, currency) reinforces them. But states and markets frequently operate in *tandem*, not opposition. This unity has helped to generate the extraordinarily complex dynamics of Europe's debt crisis, where public and private institutions have entered into a mutually destructive cycle of financial codependency. The idea that money itself is becoming more global runs against the reality that today's monetary landscape is increasingly *uneven* and *diverse*. The disintegration of the state-centered organization of money is not a moment of *transcendence* but rather of *convolution*. My analysis therefore picks up a thread from the last chapter, namely, that as Derrida suggests, money—even *territorial* money—is defined by its own *conditions of impossibility*. Nowhere is this approach more compelling, indeed, than in relation to the notion of state money.

WESTFAILURE

Scholars in the international relations field conventionally use the term "Westphalian" to describe an international order consisting of territorially bounded, independent sovereign states whose interests and goals are held to transcend those of individual citizens or rulers. The Peace of Westphalia is a term that refers to the series of treaties signed in May to October 1648 in Osnabrück and Münster, ending the Thirty Years' War (1618–1648) in the Holy Roman Empire, and the Eighty Years' War (1568–1648) between Spain and the Dutch Republic. As a model of global order, the Westphalian system is underpinned by recognition of the fundamental right of a state to political self-determination, the assumption of states' legal equality, and the principle that no state should intervene in the internal affairs of another. Territorial money, or national currency, is the analogue of this model.

In terms of politics and governance, money has a significance that can be understood in two key ways. First, it is important as an *infrastructural technology* providing crucial linkages between the state and the economy. There are clear fiscal motivations behind the state's historical monopolization of money issue (Giddens 1985). Weber argued that money made a significant contribution to the rationalization of the economic functions of the modern state (Swedberg 2000: 38). Money provides a perfect means of economic calculation, it is "formally the most rational means of orienting economic activity" (Weber 1978: 86), and it is therefore a powerful tool of capital accounting and budgeting. As a tool for calculating and settling accounts, money is important for the organization of a stable system of universal taxation, the revenues which Weber described as the precondition for the permanent existence of bureaucratic administration: "For well-known reasons only a fully developed money economy offers a secure basis for such a taxation system" (Weber 1978: 968). As a consequence, the state is "the largest receiver and the largest maker of payments in the society" (Weber 1978: 167). Taxation underpins the state's capacity to influence money economically as well as regulate it politically: "the behaviour of the state treasurers in their monetary transactions is of crucial significance for the monetary system: above all, what kind of money they actually have at hand and hence can pay out, and what kind of money they force on the public as legal tender, and further, what kind of money they actually accept and what kind they partially or fully repudiate" (Weber 1978: 167). At the same time, the widespread use of money has enabled the modern state to be less directly involved in the economy and thus to create a more hospitable environment in which rational capitalism could flourish (Swedberg 2000: 60). Helleiner, though, warns against overestimating taxation as the main motivation for states to produce their own money: besides taxation, there are also advantages to states in terms of transaction costs, macroeconomic objectives, and national identity (Helleiner 2003: 92).

The second way that money provides the state with a tool of governance is through the *monetization of public debt*. The emergence of state currency in Europe was rooted in several changes that occurred during the sixteenth to eighteenth centuries, when two distinctive circuits of money (sovereign currency and private bills of exchange) began operating in tandem. This development occurred mainly through the establishment of private central banks that were granted a monopoly over public privileges and obligations regarding the production of money. Since that time, as has been well-documented (Galbraith 1975; Davies 1994; Dodd 1994; Hart 2001; Ingham 2004b), most modern monetary systems have been organized around an amalgamation of public and private interests. These interests play out differently in specific national contexts, but the underlying logic is broadly similar. Governments rely on private interests (e.g., money markets and bond holders) to fund the national debt, and this system acts as the basis for the monetary system as a whole, which in this sense consists of monetized promises to pay. This system is administered by state agencies such as central banks, or in the United Kingdom, the Debt Management Office.

The key issue here is that in order to function as money, debt needs to be *depersonalized* and *transferable*. This step was made possible by two developments that took place in banking and trade in early modern Europe: first, the disconnection between merchants' bills of exchange and the commodities they referred to (this was known as dry exchange); and second, the separation of the bill from the identity of specific creditors and debtors. The crucial condition for the latter was the development of written contracts, enabling bilateral debts to settle a third-party debt. These paper bills were subsequently to circulate as money. At this stage, however, they were merely private tokens of debt: not until they began to circulate beyond the networks of bankers could they be regarded as forms of money. The transition to money relied on the state. Paradoxically, the institution of strong metallic standards for money provided the financial infrastructure in which credit money could thrive, providing the "secure socially and politically constructed monetary space," underpinned by a stable political system and a solid fiscal system, that Ingham regards as the crucial sociological preconditions for full-fledged credit money (Ingham 2004a: 207–208). There is an important cultural dimension to this: what underpins *any* arrangement for organizing money is a form of moral authority that Polillo describes as the *institutionalization of creditworthiness*. This institutionalization depends on socially perceived and morally loaded categories of worth that determine who has the right—and who can be trusted—to produce money. According to Polillo, the institutionalization of creditworthiness is just as much a local, or micro, process—closely linked to the creation of collective identity—as it is a question of social structure in the way that Ingham suggests. The struggle over moral authority largely takes place within the banking system: "Bankers must enforce creditworthiness on their clients and themselves, or their control over money will be contested and, at worst, usurped by organizations drawing from other sources of authority" (Polillo 2011: 454). In other words, these matters are shaped from the ground up no less than they are determined from the top down.[10]

This analysis brings together the state and credit theories we examined in Chapter 3. In Europe by the seventeenth century, a hybrid of *private credit* and *public metal* existed. Capitalist traders and states, respectively, produced these monies. They were relatively distinct and even in conflict. In England, after the 1672 default, the Stop of the Exchequer, the crucial steps toward integrating the two systems were taken. Ingham describes the subsequent consolidation of the English monetary system as a settlement among various interests: first, a *parliament* that was determined to avoid any further default and was prepared to sanction the use of tax revenues and excise duties to service loans; second, *creditors* drawn from London's mercantile bourgeoisie; and third, a (privately owned) *central bank*. Among them, these interests made it possible to turn *sovereign* debt into a *public* debt, and subsequently to monetize it (Ingham 2004a: 210–11). This step, then, was a fusion of two monies: territorial money was a hybrid from the beginning. The English government faced increasing problems with its coinage, not least through the problem of "clipping," whereby metal was shaved from the circumference of a coin, lowering its intrinsic (as opposed to face) value.

This was the context in which John Locke wrote his two famous works on money (Locke 1695, 1696), in which he argued that it was the responsibility of government to maintain the "true" value of its coinage and thereby resist the clippers' criminality. Crucially, for Locke, it was the duty of the state to support money's value not just within its own legal jurisdiction but also on the world market. Clipping was "more damaging than theft" (Caffentizis 1989: 28), an *epistemological* offense that eroded the community's conception of the reality that a coin represents. Ultimately, clipping was a crime against the state: "the use and end of the public stamp is only to be a guard and voucher of the quantity of silver which men contract for; and the injury done to the public faith, in this point, is that which in clipping and false coining heightens the robbery into treason" (Locke 1695: 144).

10   As Polillo writes in his recent study of the financial history of nineteenth century Italy and America: "Just as the political sociology of the state has moved beyond rigid characterizations of states and society to a more historically nuanced and locally focused understanding of the interaction between the two, the sociology of money should move beyond institutionalized typologies of the forms of monetary authority toward a similarly nuanced frame of analysis, attentive to variation. Under a perspective that focuses on how monetary institutions are built from the ground up, as well as from the top down, the unmistakable differentiation of money and its simultaneous homogeneity deriving from money-of-account cease to seem paradoxical. They both become tensions managed through institutional work" (Polillo 2013: 222).

When Susan Strange suggested that the era of Westphalian money was coming to an end, she meant that the world's financial flows were now being constituted by *privately issued money* that had little to do with states. She called the phenomenon "Westfailure" and suggested that it was the inevitable aftermath of the collapse of the Bretton Woods system and the emergence of new financial instruments issued by transnational banks (Strange 1999). According to Strange, the Westphalia system became the Westfailure system for three main reasons. First, it could no longer manage and control the financial system (this was a failure of *capitalism*). Second, states were failing to protect the environment (this was a failure of the *planet*). And third, the system of the states was failing to preserve a balance between rich and poor (a failure of *civil society*). One wonders what Strange would have made of the 2008 crisis. Nation-states were clearly not just relevant but crucial to the *survival* prospects of those "global" banks that, like Lehman Brothers, faced collapse. This situation was hardly evidence of "Westfailure." But on the other hand, as I pointed out at the beginning of this book, states' efforts to assist or even directly rescue the banks have indeed undermined the legitimacy of the states, damaging the notion that only states should determine who has the right to create money. This loss of legitimacy occurs because their policies in relation to troubled banks appear to provide moral support for—and, arguably, to perpetuate—huge inequities of wealth and income that have become synonymous with Wall Street. As a consequence, money has been deeply implicated in tensions between the state and civil society in a way that is at least partly consistent with Strange's analysis of more than a decade ago.

Besides Strange, scholars in international relations and international political economy—such as Sassen, Hall and Wendt (Wendt 1992)—have examined how political authority itself, which is arguably a prerequisite for operating viable currency, has been established *beyond* the state at local, national, and international levels. For example, Hall and Bierstecker write of forms of governance that lack formal state or interstate institutions. These forms include "the apparent authority exercised by global market forces, by private institutions engaged in the setting of international standards, by human rights and environmental non-governmental organizations, by transnational religious movements, and even by mafia and mercenary armies in some instances" (Hall and Bierstecker 2002: 4). Of key relevance to the discussion here is the notion of *market* authority, which in a monetary context includes banks and financial corporations, sovereign wealth funds, and various nonstate regulatory institutions. Sovereign wealth funds (SWFs) are especially interesting. These are special investment funds whose government-owned assets include international assets (Truman 2010:

10). The IMF lists five basic objectives of SWFs: stabilizing funds to insulate the budget from price swings; building wealth for future generations; managing foreign exchange reserves; building up development funds; and maintaining pension reserve funds (IMF 2008). SWFs represent a further blurring of the distinction between markets and states insofar as their investment decisions may be driven by political motivations, serving (potentially at least) as a quasiprivate extension of national security interests. Until 2008, the rapid growth of SWFs in the Middle East and Southeast Asia, especially China, attracted criticism in some Western countries, particularly the United States, around precisely these issues. Concerns about the shifting locus of global economic power from West to East was implicit in this critique, fueled by fears that SWFs "would contribute to the creation of 'sharecropper societies' in the West as foreign government investment would pour into industrial countries that had lost control of their own affairs" (Truman 2010: 2–3). But the atmosphere of paranoia that was growing up around SWFs was lessened somewhat by the crucial role they played in assisting distressed banks (e.g., CitiGroup, Merrill Lynch, UBS, Morgan Stanley, and Barclays) during the 2007–8 crisis.[11]

Seen in perspective, these arguments underline the need to reconceptualize monetary space. We need to map its different layers and dimensions, its various constituent subspaces, and the myriad interconnections among them. Taking account of these new kinds of connection, we need new metaphors for thinking about monetary space as decentered, unbounded, and diffuse.[12] Moreover, as we see in Chapter 7, what appear to be singular circuits of money are actually made up of multiple and shifting configurations of meaning that make a crucial difference to how money works in practice. Analytically, what may look from the outside like a single monetary circuit—because it is defined by one monetary form—is organized internally by multifarious networks of meaning and identity. And it is important not to overlook the fact that money flows within localized spaces, too, spaces whose connection with large-scale money might be tenuous at best. This is not the absence of geography, then, but its reconfiguration.

---

11   The major SWFs also suffered losses during the crisis. For example, the China Investment Corporation (CIC) lost 40 percent of its $5.6 billion investment in Morgan Stanley (while investing a further $1.2 billion in the bank) and fully 70 percent of its $3 billion investment in the Blackstone Group. Despite such setbacks, CIC achieved profits of $41.6 billion and $51.5 billion in 2009 and 2010, respectively (IMF 2008).

12   This type of connection means connecting money with Castells's idea of "space of flows," for example (Castells 1999), although a major weakness of his approach is its reliance solely on mapping *from above*.

NOMISMA

Most arguments about money and space focus on *land*. Yet the development of the global economy has been hugely dependent on the organization of power in relation to the *sea*. As Casarino argues: "During the emergence and consolidation of industrial capitalism, the sea became an increasingly turbulent, contradictory, and contested terrain" (Casarino 2002: 4). Nietzsche once portrayed the ocean as lying "like silk and gold and dreams of goodness" (Nietzsche 2001: 119). Gold is crucial to the history of the seas, not only in relation to trade but also to the forms of primitive accumulation that Marx described. Both the discovery of America and the rounding of the Cape of Good Hope "opened up fresh ground for the rising bourgeoisie," and trade with the colonies gave commerce, navigation, and industry "an impulse never before known" (Marx and Engels 2004: 220). Water, not just land, has always been crucial for capitalism's spatial fix. The sea is pivotal in the history of slavery (Gilroy 1993). As Frederick Douglass observed in 1852: "The arm of commerce ... makes its pathway over and under the sea, as well as on the earth. Wind, steam, and lightning are its chartered agents. Oceans no longer divide, but link nations together" (Douglass 1852: 205). Still today, more than 90 percent of the world's trade takes place by sea. The thinker who grasped the geopolitical resonance of this most clearly, perhaps, was Carl Schmitt, whose conception of the territorial division of the world—*nomos*—has important ramifications for the theory of money.

According to Schmitt, the ideal of a global economy (i.e., "an economy of free world trade and a free world market, with the free movement of money, capital, and labour") developed against the background of the invasion of the New World, subsequently shaping the territorial ordering of the world between 1492 and 1890. There is a "historical and structural relation between concepts of the free sea, free trade, free world economy, and those of free competition and free exploitation" (Schmitt 2003: 99). What made the connection between growth and free trade conceivable was the opening up of a huge land mass: a "free space, an area open to European occupation and expansion" (Schmitt 2003: 87). But the sea was crucial to this connection. As Schmitt shows, the *jus publicum Europaeum* specified that the sea "was neither state or colonial territory nor occupiable space," and it "had no borders other than coasts" (Schmitt 2003: 172). This antithesis of land and sea had been the universal foundation of international law and the site of legal debate: whereas the English viewed the sea as *res omnium* (things belonging to everybody), "a crossroad common and open to all" (Schmitt 2003: 176), the French viewed the seas as *res nullius* (things belonging to nobody). This spatial order was not derived from internal European land appropriations but rather from "the European land-appropriation of a non-European new world in conjunction with England's sea-appropriation of the free sea" (Schmitt 2003: 183). Initially the New World was *terra nullius*, or no one's land, and a space of territorial indeterminacy. It was the "designated zone of free empty space" (Schmitt 2003: 98) against which positive territorial discriminations had to be made, both legally and politically. What Hobbes described as the state of nature was not the spaceless dystopia it is often held up to be but rather a representation of the New World, and Americans were exemplars of the people he describes as having a wolf-character—*homo homini lupus est* (Schmitt 2003: 96). The discovery of the New World initiated a European struggle for territory, leading to a "new spatial order of the earth with new divisions" (Schmitt 2003: 87). Gold, imported from the Americas to Europe through Lisbon and Seville, was integral to this order (Bernstein 2004: ch. 9; Vilar 2011: ch. 8). The struggle began as a division of surface area and subsequently deepened into a practical and political project, with Europe at its center.

Schmitt describes this territorial division as the *nomos* of the Earth, i.e., its spatial ordering of law and power. As originally used by Aristotle, the concept combined senses of "orientation" and "order" to denote both an original spatial division and the creation of an order that is designed to maintain it. *Nomos* was the Greek word for the first land appropriation, understood as the first partition of space. Schmitt calls it "the primeval division and distribution" (Schmitt 2003: 67). The expression has a strong linguistic, as well as historical, resonance for money. The common Greek word for money or currency, *nomisma*, shares its root with the word for law, *nomos*. As Seaford notes: "*Nomisma* is the object or consequence of *nomisdein*, which means to acknowledge by belief or practice—whether the gods (*nomisdein tous theous*) or coinage" (Seaford 2004: 7). Aristotle remarked that money exists "not by nature but by law (*nomos*) and it is in our power to change it and make it useless" (Aristotle 2004: 1133b 1). Bodin later said that "after law itself, there is nothing of greater consequence than the title, value, and measure of coins" (Bodin 1992: 78). The sovereign must assert the right of coinage, *nummus*, just as he or she asserts the right of law, *nomos*. As there cannot be private law, there cannot be private money. The idea of fiat money (the conventional definition of legal tender) expresses this idea: "fiat" means "authoritative sanction," or in Latin, "let it be done." From the opposite direction, there is a Russian saying, "He who has money need have no fear of the law." The difference, insofar as it pertains to money, is between being *above* the law and being *outside* it. Being rich is one thing; being able to coin money is quite another. King Lear said, "No, they cannot touch me for coining[13]; I am the king himself."[14] By definition, the sovereign cannot be guilty of counterfeiting.

The idea of a zone of free empty space that Schmitt uses to describe the New World plays an analogous role to the *Ausnahmezustand* (state of exception) in his political theory. *Ausnahmezustand* involves the suspension or bracketing of "normal" law. In *Political Theology* (1922), Schmitt describes the sovereign as "he who decides on the exception" (Schmitt 2006). In the context of his work more generally, the state of exception arises because of a political or economic disturbance whose severity requires the application of special measures. Schmitt says that the exception "can at best be characterized as a case of extreme peril, a danger to the existence of the state, or the like" (Schmitt 2006: 6). It is in deciding on the exception that sovereignty manifests itself in its purest form. Crucially, it means that sovereign power cannot be subject to law all of the time. The implication of this position is spelled out by Schmitt in *Die Diktatur* (originally published in 1921, 2014 cited here): "If the constitution of a state is democratic, every exceptional suspension of democratic principles, every exercise of power autonomously from the consent of those governed can be called dictatorship" (Schmitt 2014: xl–xli).

Schmitt was writing during the crisis of the Weimar state; indeed, his work is often read as preparing the way for the Third Reich (Bendersky 1992). Significantly for us here, the economic background for his theory of exception was the then-current hyperinflation, which might be called a state of economic emergence. Although *Political Theology* (Schmitt, originally published in 1922, 2006 cited here) never mentions money, the topic does come up elsewhere in his writings, and in some interesting ways. For example, Schmitt published a study of Theodor Däubler's *Das Nordlicht* (1916) (Schmitt 1991), making use of one of its central themes ("First is the command, men come later") in *Der Wert des Staates und die Bedeutung des Einzelnen* (1914) (Schmitt 2004). What emerges from Schmitt's reading is a state whose creation depends on mistrust and a Western modernity in which *money* buys nothing but *emptiness* and *spiritual impoverishment*. There are resonances here of Benjamin's descriptions of money in "One-Way Street"—also written in the shadow of the Weimar inflation—which I mentioned in Chapter 4. All of the world's misery comes from money, Schmitt suggests, and the devastating sweep of reason ends when everything is for

---

13 To coin: to manufacture counterfeit money.
14 *King Lear*, Act 4, Scene 6.

sale (Kennedy 2004: 46–47). We need to read such remarks against the background of Schmitt's broader argument that humanitarian and moral progress has become a by-product of economic progress. The European liberal state of the nineteenth century had given way, he maintained, to a state whose overwhelming preoccupation was with economic prowess: central Europeans were "living under the eyes of Russians" (Schmitt 2007: 80). Later, in "The Age of Neutralizations and Depoliticizations" (originally published in1929, now included as a section in Schmitt 2007), Schmitt referred to an "economic catastrophe, such as a sharp monetary devaluation or a crash" as an occasion that excites "widespread and acute interest both practical and theoretical" (Schmitt 2007: 86). Unfortunately, he never elaborated on where his interest in such events might lead in terms of his own political theory.

Schmitt's political theory presupposes that a group's political identity always rests upon a friend–enemy distinction. The enemy does not need to be evil or ugly, nor in economic terms a competitor, but merely *other* "in a specially intense way, existentially something different and alien, so that in the extreme case conflicts with him are possible" (Schmitt 2007: 27). Schmitt was concerned with how different political communities with distinct identities—which are therefore potential enemies—can coexist under a shared international legal order. The function of such an order would be to align extant friend–enemy distinctions with territorial boundaries: in other words, to *spatialize* them. Money—especially the "national uniforms" it wears, to borrow Marx's phrase—is an important expression of this process of spatialization, as well as a means of reinforcing it.

Cicero said that endless money forms the sinews of war.[15] Throughout the modern era, war has placed the ever-present uncertainty of our relationship with paper money (which, ideally, would be unlimited) in stark relief. Historically, war has usually given fresh impetus to gold, whose monetary value increases whenever the geopolitical boundaries defining the validity of paper money are contested.[16] At the outbreak of the First World War, gold reserves were expected to determine the outcome, although their role in anchoring the value of money was immediately suspended just about everywhere. In France, 38,000 gold ingots and 1,300 tons of gold coins were shipped out of Paris to prearranged locations in the Massif Central and the

---

15   This was in *Philippics* (Cicero 2009: Oration V, sc. 5).
16   And as Graeber points out, bullion dominates "in periods of generalized violence," when the trust on which credit depends is obviously in short supply (Graeber 2011: 213). On top of this, gold is easier to steal.

south almost as soon as fighting began (Ahamed 2009: 71). As "sound" money, gold was meant to ensure that war could be fought without runaway inflation. Even if inflation did occur, it would be short-lived because the available resources for fueling it would be used up after about one year. But experts appear not have heeded the lessons of money's historical relationship with war, which has invariably been inflationary; states have raised funds through borrowing, taxation, and the printing presses in order to meet their escalating military costs. What stands out here is the possibility that, as with counterfeiting, money relies for its positivity on specific forms of *negativity*: not only appropriated land but free sea; not only sovereign territory but *terra nullius*; not only law but the absence of law; not only order but lack of order.

DETERRITORIALIZATION

Money does not map neatly onto territorial space; indeed, it often flows along the interstices *between* spaces. It partly takes its shape from shadows, from conduits of *financial* indeterminacy that mirror those zones of *political* indeterminacy that feature in the work of Schmitt. If money is, as Simmel said, a claim upon society, we need to rethink "society" as a more diffuse configuration, which cannot be mapped directly onto the state. Likewise, we need to rethink the monetary transactor as marginal and fluid: more *migrant* than *taxpayer*. Considered spatially, the social life of money is nuanced, dynamic, and shifting. Money is an index not just of "contained" space but also of *mobility*. The "Where's George?" website in the United States began in 1998 as an unusual and fun project: you mark a dollar bill, enter its serial number on the site, and wait for "hits" on the site by future owners of the bill who give details of where they are.[17] The movement of the bills suggests that the U.S. state boundaries no longer correlate with human behavior, at least insofar as it is expressed by the flow of money. Simmel would have enjoyed this exercise: if we follow the money, human mobility in the United States suggests that the "paradigm of spatially coherent communities may no longer be plausible" (Thiemann, Theis, et al. 2010).[18] The use of dollar bills to make this argument is crucial. Although

---

17   See http://www.wheresgeorge.com/.
18   If the United States were to be divided according to "effective borders" that correlate with actual human mobility, the authors suggest that there could be eight states, not fifty. One wonders what similar data in the Eurozone might show about the continuing relevance of

the most visible marker of money's historical connections with the state, cash—not Bitcoin—arguably remains the most difficult widely accessible monetary medium for states and their agencies to control. This is why Stowe Boyd claims that "cash is a prerequisite of a free society."[19] But today's monetary spaces are arguably more heterogeneous than they have ever been, which is why scholars have increasingly used metaphors about *flow*, derived from the work of Deleuze and Guattari (2004), to come to grips with the complexities of the monetary landscape.

Deleuze and Guattari were not system builders, and for this reason their arguments are not easy to explain. They refused to advance models that could be applied to different empirical settings and encouraged others to follow their own intellectual paths. They also doubted the value of dialectics, utopia, and social critique. Sylvère Lotringer compared them to "fugitives blowing up bridges behind them" (Lotringer and Cohen 2001: 155). They saw theory as a form of experimentation: a direct engagement with reality and a response to the present that had no preconceptions. If there is a distinct metaphysical position underpinning this approach, it is that identity does not arrive logically before difference but is rather its effect (Deleuze 2004). It is therefore surprising that Derrida's relationship to these thinkers—they were contemporaries, after all—has not been much discussed. Both philosophies focus on *difference*, although according to Patton and Protevi, whereas Derrida's version tends to be "post-phenomenological and ethical," Deleuze and Guattari's is "material and forceful" (Patton and Protevi 2003: 5). According to Smith, these philosophies also have distinctive relationships to the question of thought's *immanence*: whereas the immanence we find in Derrida is derived from Kant and Husserl (it is immanence *to* something, and therefore connected to *transcendence* in some way), the immanence in Deleuze and Guattari is not interior to anything but rather occupies a *pure outside*: "Deleuze attempts to formulate an immanent theory of Ideas and desire, while Derrida attempts to define a purely formal structure of transcendence and the passion of the double bind that it entails" (Smith 2003: 61). This difference can be seen in their treatments of money.

According to Deleuze and Guattari, the categories that we conventionally use to define identity must be derived from a multiple and never-ending series of differences. Classic liberal notions of society in which values and

---

nation-state borders. This argument presents an intriguing opportunity to review the status and role of cash (notes and coins) in the world's monetary flows.

19   See "Anonymous cash = Freedom," http://stoweboyd.com/post/2358837421/anonymous-cash-freedom, accessed May 10, 2013.

rights adhere to individuals, for example, are superseded by naturalistic ethics, similar to those found in the work of Nietzsche and Spinoza, wherein what is conventionally thought of as "morality" is the product of preindividual, unconscious forces. These forces are not, however, reducible to separate individuals. It is their analysis of money, particularly its *deterritorialization*, that mainly interests us here because money is one of the main vehicles through which deeper contrapuntal tendencies that Deleuze and Guattari discern within capitalism play themselves out. One important manifestation of this process, they argue, is the opening up of a distinction *within* money—between payment money and finance money—that corresponds to a deeper rift within capitalism itself.

Deleuze and Guattari's work in *Anti-Oedipus* (originally published in 1972; 2004 edition cited here) and *A Thousand Plateaus* (originally published in 1980; 1987 edition cited here) explores the economic, cultural, and libidinal dynamics of capital. The key philosophical argument underpinning their analysis concerns the decisive move from *representation* (which is object centered, focused on land or material money) toward *production* (which is subject centered, emphasizing not what is produced but rather the capacity to produce). Foucault put forward a similar analysis in *The Order of Things* (originally published in 1966), for example in his account of biology (Foucault 2005: ch. 7). There had been parallels shift away from object-centered representation in religion[20] and psychoanalysis[21] (Smith 2012: 162). For Deleuze and Guattari, the discovery of labor by Smith (2008) and Ricardo (1821) and the discovery of the unconscious by Freud were part of the same underlying shift from representation to production. Political economy and the libidinal economy are therefore part of the same fundamental economy. Whereas conventional psychoanalytical theory suggests that the subject must *sublimate* his or her libidinal energies to invest them in economic, social, and political activity, Deleuze and Guattari argue that libido is invested *directly* in institutions: there is no sublimation. *Desire* is now part of capitalism's infrastructure, an effect of the "unconscious libidinal investment of the social field" (Deleuze and Guattari 2004: 114). Sexuality is everywhere: "flags, nations, armies, banks get a lot of people aroused" (Deleuze and Guattari 2004: 322). Desire is therefore a positive, productive force, not a response to a lack. We find a similarly positive conception of

---

20 From Luther, who turned faith inward, to Kierkegaard, for whom faith was the very source of God.
21 For Freud, desire was no longer defined in terms of its object but rather as subjective essence, libido, or sexuality.

desire in Spinoza, Nietzsche, and Foucault. Brown's neurotic money complex (see Chapter 4) could not be farther away.

Reflecting this combination of Marxism and psychoanalysis, Deleuze and Guattari describe their work as *schizoanalysis*. This is a form of political and social psychoanalysis, whose primary unit of analysis is not the subject, but rather the *desiring machine* (Deleuze and Guattari 2004: 98). For Deleuze and Guattari, life itself is machinelike. It is constructed whenever connections are made between things, subjects, and organs. Desire produces these connections, hence the notion of "desiring-production," which is not goal-oriented production. Rather, it involves the overflow and aimless circulation of desire, the outcome of which are "machines driving other machines, machines being driven by other machines, with all the necessary couplings and connections" (Deleuze and Guattari 2004: 1). Their explanation of how capitalism emerged focuses on the decoding of flows of labor and capital, drawing heavily on Althusser and Balibar's *Reading Capital* (1968) (Althusser and Balibar 2009).

Desiring machines produce flows of biological and collective energy that embrace both the natural (or metaphysical) and social (or historical) realms. A flow is a transmission or exchange of money (value) from one pole (i.e., people, groups, or firms) to another. The poles act as *interceptors*. Deleuze and Guattari's use of the term "flow" in relation to money draws closely on Keynes's *General Theory*. Besides attributing to Keynes the first great theory of flows (Smith 2012: 164), they praise Keynes for introducing the problem of desire into monetary theory (Deleuze and Guattari 2004: 250) and for proposing a new "axiomatic"[22] of economic governance based on the regulation and stimulus of flows (Deleuze and Guattari 1987: 510). Flows must be credited and given meaning, which is a process Deleuze and Guattari refer to as *coding*. Codes are not simply applied to flows; rather, they reciprocally determine one another: no flow can be understood without its code. Codes operate through signs or signifying chains (*chaines signifiantes*), via inscription or recording, although these signs do not represent or signify; they merely "fix" the flows. This process echoes the distinction between representation and production I mentioned above. These codings operate like genetic code, which do not represent an organism but rather determine how it comes to be.[23] They do not convey a message determined in advance, like

---

22 The term "axiomatic" is used by Deleuze and Guattari to denote a method whose elements or terms do not need to be defined (Toscano 2010). The term comes from set theory in mathematics.

23 This is the idea behind *A Thousand Plateaus*, which uses a geological notion of stratification (Deleuze and Guattari 1987: 510).

Morse code or the codes that Parsons once associated with money (Dodd 1994). One could locate Knorr Cetina and Bruegger's work on "global microstructures" of financial markets here. According to them, financial markets are not like networks in any conventional sense but rather consist of a series of local settings (or, in Deleuzian terms, nodes or poles interrupting flows) in which intense and dynamic conversational interaction takes place (Knorr Cetina and Bruegger 2002: 910). The micro sociological approach taken by Knorr Cetina and Bruegger yields a rich, interactional analysis of the very dynamics that Deleuze and Guattari describe as the coding of flows.

Genetic code determines what goes into a mutation but never the precise nature of the outcome, which is always new. Codes therefore consist of an open-ended, polyvocal formation. They involve the "play of blind combinations" where anything is possible. Codes are molecular, not molar. *Molecularity* suggests a becoming other and is expressed in notions such as rhizome, pack, haecceity ("thisness"), singularity, and event. *Molarity* implies a making-the-same, stable equilibrium, and being rather than becoming and is expressed in ideas such as Oedipus, phallocentrism, and personhood. Molar organization is found at the level of the living organism, or the whole. Desire functions only at the molecular level. When capitalism *deterritorializes*, it promotes the *molecular* and the *schizophrenic*. When it needs to *reterritorialize*, it draws on the *molar* and the *paranoiac* (Holland 1999: 94). Codes ensure that flows coagulate within a particular social configuration or form. The specific forms these codings take define different historical systems of ownership and power. Deleuze and Guattari advance what could loosely be called a theory of history based on a tripartite model of social formations: primitives, states, and capitalism. Each formation is defined by the relationship between *political economy* (whose unit of analysis is the *social machine*) and *libidinal* economy (which focuses on the *desiring machine*). Like Marx, they read this history retrospectively in the sense that previous formations anticipate capitalism (Deleuze and Guattari 2004). The notions of flow and coding are crucial to this history; indeed, flow plays a similar role within Deleuze and Guattari's theory to the role that production plays in that of Marx. Deleuze and Guattari's theory of capitalism parallels that of Marx, but instead of focusing on changes in the relationship between forces and relations of production, they trace out the progressive decoding of flows. Money plays a crucial part in this history.

In "primitive" economies, flows were coded through barter; there was simply direct exchange of objects. When money was introduced into these economies through colonialism, it appeared to operate as a destructive power because of its apparent capacity to corrode existing patterns of exchange. This is, of course, a familiar theme in anthropological and historical accounts of primitive money. But it has been increasingly contested. Note, however, that according to Deleuze and Guattari, those primitive codes were operating negatively, keeping merchants in a subordinate position "so that the flows of exchange and the flows of production do not manage to break the codes in favour of their abstract or fictional quantities" (Deleuze and Guattari 2004: 168). So in this particular sense, money was a positive and liberating, not destructive, force. From here, Deleuze and Guattari seek to trace out a series of phases in money's decoding, which take the form of the emergence of progressively more abstract forms of money.[24]

A crucial stage in this sequence is the emergence of a form of money whose coding covers the entire social field. State money was a significant part of this process. States encouraged the development of money not because they were keen on encouraging free commercial activity but on the contrary, because they wanted to control it. Taxation—supported by the flawed notion (see Chapter 3) that each of us owes an infinite debt to the state—was crucial to this process. States used taxation to siphon off a portion of commercial gains for themselves: "it is taxation that monetarizes the economy; it is taxation that creates money" (Deleuze and Guattari 1987: 489). Whereas primitive debts were *finite*, debts to the state are *infinite*: we never finish paying taxes. Hence money's historical development did not simply transform commerce; it also transformed the nature of *debt*. This interpretation resonates with the arguments of Nietzsche and Benjamin that I discussed in Chapter 4. Smith draws attention to the Christian parallels: "Christianity, at least in its Pauline form, effectively 'spiritualized' this concept of infinite debt: the wages of sin is death, a debt I can only pay off by eternal damnation; God, in his mercy, decides to pay off the infinite debt to himself in our place; he redeems us, just as the Romans redeemed slaves by paying for them. In this sense, one could say that Christian theology is a spiritualized form of economics" (Smith 2012: 168).[25]

Deleuze and Guattari's arguments about money are marked by ambivalence, for example, toward its capacity to destroy outmoded and repressive

---

24 Abstract money would be a pure flow, expressing its increasing detachment from locally meaningful objects.
25 Lazzarato makes a similar point: "The infinite that Christianity introduces to religion capitalism reinvents at the economic level: the movement of capital as the self-generated movement of value, of money that makes money, and which, thanks to debt, expands beyond its limits. With capitalism, capitalist valorization and debt become infinite processes each propagating the other . . . The system of the infinite is the system of destruction/creation whose foremost expression can be found in and through the creation/destruction of money" (Lazzarato 2011: 79).

forms of organization, versus its tendency to subsume everything under the all-encompassing logic (or "axiomatic") of the market (or capital) on the other hand. Whereas despotic forms of money were incredibly powerful, they were not, in and of themselves, sufficiently extensive to lead to the development of capitalism. Before capitalism, money was merely superimposed onto *preexisting* social formations (primitive and despotic); it did not actually *define* those formations. Money had no "body" of its own; it was merely appended to other bodies that had been formed independently of it (e.g., nature, the state). For money to have its own body, it had to be capable of creating more money (as in Marx's formulation: "money begets money"). It therefore had to become capital; or more precisely, it had to be transformed into finance capital.

This argument opens out onto a deeper distinction in Deleuze and Guattari's analysis, between relations of *alliance* and relations of *filiation*. Alliances are lateral (e.g., siblings, cousins), whereas affiliations are linear (e.g., father, son). Before capitalism, money simply enabled the formation of alliances, bringing together people and things that had hitherto been separated. In order for capitalism to develop, money needed to generate its own forms of relation; in other words, it had to become filiative. Money ceased being just the conveyer of debt payments to others and became a form of debt in its own right. Recalling our discussion of Benjamin in Chapter 4, money now becomes a debt to itself, or more precisely, a debt to capital. This argument further reflects the distinctive modes of representation operating in capitalist as opposed to despotic formations. The structure of Saussurian linguistics is despotic: the signifier dominates the signified. In capitalism, by contrast, there is an oscillation between these two poles. There is no pyramid (despot at its apex, peasant at its base) but merely the free flow of goods, bodies, and images. These flows are coded not by domination and hierarchy but rather by the axiomatics of labor and capital, according to which entities are interrelated—via money—as abstract qualities. Debts to capital are infinite, and they have no aim other than the production of more capital. Money now becomes its own body, i.e., the full body of capital, wherein capital does not flow upward toward the state but merely back and forth to itself. This flow marks a new threshold in the progressive decoding, dematerialization, and deterritorialization of money.

For Deleuze and Guattari, money in this form is neither a symbol nor a thing but rather a flow. Rather than thinking of money as a series of discrete units that we accept, possess, and pass on, they suggest that each of us acts as an *interceptor of flows*, while we simultaneously produce *new* flows: "every 'object' presupposes the continuity of a flow" (Deleuze and Guattari 2004: 6). For example, we interrupt money's flow in order to consume things (e.g., by shopping or eating); we use money to join existing material flows (e.g., through traveling) and to create new flows (e.g., by investing). Money is never its own discrete flow, either, but part of a complex series of interrelated flows of people, goods, images, bodies, and ideas.[26] As Allen and Pryke observe: "In the Deleuzian spatial vocabulary, individuals and groups are made up of a tangle of lines which cross over one another in all kinds of ways, composing and decomposing lives in a manner that illustrates their subtle modifications and detours, as well as their more fixed attachments and territories" (Allen and Pryke 1999: 53). There is no center and no foundation to this "system," no site from which power originates. As subjects, we are merely points of connection and disconnection, conjunction and disjunction within these flows. For this reason, our desires are focused not on discrete objects but rather on myriad breaks, ruptures, and connections. This situation resonates with the idea of *living currency* that we discussed in Chapter 5.

As portrayed by Deleuze and Guattari, then, the monetary "landscape" is in perpetual flux. It is not divided neatly into the territorial spaces that once defined despotism, that is to say, the spatial parameters of states. In capitalism, money both *de*territorializes and, through finance, potentially creates its *own* territorial space, whose limit edge is nothing other than the entire "body" of capital itself. *In extremis*, this area would be a space without borders, regulation, or control: a space into which each of us is inserted at myriad points—not stable, never fixed, always impermanent. All of these flows still need to be coded, of course. In capitalism, the most common form of code is the accounting system, e.g., statistics relating to GDP, employment, and trade help to coagulate the flows of people, money, and goods that they purport to represent. An *un*coded flow would be unnameable, something to be feared: Deleuze and Guattari call it a "nightmarish" prospect. This nightmare is when flows simply run on and on: there is nothing *but* flow, a deluge. Economic phenomena that cannot be valued—e.g.,

---

26   On the subject of flow, Knorr Cetina and Preda make further intriguing use of the notion that financial processes are constituted by flows, which they contrast with networks: "The flow of the market reflects the corresponding stream of activities and things: a dispersed mass of market participants continues to act, events continue to occur, politicians decide and decisions have effects" (Knorr Cetina and Preda 2007: 130). In this context, the concept of flow is designed to capture the idea that financial markets are characterized by their own specific modes of temporality, *which unfold independently of space*: "The screen reality, in these markets, is like a carpet of which small sections are woven and at the same time rolled out in front of us. The carpet grounds experience; we can step on it, and change our positioning on it. But this carpet only composes itself as it is rolled out; the spatial illusions it affords hide the intrinsic temporality of the fact that its threads (the lines of text appearing on screen) are woven into the carpet only as we step on it and unravel again behind our back (the lines are updated and disappear)" (Knorr Cetina and Preda 2007: 130).

subprime mortgages in 2007, or the banks that carried them—are an example of such decoded flows.

So is money *simply* flow for Deleuze and Guattari? Not exactly. They argue that capitalist money is *dual*: "it is not the same money that goes into the pocket of the wage earner and is entered on the balance sheet of a commercial enterprise" (Deleuze and Guattari 2004: 248). There are two kinds (or inscriptions) of money: *payment* money and *finance* money. Payment money is involved in simple circulation. In this form, money is a medium of exchange, consisting of "impotent signs of exchange value" whereby money enters into a one-to-one relationship with goods in exchange (Deleuze and Guattari 2004: 248–49). Payment money is the money we use to buy things, pay our bills, give pocket money to our children, and so on. This is the transfer of existing units of currency. By contrast, finance money is the money that banks can fashion *ex nihilo* by creating debts to themselves. Whereas payment money flows through people and goods, flows of finance money involve successive acts of *creation* and *destruction*. Whereas payment money replicates the existing division of labor, finance money reconfigures those relations insofar as it can determine future production (Lazzarato 2011: 74). Financial capital is the power to command and control *time* through the creation and destruction of money.

Distinctive logics define these flows of payment money and finance money, corresponding to the distinction between relations of *alliance* and *filiation*, respectively. At its simplest, payment money connects people and things, bringing them together in ways that might not be possible without money: this is the *segmental logic of alliances*. Finance money, by contrast, entails the creation of new money and therefore defines the way in which capitalist money proliferates: this is the *linear logic of filiation*. Finance money can also be seen as a mutation of money's unit of account function (Mandarini 2006: 95 n. 41). It consists of "signs [that] have the power of capital" (Deleuze and Guattari 2004: 249). Although these concepts of payment money and finance money are defined by distinctive logics, however, they do not describe separate monetary flows. There is no prior commonality between payment money and finance money, no equivalence or instant conversions between them. This is why banks are needed, not just as the creators of finance money but also as pivotal points—or oscillators—between finance money and payment money. It is a significant weakness of Marxist economics, Deleuze and Guattari argue, that it dwells too often on "considerations concerning the mode of production, and on the theory of money as the general equivalent as found in the first section of *Capital*, without attaching enough importance to banking practice, to financial operations, and to the specific circulation of credit money" (Deleuze and Guattari 2004: 230).[27]

Taken together, payment money and finance money combine to make up what Deleuze and Guattari refer to as the *monetary mass*. The term is drawn from Susanne de Brunhoff's *L'Offre de Monnaie* ("The Money Supply") (de Brunhoff 1971). She argues that there would be no such thing as general monetary circulation without an overarching monetary system that combines the different kinds of credit and money (Deleuze and Guattari 2004: 250 n.). This is an important argument in sociological terms. For both kinds of money to work as the general equivalent—and capitalism demands that they *must*—certain social conditions have to be met. They characterize these conditions in terms of the belief (or illusion) that the various kinds of money circulating are part of the *same underlying monetary mass*. Money must not be seen as part of a myriad series of flows, in other words, but rather as constituting a singular and homogeneous entity: *money*, not *monies*. However, this singular money is a "pure fiction, a cosmic swindle" (Deleuze and Guattari 2004: 250). Banks, acting as switch points between payment money and finance money, play a key role in creating such a fiction by rendering the monetary mass homogeneous. States, too, perform a key role as "servants" to capital; they are responsible for regulating conversions between payment money and finance money, mainly by managing the credit system and acting as its ultimate guarantor.

So why is the illusion that there is a single monetary mass necessary? The idea of homogeneous money ensures that *desire is invested throughout the capitalist social field*. Unless desire is everywhere, the system breaks down. Without desire, there is no interception of flows, no breaks and disjunctions, no connections and conjunctions. Without desire, there is no investment. This is not simply a question of money but of the system's operation in its entirety. Desire does not simply focus on persons or things, but the "entire surroundings that it traverses, the vibrations and flows of every sort to which it is joined" (Deleuze and Guattari 2004: 322). Money, wealth, profit, and consumption are all part of the "voluptuous wave" of desire that makes it possible for money to produce money. Desire must be present whenever something flows and runs, even if (against our interests) it leads us toward lethal destinations (Deleuze and Guattari 2004: 115). On some

---

27   In *Negotiations* (1990), Deleuze writes: "Beyond the state it's money that rules, money that communicates, and what we need these days definitely isn't any critique of Marxism, but a modern theory of money as good as Marx's that goes on from where he left off (bankers would be better placed than economists to sketch its outlines ...)" (Deleuze 1995: 152).

level, even *economics* must arouse and fascinate everyone, including those who have no understanding of it. Even the "most disadvantaged creature" must be caught up in this wave, part of the complex of unconscious flows that surge through the system as a whole. The monetary mass must be homogeneous, too, to sustain the illusion that all dollars are equal; that the money of the financier is identical in form to the money earned by the worker; and that the difference between rich and poor is purely a question of how much money they have, not of structural dynamics shaping the way that the flows—payment money and finance money—are coded *ab initio* (see Buchanan and Thoburn 2008: 30, 153). We come back to this in our discussion of the euro later in this chapter.

As Deleuze and Guattari define it, payment money implies a commodity theory of money. It is compatible with Menger's theory of its evolution (see Chapter 1) and with Marx's account of money's emergence as the general equivalent in the first volume of *Capital* (see Chapter 2). Finance money, on the other hand, reflects the credit and debt theories of money that I discussed in Chapter 3, whose proponents specifically reject the commodity theory. Significantly, however, Deleuze and Guattari do not treat payment money and finance money as contradictory and mutually exclusive ideas but rather as part of the *same fundamental dualism of money* (Deleuze and Guattari 2004: 250). In their analysis, payment money and finance money coexist as part of the "profound dissimulation" of homogeneous money (Deleuze and Guattari 2004: 249). One theory should not be favored over another: money has to play on both boards, indeed "no integration of the dominated classes could occur without the shadow of this unapplied principle of convertibility" (Deleuze and Guattari 2004: 249) The two kinds of money are therefore in dynamic tension, as states and banks mediate between them to maintain the illusion of a homogeneous monetary mass. But although contemporary capitalism depends on the fictional homogeneity of money, it is finance money that has grown exponentially during the post–Bretton Woods era; indeed, it is the "real force" within capitalism.

This point brings us back to where the discussion in this chapter began. In its most developed, deterritorialized form, finance money is stateless. Deleuze and Guattari describe it as a multinational ecumenical organization and a *de facto* supranational power: indeed, "it could be said that capitalism develops an economic order *that could do without the State*" (Deleuze and Guattari 1987: 501, italics added). But this statement leaves open the problem of who (or what) in the global age determines the form of the monetary mass, sustaining money's fictional unity—or conversely, what happens once that unity breaks down. Capitalists, after all, may be masters of surplus value, but they do not control—because nobody *can*—the flows from which surplus value is derived (Deleuze and Guattari 1987: 249). And as we saw in 2008, banks "return" to sovereign monetary spaces whenever their survival is under threat. If there is no power regulating "global" flows of money, there is none that is capable of maintaining the illusion of the monetary mass. If neither banks nor states can do so, no supranational body exists for this purpose. In Deleuze and Guattari's terms, one possible outcome would be a particular kind of deflation: what they describe as "libidinal" investments in capitalism—*desire*—would subside as capitalist money collapses in on itself.

Deleuze and Guattari leave open the question of how the fictional homogeneity of a monetary mass might be maintained in the global age. This is hardly a new question, of course, but by framing it in terms of the distinction between payment money and finance money, we can ask it in an interesting way. Although some scholars (Strange, for example) have argued that "stateless" financial flows (i.e., finance money) have superseded national currencies and precipitated the *end of money's geography*, Deleuze and Guattari encourage a more nuanced view. This is because they do not equate *payment* money with *territorial* money (or national currency). Rather, their arguments powerfully suggest that even in a capitalist world without national currencies, there would *still* be payment money. The problem of money's "fictional homogeneity" would therefore persist, even if it were no longer a problem that could be dealt with by *states*. This prospect raises a number of important questions. What forms would payment consist of in a capitalist system in which there are no national currencies—or in which those forms no longer predominate? Which institutions—besides banks—would operate in such a world to ensure that payment money and finance money continued to operate under the illusion that they are part of the same monetary mass? Alternatively, what would the consequences be if that illusion was to break down, as some allege it has been doing as alternative currencies proliferate? One set of answers to such questions, whose proponents claim to be working in the shadow of Deleuze and Guattari, is suggested by the theory of Hardt and Negri, and I turn to this theory next.

EMPIRE

Hardt and Negri's *Empire* (2000, 2001 cited here)—alongside *Multitude* (2005) and *Commonwealth* (2009)—offers a distinctive account of globalization that embraces its political and cultural dimensions. Hardt and Negri argue that during the twentieth century, modern imperialism, with the nation-state as its focal point, gave way to a new configuration of power: a supranational order that consists not only of global markets but of regulators, too. This order is "Empire." It is characterized by a new geopolitical system whose components radically restructure the political forms of old nation-states. The emergence of Empire gives rise to new modes of warfare as well as distinctive forms of protest and opposition, which Hardt and Negri seek to theorize using Spinoza's concept of the multitude (Hardt and Negri 2005). Theoretically, their arguments also draw on notions of biopolitics (Foucault 2008a) and the assemblage (Deleuze and Guattari 1987). They also propose a reinterpretation of Marxism that could certainly be described as post-Fordist, and perhaps even as postmodernist and poststructuralist. The argument is interesting to monetary theory for three key reasons. First, they draw attention to the political—not just economic—ramifications of the increasingly global forms that have been taken by monetary and financial instruments during the past half century. Second, in exploring those forms, they establish theoretically intriguing connections between Marx's theory of capital (which frames their overarching approach) and theories of power, such as that of Foucault, which enable them to reconfigure notions of political agency insofar as it operates within the interstices among capital, labor, and sovereign power. Third, and building on this reconfiguration, they use a Spinozian concept of the multitude to grasp diffused collective agency on shifting sites of radical engagement in the global age. This Spinozian concept poses intriguing questions that resonate with our own ongoing discussion of how Simmel's characterization of money as a claim upon *society* might be recast in an era of *postnational* monies.

Empire is the political form of globalization. According to Hardt and Negri, the journey toward it involved the displacement of nation-state functions to other levels and domains (Hardt and Negri 2001: 307). Capitalist institutions have not replaced the state; rather a new form of sovereignty has emerged, composed of "national and supranational organisms under a *single logic of rule*" (Hardt and Negri 2001: xii, italics added). To understand this logic, we need to revisit arguments about what drives the spatial reconfiguration of contemporary capitalism. Although Hardt and Negri's analysis connects with Harvey's notion of the spatial fix, they also suggest that its patterns of mobility are creating a new geography that cannot be explained by capitalist accumulation alone (Hardt and Negri 2001: 397). Empire as they conceive it cannot simply be extrapolated from the old Westphalian model, as if a global metastate was in formation. In this sense, Empire is a politico-economic hybrid.

To theorize this hybrid, Hardt and Negri reach back to Polybius's *Histories*, particularly his characterization of imperial Rome in terms of the relationship among three "good powers": monarchy, aristocracy, and democracy. Polybius argued that each of these powers was a check on the other, thereby preventing monarchy's fall into tyranny, aristocracy's into oligarchy, and democracy's into ochlocracy or anarchy (Hardt and Negri 2001: 314). Empire in late capitalism is analogous to this structure. In Polybius's schema, the monarchy anchors power, giving it both unity and continuity. In the Empire as conceived by Hardt and Negri, the monarchy consists of bodies (such as the G8, NATO, the IMF, and the World Trade Organization [WTO]) that are designed to ensure the maintenance of "efficient" markets for goods, technologies, and labor power. This is a "monarchic" unity of power combined with a global monopoly of force. Polybius argued that the aristocracy defines justice, measure, and virtue. In Hardt and Negri's model, it consists of transnational corporations and sovereign nation-states. For Polybius, democracy guarantees both discipline and redistribution, organizing subjects in such a way that they are both ruled and yet still able to constrain that rule. In Hardt and Negri's Empire, democracy operates through NGOs and media organizations, the UN and religious organizations (Hardt and Negri 2001: 314). Additionally, the emergence of the new Empire gives rise to new modes of warfare, as well as distinctive forms of protest and opposition, which they theorize using Spinoza's concept of the multitude (discussed below).

Despite drawing on Polybius, there is no suggestion here that Empire is actually a throwback to imperial Rome. Rather, it represents a complex evolutionary transition. For example, the "monarchical" forms of Empire are multiple and dispersed, and their functions are sometimes fused with those of the "aristocracy" (Hardt and Negri 2001: 317). As for actors themselves, labor's cooperation has to be ensured by new forms of democratic engagement for which there is no analogue in ancient Rome. Drawing on Foucault's analysis of biopower, Hardt and Negri characterize these forms in terms of a shift from a *disciplinary* to a *control* paradigm of government that incorporates the entire social body in the apparatus of control:

> We should understand the society of control ... as that society (which develops at the far edge of modernity and opens towards the postmodern) in which mechanisms of command become ever more "democratic," ever more immanent to the social field, distributed throughout the brains and bodies of citizens. The behaviours of social integration and exclusion proper to rule are thus increasingly interiorized within the

subjects themselves. Power is not exercised through machines that directly organize the brains (in communication systems, information networks, etc.) and bodies (in welfare systems, monitored activities, etc.) toward a state of autonomous alienation from the sense of life and the desire for creativity. The society of control might thus be characterized by an intensification and generalization of the normalizing apparatuses of disciplinarity that internally animate our common and daily practices, but in contrast to the discipline, this control extends well outside the structured sites of social institutions through flexible and fluctuating networks. (Hardt and Negri 2001: 23)

Hardt and Negri argue that, in practice, the hybrid constitution that has developed within Empire combines what Polybius saw as the *good* and *bad* forms of power: its monarchy too often resembles a tyrannical international police force, its aristocracy appears to prefer financial speculation to entrepreneurship, and its democratic institutions frequently appear to be held back by special interests, or by "superstitions and fundamentalisms, betraying a spirit that is conservative when not downright reactionary" (Hardt and Negri 2001: 316). Just as Marx always emphasized points of continuity between capitalism, as he saw it developing, and socialism, so Hardt and Negri highlight the significance of new challenges to capital that Empire has helped bring into being. For example, struggles over nationalism and colonialism point to political engagements operating beyond the divisions of national, colonial, and imperialist rule (Hardt and Negri 2001: 43). Empire itself is vulnerable to new challenges at multiple points. Just as Marx once argued that labor power represents capital's most internal element ("it is always the initiatives of organized labour power that determine the figure of capitalist development") *and* its most external ("the place where the proletariat recognizes its own use value, its own autonomy, and where it grounds its hope for liberation") (Hardt and Negri 2001: 208), so it is with power within Empire, where *migration* is the specter that haunts the world (Hardt and Negri 2001: 213). As we shall see, money and finance can potentially play an important role as media through which these myriad networks of control and engagement come about. For example, money is crucial to the forms of mobility that characterize Empire as Hardt and Negri conceive it.

Within Empire, capitalist exploitation is no longer confined to work but extends across the social terrain, embracing not just commodities but "rich and powerful social relationships" (Hardt and Negri 2001: 210). This position is similar to that associated with post-Fordism and put forward by Christian Marazzi, who (like Negri) was closely linked with *Autonomia*

Operaia (see Chapter 2). This position is the view that capitalism has drawn not just economic but also qualitative, social relations into its nexus: as emotional labor, for example. "Empire is the non-place of world production where labour is exploited ... The non-place has a brain, heart, torso, and limbs, globally" (Hardt and Negri 2001: 210). Within Empire, *all* social relationships are malleable, just as territorial borders are permeable. Old, quasimetaphysical notions of natural difference and hierarchy are swept away by the political forces of globalization. Nevertheless, dialectical forces are still at play here. Taking their cue from Deleuze and Guattari, Hardt and Negri suggest that this force is simultaneously a globalization of *desire* whose consequences for capitalism are double-edged. This is globalization working against itself. To capture this ambivalence, they take on the difficult—because it is inherently speculative—task of developing a conceptual vocabulary for describing economic, social, political, and cultural forms in a post–nation-state era in order to address what kind of *society* this would be, what major forms of *association* will emerge, and how questions such as *law*, *justice*, and *citizenship* will arise. We need to grasp where money might feature in such a world.

Money has played a key role in the dynamics of globalization as Hardt and Negri conceive it. Operating on capital's *plane of immanence* through relays and networks of domination, money makes the immeasurable space of global capitalism what it is. Like the atom bomb, money is a global means of absolute control. The emergence of a world market entails the "monetary deconstruction of national markets, the dissolution of national and/or regional regimes of monetary regulation, and the subordination of those markets to the needs of financial powers" (Hardt and Negri 2001: 341). But this is a dual process, consisting both of deterritorialization as Deleuze and Guattari described, and *re*territorialization via the concentration of finance in global cities (Hardt and Negri 2001: 346). The world market, international divisions, and flows of labor that undermine center–periphery distinctions have also been eroding the boundaries between states, specifically as juridico-economic entities. This phenomenon is manifested by the emergence and increasing power of bodies such as General Agreement on Tariffs and Trade (GATT), WTO, the World Bank, and the IMF. There is no central public administration but rather several multifunctional regimes, differentiating and disseminating through networks and relays, with no transcendent center. These networks and relays are created via those very logics that are active in the construction of Empire: the police and military, the economic, and the ideological and communicative (Hardt and Negri 2001: 338).

This is not, however, a world without geography (cf. Ohmae 1990; O'Brien 1992; Agnes 2000). The movement of money and finance both creates and reinforces spatial division, e.g., by flowing to areas where labor is cheap and flexible (Hardt and Negri 2001: 326). Hardt and Negri are not alone in arguing that global capitalism is a complex, geographically textured landscape. Other scholars, too, have argued that money and finance in today's world are characterized by a distinctive geographical anatomy in which borders are not absent, but complex and overlapping (Sassen 1991, 1999; Baker, Hudson, et al. 2005). Today's monetary spaces are configured by multiple circuits connecting nodal points such as global cities (with their major financial centers and business districts) along with other major rallying points for money, such as the international art and real estate markets. In effect, these centers serve as *bottlenecks* in the global circulation of money. We conventionally think of such bottlenecks as points on the system where there is a buildup of *wealth*, in global cities and financial centers, as well as of *debt*. For example, one could map bottlenecks within today's global economy in terms of mortgage-ridden households (Iceland, United States, United Kingdom, Spain, Ireland, and central and eastern Europe); highly indebted banks (Iceland, United States, the European Union (EU), Russia, and the former Soviet Union); quasisovereign debt (Ukraine's Naftogaz and the investment company Dubai World); and the Eurozone's so-called peripheral states (Portugal, Italy, Greece, and Spain) (Roubini 2010). This mapping would offer a revealing but not conclusive picture. Other spatial formations, too, are becoming increasingly commonplace in the myriad ways we think about money. These formations are connected to *place* as well as *space*. They range from local currencies, specialized trading and exchange systems, virtual and electronic monies, and corporate incentive schemes.

Sassen has described global cities as sites of agglomeration necessitated by the territorial dispersion of economic activity in the global economy. Whereas capitalist production has been decentralized, its command and control have been increasingly centralized. But at the same time, globalization has generated new economic formations in which the heterogeneity of space remains key. Sassen (1991, 1999) identifies a dual logic of valorization within the global city whereby financial firms and their workers are overvalorized, and the legions of low-wage service workers they employ (as residential building attendants, restaurant workers, preparers of specialty and gourmet foods, dog walkers, errand runners, apartment cleaners, and childcare providers) are heavily undervalorized. This valorization shapes the complex spatial dynamics of the global city, with its contrasting areas of residential and commercial gentrification and urban deprivation. Hence globalization does not homogenize urban space but rather shapes it in conjunction with the deep economic history of particular places and the regions in which they are located. Global firms locate themselves in cities according to their own specific infrastructural requirements (Sassen 2009).

Harvey, too, underlines the role of global capital accumulation in shaping urban space. As discussed in Chapter 2, Harvey's spatial fix thesis is premised on the notion that capitalism must achieve a compound growth rate of around 3 percent per annum to maintain its own structural integrity (Harvey 2010b: 27). The strategy of accumulation by dispossession is a "solution" to this problem, and it has a significant effect on the city through the destructive dynamics of urbanization. Investment in real estate is especially well suited to financial capitalism because it is closely associated with debt. Governments, too, have promoted urbanization as a means of achieving economic development, underlining the point that states and markets are not in opposition in the spatial dynamics of money but rather operate in tandem. The property market generates capital that delays impending crises of accumulation because its return is projected into the future: this is a temporal fix, which "always runs the risk of replicating, at a much later date and on a magnified scale, the very overaccumulation conditions that it initially helps to relieve" (Harvey 2012: 42). Property developers, realtors, and landlords operate alongside banks as part of the "vast terrain of accumulation by dispossession, through which money is sucked up into the circulation of fictitious capital to underpin the vast fortunes made from within the financial system" (Harvey 2012: 53–54). *Profit* is increasingly being superseded by *rent*. Carlo Vercellone calls this situation "becoming rent of the profit" (Vercellone 2010; see also Žižek 2009: 145). The tactic, as Michael Hudson has also noted, is for banks and financial institutions to load governments, firms, and families with debt, siphon off their income in debt service, and seize their assets when they foreclose. Governments are forced to sell infrastructure, firms have to seize pension payments, and families are forced into debt peonage. The result is to centralize creditor control over society as a whole (Hudson 2012). This is capitalism of the old regime.

An important difference between Empire and *imperialism* emerges here. Rosa Luxemburg maintained that imperialism was likely to sustain capital while ultimately ensuring its demise. According to Hardt and Negri, the age in which one can speak of "peripheral" regions occupying a position outside of capital has passed (Hardt and Negri 2001: 333)—"The full realization of the world market is necessarily the end of imperialism" (Hardt and Negri 2001: 346). The old colonial binaries no longer apply. Center and periphery now coexist: *within* regions, countries, and cities. "Empire is characterized by the close proximity of extremely unequal populations, which creates a situation of permanent social danger and requires the powerful apparatuses of the society of control to ensure separation and guarantee the new management of social space" (Hardt and Negri 2001: 336–37).

Money is one of three modalities of power in this system, alongside communication and the bomb.[28] Although all three modalities of power operate through geopolitical centers of control—e.g., Washington (the bomb), New York (money), and Los Angeles (the ether)—these centers are constantly destabilized and reconfigured. Sovereignty therefore shifts from its old position of *transcendence* to the plane of *immanence* on which capital itself—and money—have hitherto belonged:

> In the passage of sovereignty toward the plane of immanence, the collapse of boundaries has taken place both within each national context and on a global scale. The withering of civil society and the general crisis of the disciplinary institutions coincide with the decline of nation-states as boundaries that mark and organize the divisions of global rule. The establishment of a global society of control that smooths over the striae of national boundaries goes hand in hand with the realization of the world market and the real subsumption of global society under capital. (Hardt and Negri 2001: 332)

Of Nixon's flotation of the dollar in 1971, Negri said that every relative parameter of values had now been dissolved. The socialist illusion that workers could be paid a wage that was commensurate to the value of what they produced had evaporated (Negri 2009: 130). We now lived in an *immeasurable world*, in which capital operates on "a smooth space defined by uncoded flows, flexibility, continual modulation, and tendential equalization" (Hardt and Negri 2001: 327). Money, as Baudrillard too was suggesting at around the same time, had no fixed anchor in this posttranscendental world (Negri 2009: 130). If money is the *perpetuum mobile*, capital "structures its mobility in a substantial way . . . determining flows which are more coalesced, ever quicker temporally and ever more integrated spatially" (Negri 2004: 255). Money's circulation is therefore synonymous with the expansion of capital's potency. Significantly, this argument collapses Deleuze and Guattari's distinction between payment money and finance money.

28   These modalities correspond to the imperial pyramid of power: to monarchy (the *bomb*), democracy (*ether*), and the aristocracy (*money*) (Hardt and Negri 2001: 335).

This view of money is consistent with what many scholars have said during the era of financialization, where money itself appears to have been financialized (Dodd 2011). The role of national currencies has been eroded in the face of the increasing power of global capital—alongside the inevitable dissolution of nation-state sovereignty (which, incidentally, Hardt and Negri see as *self-inflicted*). This is the tension identified by Susan Strange in her account of the post–Bretton Woods system, and which Barry Eichengreen characterizes as the conflict between the international monetary system (managed by states and central banks) and the international capital market. According to Eichengreen, high levels of capital mobility per se are not new. Since Bretton Woods, and increasingly since 2000, international capital mobility has returned to levels last seen before the First World War. The key difference now, he suggests, is that national governments, particularly in the West, have been placed under increasing *democratic* pressure to pursue exchange rate policies that are favorable to the domestic economy. This was less of a problem in earlier eras, especially before 1913, when it was possible to combine capital mobility and monetary autonomy. It is a chronic problem now, as it has been since 1973. The difference is political (Eichengreen 2008: 230).[29]

Significantly, Hardt and Negri suggest that it will be through *finance*—not territorial money—that new forms of global democracy will engage with economic practices and institutions. In *Commonwealth* (2009), they use Marx's account of money's dualism (see Chapter 2) to explore two faces of money. On one face (which they see as *politically neutral*), money is the universal equivalent, a medium of exchange. On the other face, money wields *command over labor*. This second face of money is an expression of power over social production (Hardt and Negri 2009: 294). By virtue of this duality, money expresses the social antagonism between the representation of the value of labor as the *general equivalent of commodity exchange* and the *real conditions of social production and exploitation* (Hardt and Negri 2009: 294). There are, they suggest, two traditional strategies for dealing with this dichotomy. The first is to destroy both faces of money, constructing an exchange system based on barter and dreaming of the return to an "antediluvian" world of use value. The second strategy is to preserve money's role as the representative of value but to destroy its power to command the social field of production (Hardt and Negri 2009: 295). This, broadly speaking, was Karatani's solution, as discussed in Chapter 2. Hardt and Negri argue for a third option, which involves conserving both faces of money but

---

29   It is open to question just how far capital controls are compatible with democracy.

wresting its control away from capital. The only means of achieving this, they suggest, is to open up money and finance to the diffuse forms of political agency that are emerging within the contested social spaces of Empire: "Might the power of money (and the finance world in general) to represent the social field of production be, in the hands of the multitude, an instrument of freedom, with the capacity to overthrow misery and poverty?" (Hardt and Negri 2009: 295).

This somewhat surprising contention puts an intriguing complexion on the conventional Marxist notion of collectivizing the means of production. In theoretical terms, the argument hinges on analytical connections between *money*, the *commons*, and the idea of the *multitude*. The concept of the multitude has been central to the work of a number of thinkers, such as Paolo Virno (2004) and Christian Marazzi (2008), with links to *Autonomia Operaia*. Most importantly for us here, the concept has been used to describe forms of political association that evade capture by conventional (state-centered) democratic structures. As a political form, a multitude is more fleeting and diffuse than a movement, while (potentially) retaining just as much influence and effect. Hardt and Negri do not provide a settled definition of the multitude; indeed, it seems to be in its nature to escape exact definition. The idea comes originally from Machiavelli and Spinoza, who distinguish between "multitude" and "people." Virno traces *people* back to Hobbes, and *multitude* to Spinoza. A *people* is characterized by unity and identity: it "belongs" to the state, which, in turn, "protects" it. The *multitude*—sometimes characterized as "mass"—is characterized by *plurality* and is essentially *unrepresentable*. Multitude is the existence of *many*, the form of *being* many. Virno argues that it is nevertheless a permanent form, not an episodic or interstitial form (Virno 2004).

As I mentioned briefly in Chapter 2, Marazzi described the multitude as an *effigy* of money, "the form of its sovereignty" (Marazzi 2008: 135). An effigy is a rough model, damaged or destroyed through protest or anger. "After having killed the god Pan, the multitude has to learn to protect itself from those momentary gods who, like little gremlins, haunt accidental events," Marazzi writes (Marazzi 2008: 135). The metaphor applies to territorial money at exactly that moment when the state that manages it is under greatest political pressure *qua* its role in economic and monetary governance. This metaphor implies that monetary sovereignty has collapsed: central banks are increasingly unable to affect monetary aggregates, leaving the state's lender of last resort function entirely subservient to financial gain. As a result, monetary policy turns into a "dependent variable of the financial markets" (Marazzi 2008: 135). Elsewhere, forms of political association developed through the Internet, especially social networking, such as Facebook and Twitter, are sometimes described in Spinozian terms. Importantly for Hardt and Negri's characterization, these are sites in which agents perform simultaneously as *producers*, *consumers*, and *conduits*—not as "citizens" or "subjects." In monetary terms, the obvious corollary of these sites—Marazzi's treatment fits here, too—are Internet-based monies and credit, such as peer-to-peer lending and Bitcoin. We examine these in more detail in Chapter 8.

According to Hardt and Negri, the European crisis of modernity that once preoccupied a range of thinkers—"From Nietzsche to Burkhardt, from Thomas Mann to Max Weber, from Spengler to Heidegger and Ortega y Gasset"—was really a sign that their own position at the center of the planet ("which they could understand only in terms of a modern mysticism") was coming to an end (Hardt and Negri 2001: 375). Likewise, Weber saw a solution to the crisis in legitimacy and sovereignty in "the irrational figures of charisma" (Hardt and Negri 2001: 377). Benjamin, too, invoked "a kind of secular eschatology [that] was the mechanism by which the experience of the crisis could be set free" (Hardt and Negri 2001: 377). Schmitt, finally, argued that "the horizon of sovereign practices can be cleared only by recourse to the 'decision'" (Hardt and Negri 2001: 377–78). All of these, however, are examples of an "irrational dialectic" that is incapable of providing an answer to the crisis these thinkers sought in their various ways to address. What is needed, rather, is a more diffuse concept of sovereignty.

Such arguments place a different complexion on the question of *monetary* sovereignty, shifting attention away from the national state (money)–global market (finance) dichotomy favored by Strange and others, toward a set of richer and more nuanced questions about how money and finance map onto diffuse configurations of economic and political agents, as well as economic forms such as peer-to-peer networks. The multitude is not a social body: it cannot be sovereign (Hardt and Negri 2005: 330). It cannot be *reduced* to a unity, and it does not *submit* to a unity.[30] If the age of Empire is the age of the multitude, this is because there is no unitary political subject, such as a party, people, or nation (Hardt and Negri 2005: 331). As they conceive it, moreover, the idea of the multitude inverts the way in which money has traditionally been held to *render all humans interchangeable*. The multitude is a *singularity* that, paradoxically, constitutes through *movement*: "Every

---

30   What this definition also misses, perhaps, is that a multitude can also reflect—sometimes quite cynically and dangerously—social differences derived from age, gender, sexuality, and race.

path is forged, mapped, and travelled" (Hardt and Negri 2001: 398). Virno described the post-Fordist multitude as a "multitude of virtuosos" (Virno 2004: 59). Virtuosos produce something that is not distinguishable (or separable) from the process of production itself; they are "simple locutors par excellence" (Virno 2004: 90). Performing from a score that he likens to Marx's concept of the general intellect (Virno 2004: 63), virtuosos are endlessly inventive (Virno 2004: 66). They do not simply *use* money, in other words, but are capable of creating it *ab initio*.

Intriguingly, this is also a description that fits Deleuze and Guattari's notion of *finance money*. Whereas payment money consists merely of "impotent money signs of exchange value" (Deleuze and Guattari 2004: 248), finance money is infinitely creative—and, literally, never-ending. Financial instruments are immaterial; nothing "real" is actually produced. In this sense, finance is virtuosic, which helps to explain why Hardt and Negri argue that, in the age of global capital it is through finance, which is "nothing but the power of money itself" (Hardt and Negri 2009: 158), that the multitude could assume its economically most radical forms. Just as the concept of abstract labor provided the focal point for constituting the industrial working class as a coherent and active collective subject, so the abstractions of money and finance can provide "instruments for making the multitude from the diverse forms of flexible, mobile, and precarious labour" (Hardt and Negri 2009: 295). Paradoxically, it is because finance eschews *direct* control over labor that it can do this:

> The key for finance is that it remains external to the productive process. It does not attempt to organize social labour-power or dictate how it is to co-operate. It grants biopolitical production its autonomy and manages nonetheless to extract wealth from it at a distance. (Hardt and Negri 2009: 289)

If money could be "reappropriated," then, it could "point in the direction of revolutionary activity today" (Hardt and Negri 2009: 295). Expressed in this way, the argument could be read against the theory that money is essentially a form of *debt*, although it is a curious feature of Hardt and Negri's work that it scarcely mentions this particular subject at all. Mitchell-Innes, whose argument are discussed in Chapter 3, suggested that each of us is capable of creating dollars simply by creating our own debt or writing out our own IOUs. Is this "virtuosic" practice of money creation what Hardt and Negri have in mind when they refer to money's reappropriation?

The multitude is a politically loaded concept, of course, so by proposing that it should create money *ab initio*, Hardt and Negri are equating money's creation with *resistance* in a way that echoes Marazzi's arguments about monetary sovereignty. But Hardt and Negri advance a positive, not only a negative, case for reappropriating money. This case comes through especially when they equate money—or more specifically, *finance*—with the idea of the *commons*. Finance, they maintain, is a "vast realm in which we can track down the spectres of the common" (Hardt and Negri 2009: 156). Through financial markets, money "tends to represent not only the present but also the future value of the common" (Hardt and Negri 2005: 151). Some sense of what they have in mind when they refer to reappropriating money is given when they state that the profits of finance capital "are probably in its purest form the *expropriation* of the common" (Hardt and Negri 2005: 151, italics added). The connection made here between finance and the commons needs to be read against Hardt and Negri's argument that the multitude "makes itself ... in the common" (Hardt and Negri 2009: x). Capitalism in its "information" phase has increasingly entailed bringing *social life in its entirety* under the command of capital (Hardt and Negri 2009: ix). At the core of post-Fordism are modes of "biopolitical" production in which subjectivity itself is produced and valorized. Marazzi calls this phenomenon *cognitive capitalism*, arguing that in its post-Fordist phase, capital produces value by extracting it from networks, the self-employed, outsourcing, and a new breed of "productive consumers" to whom are delegated functions that would usually be costs (Marazzi 2010: 52). Hence under cognitive capitalism, the notion of the accumulation of capital is transformed: "It no longer consists, as in the Fordist time, of investment in constant and variable capital (wage), but rather of investment in *apparatuses* of producing and capturing value produced outside directly productive processes" (Marazzi 2010: 55). Post-Fordist production uses information, codes, knowledge, images, and affects that require giving the producers themselves open access to the commons, for example, in the form of communication networks and information banks. Finance is central to this analysis.

Marazzi argues that finance is *cosubstantial* to cognitive capitalism. That is to say, it is integral to the production of goods and services from beginning to end, and its sources have proliferated to incorporate investment, saving, and borrowing from top to bottom of the social spectrum. In this sense, subprime mortgages were merely the logical outcome of a process that had been underway for several decades: "in order to function, this capitalism must invest in the *bare life* of people who cannot provide any guarantee, who offer nothing apart from themselves" (Marazzi 2010: 40, italics added). For Hardt and Negri, those qualities of *abstraction* that enable finance capital to be invested in "bare life" are at the same time merely the "distorted reflection" and "mystification" of the commons (Hardt and Negri 2009: 157). They draw an analogy with Simmel's argument that the metropolis—with its "detailed division of labour, impersonal encounters, time synchronicity, and so forth"—was a crucial site for cultivating the abstractions of money (Hardt and Negri 2009: 156). Just as finance's "dizzying" powers of abstraction provide a powerful means for speculating about the future, so they are equally capable of representing those social networks that are crucial to the production of future wealth: "Finance grasps the common in its broadest social form and, through abstraction, expresses it as value that can be exchanged" (Hardt and Negri 2009: 158). Negri expands on this possibility in a 2009 essay on communism. Citing Marx's statement in *Grundrisse* that money "is itself the community [*Gemeinwesen*] and can tolerate none other standing above it" (Marx 2005a: 223), he argues that money—"exchange value given a common form"—can essentially *become* community (*Gemeinwesen*). "Money has become the common land where once the Heimat [Homeland] lay, the consistency of populations at the end of the 'Gothic period,' when possession was organised into commons" (Negri 2009). *Gemeinwesen* is understood here as a totality. "It's here, it's the world, there is nothing else or other, no outside." The "revolutionary" aim of "reappropriating" finance must therefore be to penetrate these abstractions, to find within them those specters of the commons that lurk there.

Money's role in all of this is not easy to pin down, not least because Hardt and Negri's characterization of its nature appears to have shifted over time. In fact, they switch from one ambitious analogy for money, in *Empire*, to another, in *Commonwealth*. In the earlier text, they describe money as an "imperial arbiter" that is analogous to the bomb. It is a symbol of the most absolute power of all: the power to destroy. They underscore the point by invoking Aglietta and Orléan (1984, 1985, 1998), whose arguments we discussed in Chapter 1: money is *sovereign*; money is *violent*. Later, however, in *Commonwealth*, money is disarmed in order to be absorbed within a diffuse, disparate, and ever-mobile social formation. Money that once had the power to destroy life and community now has the potential to nourish the multitude. Perhaps there is no contradiction here but merely a reconfiguration of what we understand *sovereignty* to mean, above all in connection with money.

The argument that money is a distorted reflection—a mystification—of the commons resonates with Deleuze and Guattari's utopian claim that a fourth, postcapitalist socius[31] would be characterized by *economics without power*, in which debts are *finite* and *repayable* (Holland 1999: 96). This "new earth" would be a nomadic territory, free of market deterritorialization and decoding. There would—just as Hardt and Negri imply when they talk of an Empire in *permanent danger*—be a condition of perpetual crisis and revolution (Holland 1999: 109). In imagining such a future, Deleuze and Guattari wanted to rid Marx's theory of history of its traces of transcendental subjectivism and teleological reasoning. They, too, drew on Spinoza: for his eschewal of teleology, his anti-idealism, and his emphasis on striving or becoming, which they likened to the will to power. This is a Dionysian conception that recalls our discussion in Chapter 5. Time, too, is crucial to Negri's suggestion that finance—he specifically mentions derivatives—measures our striving for a collective economic future: "In stretching out within temporality, power wants to invest in the *to-come* as well" (Negri 2004: 238).

Two issues linger in this discussion. The first is about the idea of the multitude in which Hardt and Negri try to locate a diffuse notion of monetary sovereignty. The second issue concerns a distinction that appears only intermittently (and inconsistently) in their work. This is the distinction between payment money and finance money that we discussed earlier. In Deleuze and Guattari's analysis, money remains problematically dual, as states and banks struggle to maintain its fictional homogeneity, the monetary mass. Payment money has diminished in scale but not in importance. Hardt and Negri seek to avoid the oversimplifying juxtaposition of capital (finance) and state (money) that the globalization scholars and theorists of financialization tend to imply. In doing so, however, they collapse the very distinction that globalization throws into question, namely, between payment and finance money. In the next section, I turn to an example of "transnational" money, an empirical case that illustrates and operationalizes these dilemmas. This case is the hybrid, seemingly "post-Deleuzian" landscape of the Eurozone.

EUROLAND

When the euro was introduced on January 1, 1999, it was the world's second largest reserve currency, after the U.S. dollar. The Eurozone itself—often

---

31 The term "socius" is used by Deleuze and Guattari (2004) to refer to the "social body" that takes credit for production in any particular historical configuration. There are three—the Earth (for the tribe), the body of the despot (for the empire), and capital (for capitalism)—to which Hardt and Negri wish to add a fourth.

referred to as "Euroland" in its earliest days, with a mixture of affection and irony—was probably the clearest (and certainly the biggest) example of a formally homogeneous transnational monetary space. With no central political authority but only a central bank with a strict legal mandate to focus on only the technical efficiency of its currency, this was arguably deterritorialized money par excellence. But as I argue below, in practice the project of monetary integration in Europe turned out somewhat differently than its architects had hoped—and, perhaps, its critics had feared. Even the basic notion that the *same currency* would be circulating throughout the constituent member states of the Eurozone did not stand up to empirical scrutiny. In practice, the euro has never been *exactly* singular (Dodd 2005b). Moreover, its multiplicity has been more in evidence than ever during the protracted crisis that began with Greek sovereign debt and escalated when severe restrictions were placed on the mobility of euros deposited in Cypriot bank accounts. Euroland therefore provides an ideal case for discussing the arguments about territorial money that we have examined thus far in this chapter.

Before the euro's launch, there had been other monetary unions in the modern era, e.g., between Belgium and Luxemburg, a Latin Monetary Union, and a Scandinavian Monetary Union (Chown 2003). There are several monetary unions in Africa, and one has been planned for the Gulf states. The Eurozone, however, is the largest and most ambitious monetary union attempted so far, its members the most economically advanced. It was unprecedented in size, accounting for 20 percent of the world's output and 30 percent of its trade (Eichengreen 2008: 221). To some it was an anachronism, representing an outdated notion of Europe and a flawed theory of money (Goodhart 1997, 1998). It was also an elitist project, designed from the political center without considering regional variation; or insofar as such variation mattered, it was deliberately concealed. To others, the euro heralded a new world in which states were *pooling* monetary sovereignty, bringing into existence something that was unprecedented on such a scale: a currency that would be shared by people with different tax systems and governments, different languages, and distinct cultures (Dodd 2001). The euro presaged a new form of monetary cosmopolitanism in which states and nations were increasingly irrelevant. So which viewpoint has prevailed?

By 2013, it appears that both the euro's critics and supporters have finally reached a consensus: the currency cannot and will not survive in its current form. Member states of the Eurozone seem to have been irretrievably caught up in the backwash of the 2007–8 crisis, incorporated into the complex web of unredeemed debts that threaten the solvency of some of the largest banks on the continent. The problem cuts across national boundaries, as well as the border between public-sector and private-sector debt. Banks are exposed to sovereigns, and sovereigns to banks, in a complex web of cross-border obligations. Although many European banks seem to be in a condition of de facto insolvency, only a *banking* union appears capable of rescuing the *monetary* union, and even this outcome is by no means guaranteed. But if Euroland ceases to operate as a formally homogeneous monetary space, it is open to question what will replace it: a smaller Eurozone in northern Europe, a two-tier system (north and south), or complete dismantlement. Intriguingly, public sentiment within the Eurozone itself appears to be somewhat fatalistic on the issue. Whereas the citizens of several member states have rarely been exactly enthusiastic about the currency's existence, even those within the most troubled states today—Greece, Portugal, and Ireland, for example—appear skeptical about the benefits of withdrawing.[32]

From the earliest stages of planning for European monetary integration, much was made by critics of the risks involved in operating a single monetary policy in the Eurozone. There were debates, for example, over whether the Eurozone would be a viable optimum currency area (Mundell 1961; Goodhart 1998). The majority of economists believed that it would not be, although the architect of the theory in question, Robert Mundell, seemed to be broadly in favor of the euro project (McKinnon 2000). The euro convergence criteria (also known as the Maastricht criteria) based on Article 121(1) of the European Community Treaty, were designed to ensure that the Eurozone's constituent national economies were sufficiently in line to prevent the single monetary policy from working in favor of some member states and not others. The criteria were the result of compromise between French and German negotiators (Eichengreen 2008: 220), and they were subject to creative accounting (Aldcroft 2001). Just before the euro's launch in 1999 (as a virtual currency, with exchange rates fixed: notes and coins came three years later), the debt/GDP of Germany (61.3 percent) was too high, and in Belgium (122.2 percent) was more than twice as high as the entry criteria demanded, whereas that of the Netherlands ran at 70.4 percent. France's deficit/GDP was at exactly 3 percent, with Germany not far behind at 2.7 percent (Aldcroft 2001: 275). Had the Maastricht criteria been strictly applied, all countries but Luxemburg—with deficit/GDP at minus

---

32 A Pew Research Center survey conducted in March 2013 showed that in Greece, 69 percent of those polled wanted to keep the euro, as opposed to 25 percent who wanted to revert to their old national currency; the figures were similar in Spain (67/29), Germany (66/32), Italy (64/27), and France (63/37), although perhaps more noticeable here is that citizens in the strongest states appear more predisposed to exit than the others, see http://www.pewglobal.org/2013/05/13/the-new-sick-man-of-europe-the-european-union/, accessed June 15, 2013.

1.7 percent—would have had to be excluded. The Stability Pact, agreed at the Amsterdam Council in June 1997, subsequently provided for oversight into national budgets and fines for excessive deficits. This pact was breached by Portugal in 2002 and by France and Germany in 2003. All broke the 3 percent budget deficit ceiling. The pact was repeatedly "reformed" to allow for greater "flexibility" (Eichengreen 2008: 222). Earlier debates about the Eurozone's architecture, e.g., the constitution of the European Central Bank (ECB) and the stringency of its anti-inflationary stance, are now mirrored by arguments over its future, and especially over bailouts, with the same protagonists lined up (publicly, at least) on each side.

In terms of monetary policy, debates about the Eurozone's viability focus not just on the incapacity of Eurozone member states to set interest rates to suit their own domestic economic circumstances, although there were instances even early on where ECB monetary policy worked against the interests of some members states (De Grauwe 2012: ch. 9). Perhaps more important is the incapacity of member states to take advantage of the crucial connections among government spending, taxation, and credit creation. This incapacity occurs by virtue of the fact that the unit of account in which credit is created is not national. To all intents and purposes, governments spend (and borrow) in a foreign currency. From the neochartalist perspective, as discussed in Chapter 3, this means that any government spending not covered by taxes requires external financing (Wray 2006: 92–93).

To some experts and political actors, this was (and remains) a virtue, preventing states from using lax monetary policy to fund excessive spending. Such an argument misses three important points, however. First, just as most governments engaged in creative accounting to meet the convergence criteria, some would continue to do so to disguise high levels of borrowing. This appears to be what happened with Greece, where the government consistently misrepresented the size of the public debt (Tsoukalis 2012). In October 2009, the incoming Papandreou government revised the country's deficit figures, from 5.4 percent to around 12 percent of GDP. After the dissolution of the Statistical Service of Greece for producing false statistics, the figure was revised again—to 15.5 percent—in mid-2010. Second, it misses a problem that emerges from the other direction, which is that for most member states in the Eurozone, the costs of borrowing were artificially low during the first years of the project. Such was the case in Ireland and Spain, where interest rates fell to German and French levels shortly after the euro was launched (Conefrey and Fitzgerald 2010). The problem was exacerbated by the fact that inflation rates were higher, meaning that real interest rates were even lower. Thus as Eichengreen argues, "where policymakers would have liked higher interest rates to restrain demand where growth was unusually fast, monetary union delivered the opposite" (Eichengreen 2008: 223 n. 52). The effect was predictable: not only governments but also firms and households were able to borrow more. In Ireland, household debt grew from 48 percent of GDP in 1995, to 113 percent in 2004, and 176 percent in 2009 (Law Reform Commission of Ireland 2010). In Spain, household debt rose from just under 55 percent of GDP in 2000 to a peak of more than 95 percent in 2010.[33] Third, the single currency contributed to the buildup of imbalances within the Eurozone because exchange rate adjustments no longer existed to offset them (De Grauwe 2010). With around two-thirds of its exports going to other Eurozone countries, Germany benefited from a fixed exchange rate, as well as from borrowing within those very countries at levels that were subsequently deemed to be "excessive" by leading German politicians (Dumas 2010: 169–70). The negative effect of this borrowing on Germany (via the European Financial Stability Fund, and potentially outstanding liabilities within the interbank payments system, TARGET2) would not be felt until later (Sinn and Wollmerschaeuser 2011).

Knapp once said that as soon as two states agree to pool their control over money, they are no longer separate states (Knapp 1924: 41). From a similar perspective, Randall Wray described the euro as "the world's first modern experiment on a wide scale that would attempt to break the link between a government and its currency" (Wray 2006: 91). According to these definitions, when the original members of the Eurozone signed the Maastricht Treaty on February 7, 1992, they voluntarily surrendered a significant pillar of sovereignty, namely, the right to manage their own currencies. From the outset, however, the Eurozone was never a fully supranational entity but rather a hybrid. There was a central bank for the Eurozone as a whole, but no equivalent treasury. The Eurozone was sometimes compared to the United States, which also has a national central bank together with separate states that raise their own taxes. But the analogy is flawed because as witnessed during the crisis, the relationship between the central bank and separate states is more distant in the Eurozone than it is in the United States. Whereas a U.S. state in financial difficulty is likely to be bailed out by the central government, this is not the case in the Eurozone, where financial support is heavily conditional and politically problematic.

The euro was conceived as the economic vanguard of a broader political (and even constitutional) project (Habermas 2012: 1–12). After its first

---

33   Source: Economic Research, Federal Reserve Bank of St. Louis, http://research.stlouisfed.org/fred2/series/HDTGPDESA163N.

decade, however, some member states are facing debt burdens that are potentially comparable in scale—and effect—to those levied on Germany after the First World War.[34] The Eurozone's hybridity is relevant to the crisis not least because the political complexities of dealing with it have delayed important decisions and forced unsatisfying and undemocratic compromises to be made (Aglietta 2012). Although there is some evidence that some Eurozone countries are finding it increasingly difficult to make independent economic policy decisions,[35] strenuous efforts are being made to maintain a veneer of due process. The democratic costs of the crisis have been high (Streeck 2011), especially in Greece and Italy, where unelected leaders and governments were appointed to devise budgetary plans that were acceptable to holders of their public debt, as well as to other European leaders and the European Commission in Brussels. But these costs were quite high to begin with: there was barely majority support for the euro in some member states, and there was little evidence of a sense of common identity across the EU (Risse, Engelmann-Martin, et al. 1999; Risse 2003; Kaelberer 2004). These factors—democratic accountability, cultural identity, and properly coordinated governance—have been manifest in the crisis: contributing to its political intractability, driving the "blame game" being played out between weak and strong member states, and undermining the domestic legitimacy of bailouts and austerity programs that are framed in terms of either fear or guilt.

In light of this history, how should we conceptualize the Eurozone as a monetary space, and what does the crisis tell us about the future of territorial money? In terms of the arguments we have discussed in this chapter, the Eurozone appears to have assumed an increasingly *post-Deleuzian* shape during the crisis. The relationship between *finance* money and *payment* money is crucial to this change, manifesting itself as a fault line that was implicit in the system all along. From the outset, the Eurozone was designed as a *monetary* union but not a *financial* union. The Eurozone was constituted as a unified monetary space—with a *homogeneous monetary mass*, to use a phrase from Deleuze and Guattari—in the sense that there was a com-

---

34   "Germany's Carthaginian Terms for Greece," *The Telegraph*, February 12, 2012. Analogies with the period have been widely used: as a measure of the size of the debt, as an indicator of the severity of its effect on the debtor countries (Greece, Portugal, Ireland, Spain, and Italy), and as a political lever with which to pressure Germany in negotiations over how the debt should be managed.

35   The European Commission has proposed sending "fiscal inspectors" to monitor the policies of member states experiencing "severe difficulties." "Brussels plan to bring Eurozone to heel," *Financial Times*, November 22, 2011.

mon medium of exchange, i.e., payment money. But it was a fragmented financial space (finance money) with complex and uneven characteristics: diverse banking systems and bond markets and overlapping and contradictory public and private obligations for external financing (on which, as mentioned already, member states—*lacking their own currency*—would now depend above and beyond their tax revenues).

Initially, however, these fault lines were far from clear. Consider borrowing costs. Eurozone member states were able to borrow at lower interest rates because creditors (mostly bondholders) were treating them as part of a homogeneous *financial* space. That is to say, the introduction of the euro *appeared* to coincide with the unification of government bond yields across the Eurozone. Member states were borrowing at similar rates, reflecting that their debt carried a similar underlying degree of risk. It was as if a single yield curve had been established for the bonds issued by all Eurozone member states (Aglietta and Scialom 2003: 52). The effect of those lower borrowing costs on Greece was especially striking: starting with a yield of more than 11 percent in the beginning of 1998, Greek borrowing costs declined constantly to about 6 percent in mid-2000 and even further to a low at 3.3 percent in September 2005.[36] Similar examples can be seen among more recent entrants to Euroland, Slovenia and Slovakia. On joining the euro, both experienced a rapid lowering of bond rates. Indeed, almost all newly joining countries have experienced a boom upon joining the Eurozone.

If the Eurozone resembled a monetary *and* financial union during its first few years, it turned out to be an illusion. That single yield curve for sovereign bonds splintered midway through 2008, and spreads have been widening ever since. So why *have* rates diverged? One simple answer is that debt has been used in a different way since the global crisis. De Grauwe, for example, points to the "flight to safety" of investors dumping private debt and turning to low-risk sovereign debt. Crucially, this statement means that those Eurozone governments with a stronger reputation have enjoyed a lowering of rates, whereas those countries considered weaker could not draw the same benefit. Spreads have therefore increased. Some states—Greece and Ireland, particularly—saw their rates actually rise, which may simply be a direct function of a rising perceived credit risk (De Grauwe 2012: 243). Though governments, households, and firms may have benefited from

---

[36] To make matters worse, *real* interest rates were even lower than *nominal* rates because inflation rates were higher. Thus as Eichengreen notes, "where policymakers would have liked higher interest rates to restrain demand where growth was unusually fast, monetary union delivered the opposite" (Eichengreen 2008: 223 n. 52).

lower borrowing costs, the debts themselves were not shared. Each member state has its own financing arrangements, as has been made brutally plain since the crisis began. The costs of borrowing for households and small businesses have also diverged significantly during the Eurozone crisis. By February 2013, average mortgage interest rates were 2.86 percent in Germany, 3.97 percent in France, 3.94 percent in Italy and 3.26 percent in Spain. For loans under one million euros, small businesses were paying on average 2.92 percent interest in Germany, 4.35 percent in Italy, 5.17 percent in Spain, and well above 6 percent in Greece and Portugal.[37] Still now, in the heat of the crisis when, short of disbanding the Eurozone altogether, only a form of sovereign debt mutualization appears to offer a solution to the imbalances that have been building up, the idea does not enjoy wide political support (but see De Grauwe and Mosen 2009; Soros 2009). Few member state governments, let alone their domestic electorates, seem willing to countenance any form of shared borrowing, whether in the form of common bonds, another form of debt mutualization, or a permanent common rescue fund.[38] The proposals to establish a banking union support this argument because they are specifically designed to disentangle private from public debt, not to mutualize the latter.

Intriguingly, the Eurozone crisis might be seen as reversing the terms of Susan Strange's distinction between national money and international finance, with the latter (i.e., sovereign debt) remaining state-centered despite the transnationalism of the euro itself as a currency (Dodd 2011). However, the Eurozone never has been a unified *monetary* space. Although a single currency—and a single money of account—has been operating in Euroland since the currency's inception in 1999, on closer examination matters were never so simple. This argument can be made in terms of the euro's *materiality*, its operation as a *unit of account*, its *value*, and its *mobility*. Each member state (alongside San Marino, Monaco, and the Vatican State) had its own unique set of coins. Even more importantly, the euro lacked unity as a money of account, not just because there were *thirteen* such schemes oper-

---

37   See "Euro Zone Lending Rates Differ Drastically by Country," *Wall Street Journal* "Real Time Economics" blog, April 5, 2013, http://blogs.wsj.com/economics/2013/04/05/euro-zone-lending-rates-differ-drastically-by-country/, accessed May 9, 2013.

38   This is true despite the fact that some of the largest banks in Europe have a high degree of exposure to the debt of various Eurozone sovereigns: UniCredit of Italy and BNP Paribas of France hold bonds worth €80 billion each, whereas BBVA, Intesa SanPaolo, ING Bank, Commerzbank, and the Royal Bank of Scotland hold between €60 and 70 billion each. Some €47.9 billion of Greek sovereign debt is held by three French banks, BNP Paribas, Société Générale, and Crédit Agricole (BIS).

ating within the Eurozone before the launch of notes and coins between 1999 and 2002, but also because even after "real" notes and coins had replaced the old national currencies altogether, a significant number of people who used the new currency on an everyday basis were regularly *converting between* euro-denominated prices and their old currencies.[39] In this respect, the euro is comparable to other intellectual systems such as weights and measures,[40] language, and time: they are endlessly malleable, despite (or even because of) the imposition of dominant forms. Transferring permanently from one such conceptual system to another (as opposed to constantly switching between them) is sociologically complex, culturally problematic, and politically loaded. In Euroland, the process has never really been complete.

In terms of spending power, too, the phrase "a euro is a euro" has never quite applied in the Eurozone. Recently, the Eurosystem's new Household Finance and Consumption Survey (HFCS), released for the first time in April 2013, generated colorful headlines[41] because it suggested—perversely, it would seem, in light of the prevailing economic situation—that inhabitants of the Eurozone's troubled "peripheral" states (especially Greece, Cyprus, Portugal, and Spain) were *better off* than their counterparts in Germany (ECB 2013). The survey was based on data suggesting, for example, that the average net wealth of Cypriot households was (at €671,000) three

39   For small purchases, 22 percent of those surveyed were calculating prices in their old national currencies, and a further 21 percent were calculating in both currencies, and for larger ("exceptional") purchases such as a house or car, the figures were 40 percent and 29 percent, respectively. To put it another way, in 2006 only 29 percent of those surveyed were calculating prices in euros when making large purchases. Among those calculating in old currencies, most often were Belgians (65 percent), Dutch (57 percent), and Austrians (55 percent). See Eurobarometer Flash Survey No. 193, http://ec.europa.eu/public_opinion/flash/fl193_en.pdf. Five years on, in 2011, 29 percent of those surveyed were still converting prices back into their old currencies for small purchases, and 47 percent in the case of larger purchases. Bearing in mind that the Eurozone had enlarged by that time to include Malta (2008), Slovakia (2009), and Slovenia (2007), some of the established member states were still well represented among those who were calculating in their old currencies for larger purchases, with the French at 47 percent, Germans at 48 percent, Portuguese at 49 percent, and Austrians at 51 percent. The 2011 data show some strong demographic characteristics: the tendency to calculate in old currencies correlates positively with age and negatively with education; women, too, are on the whole more likely to convert prices from euros to their old currencies. See Eurobarometer Flash Survey No. 335, http://ec.europa.eu/public_opinion/flash/fl_335_en.pdf.

40   In Britain, the weights and measures question—imperialism versus the metric system—is heavily overlaid with nationalist and colonial baggage (Geyer 2001).

41   For example, "The Poverty Lie: How Europe's Crisis Countries Hide their Wealth," *Der Spiegel*, April 17, 2013, see http://www.spiegel.de/international/europe/poor-germany-it-is-time-for-a-debate-on-euro-crisis-burden-sharing-a-894398.html, accessed June 15, 2013.

times higher than that in Germany.[42] But on closer scrutiny, what the survey revealed were the consequences of using a *single unit of account* throughout an area in which there are *variable inflation rates*. In a monetary union, adjustment can only occur through real (as opposed to nominal) movements in wages and prices (not via exchange rates). In southern Europe, wages and prices have increased steadily since the euro was launched, whereas in Germany they have not. Hence, the "finding" that Cypriot households are on average wealthier than German households is a monetary illusion. What it really suggests is that euros are actually *worth* more in Germany than elsewhere in Euroland.

The Eurozone constitutes a *shared* monetary and financial space—not a *union*—in myriad complex ways. Because it lacks a corresponding infrastructure of governance and law, however, Euroland is—perhaps surprisingly—no "Empire" in Hardt and Negri's sense. Member states of the Eurozone may have embarked on a collective (albeit partial) act of self-dissolution when the Maastricht Treaty was signed, but these governments and their officials have remained key (albeit also chronically weak) players in the unfolding crisis. In the language of the "old" international relations field, overlapping debt within the Eurozone (unlike the currency itself) has been the outcome of the repeated failure to tackle problems as and when they arose.[43] In the language of Deleuze and Guattari, overlapping debt is the outcome of the increasing complexity of financial flows, as well as their opacity. According to this latter view, there is little that governments could have done anyway to prevent this situation because the Eurozone was developing according to a different logic: not of statecraft, but of *capital*.

Euroland appears to have entered a stage of *permanent economic crisis*, much as Agamben described Italy two decades ago (Agamben 2000). There is nothing particularly unusual about this situation, of course. Many countries in the global north have been crisis-ridden since 2007–8. But what makes the situation in the Eurozone intriguing is that its member states lack control over the medium that governments invariably turn to when facing an economic crisis. In Schmitt's terms (Schmitt 2006), *money* plays a crucial role in the politics of exception, especially in relation to *sovereign*

---

42 The survey drew criticism for inconsistencies in the way the data were compiled. For example, median rather than mean values were used, which skews the study toward homeowners, of which there are relatively few in Germany, see Wolfgang Münchau, "The Riddle of Europe's Single Currency with Many Values," *Financial Times*, April 14, 2013.

43 Susan Strange sometimes used the term "non-decisions" to describe political inaction that nevertheless has significant consequences; indeed, it was central to her account of the development of the international monetary system (Strange 1986: ch. 2).

insolvency. Throughout a series of financial crises during the past two decades—from emerging markets, to South American and other sovereign defaults, through to the current Eurozone crisis—the problems are invariably worse when countries borrow in foreign currency. It is less risky for a government to borrow in its own currency: from the perspective of both the *lender* (avoiding shocks from currency mismatches) and *borrower* (since defaulting in the domestic currency is politically disastrous). In the Eurozone, the state cannot directly monetize; it has no power to do this independently. Money, then, is critical to the exception that sovereignty fundamentally entails, and it is precisely the *absence* of this sovereignty within the Eurozone that has left some of its member states resorting to repressive policy measures—forms of financial as well as literal violence—to make the necessary adjustments and accommodations to the Eurozone itself as a hybrid monetary space. The fiction of the euro as homogeneous money is at the heart of this violence. In Schmitt's terms, the power of exception within the Eurozone, insofar as it applies to a country such as Greece, has been appropriated by the so-called *Troika*, i.e., the International Monetary Fund, the European Central Bank, and the European Commission.

Schmitt argues that the threshold of territorial space, the margin between inside and outside, is one of sovereignty's most important conditions of possibility. This recasting of political theory around *exclusion*, not inclusion, allows us to see the project of European monetary integration in a different way. Sovereignty establishes itself on this very border, where violence often arises because of its maintenance. According to Balibar, Schmitt's theory, elaborated during the "European civil war" in the early twentieth century helps to capture European integration at precisely such a conjuncture, in which borders are key. In *We, The People of Europe?* (2004), Balibar uses Bodin's *Six Books of the Commonwealth* (originally published in 1576, 1992 cited here) to theorize the distinction between *absolute* and *popular* sovereignty. The aspect of his account that is of interest to us is where Bodin refers to two "limitations" of sovereignty. A limitation is on the *outside* of sovereignty, according to Balibar: it is "where the absoluteness of its power comes to an end" (Balibar 2004: 145). By Bodin's reckoning, it does so by virtue of religion and money. About the question of money, Balibar picks up the old name for the administration of finances, the *fiscus*.[44] This term refers to questions of who monopolizes the coinage, who can be taxed, how much, and so on. As Balibar sees it, the question of the *fiscus* (who controls

---

44   Latin for "basket," the *fiscus* was the treasury of the Roman emperor, so-called because the money was stored in baskets.

money and finance) alongside the question of *religion* (who controls manifestations of religious belief), define the limit of sovereignty.

As noted earlier, Bodin maintained that the sovereign should assert the right of *coinage* (*nummus*) just as he or she asserts the right of *law* (*nomos*): there cannot be private money. However, taxes are a "delicate" matter: the idea of the sovereign having to seek "consent" to the levying of new taxes is a clear limitation on sovereignty. Bodin invokes what Balibar calls a "prudential" rule, i.e., that "taxes imposed on the people against their will either are never collected or cause revolts capable of endangering the state itself" (Balibar 2004: 146). As a consequence, *fiscus* affects the whole of sovereignty, piece by piece: it "forms a totality in which monetary policy and tax policy must balance ... because the mastery of finances is the condition of the autonomy of the political in all other domains (just as the mastery of beliefs is the condition of obedience to power and to the law in general)" (Balibar 2004: 146). As far as *absolute* sovereignty is concerned, money is one of its fundamental limits—not its foundation:

> sovereignty will only be truly absolute if, by regular means (thinkable as the development of its own order, and thus excluding dictatorship or the state of exception), it manages to interiorize its own limits, that is, to incorporate in the field of the political what at first seemed to escape it, showing the persistence of a remainder: the regulation of beliefs (whose type is constituted by religious faith and its intellectual, moral, and cultural continuations) and the regulation of economic processes by way of the *fiscus* (monetary and fiscal policy, unified by taxation and the public debt). (Balibar 2004: 147)

What, then, of *popular* sovereignty? This is Balibar's "perilous leap," when sovereignty "passes from a princely to a popular form, that is, to emerge as truly state sovereignty" (Balibar 2004: 145). The argument is complex but especially interesting where he maintains that the two fundamental limitations of absolute sovereignty—religion or *Bildung* (nowadays, culture: "morality and education" have "taken over from religion," he says (Balibar 2004: 152)), and money or *fiscus* (or crucially: finance)—are sites on which civil society and state codetermine each other. Regarding *Bildung*, this is a question of "finding forms of cultural communication within the people" (Balibar 2004: 152). Regarding *fiscus*, this is "the sense in which mastery of public finances allows the tendency towards 'savage' capitalism to be checked, at least in internal space, by a combination of monetary and social policies" (Balibar 2004: 152–53). A little further on, Balibar describes this function as providing "forms of social mediation of class antagonisms that are not pure show" (Balibar 2004: 153).

The theoretical context of Balibar's discussion is a particular understanding of European integration as a conjuncture in which borders are key. The danger, he argued a decade ago, is that the EU would contribute to the formation of a kind of apartheid. For example, by defining European "nationals" (versus "immigrants") more strictly than had been the case hitherto, the Maastricht Treaty created "a new discrimination that did not exist within each national space" (Balibar 2004: 44). The euro has added an economic dimension to this discrimination—reinforcing, mediating, and transgressing the boundaries of which Balibar speaks. In these terms, the very existence of the euro has reconfigured not only Euroland itself but also "Europe," in three important ways.

First, the euro has *subdivided the EU*, between core and periphery. But this is not a simple division between where the euro circulates and where it does not: 20–25 percent of euros circulate outside the Eurozone; in Montenegro and Kosovo (both EU), Mayotte, Saint Pierre, Miquelon, Akrotiri, and Dhekelia (all non-EU) the euro is the sole currency. Membership is a question of rights and representation, of having a vote on the board of the European Central Bank (ECB), for example. It is also, as we are seeing now, a question of possible redistribution. Strikingly, the Eurozone crisis has often been framed in imperialist language, using terms such as "core" and "periphery" to capture the imbalances that underpin it. The so-called core consists of Germany, France, and other (mostly) northern European states, whereas the periphery consists of the so-called PIIGS (Portugal, Italy, Ireland, Greece, and Spain), which are mainly southern European states. Hardt and Negri argue that such language is outdated. Transnational space is inclusive: that threshold between the inside and the outside that was such a crucial vantage point for social critique no longer exists (Hardt and Negri 2001: 183), and its periphery has been internalized. The world is no longer divided into opposing camps (e.g., center vs. periphery, First vs. Third World) but is made up of "partial and mobile differences" (Hardt and Negri 2001: 144). This is surely right. Even in the Eurozone today, which appears internally divided, we are as likely to find peripheral and marginalized spaces inside Berlin as on, say, the southern borders of the Eurozone as a whole. Within Empire as Hardt and Negri conceive it, extremely unequal populations often exist in close proximity of each other, creating a situation of "permanent social danger" that frequently requires the oppressive management of social space (Hardt and Negri 2001: 336).

Second, the Eurozone has *created its own economic marginals*, i.e., states that did not qualify for membership according to a set of rules (the Maastricht convergence criteria) that were contested and negotiable and that have been "broken" several times since then—new members, potential members, and perhaps soon, ex-members. From the beginning, Greece was the most marginal case on entry, allegedly requiring the accountants' sleight of hand to be included in the original euro grouping, slightly late but before the introduction of notes and coins, in 2000. It is ironic that those similar accounting "tricks" are being blamed now as the Greek government is accused of covering up its fiscal difficulties.

Third, Euroland *created its own monetary borders*, i.e., zones of indeterminacy where money flows beyond tax and regulation, and where states prohibit trafficking in certain people and goods. Money, like language, flows into border zones, where it is more difficult to exclude, and indeed it may help lubricate the flow of people and goods beneath and around the fiscal state. When the finance minister of the euro's core state—its major surplus state—argues that another state ought to be "allowed" to go bankrupt, he implies that bankruptcy is a necessary precondition for withdrawal of a state from the Eurozone.[45] This bankruptcy would mean the state's downgrade not from core to periphery but from inside to outside, to marginal status—its relegation to the economic hinterland of the Eurozone, but perhaps not of the EU. An extreme version of this interpretation would be to imagine Eurozone membership as a revolving door, granted and withdrawn according to regular measures of good behavior—this is not something that was ever envisaged, not anything that could remotely work. Schäuble (2010) surely did not mean this—but his logic implied it.

In narrow terms, the euro has threefold significance for what Balibar has to say. First, it is often pointed out that the entailed monetary integration without any other kind of integration—cultural or political, for example—would be something like an integration of *fiscus* but not of *Bildung*. But the euro actually divided the *fiscus*, and we are seeing the consequences of this division. Second, it is ironic to find that the Eurozone—where, precisely, issues of sovereignty have been placed in question for more than a decade—is

---

45   I refer to Wolfgang Schäuble, who as German Finance Minister wrote in March 2010: "Emergency liquidity aid may never be taken for granted. It must, on principle, still be possible for a state to go bankrupt. Facing an unpleasant reality could be the better option in certain conditions. The *monetary union* and the euro are best protected if the eurozone remains credible and capable of taking action, even in difficult situations. This necessarily means suspending an unco-operative member state's voting rights in the Eurogroup. A country whose finances are in disarray must not be allowed to participate in decisions regarding the finances of another euro member. Should a eurozone member ultimately find itself unable to consolidate its budgets or restore its competitiveness, this country should, as a last resort, exit the monetary union while being able to remain a member of the EU" (Schäuble 2010).

the site on which we are now witnessing what has been referred to as a "sovereign" debt crisis. And third, Balibar's "Keynesian" interpretation of popular sovereignty involves (in the economic field) the principle of generating "fiscal" institutions that can mediate the relationship between state and civil society. These are institutions he describes as, first, protecting society internally from the savagery of capitalism from the outside, and second, mediating society's class antagonisms.

After the Cypriot banking crisis in March 2013, capital controls were introduced in Cyprus to circumvent the outflow of euros from local bank accounts (including what would be left of the larger accounts once the "bail-in" levy had been applied).[46] From the end of March 2013, every bank account in Cyprus was subject to a monthly transfer limit of €5,000. To all intents and purposes, then, Cypriot euros are now a *parallel* currency. They are exchangeable with non-Cypriot euros at a rate of one to one only up to a limit. They are, in this sense, the special purpose money of the Eurozone. Similar issues have arisen elsewhere in Euroland during this crisis. In Greece, a "slow motion bank run" has been underway since the country's sovereign debt crisis blew up in late 2011. Here, the onus is on moving funds *out* of the Greek banking system and into safe haven elsewhere in the Eurozone. At its height, Greek banks were reporting €30 million of outflow of funds into other Eurozone member states. This was not a conventional bank run, fueled by fear of bank failure, but a run caused by prevailing concerns about exchange rate risk, and more specifically, about the prospect of an instantaneous devaluation of Greek deposits should the country exit the Eurozone altogether.[47] Here too, then, not all euros were equal: not because they could *not* move but because of an overwhelming sense that they *had* to.

If, in Schmitt's terminology, money is itself the *exception*, then in principle, as I have already argued, the power to invoke it within the Eurozone now lies not with the sovereign state but with the *Troika*. But legally, the ECB has been prevented from acting as a central bank normally would under such circumstances. According to Article 123 of the 2007 Lisbon Treaty, the ECB is prohibited from providing credit facilities directly to public bodies. Likewise, the bank is deprived of the means to intervene lawfully in bond markets. The Eurozone therefore provides an especially powerful

---

46   After initially proposing a levy or tax on all deposit accounts—9.9 percent for those too big to be covered by the EU-mandated €100,000 deposit guarantee, and 6.75 percent for the smaller depositors—the government reached a compromise whereby only larger depositors would be hit.

47   See Gavyn Davies, "The Anatomy of the Eurozone Bank Run," *Financial Times*, May 20, 2012.

and surprisingly clear-cut example of money beyond the state. Although the euro is a transnational currency, it is not a currency into which the sovereignty of Eurozone member states has effectively been displaced. Not only are those states deprived of the power of exception that money makes possible, but also there is no other corresponding transnational body that is empowered in this way. The "sovereignty" that member states surrendered was not a contractual relationship—characterized by belonging, community, and inclusion—but the very power of suspension in which sovereignty ultimately resides.[48] As a consequence, they enfeebled themselves as debtors.

CONCLUSION

In *Time for Revolution*, Negri draws on Schmitt to define a particular mode of temporality, which he calls the time of command (2004). He suggests that Schmitt's classic formulation ("The sovereign is he who decides on the exception") applies not only to the state of war, but also to *economic* crisis. Likewise in *Means Without End* (1996), Giorgio Agamben argues that "crisis ... constitutes the internal motor of capitalism in its present phase, much as the state of exception is today the normal structure of political power" (Agamben 2000: 133). The state of exception "requires that there be increasingly numerous sections of residents deprived of political rights." Likewise, economic crisis "demands not only that the people of the Third World become increasingly poor, but also that a growing percentage of the citizens of the industrialised societies be marginalised and without a job" (Agamben 2000: 133). Consider the analogy more closely now: to be deprived of political rights is a process whose "outer limits" consist of the condition whereby citizens are "reduced to naked life" (Agamben 2000: 133). This is bare life, *la nuda vita*, a concept Agamben appears to have taken from Benjamin, whose notion of *das bloße Leben* is invoked in two early essays, "Fate and Character" (1921) and "Critique of Violence" (1921), and sometimes translated as *mere life*. "For with mere life," Benjamin writes, "the rule of law over the living ceases" (Benjamin 1996b: 250). As we saw above, Marazzi also used the expression in his description of subprime lending, when he said that capitalism must invest in "the *bare life* of people who cannot provide any guaran-

---

48   Following Schmitt, Agamben defines sovereignty in terms of the capacity to suspend the rule of law. He describes the declaration of a state of exception: the ban. It is an idea that "calls into question every theory of the contractual origin of state power and, along with it, every attempt to ground political communities in something like a 'belonging,' whether it be founded on popular, national, religious, or other identity" (Agamben 1998: 181).

tee, who offer nothing apart from themselves" (Marazzi 2010: 40, italics added). In Agamben, it is the ban—the exception—that produces bare life, creating a zone of indeterminacy between *bios* (or life as defined in relation to the *polis*) and *zoē* (or life as defined in relation to *oikos*). In law, this zone is created by a suspension of human rights: the person who is subjected to it is placed at the threshold of the law and rendered as an outcast, a refugee.[49] These two logics, exception and crisis, meet in political protest, in those makeshift camps that form the amorphous Occupy movement.

The insolvent state is the state that fails to pay its debts. An insolvent state that lacks the capacity to create its own money is—in relation to the international monetary system—in a position that is analogous to the outcast. Its debts are entered into through bonds taken out as if between private parties: the state is essentially treated as a debtor, much as a firm or household would be. According to Deleuze and Guattari, this is a problem associated with finance money. By contrast, collective or socialized debt is the mechanism for moving surplus around the group, similar to gift exchange as Mauss described it, through the incurring and meeting of obligations—or as Simmel would say, "claims upon society." This is a problem associated with payment money. Such a group cannot be insolvent other than through the collapse of its own internal structures. The Eurozone crisis exposes the logical conflict that arises here: debts cannot be transformed from one logic (private debt) to another (collectivized debt). Arguments about the Eurozone becoming a "transfer union" reveal the gap that has opened up between two flows—payment money and finance money—that central mechanisms such as the stabilization fund and the banking union have been conceived to fill. But in principle, such a gap is present in *all* modern monetary systems. Two forms of sovereignty can disguise the gap: first, the state's monopoly over *law* (the state defaults and its debts are restructured); and second, its monopoly over *money* (devaluation). Where the Eurozone is distinctive, arguably, is that these measures of sovereignty have fallen out of line.

When Goethe envisaged humanity above the nations, he implied that people could cohere in spite of their supposed allegiance to the state, around more abstract ideals such as their common humanity. At its most

---

49   As Agamben describes it, the camp is a piece of land that is "placed outside the normal juridical order, but is nevertheless not simply an external space" (Agamben 2000: 133). Compared to the Weimar Republic in which Schmitt was formulating his theory of sovereignty, however, the camp, and the exception in general, have become normal. This is a "new juridico-political paradigm in which the norm becomes indistinguishable from the exception" (Agamben 1998: 168–69). The territorial aspect of Agamben's characterization is important because it recalls what Schmitt said about the New World as a designated zone of "free" space.

lyrical, perhaps this is what the idea of the multitude is meant to convey, besides the more radical idea that its members (by definition) refuse to be political subjects. Simmel, too, might have had something similar in mind when he insisted, *contra* Durkheim, that society is a conceptual abstraction much more than it is an empirical reality: which begs the question, of course, as to what he meant when he described money as a claim upon society. Simmel preferred the concept of sociality as the focal point of sociology, which denotes something like an intermingling, a process of *being* social as opposed to a state of *belonging* to society. This is what I have been trying to capture when referring to the *social life* of money. The discussion in this chapter suggests that this more fluid conception of sociality—and, alongside it, notions such as Spinoza's multitude—might shed light on some of the most significant and intriguing ways in which money is advancing beyond the state. What I have in mind here is not an *Über*-currency—the euro fits that description well enough, as, arguably, would a global currency—but rather forms of money that are actively created by their users, as part of the commons. This might seem like a naively utopian prospect. But before addressing that very possibility, we first need to come to grips with its conceptual implications. Besides the political issues that such a prospect throws up, some of which have been considered in this chapter, the idea of a user-driven money suggests that we need to reconfigure notions of agency and culture in relation to money. This will be our aim in the next chapter.

7 CULTURE

> Certainly money means something very different in the minds and the behaviour of people of different cultures. It may be difficult or impossible to reduce its *cultural significance* to a common denominator for different periods. But this kind of interpretation of meaning is not what concerns monetary science. For the latter, what is involved is rather—if we must speak of "meaning" at all—*that* meaning which lies in the *function* of money in the economic process. For *this* meaning the *other* ("cultural significance") is relevant only insofar as it influences the actual behaviour of people with respect to money; and here it is again a question of performance (to be answered in the individual case) whether one succeeds in grasping these elements of a given cultural environment which are essential for the explanation of monetary history.
> **JOSEPH SCHUMPETER, "MONEY AND CURRENCY"**[1]

Schumpeter's insistence that culture is "not what concerns monetary science" typifies a way of approaching money in classical social and economic thought that has never really gone away—even though it has been persuasively challenged by scholars in sociology and anthropology. Revealingly perhaps, though many of the discussions so far in this book have touched upon the question of money's relationship with culture, none has focused on it explicitly and directly. As Schumpeter implies, that relationship is important because it deepens our understanding of how money is used in different social contexts. Culture is important to understanding the ways in which people shape money for themselves, bending it to their own purposes and resisting its capacity to homogenize everything it touches. This idea ought to be compelling to "monetary science," not least because culture influences what money actually *does*.

1   Schumpeter 1991: 521–22.

CHAPTER 7

The importance of culture to money is demonstrated by returning to the discussion of the euro from the last chapter. When the Eurozone was established, a paradox was revealed that illustrates both the importance of money's cultural context and the fact of its glaring absence from mainstream monetary debate. Both critics and architects of the euro took seriously the prospect that the new currency might eventually contribute to the formation of greater levels of social and political cohesion across member states of the Eurozone. Within academia, the view was advanced that the euro might even be a tool of identity creation (Risse, Engelmann-Martin, et al. 1999; Helleiner 2001; Risse 2003; Kaelberer 2004). In its practical design, however, the Eurozone was made to conform as far as possible to the classical view of money reflected in Schumpeter's remarks as quoted above: namely, as a *thing* that operates purely on the basis of rational self-interest. For example, the European Central Bank was directed to focus on the purely technical question of price stability, free from cultural or political considerations. The ideal of a one-size-fits-all monetary policy applicable to all member states seemed entirely in keeping with this sanitized view of money as a culturally neutral landscape. If the euro was implicitly culturalist in its *aspirations*, then, it was dogmatically Mengerian in its *design*. In practical terms, it was as if the project had been steered by the classical, nineteenth century view of money as a radical leveler that bleaches all color from the world and corrodes every distinction it encounters (Helleiner 2001: 1–2).

The belief that money is like a cultural acid that modern society mystifyingly inflicts upon itself still has populist appeal, which has if anything increased in the wake of the 2008 crisis. In *How Much Is Enough?* (2012), Skidelsky and Skidelsky argue that modern capitalism embarked upon a Faustian bargain whereby capitalist money making has been "stripped of its ethical opprobrium" (Skidelsky and Skidelsky 2012: 50) and valued as a tool to alleviate economic poverty, but at the price of greater cultural poverty based on the belief that "all creativity and innovation ... needs to be stimulated by money" (Skidelsky and Skidelsky 2012: 9). Similarly, in *What Money Can't Buy* (2012), Michael Sandel complains that "We live at a time when almost everything can be bought and sold." He continues: "We need to ask whether there are some things that money should not buy" because "commercialism erodes commonality" (Sandel 2012: 5, 7, 202). Pope Francis, too, has joined the chorus of complaint against the cultural damage that has been inflicted by money in the neoliberal age.[2] Seemingly keen to promote

---

2   See *Il Fatto Quotidiano*, May 16, 2013, http://www.ilfattoquotidiano.it/2013/05/16/papa-francesco-basta-con-feticismo-del-denaro-corruzione-e-evasione/595811/, accessed June 16, 2013.

the austere image projected by his chosen papal name, Francis attacked the "dictatorship of an economy without purpose nor truly human face,"[3] arguing that "the worship of the ancient golden calf has found a new and ruthless image in the fetishism of money."[4] Money, he concludes, must "serve and not govern."[5] These are all familiar arguments that one could easily find in classical social thought; one could even be forgiven for considering them banal.

The discussion in this chapter deals with two sides of the argument about the relationship between money and culture. The first looks at how *money shapes culture*, and the second considers how *culture shapes money*. The dichotomy derives from competing interpretations of money's capacity to turn quality into quantity. In classical thought, this function gave rise to a starkly modernist view of money as culturally neutral at best, and at worst, culturally corrosive. The approach is typified in the writings of Marx, Nietzsche, Simmel, and Polanyi. Against this, a strong literature has developed, mainly during the last quarter of the twentieth century, which advances the view that money is richly embedded in and shaped by its social and cultural context. What is needed, according to this view, is a theory of money's *qualities*, not simply an account of its role as a *quantifier*. Such a theory needs to focus not only on how money is "marked" by cultural practices from the outside but also on a deeper level, on the way in which those practices shape money *from within*, for example, by defining its scales of value. Moreover, these approaches view money as multifarious, as *monies*, rather than as a unitary phenomenon, as *money*.

Examining the way in which *culture shapes money* is important for several reasons. First, it draws attention to money's multiplicity, i.e., the variety of material forms it takes, as well as the range of accounting systems it uses, often in the same social settings. Secondly, cultural factors are crucial in determining why and how these media and accounting systems are adopted as money in the first place. Third, analyzing money culturally enables us to focus on the practices and meanings that shape money without reducing them to economic functions and institutions: such an approach makes it impossible to reify money as an autonomous and mechanistic *thing* and demands that we see it instead as an inherently social *process*. Fourth, exploring cultural factors in money's reproduction points to

[3]   "La dittatura dell'economia senza volto né scopo realmente umano."
[4]   "L'adorazione dell'antico vitello d'oro ha trovato una nuova e spietata immagine nel feticismo del denaro."
[5]   "Il denaro ... deve servire e *non governare*."

noninstitutional dynamics in money's development, directing us away from states and banks and toward social relations that are equally important to the formation of monetary circuits. There may be important tensions here, too, not just between states and classes but also between distinctive systems of meaning and modes of valuation. These are tensions that take on a special importance and dynamism where several monies circulate alongside each other. Fifth, culture enables us to connect money with broader social and political questions about identity formation, ethnicity and race, gender and power.

Defining culture is, of course, not easy, and it is important not to treat culture merely as an adjunct to the supposedly more "essential," i.e., "economic," features of money. The one sociologist whose work has blazed a trail in resisting such a treatment is Viviana Zelizer, and I adopt her definition of culture—"shared understandings and their representations in symbols and practices" (Zelizer 2011: 2)—as my baseline throughout this discussion. Culture—shared meanings, and our representations of them—is not merely an add-on or extraneous property of money, which adds color or variety to a preexisting "thing." As I argue, money is a process, not a thing: it *consists* of social relations, and shared understandings are crucial to these. Culture is not simply part of the "symbolism" of money—the "nationalism" of the British pound, for instance—but is integral to its *modus operandi*, for example, the accounting systems on which it depends. Understood in such terms, culture does not simply leave an indelible mark upon money. It shapes what money has variously come to be.

These arguments are crucial to our broader assessment of money's capacity for reinvention, which is perhaps the most significant reason for considering them in detail here. As I have suggested in earlier chapters, a specific set of arrangements for producing money (organized around the state and banking system) has been *naturalized* in much of the discourse that surrounds money. Set against this understanding, the argument that money—for example, the right to *produce* it, the obligation to *regulate* it, the capacity to *lend* and *borrow* it, the freedom to *use* it in various ways—can be reappropriated by everyday users (as opposed to states and banks) is too easily dismissed as naive and overly optimistic. But a closer look at the scholarly literature on money and culture, and research that addresses money's role within the human economy, reveals myriad ways in which money *already is* actively created by ordinary users—even those monies that states and banks produce. Money, in other words, is considerably more *malleable*, and more capable of *reinvention*, than most mainstream theories of money have led us to believe.

MONEY AND CULTURAL ALIENATION

Zelizer once berated the classical theorists for adopting a culturally indifferent view of money: "Impressed by the fungible, impersonal characteristics of money, traditional social thinkers emphasized its instrumental rationality and apparently unlimited capacity to transform products, relationships, and sometimes even emotions into an abstract and objective numerical equivalent. But money is neither culturally neutral nor morally invulnerable" (Zelizer 2011: 97). But if anything, classical social thought was shaped by a view of money as culturally *malevolent*, not neutral. Marx's association of money with estrangement and commodity fetishism, Nietzsche's argument that money had replaced God as the focal point of human moral conscience, and Simmel's placement of money at the locus of his analysis of the objectification of *all* culture—each conveys money as a medium that is responsible for corrupting social relations and hollowing out modern cultural life. These thinkers portray money as a *quantifying* force, in opposition to the *qualitative* features of those social relations it comes into contact with. Money is seen as an alien *and alienating* presence in social life, bringing people together simply by rendering them as tools for each other.

In Chapter 2, I examined Marx's theory of the contradictory character of money, i.e., the tension between its status as the *universal* expression of abstract exchange value and its role as a *particular* commodity with its own specific use value. His understanding of money's cultural destructiveness focuses on the first of these properties and is a central feature within his broader theory of alienation. Marx puts forward a speculative and philosophical account of money as alienation in "On James Mill" (written 1844, published 1932, 2000b cited here) and *Grundrisse* (originally published 1939, 2005a cited here). In "On James Mill," he presents money as the lost and estranged essence of private property: it is property that is alienated and external to itself. He compares money to Christ's representation of men before God. Just as Christ is both alienated God and alienated man, so money is the alienated manifestation of the relationship between producers. Or more specifically, just as God only has value insofar as he represents Christ, so men's products only have value insofar as they are represented by money. Credit is "the economic judgement on the morality of a man [who] himself has been changed into money or money become incarnate in him" (Marx 2000b: 118). In *Grundrisse*, Marx writes that money is the "divine existence of commodities, while they represent its earthly form" (Marx 2005a: 221). Money symbolizes the domination of *things* over *people*. Society itself is thereby reduced to relations between things; people themselves are reduced to things; they are the property of things.

Just as money expresses estrangement as an *object* in its own right, so—as a *medium*—it alienates human beings by dividing, separating, and then comparing everything it comes into contact with, distorting natural and social relations by draining them of their specific meaning and color. In *Grundrisse*, Marx argues that people have faith in money only because they have objectified their relations with each other: money appears as a thing only for this reason. Monetary relations only *appear* to be abstract: "The abstraction, or idea, however, is nothing more than the theoretical expression of those material relations which are their lord and master" (Marx 2005a: 164). In *On the Jewish Question* (originally published in 1843, 2012 cited here), he describes money as the god of practical need and self-interest. Money is the jealous deity that refuses to accept the existence of any other gods, thus degrading them by transforming them into commodities. As the universal equivalent, i.e., the measure of the value of all things, money robs everything of its own specific value. When it becomes valued in its own right, as inevitably it does, money is merely the expression of our alienated existence. As a god, money is worshipped, i.e., desired and hoarded. It is the estranged essence of work. It has thus acquired power over commodities and the human beings producing and exchanging them. Money, in other words, turns social processes into objective things. It does not simply conceal culture's role in economic life, but it also destroys it.

All through Marx's writing on money, his frequent use of religious metaphors is striking and indicative of what he believes is money's corrosive effect on culture: money is compared to a divine power, and its relationship with commodities is likened to the relationship between God and Christ. Nietzsche, too, used religious metaphors in relation to money. But as we saw in Chapter 4, whereas Marx drew on religion to underline money's inescapable power, Nietzsche did so also to diminish religion and thereby underscore his thesis about the transvaluation of values. Nietzsche's apparent contempt for money stems from the belief that it flattens everything it touches, particularly from its association with a shallow bourgeois morality that seeks to place everyone on the same level, reducing humanity to its lowest common denominator rather than its most elevated example.

The work of Simmel is usually held up as the example par excellence of a classical view of money as both the symptom and cause of a profound cultural alienation. Habermas described the book's final chapter as a "philosophy of culture" that "inspired [Walter] Benjamin to observations on the overflow of stimuli, the density of contact, and the acceleration of movement in the metropolitan space of experience" (Habermas 1996: 408). Simmel made some important preliminary remarks about the relationship between money and culture in his 1896 essay, "Money in Modern Culture." There is no denying that here, as in *The Philosophy of Money*, he says more about money's cultural destructiveness than anything else. Money, he says, makes us overlook the unique value of things, and as a consequence, allows the meaning of life to slip through our fingers as "definitive satisfactions become even rarer" (Simmel 1991a: 23). Simmel reaches the more general conclusion in this essay that everything substantial and stable in modern culture is being rendered more fluid and unstable through money: "we are dispensing with the absolute truths that would be contrary to all development, and gladly sacrificing our knowing to continual reshaping, duplication and correction," a state which he associates with increasing empiricism (Simmel 1991a: 29). Money levels all values to their lowest common element and encourages us to be ethically lax and thoughtless toward others (Simmel 1991a: 24, 29). Despite its colorlessness, money is increasingly craved on its own, introducing a restlessness and feverishness into modern life (Simmel 1991a: 27). Like Marx and Nietzsche, Simmel is also drawn to analogies between money and religion. Money's elevation above the individual, its status as the center of everything that may be alien and distant, and its ability to unite the diversity of the world into a single unit—in all of these respects, money can engender feelings analogous to the belief in God. He specifically cites Hans Sachs's remark that money is the "secular God of the World" (Simmel 2004: 238).

Through money, Simmel advances a theory of *cultural alienation* that bears comparison with the young Marx, suggesting that money appears to exist as autonomous exchange value, and its circulation appears guided by its own laws (Frisby 2002: xxxii).[6] There are echoes of Marx, too, in Simmel's argument that the increasing objectification of culture has its roots in specialization: the more differentiated the means of production, "the less is the worker able to express his personality through them" (Simmel 2004: 459). This nondifferentiation brings about a growing sense of estrangement between "the subject and its products" that "ultimately invades even the more intimate aspects of our daily life" (Simmel 2004: 459). Simmel also

6   Simmel's approach also influenced Lukács, who went to his lectures in 1909–10 and regularly attended Simmel's private seminars, later praising *The Philosophy of Money* as laying foundations for the sociology of culture. Frisby suggests that Lukács's own theory of alienation (Lukács 1971) owed a debt to Simmel before Marx, although of course, Lukács's work takes in aspects such as class analysis and ideology that are missing from Simmel's book (Simmel 2004: 15–21).

maintains that this process of specialization made possible by money, including industrial and military machinery, results in the development of "an increasingly conscious *objective mind*", and to the "strange phenomenon" whereby "the cultural growth of the individual can lag considerably behind the cultural growth of tangible as well as functional and intellectual objects" (Simmel 2004: 463, original emphasis). A decade or so later, Simmel converts this essentially modern phenomenon into a more general "fate" that he calls the "tragedy" of culture (Frisby 2002: 110).

Simmel's arguments about money's effect on culture are by no means as uniformly negative as some critics and commentators suggest, however. Though as we have seen, some of what he had to say is negative, it is not the whole truth because he sometimes maintains that culture played a key role in shaping the nature of money. This idea is made clear, for example, when he contrasts his own conception of money to the theory of money derived from historical materialism. Describing *The Philosophy of Money* as an attempt to "construct a new storey beneath historical materialism" (Simmel 2004: 56), Simmel states that it would be both an enquiry into "the incorporation of economic life into the *causes* of intellectual culture" and an analysis that views economic forms "as the *result* of more profound valuations and currents of psychological or even metaphysical pre-conditions" (Simmel 2004: 56, italics added). Although Simmel describes the book's second part ("Synthetic Part") as an attempt to understand money's "effects upon the inner world—upon the vitality of individuals, upon the linking of their fates, upon culture in general" (Simmel 2004: 54), he does *not* simply reduce "culture" to a passive, weakened, and defensive role in the face of an active, aggressive, and corrosive phenomenon called "money." If anything, Simmel sees money as a microcosm through which modern culture can be explored, without suggesting that the relationship between money and culture operates only in one direction.

The deeper problem that Simmel focuses on in his writings concerns the tension between objective and subjective culture. But although money *expresses* this tension,[7] it does not necessarily *cause* it. For example, Simmel argues that the "fundamental re-orientation of culture towards intellectuality . . . *goes hand in hand* with the growth of a money economy" (Simmel 2004: 152, italics added). In short, his account of the relationship between money and culture is not uniformly bleak and not always unidirectional. The work of Norbert Elias is also worth briefly mentioning here because in his history, money could have a "civilizing aspect" *by virtue* of the fact that it

---

7 As Frisby puts it, in Simmel's analysis "the effects of money and the money economy become the fate of all culture" (Simmel 2004: 33).

is impersonal. Elias drew particular attention to the "peculiarly opaque nature of the control and foresight, the restraint of inclination... that any involvement in money chains imposes on people" (Elias 1994: 320–21). In this sense, money was closely bound up in the discipline of court society, whereas monetary restraint—frugality—was an essential part of bourgeois *économie*. This view would surely have intrigued Simmel because it suggests that the network of social relations and obligations that money imposes upon its holders helped to cultivate those forms of social distance and self-control that were essential to the civilizing process as Elias conceives it.[8]

Although Simmel accepts that money's presence as a mediator in exchange relationships fosters an increasing distance between personality and property and creates a clean separation between a person's "objective economic activity" and his or her "individual colouration" (Simmel 1991a: 21), he also maintains that money provides a common basis of direct mutual understanding, creates an "extremely strong social bond" among the members of an economic circle, and makes it possible to enter into a widening sphere of economic relations. He writes: "it is ultimately money which establishes incomparably more connections among people than ever existed in the days of feudal associations or the arbitrary unifications most highly praised by the guild romantics" (Simmel 1991a: 20). Likewise, whereas the freedom money gives to its holder can render life vapid and insubstantial, it liberates us from possessions by loosening our emotional attachment to them (Simmel 1991a: 23). What is at stake here, just as it is throughout *The Philosophy of Money*, is Simmel's emphasis on the cultural influence of money *as an idea*. Money's effect on modern culture transforms not only relations between people and things but also the way in which they *think* about those relations. According to Allen and Pryke, this phenomenon remains just as true one hundred years later when a broader range of monetary instruments is in circulation. Derivatives, they suggest, are just as capable of transforming cultural life and identity as the monetary forms Simmel was writing about; indeed they "can best be understood as serving to pull distant spaces into centres of rhythmic coordination which coordinate exchange in a new form of monetized space-time" (Allen and Pryke 1999: 52). The major difference today, they suggest, is that money is increasingly heterogeneous, compared to Simmel's time. It is therefore more appropriate to

---

8   Money's "civilizing influence" was by no means inevitable, according to Elias. For example, he conceded that the very length of the chain of functional dependencies into which money sometimes drew its holder could conceal those economic inequities that they helped to perpetuate (Newton 2003; Pixley 2012b).

refer to money *cultures*, not the single "money culture" that Simmel identified. These cultures "operate through shifting codes of meaning in relation to movement, pace, and instantaneity" (Allen and Pryke 1999: 52). They consist of people who position *themselves* in relation to money's circulation, as well as being positioned *by* it. Our experience of money, and therefore its effect upon our outlook and identity, is never uniform because it depends on our points of attachment with it, which are multiple.

Suggestively, Simmel distances himself from historical materialism by virtue of the fact that Marx—he alleges—"makes the *entire cultural process dependent on economic conditions*" (Simmel 1991a: 30, italics added). Simmel accepts this notion: "the consideration of money can teach us that far-reaching effects on the entire psychic and cultural state of the period do indeed emanate from the formation of economic life" (Simmel 1991a: 30). But at the same time—and crucially, I think—he also describes the monetary system as "a branch from the *same root that produces all the other flowers of our culture*" (Simmel 1991a: 31). Again, the language is revealing. To characterize money alongside other *flowers of culture* hardly suggests a negative view of money itself; indeed his description of money as a *branch* derived from the *same root* seems much more in keeping with his description of money as an example of what he considers to be "the *most idealized powers of existence* [and] the *most profound currents of individual life and history*" (Simmel 2004: 55, italics added). On the other hand, nobody can deny the negative implication of the following sentence, later on in the text: "The complete heartlessness of money is *reflected* in our social culture, which is itself *determined* by money" (Simmel 2004: 346). In the end, perhaps the best that can be said is that Simmel's position on the relationship between money and modern culture, rich and suggestive though it is, remains elusive and ambiguous. Although this is hardly a satisfactory conclusion, it warns against a simplistic, one-way reading of Simmel's remarks on the relationship between money and culture. But as he himself suggests, to know more about money's effect on culture may actually help us to solve some of the problems that money itself creates, for money is "capable of healing the wounds it inflicts" (Simmel 1991a: 31). This is a possibility we will return to in the next chapter.

POLANYI AND THE PROBLEM OF EMBEDDEDNESS

Scholars have increasingly challenged the image of money as a culturally destructive force that we tend to find in classical social thought, and I want to focus on this challenge in the remaining sections of this chapter. We begin with the work of Karl Polanyi, whose notion of *embeddedness* has influenced much of the contemporary literature on moral economy and—especially—the anthropology of money. As I am about to argue, Polanyi's work is somewhat ambiguous in its implications for understanding the connections between money and culture. His distinction between special-purpose and general-purpose monies offers a rich and suggestive way of exploring the cultural context in which monetary transactions take place, as well as the historical conditions under which the market economy has shaped the monetary system. On the other hand, however, that very distinction supports a view of contemporary forms of money from which culture is conspicuously *absent*. This view of money is implicit in the critical analysis of market society laid out in Polanyi's book, *The Great Transformation* (originally published in 1944; 1957b edition is cited here), which is the text I begin with here.

Polanyi's early engagement with the effect of "market money"—he later calls it general-purpose money—comes as part of a broader investigation of the development of market society that has subsequently influenced a number of fields, including the new economic sociology, international political economy, economic anthropology, and the voluminous literature on globalization. It is a puzzling, contradictory text because Polanyi appears to shift between a portrayal of the market as a cold and anonymous space that constitutes a *threat to society* and a more complex view of the market as necessarily *embedded within society*. According to Fred Block, one explanation of the discrepancy might be that Polanyi shifted his own position while writing the book, away from a Marxist examination of contradictions in market society and toward a more nuanced treatment of the embedded economy (Block 2003). His portrayal of money as a *fictitious commodity* was pivotal to this shift.

The book's central thesis addresses the societal, political, and cultural tensions that arise when markets are allowed free reign in the organization of society. The "great transformation" of its title refers to the social and political upheavals in England during the institutionalization of a market system in the nineteenth and early twentieth centuries. Polanyi portrays this process as the flawed, and ultimately failed, birth of the self-regulating market. The idea of such a market—detached from the wider society, operating according to its own laws, and therefore best left to its own devices, free from regulatory interference—was not just morally questionable, he argues, but unattainable. At the heart of his analysis is a particular understanding of money and its relationship with society.

Polanyi argues that the development of market society stalled around the failure to completely marketize the "fictitious" commodities of land, labor, and money. These are fictitious in the sense that they are not directly produced for sale but are derived from the very organizing principles of society itself. *Labor* is simply a name we give to a human activity that is integral to *life*. *Land* is but another name for *nature*. And *money* is merely a token of *society's purchasing power*. To subject any of these "commodities" purely to the forces of supply and demand—to offer them for sale in free markets—would result in the "demolition of society" (Polanyi 1957b: 76). Fictitious commodities cannot be organized through market mechanisms alone: human beings would perish through "vice, perversion, crime and starvation," nature's power to produce food and raw materials would be destroyed, and a surfeit of money would periodically liquidate business, just as floods did in traditional societies. Historically, this problem triggered what Polanyi calls the *double movement*, as society "protected itself against the perils inherent in a self-regulating market system" (Polanyi 1957b: 80). Although incoherent and unplanned, this countermovement led ultimately to a paradoxical situation whereby the only way of realizing the "stark utopia" (Polanyi 1957b: 218, 250) of the self-adjusting market was through the support of a strong interventionist state. He wittily describes this system as *planned laissez-faire* capitalism: "There was nothing natural about laissez-faire, free markets could never have come into being merely by allowing things to take their course ... laissez-faire itself was enforced by the state" (Polanyi 1957b: 145).

The double movement that Polanyi describes consists of the *reembedding* of market institutions within society. It is important to bear in mind that Polanyi's use of the term "embeddedness" differs quite significantly from its subsequent use in economic sociology. Whereas Granovetter's widely cited treatment of the concept focuses on networks of social relations (Granovetter 1985), in Polanyi's hands, embeddedness is closely associated with the analysis of institutions (Beckert 2007). As Krippner notes, for Polanyi markets are "fully social institutions, reflecting a complex alchemy of politics, culture, and ideology" (Krippner 2001: 782). More importantly for our discussion, he argues that, compared to labor and land, money has a special status as a fictitious commodity because its subjection to the self-regulation market involved nations *in toto*. By contrast, the subjection of land and labor to market forces set class against class *within* nations. This situation means that money could not be completely surrendered to market processes without—in effect—putting society as a whole up for sale. Polanyi's analysis of this issue focuses on the gold standard, which he describes as "an attempt to extend the domestic market system to the international field" (Polanyi 1957b: 3). Currency was the "pivot of national politics," and gold was the "faith of the age" (Polanyi 1957b: 25, 26). Between the two world wars, this very combination of *politics* and *faith* undermined money's status as a fictitious commodity as the national costs of maintaining the gold standard—its effect on economic growth and unemployment—became increasingly impossible to conceal. Far from being left to the mercy of the self-regulating market, monetary policy became mired in the *realpolitik* of import quotas, bilateral treaties, embargoes, and exchange equalization funds: an arsenal of restrictive measures that were designed to maintain money's status as the medium of free trade (Polanyi 1957b: 28). But for Polanyi, it is the connection between money and society as a whole that cuts most deeply of all: the "final failure of the gold standard"[9] was the "final failure of market economy" (Polanyi 1957b: 209).

Polanyi depicts the self-regulating market as a socially emaciated space that "could not exist for any length of time without annihilating the human and natural substance of society" (Polanyi 1957b: 3). Society was "discovered" in the age of industrialism, through the double movement whereby the dystopia of the self-regulating market was resisted. Nevertheless, his thesis suggests only a partial revision of the argument we found Simmel making about the spread of the money economy. Simmel's worst fear was that this spread would lead to the *objectification of culture*, drawing people into social relations that were increasingly shallow and instrumental. At the heart of it all would be individuals who find themselves increasingly isolated and estranged from others, unable to enjoy the apparent freedom that money enables people to have simply because they lack the sense of self and integrity that would enable them to use it properly. Although he does not cite Simmel, Polanyi seems broadly to share this fear (Steiner 2008). Where he differs from Simmel is in arguing that the social and moral erosion that was predicted in *The Philosophy of Money* would not be allowed to run its course. Society, in the form of its core political and regulatory institutions, would lead a great countermovement.

But this situation leaves us in an ambiguous position as far as money is concerned. Like Simmel, Polanyi was by no means a straightforward critic of market institutions and money and was not advocating their abolition. On the contrary, he maintained that market structures should continue "to ensure the freedom of the consumer, ... to influence producers' income, and to serve as an instrument of accountancy, while ceasing altogether to be an organ of economic self-regulation" (Polanyi 1957a: 260). It all depended on

---

9   He was referring specifically to its relinquishment by Britain in 1931 and by the United States in 1933.

ensuring that markets and money were properly institutionalized and regulated. Once they were, they would play an important role in shaping an equitable social democratic order (Beckert 2007; Hann and Hart 2009).[10] This notion implies that full market money is *never* completely viable because society necessarily rejects it. As I move on to argue now, however, Polanyi's position in *The Great Transformation* is at odds with the distinction he drew later on between special-purpose and general-purpose money.

Polanyi made a significant effect on monetary scholarship during the 1950s and 1960s with his distinction between special-purpose and general-purpose monies (Polanyi 1957a, 1968; see Dalton 1965: 48–49). Special-purpose money is used in the nonindustrial world, or nonmarket society, and can only be exchanged for a limited range of goods. General-purpose money, by contrast, is used in the industrial world, or market society, and can be used to purchase just about anything. There is an important cultural aspect to Polanyi's argument. The underlying thesis is that special-purpose monies circulate where systems of exchange are *culturally embedded*, for example, within kinship systems. They are sometimes referred to as "primitive" money. The concept of primitive money is epitomized by Paul Einzig's fascinating study, *Primitive Money*, published in 1949 (Einzig 1966). Einzig lists a remarkable range of objects as examples of monies used in premodern societies, including mats, teeth and tusks, rats, stones, beads, pigs, feathers, shells, yams, rice, drums, bronze, beeswax, buffaloes, cattle, cauldrons, axes, jars, tin, gold dust, silver, lead, tea, coconuts, grain, reindeer, tamarind seeds, camels, iron, salt, calico (cotton cloth), slaves, brass, fur, alcohol, wampum, cocoa, maize, arrows, and guns. Significantly, he rejects the Mengerian view that the monies he lists must all have emerged from barter. According to Einzig, it seems more likely that the objects came to be used as money through associations with matrimonial, political, or religious payments (Einzig 1948: 984). This idea suggests that money is not, in and of itself, a commercial institution but is bound up with a repertoire of social practices, rituals, and customs. Graeber, for example, suggests that many of the monies such as those Einzig lists were forms of adornment linked to displaying wealth (Graeber 2001; cf. Simmel 2004: 142). These adornments, according to Polanyi, are special-purpose money.

As Polanyi describes them, general-purpose monies circulate in market societies where money has already cut through cultural barriers to exchange. Notably, Polanyi refers to the semantics of money *uses*, not simply to its *functions*, as they are conventionally described in economics. The key argu-

---

10 In the next chapter, I explore which aspects of money lend themselves to such a role.

ment here is that *all* such uses must be *institutionalized separately*: the fact that money is used for one purpose in a particular context does not mean that it can be used for another. Likewise, particular monetary instruments may be eligible for one use but not for another. This is significant, too, because whereas in market societies (general-purpose) money is used mainly for *exchange* purposes, in nonmarket societies (special-purpose) money is more often used as a means of *payment*, e.g., for fines, taxes, and sacrifice. As such, money in such contexts is closely linked to social reproduction, that is to say, the changing status of human beings and their place in society through birth, death, marriage, and compensation. Payment use connects money intimately to power because it typically involves transactors of different social standing. Payment monies are *socially codified* and *ranked*. In a similar vein, Mary Douglas once argued that money acquires a sacred character whenever it is used to *amend* social status (Douglas 1967). We come back to this in a moment, when the discussion moves on to Bohannan.

Georg Thilenius examined similar issues about possible differences between kinds of money according to their range of function or degree of abstraction in 1921. He distinguished between *Nutzgeld*, or useful objects used in exchange, and *Zeichengeld*, or objects of conventional form, practically useless, mere tokens of value (Thilenius 1921; Quiggin 1949: 3). Quiggin notes further relevant distinctions, such as those drawn by Albert Terrien de Lacouperie (1845–1894) between *Naturgeld*, *Handelsgeld*, und *Industriegeld*, and by George Montandon (1879–1944)—an advocate, incidentally, of scientific racism—between *natural money* and *money of civilization* (or "cultural money"). Tellingly in light of our discussion of origin myths in Chapter 1, each distinction seems to be grappling with the idea that some forms of money are *closer to nature*, or to what is *essentially useful*, whereas others tend to be *closer to civilization*, and are *abstract*. It is an intriguing point because it seems to reverse the idea, which Polanyi seems to perpetuate, that only earlier (limited-purpose) monies possess sufficient cultural richness to constitute objects of anthropological research in their own right, whereas later (general-purpose) monies correspond to the culturally neutral, colorless media of exchange one finds in economics textbooks—or in Simmel.

The notion of ranked money was taken up and developed by Paul Bohannan in his path-breaking study of money uses among the Tiv in Nigeria (Bohannan 1955; Bohannan and Bohannan 1968). The Tiv organized their monetary exchanges according to a hierarchy of three distinct spheres of exchange, each with its own special-purpose money. This money served to separate various classes of goods. At the bottom of the hierarchy were subsistence goods such as food. In the middle were luxury and prestige goods such as cloth, cattle, and slaves. At the top were rights of exchange over people, mainly women who were exchanged in marriage. Bohannan's study shows that these spheres of exchange—corresponding, in Polanyi's terms, to distinct uses of money—were incommensurate. Though the money intended for use in one sphere could not be used in another, conversions from one sphere to another were possible. Conversion upward (i.e., exchanging goods in one tier for goods in a higher tier) was generally viewed as desirable, but conversion downward was regarded as disgraceful. Significantly, it was the *specificity* of the monies in circulation that reinforced social boundaries between the spheres. However, when a more generalized form of money *did* eventually begin to circulate among the Tiv, Bohannan suggests that the consequences were disruptive: insofar as barriers were eroded, traditional culture was undermined. People could accumulate money by selling goods lower down in the hierarchy and then buy their way into marriage circuits, circumventing elders. Similar lines of demarcation between money are explored in Hutchinson's study of the Nuer of southern Sudan. Here among market traders, a sharp distinction was drawn between money made from strangers for products sold at the local market, which they called "money of shit," and monies received for cattle from other Nuer, which were themselves defined in subtly nuanced ways (Hutchinson 1996: 86–87; see also Hutchinson 1992).

Bohannan's work has attracted its fair share of criticism. Some historians allege that he got his facts wrong, and anthropologists have accused him of theoretical naiveté (Hann and Hart 2011: 59). Some argue that he paid too much attention to exchange spheres as opposed to relations of production, overestimating the importance that *money alone* can have in the reproduction of traditional culture. Others discern a degree of romanticism in his approach. Hart wryly observes that academics seem more inclined than most to "line up with Tiv elders in bemoaning the corrosive power of modern money and vainly insist that traditional culture should prevail" (Hart 2005b). Bohannan's arguments—like those of the classical thinkers discussed in the previous section, to a degree—appeal to the suspicion that there is something *inauthentic* about general-purpose money. It symbolizes a world we would rather reject. Here, his approach seems to echo that of Polanyi in *The Great Transformation*.

Polanyi's main criticism of orthodox treatments of money is that they are too narrow. It seems significant, however, that he based this critique on evidence from *non*market societies. The implication is that orthodox approaches to money are valid in the context of market society. This corresponds to the separation Polanyi makes between two meanings of "economy," i.e., formal and substantive. The *formal* meaning presupposes that economic behavior follows a universal rule defined by the logical relationship between means and ends. The *substantive* idea defines the economy according to the empirical content of the societal systems through which material wants are provided. This idea is closer to the position generally taken by economic anthropologists, who maintain that economic systems do not follow universal laws but vary from culture to culture. In drawing such a distinction, Polanyi suggests that whereas all premodern economic systems should be characterized according to the substantive definition, modern economic systems conform to the formal definition. Many anthropologists—and sociologists, for that matter (Barber 1995; Krippner 2001)—do not accept this position; indeed, Polanyi's analysis opened up a protracted and ultimately unresolved debate between formalists and substantivists in anthropology. There is no need to rehearse the two sides of the debate in detail here because it has been so widely covered elsewhere (Scott 1966, 1969, 1973; LeClair and Schneider 1968; Dalton 1969; Godelier 1972, 1988; Prattis 1973; Isaac 1993). In essence, the argument was about the possibility of using neoclassical economic theory to understand premodern, or "primitive" forms of production and exchange. As Hann and Hart note, the debate carries echoes of the nineteenth century *Methodenstreit*, or battle of methods: "one side [were] claiming the economy is always the same and the other that it is different" (Hann and Hart 2011: 70).

The main insight that comes out of Polanyi's argument about the semantics of money uses concerns the diversity of monetary *practices*. He suggests that this diversity is a consequence of money's embeddedness in specific cultural practices and relations of power. Money is not *neutral* and *colorless*, but *ranked* and *codified*. According to this "substantivist" view, money therefore does not *corrode* social and cultural distinctions but *reinforces* them. But as I have just suggested, this argument comes with a significant (and problematic) caveat, namely, that Polanyi's understanding of money's diversity is based on examples derived from *outside* of the market sphere. In other words, his distinction between general-purpose and limited-purpose money does not *challenge* the classical conception of money in any fundamental way. Rather, both Polanyi and Bohannan could be read as suggesting that earlier forms of money—special-purpose money—are merely *emaciated* versions of general-purpose money. They are *partial* monies, limited in function and lacking in cultural sophistication (Davies 1994: 23). Although the idea of special-purpose money is still used today to describe supposedly small-scale or specialist forms of money, such as local currencies

(Ingham 2004b), it is the notion of general-purpose money that is increasingly discredited. To a degree, *all* forms of money conform to the limited-purpose definition: even a major currency, like the euro (Dodd 2005b). In the face of empirical evidence about the diversity of all monies, even those defined as general-purpose monies, Polanyi's original distinction begins to break down. There is a lingering sense, then, that Polanyi's dualistic conception of money does not really withstand closer scrutiny. As I have suggested here, it seems to have been guided by those very assumptions about the relationship between money and market society that he cautioned against in *The Great Transformation*. Zelizer mounted the most significant challenge to Polanyi's idea that all modern monies are general-purpose—although, curiously, she seldom cites Polanyi himself. I examine this position next.

RELATIONAL MONIES

Perhaps the main conclusion we should draw from the discussion of Polanyi just now is that to sustain the classical argument that money homogenizes everything it touches, we must first homogenize money itself. This is far more difficult to do than it first appears; indeed, it is unsustainable in the face of clear evidence that people themselves differentiate the money they come into contact with, transforming it into *monies*, not money. One could counter this view by arguing that money is such a powerful homogenizer that it eventually absorbs such efforts, just as a dominant cultural industry absorbs alternative subcultures. Such an argument would be illogical, however: if people can and do differentiate their monies, money simply cannot homogenize everything it touches. We can transform it and bend it to our own ends and impute our own structures of meaning to its varying forms. This, essentially, is the position taken by Zelizer. Her core thesis about earmarking suggests that *all* forms of money are differentiated according to use and fungibility in ways that, according to Polanyi, were characteristic of special-purpose monies alone. By contrast, Zelizer argues that all forms of money—primitive and modern, local as well as state fiat currencies, and cash alongside virtual money—are shaped from the inside by the social practices and cultural values of their users. Polanyi represents what she calls the moral critique of the "boundless market" (Steiner 2008: 99). She rejects this critique because in offering no alternative model of the market, it simply reproduces the idea that markets are powerful and autonomous forces that we can only obstruct, not reconfigure. Besides Polanyi's double movement thesis, other examples of such an approach include Richard Titmuss's study of blood donation and Fred Hirsch's work on the "commercialization effect" (Titmuss 1971; Hirsch 1978). According to Zelizer, all of these thinkers unnecessarily dramatize the moral dangers of the market with "nightmarish visions of a fully commoditized world" (Zelizer 2011: 370).

Zelizer argues that culture is not exogenous to money. Rather, money is the site on which culture and economy reciprocally interact. This is the basis of her critique of Simmel: "Suffering from a sort of intellectual colour blindness, Simmel's brilliant analysis of money failed to capture the rich new social hues emerging in a monetary economy as people improvised different ways to personalise and differentiate monies" (Zelizer 1997: 201). This image of market money, alongside that of Marx, is based on several flawed assumptions (Zelizer 1997: 11–12).[11] First, it suggests that money's unique suitability as a tool of market exchange is based on features (e.g., lack of quality, homogeneity, divisibility, and liquidity) in relation to which money's symbolic meanings, insofar as they exist, are wholly incidental. Second, it assumes that in modern society, all monies are the same: any differences between them are quantitative, not qualitative. Third, it presumes that nonpecuniary values—i.e., values connected to personal, social, or sacred life—are entirely distinct from monetary values, which are profane and instrumental. Fourth, it suggests that relationships mediated by money inevitably expand and corrupt other areas of social life and, increasingly, society in general. And fifth, it assumes that whereas money can (and does) transform nonpecuniary values, the reverse is unlikely: money is rarely affected by values, practices, and beliefs that emanate from "outside" the market economy.

A fallacy runs through the classical treatment of money, which holds that, by drawing an increasing number of social relations into its compass, money spreads "uniformity, precision, and calculation" throughout modern society (Zelizer 1997: 12). The analysis covers two distinct forms of homogenization: the homogenization *of* money and the homogenization of social life *by* money. It is important not to run these together. The second kind of homogenization involves a broader and more complex set of causal relations than the first. As for the first kind, Zelizer argues that money must be seen as multiple (not as homogeneous) because of the way it is always earmarked by users. By allocating specific quantities of our income to manage a domestic budget, or by setting aside currency received as a gift for a specific purchase,

---

11   Zelizer also claims to find such assumptions, variously, in the work of Coleman, Cooley, Giddens, Habermas, Marshall, Marx, Mitchell, Parsons, Schumpeter, Simmel, and Weber.

we impute meaning to currency and thereby ensure that "not all dollars are the same" (Zelizer 1997: 11). Against the second kind of homogenization, Zelizer maintains that money is *reciprocally influenced* by cultural and social structural factors that exist "outside" the market. These factors shape money's uses, its users, the allocation system in which it is used, the way it is controlled, and where it comes from.

Zelizer rejects the idea that markets (economy) and morals (culture) are hostile worlds that clash whenever they come into contact: on one side, a world of rationality, efficiency, and impersonality; on the other, a world of self-expression, cultural richness, and intimacy (Zelizer 2011: 429). On the contrary, money and markets are shaped *from the inside* by those very forces that scholars such as Polanyi argue were resisting them *from the outside*. By the same token, Zelizer does not propose *reducing* money and markets to culture. Such an argument is often used to counter the view that economy and culture are hostile worlds but is taken too far when markets are portrayed as "nothing but economic rationality, nothing but culture, and nothing but politics" (Zelizer 2011: 314). Rather than trying to resolve false dichotomies by reducing one term to the other, the relationship between culture and economy needs to be understood as a mutual interaction, consisting of "multiple forms of connections between complex social processes and their economic components" (Zelizer 2011: 408).

Zelizer's proposed alternative to these "nothing but" approaches focuses on the multiplicity of markets and money. Theoretically, this middle course is designed to capture the interplay among economic, cultural, and social-structural factors by identifying "types and patterns of social-structural and cultural variation in 'multiple markets'" (Zelizer 2011: 377). We therefore need a richer treatment of money that captures its heterogeneity. Zelizer first developed such a perspective through an analysis of domestic money in the United States during the late nineteenth and early twentieth century, when rising real incomes and the increasingly widespread use of money meant that families were reevaluating how they managed their finances, how household income should be allocated, and what it meant to spend well. As a consequence, the money that made up the homogeneous household budget was broken up, differentiated, and individualized in ways that reflected both gender and class differences. This was a cultural coding of money, its subjection to domestic as opposed to market rules (Zelizer 2011: 114). In *Pricing the Priceless Child* (1985), Zelizer examines how insurance raises fundamental questions about how human existence can be priced, how the value of different lives can be compared, and whether monetary compensation for injury or death is a proper recognition of loss or is morally corrupting. The growth of a market in childrens' life insurance was shaped by changes in the way that children themselves were valued: these began as a means of giving the "sacred" child a proper burial, later becoming a means of investing in their future education (Zelizer 1985, 1981). Neither life nor childrens' insurance was a straightforward case of commodification or an instance of the encroachment of market values onto terrain whose moral fabric they immediately destroyed (Zelizer 2011: 378).

Zelizer argues that monetary values can be incorporated into intimate relationships without corrupting them (Zelizer 2005b, 2006b). Others, too, have drawn attention to the strong emotional associations of money. According to Krueger, for example, "money is probably the most emotionally meaningful object in contemporary life; only food and sex are its close competitors as common carriers of such strong and diverse feelings, significances, and strivings" (Krueger 1986: 3). The interaction between economics and intimacy frequently takes the form of differentiation strategies as lines are drawn between roles (wife, lover, lawyer, parent, friendship, business) and kinds of payment (gift, wage, allowance) that often overlap in the intimate economy. This is a "relational" approach to money, which assumes that social relations are characterized by the boundaries that people erect around meaningful relationships (Zelizer 2012). This approach involves designating which kinds of economic and monetary transactions are appropriate for different forms of relation. Zelizer calls this "relational work," a term designed to draw out active, creative, and dynamic features of economic transactions that more conventional analyses of "economic embeddedness" tend to overlook. This idea echoes a more general view that the "embeddedness" argument does not go far enough in challenging orthodox economic models (Krippner and Alvarez 2007). According to Zelizer, the idea of embeddedness directs our attention toward that which economic processes are embedded *in* and therefore leaves those processes themselves unexamined (Zelizer 2012).

An especially intriguing case study of what Zelizer calls monetary differentiation through relational work can be found in the "financial diaries" of impoverished villagers and slum dwellers in Bangladesh, India, and South Africa that were recorded for research by Daryl Collins and his colleagues, and written up in *Portfolios of the Poor* (2010). As they point out, poverty makes "managing your money well ... absolutely central to your life" (Collins, Morduch, et al. 2010: 4). This is not, however, simply a question of leading a frugal, desperate existence. On the contrary, money management in the 250 diaries collated by Collins et al. involves navigating one's way through a complex set of social ties: juggling savings and loans with friends and family members, participating in savings and insurance clubs, and borrowing from local "moneyguards" and shopkeepers. Take the example of Hamid and Khadeja, a couple with one child who were managing a family budget of 78 cents per person per day:

> Far from living hand-to-mouth, consuming every *taka* as soon as it arrived, Hamid and Khadeja had built up reserves in six different instruments, ranging from $2 kept at home for minor day-to-day shortfalls to $30 sent for safe-keeping to his parents, $40 lent out to a relative, and $76 in a life insurance savings policy... They are borrowers, with a debt of $153 to a microfinance institution and interest-free private debts from family, neighbours, and employer totalling $24. They also owed money to the local grocery store and to their landlord. Khadeja was even acting as an informal banker, or "moneyguard," holding $20 at home that belonged to two neighbours seeking a way to keep their money safe from their more spendthrift husbands and sons. (Collins, Morduch, et al. 2010: 8–9)

Through such relational work, a complicated patchwork of social relations is built up through money. Sociologically speaking, one might say that financial management among the world's poor is considerably more sophisticated than it is among the world's wealthiest. And crucially for our discussion here, *social relations themselves* are the "financial tools" used to manage money in extreme poverty. This, essentially, is culture shaping money.

As Zelizer herself has noted (Zelizer 2012: 14–18), there are some suggestive parallels between the process of monetary differentiation that takes place through what she calls earmarking, and the phenomenon that is known by behavioral economists as mental accounting. Mental accounting—defined by Richard Thaler as "a set of cognitive operations used by individuals and households to organize, evaluate, and keep track of financial activities" (Thaler 1999: 183)—takes place when individuals allocate different portions of the monies they possess to distinct cognitive spaces according to how those monies will be used. According to Thaler, people do this primarily because it is more efficient: they save time and effort through not having to think about certain choices where specific portions of their monies are concerned. Others suggest that emotional issues may also be involved: mental accounting becomes emotional accounting when particular monies are given "affective tags" (Levav and McGraw 2009). As Zelizer points out, however, this approach fails to treat social relations as playing a constitutive—as opposed to merely contextual—role in money's differentiation. Even apparently selfish forms of mental accounting take others into consideration; indeed, they invariably emerge from social interactions—and social histories—of one kind or another. This consideration is why Zelizer prefers the notion of *relational* accounting to mental accounting, because monetary differentiation is closely linked to the ways in which we manage our ties to others.

Zelizer's approach is richly suggestive as a critique of mainstream monetary thought, and she opens up some intriguing questions and possibilities. For example, there are several possible interpretations of what earmarking means and thus of its implications for the analysis of money. The first ("weak") version of the idea suggests simply that we need to *view money in a different way*. To focus on earmarking is to take a micro as opposed to a macro approach to the analysis of currency, to view money from below, not from above: from the perspective of money's users, not its producers. A second ("moderate") version of Zelizer's thesis is that *social practices modify money* by restricting its use, regulating its allocation, or modifying its appearance. As Zelizer herself puts it, here the focus is on "social practices that sort otherwise identical media (for example, two $100 bank notes) into distinct categories" (Zelizer 2012). To say that a currency is diverse in terms of its social meaning is to describe the way in which it is variously handled and interpreted by its users. Crucially, as we have seen, these practices are found especially where money is used outside of the market, e.g., in the household and the intimate economy and in relation to morally ambiguous financial practices such as life insurance. This interpretation often seems to be how Zelizer's work is read, both by her critics (e.g., Fine and Lapavitsas 2000) and those who are more sympathetic to her approach. Both of these interpretations suggest a valid and important complementary perspective in relation to the treatments of money that were discussed earlier in this chapter, but they would leave those arguments unchallenged because little is said about those very processes—defined by commodification and market exchange—about which thinkers such as Marx, Nietzsche, Polanyi, and Simmel were so pessimistic. For example, Philippe Steiner suggests that Zelizer underestimates the dangers of the "marketization" of society that Polanyi had so obviously feared: the risk is that the theory of "connected lives" provides no basis from which to mount a rigorous critique of neoliberalism (Steiner 2008: 103; see also Esparza and Lapegna 2007). For Zelizer, on the other hand, the question should not be *whether* markets have harmful effects on human relationships, but rather, *when*. This, always, is a research question: "When, and why, we should ask, do certain economic arrangements produce injustice and which enhance welfare?" (Zelizer 2011: 359).

But there is a third ("strong") interpretation of Zelizer's approach, which is more radical and incisive than either of these two versions would allow. It is, moreover, consistent with her own suggestion that surely "the world of social monies extends beyond the doorsteps of households and charities" (Zelizer 1997: 34). Zelizer's earlier work on earmarking opened up the important issue of monetary multiplicity, but it is through her later work on "circuits of commerce" (or so-called Zelizer circuits) (Zelizer 2004, 2005a) that Zelizer moved the analysis on to embrace not just the *marking* but the actual *production* of money, e.g., through the creation of completely new currencies (e.g., virtual monies such as Facebook credits and Linden dollars, local currencies, gambling chits, and Bitcoins) and through the transformation of various objects (e.g., cigarettes and chewing gum) *into* monetary media. Circuits of commerce describe the micro foundations of economic life and are distinct from economic formations such as markets, networks, or firms. This is the active creation of money through relational work. Randall Collins views it as an example of money's use to "enact" social structure (Collins 2000).

According to Zelizer, circuits are configured around shared economic activities carried out through economic relations between individuals. They have their own accounting systems for evaluating exchanges, including schema of moral valuation, which are derived from shared understandings of the meaning of transactions within the circuit. A circuit is maintained via a boundary separating members from nonmembers of the circuit, and there are often mechanisms for controlling any transactions that cross this boundary. The idea recalls the arguments of both Polanyi and Bohannan about money that is ranked: each circuit incorporates its own money, consisting of a particular material object, money of account, or both (Zelizer 2004: 125; 2011: 305). Circuits of commerce can emerge in many different kinds of location but often go unnoticed because they tend not to fit our conventional expectations about economic structure. The idea is useful as a means of exploring the multiplicity of economic arrangements growing up in the present day: "Internet peer production, microcredit arrangements, barter groups, local currency systems, gift-exchange communities, investment clubs, corporate work teams, mutual aid associations, garage sales, and more" (Zelizer 2011: 304). They can be compared to Weber's notion of "spheres" (Weber 1958), Bourdieu's idea of "fields" (Bourdieu 1993), Latour and Callon's model of actor networks (Callon 1986; Latour 2005), and Florence Weber's concept of *"scènes sociales"* (Weber 2001). Zelizer suggests that the circuits idea also applies to Bohannan's analysis of spheres of exchange among the Tiv (Bohannan 1955; Bohannan and Bohannan 1968), Pryor's work on exchange circuits (Pryor 1977), Morrill's work on cultures within firms (Morrill 1995), Akin and Robbins's discussion of Melanesia's differentiated money spheres (Akin and Robbins 1999), Blanc's idea of parallel currencies (Blanc 2000), Knorr Cetina and Bruegger's analysis of connections between financial traders (Knorr Cetina and Bruegger 2002), Velthuis's study of art markets (Velthuis 2005), and Goffman's work on relations among the urban poor (Goffman 2009). She also applies the idea in her own analyses of local currencies (Zelizer 2005a) and remittances (Zelizer 2006a).

The circuit idea has important ramifications for a question we have visited a number of times in this book: namely, in what sense can money be described as a claim upon society? In the last chapter, I considered Spinoza's idea of the multitude—as taken up by Hardt and Negri—as a potential stand-in for "society," which allows for a more pluralistic and flexible interpretation of money's collective foundations than "nation-state." The concept is certainly suggestive, especially in relation to digital currencies, and Zelizer's circuits idea is similarly promising. At the same time, the idea of the multitude has a number of weaknesses when applied to money, which Zelizer's approach appears to address. For example, a multitude is arguably *too* temporary and diffuse to be applied persuasively to money, simply because the collective guarantees that *underwrite* money necessarily extend over time and space, and with a certain degree of consistency. Moreover, a multitude tends to be *oppositional* in character, whereas many alternative currencies (such as LETS tokens and time dollars) are likely to be based on positive associations, and a sense of belonging, with an identifiable community or group. Zelizer's concept of the circuit may be better suited for describing such forms. The circuit generates its own specific mode of sociality: it has its own internal culture, so to speak. It is similar, in fact, to what Steiner calls an "economic culture" (Steiner 2008). For example, the very creation and coordination of local currencies—e.g., through meetings, the creation of standards, or newsletters—creates distinctive circuits of interpersonal relations. Although the aims of these schemes vary considerably, ranging from forging local ties, to building alternatives to capitalism, to radical libertarianism (Zelizer 2011: 326), the important point is that the process of their very establishment is integral to the realization of these aims. Much the same might be said of remittances: payments of money, food, clothing, and various other gifts sent by migrant workers back to their home communities, usually to family members. For Zelizer, these payments create complex circuits through which remittances flow, closely coordinated arrangements that rarely seem to malfunction, despite the long distances involved. However, the circuits are not fixed, and the roles that constitute them are continually negotiated, contested, and reshaped, although the circuit itself exerts an important degree of collective control over its members (Zelizer 2011: 350).

Circuits of commerce are not spontaneous, although they may be short-lived. Typically, they straddle conventional boundaries between societies, states, firms, or markets. They tend to occur across existing social settings. Even in the case of local currencies, circuits are not self-contained communities in their own right; they do not constitute closed-off or all-encompassing social relations. Their members usually participate in more than one circuit. Commercial circuits also seem to fall between tighter groupings based on kinship, ethnicity, or religion (although they often form in relation to these) on one side and more anonymous and disparate networks on the other. Circuits are often constructed as a response to collective problems of trust in the absence of central authorities, problems that can be especially acute when child care, family formation, long-distance trade, or credit is at stake. And crucially, circuits are just as likely to be found in market as in nonmarket settings. There are other nuances, too, which resonate with the arguments that we discussed in the last chapter about the development of postterritorial monies. The relational monies that Zelizer describes are less a symbolic expression of positive identity (i.e., social class, national state, or local community) and much more a practical, finely grained *index of difference*. As Zelizer puts it, people perform relational work "by means of multiple monetary distinctions" (Zelizer 2012: 158). To focus on monetary practices in this way suggests that money is not as a *thing* that is simply mapped onto social and cultural spaces but rather a *process* through which various kinds of human association are actively created and valued. This notion of money as a process requires further discussion, however. If money is a process and not a thing, what does its creation involve in practice? I turn to this question next.

SCALES OF VALUE

In the last section we considered the argument that, *contra* Simmel and Polanyi, pecuniary and nonpecuniary values can reciprocally interact through the very social practices that produce money. This argument suggests that money and culture do not simply act upon one another from the outside but are mutually constitutive. The anthropology of money has gone in this direction increasingly. Work in this field suggests that culture does not simply "resist" money's encroachment in the way that Polanyi implied. On the contrary, shared meanings—their expression in social practices and their representation in symbols—actively shape money as a *tool of calculation*, as a *material form*, and as a *means of creating and sustaining differences in social hierarchy and rank*. Money is treated as an open site in this empirically varied field. Inevitably, and quite rightly, there are no theoretical accounts of money in anthropology that unify the field. Providing an overview of work in this area is therefore difficult. I want to focus on one particular issue because it demonstrates the analytical power of prizing open what appear to be objective and invariant (and noncultural) features of money, namely, its properties as a system of *valuation* and *calculation*. This work is significant for the broader discussion of monetary diversification because it underlines the cultural richness and specificity of the modes of calculation that these various monetary forms involve. To put the matter bluntly: far from being culturally corrosive, these modes of calculation are cultural practices in their own right.

As we discussed earlier in this chapter, the argument that money is a force of cultural destruction usually relies on the straightforward view that money transforms *quality* into *quantity*. For classical thinkers such as Marx, Nietzsche, and Simmel, money's effect on culture was mainly caused by its transformation of qualitative relationships between people and things into measurable quantities. In the *Economic and Philosophical Manuscripts of 1844*, Marx portrays money as the "the general confusion and inversion of things; it makes impossibilities fraternize." (Marx 2000a: 118). Money is an inverting power, a calculating force that turns the world upside down. In *Capital*, he defines money as a "radical leveller" that "extinguishes all distinctions" (Marx 1982: 229). Nietzsche argued that "setting prices, estimating values, devising equivalents, making exchanges . . . constitutes *thinking as such*" (Nietzsche 1996b: 51, italics added), whereas for Simmel, money inherently encourages psychological attitudes that are calculative and intellectualizing: "The money economy enforces the necessity of continuous mathematical operations in our daily transactions . . . Gauging values in terms of money has taught us to determine and specify values down to the last farthing" (Simmel 2004: 444).

All of these thinkers tend to leave the calculative practices that money involves safely sealed inside a black box. That is to say, calculation pertains to a "technical" feature of money that is not traditionally seen as being open to empirical investigation, above all by anthropologists and sociologists. Arguments about opening the black box of calculation and subjecting it to sociological investigation have featured in the social studies of *finance* but much less so in the sociology or anthropology of *money*. Moreover, ethnographic work on practices of calculation has moved beyond seemingly exotic, non-Western spaces and into fields such as banking, where one might expect to find technically sophisticated systems of calculation that have relatively little to do with culture. Maurer even wonders whether—paradoxically—financial markets have become the "new exotic" for anthropologists (Maurer 2006: 18). William Desmonde made a similar point in *Magic, Myth, and Money*, published in 1962:

> to many of us, money is a mystery, a symbol handled mainly by the priests of high finance, and regarded by us with much of the same reverence and awe as the primitive feels toward the sacred relics providing magical potency in a tribal ritual. As if in a higher plane of reality, the symbol seems to operate in an incomprehensible, mystical way, understood and controllable only by the magic of brokers, accountants, lawyers, and financiers ... like spellbound savages in the presence of the holy, we watch in wonder the solemn proceedings, feeling in a vague, somewhat fearful way that our lives and the happiness of our children are at the mercy of mysterious forces beyond our control. (Desmonde 1962)

Not all work in this area, it must be said, contradicts the classical view of money's cultural destructiveness. LiPuma argues that the proliferation and ascendance of quantitative finance in contemporary capitalism has transformed social imaginaries (LiPuma 1999), and Poovey suggests that finance is eroding "humanism" by excluding all value that cannot be brought into the calculative apparatus (this idea is very close to Simmel) (Poovey 2001). Maurer, however, sees a deeper "anxiety about number" in the argument that money works like acid, stripping social life away from everything it touches. This view plays up to the "folk theory that presumes that whenever we see numbers and math we see something that counts, calculates, equates, desacralizes, and rationalizes" (Maurer 2006: 24). Quantity is "simultaneously a quality of things," something missed when money is simply viewed as enforcing a "colonizing quantification" (Maurer 2006: 25).

Broadly speaking, the anthropological literature on calculation cleaves into studies of the cultural effect of financial techniques (Zaloom 2003) and work that focuses on calculative technologies (Miyazaki 2005). Studies falling into the second category draw on actor–network theory to explore the distribution of calculation among humans and material devices, further drawing attention to feedback loops whereby the techniques used influence and shape the "reality" that the numbers are supposed to represent (MacKenzie 2008, 2011). In monetary scholarship, emphasizing money's role as an accounting scheme is commonplace, above all, in approaches that have been shaped by Keynes (Wray 1998; Ingham 2004b). But the accounting scheme itself is rarely subjected to further interrogation: all that matters is the state's role in determining what the scheme should be. Even if the classical thinkers were justified in arguing that money renders everything calculable, they overlooked the representationally complex nature of the calculations that varying forms of money actually entail. Money's quantitative functions, and above all the creative practices behind them, are not culturally neutral but are shaped by both culture and context. Even when money enters social fields where it was previously absent, its calculative functions are not simply resisted. Boundary work takes place, much of it morally fraught, that disrupts and modifies the calculation (Strathern 1992). These complexities pose deeper questions about money, number, and quantification (Crump 1981, 1992). Money's numbers can signify "the divine, the transcendent, the ineffable" (Maurer 2006: 23). Monetary calculation can be used for new ends, such as when people use money to calculate other, non-monetary aspects of their lives.

Polanyi once described money as a "semantic system similar to speech, writing or weights and measures" (Polanyi 1968: 175), and cultural anthropology is replete with examples of the cultural complexity that lies behind money's calculative functions. Helen Codere constructed a "semiotics" of money based on the argument that money is usually integrated with other symbolic systems such as number, weights and measures, and writing: "Much has rightly been made of these other symbolic systems in writings on the history of science," she argues, "far less in the writings of economic historians" (Codere 1968: 561). Though the essence of any accounting system is to symbolize quantities, these quantities have their own cultural histories, which are rooted in our intellectual existence and thereby shaped by "given states of knowledge and technology and their levels and processes of growth and development" (Codere 1968: 574). Money is an intellectual system, which is comparable to mathematics in its range of development: "from the most rudimentary calculations and systems to the most elegant and diversified refinements" (Codere 1968: 574). In Polanyi's terms, Codere is proposing an "anti-formalist" theory of money: "It is substantive or realist because it is empirical and because it deals with money as a substantivist would deal with any economic fact—not as something that can be separated out of general human existence by the test of whether scarce means are being applied to alternative ends but as something that in the overwhelming number of cases is likely to be decisively related to technological, social, moral and political contexts and opinions" (Codere 1968: 575–76).

Although Codere casts doubt on the notion that the presence of money in any society or social setting automatically fosters homogenizing calculating attitudes, other scholars have examined the interaction between different numerical scales when distinct monies or modes of monetary calculation coexist, for example, in the calculation of loan payments. Money's connections with *time* offer especially rich examples of the creative work that takes place in monetary calculation under these circumstances (Gell 1992). When loans are calculated not in incremental time (as they would be in most Western contexts, i.e., month by month) but rather in *thresholds* or *seasons*, the apparatus of credit and debt functions in a radically different way (Austin 1993; Clark 1994; Shipton 1991, 1995; Berry 2001). The dynamics involved when money's calculative functions interact with culture have come to light particularly in studies investigating what happens when distinctive monetary systems, and therefore different accounting schemes, come into contact with one another. Two contrasting anthropological studies provide significant insights into this question: Gregory's *Savage Money* (1997) and Guyer's *Marginal Gains* (2004), and I look briefly at their arguments now.

A QUALITY THEORY OF MONEY

Gregory's arguments are based on fieldwork undertaken in the Bastar District of India, but its focus is broader: the notion of "savage money" describes the world's monetary landscape after Bretton Woods, in a global economic system he describes as "disorganized capitalism." What Gregory calls savage money has been wrenched from political control and appears to circulate with no relationship to material goods or labor. It is similar to the "mad money" that Strange was describing at around the same time (Strange 1998a). Gregory argues that the U.S. decision to suspend convertibility was related to its military expenditure overseas, and the Vietnam War in particular. The effect of the *de facto* revaluation of gold reserves was to transfer the cost of the war to the dollar-holding developing countries (Gregory 1997: 273). He is particularly interested in the *symbolism* of world money. Symbolic analysis "is a matter of grasping a material object in its historically specific concreteness and asking: 'What material object was formerly united to this one?' 'What invisible value relation binds the two parts together today?' 'Who are the valuers behind this relation and what is the political nature of their relationship?'" (Gregory 1997: 299). In his discussion of the era of gold and world money (1934–71), where the political relationship is "paramount power," the material object in question used to be *gold* and subsequently became *paper*: "The power of the U.S. government maintained the former; free market anarchists control the latter and their power grows as they succeed in destroying yet more instruments of state control and in creating yet more new markets for symbolic objects that did not previously have a price" (Gregory 1997: 300). The process Gregory describes resembles the financialization of territorial money that we discussed briefly in Chapter 6. He calls it commodity fetishism in its highest form, wherein traders profit "by observing the actions of the central banks, decoding their intentions, and doing, in most cases, precisely the opposite so that the aims of the banks are thwarted" (Gregory 1997: 300). Intriguingly, Gregory warns against too *much* "culturalism" in the analysis of money: "A culturalist approach to the theory of commodities that persists in dissolving historically specific unifying values into endless cultural diversity by appeal to the notion of 'indigenisation' . . . will never understand the symbolism of the money tokens that pass through their hands on countless occasions each and every day. Indigenisation is, of course, a factor in the world today but so too is 'Americanisation.' These are not opposing tendencies but complementary expressions of the one underlying value: free market anarchism" (Gregory 1997: 300–301).

Against this historical background, Gregory develops the notion of *subalternate* (as opposed to *superalternate*) money, in order to capture alternative monetary forms that operate on the margins, and within the interstices, of these dominant monies. The phrase comes from his distinction between superalternate and subalternate values: "superalternate" values are those of master, landlord, husband, or parent; "subalternate" values are those of the slave, tenant, wife, or child. Empirically, the categories are fluid: people "create multiple value systems for themselves and are constantly switching between them according to the dictates of the moment" (Gregory 1997: 8). To come to grips with subalternate money, he proposes a "quality" theory of money, which is opposed to the "quantity" theory of money that dominates orthodox monetary theory. The premise of the quality theory is that the value of money is a signifier that has *iconic*, *indexical*, and *symbolic* meaning that is intimately connected to power. "Many historians and economists have failed to understand the symbolism of money, with the result that their theories become apolitical and objectivist" (Gregory 1997: 262). To grasp this meaning, we need to understand the "invisible chains" that bind monetary objects (and signifiers) together (Gregory 1997: 262). Superalternate money—underpinned by gold during the Bretton Woods era—was an index of the coercive power of the state (Gregory 1997: 256). Gregory's argument on gold echoes that of Polanyi: to maintain the standard, states had to "fix" the price of gold, for example, by denying ordinary citizens the right to trade in it. Since Bretton Woods, however, attempts to replace gold with a theoretical idea—the dollar standard, for example—have failed.

The natural properties of monetary objects—whether cowries, paper dollars, or gold—provide no clues as to their iconic, indexical, or symbolic significance. But it is here, in money's symbolism, that we can find the invisible chains that bind monetary objects and relations together. Gregory's analysis is especially intriguing when he examines situations in which two standards of monetary accounting clash: he calls these the dominant standard (**Sd**) and the subordinate standard (**Ss**). In such cases, the question of which standard of value prevails in economic transactions is a "struggle for prestige, a question of politics" (Gregory 1997: 259). He explains the struggle in terms of a quality, as opposed to quantity, theory of money. From the perspective of the traditional quantity theory of money, the transition from **Ss** to **Sd** would appear to be caused by an objective economic law, e.g., a loss of value caused by excessive supply. From the perspective of Gregory's *quality* theory, by contrast, it is the power of the dominant money that *dictates* supply in the first place: the demand for the subordinate standard falls because those in power *demand* **Sd** (Gregory 1997: 260–61). There is no "natural" tendency for superalternate standards of value to oust subalternate standards or for general-purpose monies to replace special-purpose monies. It is a question of power, not economic logic (Gregory 1997: 263). For Gregory, then, it is not (*contra* Wray) tax that "drives" money but rather *coercion*, reinforced by *law*: "a constant price (or quality) of money is an index of the dominance of an imperialist state" (Gregory 1997: 257).

Whereas Gregory's approach focuses on the large-scale effect of a major currency on local monetary systems, the work of Guyer takes a more detailed look at the monetary practices that take place when different currencies—even those of unequal status—circulate side by side. Number is an important variable in this picture, too, although Guyer suggests that the distinction between the quality and quantity theories of money must not be drawn too sharply. Moreover, the idea of two opposing standards of value—"two major actors, two currency modes" (Guyer 2004: 12)—is too simplistic. Using ethnographic research from Cameroon and Nigeria and focusing on an indigenous commercial civilization in West and Central Africa that is more than 300 years old, Guyer offers an account of this intermixing of quantity with quality that is necessarily unsystematic and "wild"—somewhat like the monetary practices she describes. For Guyer, it is not a question of quantity *versus* quality: both "sides" of Gregory's distinction are implicated within the monies she explores, as closely intertwined and dynamically interdependent standards of value. Given that the authorities largely failed to impose a single accounting standard for money, the result was a constant switching *between* calculative schemes across a wide range of monetary transactions. Whereas orthodox Western monetary theories are difficult to apply to this region, Guyer resists the idea that in such contexts we are necessarily dealing with "traditional" or "primitive" (and therefore weak) monies and monetary practices. Rather than setting up a simple dichotomy between non-Western and Western currencies (superalternate versus subalternate monies, for example), we need to grasp that there are overlapping and *mutually constitutive* monetary histories at work. Having said this, Guyer resists proposing a binary distinction between the local monetary practices she is describing and a broader based global system. There are overlapping histories at work here that must be seen as mutually constitutive. Cameroon and Nigeria have been thrust into modern world history in powerful and long-lasting ways. But at the same time, slave and tropical commodity trading have transformed that history:

> Universalist European theory does not easily apply because its coherent models and calculative practices orient to its own frontiers of innovation, taking the institutional frameworks as given. The convoluted history of those Western institutions and practices that created the monetary experiences of others was almost completely erased. (Guyer 2004: 14–15)

Guyer's argument resists straightforward summary and analysis, and most critical engagements with her work tend to be from the perspective of other fieldwork where the aim is to add complexity and build comparison. The discussion is especially compelling in highlighting the workings of asymmetrical exchanges involving money. These are exchanges between non-equivalents where the asymmetries involved are not simply explained away, masked, or eliminated but rather negotiated, manipulated, and exploited: "People gained familiarity with negotiating intervals, performing precedence and exchanging goods and services that were explicitly not the match of each other while still measuring value on a monetary scale" (Guyer 2004: 47). There is wide variation in modes of calculation and accounting: for example, multiple scales (ratio, ordinal, interval, and nominal) are often used creatively as an occasion for arbitrage. Rather than simply being seen as a threat, they are an opportunity for marginal gains: "When one scale is not exactly reducible to the terms of another, a margin for gain lies in the negotiation of situational matching. The gain can be either conventionalized or singularized, recognized or concealed, foregrounded or backgrounded, depending on context" (Guyer 2004: 51). Different monetary scales provide a varied repertoire for those engaged in commercial and financial transactions. Orthodox Western theories of money fail to explain the workings of such a repertoire because they are based on assumptions (e.g., about the exchange of equivalents, the presence of banks, and the importance of the state) that do not apply: "People preserve the repertoire, rather than 'rationalizing' it into a system, Weberian style" (Guyer 2004: 98).

From a sociological perspective, one of Guyer's most intriguing findings is that the majority of monetary valuations she found express a ranked view of the social world (Guyer 2004: 82). This finding recalls Bohannan's work, as well as some remarks we made about the history of *Wergild* in Chapter 1. According to Guyer, the nature of the ranking system in operation can have a profound effect on monetary practices such as lending and borrowing. We should therefore avoid classifying most uses of money as forms of consumption, with the residual as savings and investments. Rather it is more appropriate to think of almost every monetary transaction as a kind of investment, a "performative conversion, a devotion of present income to the hope of future gains" (Guyer 2004: 99).

A similarly rich picture of monetary calculation emerges from Haiti, which was the site of Sydney Mintz's study of the use of complex accounting measures in the Fond-des-Nègres marketplace (Mintz 1961, 1967). Although only one currency was used in Haiti, different sorts of measures were used for different products, resulting in constantly changing prices in response to the irregularities of local trade. An extraordinarily complex range of measures were in use, both in this particular market and in others:

> Scales are not used in local trade and solids and liquids are not sold by familiar numbered unit measures of any sort. Measures vary considerably from market region to market region; many products are sold neither by number nor by weight; the same number will be used for measures of different sizes, and vice-versa. The total effect upon the outside observer is likely to be one of whimsicality and arbitrariness. (Mintz 1961: 23)

This was the "creolization" of rural economic life, as local accounting systems were actively blended within the common economic and structural framework of colonial Caribbean societies in what could be seen as an early example of globalization (Browne 2005; Mintz 2012). The effect of such complexity upon money has been long lasting. Still today, two systems of accounting coexist in Haiti—the dollar and the gourde—despite the fact that only one official currency (the gourde) actually circulates. Though mainstream businesses routinely calculate in the gourde, Haitians themselves use a dual system; the dollar is a throwback to the era (before 1989) when the gourde was fixed to it at a rate of five to one. It is common for single transactions to take place in both systems, with prices measured in one currency and change calculated in another.

Just as Guyer observes in her work, here too the difference between accounting systems provides frequent opportunities for arbitrage, or "marginal gains." Thus, although these practices demonstrate the cultural richness of the repertoires used for monetary calculation, economic incentives are never too far away in shaping the way these repertoires are actually used. Echoing Mintz, a system that can appear chaotic and unfathomable to outsiders has its own internal structures. Baptiste, Horst, and Taylor understand Haitian monetary practices as a system of distinct but interrelated *monetary ecologies* (Baptiste, Horst, et al. 2010). Following LaGuerre's schema (LaGuerre 1982), they argue that these are organized around three economic systems, each of which constitutes a particular sociocultural context in which multiple currencies flow. These are the *market* system examined by Mintz, the *borlette*, which consists of the neighborhood gambling and lottery (Wilson and Levin 2010), and the *Sangue*, or rotating credit associations (Baptiste, Horst, et al. 2010: 3–4). Besides these, a range of financial service providers, banks, microcredit institutions, and money transfer services operate, albeit unevenly. The picture portrayed in this study is of an extraordinarily complex series of monetary circuits that depend on informal social networks, family ties, church groups, and international aid and nongovernmental organizations—as well as banks and other formal financial institutions that control access to money through their own complex rules and regulations. Of necessity, the Haitian monetary system combines two worlds: "a formal one that operates mostly in French and requires a knowledge of office culture, and an informal one that operates in Haitian Creole based on social networks and personal relationships where trust is the main currency" (Baptiste, Horst, et al. 2010: 6–7).

The work of Guyer and others brings out the importance of culture to the *interstitial* qualities of money, that is to say, its capacity to slide beneath borders and exploit—often for economic gain—those distinctions that exist on the margins of culture and society. It is therefore not surprising to find these themes in work that explores the monetary dynamics of economic (and social and political) transactions in and around geopolitical borders. For example, Sarah Green's work on the Greek–Albanian border draws attention to the singular status of EU development money within the social networks of Epirus (Green 2005). Recalling Hutchinson's study of the Nuer, to which I referred earlier, Green argues that EU money was considered to be "elite" money—in terms of its quantity and complexity, for example—which had to be mediated in a certain way in order to have any meaning at all. EU money was richly laden with metaphor, for example, when corrupt practices were often associated with eating seed money, rather than using it effectively:

> It is easy to see how people in Epirus related that to the idea of "eating": "eating" the seed money was explicitly understood as a means to destroy, rather than to help plant, these "seeds." "Eating" development money was understood as an activity that caused the eater to get fat, while also destroying the (re)productive potential of the money, and thereby destroying any possibility of the EU policy "bearing fruit." (Green 2008: 272)

Complex bureaucratic procedures had to be undertaken when applying for this money, and in accounting for its use, that were for the most part baffling to the majority of the population in Epirus: "only a small number of people with special skills could negotiate this minefield of paperwork" (Green 2008: 270). The marginal status of the euro itself, moreover, was regarded as highly distinctive by Epirots: wavering precariously between statelessness and joint Greek–EU origin, "this money made the external origins of EU development funding (and therefore its different interests) particularly explicit and visible" (Green 2008: 270).

In a similar vein, Gustav Peebles, in *The Euro and Its Rivals* (2012) investigates what European integration means by exploring money's status within interstitial economic and social spaces. In Peebles's case, that space consists of the Øresund Region between Denmark and Sweden, which separates Zealand from Scania. Peebles treats this space as a microcosm of the Eurozone; it is a region whose efforts to forge its own transnational (or, more precisely, *bi*national) identity were organized around the reinvention of its monies. Peebles locates the project within a lineage of "utopian" schemes that have sought to perfect *money* in order to perfect *society*. Most striking, perhaps, this region was meant to be a scientific—neoliberal—utopia in which monetary values were torn away from human values and phenomena such as bankruptcy were judged solely according to the former. But as Peebles shows, the tensions that were experienced by the inhabitants (and architects) of Øresund were frequently expressed through the interplay of monetary sameness and cultural difference in which the former—money's supposed uniformity and indifference to culture—was continuously renegotiated, questioned, and evaded. This transition frequently took place on the boundary between the public and private sphere:

> the Swedish moral injunction to do right by oneself . . . involved proving that one could indeed control one's money, that one could approach it

with all the rigor of a scientific accountant, which explains the importance in Sweden of the receipt and the refusal to accept minor everyday gifts. The successful control of money announced one's status as a modern and independent individual. Yet, with the national border in Øresund as a backdrop, this moral injunction has been shown to be spatially bounded; at various times, people slipped outside its scientific rigors and embraced the distinctly unscientific attitude of vagrancy and receiptless, spendthrift ways. There still remains a bedrock moral structure underneath all these scientific claims and projects ... Practices that came under the gaze of the scientific state in the modern home were abandoned to the whims of monetary valuation in the external sphere of the neoliberal market. Once one notes the congruence in moral critiques against illegal immigrants and hoarders of money abroad with the past indictments of vagrants and bankrupts, one sees clearly the continual ability to delimit borders of inclusion and exclusion via daily monetary practices and exchange regulations. (Peebles 2012: 159–60)

What these studies show is that cultural variation does not simply add color to forms of money that would otherwise conform to the drearily grey—predominantly classical—view of it as a homogeneous instrument that promotes standardized practices of calculation. Rather, cultural practices are a central feature of money itself, shaping it *from within*. This notion suggests that money is not just "earmarked," but continually invented and reinvented by its users. Such a perspective yields a radically different understanding of the nature of money—in relation to key categories such as capital and finance, credit and debt, society and state—than those we have been discussing so far in this book. In the next section, I begin to explore the normative implications.

REPERSONALIZING IMPERSONAL MONEY

An important strength of the approaches discussed in this chapter is in drawing attention to the varied forms that money can take and the myriad ways in which it reciprocally interacts with the values and cultural repertoires of its users. There is a danger, however, of forcing yet another dichotomy onto our understanding of the field, namely, between *structural* accounts of money and *agent-centered* approaches: or in other words, between a theory of money that is *determinist* and one that is *voluntarist*. One approach sees money as an objective and objectifying force: *in extremis*, it is a vehicle and expression of profound human alienation. The other sees money as the active and ongoing creation of its users. Or to express the contrast in a slightly different way, whereas the first approach privileges accounts of money that are largely technical and informed by "expert" theory, the second pushes us toward accounts that are more practical and informed by "lay" theories. The classical thinkers, and later Polanyi, might have exaggerated their fears about the destructive colonization of society by money, but this does not mean that such fears were altogether unfounded. Likewise, coming to grips with the creative ways in which money's users can mold and even reinvent money itself does not mean that we can dispense with the need to understand the broader structural conditions of production of particular monies. What is needed, ideally, is a strategy that avoids treating such options (alongside the other dichotomies mentioned here) as mutually exclusive. This is the approach taken by Keith Hart.

As we have discussed several times in this book, orthodox monetary theory is defined by two interconnected dichotomies: *commodity* versus *credit* theories of money's value, and historical accounts that prioritize the *market* versus the *state* as key sites of money's emergence and development. These simple dichotomies need to be broken down to produce a more nuanced view of money's nature, value, and history. According to Hart, the most powerful and misleading dichotomy of all is that between *market* and *state*. Rather than duplicating the dichotomy by opting for one or the other, we should think of states and markets as part of the same fundamental dualism—heads and tails—through which money is created. On the *state* side of the coin (heads), money expresses political hierarchy and authority: this side shows how much the coin is worth in exchange and reminds us that states underwrite money's value. This side corresponds to Polanyi's emphasis on money's role as a form of *payment* and not just exchange, and also to Gregory's arguments about the relationship between money and *power*. As Hart himself has said, this approach corresponds to Polanyi's depiction of money as a token domestically and a commodity internationally. On the market side (tails), money is shaped through horizontal relationships such as market exchange: money is in this sense a commodity. Hart argues that these two sides of money correspond to deeper political, moral, and philosophical streams in Western thought, which he further subdivides in terms of Kant's analytic of *form* and *substance*. The state theory of money divides into an emphasis on (a) the formal dependence of money on law and policy versus (b) its substantive dependence on elements of nation, *Volk* or *navod* ("populism"). Market theories cleave into (c) formal economic theory as opposed to (d) substantive theories of money's dependence on trust (Hart 1986: 645).

Monetary systems are dynamic; they vacillate between state regulation and market mediation. Such differences go back to archaic civilization, to popular revolutions against debt bondage and usury in the ancient Mediterranean. Monetary thought's long-standing theme is that heads and tails are irreconcilable: "Oscillations between the two produced both revolutions and institutions designed to contain the contradiction" (Hart 1986: 650). The shifts can be in response to fluctuating supply and demand (of monetary instruments) and changes in the political order. Far from being mutually exclusive, as mainstream thinking about the economy suggests, states and markets are part of the same basic configuration; they form an "ambiguous unity" (Hart 1986: 638). The relatively short-lived predominance of nation-states in the production and management of currency is giving way to a phase where money markets, offshore banking, and electronic payment systems are undermining the monetary sovereignty of nation-states (Hart 2001: 235). Money is as plural and dynamic today as it has ever been: "The money form is not standing still" (Hart 2001: 237).

What distinguishes Hart's approach is that it deals not with the difficulties that the erosion of state fiat money presents to governments but rather with the opportunities it presents to everyone else. He focuses particularly on digital money, which he regards as a potentially decentralizing force within markets for both consumer goods and financial products. Mainly through the Internet, consumers are being offered a diverse range of media through which to pay for goods or attain credit. Crucially for Hart, digital money is increasingly being manifest as *personal* credit. Money is thereby being transformed into an entity whose production—potentially, at least—we can actively control. This argument presents an interesting challenge to conventional understandings of economic agency: power is being transferred from the producers of money to the users themselves. As he states, the "great potential of the Internet is not restricted to the money form in a narrow sense, but lies rather in the expansion of electronic markets, in borderless trade at the speed of light. For electronic money will develop to the extent that it is needed for such trade" (Hart 2001: 276). Hart thereby builds on and extends the argument that money is neither opposed to nor merely embedded in, but actively and creatively constituted by social relations. His treatment of this argument is especially interesting because it focuses mainly on seemingly *im*personal Internet currencies, thereby lifting the relational perspective on money beyond face-to-face contact and beyond kinship relations, too.

Hart argues that just as money does not necessarily require the support of a sovereign political body (or a single overarching "society") to be widely accepted, so monetary relations are not inherently impersonal. He therefore sees money much as Durkheim saw religion: as a means for bridging the gap between our everyday personal experience and our broader social groupings. Although he agrees with Zelizer that money is not lifeless but the active creation of human beings, Hart refuses the dichotomy between impersonal and personal money that the notion of earmarking sometimes implies. Money has to be impersonal in order to connect people with wider relations, although as Zelizer has shown, people continuously make it personal. We are thereby forced to engage in a form of dualistic thinking in our monetary lives, dividing ourselves between social relations that are putatively characterized by the absence of money (the family, the inside, the home), and social relations (impersonal society, the outside, the market) in which money is expected to dominate. For Hart, the contrast usually drawn between these two spheres—between a (nonmonetary) private sphere that stands for personal integration and free association and a public (monetary) sphere that signifies alienation and detachment—is false. In rejecting the dichotomy, he maintains that money can and must be central to any attempt to "humanize" society. Though money surely is a source of our vulnerability in society, it is also a practical means of rendering the impersonal world more meaningful.

What makes this argument especially intriguing is that the case is advanced through an analysis of the *properties*—not just the *use*—of digital money. One of the most important characteristics of electronic money is the way in which it conveys information. In economics, the information that is transmitted by money has conventionally been understood as consisting of abstract price signals that enable markets to work. But of course, there is potentially much more substance to monetary information than this. Just as Gregory views money as a symbolic index of the coercive power of the state, Hart argues that digital money is an index of personal information about its users that is not present with traditional forms of money, such as cash. The classical conception of money as an *anonymous* medium of exchange has been undermined by a fundamental change in the nature of the monetary form. For better or worse, monetary transactions are increasingly *traceable*: not just in terms of the amount changing hands and the flow of funds involved, but also in terms of the preferences and routines of transactors themselves. Loyalty cards offer an outstanding example of this development, enabling corporations to manipulate sophisticated detailed data about their customers' buying behavior. This, in the end, is as close as Hart comes to providing a general definition of money: it is an instrument of *collective memory* (Hart 2001: 234), a "memory bank" that tracks a diverse range of social exchanges that are mediated by increasingly specialized monetary forms: "we should look for the meaning of money in the myriad acts of remembering that link individuals to their communities" (Hart 2001: 318–19).[12]

According to Hart, the application of this technology within decentralized markets has the potential to transform money from an impersonal medium of exchange to "an act of remembering, a way of keeping track of the exchanges we each enter into" (Hart 2001: 234). If such a potential is realized, money will act as a perpetually mobile testimony to our participation in a diverse range of specialized (and, to some degree, *re*personalized) payment networks. He thereby invites us to imagine myriad potential ways in which money might be appropriated by individuals and communities. His primary aim is to wrench our understanding of money away from a particular conception of the market itself as autonomous, and by doing so, to encourage more creative interpretations of the nature of money itself. Significantly for the discussion in this book, he seeks to decouple our interpretation of money from a particular conception of *society*. He agrees that money is a "token of society," much as Simmel suggested (Hart 2001: 235). But Hart uses a *differentiated* concept of society to elaborate the idea. Society has three distinct senses within the sociological and anthropological literature on money: as *state*, *nation*, and *community*. Applied to money, all three senses of "society" suggest that "money is a symbol of something intangible, an aspect of human agency, not just a thing" (Hart 2001: 252). More importantly, however, each concept of society yields a distinctive conception of the interrelationship between money and social structure. When viewed as a creature of the *state*, money is conveyed as a tool of power that expresses "vertical relations between unequals, rulers and ruled, like the top and bottom two sides of the coin, heads and tails" (Hart 2001: 252). By contrast, when society is taken to mean *community*, money's dependence on *trust* is underlined. This interpretation locates the source of monetary value within "horizontal" relations between members of a community. Finally, the association of money with *nation* combines these vertical and horizontal interpretations, i.e., "the formality of the state with the informal substance of community" (Hart 2001: 252). Hart's own analysis of digital money leans strongly toward the interpretation of society as community. But he does not

---

12   Kocherlakota, incidentally, puts forward a rather different version of this view of money as memory, arguing that "the role of money is to serve as a (typically imperfect) form of memory," and providing an economic theory that seeks to explain money's existence in these terms (Kocherlakota 1998).

exclude the other two senses of the term. In other words, Simmel's characterization of money as a claim upon society remains valid even today, as long as the meaning of "society" is never fixed but is allowed to flex according to the scale of monetary form in question.

Inevitably, such arguments are speculative. For example, the contention that the growing range of available ways to pay with (and borrow) money necessarily equates with a transfer of economic power away from states and corporations requires detailed empirical scrutiny. The argument that digital money is a device for *remembering* cannot be divorced from the criticism that it is also a vehicle for political and commercial *surveillance*, above all, as long as the technology involved is controlled by corporations and states. And as we see in the next chapter, the main attraction of Bitcoin for many of its users is precisely that people using it are *not* traceable. Although Hart is encouraged by the potential of the Internet for reinventing money, one also wonders just how far this can affect large-scale banks and financial markets. As Hart himself makes clear, however, he is not suggesting that money is being repersonalized in all of its forms. State currency is and will remain the dominant form of money, although it is undoubtedly losing its monopoly over the world's monetary system. If anything, the analysis he proposes is a dialectical one. That is to say, the development of electronic money can act as a counterweight to the growth of financial markets, generating a form of currency competition driven by consumers, not institutional elites. More personalized forms of money will coexist with other, more traditional forms. Quite what such diversity means when trying to come to grips, not just with the future of money per se but also with its potential role in society's human and moral economy, is a question I explore in the next chapter.

CONCLUSION

In this chapter, we have examined various ways of contradicting, and countering, the assumptions underpinning Schumpeter's claim that culture is of no interest to monetary science. As we have seen, there is a rich body of research on cultural aspects of money. Broadly speaking, its main findings are that culture (i.e., shared meanings and practices, and their symbolic representations) should be seen neither in *opposition* to money nor as *exogenous* to it. There are many ways in which money's value, its function as an accounting system, its commensurability with persons and things, the practices associated with lending and borrowing it, as well as broader connections between monetary values and social hierarchy, are constituted by factors that have conventionally been viewed as part of an entirely separate world in which money has no natural place. But as I argued earlier in this chapter, we should also avoid caricaturing the work of classical thinkers such as Marx and Simmel as overly narrow and economistic. Both were centrally concerned with how money's key features are socially reproduced, not simply "given" as the objective properties of money. Neither one of these thinkers lacked what subsequently came to be called a sociological imagination. However, there is a strong case to be made that their depictions of money were lacking the texture and color that researchers have subsequently discovered.

The work of Polanyi underlines the critical potential of taking such a view. His "double movement" thesis suggests that money requires protection from society to no less an extent than do nature and human life. To express this in another way, society needs to be protected from itself in the way that it seeks to incorporate these phenomena as fictitious commodities (labor, land, and money) that can be organized and distributed through the mechanisms of the self-regulating market. But as I argued above, Polanyi leaves us with a lingering sense that any "culturalist" view of money that is derived from his work would remain parasitic upon narrower, market-based approaches to money. Culture is important not only in grasping what money does but also what it might *become*. We therefore need to grasp not just the ways in which money is "resisted" by its users, but more positively, how they actively *create* it. Money's value, potentially, is not simply what it can be exchanged for, but also the role it might play in enriching economic life. This utopian idea is the focus of discussion in the next chapter.

8 UTOPIA

> Man proposes and disposes. He and he alone can determine whether he is completely master of himself, that is, whether he maintains the body of his desires, daily more formidable, in a state of anarchy. Poetry teaches him to. It bears within itself the perfect compensation for the miseries we endure. It can also be an organizer, if ever, as the result of a less intimate disappointment, we contemplate taking it seriously. The time is coming when it decrees the end of money and by itself will break the bread of heaven for the earth! There will still be gatherings on the public squares, and *movements* you never dared hope participate in. Farewell to absurd choices, the dreams of dark abyss, rivalries, the prolonged patience, the flight of the seasons, the artificial order of ideas, the ramp of danger, time for everything!
>
> **ANDRÉ BRETON, MANIFESTOES OF SURREALISM**[1]

Frederick Jameson described the proposal to abolish money—and, alongside it, private property—as "the grandest of all the ruptures effectuated by the Utopian Imagination" (Jameson 2007: 229). Thomas More in 1516 instigated the rupture he had in mind. For More, the end of money would mean the end of "all those types of criminal behaviour which daily punishments are powerless to check: fraud, theft, burglary, brawls, riots, disputes, rebellion, murder, treason, and black magic" (More 2004: 111–12). Money's abolition would resolve problems such as "fear, tension, anxiety, over-work, and sleepless nights," and even poverty itself "would promptly disappear if money ceased to exist" (More 2004: 111–12). More was part of a distinguished line of monetary abolitionists stretching back to Plato—who envisaged a society with neither gold nor silver, profits from mechanical crafts, usury, or the "raising of sordid beasts" (Plato 2000: 1328)—and forward, via Proudhon, to modern anarchism and nonmarket socialism (Nelson and

1   Breton 1969: 18.

313

Timmerman 2011).[2] "Let all merchandise become current money," Proudhon declared, "and abolish the royalty of gold" (Proudhon 1927: 46). Breton's prediction that—of all things—*poetry* would decree the end of money is merely one of the more unusual examples of its kind. Incidentally, the only known original copy of Breton's manifesto was eventually sold, alongside a selection of his personal effects, for €3.9 million in 2008. As it happens, Breton's idea resonates with Goethe, who in the Masquerade scene of *Faust II* likened poetry to a spendthrift. In response, Hörisch interprets poetry and squandering as transgressions of the mentality associated with the modern money economy (Hörisch 2000: 153–58).

There is another line of thought besides abolitionism, which is perhaps richer, consisting of various *reimaginings* of money. These are images of Utopia defined not by money's absence but rather by its radical transformation. There are some notable scholars here, too, such as Aquinas and de Azpilcueta, who advocated the principle of just pricing (Grabill 2007; Alves and Moriera 2010; see Schumpeter 1986: 91–92), and Ruskin, who advocated labor money (Ruskin 1997: 215). For such thinkers, the problem is not that money exists at all but rather that it has been badly designed. They have all made important contributions to a tradition of practical schemes that use innovations in the design of money and the price system to improve economic conditions, including proposals by renowned economists, such as Irving Fisher's stamp scrip (Fisher, Cohrssen, et al. 1933) and Robert Shiller's baskets (Shiller 2008). Finally, there are now several thousand alternative monetary systems in operation worldwide, using a range of different media and accounting schemes designed to foster local economic growth, resist financial exclusion, and even challenge what many believe to be the persistent and damaging hegemony of states and banks in the way that money is produced and managed. There are, then, whole hosts of ways in which, to use Simmel's memorable phrase, war has been declared on the monetary system.[3] Although not all such skirmishes involve the construc-

---

[2] The idea of a moneyless world usually breaks down over the prospect of finding people to barter with (the double coincidence of wants problem), but some commentators believe that this hitch is much *less* of a problem in the computer age. For example, David Birch argues that "we can resolve the long chain of intermediate coincidences, minimising each step by search, in a few milliseconds. In this way, it is possible to imagine trades taking place with Google replacing Bank of England notes," see "Imagine there's no money," http://fw.ifslearning.ac.uk/Archive/2011/October/Comment/Imaginetheresnomoneydavidbirch.aspx, accessed May 10, 2013.

[3] Simmel uses the phrase in relation to socialism: "For by declaring war upon this monetary system, socialism seeks to abolish the individual's isolation in relation to the group" (Simmel 2004: 346).

tion of utopian programs, many of them are triggered by what Jameson, after Bloch (Bloch 2000), called the utopian spirit. It is this spirit, insofar as it applies to money, that this chapter sets out to explore.[4]

The chapter begins by considering two examples of Utopia in which there *is* a role for money, albeit one that can only be glimpsed. They are rarely discussed, which (besides their inherent interest) is a good reason for bringing them to light now. The first appears in the work of Simmel, the notion of "perfect" money that he introduces in *The Philosophy of Money*. I argue that Simmel's concept of perfect money can be understood as utopian in two senses, conceptual and ethical, that correspond to the two interpretations he develops, in *Soziologie* (Simmel 2009), of the idea of a perfect society. This concept sheds light on an aspect of his writings that has attracted relatively little attention, namely, his views on the relationship between money and socialism. Second, I examine Erich Fromm's case for a "humanistic" utopia (Fromm 1976). This was meant to supersede the "technical utopia" that, so he argued, Western societies had been slavishly pursuing since the Enlightenment. His argument is intriguing now because it was conceived in the teeth of the capitalist crises of the 1970s, which arguably presaged many of the financial problems we are witnessing today. His key distinction, between *having* and *being*, proposes a particular understanding of two coexisting orientations to being human. Money straddles both orientations. As I argue below, Simmel and Fromm raise profound questions about money's role in both shaping and mediating human economic relations. In the remaining sections of this chapter, I explore these questions in a more practical way by relating them to other utopian schemes for reforming money, both as advanced by great social reformers such as Ruskin and Proudhon and as proposed by those who are more narrowly engaged with the technical features of money. I also relate these arguments to several "real-life" monetary (and financial) utopias, such as local and complementary currencies, mobile money, and Bitcoin.

---

4   Utopianism is by no means unambiguously positive, of course, and what seems utopian from one perspective can be dystopian from another. Neoliberalism can be seen this way: as a libertarian paradise as envisaged by Ayn Rand in *Atlas Shrugged* (Rand 2007: 752–815)—one chapter of the book is called "The Utopia of Greed"—or as the bleak free market dystopia portrayed by Thomas Frank in *One Market Under God* (Frank 2001). Taking account of both views, Jocelyn Pixley writes of a "finance utopia"—rooted in the idea of a self-correcting market—which is not partial and modest as utopian projects ought to be (if they are realizable), but all-embracing: "The 'market' utopia is 'total' in dismissing and manipulating everything else, democracy notably. 'Money capitalism' dominates the world's wealth; the sector acts through mindless competition that pulls the world apart. Authoritarian mediocrity rules" (Pixley 2012a: 226).

SIMMEL'S PERFECT MONEY

When exploring the intellectualization of modern culture, Simmel (Simmel 2004: 437) cites Comte's proposal (Comte 1896: 194) "to place bankers at the head of secular government in his utopian state"—because of their capacity for abstract thought—without irony. Although he could scarcely have imagined the size of today's banks, Simmel did predict that the monetary system would increase in scale: "Progressive development strives in reality for the expansion, and consequently the centralization, of the institutions and powers that guarantee money values" (Simmel 2004: 183). The utopian impulse seems never too far away from this trend. But if we apply Simmel's own logic to this situation, we must immediately cast our eyes in the opposite direction to look for a contradictory movement. Evidence of the progressive *de*centralization of money can be found as alternative monetary forms. They include local schemes that use a common accounting system to exchange goods and services such as LETS, time dollars, mutual credit, peer-to-peer (P2P) lending schemes such as Whuffie and Kiva, and digital currencies such as Ripple, Ven, Pecunix, and Bitcoin. In Argentina, a spate of such schemes—*Trueque*—emerged during the 1999–2002 crisis (North 2007). Alternative monies are of particular interest now in the wake of the financial crisis, as we look for new ways of organizing money and credit that are not controlled by states and banks. But though there is evidence that these alternatives are gaining ground, it is open to question what Simmel would make of them. As we shall see, on the basis of these arguments, he develops a notion of "unequal pricing" that, by his lights, would be the realization of the utopia of perfect money—and the logical correlate of the perfect society.

Simmel was neither an abolitionist, nor a reformist, of money. But there is a utopian impulse underlying his analysis, which surfaces at various points in *The Philosophy of Money* (Simmel 2004), most notably in his enigmatic remarks on formal affinities between money and socialism, and when he examines various schemes (such as labor money) for reconfiguring money as a progressive social technology. These projects intrigue Simmel because they carry specific *ideas* of money to their logical extremes, thereby enabling us to see money's significance from a number of different perspectives. His treatment of these ideas should therefore help us to reach a balanced appraisal of normative dimensions of his analysis of money. In the extant literature, a rather narrow, economic interpretation of Simmel's book is sometimes advanced as the epitome of a conception of money that is excessively utilitarian and therefore socially corrosive. On the other hand, he is sometimes accused of producing an overly "culturalist" account of money that neglects social structure (Ingham 2004b: 66). As my argument in Chapter 7 suggested, neither reading is fully justified. In what follows, I hope to develop a more balanced view that takes account of ethical dimensions of Simmel's work that have not been widely discussed, for example, his views on money and socialism.

The idea of perfect money comes up several times in Simmel's book. In the first chapter, he refers to a form of "conceptually correct" money that is detached completely "from every *substantial value* that limits the quantity of money" (Simmel 2004: 165, italics added). Understandably, most commentators assume that he means *token* money, consisting of paper (Ingham 2004b: 64). But Simmel's language is strange: the phrase *conceptually correct* money suggests a *theoretical* position against which a certain form of money should be deemed to be correct or complete. Elsewhere, he also refers to a *pure concept* of money (Simmel 2004: 119, 121, 127, 129, 167, 168) and to *perfect* money (Simmel 2004: 128, 221, 235, 277, 349, 485). These, I would argue, are formulations of the same basic idea: correct, pure, or perfect concepts in Simmel's work are *fictions*. They are comparable to Weberian ideal types in the sense that they guide and delimit our thought. They are the tools against which we can interrogate our empirical observations, or in other words, *conceptual* utopias. By calling money a fiction, Simmel suggests that the idea of money that underpins its use in society never actually corresponds to the empirical forms of money that we encounter there. Crucially, he means that it is a *generic* fiction: all empirical manifestations of money are a variation on an idealized form that he sometimes calls perfect money. He does not regard money, in this abstract sense, as a real entity. Rather, he sees it as an *idea*. As such, it presents the conceptual limit against which all monies take shape as amalgamations of qualitative and quantitative features (Dodd 2005a, 2007, 2008).

Besides the methodological relevance of conceptually correct money as a tool for thought, I want to suggest that Simmel also gives the idea an intriguing *ethical* dimension, which concerns the deeper social, political, and cultural tensions within money that we have discussed elsewhere in this book. These are tensions that, typically, he does not seek to reconcile but rather to hold in suspension. So what is perfect money, or what would it be? When he states that conceptually correct money is detached from "every substantial value," Simmel refers not just to money's intrinsic value, but also to the "essential fiction" that its value *remains unchanged* (Simmel 2004: 191). Perfection, then, is a property of *stable* money. On close inspection, however, it seems that Simmel had not just low inflation in mind. "Stable" money also means money that *does not disturb the structure of the society in which it circulates*. As we shall see, what he has in mind here is not the more conventional idea of "neutral" money that is associated with classical economics but a condition whereby prices express the specific relationship an *individual* has to *society*. This is an important theme throughout Simmel's work and was crucial to his reading of Nietzsche, which we discussed in Chapter 4.

Simmel's argument rests on an equation between (a) the total quantity of *money* in circulation and (b) the total quantity of *commodities* on sale. Prices are the numerical expression of a proportion between (a) and (b). These observations are consistent with Simmel's relationist theory of value, according to which nothing has value in its own right, but only in relation to other things (Canto-Mila 2005). Stable money appears to have two distinct meanings in Simmel's text. First, it means that all prices must be constant *relative to each other*, even when the overall totals (of money on one side and commodities on the other) change. In other words, any alteration in the money supply must affect all prices equally: if the money supply doubles, all prices must do so. Only once this condition is met is it possible to regard money as stable, and therefore as perfect, or conceptually correct. This looks like the quantity theory of money, rooted in the sixteenth century and traditionally attributed to Jean Bodin's *Response to the Paradoxes of Malestroit* (originally published 1568, 1997 cited here) (Spiegel 1991: 86–92) and was the prevailing orthodoxy in economics at the time that Simmel was writing (Spiegel 1991: 589–90). But Simmel advances a second interpretation of the idea of stable money, whereby any change in the money supply would affect not only all *prices* equally but also all *persons* in the same way (Simmel 2004: 161). This idea is premised on the argument that, even distributed proportionately, any increase in the money supply would have an unequal effect across society, according to wealth. These are commonplace concerns in the monetary literature. In his 1923 essay, "Social Consequences of Changes in the Value of Money," Keynes discusses the idea that inflation—not the money supply per se—affects different groups in society according to their wealth. He states that "when the value of money changes, it does *not* change equally for all persons" (Keynes 1972:80), and on this basis, famously describes inflation as "unjust" and deflation as "inexpedient" (Keynes 1972: 103). Later, in *Human Action* (1949), Ludwig von Mises would agree: "As money can never be neutral and stable in purchasing power, a government's plans concerning the determination of the quantity of money can never be impartial and fair to all members of society" (von Mises 1998: 419). But the fact that Simmel frames the problem of "conceptually correct"—or *perfect*—money in these terms is worth investigating further because he advances what seems to be a quintessentially *sociological* interpretation of the idea of neutral money. And this interpretation, as we shall see, is crucial to the spirit of utopianism that runs through his work.

When Simmel speculates about what the effect of a sudden change in the money supply might be on different groups in society, he describes three individuals whose income consists of one, ten, and a hundred thousand marks, respectively: "In the first case there would be, perhaps, an improvement in nutrition, in the second a refinement of artistic culture, and in the third a greater involvement in financial speculation" (Simmel 2004: 163). In a similar vein, in his 1899 lectures as transcribed by Park (Park 1931), Simmel characterizes a tripartite division between classes in terms of money: "some possess no money at all (lowest), others save something (middle), a third class can live permanently from its interest (highest strata)" (cited in Simmel 2004: xviii). But most importantly of all for our discussion, Simmel extends the argument by claiming that stable money is only possible in an *ideal social order* (Simmel 2004: 191). Oddly, this striking remark has hardly ever been picked up in the extant secondary literature, although it was highlighted in G. H. Mead's review of the first edition of *The Philosophy of Money*, published in 1900. Intriguingly, Mead read the passage in similar terms to those I am proposing here:

> Under ideal conditions ... there would be no necessity that money should have any inherent value. It would be only an expression of the relation between the values of goods stated in the form of a fraction. Money would be purely symbolic ... The failure to reach the ideal is the result of the *inability of the community* to make its equation between its different goods and the sum complete and perfect. In the presence of this uncertainty the individual reverts instinctively, especially in periods of panics, to an equation between the commodity and an intrinsically valuable thing. That money still has, to some degree, independent value is an indication of our failure to reach completely the ideal of economic organization. (Mead 1994: 146, italics added)

As Mead suggests, what first appears to be quite a narrow technical argument about relative prices carries a strong ethical undercurrent insofar as such an order depends on the ability of the *community* to make the equation between money and commodities "complete" and "perfect."[5] So in what

---

5 Note that the social order Simmel has in mind does not depend on the *elimination* of inequality but rather on its *stabilization* vis-à-vis money.

kind of social order would the structure remain undisturbed by a change in the money supply? Under what conditions, and with what form of money, might such an increase affect everyone equally? Might there, in fact, be a perfect *society* that corresponds to Simmel's notion of perfect *money*?

As it happens, Simmel does use the idea of a perfect society elsewhere in his work, namely, in the excursus from Chapter 1 of *Soziologie* (1908), "How Is Society Possible?" (Simmel 2009: 40–52). Here, he proposes a "Kantian" theory of society as a process that is produced through the synthesizing activities of its members. Simmel suggests that these activities involve a series of fictions (these resemble his pure concept of money). One example of such a fiction that occurs in societal synthesis is the process of forming an ideal picture of another's individual qualities. This is the picture we would see were that person to reach his or her fullest potential as a distinct individual (Simmel 2009: 44). Simmel argues that a similar process of idealization is necessary at the level of *society as a whole*, which "simply continues as if every one of its members were fully relationally integrated, each one dependent on all others and all others on the one, just because each one is individually a part of it" (Simmel 2009: 50). What he has in mind here is a form of integration whereby each person discovers his or her own unique location within society, which he likens to their *vocation*. This is the position through which one's particular qualities as an individual find their fullest societal recognition; indeed, this is the condition for his or her realization. Crucially, for Simmel, those very qualities that make individuals unique, and therefore distinct from one other, do not *obstruct* social life but are rather the very *precondition* for harmonious social existence (Pyyhtinen 2010: 96). In making this argument, Simmel draws a further distinction, between "the *perfect* society and the perfect *society*" (Simmel 2009: 51, original italics). This distinction yields two notions of perfection, ethical and conceptual, that help us to explore the argument about conceptually correct money still further.

Simmel associates ethical perfection (the *perfect* society) with a form of *absolute* equality whereby individuals are treated as identical. Besides absolute equality, he also refers to *complete* equality and *communistic* equality (Simmel 2004: 163, 336, 346). The form of equality he associates with conceptual perfection, conversely, is *relative*, i.e., it based on individual difference: "Society is a construct of unlike parts" (Simmel 2009: 49). Simmel invokes both forms of equality—absolute and relative, respectively—when contrasting an earlier individualism ("The viewpoint of Christianity, the Enlightenment of the eighteenth century (including Rousseau and Kant), and ethical socialism) with a later individualism that he associates with "the nineteenth century since the Romantics" (Simmel 2004: 362). Though the first kind assumes that "value lies in human beings merely because they are human beings ... the absolute value of all men is the same," the second emphasizes "the differences between individuals and their qualitative peculiarities" (Simmel 2004: 362). When considered in terms of their qualities, individuals are necessarily unequal "because of their different natures, life contents, and destinies" (Simmel 2009: 49). If this form of equality were achieved in society, it would constitute a form of conceptual perfection, i.e., a perfect society consisting of a structure composed of *unequal* elements. Equality, in this sense, is not synonymous with equivalence: it is a form of relative, not absolute, equality.

The distinction Simmel draws here between relative and absolute equality is also implied in an earlier essay, "Sociological Aesthetics" (1896). Here, Simmel distinguishes between aesthetic and political forms of equality, and this distinction has an important bearing on our discussion of money and socialism.[6] The difference hinges on the idea of *symmetry*. Aesthetically, symmetry "gives meaning to everything from one single point" (Simmel 1968). There is a balance between part and whole that appeals innately to the eye: "The various parts of the whole must be balanced against one another, and arranged evenly around a centre" (Simmel 1968: 71). However, as aesthetically pleasing as symmetry might be, in Simmel's estimation it is not politically satisfying. Symmetry in art is one thing. Symmetry in *society*, he suggests, favors tyranny: "The charm of symmetry, with its internal equilibration, its external unity, and its harmonic relationship of all parts to its unified centre, is one of the purely aesthetic forces which attracts many intelligent people to autocracy, with its unlimited expression of the unified will of the State" (Simmel 1968: 73). Simmel advances similar claims in *The Philosophy of Money*, arguing that both socialism and despotism possess a strong inclination toward the symmetrical constructions of society. Both imply a strong *centralization* of society that "requires the reduction of the individuality of its elements and of the irregularity of its forms and relationships to a symmetrical form" (Simmel 2004: 489). Bringing objects and people "under the yoke of the system" by arranging them symmetrically is the best way of subjecting them to rational administration. Historically, this logic has been played out in architecture: with Louis XIV's symmetrical windows and doors; in Campanella's sun-state with its mathematically de-

---

6   Frisby suggests that there is a shift in Simmel's work around the mid-1890s from ethical to aesthetic concerns and cites a review of *The Philosophy of Money* by Rudolf Goldscheid that maintains that the "ideal" that lies behind the book is aesthetic, not ethical (Frisby 1992: 12).

signed capital and finely graded spatial arrangements of citizens; within the cities of myriad socialist utopias, with their symmetrical organization of buildings and localities into circles or squares; and in Rabelais' order of Thelemites with its gigantic central building "in the shape of a sextangle, a tower at each corner, sixty steps in diameter" (Simmel 2004: 489).

By contrast, the "conceptual" perfection that Simmel conceives in "How Is Society Possible?" consists of an asymmetrical arrangement. This arrangement is one of *relative* equality. Simmel suggests that although this arrangement might be aesthetically displeasing—the whole "looks disorganized and irregular"—political asymmetry brings the inner life of the state, that is, the life of its constituent individuals, to its "most typical expression and its most harmonic form . . . Asymmetrical arrangements permit broader individual rights, more latitude for the free and far-reaching relations of each element" (Simmel 1968: 74–75). By contrast, the "despotic compulsion culminates in symmetric structures, uniformity of elements and avoidance of anything that is improvised" (Simmel 2004: 338). Asymmetry may offend his taste, but it clearly appeals to Simmel's political sensibilities.

Money, Simmel says, has an inherent tendency of "making the individual more and more dependent on the achievements of people, but less and less dependent on the personalities that lie behind them" (Simmel 2004: 296). Here, his argument touches on broader themes in the history of modern thought, which we also find in Simmel's treatment of Nietzsche. These themes resonate with the subsequent work of thinkers associated with the Frankfurt School. Specifically, they relate to the problem of reconciling our personal striving for *uniqueness* and *distinction*, which money and economic liberalism appear to nurture, with the conflicting tendencies of modern society (and the mature money economy) toward *leveling*. If the tendency of money to render our social relations increasingly functional were carried through to its logical extreme, it would encourage a form of life which has "a profound affinity to socialism, at least to an extreme state socialism" (Simmel 2004: 296). Such a form of socialism, Simmel writes, transforms "every action of social importance into an objective function" (Simmel 2004: 296), constructing a society in which the order of functions stands above the psychological reality of man "like the realm of Platonic ideas above the real world" (Simmel 2004: 297). If this is a perfect society, it is one that has been synthesized *from the outside*, "conceived in accordance with a completely objective standpoint" in which "the personality as a mere holder of a function or position is just as irrelevant as that of a guest in a hotel room" (Simmel 2004: 297).

Simmel suggests that his critique of the tragedy of modern culture uncovers a "secret restlessness, this helpless urgency that lies below the threshold of consciousness" that "drives modern man from socialism to Nietzsche" (Simmel 2004: 484). This statement testifies to his underlying Nietzschean sympathies, particularly toward the latter's emphasis on the distinctive qualities of the single individual. For Nietzsche, it is the single highest example of its individuals that determines the value of an era. When Simmel describes society as "the universal which, at the same time, is concretely alive" (Simmel 2004: 101), the life he is referring to here is expressed through *exchange*, which makes possible that interaction through which an object is raised from isolation into the sphere of economic value. Simmel is drawn to the fact that Nietzsche does not *dissolve* the individual into the group: "Man follows a single line to oneself" (Simmel 1991b: 146). Simmel connects these arguments to Nietzsche's antipathy toward money: the noble person is uninterested in price, indeed "the style of aristocratic life is diametrically opposed to that of the money economy where the value of things tends increasingly to be so identified" (Simmel 1991b: 166). Nobility in this context stands for that singular quality which, as we saw in Chapter 4, Nietzsche associates with the single highest example of the value of an era. By contrast, the money economy is based on an extreme *esteem* for money—which Simmel, like Nietzsche, decries.

Simmel's statement that relative equality could never be achieved through symmetry in society could easily be read as a critique of socialism. But this must be squared with his various remarks about money's formal *affinities* with socialism (Simmel 2004: 296). Whereas money played a crucial role in the development of "the individualistic society of England . . . through the growth of its financial system," it is also the precursor of "socialistic" forms of society (Simmel 2004: 495). Money nurtures socialism in two ways that are of interest to us here: first, because specific monetary conditions present the "blueprint or type of social form that socialism strives to establish," and second, "through the dialectical process of *turning liberalism into its negation*" (Simmel 2004: 495, italics added). This point can be illustrated by considering Simmel's argument about the pure monetary association. This association is a liberal order in which only the money interests of its members come into play. Freely entered into, this order rests on the complete separation of the two sides of the individual (the personal and the functional) that socialism conflates. This separation enables "a unification of people who, because of their spatial, social, personal and other discrepancies in interests, could not possibly be integrated into any other group formation" (Simmel 2004: 347). Monetary associations appeal to him politically, if not aesthetically, because they nurture individual freedom, enabling us to commune with others without giving up our "personal freedom and reserve" (Simmel 2004: 344). Of the workers' associations formed in post-

1848 France, he remarks: "they found a way of realizing the existing unity of their interest in that communality through the mere possession of money" (Simmel 2004: 344). But just as liberalism becomes its own negation if taken too far, the monetary association generates "irregularity" and "unpredictability"—conditions under which individuals are increasingly self-estranged (Simmel 2004: 332). Hence Simmel's remark that "the deeper connection of the money economy with the tendencies of liberalism" helps to explain "why the freedom of liberalism has brought about so much instability, disorder and dissatisfaction" (Simmel 2004: 404). Without a counterpoint, then, the liberal monetary association destroys everything that, *in moderation*, it nurtures—like the family that "has become almost nothing more than an organization for inheritance" (Simmel 2004: 345). Here, Simmel's lack of any clear political affiliation shines through.

Simmel argues that—*in extremis*—both the "socialist" division of labor *and* the "liberal" association of monetary interests undermine our quest for individual distinction. Just as the former denies and destroys the individual personality, the latter cuts it adrift. The outcome is essentially the same: an excessively *rational* order—liberal *or* socialist. As an ideal, socialism inspires "all the innermost and enthusiastic sympathies for the group that may lie dormant in the individual." As such, it has strong affinities "with the hollow communistic instincts that, as the residue of times long since past, still lie in the remote corners of the soul" (Simmel 2004: 346). But when taken too far, such ideals all too easily lead to a soul-destroying rationalism, which permits the "control of life's chance and unique elements by the law-like regularities and calculations of reason" (Simmel 2004: 346). Simmel's argument powerfully suggests that the "complete" realization of socialism always produces conditions diametrically opposed to those for which the socialists actually strive.

In *Soziologie*, Simmel approvingly cites the Familistère de Guise as something approaching a socialistic form of organization. This was a cast-iron factory founded by a disciple of Fourier on the principle of providing "complete sustenance for each worker and his family, guaranteeing a minimum subsistence, care and education of children at no cost, and collective provision of the necessities of life" (Simmel 2009: 54). Significantly, the factory was small, employing only around 2,000 people, and was surrounded by a society living under very different life conditions.[7] When Simmel states

---

7   In "On the Significance of Numbers for Social Life," Simmel suggests that socialism works best in "small, and therefore undifferentiated groups"—"The contribution of each to the whole and the group's regard to him are visible at close range; comparison and compensation are easy" (in Wolff 1950: 88).

that "completely or approximate socialistic arrangements until now were feasible only in rather small groups, but are ever frustrated in large ones" (Simmel 2009: 53), a parallel is suggested with today's local currency movements, which operate as what Polanyi would call special-purpose monetary circuits serving specific needs (for specialized credit, local trade, and so on) within much larger circuits of general-purpose money. The stated aim of such movements is rarely (if ever) to *replace* mainstream (general-purpose) money. Rather, it is to provide a *counterweight* to it, that is to say, a set of monetary arrangements that can make up for the shortcomings of mainstream money, such as financial exclusion (Dodd 2005b). Likewise, socialism appeals to Simmel not *tout court*, but rather as a corrective, i.e., a tendency that resists the equally complete realization of the form of individualism he identifies with economic liberalism. If anything, socialism would work most effectively only from *within* a liberal market order.

Simmel's arguments about socialism and liberalism are taken further in his critique of *just pricing*. This is the principle espoused in Aquinas's argument that "no man should sell what is not his" (Aquinas 2000: IIa, IIae q. 77 a. 1). The idea is also mentioned in E. P. Thompson's "The Moral Economy of the English Crowd in the 18th Century," which describes rioting against those merchants and traders who raised the price of grain to exploit shortages (Thompson 1971: 78–79). More recent examples include various forms of price regulation such as the minimum wage, trade tariffs, price gouging, and antidumping laws. In the financial sector, attempts to regulate interest rates—capping payday loans, for example—might be seen as examples of just pricing. The just price is considered by Aquinas to be *objectively fair*. It is both "fixed" and "real." According to Simmel, however, the principle merely "corresponds with the substantialist-absolutist world view" that was characteristic of the Middle Ages, which assumes that there is an objective relationship between an *object* and its *price*. For Simmel, far from being objective, such a price is "subjective in the worst sense of the word" and therefore arbitrary: it is an "inadequate valuation that made a momentary constellation [of value] into a fetter for future developments" (Simmel 2004: 317). Just pricing leads ultimately to *leveling*, which we have seen, Simmel associates with "extreme" socialism. Aquinas's proposal therefore conflicts with Simmel's image of a society that comes "concretely alive" through the intermingling of individual interests through exchange.

These arguments raise some broader theoretical questions about *value*, specifically about whether any element of value exists *before* exchange. For example, value that inheres in gold, or can be measured against time (labor money) or weighed against an abstract standard such as justice. This idea takes us back to Simmel's relationist conception of value, which we explored in Chapter 1 (Simmel 2004: 124–25). According to Simmel, value and price (they are identical) are the product of a synthesis of subjective valuations that are neither fixed nor objective, but in flux. Value emerges from the continual interplay of exchange relations. No price that is considered to be an objective and independent representation of value (like a Platonic realm of values) can be "just." Just price theory belongs to the same premodern world as labor money and reflects an outlook that is "particularly appropriate to a barter economy" (Simmel 2004: 126).

We now reach a critical stage in Simmel's argument. Against just price theory, he counterposes the idea of a pricing system that is both *ethically* defensible (because it embraces the ideal of personal distinction) and—crucially, bearing in mind the discussion just now—*analytically* consistent with the relationist theory of value. Such a system, Simmel suggests, must be derived from the *unequal price*. This is the price that takes account of "the overall state of the economy, the many-sided forces of supply and demand, [and] the fluctuating productivity of people and objects" (Simmel 2004: 317). The unequal price must take account of the capacity of consumers to pay and is therefore a price that embraces the principle of relative equality (Simmel 2004: 318–19). Theoretically, this notion of perfect *money* corresponds with Simmel's idea of a (conceptually) perfect *society*. The unequal price is the conceptually correct price, whereby that harmonious connection between part and whole (individual and society) that Simmel looks for in the perfect society is expressed through money. "Individuals' circumstances, too," Simmel writes, "are objective facts that are very important for the carrying out of individual purchases. However, in principle they do not find any expression at all in price formation" (Simmel 2004: 317).

This, then, is Simmel's monetary utopia: the world of conceptually correct—or perfect—money. In such a world, prices would be shaped by a "thoroughgoing ideal of fairness" (Simmel 2004: 317). Through perfect money, *individualism* gains recognition through *price*. But it is important to grasp the difference between what Simmel is advocating on one side and conventional economic liberalism on the other. A monetary system that is premised on everyone paying the *same* price merely allows for the expression of what the Frankfurt theorists later called *pseudoindividualism* (Adorno and Horkheimer 1997: 154). That is to say, it promises to bring about a form of standardization in which anything *but* the uniqueness of the individual is recognized. His analysis thereby anticipates a strong undercurrent in the work of subsequent critical theorists, who argued that antithetical forms of economic and administrative reason (underpinning the formation of market and state, respectively) had become fused inside a technological or instrumental rationality in which the individual is powerfully ensnared and freedom is assaulted from all sides (Habermas 1987; Marcuse 1997). Habermas later describes Simmel's relationship with critical theory as a "contagion" through which one can discern a similar journey to the one Simmel himself took, from Hegel to Schopenhauer (see Simmel 2004: 484). This, he suggests, was the path taken by critical theory, "from the railroad timetable to the bankruptcy note" (Habermas 1996: 413).[8]

Simmel proposes a society of "unlike parts." This is exactly the reverse of the logic that operates when prices are equal. In a system of equal pricing, the poor pay proportionally *more* for commodities than the rich. In a system of unequal pricing, by contrast, the poor would pay proportionally *less*. The price that is fixed, the *equal* price or the *just* price, is "the superadditum of wealth": a tax on the poor. Simmel's phrasing intrigues—and cuts, too, if Aquinas was his target. The *donum superadditum* denotes a gift of God that is "superadded" to those gifts we naturally possess, similar to divine grace. In medieval theology, the "extra gift" of intellectual and physical powers was given to Adam and Eve—but lost at the "fall" (González 2005: 48). Equal prices, even "just" ones, merely reinforce a sense of wealth as divine entitlement.

By factoring into price not simply the conditions of *production* (as is usually the case) but the (unique) circumstances of each individual *consumer* too, Simmel suggests that unequal pricing would adequately express "at every sale" *all* the circumstances that go into every exchange: "The new equation [unequal pricing] is no less objective than the old one [equal pricing]; it is only that it also incorporates personal circumstances among its elements" (Simmel 2004: 318). Through the unequal price, "everything *subjective* would have become an *objective-legal* element of price formation" (Simmel 2004: 319, italics added). Here, production and consumption unite in the formation of the conceptually correct—*utopian*—price. And for Simmel, this is the price that would correspond to a "philosophical view of the world which sees all original *objective* data as *subjective* formations" (Simmel 2004: 319, italics added):

---

8   Habermas criticizes Simmel for advancing a diagnosis that attributes the "tragedy of our times" merely to "estrangement between the soul and its forms," which detaches the problem from its concrete historical connections. Intriguingly, he cites Simmel's sympathies with the reformers, Ruskin and Morris, as evidence of an implicit "yearning for undifferentiated, overseeable totalities" (Habermas 1996: 413). Ruskin's proposals for monetary reform are discussed later. As we will see, Simmel did not sympathize with the concept of labor money.

through this absolute retracing to the Ego, [unequal pricing] would gain the unity, cohesion and palpability that give meaning and value to what we call objectivity. Just as in this case the subject would transcend its antithesis to the object which it has completely absorbed and transcended, so, in the other case, the antithesis is overcome by the fact that the objective behaviour has swallowed up all subjectivity without leaving a residue upon which the antithesis could survive. (Simmel 2004: 319).

Simmel suggests that unequal pricing would be an ideal social formation that is made possible by the notion of conceptually correct—or perfect—money (Simmel 2004: 318–19). In theoretical terms, it is as if the principle of the relationism of values, i.e., their irreducibility to one *primary* value such as *nature* or *labor*, were being crystallized by money as a primal form. If so, this irreducibility is similar to the *Urphänomen*—which is a conceptual utopia, of sorts—that Simmel finds in Goethe (Dodd 2008). This form embraces diversity and flux, making possible "the most adequate realization and effectiveness of every individual complication through the equalization of the greatest diversity—as if all specific forms must first be returned to the *common primary element* in order to secure complete freedom for individual reorganization" (Simmel 2004: 319, italics added). Unequal pricing, Simmel says, is "utopian, but logically possible" (Simmel 2004: 319). Moreover, it is logically *complete*.

Although he demonstrates that a system of unequal pricing would be *philosophically* consistent with the idea of perfect money, Simmel offers few clues as to how such a system might work in practice—or even whether it *could*. He suggests that unequal pricing has "recently been declared a general remedy in social policy" (Simmel 2004: 318): but by whom, and in what context, he does not say. It is difficult to imagine how the scheme would have operated in his time, at least beyond a small-scale economy in which there is hardly a need for money at all. Simmel does, however, note some empirical manifestations of the logic behind unequal pricing as he conceives it: the patient who pays the doctor a fee whose magnitude varies according to his or her circumstances; the citizen who pays less for indispensable services provided by the state; and fines that take account of income. Today, one can certainly think of examples of *variable* pricing, such as the pricing of airline tickets and bulk pricing, but not of *unequal* pricing in exactly the form that Simmel conceives it. The main difference between such schemes and his is that most cases of variable pricing are either geared solely to conditions of supply (as with airline tickets) or actually work *against* those on lower incomes (as with bulk pricing). But more modest or limited forms of unequal pricing that have a progressive rationale are not altogether uncommon, such as tiered membership fees for unions and professional associations. Intriguingly, means-tested pricing seems to be used quite frequently within groups that resemble the guilds in which Simmel expected socialism to thrive as a counterweight to economic liberalism.

Of course, none of these instances fulfils Simmel's idea in its purest form. Even if we had enough computational power to organize a system in which each monetary value would be tailored to individual conditions of production and consumption, it seems unlikely that the information on which such a system depends could ever be compiled in the face of evasion, as is common with income tax. It is striking, too, how closely such a system would resemble the "machine dream" of a perfectly rational, centrally coordinated system of prices that once featured in the socialist calculation debate. Moreover, the idea raises the question as to how a monetary system would operate in which the incentive to *accumulate* money has effectively been removed. In such a system, money would be confined to the role of a signaling device, and though this step is crucial to almost every theory of money's functions in the economy at large, it is curious to see just how far removing the "money motive" from economic life seems tantamount to abolishing money altogether—which, perhaps, was Simmel's essential point.[9] We return to this issue in a moment, when discussing Fromm.

Simmel suggests that unequal pricing would "possess the *advantages* of socialism without its *shortcomings*" (Simmel 2004: 318, italics added). Through unequal pricing, it seems, money could help to realize that "third term" he craves, *between* liberalism and socialism. Money presents such a prospect because, through its circulation, the "fiction" is posited with which this discussion began: that is, the pure *concept* of money, which is an embodiment of value whose invariant stability stems from the equation between the totality of commodities on one side and the total sum of money on the other. This fiction underpins perfect money, enabling it to stand outside the perpetual flux of exchange relations. It suggests a fusion of terms—the *conceptual* fiction of perfect money alongside the *ethical* ideal of unequal pricing—that would correspond to Simmel's own when he writes about the two kinds of perfect society. Simmel's treatment of perfect money is rooted in his own personal concerns with the ambivalent fate of the

---

9   Indeed, this is one of the arguments he deploys against the idea of *neutral* money: "If what the above theory presupposes were true—namely, that an increase in the volume of money would leave the relations of people to each other and the relative prices of commodities completely unchanged—there would be no ... *stimulation of work energies*" (Simmel 2004: 163, italics added).

individual in the mature money economy. Unequal pricing is the only rational way of ensuring the interest and personal striving of individuals—both in their quantitative aspects and qualitative aspects (Simmel 2004: 317)—come into line with their objectified societal existence. This is *relative* equality: *one price for each*.

We come full circle: from money's status as a conceptual utopia, through to its potential as a social technology through which we might achieve an ethical utopia—a perfect money that fulfils Simmel's idea of the perfect society. Such an alignment would be possible only if the two currents whose conflict modern money "tragically" conveys—subjective desire and creativity on one side, objectification and estrangement on the other—were to reach a settling of accounts. The ethical and practical variety of the examples Simmel uses to explore how this settlement might be achieved and the rather different economic and political interests they may serve provide an ironic but logically exact demonstration of the very point he himself makes so compellingly throughout *The Philosophy of Money*: that to all practical intents and purposes, there really is no single, workable solution to the puzzle of perfect money.

FROMM'S HUMANISTIC UTOPIA

The correspondence between Simmel's notion of perfect money and his arguments about the perfect society hinge on his unusual conception of the relationship between the individual and society. According to this view, *eudaemonia*—happiness, or welfare—depends on what makes us different, not similar. Money can make a contribution to this happiness insofar as it can express these differences, but it must not determine them artificially. In this section, we turn to a different utopian project in which money can also play a significant part, namely, the "humanistic" utopia as conceived by Erich Fromm. Whereas Simmel's arguments focus on money's mediation of the relationship between society and the individual, Fromm's treatment deals with money in terms of the relationship between the subject and object. Fromm wrote his utopian tract, *To Have or To Be?* (1976), just as the postwar welfare system and the Keynesian economic policies that sustained it were irretrievably breaking down. Milton Friedman, who argued that the solution to these problems lay with monetarism and small government (Spiegel 1991: 589–90)—and who has sometimes been labeled as something of a utopian himself—was awarded the Nobel Prize in the same year that Fromm's book was published. Fromm's humanistic utopia could hardly have been more different from Friedman's libertarian—essentially neoliberal—image of wholesale market deregulation (Eichengreen 2007). In this discussion, I want to examine its implications for money.

Fromm's thesis is an elaboration of arguments he had made in earlier works on freedom and human character, such as *Escape from Freedom* (originally published in 1941, 1994 cited here) and *Man for Himself* (Fromm 1947). Throughout these writings, he seeks to combine insights from Marxism and critical theory, social psychology, and theology. His analysis pivots around a distinction between two fundamental modes of human existence, *having* and *being*, which he characterizes as two distinctive orientations toward self and the world and "two different kinds of character structure" (Fromm 1976: 33). He applies the distinction to important sociological and philosophical questions relating to economy, politics, and religion, as well as to a range of social psychological examples such as learning, remembering, conversing, reading, exercising authority, knowing, faith, and loving.

Breton suggested that poetry's form, its sense of anarchism, might one day bring about the end of money. With Fromm, it is poetry's *content* that expresses what is essential. The difference between the two modes of existence (having and being) is expressed by two contrasting poems. Alfred Tennyson's "Flower in the Crannied Wall" presents nature as an object of human possession ("I hold you here, root and all, in my hand") and intellectual speculation ("*if* I could understand / What you are ... I should know what God and man is"), and suggests that what nature contains must be *killed* in order to be both *possessed* and *known* ("I pluck you out of the crannies"). This statement expresses the orientation to *having*: Tennyson "may be compared to the Western scientist who seeks the truth by means of dismembering life" (Fromm 1976: 26). By contrast, a haiku by the seventeenth century Japanese poet, Bashō, presents an almost identical situation; only the poet merely *contemplates* the flower ("When I look carefully"), without touching it. Whereas Tennyson needs to *possess* and *destroy* nature to understand it, Bashō merely wishes to see and "to be at one, to 'one' himself with it—and to let it live" (Fromm 1976: 27). This is the orientation to *being*, "in which one neither *has* anything nor *craves to have* something, but is joyous, employs one's faculties productively, is *oned* to the world" (Fromm 1976: 28, italics in original). Fromm cites Goethe, too, as an example of this orientation—"the great lover of life, one of the outstanding fighters against human dismemberment and mechanization" (Fromm 1976: 28). It was Goethe who sought to develop a nonmechanistic understanding of nature through imagined archetypes such as the "primal plant." There are some rich and fascinating connections between this method of relating to nature and Benjamin's mode of engagement with history and the concept of origin, and Simmel's with value and the *idea* of money (Dodd 2008).

The distinction between having and being is the difference between a society centered around *persons* and one centered around *things*. Language, too, is an expression of the having modality that prevails within Western industrial capitalism; for example, in the frequent substitution of noun ("I have a problem") for verb ("I am troubled"), which, by eliminating subjective experience from speech, "betrays a hidden, unconscious alienation" (Fromm 1976: 31). "Being" concerns the essence of a person, not his or her appearance: it is his or her very existence insofar as it derives from an authentic relationship with the world. Of crucial importance here is the idea of being as a *process*.

"Having" is the existential modality wherein our relationship with the world is one of ownership and property. I *am* what I *own*; I *am* what I *consume*. Within the having modality, happiness consists in superiority over others, our own power, and our ability to conquer. That is to say, the subject is defined not by what he or she *is*, but by what he or she *has*. Whereas the having orientation—which, as we shall see, finds its quintessential expression in the money incentive (Fromm 2002: 285)—is characteristic of Western industrial capitalism, the orientation to being can be found in a number of "less alienated" societies (e.g., medieval society, the Zuni Indians, African tribal societies); indeed, it was a characteristic way of life long before capitalism. Within the being modality, happiness consists in loving, sharing, and giving—the ability to transcend the isolated ego. After decades of industrialization, Japan may have its Tennyson, too, of course. "It is not that Western Man cannot fully understand Eastern systems . . . but that modern Man cannot understand the spirit of a society that is not centred in property and greed" (Fromm 1976: 29).

Although Fromm advances this argument through ancient theological texts, this is not, per se, a theological argument. As Fromm writes about the bible in *You Shall Be as Gods* (1966): "It is a book which has proclaimed a vision for men that is still valid and awaiting realization. It was not written by one man, nor dictated by God; it expresses the genius of a people struggling for life and freedom throughout many generations" (Fromm 1966: 10). He finds examples of the distinction between having and being in the New and Old Testaments, the Talmud, the writings of the late thirteenth and early fourteenth century theologian, Meister Eckhart, as well as in Spinoza, Marx, and Freud. His reading of the Old Testament focuses on the story of Moses, which he depicts in terms of a deep underlying connection between *being* and *freedom*. "One of the main themes of the Old Testament,"

Fromm writes, "is: leave what you have; free yourself from all fetters: *be!*" (Fromm 1976: 55). In *You Shall Be as Gods*, he uses the story to illustrate the paradox that "the enslaved man has no concept of freedom—yet he cannot become free unless he has a concept of freedom"(Fromm 1996: 74). The role of Moses as a liberator suggests a people whose apparent *fear* of freedom— "they had no overseer and no king and no idols before whom they could bow down" (Fromm 2002: 86)—is expressed through their willingness to sacrifice their *money*, specifically gold, to gain what they believe to be old certainties. This is the story of the golden calf, the idol made by Aaron to placate the Hebrews when Moses went up to Mount Sinai. So in place of Moses, a "living God," Aaron fashions for them an idol made of gold, which cannot walk before them because it is dead. Fromm suggests that they "pay for God's error in having permitted them to take gold and jewellery out of Egypt," thus carrying within themselves the craving for wealth. In the hour of their greatest despair, "the possessive structure of their existence reasserted itself" (Fromm 1976: 58). As we will see in a moment, this question of *taking* one's property, rather than leaving it behind, is for Fromm a major aspect of the having orientation. The Hebrews subsequently transformed their democratic tribal life into Oriental despotism: "The revolution had failed; its only achievement was, if it was one, that the Hebrews were now masters and not slaves" (Fromm 1976: 59).

Fromm's interpretation of the Old Testament fascinates for its intricate and subtle interweaving of money into a broader sociological discussion of space, possession, mobility, and time. Take, for example, his exploration of the *desert* as a symbol of the very freedom that the Hebrews came to fear. The desert was not, speaking in our own terms, a *home*: it was not a *country*; it had no *city*, and no *riches*. The desert was the "place of nomads" who own what they need, and what they need "are the necessities of life, not possessions" (Fromm 1976: 55). Indeed, nomadic themes run throughout Fromm's analysis as symbols of an unfettered, nonpropertied life: unleavened bread, for example—the bread of the wanderers—and the *suka* (or tabernacle) in which nomads live, the tent that is easily built and easily taken down. The Talmud calls it the "transitory abode"—an abode to be lived in, not owned. Mobility matters to Fromm because he believes that being is necessarily *becoming*, involving activity and movement. He cites Simmel, as well as Heraclitus and Hegel, when arguing that living structures can exist only if they change (Fromm 1976: 55–56). As a template from which to construct his humanistic utopia—despite, or perhaps because of, the fact that it is exactly this that the Hebrews fear—the desert is therefore a *non*place (*ou topos*) in a specific sense. It represents freedom and the propertyless life, where Fromm finds formulated "for the first time" Marx's core principle, "to each according to their needs" (Fromm 1976: 56). The New Testament continues this "protest against the having structure of existence" (Fromm 1976: 60). For example, Satan and Jesus are further expressions of the distinction between having and being, whereby Satan represents material consumption and power of *having* over nature and humankind, and Jesus stands for *being*, and the idea that not-having is the premise for existence itself. "The world has followed Satan's principles, since the time of the gospels," Fromm suggests (Fromm 1976: 63).

From Eckhart, Fromm draws on the notion of spiritual poverty, described as a state of emptiness or inner poverty. This is not, it should be emphasized, a poverty of *things*. The person who is in a state of spiritual poverty makes a positive decision to *want* nothing, *crave* nothing, and be *attached* to nothing (Fromm 1976: 91). For Eckhart, human freedom is only possible to the extent that we can free ourselves from the orientation toward having. Anything can be the object of craving. Nothing is *intrinsically* bad; it merely becomes so because when we *crave* it, it becomes a *fetter*. Money often expresses the having orientation for precisely this reason. Fromm argues that Freud's equation between money and feces—we explored this in Chapter 4—is an implicit critique of bourgeois society, comparable to Marx's discussion of money and fetishism in the *Economic and Philosophical Manuscripts* (Fromm 1976: 66). Fromm reads Marx as arguing that the less you are and the less you express your life, the more you have and the greater is your alienated life: "Everything the economist takes away from you in the way of *life* and *humanity*, he restores to you in the form of *money* and *wealth*" (Fromm 1976: 88, italics added). Marx's notion of the "sense of having" corresponds to Eckhart's idea of "egoboundedness." What Marx calls unalienated existence resembles what Fromm sees as the "being" mode of existence, i.e., "the active, unalienated expression of our faculty towards the corresponding objects" (Fromm 1976: 155).

Fromm further illustrates the distinction between having and being through a discussion of the institution of the Shabbat, or Sabbath. Economic themes are crucial here, too. Its central importance is expressed by the fact that it was "the only strictly religious command in the Ten Commandments," and its observation has persisted—in spite of extreme hardship and difficulty—through two thousand years of diaspora life. Fromm suggests that the Sabbath is central in Jewish law because it expresses the central idea of Judaism: "the idea of freedom; the idea of complete harmony between man and nature, man and man; the idea of the anticipation of the messianic time and of man's defeat of time, sadness, and death" (Fromm

2002: 153). The Shabbat is not, per se, a day of rest, in the sense of there being inactivity. Rather, it is the day on which complete harmony between humans and nature is reestablished, when nothing can be destroyed or built. It is "a day of truce in the human battle with the world" (Fromm 1976: 57). The theme of *mobility* enters Fromm's analysis here, too, and as with his discussion of the desert as the space of freedom and not-having, its relationship to *possession* is crucial. Nothing can be carried in the street on the Sabbath: not because it would involve work, but rather because it implies the transfer of property from one private place to another. On the Shabbat, one must live *as if one has nothing*. One is simply being: praying, studying, eating, drinking, singing, and making love.

Messianic time is anticipated here, as the never-ending Shabbat when time is defeated and "pure being rules" (Fromm 1976: 57). The concept of Messianic time has a rich tradition of literature and debate devoted to it (Scholem 1971). Besides Fromm, Walter Benjamin is another social thinker for whom the idea of Messianic time—which he understands as a politically charged historical awakening (Benjamin 2003b)—yields potentially radical historiographical insights. For Fromm, Messianic time is also the time of utopia—"the golden age of the future" (Fromm 2002: 98)—in which the aim of living is the expression of our essential powers. Time connects with the distinction between having and being in some intricate and intriguing ways. The fear of dying is linked to the having mode, for example, because it is a fear of *losing what one has*: Fromm quotes Spinoza, saying in *Ethics* that "the wise think about life, not death" (Fromm 1976: 58). A richer translation of this passage from Spinoza would be: "A free man thinks of nothing less than of death, and his wisdom is a meditation on life, not on death" (Spinoza 1996: 151). According to Fromm, the being mode exists only here and now (*hic et nunc*): not in the sense of being outside of time, but rather in being not *governed* by time. Those who exist within the modality of being respect time but do not submit to it, as in the phrase "time is money." The here and now is eternity: timelessness, but not indefinitely prolonged time (Fromm 1976: 126–27). Those who are dominated by the having orientation view the past as dead, whereas to experience the past in the being mode means relating to it as if it were still fresh. Expressing its deeper connections in his thinking with the idea of not-having, place, and the Shabbat, Messianic time is a return to home in the specific sense in which Fromm conceives of it. When humans were expelled from paradise they lost their home. In Messianic time, they will be at home again: *in the world* (Fromm 2002: 98).

Fromm argues that the orientation to having dominates Western society. It is not natural. The predominance of orientation to having has its own specific historical trajectory and derives from fundamental differences in the nature of society. It is a product of industrial capitalism and the modes of socializing individuals that operate there. In psychological terms, the orientation to having—experienced *in extremis*—can lead to neurosis, just as, sociologically, it sets us on the path toward the neurotic society. This is a construction, in Fromm, with which Norman Brown (Brown 1959) would surely have sympathized. The orientation to having is intimately associated with private property, and in particular, the *hoarding of money*. Although private property is only one mode of our relationship with things, Fromm argues that in modern society it has come to be seen as the most *natural* kind, wherein it is believed that individuals are defined not by what they *are*, but rather by what they *own*. This is a contradictory, neurotic mode of human existence. The etymology of private—*privare*, to deprive of (Fromm 1976: 34)—underlines the paradoxical nature of an economic system, capitalism, which both encourages us in the wish to acquire property while at the same time preventing the majority of us from doing so. Psychologically, the human consequences are damaging. Those deprived of property channel their acquisitiveness toward friends, lovers, health, travel, art objects, God, and the ego (Fromm 1976: 75). Patriarchy is one expression of this deprivation. The having orientation, which private property expresses, leads us into dead relationships with people and things (Fromm 1976: 77). Freud reveals further dimensions of the having mode: the anal character is a person whose main energies in life are directed toward saving, and hoarding, money and material things—together with feelings, gestures, words, and energy (Freud 1908). Having and being, then, are the two fundamental modes of existence, alternative orientations toward self and the world, which Fromm uses to propose a distinctive interpretation of the human condition and social history, as well as a radical—utopian—vision of an alternative future (Fromm 1976: 28).

Having and being are not mutually exclusive in Fromm's theory. There is an element of having that is compatible with being, and indeed they are essential to each other as contrasting orientations whose balanced coexistence is the precondition for good living. What Fromm finds problematic in advanced Western capitalism is not the existence of the having orientation per se but rather the fact that this particular socioeconomic system has encouraged the existence of this orientation in an extreme, pathological form. In order to make this argument, he introduces a further distinction between two subcategories of having, "existential" and "characterological" (Fromm 1976: 83). Existential having is concerned with survival and necessity and is rooted in human existence. Characterological having is about possessing and keeping what is not innate; this type of having has developed in conjunction with social conditions, not nature. Existential having is not incompatible with being but rather essential to it. The being orientation involves a dynamic relationship with the external world. Strictly speaking, it is indescribable because "the living human being is not a dead image and cannot be described like a thing" (Fromm 1976: 89). The being orientation is not, however, equivalent to asceticism, which may consist merely of the negation of the having orientation. *In extremis*, this orientation would be a case of denial by overcompensation (Fromm 1976: 90).

A fundamental characteristic of the being modality is to be active: not in the sense of being perpetually busy but in the sense of exercising our inner activity, using our human powers productively through nonalienated activity, in which we experience ourselves as the subject: "It means to renew oneself, to grow, to flow out, to love, to transcend the prison of one's isolated ego, to be interested, to 'list', to give" (Fromm 1976: 92). Nonalienated activity is a process of "giving birth" to something. This activity includes contemplation, which both Aristotle and Aquinas saw as active, not passive. Fromm also cites Spinoza in this connection, i.e., his opposition between (a) activity, reason, freedom, well-being, joy, and self-perfection, versus (b) passivity, irrationality, bondage, sadness, powerlessness, and strivings contrary to human nature (Fromm 1976: 94–98). For Marx, accumulated capital—arguably the most extreme, pathological case of the orientation to characterological having—represents the past: it is, as Marx says, *dead* labor. Likewise for Fromm, the fight between capital and labor is the fight between deadness and aliveness, "the present versus the past, people versus things, being versus having" (Fromm 1976: 99). Marx's idea of socialism was rooted in the idea of restoring human self-activity to its fullest powers in *all* spheres of life. However, this need can reinforce either the having or the being mode. According to Fromm, the possibility for realizing this potential rests on human unity and our need to be part of a bigger "we."

Writing through the white heat of economic crisis in the 1970s, Fromm argued that a profound paradigm shift was needed: not just in economic and monetary policy but also in the philosophy and ethics underpinning capitalism. He maintained that the only alternative to psychological, economic, and environmental catastrophe would be a radical change in human character.[10] In order for humankind to achieve eudemonia—good living—

---

10 Fromm's treatment of this idea seeks to marry elements of the Four Noble Truths of Buddhism (we are suffering and aware of it; we recognize the origin of our ill-being; we recognize that there is a way of overcoming this; we accept that we must therefore follow certain norms for living) together with Marx's idea of salvation (Fromm 1976: 165–67).

but in fact in order to *survive*, there needs to be not only what Fromm describes as a radical transformation of the human heart but also a radical transformation of the socioeconomic system. Hence the socioeconomic, characterological and religious structures of each modality of existence, having and being, are inseparable, for Fromm. That is to say, society produces a "social character" by establishing a dominant pattern; nobody wants to be an outsider (Fromm 1976: 108–109). A society that unifies around the having modality is likely to be conflictual and warlike: once "locked into" extreme forms of characterological having, it is impossible to be satiated, leading to envy and hostility toward our neighbors, and this statement is as true for nations as it is for individuals. In the being mode, by contrast, enjoyment can be shared, which is "one of the deepest forms of human happiness" (Fromm 1976: 116). Hence *joy* must be a crucial feature of both Shabbat and Messianic time. Spinoza says that joy "is man's passage from a lesser to a greater perfection" (Fromm 1976: 120). Money—I want to suggest—must be strongly implicated in this transformation.

In concrete terms, Fromm advances a program for achieving what he calls a humanistic utopia.[11] The underlying premise of this program, he argues, must be that the free-market economy is a fiction, and its model must be the subject who lives according to the principles of being and existential having as outlined above. At the heart of this program is the objective of abandoning the goal of unlimited growth without risking economic disaster and creating working conditions that foster nonmaterial satisfactions and nonmonetary motivations. Viewed from the perspective of the twenty-first century, Fromm's proposals provide an intriguing—and ironic—commentary on three subsequent decades in which that very free-market "fiction" he derided as exhausted has actually dominated policy discourse. Unsurprisingly, consumption features at the core of what Fromm has to say: he proposes the goal of "sane" or "healthy" consumption (premised on a notion of value geared toward well-being) and advocates the principle of *militant consumerism* in order to realize it. Economic democracy, too, figures prominently in Fromm's program, alongside decentralization in both industry and politics and a form of "humanistic" as opposed to bureaucratic management. Wider and more effective processes for disseminating information were, he argued, basic prerequisites for these more open and partic-

---

11   This utopia is in contrast to the *technical* utopia that has characterized social, political, and economic thought since the Enlightenment. Fromm draws a further distinction between utopian *daydreaming*, which involves thinking up impracticable and static blueprints, and *genuine* utopian thinking, which is focused on the practicable.

ipatory forms of governance. More broadly, Fromm argued that the gap between the richest and poorest nations had urgently to be closed; and most radically, he put forward the idea of a universal guaranteed income premised on the unconditional right of everyone to a minimal standard of living. In this way, social life itself might be elevated to an end in its own right: "We are not confronted with the choice between selfish materialism and the acceptance of the Christian concept of God. Social life itself—in all its aspects in work, in leisure, in personal relations—will be the expression of the 'religious' spirit, and no separate religion will be necessary" (Fromm 1976: 197).

Little that Fromm said in 1976 would be out of place in contemporary debates about "ethical" finance and the corrosive local effect of global inequalities as, once again, we find ourselves trying to come to terms with the failure of some of capitalism's most profound underlying beliefs. He was no dogmatic socialist, either, but argued that the notion of the "dictatorship of the proletariat" is just as nebulous and misleading as the idea of the "free-market economy" (Fromm 1976: 172). Nor was Fromm a monetary abolitionist: it would be misleading to assume that money can be located on just one side of the distinction between having and being. If this were so, then the humanistic utopia that he develops out of his critique of Western capitalism, like that of More, would be defined by money's absence, and Fromm could be added to the distinguished line of monetary abolitionists with which this chapter began. On closer inspection, however, most of his examples serve to caution us against a specific *idea* of money: the economic activities it encourages and the forms of social life that it reflects. This is not simply a question of money's existence, but of using it—or, rather, *having* it—for the sole purpose of possessing objects and (especially) people. At stake here is the question that emerged from the discussion of Simmel's concept of perfect money, namely, the *money motive*. Fromm's critique is directed toward money's alignment with characterological having, not toward money per se. Simmel, as we saw earlier, sees the individual's striving to earn more and more money as of "the greatest socioeconomic significance" (Simmel 2004: 165) and suggests that monetary reforms that failed to take account of this situation were likely to fail.

By contrast, Fromm does not regard the striving for *more* money as psychological and sociologically fixed in the way that Simmel appears to do. Fromm points out that a common misreading of Marx, for example, is that he "had meant that the *striving for gain* was the main motive in man" (Fromm 2002: 254). The point of Marx's analysis, according to Fromm, was to show that the origins of the money motive were sociological, not psychological;

indeed, "the wish for more money is constantly fostered by the same industry which relies on money as the main incentive for work" (Fromm 2002: 285). Likewise in "Medicine and the Ethical Problem of Modern Man" (1957), Fromm distinguishes between the motivation to work purely for money and other kinds of motivation. The medieval artisan earned money, "but he worked because he loved his work, and many times he would have preferred a smaller income to a more boring type of work" (Fromm 1963: 187). Doctors, too, claim that "they do their work out of interest for the patient, and earn money only incidentally" (Fromm 1963: 187). Of course, both these forms of work have not yet been subject to the same degree of depersonalization as one finds in many other forms of labor, whereas the relatively high remuneration "incidentally" received by most doctors doubtless makes their apparent indifference to money somewhat easier to bear. But cynicism aside, there is an important analytical point underpinning Fromm's argument, and it is this: what distinguishes the stance of the artisan and doctor is their realization that *man is not a thing* (Fromm 1963: 187).

The concept of "man as thing" recalls Marx's notion of commodity fetishism. Fromm sees this orientation as a form of idolatry, which he opposes to the worship of God. We transfer our passions and qualities to idols, as our alienated forms. The more we impoverish ourselves, the stronger becomes our experience of the idol (Fromm 2002: 37). Like the golden calf, the idol is a lifeless thing: "The goldsmiths make it a god—a god that cannot move, nor answer, nor respond; a god that is dead; one to whom man can submit, but to whom he cannot relate" (Fromm 2002: 37–38). There are echoes, here, of Nietzsche's complaint that "What one formerly did 'for the sake of God,' one now does for the sake of money" (Nietzsche 1997a: 123). The target of Fromm's critique is not simply the desire to earn money—he never disputes that "fear of starvation" is the sole incentive to earn money in many cases (Fromm 2002: 283; Einzig 1948: 283)—but rather the singular wish to *hoard* it. According to Fromm, hoarding is the quintessential expression of egotistic individualism and the belief that "my property is me" (Fromm 1963: 176). He cites Matthew from the New Testament (6:19–21): "Do not lay up for yourselves treasures on earth, where moth and rust consume and where thieves break in and steal, but lay up your treasures in heaven" (Fromm 1976: 61). Whereas Marx saw such advice as evidence in support of his characterization of religion as an opiate, Fromm reads it as an expression of fundamental opposition to the having orientation.

The "industrial religion" of Western capitalism elevated profit, property, and power to the status of sacred objects, whereas the damage they cause to human freedom and individualism are masked by Christian terminology. In more advanced forms of capitalism, Fromm finds evidence of a new emphasis on "marketing" that has overtaken hoarding: "the greed to have and to hoard has been modified by the tendency to merely function well, to exchange oneself as a commodity who is—nothing" (Fromm 1976: 128). The marketing characters buy and consume but show remarkably little attachment to what they have bought. Having first introduced the idea in *Man for Himself* during the 1940s (Fromm 1947), Fromm's analysis of the marketing character resonates with discussions of post-Fordism in the 1970s (see Marazzi 2008). Here, too, emphasis is placed on the idea of "man as thing." For the marketing character, the personality is the basis of exchange value, and human identity rests entirely on the capacity to become a selfless instrument of the corporate machine (there is no authentic self, just an ego that changes according to corporate requirements) (Fromm 1976: 195). This idea, Fromm argues, explains the ephemerality of consumerism: we do not develop deep or prolonged attachments to the things we buy; they are just as expendable as we are (Fromm 1976: 147). The marketing character has a manipulative intelligence, which is entirely cerebral, not emotional. Fromm links it to Marx's discussion of the alienated character (Fromm 1976: 148).

There are two important aspects of existential having that do not contradict the orientation to being as Fromm defines it. The first is a sense of having that is closely connected to *necessity*, to what Fromm sees as the mode of existence wherein we are actively and creatively engaged in an authentic relationship with the world and each other. The second is a form of having that is both *changing* and *finite*, and which—like the Sabbath—can free us from the "chains of time" (Fromm 2002: 155). At no stage in his analysis does Fromm suggest that money per se is incompatible with either condition. Rather the key message from his argument is that although we clearly need money, money *does not matter*; we need money *in order to* live, just as we need food, shelter, and various tools, but we do not have to live *for* money. If this is a monetary utopia, it operates like a photographic negative, inverting those values Fromm finds most problematic in industrial capitalism. What he calls for is not money's abolition but rather a transformation of money that he believes will be achieved through a synthesis of "the spiritual core of the Late Medieval world and the development of rational thought and science since the Renaissance" (Fromm 1976: 197). He calls this nonplace the "city of being."

So what kinds of money might correspond to these principles? Simmel's notion of perfect money is one possible answer: as we have seen, this form of money would respond to need and equate it with capacity to pay. But more than anything else, Fromm's arguments suggest that money within a humanistic utopia conceived in his terms must relate to *time* in a specific way. This would be a *living* currency in the particular sense of a form of money whose value is intrinsically linked to its existence *through* time. There are some intriguing analogies between this idea and some of the arguments we have been discussing in this book, such as accumulation and waste (Chapter 5), mobility and flow (Chapter 6), and cultural alienation (Chapter 7). Fromm's treatment of the Sabbath resonates with Benjamin's arguments in "Capitalism as Religion" (Chapter 4), suggesting that debt has been locked into a particular conception of history that is premised on a denial of capitalism's inevitable decay. There are further echoes of Fromm in Brown's description of the people who have liberated themselves from the neuroses attached to the money complex: they have the courage to die. In what remains of this chapter, I take forward these various "utopian" treatments of money in a search for more practical historical and contemporary examples of monetary reform. Fromm insisted that he was arguing for an "awake" utopia: we must be hardheaded realists, he said, shed of all illusions (Fromm 1976: 170). So how real, and how *realistic*, might a monetary utopia actually be?

GIVING TIME FOR TIME

Labor money is one of the oldest and most powerful attempts to unleash the utopian spirit from inside money. Historically, the idea has appeared in a number of guises, including the labor voucher that was advocated by Robert Owen and Josiah Warren during the early nineteenth century, and more recently, the time dollar as conceived by Edgar Cahn. The fundamental principle behind labor money is simple: an hour of a person's time is worth exactly the same as an hour of any other person's time. In practice, though, there are some considerable complications, as we shall see. Before turning to these, let me first examine the argument in favor of labor money. One of the most influential and intriguing can be found in the work of John Ruskin.

Ruskin's case for labor money rests on his characterization of money itself as an expression of *right*, not a means of circulation. Money is not wealth as such but rather a sign of *entitlement* to it (Ruskin 1928: 168). What matters to money is not what it contains, but what it can acquire: specifically, this is power over labor (Ruskin 1928: 169). Issuing money based on its intrinsic value is barbaric, Ruskin says, a remnant of barter, "which alone can render commerce possible among savage nations" (Ruskin 1928: 169). The practice will cease in proportion to the "extension of civilization" and an increase of trustworthiness in governments. Hence for Ruskin, morality is not merely an additional element of wealth; it is integral to it. The "final and best" definition of money, Ruskin concludes, is as follows: "a documentary promise ratified and guaranteed by the nation to give or find a certain quantity of labour in demand" (Ruskin 1997: 185 n.). In short, money gives its possessor power over others. Thus when money circulates, it is not value or goods, but *people*, who are manipulated by those who have it. There are resonances with Fromm here: Ruskin follows Chaucer (*The Pardoner's Tale*) in viewing money as a metaphor for death (Henderson 1999: 137), whereas by contrast, the vitality of labor places it at the center of his analysis of capitalism. Invariably, national wealth has a moral sign attached to it, which reveals its real value. The essential difference is between wealth that is indicative of "faithful industry, progressive energies, and productive ingenuities" and wealth that stands for "mortal luxury, merciless tyranny, [and] ruinous chance" (Ruskin 1997: 187). Wealth arises from *creation* in the former instance, as opposed to *destruction* in the latter.

Ruskin argues that injustice arises in the use of money to acquire labor in two ways: whenever the worker is underpaid or overpaid. Lying between these is the *right* or *just* payment, which Ruskin measures in terms of "giving time for time" (Ruskin 1997: 195). Abstractly, a just wage "will consist in a sum of money which will at any time procure for him at least as much labour as he has given" (Ruskin 1997: 196).[12] Complexities inevitably arise, such as the problem of determining the monetary value of skill, whether defined by experience, intellect, or passion. But the basic principle of giving time for time, Ruskin argues, is perfectly sound, and people should therefore strive to follow it, even if all they actually achieve is a practically serviceable approximation. By doing so, Ruskin argues, the power of wealth is automatically diminished, partly because it mitigates against its concentration in the hands of a few and also because it "gives each subordinated person fair and sufficient means of rising in the social scale," hence removing the "worst disabilities of poverty" (Ruskin 1997: 199–200). Ruskin views wealth not simply as a consequence of money's accumulation but also of ensuring that others have less. He calls this "the art of contriving the maximum inequality in our favour" (Ruskin 1997: 182).[13]

---

12   A similar principle is expressed by Proudhon's idea of the Equality of Functions. In *The Creation of Order in Humanity*, he argues: "Yes, the price of everything is the labour necessary to produce it; and, since each labourer is individually paid by his own product, the product of one ought also to be able to pay the labour of another; the only difficulty is to find a comparative measure of values" (cited in Dana 1927: 15).

13   One is reminded of H. L. Mencken's definition of wealth as "any income that is at least one hundred dollars more a year than the income of one's wife's sister's husband."

Neither Marx nor Simmel, it must be said, thought much of the idea of labor money, or indeed any other time-based currency. Simmel's analysis of labor money builds on his argument, pursued in the context of a broader engagement with Marx, that the labor theory of value—although "philosophically, the most interesting" attempt to come up with a unified conception of value (Simmel 2004: 410)—is fundamentally flawed. Labor cannot provide a common measure of value because some forms of labor are more *useful* than others, whereas the idea of labor money presupposes that there is "unconditional interchangeability" between *all* forms of labor (Simmel 2004: 427). At a minimum, labor money is "technically possible," but only in a subsistence economy where "only the immediately essential, unquestionably basic life necessities are produced" (Simmel 2004: 427). Empirical research on LETS and time banks lends some credence to Simmel's remarks: their membership tends to be homogeneous, skewed toward those on low incomes with time to spare, and what Simmel calls the "higher spheres" of labor—the professions, in our lexicon—tend to be underrepresented. As a consequence, such schemes offer a narrow range of services and tend to have quite a limited application and life span (Seyfang 2001; Collom 2007). As for the theory of value that labor money implies, Simmel remarks that it is here that "all the threads of the deliberations on socialism intertwine" (Simmel 2004: 427). That is to say, only within a "completely rationalized and providential economic order" could labor provide a truly *universal* equivalent. Such an order would be a "*scientific* utopia" (Simmel 2004: 418, italics added)—presumably, Simmel is using the term in a pejorative sense—based on the principle of *absolute* equality that, as we have seen, he is at pains to dismiss.

Had Simmel been able to read Marx's *Grundrisse* (completed in 1858, published in 1939), he would surely have been drawn to its discussion of monetary reform. Marx doubts whether "the different civilized forms of money—metallic, paper, credit money, labour money (the last-named as the socialist form)—can accomplish what is demanded of them without suspending the very relation of production which is expressed in the category money" (Marx 2005a: 123). We may make piecemeal reforms to money, he says, and "one form may remedy evils against which another is powerless," but no single solution is capable of "overcoming the contradictions inherent in the money relation, and can instead only hope to reproduce these contradictions in one or another form" (Marx 2005a: 123). We discussed these contradictions in Chapter 2, and Simmel would surely have found much to agree with in Marx's argument that there is no single solution to the contradictions expressed in and through money. As for labor money itself, Marx argues that the distinction between value and price—"between the commodity measured by the labour time whose product it is, and the product of the labour time against which it is exchanged"—calls for a "third commodity to act as a measure in which the real exchange value of commodities is expressed" (Marx 2005a: 139–40).

According to Makoto Nishibe, the principle behind LETS is "immune" to Marx's critique. First and foremost, the value of LETS tokens are derived not from labor—as is the case with time dollars—but rather existing units of national currency, such as the Canadian dollar. The purpose behind LETS, Nishibe argues, is not to fulfill egalitarian principles by using labor time as a leveler. The aim, rather, is to "rebuild cooperative and mutual-aid human relationships, based on the idea of reciprocal exchange" (Nishibe 2006: 102; see also Nishibe 2001). Nishibe characterize LETS as an "associative credit system" in which participants mutually provide credit by virtue of their membership in the association or scheme: "They only have to promise to return their 'debit' back to the association by making 'credit' on future sales of products and services" (Nishibe 2006: 103). As we saw Karatani arguing in Chapter 2, Nishibe also suggests that money associated with a LETS cannot transform itself into capital because the credit that is created through the system "gradually vanishes through multilateral cancellation among participants" (Nishibe 2006: 103). In other words, LETS makes the building up of a surplus impossible by canceling debts. One imagines that Fromm would approve.

As both Marx and Simmel suggested, labor or time-based currencies have been controversial mainly because of the difficulties that arise when comparing an hour of one person's labor with that of another. This is not just a question of skill but arises for example when workers are carrying out the same task: one with effort and enthusiasm, the other without. Ruskin argued that in such cases the "natural and right system" would be for all workers to be paid at fixed rates: the "bad" worker must simply remain unemployed, not paid at a lower rate (Ruskin 1997). According to Ruskin, greater difficulties arise because of "sudden and extensive inequalities of demand" because these inequalities inevitably generate the need for higher wages to compensate for periods of involuntary unemployment. It is therefore intriguing to find full (or at least fuller) employment listed as one of the key objectives of the time dollar system, which is the most recent incarnation of Ruskin's idea, while remaining at odds with it in this crucial respect (Cahn 1999). On the other hand, time-based currency schemes automatically demand a reappraisal of what constitutes paid work, as domestic and community-based work are brought into its compass. Many time dollar schemes tend to suffer from an imbalanced supply of labor skills, with those not in formal employment and the socially excluded significantly overrepresented among active members (Seyfang 2002, 2004a). For a conventional economist, this would surely be seen as an outcome of the fact that fixed and uniform rates of pay inevitably distort the conventional dynamics of supply and demand when rates are flexible and money acts as an incentive, not a leveling device.

In theory, time-based currencies lie on one side of Simmel's distinction between *absolute* and *relative* equality. Ruskin's insistence on what is "natural" and "just" in paying fixed rates for labor would be labeled as utopian by Simmel, but in a negative way. In his terms, labor money extends the principle of absolute equality to such a degree that it destroys the principle of relative equality. In practice, many such schemes have sought compromise, for example, by awarding double rates for work that is in short supply. In addition, it should be said that time-based currencies are pursued for more varied reasons, not just equality: for example, time dollars have been used quite effectively to foster community networks, putting those who are out of paid employment in touch with and working for each other (Seyfang 2004b). As this situation suggests, and as Simmel himself remarked, monetary reforms are best looked at as piecemeal ways of addressing much larger problems, where wholesale solutions to such problems are likely to be flawed and to fail. Potentially, they are part of a larger repertoire of monetary reforms. It therefore remains to be established what other schemes such a repertoire might contain.

ROTTING MONEY

Besides the issue of equality, the question of *incentive* leaps out from the above consideration of time-based currency. As Fromm observed, the monetary incentive is not simply a case of working *for* money but rather of working for *more* money. This is where money is aligned with "characterological" having and is treated as an object of possession in its own right. In Simmel's terms, this is when money ceases being used as a means to an end and becomes sought after as an end in itself: miserliness is the most extreme (and pathological) form of this outlook. Tellingly, Simmel sees what many of us might regard as the antithesis of the miser—the spendthrift—in a similar way, because both are attracted to money's power to buy things without being able to look beyond that power at what money *actually* buys. The only difference is that whereas the miser is attracted to this power when it is stored up, the spendthrift enjoys its release. Though psychologically intriguing, however, from the perspective of monetary governance, Simmel's success in transcending the dichotomy between the miser and the spendthrift is of limited value. The effect of the miser on the operation of a monetary system, not just on the individuals who use it, is quite different from that of the spendthrift. Hoarding is a problem for money in a number of ways, not the least of which is that it is inherently deflationary. Countering it by keeping money in circulation is therefore a significant theme in the literature on monetary reform.

The danger posed to our collective economic well-being by individual thrift (or hoarding) is often referred to as the paradox of thrift. The paradox exists by virtue of an elementary fallacy of composition. Behavior that looks beneficial from the individual's perspective can be collectively harmful when others adopt the same behavior: if everyone saves, the economy stands still. Mandeville captured the idea in *Fable of the Bees* (1705)—"Bare Vertue can't make Nations live / In Splendour" (Mandeville 1989: 76)—and Keynes popularized it when, citing Mandeville, he drew an explicit connection between the "evils of unemployment" and the "insufficiency of the propensity to consume" (Keynes 2008: 326). Other economists, too, remarked on a similar phenomenon, each emphasizing the disparity between part and whole: for example, Adam Smith (as Keynes reads him) when remarking that "What is prudence in the conduct of every private family can scarce be folly in that of a great Kingdom" (Smith 2008: 293); John Robertson in *The Fallacy of Saving* (1892) when he states that "Had the whole population been alike bent on saving...industrial paralysis would have been reached" (Robertson 1892: 125); and William Foster and Waddill Catchings in *The Dilemma of Thrift* (1926) (Foster and Catchings 1926). Invariably, the paradox of thrift tends to be discussed most urgently during an economic depression: Irving Fisher wrote about the problem during the 1930s (Fisher 1933), and Paul Krugman (among others) has drawn attention to it in relation both to Japan's "lost decade" (Eggertsson and Krugman 2012) and the aftermath of the 2008 global banking crisis (Krugman 2012: 51–52).

Keynes once asked: "Why should anyone outside a lunatic asylum wish to use money as a store of wealth?" (Keynes 1937: 116). To answer his own question, he developed the notion of the liquidity premium, i.e., what people are prepared to forego (e.g., interest payments) for the sake of having an asset in their possession (e.g., cash as opposed to other financial assets) that can immediately and easily be used to settle future liabilities (Keynes 2008: 215). Money, he said, is a "subtle device for linking the present to the future" (Keynes 2008: 269). Its liquidity premium is problematic because it encourages people to hold onto it, rather than to spend it, under conditions of economic uncertainty. Note the connection with Marx here, who as we saw in Chapter 2, argues that there is a contradiction between money's status as the *universal* representative of value on one side and as a particular *commodity* on the other. The problem of hoarding arises by virtue of our attachment to the latter at the expense of the former. In Deleuze's terms (see Chapter 6), our desire *coagulates* money's flow: this is desire expressed *in* money, not *through* it.

When Keynes wrote about the paradox of thrift, he cited not only Mandeville's well-known fable but also a work by a lesser known advocate of monetary form, Silvio Gesell. Gesell (1862–1930) was a theoretical economist as well as a social activist, whose major work, *The Natural Economic Order* (originally published in 1906, 2007 cited here) contained long and detailed sections on "free" money, or as he put it, "money as it should be." Gesell published several other writings on the subject, including *Currency Reform as a Bridge to the Social State* (1891) (Gesell 1951) and *The Nationalization of Money* (Gesell 1892), as well as founding a monthly periodical, *Geld- und Bodenreform* (*Monetary and Land Reform*) in 1900. He defined free money as "an instrument of exchange and nothing else," whose sole test of usefulness was the "degree of security, rapidity and cheapness with which goods are exchanged." Good money, as Gesell understood it, should *secure*, *accelerate*, and *cheapen* the exchange of goods. By contrast, the introduction of the gold standard to Germany had been a "disaster" because it had "overimproved" money, considering it only from the point of view of its holder. Gold's problem was that it was just as satisfying to hold onto—if not more—as to spend: "The possession of a gold coin is incontestably more agreeable than the possession of goods." For that reason, demand for goods was placed at the discretion of the owners of money and "delivered up to be the sport of caprice, greed, speculation and chance." Ironically, the German monetary reforms had paid too much attention to money itself and not enough to the purposes to which the money would be put, namely, the exchange goods.

Gesell's proposed resolution to the problem alluded to in the paradox of thrift, and by Keynes's notion of the liquidity premium, was disarmingly simple: make money less attractive to hold onto. Money, he argued, should *age*, just like commodities. The latter, he observed, have a definite—material— relationship with time: for example, they *rot*, *decay*, *break*, and *rust*. Money must have the same properties: it, too, must go out of date like a newspaper, rot like potatoes, rust like iron, and evaporate like ether.[14] If it does not, the

---

14   Organizers of Freicoin (discussed below) use the metaphor of hot potatoes to describe a money "that is passed around as quickly as possible, in a virtuous cycle of investment and consumption"; see http://freico.in/about/.

relationship between money on one side and goods on the other will always be asymmetrical—and insofar as people prefer money to goods, they are more likely to hoard it. "Commodities in general, straw, petrol, guano and the rest can be safely exchanged only when everyone is indifferent as to whether he possesses money or goods, and that is possible only if money is afflicted with all the defects inherent in our products. That is obvious." Gesell concludes that money ought to be made *worse* as a commodity if it is to be *improved* as a medium of exchange. The gold standard achieved precisely the opposite.[15]

For Keynes, however, there were some crucial flaws in Gesell's theory. Once money's "advantages" are taken away and it loses its special liquidity premium, money substitutes—e.g., "bank-money, debts at call, foreign money, jewellery and the precious metals generally" (Keynes 2008: 326)—would inevitably take its place. Good money, in this sense, would drive out bad. Nevertheless, Keynes thought that Gesell's ideas could be applied on a modest scale. Indeed they have, albeit not always for the exact reason he had in mind. The practice of deliberately reducing money's value over time unless stamped is known as *demurrage*. Gesell himself never used this term, which may have been derived from the French, *demeurer*, to remain. The expression is also used in shipping to denote the fee paid by the charterer of a vessel for extending their use of it beyond the contracted time. Similar terms include rusting money, melting money, disappearing money, cost-bearing money, carrying costs, and ambulatory tax. The idea is to charge a fee for not using money within a specified time, i.e., hoarding. Although Gesell's scheme was intended for national currency, the practice has been widely adopted within alternative currency schemes, whereas Irving Fisher's idea of stamp scrip (Fisher, Cohrssen, et al. 1933)—his coauthor, Hans Cohrssen, was a follower of Gesell—was introduced not as a permanent feature of money but rather as a temporary measure designed for use with state currency during the Great Depression. The central notion was that money should lose one-thousandth of its value per week (about 5 percent per year) unless its holder purchased a small currency stamp, attaching it to the note in question. The "unfair privilege" enjoyed by money compared to

---

15   There is a strong nationalistic tenor to Gesell's arguments, which is worth noting even though it is incidental to what he says about demurrage. He argues that a country's money supply should be insulated from "foreign, often hostile, influences," which can (if not successfully managed) lead to currency inflows and outflows that destabilize prices. For this reason, he argues that the bank of issue should retain a monopoly over the money supply. This is an issue about which many of Gesell's followers, such as the organizers of Freicoin, disagree with him.

goods—indestructibility—would thus be eradicated at a single stroke. Gesell had predicted that, as a consequence, people would avoid the expense by therefore passing their money on as quickly as possible. Hoarding would cease being a significant problem because "the circulation of money is subjected to pressure."

Demurrage was taken up in a number of schemes during the Great Depression, albeit not at the level of state currency. In Germany, Austria, Switzerland, and France, and in a number of American towns, demurrage-based "emergency money" was issued. Rates of depreciation varied, although the precise level appeared to make little difference to whether a specific scheme succeeded or failed. The central measure of perceived success in most cases was whether the velocity of money increased, stimulating the local economy. The results were mixed. Godschalk lists four American schemes—in Santa Cruz, California; Okmulgee, Oklahoma; Mason City, Iowa, and Carmel, California—in which money's velocity does appear to have increased significantly as a result of demurrage (Godschalk 2012). Demurrage subsequently returned on a widespread scale with the expansion of the LETS movement during the 1990s; it was used in the Austrian Waldviertler system, Regiogeld in Germany, Abeille in France, and the Stroud Pound in the United Kingdom. In Germany, the Bavarian Chiemgauer applies demurrage to cashless currency via a negative interest rate. Again, these monies often have a velocity of circulation that is notably higher than that of mainstream currencies (as measured by M1) such as the euro (Gelleri 2009; Godschalk 2012).

There are versions of demurrage in fictional dystopias. In Nea So Copros, as portrayed by David Mitchell in *Cloud Atlas* (2004), hoarding is outlawed as an "anti-corpocratic crime," and enrichment laws demand that people must spend a fixed amount of dollars per month according to their social strata. As one character put it, "He said his mum feels intimidated by modern gallerias, so Hae-Joo usually works through the quota" (Mitchell 2004: 227). Nevertheless, the ideas behind Gesell's proposals would almost certainly have appealed to Fromm, had he known of them, for deeper reasons. In Fromm's terms, money that decays resists being taken over by the having orientation, wherein the link between money and immortality—between the self and the sense of permanence that possession (however empty) brings—is key. His opposition to hoarding suggests corresponding support for a scheme in which money keeps circulating. The analogy between *demurrage* in relation to currency on one hand and to shipping on the other is equally suggestive in relation to Fromm's distinction between having and being. Money that is designed to circulate continuously cannot, in and of itself, be the object of the having orientation, as Fromm describes it. Such money cannot be *owned* but is merely *used*, passed along through a sequence of exchanges. Likewise, the idea of a form of money that decays contrasts with the depiction of money as sublimated filth that we explored in Chapter 4. The money that Brown refers to in relation to the money complex is unlikely to have been what Gesell calls rusting money. In terms that Nietzsche recognized in *Zarathustra*—and that Klossowski might also recognize (see Chapter 5)—money that rots and dies is money that *lives*. It is the antithesis of money that feeds off what Brown called the neurotic money complex, shaped as this is by the very refusal of death and decay. Quite possibly, rotting money is as close to the notion of *Dionysian* money—in material form, at least—as we are likely to find.

PROUDHON'S BANK

Throughout this book, I have referred to the relationship between money and society—reconfigured in terms of the social life of money—as a key problem in monetary scholarship. As I suggested in Chapters 6 and 7, the notion of "society" that is generally used in relation to money needs to change—specifically, it needs to be more fluid, flexible, and varied. Marx and Simmel used the same word, *Gesellschaft*, when describing the relationship between the individual who holds money and the wider social group whose members accept it. Marx wrote in *Grundrisse* that, in money, "the individual carries his social power, as well as his bond with society, in his pocket" (Marx 2005a: 157). Fifty years later, Simmel described money as a "claim upon society" (Simmel 2004: 177). As we have already seen, the notion of *society* that is used in conjunction with money can actually mean a number of different things. Marx appears to have intended it to express the concept of *exchange value* that money represents, and thereby the power over others that money grants to anyone who owns it. Specifically, he states that "the power which each individual exercises over the activity of others or over social wealth exists in him as the owner of *exchange values*, of *money*" (Marx 2005a: 157). Simmel's formulation is sometimes taken to equate *society* with *nation-state*. But as I discussed earlier in this chapter, it makes better sense when read in terms of his own concept of sociation (*Vergesellschaftung*), and in light of the specific notion of the "*perfect* society" that he was developing at around the same time, in *Soziologie*. More recently, as we have seen, money's links with "society"—or rather, social life—have been understood in terms of the concept of the *community* (Hart), the *multitude* (Hardt and Negri), and the *circuit* (Zelizer). What matters in all of these treatments of the term is to avoid conveying society in *hierarchical* terms. Most key problems with money and credit systems as constituted during the modern era, according to this line of thought, derive from their dependence arrangements that place core institutions (e.g., the state and/or banks) at the top of a hierarchy, responsible for issuing and regulating money. Critics of such a system advocate a horizontal arrangement. Proudhon's proposal for a Bank of the People is a good example. His arguments are intriguing because they touch upon one of the most prominent and controversial themes in contemporary discussions of financial regulation and monetary reform, namely, the issue of *disintermediation*.

Proudhon proposed his scheme for two banks—a Bank of Exchange and a Bank of the People—in *Solution of the Social Problem*, completed one year after the 1848 revolutions in France. Although he had participated in those revolutions, Proudhon had misgivings about the provisional government, which he believed was neglecting vital economic questions. "Utopia needs for its realization capital accumulated, credit opened, circulation established and a prosperous state," he wrote (Proudhon 1927: 45). Broadly speaking, his aim was to hand control over economic relations to workers, taking power away from capitalists and financiers. The notion of social or mutual credit was at the core of his proposals. Proudhon envisaged the Bank of Exchange as a replacement for the existing central bank, the Bank of France.

"Money hides itself," Proudhon claimed, and the only solution would be to "Let all merchandise become current money, and abolish the royalty of gold" (Proudhon 1927: 46). The Bank of Exchange, he said, would dispense with metallic money altogether. Proudhon's argument was premised on the view that money is central to the property rights on which capitalism depends. Without money, he reasoned, there would be no means of extracting interest through borrowed capital. Proudhon's proposal amounted not so much to *abolishing* money, however, but rather to *bypassing* it. If workers could borrow without paying interest—if credit was free—then there would be no market for interest-bearing capital. What was required, Proudhon argued, was a transformation in the understanding of what money essentially is: not capital, but a medium of exchange. Money is not something that needs to be amassed (as capital) because of what it earns (interest). Rather it needs simply to be used: that is to say, exchanged and passed on. Banks should therefore issue exchange notes (i.e., a coupon or mortgage note) rather than traditional banknotes. These exchange notes represent loans against property. The loan is set for a number of years, whereupon it becomes repayable to the bank by the original borrower. In the event of default, the property on which the note is secured can be sold, and the rights over it passed to the last holder of the note. Compared to traditional banknotes, what goes missing with such an arrangement is the "parasitic middleman, usurping, like that State, the rights of the labourer, and absorbing, like the capitalist, a part of his product" (Proudhon 1927: 92).

The purpose of exchange notes is "to convert property itself into money; to free it, to mobilize it, to make it circulable like money" (Proudhon 1927: 90). The difference between Proudhon's exchange notes and traditional banknotes is important. Whereas a banknote contains a guarantee that it could be redeemed in metallic currency, an exchange note is really just a credit note being passed around and accepted—this is key—at face value. For this reason, exchange notes might have a more limited sphere of circulation than traditional banknotes, i.e., they would be restricted merely to clients of the bank. Moreover, they would be more reliant on maintaining certain levels of confidence across the bank's clientele. But for Proudhon, such notes are to all intents and purposes money. And credit is reduced to a "simple exchange in which one of the parties delivers his product at one time, the other remits his in various instalments, without interest, without any other costs than those of accounting" (Proudhon 1927: 93).

Proudhon's proposals were premised on a particular understanding of property, labor, and capital. Capital, he said, is unproductive. Rent and interest—and profit in general—are merely forms of theft (Proudhon 1927: 88). Mutual credit, he argued, would be the best means of abolishing rent and interest because it would make the whole idea of capital, and thus the capitalist himself (or herself), redundant. The contrast between traditional credit and mutual credit is crucial to this organization. In a system of interest-bearing property, credit involves a unilateral relationship between lender and borrower. The lender is essentially a parasite, to which the borrower (the laborer) has to pay "tribute" in order to use capital, which the worker ultimately owns. In a mutual system, with no intermediary lender extracting usury, credit is the giving of the product of one's labor in consideration for the product of another's future labor. In the interest-bearing system, there is only one debtor and one creditor. In the mutual system, "every creditor or mortgagee becomes a debtor in his turn" (Proudhon 1927: 85). According to this view, credit is exchange, and the consumer "becomes the sleeping partner of those who, not having any products to offer for exchange, ask either for work or for instruments of labour" (Proudhon 1927: 86). There are striking similarities between Proudhon's idea of money and credit, and Mitchell-Innes's characterization of money as a privately issued IOU. Just as Proudhon states that credit is thus bilateral—"workers mutually pledge each other their respective products, on the sole condition of equality in exchange" (Proudhon 1927: 85)—so Mitchell-Innes argues that "Everybody who incurs a debt issues his own dollar" (Mitchell-Innes 1914: 55). In light of this comparison, it is all the more surprising—as noted in Chapter 3—that Mitchell-Innes is so often cited as a leading light for the *state* (not just the credit) theory of money.

In terms of contemporary debates about the future of money and banking, the key to Proudhon's analysis therefore lies with the question of *mediation*: "Between the producer and the consumer, the current view places the capitalist; between product and product, it puts money; between the worker and the employer, that is to say, between labour and talent, it puts capital, property" (Proudhon 1927: 86). In contrast to the traditional bank, the mutualist association as Proudhon conceives it has no capital; it does not produce anything but exists for exchange alone; its membership is unlimited; it is perpetual (like humanity itself); it does not bind its members to each other (there is no joint liability but only general insurance); and it makes no profit because, after all, "labour produces everything out of nothing" (Proudhon 1927: 87–88). Proudhon describes this arrangement as a system of social economy based on two key principles: first, production without capital, and second, exchange without profit. In such a system, credit is taken out of the hands of unproductive intermediaries and placed directly into the hands of producers. In this way, credit is restored to its proper social function: it is no longer a tool of speculation whereby borrowers are forced to give up part of their product to the capitalist, but would be managed by the community of producers. Such, according to Proudhon, is the principle of *mutualism*. As with nature, which is beautiful and luxuriant, wealth comes purely from within the community—not from capital, but essentially from nothing.

Besides the Bank of Exchange, which never actually came to fruition, Proudhon's other key proposal was for a Bank of the People, and he set up a society of this name on January 31, 1849. There are some notable technical differences between the Bank of Exchange and the Bank of the People, as Proudhon conceived them. Presumably, most of them reflect practical considerations. Whereas the Bank of Exchange would lend at zero interest, the Bank of the People would simply lend at low rates of interest (initially fixed at 2 percent, falling to a minimum of 0.25 percent). The Bank of Exchange was to have no capital; by contrast, the Bank of the People would begin with 5 million francs of capital, divided into shares of 5 francs each. As for money, the Bank of the People would issue notes in exchange for specie: unlike ordinary banknotes, these would not be notes payable in coin, but simply "orders for delivery, invested with social character, made perpetual and payable at sight by every member or support in the products of services of his industry or profession" (Proudhon 1927: 99).

Proudhon described the Bank of the People as the *translation into economic language* of the principles that had underwritten modern democracy and the French Revolution: liberty, equality, and fraternity (Proudhon 1927: 94). The Bank of the People promised to be a realization of the financial formula of the principle of reciprocity itself. Although Proudhon intended that the Bank of the People would eventually be turned into a joint-stock company, in the first instance it had to operate as a partnership, with a general manager, a supervising council consisting of thirty delegates, and a general assembly with one thousand members. Should the Bank of the People fail, assets would be divided "among those who are entitled to them" (Proudhon 1927: 112). And, indeed, the Bank of the People was short-lived. By early April, he announced that the experiment was coming to an end: events, he said, had "proved too strong for it."

Perhaps the crucial difficulty with Proudhon's scheme was its scale. By March 1849, the Bank of the People had almost 12,000 subscribers but only 18,000 francs in capital. In monetary terms, it would seem that "utopia" is much more likely to be realized by treating money as an open site, offering a repertoire of monies, not a single form. As Simmel described socialism, each of these monies serves as a counterpoint within a prevailing order—none should seek to dominate. Proudhon's ideas still resonate in later schemes—more modest—that were based on the ideals of mutualism. But the next major advocate of these ideals—Clifford Hugh Douglas, an Englishman who sought to apply engineering principles to the flow of money—was just as ambitious as his French counterpart had been. In *Economic Democracy* (1920) and *Social Credit* (1924) (Douglas 1974, 1979), Douglas advanced an "engineer's view of an ideal society" in which money featured centrally as the means by which the flaws of actually existing society could be corrected. Douglas's proposals correspond to contemporaneous intellectual developments such as scientific management (Martin-Nelson 2007). Douglas likened the relationship between factory cost and money released as a *conversion*, analogous to the conversion of mechanical energy into electricity or heat. What was left over he described as *dispersion*, which in the present system was being charged to the consumer rather than set against the value of the product. The crucial thing, he said, to keep a balance, was that products should absorb the dispersion through price, not the consumers who buy them. This was not, for Douglas, a question of justice, but rather of basic engineering:

there was insufficient money in circulation. One of the targets of Douglas's critique was a belief that he parodied as "super-production." This was the notion that a high and increasing level of production was an end in itself, without reference to human need. In 1918, he wrote: "There is no more dangerous delusion abroad in the world at this time than that production *per se* is wealth—it is about as sensible as a statement that because food is necessary to man he should eat continually and eat everything" (Douglas 1918).

Douglas's proposals were provoked by the observation (which he made during the First World War) that wages were always insufficient to cover the costs of goods actually produced. Simply put, workers had insufficient purchasing power. Workers were suffering as consumers, not because they were lazy or lacking in technical knowledge but rather because the financial system was imposing artificial restrictions upon the flow of money. He proposed overcoming this problem and bridging the gap between goods produced and wages earned, with debt-free credit, as well as a price adjustment mechanism (which he called the Just Price), whereby prices would be reduced in line with the growing efficiency of production. Debt-free credit would be created by means of a national dividend: a minimum payment to all workers that was offered as an immutable right. The idea is similar to Fromm's later proposals for a guaranteed yearly income. Although he never framed it as a form of credit, or as a new form of money, Fromm saw the idea as perfectly natural, liberating the individual from the kind of surveillance that means-tested welfare entails. Although Simmel, as we have seen, would regard this as a step too far in the direction of absolute (as opposed to relative) equality, both Douglas and Fromm argue that the principle is a precondition for individuals to realize the very freedom—and, at root, human dignity—that Simmel held dear. "The core of this idea," Fromm wrote, "is that all persons, regardless of whether they work or not, shall have the unconditional right not to starve and not to be without shelter" (Fromm 1976: 185).

As for just prices—Douglas also called them true prices—several practical ideas were proposed. One involved the state calculating the difference between actual and true prices, with banks periodically reimbursing consumers for that sum on presentation of their receipts. Another idea was that retailers would seek reimbursement, so that consumers paid true prices from the outset. It is intriguing that Douglas was unable to envisage a system whereby producers made the adjustment at the source. Nevertheless, the notion that prices could be set—fixed or adjusted—in some way to reflect conditions on both sides of supply and demand bears some resemblance to Simmel's notion of perfect money. The key difference is that whereas Douglas's prices reflect a general discrepancy between the supply of money and the cost of goods, Simmel started with this equation but went on to imagine how prices could be tailored to the unique individual circumstances of each consumer.

There are some wider resonances between these varieties of mutualism—that of Proudhon and that of Douglas—and political philosophy, which are important to bear in mind when weighing their significance for the idea of utopian money. Mutualism, as Proudhon conceived it, involves removing the *state* from the credit system (removing banks is a different issue, and I will move on to it). Proudhon resorted to anarchist principles as justification for his banks: "The economic idea of capitalism, the politics of government or of authority, and the theological idea of the Church are three identical ideas, linked in various ways," he argued in *Les Confessions d'un Révolutionnaire* (1851): "What capital does to labour, and the State to liberty, the Church does to the spirit" (cited in Nettlau 1996: 43–44). In 1867, Bakunin made the same point through the corresponding concepts of federalism, socialism, and antitheologism, and Spanish and Italian Internationalists subsequently used the formulation of anarchism, collectivism, and atheism (Nettlau 1996: 44). By contrast, social credit as envisaged by Douglas relied heavily on the state to manage the distribution of credit, as well as the difference between actual prices and true prices. Douglas, then, was a different political animal, although he was arguably more successful than Proudhon. Whereas the latter cast himself as a revolutionary—mainly through advocacy of radical, although peaceful, reform—Douglas advanced the social credit cause by forming various working groups in Britain and giving lectures in Canada, Japan, New Zealand, and Norway. In this way, he inspired the formation of the Canadian Social Credit Movement (in which William Aberhart, a Douglas follower, played an important role), the Douglas Credit Party in Australia, and New Zealand's Social Credit Political League. Most importantly of all, Douglas envisaged the state as taking a central role in the future of money and credit, whereas in Proudhon's schemes it was the state's *absence*—above anything else—that should define the future of money. In this respect, it was Proudhon, not Douglas, who turned out to be most in tune with the majority of monetary reformists throughout the twentieth century.

One recent noteworthy manifestation of mutualist principles has been the microcredit movement, and in particular, the Grameen Bank founded in Bangladesh by Muhammad Yunus in 1976. The principle behind microcredit is to provide loans that would normally be too small for ordinary banks. The idea of collectivism is built into the very structure of the loan, which is made to a "solidarity group": if one person defaults, the credit record of all group members is tarnished (although other group members are not actually liable for that portion of the loan).[16] Besides encouraging collectivism, the principle behind microcredit is that, when compared with charity, lending—within limits—can be empowering. Critics, on the other hand, argue that microcredit amounts to little more than the privatization of welfare, draws many borrowers into a debt trap, and reinforces extant gender inequalities (Rankin 2001; Karim 2008; Faraizi, Rahman, et al. 2010). The microcredit movement (including global organizations such as Kiva) has been enormously successful: solidarity lending now operates in forty-three countries worldwide. The Grameen Bank, principally owned by its borrowers, has spawned a large network of organizations, such as trusts and nonprofit ventures, including Grameen America, which made more than $85 million worth of loans between 2008 (when it was founded) and 2013.[17] However, microfinance recently underwent a crisis of its own, analogous perhaps to the subprime crisis.[18] The problem, to a degree, was one of scale: microcredit was becoming a victim of its own success as new companies were attracted to the system for commercial, rather then ethical, reasons: some of these were engaging in lending practices that resonate with subprime, such as failure to conduct proper credit checks and lending unrealistic amounts (Wichterich 2012). Having seen growth from 1 to 26.7 million microloans between 2003 and 2009, the microcredit system in India went into meltdown during 2010, amid accusations of predatory lending, excessive interest rates, and coercive collection tactics.[19] Inevitably, government intervention has followed—not only in India but elsewhere, such as Mexico and Peru—with tighter regulation of organizations that have evolved from a quasicharitable to a more commercially driven form. As microfinance scales up, in other words, its similarity to conventional banking appears proportionately to increase.[20]

16   The majority of such loans have been made to women: 97 percent in Bangladesh.
17   See http://grameenamerica.org/financial-info.
18   Chris Gregory, for example, calls the Indian crisis a "a collapse of the classic subprime lending kind" (Gregory 2012: 394).
19   See "Microfinance: Small Loan, Big Snag," *Financial Times*, December 1, 2010.
20   In an intriguing aside that resonates with our discussion of the moral economy of debt in Chapters 3 and 4, Gregory suggests that as the problems associated with microcredit have emerged, so has the language used to describe it change: micro*credit* has increasingly become micro*debt* (Gregory 2012: 394). He writes of Yunus: "Yunus is a village money lender who lends money on interest to the poorest of the very poor. What distinguishes him from other village money lenders is his success both financially and socially: he is probably the biggest village money lender in human history (8.32 million borrowers in 2010) and perhaps the only one in human history who is not looked down upon as an exploiter of the human misery of the masses. Thus he is the managing director of a village *bank*, not a village *moneylender*; the 20% he charges for income-generating loans is called *interest* not *usury* as any rate

An explanation of the possibilities that might be created for improving society though money once it has been freed from government *and* big banks can be found in the work of Edwin Riegel, who proposed private enterprise money as the foundation for a "non-political" monetary system (Riegel 1944). Riegel's monetary theory rests on the distinction between the *objective* and *subjective* idea of money. The objective idea views money as an entity with an independent existence: it can be created by law, apart from trade, and can—or even should—therefore be issued by governments. The subjective idea views money as a relationship (or process) that "can spring only from trade" (Riegel 1978: ch. 2), for there has never been and can never be an issue of money "except by a buyer in the act of purchase" (Riegel 1944: ch. 2). Although this idea initially appears similar to Menger's argument—like Menger, Riegel argues that money originated in barter—it turns out to more closely resemble the concept of money as a form of privately issued debt. It is thus Mitchell-Innes, not Menger, who is the closest comparator here. Just as Mitchell-Innes argues that the "whole theory of money" can be summarized as a chain of cancelled debt—"A's money is B's debt to him, and when B pays his debt, A's money disappears" (Mitchell-Innes 1913)—so Riegel describes money in terms of a "circle from issue to redemption" in which the "creditors (money holders) displace each other" (Riegel 1978: ch. 2). One important difference is that whereas Mitchell-Innes regards each transaction as the incurrence of a separate debt that is canceled by the next transaction, Riegel suggests that the original debtor "remains until, in due course, he makes a sale (delivers value to the market), thereby capturing the money with which to liquidate his 'loan'" (Riegel 1978: ch. 2).

Riegel attacks conventional theories of money from two sides. Against the traditional view of money as a commodity such as gold or silver, he maintains that even the most cursory comparison between the total supply of the commodity in question and the total value of money that is actually involved in trades reveals that the "spirit" of money is that it is an accounting system and a "representative of value in all commodities" (Riegel 1944: ch. 1). Against the state theory of money, on the other hand, Riegel argues that money is simply a "receipt for value" that can only arise out of exchange, not political fiat. This notion puts him at odds with both chartalism (Knapp) and neochartalism (Wray). As we saw in Chapter 3, both Knapp and Wray suggest that the government's monopoly position as the recipient of tax

---

over about 8% was called in the good old days; the loans he gives are called *micro-credit* rather than *micro-debt*; the people to whom this micro-credit is extended are called *borrowers* not debtors" (Gregory 2012: 385).

payments underpins its capacity to declare what "money" is. This situation is exactly what Riegel objects to: "A money issuer must be a seller who bids for money, not a taxer who requisitions it in whole or in part, as politically expedient and without a quid pro quid" (Riegel 1944: ch. 1).

Riegel's ideas are sometimes cited as important precursors for latter-day complementary schemes such as the LETS movement (Greco 2009: 5–6). This is a questionable claim. With LETS, there are important social considerations: primarily, money is seen as a means of community building. Such considerations are missing from Riegel's analysis, which is rightly invoked by libertarians as an exemplar of "free market money" (Browne 1974: 27, 30, 379). Whereas Riegel's proposals were antistatist, they also reveal an underlying commitment to an *individualist* account of money's evolution and reproduction. This idea, too, contradicts many of today's local currency movements. Riegel thus shares considerably more common ground with Hayek than with Proudhon. He was also a globalist, as the following passage, from *The New Approach to Freedom*—published the same year as Hayek's *Denationalization of Money* (Hayek 1976)—makes clear:

> When the people of the world have a common monetary language, completely freed from every government, it will so facilitate and stabilize exchange that peace and prosperity will ensue even without world government. With the state denied its money diluting power, the ills that lead to strife and war will be removed. A union of peoples rather than a union of political governments is what this world needs. (Riegel 1976: 28)

Riegel was part of a Private Enterprise Money Committee, which in 1944 produced the Money Freedom Declaration. The declaration condemned the "power in government to control the affairs of the people through the power to issue money" and asserted that it is a sovereign right of every individual to issue their own private money through the interchange of goods and services. The declaration envisaged a nonprofit, nonstock organization issuing money purely through trade using *valuns*, defined as tokens of mutual credit. This system would be a step further than Proudhon's Bank of the People[21] because there was no initial capital, nor any movement of conventional money into the scheme. Instead, the system would truly start from nothing, relying on its intrinsic superiority to grow as "more persons and corporations will join it and thus more and more trading will be done with valuns and less with dollars, pounds, francs and the scores of other

---

21   Riegel does not cite Proudhon; neither does Greco.

political money units." Once again, we are left wondering where money—or more specifically, the value of money—comes from. The answer here, as it was for Proudhon, is disarmingly simple: from the trust and endeavor of those who live and work within the social space in which it circulates. Money's value, as I have suggested a number of times already in this book, comes from its *social life*.

Riegel's ambitions extended far beyond the monetary sphere. The system would, the declaration said, raise wages to their highest possible level; maintain constant employment; prevent both inflation and deflation; abolish bureaucracy and government centralization; defeat fascism and communism; ensure freedom, prosperity, and democracy; and preserve peace. Beneath the declaration, as published, were listed various tributes to Riegel's book: its criticisms of conventional monetary theory were "devastating" and "irrefutable" and proved that totalitarianism would be impossible if governments had no control over the monetary system; Riegel's text was bound to be more influential than Marx's *Capital*, moreover, not least because it exposes "how a political and coercive money system is bound to destroy free enterprise—to corrupt free citizens into subjects and slaves." But unlike Proudhon's Bank of the People, Riegel's system never actually got off the ground.

In September 2011, a rather different monetary declaration was published, as part of the "Utah Monetary Summit." This declaration, too, insisted that monopolistic monetary systems were inherently damaging, engendering currency debasement that would result in lost purchasing power, inequitable wealth redistribution, misallocation of productive resources, and chronic unemployment. Echoing Riegel, the Utah declaration stated that the right to choose between alternative media of exchange—like the right to choose between suppliers of goods and services—is a cornerstone of a free market and society. However, whereas Riegel had insisted that money was not a thing but an accounting system, the Utah declaration referred to "natural money" as precious metal coin and argued that, because its value had remained steady, it was best able to serve society's needs by reducing inflation risk, encouraging saving, and attracting foreign investment in the region in which it circulates. Moreover, people should be free to hold as much money as they wanted to, with whichever financial institution they wanted to, without any obligation to disclose those holdings. The summit's sponsors included the Secure American Gold Exchange, the Old Glory Mint, and the Utah Gold and Silver Depository. People should be allowed to use whatever forms of money they wanted, the declaration said, "especially gold and silver coin." The "royalty" that Proudhon had sought to abolish was to be crowned once more.

VIRES IN NUMERIS

For its principle designer, Bitcoin's goal was to establish a form of money in which there is no need for trust. If money's users no longer have confidence in banks or states—or, perhaps, each other—to regulate and preserve the value of money, Bitcoin dispenses with the need for it by building trust into the software. On the face of it, the underlying rationale of Bitcoin is to ensure that money has anything *but* a social life. It is a techno-utopia that rests, quite literally, on a technology of mistrust. There are further curiosities to Bitcoin as a theory of money. Although it is a virtual currency, the philosophy behind Bitcoin implies that we must think of money as a *thing*: an asset whose value must be zealously protected over time. Of all the ideas we have been discussing in this book, the theory of money behind Bitcoin is broadly Mengerian; indeed, one could say that Bitcoin is a virtual form of gold—only moreso, because in theory at least, its supply is *absolutely* fixed. For these two reasons—the absence of trust and the view of money as a thing—Bitcoin arguably relies on an extraordinarily old-fashioned, even reactionary, image of money. This is what makes its development so interesting because it seems to excite people for reasons that are anything *but* reactionary.

There have been other versions of free market money whose soundness is derived not from gold itself but from an electronic analogue of gold. Bitcoin, however, is one of the most intriguing and controversial cases. The project started in several different ways, with ideas that finally came together in 2009 when the Bitcoin network was launched. One of the most important elements of the Bitcoin project is cryptography, which in its modern form is a science of secret writing that, since World War I, has become increasingly dependent on computer science. Bitcoin was developed when cryptographic techniques were combined with a monetary philosophy that was derived from Menger, although many supporters of "Austrian" economics tend to be critical of Bitcoin. This suspicion comes from two main reasons: first, because Bitcoins are not *actually* gold—indeed, according to this view, they have no intrinsic value; and second, because Bitcoins did not evolve as money because of their high use value, as Menger's theory would suggest. On the other hand, Bitcoin's supporters argue that, despite the efforts of hackers, the virtual currency is a more secure store of value than gold, which unless you are actually storing it, is subject to political manipulation and even confiscation. For less theoretically driven supporters of gold, as well as diehard deflationists, Bitcoin may actually have advantages over the yellow metal because whereas there is always the possibility of discovering and mining more gold, the total quantity of Bitcoins is set to reach a hard limit of 21 million Bitcoins during 2140: by design, there will *never* be more than this number in circulation.

The basic concepts underlying the idea of Bitcoin were prefigured in several academic papers and other initiatives over a period of more than two decades. In 1982, David Chaum presented a conference paper, "Blind Signatures for Untraceable Payments" (Chaum 1983), in which he envisaged a payment system that could combine one of the main advantages of cash—anonymity—with some of the key benefits of electronic banking, namely, security. In the late 1990s, Wei Dai (also an expert on cryptography) proposed the idea of "B-money," which would be used within a community inspired by Timothy May's notion of crypto-anarchy (May 1992; Kelly 1995: ch. 12; Dai 1998).[22] The cryptoanarchist community consists of participants who cannot be linked to their true names or physical locations. It is defined by cooperation, and the idea of B-money answers the requirement for there to be a medium of exchange and a method for enforcing contracts that does not rely on government. Dai's proposal was significant because it specifically advanced the idea that—as with mutualism—money can be created out of nothing, i.e., from *within the network itself*. Technically, this was made possible by a subprotocol that ensured that only a finite quantity of money is created within any given time period. This latter feature is crucial to Bitcoin. At around the same time, Nick Szabo developed the notion of "bit gold" (Szabo 2008), widely seen as the precursor to Bitcoin. Like B-money, bit gold sought to use secure cryptography that made it possible to combine anti-inflationary monetary creation (it would be strictly limited and controlled) with the principle of disintermediation. In other words, bit gold as Szabo conceived it would consist of valuable electronic bits (created through a "proof of work" generated from a public string of bits, called a challenge string) that cannot be forged, and whose creation is both finite and independent of any third party such as government or a central bank. The technical problems that need to be overcome to achieve this combination are considerable. Two key dangers have to be avoided: the low-cost producer who can flood the market with bit gold (or, subsequently, Bitcoins) and the profiteering "bit gold miner" who uses

---

22   At around the same time, Neal Stephenson's *Cryptonomicon* was published. Stephenson mixed the genres of historical novel (one of the book's central characters was based on Turing, whose work in cryptography was crucial to Allied efforts during the Second World War) and science fiction thriller. One of the key story lines tells of an attempt to establish a data haven in Southeast Asia, partly funded through a digital currency using powerful encryption and backed by gold (Stephenson 1999).

optimized computer architecture. The history of Bitcoin suggests that the latter has proven more difficult to avoid than the former.

Satoshi Nakamoto—a pseudonym for an individual or a group—introduced the idea of Bitcoin in a 2008 paper (Nakamoto 2008). He characterized the scheme as a system for electronic transactions that did not rely on trust, a possibility that in his view specifically required the elimination of opportunities for double spending. Double spending exists as a problem in electronic payment systems because each owner of a coin has no means of knowing whether or not the previous owner of the coin used it twice. The common solution had been to rely on a trusted authority, or mint, that would check every transaction. According to Nakamoto, however, the trust-based model for electronic transactions suffers from inherent weaknesses associated with increased transaction costs, e.g., small, casual transactions are discouraged:

> The root problem with conventional currency is all the trust that's required to make it work. The central bank must be trusted not to debase the currency, but the history of fiat currencies is full of breaches of that trust. Banks must be trusted to hold our money and transfer it electronically, but they lend it out in waves of credit bubbles with barely a fraction in reserve. We have to trust them with our privacy, trust them not to let identity thieves drain our accounts. Their massive overhead costs make micropayments impossible.[23]

Nakamoto's proposals sought to get rid of this central authority by using a block chain (shared by all computers or nodes within the network) through which the transaction history of each coin could be publicly known.[24] Privacy would be maintained, meanwhile, by encrypting the public keys, ensuring that the history of every "coin" is anonymized. Most Bitcoins are not really coins, of course: this is a ledger-based monetary system.[25] There are physical Bitcoins, too, called Casascius coins. In a nice reversal of the usual distinction between the material and the virtual, these are collectible coins with a "real" Bitcoin—the address and redeemable private key—embedded inside, hidden beneath a hologram.[26]

---

23   See http://p2pfoundation.net/bitcoin.
24   See http://blockchain.info/. This is a transaction database shared by all nodes participating in the system.
25   But unlike credit and debit card transactions, where the bank or card company manages the ledger, Bitcoin ledgers consist of block chains.
26   See https://www.casascius.com/.

Bitcoin was launched in January 2009, using open-source software, as a peer-to-peer payment network that combined the principles discussed above: Bitcoins were created within their network; their creation was strictly controlled without being governed by a central issuing authority. The network is programmed to ensure that the total number of Bitcoins in existence will never exceed 21 million: half of that total supply was generated by 2013. Bitcoins are created through dedicated rigs (PCs), which mine for new coins through a series of computations that require considerable computational power. The network is designed to produce a fixed number of Bitcoins per unit of time: 25 new Bitcoins will be generated every ten minutes until 2017, and that number will subsequently be halved every four years after that. Thus the more people (or rigs) there are mining for coins, the harder they will be to produce: only the most powerful rigs, i.e., several computers working together, will be able to create new coins. For this reason, rigs are expensive: a powerful rig sells for around a thousand dollars secondhand. Potentially, this could be a flaw in the system. Given the fact that coins are harder to mine the more miners there are, an inbuilt incentive exists for the most powerful miners to scale up their operations until it becomes unprofitable for others to mine. Although the system was designed to ensure that no single entity would be able to control more than half of the computational power devoted to mining, it may be feasible that one single miner could control all of it. This is one potential weakness of the system resulting from the hard limit on Bitcoin supply. The other failing—much more widely discussed—is an inevitable function of its success, that is to say, its proneness to bubbles and crashes.

Since its launch, the Bitcoin network has grown rapidly to become the most widely used alternative money system. Various retailers of material goods, music download websites, game providers, gambling sites, software providers, and high-profile online businesses such as WordPress, Reddit, Namecheap, and Mega, accept Bitcoins. The bitcoinstore.com sells a wide range of consumer goods.[27] There are Bitcoin gift cards, dedicated payment system and debit cards, and a series of exchanges (such as Bitcoin-Central and Bitcoin-24.com) in which Bitcoins can be traded for major currencies in real time. In December 2012, a French bank, Crédit Mutuel, together with the payment service company Aqoba, entered into an agreement with Bitcoin-Central to provide banking and payment services denominated in Bitcoin. In early 2013, a Bitcoin-specific HTML5 scheme was white-listed, meaning that the currency was on its way toward becoming

---

27 For example, on April 15, 2013, an Asus laptop was available for 6.2271 BTC, which the website states was equivalent to US$629 (see https://www.bitcoinstore.com/).

standard on all web browsers.[28] Silk Road, an online marketplace for buying and selling drugs,[29] took full advantage of the untraceability of Bitcoins, in combination with the anonymizing tool, Tor. The site opened in February 2011; after two years, the site was generating $1.7 billion of sales per month. For critics (as well as some supporters) of Bitcoin, Silk Road was the perfect storm, demonstrating the currency's capacity to evade state regulation of criminal as well as financial activity. The FBI closed down the site on October 2, 2013. Silk Road 2.0 opened a little more than a month later.

Bitcoin could almost be a mirror image of the state's increasing use, post-9/11, of the mainstream financial system for security purposes (de Goede 2012). As such, Bitcoin has attracted a barrage of criticism. For example, "Because Bitcoins are totally independent and not regulated by authorities, it proved the perfect monetary instrument for an anonymous community which had a mutual interest in maintaining anonymity as well as an alternative underground store of value" (*Financial Times*, April 3, 2013); "The FBI sees the anonymous Bitcoin payment network as an alarming haven for money laundering and other criminal activity—including as a tool for hackers to rip off fellow Bitcoin users" (*Wired*, May 9, 2012); "below the 'real' economy of legal tender and federal reserves, Bitcoins fuel a shadow economy that connects students, drug dealers, gamblers, dictators and anyone else who wants to pay for something without being traced" (*The Guardian*, March 4, 2013). Few critics pointed out that the other monetary form that is uniquely well suited to secret transactions is cash. The *Financial Times* has been particularly prominent in the debate, carrying a series of mainly critical articles about Bitcoin during its early 2013 boom, and inevitably, whenever the system has run into difficulties. After the bankruptcy of Mt. Gox, for example, John Gapper portayed Bitcoin as *l'enfant terrible* of alternative currencies, accusing its supporters of naively wanting to conquer the world's monetary landscape while simultaneously resisting proper regulatory oversight: "You cannot challenge fiat currencies and disrupt the global payments industry while reacting to any uninvited scrutiny like an adolescent whose parent has opened the bedroom door without knocking" (*Financial Times*, March 12, 2014). One year earlier, when the price of Bitcoin was booming, John Kay referred to those supporters as "cranks . . . who espouse schemes

---

28 See "Bitcoin takes an important step toward becoming part of every web browser on the planet," http://qz.com/78014/bitcoin-is-now-part-of-the-web-sort-of/, accessed May 10, 2013.

29 Around 70 percent of items sold on Silk Road are drugs; other items include erotica, books, and fake IDs.

for securing peace and prosperity by reforming the world's money" (*Financial Times,* April 16, 2013). I would prefer to call them utopians.

Bitcoin uses a considerable amount of electricity, and its critics have been fast to point this out, too. During the Bitcoin boom in April 2013, *Bloomberg* published a piece calling Bitcoin a "real-world environmental disaster" and came up with the "measurement" that Bitcoin mining uses up 982 megawatt hours a day: "That's enough to power roughly 31,000 U.S. homes," it said.[30] Krugman joined the chorus, dismissing people who "think it's smart, nay cutting-edge, to create a sort of virtual currency whose creation requires wasting real resources."[31] Of course, none of these critics tried to measure the environmental costs associated with the production and use of more conventional money, such as paper bills and plastic credit cards. As with critics of Bitcoin's role in the "illegal" economy, this was less a serious debate about the merits of Bitcoin—although, as we shall see, there are serious questions to be asked about the theory behind Bitcoin, and about its viability as a form of money—than a campaign simply to discredit the currency.

During July 2012, a rack of seven interconnected mining rigs was being advertised on YouTube. "At today's exchange rate $11.10 per Bitcoin you can make over $850 a month with this setup," the ad claimed.[32] This claim gives one of the most crucial aspects of the Bitcoin boom away. The rate had been more than $30 a little more than a year earlier, before crashing in June 2011, and has been fluctuating ever since. The value of Bitcoins grew dramatically during late 2012 and early 2013 (for reasons I will discuss in a moment), rising from $12 and topping out at $266 in April before falling back to $130 in the face of apparent difficulties at Mt. Gox, the main Bitcoin exchange, in coping with demand. The currency's value rose dramatically again during late 2013, reaching a trading high of $1,242 by the end of November before wildly fluctuating again, falling from $1,200 to $600 between December 6 and 7, 2013. Security breaches, including various malware attacks aiming to steal Bitcoins,[33] are among the major reasons most often cited for these

---

30   See http://www.bloomberg.com/news/2013-04-12/virtual-bitcoin-mining-is-a-real-world-environmental-disaster.html.
31   See http://krugman.blogs.nytimes.com/2013/04/12/adam-smith-hates-bitcoin/?smid=tw-NytimesKrugman&seid=auto.
32   See http://www.youtube.com/watch?v=wYHoE21kUcs.
33   One version of Bitcoin malware used Skype to turn infected computers into "slaves" of a Bitcoin generator (see http://www.securelist.com/en/blog/208194210/Skypemageddon_by_bitcoining).

368   CHAPTER 8

periodic crashes:[34] for example, in 2011 a user claimed that he had half a million U.S. dollars worth of Bitcoins stolen from his computer by malware. Another cause was that the very feature that was meant to ensure that Bitcoins were sound money (just like gold) in the first place—their finite supply—became a source of speculation, and a Bitcoin bubble.[35]

Arguably, Bitcoins were being mined primarily not in order to be used but rather to be hoarded. This phenomenon prompted some critics to liken the currency to a Ponzi scheme. The comparison seems flawed: unlike entrants to a Ponzi scheme, holders of Bitcoins are not—per se—victims of fraud. But according to Eric Posner, Bitcoin "investors" are likely to suffer the same fate: "Bitcoin will collapse when people realize that it can't survive as a currency because of its built-in deflationary features, or because of the emergence of bytecoins, or both. A real Ponzi scheme takes fraud; Bitcoin, by contrast, seems more like a collective delusion."[36] Viewed simply as a currency, Bitcoin's biggest pitfall is likely to be price deflation (and, *in extremis*, hyperdeflation), not inflation. This would be the conclusion reached about Bitcoin from the perspective of modern monetary theory, as discussed in Chapter 3. As the blogger "Lord Keynes" notes, "without relative price stability and an elastic supply, Bitcoins are not a viable monetary unit for any large capitalist system."[37] Although almost every monetary scholar would agree with the point about price stability, those of a more "Austrian" persuasion—not to mention the designers of Bitcoin themselves—would disagree about elastic supply: the Bitcoin software is designed to avoid such elasticity, which is regarded as a weakness of the fiat monetary system.

As a form of money, Bitcoin shares many of the flaws associated with gold, namely, its attractiveness to speculators and its inflexibility *qua* money. And yet Bitcoin is unlike gold in a number of crucial respects. One of the main reasons for its novelty is the open-source software on which it is based. Strictly speaking, no individual or organization controls Bitcoin. There is a

---

    34   The December 2013 crashes were linked to new Chinese government restrictions on Bitcoin transactions, see "China Bans Banks from Bitcoin Transactions," *Financial Times*, December 5, 2013. China has the largest market in Bitcoins. Other major falls in Bitcoin's value occurred from June 8 to 12, 2011 (when the price fell by 68 percent), on January 17, 2012 (36 percent), from August 17 to 19, 2012 (51 percent), between March 6 and 11, 2013 (33 percent), and on April 10, 2013 (61 percent). See *Forbes*'s "An illustrated history of Bitcoin crashes," http://www.forbes.com/sites/timothylee/2013/04/11/an-illustrated-history-of-bitcoin-crashes/.

    35   The total value of all Bitcoins in the world exceeded $1 billion for the first time in March 2013.

    36   See *Slate*, "Fool's Gold," http://www.slate.com/articles/news_and_politics/view_from_chicago/2013/04/bitcoin_is_a_ponzi_scheme_the_internet_currency_will_collapse.html.

    37   "Bitcoin Is No Great Mystery," see http://socialdemocracy21stcentury.blogspot.ie/2013/04/bitcoin-is-no-great-mystery.html, accessed April 15, 2013.

group of administrators, the Bitcoin Foundation, which is run on similar lines to the Linux Foundation, funded through grants via for-profit companies such as Mt. Gox and CoinLab. The Bitcoin Foundation employs a salaried chief scientist, who works full-time on maintaining the open-source code. As a monetary system, Bitcoin is designed to be genuinely open and "democratic" in the sense that its supply is neither controlled nor controllable by any single entity. One curious feature of Bitcoin, however, is the degree of centralization that can evolve within the system. As I have already noted, it is mathematically conceivable that a powerful miner does control more than 50 percent of Bitcoin production.

The Bitcoin "boom" that occurred during the early months of 2013 drew greater levels of publicity to the system than hitherto, not least because it coincided with a series of events in the mainstream monetary and banking system: first, the Cypriot banking crisis, with the initial plan to "bail-in" small depositors, overriding deposit insurance; second, Russia's call for a repatriation of offshore capital; and third, the Japanese currency debasement. Though it remains doubtful whether Bitcoin's price rise was actually driven by these events, the coincidence was enough to fuel debate about the future of state money and mainstream banking, and the potential role of Bitcoin as an alternative currency that appeared to be free from political manipulation, and in relation to which general issues of "trust" (which had been shattered in Cyprus) did not appear to arise. For a while at least—whatever John Kay might have said about "cranks"—monetary utopianism seemed to be catching on.

The social foundations of the Bitcoin system—or, rather, the apparent lack of obvious social foundations—are underpinned by the math behind it:[38] in principle, "crypto proof" replaces trust. *Vires in Numeris*—"strength in numbers"—is the motto on the physical Bitcoins that are produced by Mike Caldwell, who argues that "if you accept bitcoin in exchange for your goods or your work, that is a vote for economic fairness." According to this view, Bitcoin's strength lies in its very diffuseness, the lack of any central governing principle. Gavin Andersen, Bitcoin's chief scientist, believes that

38   Sociologically, on the other hand, the image we have of the "average" Bitcoin user is rather predictable. According to a Bitcoin users' survey that ran between February and April 2013 (with 1,087 responses), the "average" Bitcoin user is overwhelmingly male (95.2 percent) (for a discussion of Bitcoin and gender, see Scott 2014), 32.1 years old, libertarian or anarcho-capitalist (44.3 percent), nonreligious (61.8 percent), with a full time job (44.7 percent), and is in a relationship (55.6 percent). Some 36.7 percent of users do not drink, smoke, gamble, or take drugs, and more people have used Bitcoin for donations than for illegal transactions (see http://simulacrum.cc/2013/04/13/overview-of-bitcoin-community-survey-feb-mar-2013/).

CHAPTER 8

even if he were forced by the U.S. government to stop working on the software, the system itself would be impossible to close down:

> ... there are people all over the world who could pick up and reimplement it, for example in different programming languages; if you browse the Bitcoin forums you've seen the enormous chaos and energy there. There's all sorts of people doing all sorts of things—many of them crazy things that will never succeed, but some of those will be the next big things in Bitcoin.[39]

Hoarding, though, remains a key issue with Bitcoin. As we have discussed a number of times in this book, hoarded money is of limited usefulness *qua* money. The very feature of Bitcoin that renders it attractive as an open and democratic monetary system that is free from asymmetrical power structures—the software that controls exactly how many Bitcoins will be produced—undermines its operation as a form of money.

Reflecting some of these concerns, a new variant of Bitcoin is under development, which exploits its perceived virtue of disintermediation while specifically seeking to avoid hoarding.[40] This is Freicoin, which is essentially Bitcoin plus demurrage. The new currency is being promoted through the Freicoin Foundation, which is linked to Occupy Wall Street. Although having such an organization at the "center" of a P2P currency seems odd, its organizers claim that there is no other way of dispersing coins across society.[41] Freicoin uses a combination of organizational modes: vertically, the foundation distributes coins through grants; horizontally, the coins are mined through a network of rigs. The vertical aspect underlines Freicoin's commitment to proactive *social* reform through monetary innovation: the meme of the 99 percent is ever-present in its narrative.[42] Like Bitcoins, Fre-

---

39   Quoted in "The Bitcoin Boom," *The New Yorker*, April 2, 2013, see http://www.newyorker.com/online/blogs/elements/2013/04/the-future-of-bitcoin.html.

40   There are several other alternatives to Bitcoin, such as Litecoin, Namecoin, PPCoin, and Dogecoin. As of January 2013, there were more than seventy digital currencies listed on http://coinmarketcap.com/. Each offers its own distinct variation on (and reputed advantage over) the Bitcoin theme. For example, Litecoin can be mined using consumer-grade hardware (see https://litecoin.org/), while PPCoin is designed to be more secure (see https://en.bitcoin.it/wiki/PPCoin). Dogecoin, using the Shiba Inu dog as its mascot, is based on Litecoin. In 2014, a new digital currency called Coinye West—the name is inspired by the rapper, Kanye West, although he has no direct links with the project—was due to be launched, reputedly for use in the music industry.

41   See http://freico.in/faq/.

42   For example, "For the 99% who live paycheck-to-paycheck, the loss from demurrage is minimal and would be compensated for in wages and pricing. For those who manage to

icoins will be mined through proof-of-work block chains. Algorithms are meant to ensure that monetary growth is smooth until circulation stabilizes at 100 million coins. Bearers of these coins will pay the 5 percent "holding fee" automatically, with that slice being used through miners to pay for operating costs. Whereas Bitcoins are used for Internet payments, the designers of Freicoin ultimately intend it to be used in "real" transactions. But the biggest major difference between Bitcoin and Freicoin is demurrage. According to Freicoin's advocates, demurrage achieves two things: first, it mitigates against hoarding: "Banks, financiers, and large corporations can no longer hoard money waiting for higher interest rates or a more favorable investment climate as the demurrage acts as a tax on stagnant money."[43] Second, demurrage means that the maximum supply of Freicoins is never reached, hence "there will be a perpetual reward for miners that comes from compensating for the coins 'destroyed' by the demurrage fees."[44] Freicoin and Bitcoin are not in competition, their advocates claim. They reject Gesell's view that money is a natural monopoly.

Perhaps this rejection reveals something interesting about Bitcoin as a techno-utopia, because for all that the currency seeks to eliminate the nuances of social life—i.e., trust, incompetence, and political expediency—which Bitcoins founders took to have undermined conventional monetary systems that were run by governments and central banks, it seems that greater social intervention, specifically in the form of regulation, may be the precondition for Bitcoin's future success. If Bitcoin's initial appeal was rooted in the promise of machines, its subsequent life looks just likely to be marked by the reemergence of the social life of money. This situation ought not to be surprising. As sociologists of science and technology have been arguing for a long time, technological artifacts cannot simply enact organizational forms—in this instance, a monetary system—on their own. Human, social, and political factors inevitably emerge as those who interact with and use these artifacts both shape and are shaped by their practical use (Winner 1985). In Bitcoin's case, there is a close analogy between the underlying view of money as a "thing" in itself and the notion that technology is capable of

---

accumulate some savings and for the 1% who receive much more income than they reasonably spend, they can either save real wealth (gold, silver, Bitcoins, real estate, artwork and fine wine, for example) and accept the obvious limitations of wealth saving (loss, storage, theft, rot, fire, insurance premiums, etc.), or they can loan it out to borrowers at what ends up being near-zero basic interest. With sustainable 0%-APR interest loans the order of the day, business will boom and the economy will grow in a virtuous cycle," see http://freico.in/about/.

43   See http://freico.in/about/.
44   See http://freico.in/about/.

shaping a social system—in this instance, money—all by itself, free from human intervention. Most importantly for our discussion in this book, the idea behind Bitcoin is premised on denying—or circumventing—the social life of money, and on treating money as a *thing*, not a *process*. As I have repeatedly argued, however, neither idea withstands close scrutiny.

TOWARD A MONETARY COMMONS

This journey through various iterations of monetary freedom—from Paris to Utah, from Proudhon's mutualism, through Douglas's social credit and Riegel's private enterprise money, to gold in both its literal and virtual forms—has been a journey from the Left to the Right: from a fear of monetary shortage and economic sclerosis on one side to the fear of monetary abundance and inflation on the other; from a monetary system in which trust is crucial both as money's precondition and as something money can nurture, to a system that rests on the elimination of any requirement for trust whatsoever; and from an orientation to money as a process, coming into being purely for the purpose of being passed on, to a notion of money as a thing—even a *virtual* thing—whose essential truth lies in its value over time. In the journey we have taken, the differences elaborated here are implied by Riegel's distinction between the objective and subjective view of money. As soon as money is viewed as an independent entity, something that *possesses* value, which in turn is *possessed* by its owner, the freedom associated with it becomes largely a negative freedom: a freedom to hold on to one's property without interference. By contrast, the freedom to use money through creating it in the first place is characterized as a positive freedom in Fromm's sense, i.e., the freedom to enter into the web of exchanges. Fromm surely had a point: once it is treated as a thing and hoarded, our orientation to money is a relationship with the dead.

When Polanyi called the self-adjusting market a stark utopia, he conjured the image of a socially emaciated space that "could not exist for any length of time without annihilating the human and natural substance of society" (Polanyi 1957b: 3).[45] As we have seen, advocates of alternative monies often envisage a set of exchange relations in which money creates rather than erodes binding social ties (Blanc 2000; Lietaer 2002; Greco 2009; Hallsmith and Lietaer 2011; Lietaer and Belgin 2011). But local association does not only underwrite the value of such monies. It restricts it, too. One major

---

45   Polanyi also described economic liberalism as a utopia (Polanyi 1957b: 218, 250).

practical difficulty of such monies is their limited-purpose quality (Ingham 2004b: 184–88). Their value evaporates beyond the community, and their validity can be partial even within its borders. Such self-imposed limits of local monetary orders, though a source of richness and strength, tend to undermine their efficacy over time (Collom 2007). Digital currencies may help to resolve this problem (Hart 2001; Dodd 2005b), although arguably at the expense of the rich social ties on which more local systems appear to thrive. The underlying tension here, in Simmelian terms, is between *quality* and *quantity*: between the depth of associations facilitated by local currencies on one side and the breadth of the exchange relations that any given monetary form makes possible on the other (Evans 2009: 1037–38). Peter North refers to this tension in terms of the alignment of the moral and economic scale of local currencies (North 2005).

The obvious solution to such dilemmas is to develop not just one alternative form of money but rather several: this solution would be not so much a "real" utopia—an idea that is focused mainly on practical design problems (Spannos 2008; Wright 2010)—as a "realistic" utopia of the pragmatic and limited kind favored by Rawls in the context of political philosophy and international relations (Rawls 2001; Brown 2002). The idea of having distinct currencies circulating alongside each other is hardly new, of course; indeed, one could say that it accurately describes the existing state of affairs throughout the history of money. As we discussed in Chapter 7, Zelizer argues that multiplicity is an inherent feature of even apparently singular, monolithic monies, such as national currencies. But the positive advocacy of monetary multiplicity is rarely found in the literature on monetary reform, which, as we have seen, tends to get hooked onto specific fears (e.g., stagnation or inflation) that generate formulaic and sometimes self-defeating solutions to complex problems. When the Bank of England published an article on local currencies in its last *Quarterly Bulletin* of 2013, its recognition of the potential of such monies to enhance local economic development—the article refers to a local multiplier effect, for example (Naqvi and Southgate 2013: 5)—was tempered (if not entirely undermined) by the underlying question, which was whether local currencies posed any threat to the stability of "proper" banknotes.[46] As an acknowledgment by a state agency of money's multiplicity, this was somewhat double-edged.

---

[46] The authors conclude that local currencies are probably too small to make a difference in this regard: "Given that the schemes currently operating in the United Kingdom are at present small (both individually and in aggregate) relative to aggregate spending in the economy, and are typically backed one-for-one with sterling, they are unlikely to present a risk to the Bank's monetary or financial stability objectives. Nevertheless, a risk could arise if consumers

Richard Douthwaite proposed something along the lines of a multiple currency system in *The Ecology of Money* (2006). In accordance with its environmentalist language, Douthwaite's position, too, is based on a certain kind of fear, namely, of the contribution that extant forms of money have been making to the emergence of our "unsustainable, unstable global monoculture" (Douthwaite 2006: 2). On this particular connection, Douthwaite's argument—in common with the New Economics Foundation in Britain (Ryan-Collins, Greenham et al. 2012)—is that the monetary system as it is currently configured in advanced capitalist countries (with banks creating money as they create loans) supports an economic system that is underpinned by the belief (and corresponding policies) in perpetual growth. Given that interest payments are necessary to service the debts that money consists of, "the economy must grow continuously if it is not to collapse," and continual growth is unsustainable (Douthwaite 2006: ch. 1). We discussed an analogous logic in David Harvey's work, discussed in Chapter 2. And as we saw earlier, this argument was also the cornerstone of Fromm's proposal for a humanistic utopia.

Douthwaite's argument focuses on money creation, which, he states, is currently in the hands of three distinct groups in society: commercial institutions (or banks), governments, and users (i.e., communities, etc.). Contrary to monetary theorists such as Ingham and Wray who maintain that these different forms of money are essentially part of the same generic monetary system—defined by the unit of account that a government declares it will accept in payment of taxes—Douthwaite insists that these are distinct monetary *forms* that meet different *needs* and therefore fulfill different social *functions*. He identifies four such needs in particular (Douthwaite 2000: ch. 4): first, an international currency is required that can play the role that used to be performed by gold; second, there is a need for a national or regional currency that is related to the international currency; third, localized monies are required, which are voluntarily created by their users to mobilize resources left untapped by national or regional systems (these are like Zelizer's circuits of commerce); and fourth, a secure long-term store of value is needed by those who want to hold their savings in a liquid form.

---

mistakenly associate local currencies with banknotes. Such a perception could generate a spillover effect if, for example, a successful counterfeit attack on a local currency were to reduce confidence in banknotes or, in the event of failure, if consumers were to incorrectly expect recompense from the Bank. Bearers of local currency vouchers do not benefit from the same level of consumer protection as banknotes issued by either the Bank of England or the authorised commercial issuing banks in Scotland and Northern Ireland" (Naqvi and Southgate 2013: 1).

Substantively, Douthwaite's work stands out for the proposal he makes in relation to international money. Instead of using gold, a major currency, or a currency basket as the international reserve currency, he suggests adopting energy-backed currency units. These units would be like ration coupons, with a finite supply administered by a transnational body such as the IMF and allocated to governments on a per capita basis. These coupons could then be used to purchase energy emission rights and distributed both to citizens and corporations domestically. This "money" would be an "ecological" money because rather than the world's monetary system (and its economies) being governed through the supply and demand of credit—whose environmental effect would just be seen as an externality—the relationship between economic activity and energy consumption would be directly expressed by (and could be controlled through) the flow of international money. The principle would be that economies can expand only to the extent that they become more energy efficient: using up too much of a country's energy quota would be like running up too much debt, with domestic "inflation" eventually forcing it to contract.

Douthwaite's proposals represent a utopian pricing system, which uses a chosen scarce resource—energy, as opposed to labor or time, for example—to underpin the value of money. In such a system, the price mechanism is meant to achieve a more equitable distribution of the resource in question. In all such instances—gold, labor money, time dollars, and energy units—the logic is that by holding money's value to a commodity that is in finite supply, prices have to stabilize over time. With gold, the aim is to hold prices steady. With labor and time, the objective is to ensure that those who provide goods and services are rewarded more equitably because by definition, the prices people pay as consumers are equivalent to the efforts they expend as producers. Because he expects prices (and, especially, price inflation) to influence both the supply *and* demand for energy, Douthwaite's scheme bears a closer resemblance to Simmel's perfect money: the aim, after all, is not to redistribute energy, but rather to distribute it as fairly as possible, although only according to the principle of absolute equality (energy use per capita), not the principle of relative equality that Simmel found so important.

Although the notion of ecological money is intriguing in its own right, perhaps of greater interest to Douthwaite's argument is the prospect that energy units merely make up one tier of a four-tier monetary system in which each money is expected to answer a specific set of needs. The principle behind the idea is simple and ought to be self-evident after even the most cursory encounter with the history of money. Throughout that history, distinct monies have circulated side by side, being created and used according to need. Even during the modern era, in which states supposedly monopolized the right to name money and to control its production and supply, supplementary monies have existed and often thrived. Whereas user-controlled currencies such as LETS tokens or time dollars often fulfill an important countercyclical function—e.g., by enabling people to pay for goods and services even when their supplies of conventional money are depleted—this is hardly a good basis for holding them as a relatively liquid store of value. Indeed, as we discussed earlier in this chapter, being held for any length of time is the kiss of death for such countercyclical currencies, which, as Gesell rightly pointed out, are better off being made to rot. Whether it is desirable to have any form of money whatsoever that is designed for being hoarded is a separate question, to which Fromm's answer, as we have also seen, would be a resounding no.

Nevertheless, there is something intuitively appealing about Douthwaite's approach: if not to the idea of energy units, then certainly to the argument that any viable—and, even, utopian—monetary system should be a field of variation, consisting of a repertoire of different ways for organizing money. To recall our discussion from Chapter 1, if only one particular aspect of money is allowed to hold sway at the expense of all others, it is likely that predictable and perfectly avoidable problems will arise: for example, sclerosis in the case of commodity-based money, and inflation in the case of credit money. Sociologically, too, we need to develop a more rounded understanding of the variable effect of different forms of money on society itself in order to come to grips with the fact that, *contra* Simmel, there is actually no such thing as perfect money.

Most of the utopian images of money we have seen in this chapter are concerned with money's substantive features: the source of value it represents, its effect on social inequality and human freedom, its potential as a social technology for addressing resource depletion, and its role in forging sustainable local economies. In *The Diamond Age*, Neal Stephenson conjures up an image of future money—most would probably see it as dystopian—that is striking because it focuses not on value, but rather on *process*. His protagonist, Bud, secures a new line of credit from an individual calling himself the Peacock Bank. The credit is implanted in the iliac crest of Bud's pelvis—although he could have opted for the mastoid bone in the skull, or indeed anywhere a big bone was close to the surface. The tiny card communicates through radio waves. "Then you could go around and buy stuff just by asking for it; Peacock Bank and the merchant you were buying from and the card in your pelvis handled all the details" (Stephenson 1994: 10). The idea that you can "buy stuff just by asking for it" suggests a world in which we could behave *as if money did not exist*. If one could get credit in one's bones, a whole host of practical problems—losing your card, having it stolen, verifying your ID—would evaporate. It is striking how close Stephenson gets to the spirit of what money has become: forms of mobile money such as contactless payment or Wave and Pay appear to render money as inconspicuous as it can possibly be—short of having your credit limit injected into your pelvis. In 2004, the Baja Beach Club in Barcelona launched a new payment system for its VIP members: a VeriChip implant lodged inside a 1-mm-diameter glass capsule injected beneath the skin. "We are the first discotheque in the world to offer the VIP VeriChip. Using an integrated (imbedded) microchip, our VIPs can identify themselves and pay for their food and drinks without the need for any kind of document," the club announced. The scheme was subsequently criticized when the chips proved difficult to remove.[47]

It has become easier to pay than ever as innovative ways of conveying money from one transactor to another through cards, terminals, and electronic circuits emerge with exhilarating frequency. Given such developments, one might imagine that the world in which multiple monies thrive is upon us. But these are multiple ways of *paying*. The monies themselves, and the circuits being used to convey money from one node to another, do not present quite such an array of choice as might initially appear to be the case. Many of the new payment systems that are available involve partnerships with established financial services companies: wave and pay operates through Visa, for example; Google Wallet works in partnership with Visa, MasterCard, American Express, and Discover; iZettle works with American Express and MasterCard. It is therefore worth pausing to ask why there has been such an explosion of payment services in recent years, before discussing what it might mean for the future of money.

Google Wallet and Wave and Pay are forms of "mobile money" that have been developing alongside the growth of alternative monies. Mobile monies appeal to users because they remove from the act of payment the inconveniences and impositions associated with traditional banking. Some forms of mobile money do this explicitly. Take the M-Pesa system, which mainly operates in Kenya, Tanzania, Afghanistan, South Africa, and India. M-Pesa[48] uses mobile phones to transfer money, advertising itself as a cheap and easy

---

47   See http://www.prisonplanet.com/articles/april2004/040704bajabeachclub.htm and http://edition.cnn.com/2004/WORLD/europe/06/09/spain.club/index.html.
48   *M* is for mobile; *pesa* is Swahili for money.

way to move money without needing banks (or, in many cases, not visiting bank branches). Other forms of mobile money, such as Square Wallet, still use banks but eliminate most of the aggravation that usually come with banks.[49] With Square, once a merchant and a customer have both registered for the service, the merchant needs only the customer's name; the customer's photograph appears on the merchant's terminal while the system manages the details, sending the customer a text message to confirm. This is not quite payment by pelvis but close enough. "Feel like a regular every time you pay," the advertising says, conveying a combination of speed and *Gemeinschaft* that Simmel would surely have found compelling.

What we gain in convenience with transactions like this, we lose in the discount the merchant has to pay to the provider of the payment service in question. This is the "cut"—usually between 1 and 4 percent—that is sliced from an increasing number of everyday transactions: not just those involving credit and debit cards but virtually all cashless forms of payment that we make. Those forms of payments that seem to liberate us from the clutches of banks and large corporations base their attractiveness on an underlying sense that they are enabling us to escape from the old vested interests that were present—somewhere in the background—whenever we used money. The classic expression of such interests, of course, is *seigniorage*, which used to be the difference between the value of money and what it cost to produce. Seigniorage was classically seen as a tax—economists called it an inflation tax—because it was usually the state (via its central bank) that produced the notes and coins in question. Today, however, the "tax" on the everyday use of money is paid not to the state but to the providers of the payment networks. These are the very providers—PayPal, Square, Google, and M-Pesa—whose primary attraction lies in the fact that they are *not government*. This phenomenon is the new, private, seigniorage.[50]

The expansion of mobile money has proceeded hand in hand with the development of increasingly sophisticated ways for private corporations to "mine value in the act of payment" (Maurer 2011: 10). The payment services "industry" is still dominated by the credit card companies, but they are increasingly being joined by social networking platforms and mobile phone companies, all vying for the 1 to 4 percent slice that gets extracted from virtually every payment made. What this slice amounts to, essentially, is a

---

49   https://squareup.com/wallet.
50   Although it is not *exactly* seigniorage, the term goes some way toward capturing the idea that this is essentially a fee that is charged for the mere use of money, like the opposite of demurrage. As Maurer points out, "We may need a better vocabulary for fees, rents, taxes, tribute—not everything, as the Islamic bankers remind us, is usury" (Maurer 2011: 11).

significant "grab" for a major part of money's infrastructure, the global payment networks, by private capital. There is an important irony here because although the emergence of mobile money appeals to money's users for a mixture of reasons—speed and convenience are two—a significant part of their selling point is the appearance that mobile money is loosening the grip of the state over money, primarily by undermining its capacity to exploit its formal rights over money's creation for financial advantage—otherwise known as tax. From this point of view, cash is the enemy of human freedom (Wolman 2012): never mind that it is corporations such as Visa who are in the vanguard of the "struggle" against this "enemy."

If we were to liken money's infrastructure to a road system, the emergence of mobile money is roughly equivalent to a takeover of the highways by private corporations. We still pay a toll for using the road; indeed, we may be paying more than before. It is merely the corporations, not government, that take the proceeds. If a major advantage of this system is the damage it does to the privileges of the state, a significant potential disadvantage is that an important aspect of money's infrastructure is potentially being taken further away from, not closer toward, the civic benefits that are meant to accrue from the emergence of alternative monies. Mobile forms of money only appear to represent a major step forward in the disintermediation of the monetary system itself. Though they may weaken the role of the state, they strengthen the hand of the banks. If such developments are the harbinger of a new pluralism in money, it is a kind of pluralism that seems likely to exclude precisely those monetary forms that are being held up as exemplars of a world in which money is no longer in the grip of the financial system.

Returning to the analogy with roads, one could argue that two different systems dominate the world's monetary flows. One, which is by far the largest, consists of forms of money that are produced by *hierarchical* systems, banks and governments, and are strongly mediated. This is a global system, hugely complex in its structure but possessing a sufficient level of coherence for its collapse to seem highly likely during the 2007–8 banking crisis. The other, smaller, and more disparate system is a group of roads where there is little if any mediation and virtually no hierarchy to speak of. These are *horizontal* systems consisting of monetary networks or circuits of one kind or another. There are many different forms of money in such systems, some with rationales—as we have seen with Bitcoin—that speak to opposite ends of the political spectrum. Nevertheless, the prime characteristic of the forms of money that are being used within this system is that they are organized horizontally, using modes of issuance that come close to realizing the conviction of the great monetary reformers and thinkers that money is essentially a *social agreement between its users*. Nobody should have a monopoly over its production and supply. In an ideal world, these road systems would be linked, like a system of highways and local roads. The highways link large centers of population and cross state borders, together with a complex system of local roads, tailored to more specific, often more localized, terrain. But the pluralistic monetary landscape that is emerging today is flawed because a major part of its infrastructure—involving the "mainstream" payment system, the highways—is being privatized as major banks and corporations extract a profit from every transaction that their systems convey.[51] This is not simply a question of global or national monies versus local monies. Monetary forms such as Bitcoin, and forms of social lending such as Kiva, are not local monies.

There are two key issues here. The first concerns *ownership* and *governance* of the payment networks themselves. They are money's infrastructure. Though there can be no guarantees, a pluralistic future for money seems more likely if this crucial part of its infrastructure is treated as part of the commons. This goal may not be as ambitious a concept as Hardt and Negri's vision of the financial commons (see Chapter 6), but it is arguably more realistic and achievable. The increasingly private character of payment systems militates against this situation and explicitly encourages a form of profiteering from money's mere use, which is arguably no more logical or ethically defensible than usury. Since the 2007–8 crisis, most public debate about the nature and purpose of the monetary and financial system has been preoccupied with debt. But the "new seigniorage" has all of the potential to be an equally corrosive feature of the world's monetary landscape. The second key issue is connected to the first. It concerns the relationship between the two main payment networks I have been discussing here. At present, the two road systems meet in various ways, or in many instances not at all. Local currencies such as London's Brixton Pound are only exchangeable in specific places in a delimited area. To some degree, this is exactly the point: such currencies are designed to keep value within the community in which they circulate, so it makes little sense to expand their circulation, even though their spatially limited nature undermines the success of such currencies. But even globally extensive monies such as Bitcoin are undermined by the fact that they cannot be spent as freely as main-

---

51   Payment service providers wield significant power in other ways, too, as exemplified by the involvement of Bank of America, VISA, MasterCard, PayPal and Western Union in the WikiLeaks case.

stream currencies: they become niche currencies in the wrong way, appealing either to those with a particular level of technical knowledge and equipment or to speculators. Alternative monies remain stubbornly outside the mainstream: enriching the monetary landscape, but nowhere near as much as they should. These two issues are related, of course, because as long as private institutions stand to gain from the mere flow of certain monies, they will seek to control which particular monies flow along which particular networks. Such barriers need to be broken down, whereas the particular "opening up" of payment networks we are witnessing with the development of systems such as Google Wallet is merely transferring the role of gatekeeper from the state to private corporations.

CONCLUSION

Alternative monies are by no means new. Besides the quite well known reformers we have been discussing here—from Ruskin and Proudhon through Gesell and Riegel to Nakamoto—there is a whole host of committed monetary radicals who argue not only that it is possible to create better and alternative monies than those we already have but also that these monies genuinely enrich our social and economic existence. The chorus of voices calling for monetary reform has certainly grown since the 2007–8 banking crisis. But it had been growing steadily already, particularly since the emergence of local currency schemes during the mid to late 1980s. The LETS model can be found in Russell's science fiction novel, *The Great Explosion* (1962) (Russell 1993), which describes an anarchist-libertarian utopia where a system of barter and gift exchange operates, using a measurement called *obs* (obligations) as its unit of account. Other fictional precursors to alternative monetary and credit systems include Cory Doctorow's *Down and Out in the Magic Kingdom* (2003), which provided inspiration for Whuffie. Although varied in form, scale, and design, most alternative money and credit systems have a discernible set of normative goals that could certainly be described as utopian in spirit: to foster a sense of community, to build local wealth without allowing it to be siphoned off by large corporations and banks, and to provide "free" banking. Such schemes appear to work against any idea of money as "soulless": they are designed to enrich, not erode, civic life. On the other hand, some of the schemes we have been discussing in this chapter appear to work in the opposite direction, for example, by using measures to obviate the need for trust at the level of the monetary system as a whole.

Simmel once disparaged socialism for its "trait of wishing to solve all riddles and difficulties of things with a single formula or a single stroke" (Simmel 1997: 271), likening it to the "shibboleth" of Hegelian philosophy. Just as Hegelianism was superseded by the "patient work of gaining knowledge from the individual elements of the world," so we need to learn to pursue social improvements in a more piecemeal fashion: "worker protection and worker insurance, general and unrestricted education, gradual work towards a standard working day and a minimum wage" amount to a "gradual levelling of social distinctions" (Simmel 1997: 271–72). To avoid this leveling, he said, socialism itself should be seen as a pure concept, just like money. As such, it is "an inference from ideal convictions and an expression of a developing conception of society which strives toward perfection" (Simmel 2004: 166). As with perfect money, we are better off on the *road* to completion. Were we ever to reach journey's end, our goal would in all likelihood invert. For Simmel, then, socialism and liberalism would ideally coexist as countervailing tendencies, each keeping the other in check. As monetary reform in general is concerned, Simmel was probably right. The future of money is best viewed in terms of a rich field of variation: a repertoire of possibilities, not a single formula. In utopia, money would be genuinely multiple.

We have touched on a wide range of monetary reform issues in this chapter: from idealistic schemes (such as those of Proudhon and Simmel) that are designed to address fundamental problems of social inequality, to theories (such as those of Gesell and Fromm) that focus mainly on our relationship with money, to a series of practical proposals for developing forms of money and credit that answer specific social, ethical, and political objectives. In the end, we have no utopia. Most monetary reform proposals have been framed as much by apprehension as by aspiration. Proudhon and Douglas feared economic stagnation as much as they strove for the social benefits of mutualism, whereas Riegel and Nakamoto were as anxious about liberating money from the inflationary dangers of monopolistic institutions as they were encouraged by the political benefits of monetary freedom. On both sides, these arguments reverberate in present-day, postcrisis concerns about the harmful effects of monetary austerity and the social damage caused by large banks and the state agencies they have captured.

Be careful what you wish for: pushed to their farthest logical extremes, both mutualism and libertarianism are capable of bringing monies into existence that negate any initial benefits they might bring. A currency whose value fluctuates wildly through speculation is just as incompatible with what libertarians define as monetary freedom as a currency issued by government fiat. Likewise, mutualism can become just as stagnant as metallism if confidence in money's redeemability is undermined and there is no underlying source of value for circulating tokens of personally issued credit. With money, every imaginable utopia appears to imply a corresponding dystopia. Simmel never used the term dystopia. Had he done so, it would probably describe the condition in which either of two tendencies, liberalism or socialism, were to achieve completion. His argument could equally apply to neoliberalism. This is an ideology whose faith in *laissez-faire* markets and minimalist regulation replicates that selfsame error that Simmel associates with socialism: namely, of wishing to solve all riddles with one formula.

There is no single solution to the problems money poses in today's world because there is no single set of problems. Simmel warned against extreme solutions, choosing to prefer versions of political creeds such as liberalism and socialism that only ever operate as a counterpoint, never as an absolute set of guidelines to live by. Such "middle-range" pragmatism refuses to imagine that the perfect world is necessarily the antithesis of everything that worries us about the world we currently inhabit. In monetary terms, the Simmelian pragmatist would not argue for a debt-free existence; nor for a return to gold; nor for a world consisting only of state-free money; nor—even—for a world without banks. Rather, he or she would argue for a genuine monetary pluralism in which as full a range of monies is available, circulating in networks that are free to all, for individuals to use according to need and circumstance. This world would not be one in which the public infrastructure of an entire society is allowed to wither in order to defend the value of the one officially sanctioned money in which they are allowed to pay their taxes. Above all, it would be a world in which people never feel compelled to hide their money in freezers.

CONCLUSION

> I turned the corner; the dark octagonal window indicated from a distance that the shop was closed. In Calle Belgrano, I took a cab. Sleepless, obsessed, almost joyful, I reflected on how nothing is less material than money, inasmuch as any coin whatsoever (a twenty-centavo piece, let us say) is, strictly speaking, a repertory of possible futures. Money is abstract, I repeated, money is future time. It can be an evening in the suburbs, it can be the music of Brahms, it can be maps, it can be chess, it can be coffee, it can be the words of Epictetus teaching us to despise gold. Money is a Proteus more versatile than the one on the island of Pharos. It is unpredictable time, Bergsonian time, not the obstinate time of Islam or the Portico.
> **JORGE LUIS BORGES, *THE ZAHIR*[1]**

On May 24, 2010, an American lawyer known online as Beowulf posted a comment on a discussion thread suggesting that the U.S. Treasury could, if it wanted, mint twelve $1 trillion platinum coins and deposit them at the Federal Reserve in order to "pay off the national debt by lunch."[2] It was able to do this, he claimed, because of a legal anomaly that gives the Secretary of the Treasury power to fix the denomination on a platinum coin at any level he chooses.[3] Less than three years later, Beowulf's idea of the $1 trillion platinum coin took on emblematic significance. Its use was widely discussed as a means of evading political efforts to impose a ceiling on U.S. public debt. A Twitter campaign to promote the idea, #MintTheCoin, became a matter of passionate public debate and generated fierce doctrinal

1 Borges 1968: 131.
2 See http://moslereconomics.com/2010/05/14/marshalls-latest/.
3 According to U.S. Code, "The Secretary may mint and issue platinum bullion coins and proof platinum coins in accordance with such specifications, designs, varieties, quantities, denominations, and inscriptions as the Secretary, in the Secretary's discretion, may prescribe from time to time," see http://www.law.cornell.edu/uscode/31/usc_sec_31_00005112—000-.html.

disputes between monetary experts about whether Beowulf's initial idea was theoretically possible and legally permissible, and if so, what its economic and political consequences might be. Many observers dismissed the idea as juvenile and batty. "Where will we get the platinum?" asked *The Guardian*'s Heidi Moore.[4] Some saw the coin as simply a genuine, last-ditch, means of avoiding America's fiscal cliff, whose inflationary potential could be offset by borrowing against it. Others read in the coin a Baudrillard-style subversion of monetary realism. Beowulf himself said that the idea began as a "silly question" and a deliberate absurdity: "There's really no reason for a trillion dollar coin, it's kind of sad that it's gone this far."

Was #MintTheCoin utopian? Perhaps it was, but surely no less so than believing that America's $16 trillion debt *would* eventually be repaid, just as if it were a personal bank loan or a credit card bill. Though our national monetary systems were once captive to this premise, it is becoming increasingly difficult for governments and banks to sustain the illusion that money is a thing: an entity that can be acquired, accumulated, and stored up, ergo, something a country simply runs out of. A monetary crisis almost invariably exposes the social life of money, i.e., the complex and dynamic configuration of social, economic, and political relations on which money depends. These relations, concealed as long as money is viewed as an independent thing, are laid bare when the illusion that money has "real" value becomes unsustainable. But a crisis does not simply show money up for "what it really is." More importantly, it reveals money for *what it is not*: that is to say, it is not an objective entity whose value is independent of social and political relations. This is the underlying significance of the debate about the $1 trillion coin: the very possibility that such a coin could be minted, and that it could indeed be used to redeem some of America's public debt, seemed to reinforce the argument that money is a *process*, whatever material (or immaterial) form it takes in practice. What it requires is not the anchor of its material reality, but rather the backing of others: faith.

According to its critics, utopian thought is too idealistic and too closed: it involves planning a future on the drafting table where the practicality of theoretical ideas is never properly tested. The results can be disappointing, and even disastrous. Alternatively, utopianism can be open-ended, oriented less to a set of goals than to putting in place the *means* by which people are

---

4   Moore argued that the United States only produces 3,700 kilograms of platinum per year. "The mint could, on the direction of Treasury, just make a platinum-finished coin that bears the face value of $1tn, but that would just create a nonsensical level of inflation in the value of the US dollar," she concluded, see http://www.guardian.co.uk/business/2013/jan/04/minting-platinum-coin-option-treasury.

free to choose goals for themselves. This is where money fits in: not as an end in itself but rather as a means through which a greater range of options is opened up for organizing production, exchange, credit, and debt. To support a narrow view of the monetary system as a creature of the state whose operation *must* be administered by large, profiteering private banks is to deny these options. To dismiss those who argue that there are alternatives as "idealistic" is either to suffer from a lack of imagination or to support a system that demonstrably operates in favor of a rich minority. To support a more open, multifarious, and flexible monetary system—a society of *monies*, not *money*—is hardly unrealistic. Rather, it describes the state of the monetary landscape in which we are increasingly finding ourselves, where alternatives to the dominant state fiat money system are proliferating. Whether any specific type or a combination of these alternatives genuinely constitutes a *threat* to that dominant system is open to question and, I would argue, beside the point.

"Attitudes towards money proceed in long cyclical swings," Galbraith said; "when it is good, they think of other things" (Galbraith 1975: 3). When it is bad, they think of little else. Those who in early 2013 were urging the U.S. government to mint a $1 trillion coin to relieve the national debt were challenging the arguments of monetary realists who insist that the country has run out of money. They can be lined up alongside those who urge Greece or Italy to default on their debts and begin again with their money, with "new drachmas" and "new lire."[5] Perhaps #MintTheCoin was "utopian." Perhaps the skeptics were right when they warned that had it been carried out, the effect on inflation and on the confidence of international creditors would have been disastrous. The argument that what many of us use as money actually *consists* of public debts remains as ideologically divisive as ever. Likewise, the concept of "paper" money and of "printing" money are frequently used (alongside images of wheelbarrows laden with worthless banknotes) to symbolize perceived dangers of a system in which money is not a thing with "real" value but an *obligation* and a *process* that depends on *confidence* and *trust* (Coggan 2011). Weimar inflation has been the most overused and misused historical comparator throughout the post-2008 period.

5   Of the two, the new drachma has seemed the likelier prospect by far, as suggested by Bloomberg's decision to designate a code (XGD) for it, see "Bloomberg Tests Post-Euro Greek Drachma Code," *Wall Street Journal*, June 1, 2012, http://blogs.wsj.com/eurocrisis/2012/06/01/bloomberg-tests-post-euro-greek-drachma-code/. On the new lira, see "Berlusconi says Italy may be forced to leave the euro zone," *Reuters*, December 18, 2012, see http://www.reuters.com/article/2012/12/18/us-europe-italy-berlusconi-idUSBRE8BH15U20121218.

Amid widely circulating fears that public debt will be downgraded should a country's capacity to pay seem questionable, most Western governments that ran up large debts to cope with the aftermath of the crisis and directed their central banks to use monetary policy in order to convert bad private debts into enduring public obligations have resorted to austerity programs to maintain the illusion—discussed in Chapter 4—that all debts must be repaid. Eurozone governments, unable to use monetary policy directly themselves, have resorted instead to internal devaluation to keep what is being portrayed as a sovereign debt crisis (but actually entails more complex issues about imbalances within the Eurozone as a whole) from spiraling out of control. These are the "collective sacrifices" that Agamben feared. He predicted that they would be docilely entered into whenever the creditor class waves the scarecrow of a generalized economic crisis in the faces of those already paralyzed by debt (Agamben 2000: 133). Monetary realism—the belief that money is a thing, or at the very least must be governed *as if* it were a thing—is invariably invoked to justify such policies.

It makes intuitive sense to compare a country's debts with the debts of a household, which may explain why monetary realism still has the power to persuade. It remains the most commonly used argument against Bitcoin, for example, that the digital currency *has no underlying value*. What, though, *is* the underlying value of money? Given that it is no longer possible to answer "gold" (or any other material substance), critics of Bitcoin (and other digital currencies) opt for an economic variable such as "output,"[6] or a political one such as "legitimacy" or "law,"[7] to argue that the currency lacks anchorage in "real" value. It is a curious strategy, because as we have seen, the Bitcoin system is intended to replicate the condition whereby the supply of a material currency is naturally scarce. In other words, the system is designed to be as close to monetary realism as it is possible to be. The placard in Paternoster Square that read "we are the true currency" captures the notion of a collective "will" underpinning money's production (once it has been stripped away from the machinery of the state and banking system). It is the obverse side of Klossowski's living coin: money as an *embodiment of collective life*. Indeed, money *is* social life, in this specific sense. What it requires is not the anchor of its material reality but rather the backing of

---

[6] See "Thoughts on the 'value' of fiat money," April 11, 2013, http://pragcap.com/thoughts-on-the-value-of-fiat-money, accessed May 10, 2013.

[7] See "Bitcoin Has No Intrinsic Value, And Will Never Be A Threat To Fiat Currency," April 11, 2013, http://www.businessinsider.com/bitcoins-have-no-value-2013-4, accessed May 10, 2013.

others. But faith, of course, is an extraordinarily complex, deeply social phenomenon, most especially where money is concerned.

Throughout this book, we have been examining theories of money that offer variations on and alternatives to Simmel's description of it as a claim upon society. It is striking that almost every enquiry about money's role in society, e.g., about its effects in perpetuating or alleviating social inequality, returns to basic questions about the nature of money's existence, and as I argued in Chapter 1, about its origins. Increasingly, the argument that money's origins are to be found not beneath the ground but in *various kinds of social practice*—e.g., gift exchange, political and religious obligation, sacrifice—is gaining widespread acceptance. The realization that money is not a material *thing* but a social *process* is, in formal terms, a moment of disenchantment. It represents a stage in what Aglietta (1986) described as money's *desacrilization*. It is, perhaps, a moment of crisis in its ancient Greek sense, κρίσις, meaning "a separating, power of distinguishing, decision, choice, election, judgment, dispute." This takes us back to the arguments about money's quasireligious character that were explored in Chapter 4. Recall Brown, who argued that that our illusion is not that money *is* sacred (and depends on faith), but rather that it is not.

When Nietzsche suggested that money had replaced God as an object of everything that gives the highest feeling of power and good conscience, he "meant to imply all that ever has been or ever could be subsumed in the name of 'God', including all God-substitutes, other worlds, ultimate realities, things-in-themselves, noumenal planes and will to live—the entire 'metaphysical need' of man and all its products" (Hollingdale 1999: 70). All that remained after the death of God was the bad diet of the modern age and its "contemptible" money economy. This is home to bourgeois man, the banker with *faux* Christian ethics who is unable to tell the difference between financial obligation and moral guilt. For many commentators, "what Nietzsche meant" was fundamentally concerned with the emergence of a "man" who must create his (or her?) own values to live by. Foucault's suggestion that Nietzsche's pronouncement was a precursor to the subsequent death of "man" is especially intriguing in this context because the "man" he is referring to is the *economic* man, the measuring animal, whom Nietzsche held in such contempt (Foucault 2008b: 124). According to Foucault, this Godless, empirical, man was subsequently caught within a philosophical paradox opened up by the death of God. In philosophical terms, this is a human who is caught within the paradox of being both *knower* and *known*. On one side, just as Nietzsche suggested, "he" has constituted "himself" as the transcendent knower, infinite and therefore analogous to God. Yet on the other side, by virtue of what "he" knows, "he" is not transcendent but empirical, not infinite but finite. In economic terms, this is the human whose needs are a source of self-estrangement, not the foundation of self-knowledge (Foucault 2005: 422). In that same text, Foucault portrays the human who ushers in Nietzsche's declaration as the *homo economicus* of nineteenth century economics. This is not the human the economists wanted him or her to be, i.e., the human who is aware of his or her own needs, who can represent them to him or herself, and who is able to produce the objects that satisfy them. Rather, it was "the human being who spends, wears out, and *wastes his life* in evading the imminence of death" (2005: 280, italics added).

The question that Foucault asks is inextricably bound up with this era—*Was ist der Mensch?* ("What is man?")—and reverberates with a question we have returned to repeatedly in this book: *Was ist Geld?* ("What is money?"). The analogy between these questions is striking. Both hang on a logical contradiction. In the case of "man," it is the paradox that "man" is simultaneously (transcendent) knower and (empirical) known. That is to say, "man" is both the condition for "his" own knowledge and the object of that knowledge. This state, Foucault suggests, gives rise to the "web of confusion and illusion" in which anthropology (as the empirical study of humans) and philosophy (as the study of being) are tangled (Foucault 2008b: 121). With money, a similar paradox is found wherein money is both outside the sphere of economic value as its external measure and inside that sphere as a value in its own right. Money is both *outside* and *inside* the realm of values from which it derives what Wittgenstein once called its "life" as money (Wittgenstein 2007: 144). This tension arises in Marx, for example, when he posits a contradiction between money as a universal measure of value and money as a particular commodity. Harvey called it the conflict between money as *fixity* and money as *flow*: money gets fixed when it is withdrawn from circulation and taken outside the monetary system. Simmel, also, remarks on the paradox whereby money is both *measure* and *measured*, as did Godelier when he remarked that money is "both swept along by the movement of commodities and immobilized as a point around which all this machinery begins to revolve and whose volume and speed it measures" (Godelier 1999: 29). With debt, too, money both *transcends* debt (human as knower) and *is* debt itself (human as known).

It is perhaps no accident that Benjamin invoked Nietzsche's money in order to suggest that "man" is in debt to himself, just as God was. Both sets of questions (about "man" on one side and money on the other) turn on key arguments about origin. As we saw in Chapter 1, any inquiry into the origins of money is as likely to lead to circularity and regress in the case of money, as Foucault alleges it does whenever "man" is its object. Foucault argued that Nietzsche's enterprise was not simply to kill God, but *also* "man": "it is in the death of man that the death of God is realized" (Foucault 2008b: 124). This is the very same death that Foucault himself conveys in terms of the emergence of a language that no longer represents—and can therefore no longer represent "man" as an object for himself—but is pure formality and self-referential signification. In Chapter 1, I examined theories in which money is portrayed through language, and language through money. This is a view that, *in extremis*, portrays money as nothing more than empty signs commuting with empty signs.

In a note added to the third edition of *Capital*, Engels described a "special sort of monetary crisis," appearing independently of other kinds of crisis, whose sphere of impact is the banking system and which "affects industry and commerce by its backwash" (see Marx 1982: 236 n. 50). In the era of financialization, such a crisis is no longer special, but normal. And the backwash has become a tsunami. This is a crisis within a financial sector that operates as self-referential language: a cancerous outgrowth of capital, in which skillfully engineered financial instruments circulate as *faux* money according to their own internal dynamics. With a grotesque reflexivity, financial speculation becomes nothing more than a form of speculation about speculation itself. This is the era of what Baudrillard (1993) called "cool" money, wherein financial instruments flow within an independent sphere, seemingly detached from the real economy, as if finance was its *own* self-perpetuating reality. But as I have argued in this book, this sphere is never sealed off from economy and society, or from humanity in general. Every significant crisis unveils the social life of money, i.e., the complex assemblage of social and political relations upon which money and finance feed.

Money makes universal debtors of us all, living in the shadows of the *Übermensch* that Benjamin described, projected upward through the sky by unredeemed obligations before coming face to face with his creditor. The banking system that was meant to sustain money has been destabilized by its own relentless production of risk, starting on its periphery but generating financial obligations at its core that must be monetized in order to be paid off: both literally, and through its own violent cycles of debt, default, and deflation. This time ought, then, to be a moment of decision, and it is striking that Simmel's interpretation of Nietzsche's ideas stresses the strong moral imperatives they suggest for the individual in modern society (Frisby 1985: 35). For Simmel, both the *Übermensch* and eternal return are "norms of and challenges to our conduct" (Simmel 1991b: 174). All money may be *virtual*, and not a *thing*, but at the same time, it is not *nothing*. Although money's underlying values may not be "real" in any material sense, undeniably they are human, social values. These are the values upon which money as a process depends and which sustain the social life of money. If Benjamin's image of the universal debtor, the *Übermensch* whose inexorable rise coincides with the inherent destructiveness of financial capitalism, stands for anything here, it is not contempt for money but rather the urge to devise a form of it that can facilitate and express the creation of new values.

Citibank Chairman Walter Wriston (1919–2005) once said that countries cannot go bankrupt: "Countries don't go out of business—the infrastructure doesn't go away, the productivity of the people doesn't go away, the natural resources don't go away. And so their assets always exceed their liabilities, which is the technical reason for bankruptcy. And that's very different from a company."[8] He might have been talking about the capacity of any country to create its own version of the $1 trillion coin. But more profound issues are at stake here. As long as there are human values such as productivity, and an infrastructure, no country is "bankrupt" other than in the narrowest sense of defaulting on its debts. Money, in these broad terms, is underpinned by human—*social*—values and not by bonds or the power of the mint. When Argentina was declared bankrupt in 2001–2 because it defaulted on its public debt, a host of new currencies emerged, each based on forms of value that were derived from the human beings producing them. This solution was the philosophy of social credit, played out among people who had been excluded from global finance. It was a "grassroots" reinvention of money by those very communities that had been declared insolvent and cut off. There is nothing romantic about this story. Many of the currencies failed, and those that were successful were often short-lived. Much of Argentina's debt has since been written off, but some hedge funds have acquired it at below face value in order to aggressively pursue redemption. Strange feared that the growth of the financial sector would lead to the death of money. But the Argentine insolvency demonstrates that any large-scale financial failure is likely to be followed by a localized reinvention of money. Money is dead; long live money.

Just as states like Argentina seem unable to escape from the logic of international finance, so individuals and households have become increasingly trapped in debt. The hold of banks and the financial sector over the

---

8   Cited in "Money Matters: An IMF Exhibit—The Importance of Global Cooperation: Debt and Transition (1981–1989)", see http://www.imf.org/external/np/exr/center/mm/eng/mm_dt_01.htm. Also cited in Buckley (1999: 14).

economy—not only through debt, but also through rent-seeking[9]—has arguably been increased, not weakened, by the financial crisis. It will be increasingly difficult for individuals to sever their links with mainstream finance, particularly when they are drawn into financial obligations as debtors from an increasingly early age, for example, as students. For the foreseeable future, opportunities to escape debt peonage are likely only to be piecemeal and small scale. But as #MintTheCoin suggests, there is considerable political life in the notion that money can be reclaimed from the grip of the banking system, albeit mostly in piecemeal fashion. Plausible resistance to debt peonage is possible via various forms of empowerment through money. Ultimately, money's value is derived from the value of the human lives on which the economy—and the *social* life of money itself—depend. There are as many different possible versions of this future as there are manifestations of the past in Borges's coin. Just as there is no single model of money that captures the meaning of the Zahir (Borges 1968), so there is no grand vision of a monetary future that will answer all the demands we are likely to place on it. Money and credit must be seen in terms of a repertoire of choice.

I began this book by asking a question that has lingered in the background of most academic discussions of the financial crisis, namely, where does the crisis leave money? In the platinum coin, we had an answer of sorts, which is both technical and political. What began as a torrent of real estate foreclosures and distressed debt led tangentially to detailed analyses of the U.S. law on minting platinum coins. However we read this episode—as a real solution, an accounting trick, a distraction, or merely as satire—it evokes money's singular power as the exception by which debt's certainties can be placed in suspension and held, however briefly, in check. But in the aftermath of the crisis, there remain deep confusions about the reality of money and its connections with debt; pressing questions about who has the right to declare what money is on behalf of the society in which it circulates; and, perhaps above all, an underlying atmosphere of absurdity in discussions that try to resolve these matters by imagining that money is a *thing* with a stable meaning and functions are constant. In this book, I have argued that money is no such thing. It is a *process* that is inextricably social, inherently dynamic, and complex, whose meaning is contested and unstable.

---

9 This point is where one would want to correct Walter Wriston. Although a country's infrastructure may not "go away," it may well be appropriated by private interests and turned into a source of rent: this is one of the most corrosive underlying logics of accumulation in the age of financialization. We discussed this in Chapters 3 and 6.

There is no unique sociological angle that illuminates the nature of money. There may, however, be several. Trying to "fix" money, both in theory and in practice, is misleading and potentially destructive. We ought to take an intellectually open view of competing monetary theories. Borges believed that he saw in the Zahir a symbol of "all the coins that forever glitter in history and in fable" (Borges 1968: 130). Just as money, for him, did not belong to the world of obstinate time, so it cannot possess that singularity of form that would lend itself to the construction of a unified general theory. As Hart describes it, money is not "one static thing or idea" (Hart 2001: 233). He is surely right about the status of money as a thing. But as an *idea*, money is remarkably durable in one vital respect. Money is *social*: it is a claim, if not on "society," then on *varying modes of shared existence and experience*. Money has a social life, then, in myriad different ways. Its sociality can be found in its role in the reproduction of conflict and inequality (Chapter 2), its inherent connections with credit and debt (Chapter 3), its sacred or quasisacred properties (Chapter 4), its expression of society's capacity (and incapacity) to deal with surplus and waste (Chapter 5), its shadowy existence within and on the interstices of geopolitical space (Chapter 6), its inherent (and constitutive) cultural properties (Chapter 7), and its reformist, utopian spirit (Chapter 8). These are distinctive and frequently contradictory aspects of money. I have explored a wide range of theory—both specialist and nonspecialist—that can inform our understanding of the *idea* of money, its historical effect on society, its utopian potential, and the different forms that money will take in the future. "Perhaps I will manage to wear away the Zahir by force of thinking of it and thinking of it. Perhaps behind the Zahir I shall find God" (Borges 1968: 137). Money's protean character—its capacity to be myriad possible futures, as Borges saw—will always encourage a sense of adventure in the way we give form to our lives. Money is utopian in *this* sense. It is a nonplace where form and idea endlessly coalesce. Little wonder that it has proved so elusive for those who have sought to encapsulate it in theory.

BIBLIOGRAPHY

Abraham, K. (1917). "The Spending of Money in Anxiety States." *The Psychoanalysis of Money*, E. Borneman, Ed. New York, Urizen Books: 99–102.
Ades, D., S. Baker, et al., Eds. (2006). *Undercover Surrealism: Georges Bataille and Documents*, London, Hayward Gallery Publishing.
Ades, D. and F. Bradley. (2006). "Inroduction." *Undercover Surrealism: Georges Bataille and Documents*, D. Ades, S. Baker, et al., Eds., London, Hayward Gallery Publishing: 11–16.
Adorno, T. W. (2007). "Theses Against Occultism," *The Stars Down to Earth*, London, Routledge: 172–80.
Adorno, T. W. and M. Horkheimer (1997). *Dialectic of Enlightenment*, London/New York, Books.
Agamben, G. (1998). *Homo Sacer: Sovereign Power and Bare Life*, Stanford, CA, Stanford University Press.
Agamben, G. (2000). *Means Without End*, Minneapolis, University of Minnesota Press.
Agamben, G. (2009). *Signature of All Things*, Cambridge, MA, MIT Press.
Aglietta, M. (1986). *La Fin des Devises Clés*, Paris, La Découverte.
Aglietta, M. (2012). "The European Vortex." *New Left Review* 75: 15–36.
Aglietta, M. and A. Orléan (1984). *La Violence de la Monnaie*, Paris: Presses universitaires de France.
Aglietta, M. and A. Orléan, Eds. (1985). *Souverainté, Légitimité de la Monnaie*, Paris, Association d'Économie Financière.
Aglietta, M. and A. Orléan (1998). *La Monnaie Souveraine*, Paris, Jacob.
Aglietta, M. and L. Scialom (2003). "The Challenge of European Integration for Prudential Policy." LSE Financial Markets Group Special Paper. London, London School of Economics, 152.
Agnes, P. (2000). "The 'End of Geography' in Financial Services? Local Embeddedness and Territorialization in the Interest Rate Swaps Industry." *Economic Geography* 76 (4): 347–66.
Ahamed, L. (2009). *Lords of Finance: 1929, The Great Depression, and the Bankers Who Broke the World*, London, Windmill Books.
Akin, D. and J. Robbins (1999). *Money and Modernity: State and Local Currencies in Melanesia*, Pittsburgh, Pittsburgh University Press.
Aldcroft, D. H. (2001). *The European Economy 1914–2000*, 4th ed., London, Routledge.
Alexander, J. C. (2011). "Market as Narrative and Character." *Journal of Cultural Economy* 4 (4): 477–88.
Allen, J. and M. Pryke (1999). "Money Cultures after Georg Simmel: Mobility, Movement and Identity." *Environment and Planning D: Society and Space* 17 (1): 51–68.
Althusser, L. and E. Balibar (2009). *Reading Capital*. London/New York, Verso.
Altunbas, Y., L. Gambacorta, et al. (2009). "Securitisation and the Bank Lending Channel." *European Economic Review* 53: 996–1009.
Alves, A. A. and J. M. Moriera (2010). *The Salamanca School*, New York, Continuum.
Amar, A. (1956). "A Psychoanalytc Study of Money." *The Psychoanalysis of Money*, E. Borneman, Ed. New York, Urizen Books: 277–91.

Amar, M., D. Ariely, et al. (2011). "Winning the Battle But Losing the War: The Psychology of Debt Managament." *Journal of Marketing Research* 48 (Special Issue): 38–50.
Amin, S. (1974). *Accumulation on a World Scale. A Critique of the Theory of Underdevelopment,* New York, Monthly Review Press.
Amis, M. (2011). *Money: A Suicide Note,* London, Vintage.
Ansell-Pearson, K. (2005). *How to Read Nietzsche,* London, Granta Books.
Aquinas, T. (2000). *Summa Theologica,* Allen, TX, Resources for Christian Living.
Arena, R., A. Graziani, et al., Eds. (2004). *Money, Credit, and the Role of the State: Essays in Honour of Augusto Graziani,* Farnham, U.K, Ashgate Publishing.
Arendt, H. (1951). *The Origins of Totalitarianism,* New York, Harcourt Brace and Co.
Aristotle. (2004). *The Nicomachean Ethics,* Harmondsworth, U.K., Penguin.
Arrighi, G. (2005a). "Hegemony Unravelling—1." *New Left Review* 32 (March–April): 23–80.
Arrighi, G. (2005b). "Hegemony Unravelling—2." *New Left Review* 33 (May–June): 83–116.
Arrighi, G. (2009). *The Long Twentieth Century: Money, Power and the Origins of Our Time,* London/New York, Verso.
Arrighi, G. and B. J. Silver (1999). *Chaos and Governance in the Modern World System,* Minneapolis, University of Minnesota Press.
Aschheima, J. and G. S. Tavlas (2004). "Academic Exclusion: The Case of Alexander Del Mar." *European Journal of Political Economy* 20: 31–60.
Aspers, P. (2007). "Nietzsche's Sociology." *Sociological Forum* 22: 474–99.
Atwood, M. (2008). *Payback: Debt and the Shadow Side of Wealth: Debt as Metaphor and the Shadow Side of Wealth,* Toronto, Anansi Press.
Auster, P. (1989). *Moon Palace,* London, Faber and Faber.
Austin, G. (1993). "Indigenous Credit Institutions in West Africa, c. 1750–c. 1960." *Local Suppliers of Credit in the Third World, 1750–1960,* G. Austin and K. Sigihara, Eds. London, St. Martin's Press: 93–159.
Bailey, S. (1825). *A Critical Dissertation on the Nature, Measure, and Causes of Value: Chiefly in Reference to the Writings of Mr. Ricardo and His Followers. By the Author of Essays on the Formation, etc., of Opinions,* London, R. Hunter.
Baker, A., D. Hudson, et al., Eds. (2005). *Governing Financial Globalization: International Political Economy and Multi-Level Governance,* Abingdon, U.K., Routledge.
Balibar, E. (2004). *We, the People of Europe? Reflections on Transnational Citizenship,* Princeton, NJ, Princeton University Press.
Baptiste, E., H. A. Horst, and E. B. Taylor (2010). "Mobile Money in Haiti: Potentials and Challenges." Institute for Money, Technology and Financial Inclusion Report, April 2011. www.imtfi.uci.edu/files/imtfi/docs/2012/taylor_baptiste_horst_haiti_mobile_money.pdf, accessed March 3, 2014.
Barbalet, J. (2008). *Weber, Passion and Profits: "The Protestant Ethic and the Spirit of Capitalism" in Context,* Cambridge, U.K., Cambridge University Press.
Barber, B. (1995). "All Economies Are 'Embedded': The Career of a Concept, and Beyond." *Social Research* 62: 387–413.
Barr, B., D. Taylor-Robinson, et al. (2012). "Suicides Associated with the 2008–10 Economic Recession in England: Time Trend Analysis." *British Medical Journal* 345, Aug. 14, doi: http://dx.doi.org/10.1136/bmj.e5142.
Barthes, R. (1977). *Roland Barthes by Roland Barthes,* Berkeley, University of California Press.
Bataille, G. (1933). "The Notion of Expenditure." *Visions of Excess,* A. Stoekl, Ed. Minneapolis, University of Minnesota Press: 116–29.
Bataille, G. (1985a). "The Psychological Structure of Fascism." *Visions of Excess,* A. Stoekl, Ed. Minneapolis, University of Minnesota Press: 137–60.
Bataille, G. (1985b). "The Use Value of D. A. F. de Sade (An Open Letter to My Current Comrades)." *Visions of Excess,* A. Stoekl, Ed. Minneapolis, University of Minnesota Press: 91–102.

BIBLIOGRAPHY 397

Bataille, G. (1986). *Eroticism, Death and Sexuality*, San Francisco, City Lights Books.
Bataille, G. (1988a). "The College of Sociology." *The College of Sociology, 1937–39*, D. Hollier, Ed. Minneapolis, University of Minnesota Press.
Bataille, G. (1988b). "The Sorcerer's Apprentice." *The College of Sociology 1937–39*, D. Hollier, Ed. Minneapolis, University of Minnesota Press: 12–23.
Bataille, G. (1991). *The Accursed Share, Vol. 1*, New York, Zone Books.
Bataille, G. (1992). *On Nietzsche*, London, The Athlone Press.
Bataille, G. (1996). *The Trial of Gilles De Rais*, Los Angeles, Amok Books.
Baudelaire, C. (1970). *Paris Spleen*, New York, New Directions.
Baudelaire, C. (1995). *The Painter of Modern Life and Other Essays*, London, Phaidon.
Baudelaire, C. (2006). *Intimate Journals*, Mineola, NY, Dover Publications.
Baudrillard, J. (1981). *For a Critique of the Political Economy of the Sign*, New York, Telos Press.
Baudrillard, J. (1983). *Simulations*, Los Angeles, Semiotext(e).
Baudrillard, J. (1990). *Seduction*, Montreal, New World Perspectives/CTheory Books.
Baudrillard, J. (1993). *Symbolic Exchange and Death*, London, Sage.
Baudrillard, J. (1997). "Global Debt and Parallel Universe." *Digital Delirium*, A. Kroker and M. Kroker, Eds. New York: St. Martin's Press: 38–40.
Baudrillard, J. (2001). *Impossible Exchange*, London/New York, Verso.
Baudrillard, J. (2002). *Screened Out*, London/New York, Verso.
Baudrillard, J. (2003). *The Spirit of Terrorism*, London/New York, Verso.
Baudrillard, J. (2009). *The Transparency of Evil: Essays on Extreme Phenomena*, London/New York, Verso.
Beckert, J. (2007). "The Great Transformation of Embeddedness: Karl Polanyi and the New Economic Sociology." Discussion Paper 07/1, Cologne, Germany, Max Planck Institute for the Study of Societies.
Beckert, J. (2011). "Where Do Prices Come From? Sociological Approaches to Price Formation." Discussion Paper 11/3, Cologne, Germany, Max Planck Institute for the Study of Societies.
Beckert, J. (2013). "Capitalism as a System of Expectations: Toward a Sociologiocal Microfoundation of Political Economy." *Politics and Society* 41 (3): 323–50.
Bendersky, J. W. (1992). *Carl Schmitt: Theorist for the Reich*, Princeton, NJ, Princeton University Press.
Benjamin, W. (1996a). "Capitalism as Religion." *Selected Writings, Vol. 1: 1913–26*, M. Bullock and M. W. Jennings, Eds. Cambridge, MA/London, The Belknap Press of Harvard University Press: 288–91.
Benjamin, W. (1996b). "Critique of Violence." *Selected Writings, Vol. 1: 1913–26*, M. Bullock and M. W. Jennings, Eds. Cambridge, MA/London, The Belknap Press of Harvard University Press: 236–52.
Benjamin, W. (1996c). "Fate and Character." *Selected Writings, Vol. 1: 1913–26*, M. Bullock and M. W. Jennnings, Eds. Cambridge, MA/London, The Belknap Press of Harvard University Press: 201–206.
Benjamin, W. (1996d). "The Meaning of Time in the Moral Universe." *Selected Writings, Vol. 1: 1913–26*, M. Bullock and M. W. Jennings, Eds. Cambridge, MA/London, The Belknap Press of Harvard University Press: 286–87.
Benjamin, W. (1996e). "One-Way Street." *Selected Writings, Vol. 1: 1913–26*, M. Bullock and M. W. Jennings, Eds. Cambridge, MA/London, The Belknap Press of Harvard University Press: 444–88.
Benjamin, W. (1999). *The Arcades Project*, Cambridge, MA/London, The Belknap Press of Harvard University Press.
Benjamin, W. (2003a). "Central Park." *Selected Writings, Vol. 4: 1938–40*, H. Eiland and M. W. Jennings, Eds. Cambridge, MA/London, The Belknap Press of Harvard University Press: 161–99.
Benjamin, W. (2003b). "On the Concept of History." *Selected Writings, Vol. 4: 1938–40*, M. P. Bullock, M. W. Jennings and H. Eiland, Eds. Cambridge, MA/London, The Belknap Press of Harvard University Press: 389–400.

Benjamin, W. (2009). *The Origin of German Tragic Drama,* London/New York, Verso.
Bernstein, P. L. (2004). *The Power of Gold: The History of an Obsession,* Chichester, U.K., John Wiley and Sons.
Berry, S. (2001). *Chiefs Know Their Boundaries: Essays on Property, Power and the Past in Asante, 1896–1996,* Portsmouth, NH, Heinemann.
Besharat, A. (2012). "Essays on Mental Accounting and Consumers' Decision Making." Ph.D. thesis, Tampa, FL, University of South Florida.
Binswanger, H. C. (1994). *Money and Magic: A Critique of the Modern Economy in the Light of Goethe's "Faust,"* Chicago, University of Chicago Press.
Blackburn, R. (2010). "Socialism and the Current Crisis." *Dissent* 57 (3): 29–32.
Blanc, J. (2000). *Les Monnaies Paralleles,* Paris, L'Harmattan.
Bloch, E. (2000). *The Spirit of Utopia,* Stanford, CA, Stanford University Press.
Block, F. (2003). "Karl Polanyi and the Writing of 'The Great Transformation.'" *Theory and Society* 32 (3): 275–306.
Bodin, J. (1992). *On Sovereignty: Four Chapters from The Six Books of the Commonwealth,* Cambridge, U.K., Cambridge University Press.
Bodin, J. (1997). *Response to the Paradoxes of Malestroit,* London, Thoemmes Continuum.
Bohannan, P. (1955). "Some Principles of Exchange and Investment among the Tiv." *American Anthropologist* 57: 60–70.
Bohannan, P. and L. Bohannan (1968). *Tiv Economy,* Evanston, Ill., Northwestern University Press.
Boltanski, L. and L. Thevenot (2006). *On Justification: Economies of Worth,* Princeton, NJ, Princeton University Press.
Borges, J. L. (1968). *A Personal Anthology,* London, Jonathan Cape.
Bourdieu, P. (1990). *The Logic of Practice,* Cambridge, U.K., Polity Press.
Bourdieu, P. (1992). *Language and Symbolic Power,* Cambridge, U.K., Polity Press.
Bourdieu, P. (1993). *The Field of Cultural Production: Essays on Art and Literatire,* Cambridge, U.K., Polity Press.
Brass, T. (2011). *Labour Regime Change in the Twenty-First Century: Unfreedom, Capitalism and Primitive Accumulation,* Leiden, Netherlands, Brill.
Brender, A. and F. Pisani (2010). *Global Imbalances and the Collapse of Globalised Finance,* Brussels, Belgium, CEPS.
Breton, A. (1969). *Manifestoes of Surrealism,* Ann Arbor, University of Michigan Press.
Brodersen, M. (1996). *Walter Benjamin: A Biography,* London/New York, Verso.
Brown, C. (2002). "The Construction of a 'Realistic Utopia': John Rawls and International Political Theory." *Review of International Studies* 28 (1): 5–21.
Brown, N. O. (1959). *Life Against Death: The Psychoanalytical Meaning of History,* New York, Vintage Books.
Brown, N. O. (1992). *Apocalypse and/or Metamorphosis,* Berkeley, Cal, University of California Press.
Browne, H. (1974). *You Can Profit from a Monetary Crisis,* New York, Ishi Press International.
Browne, K. E. (2005). *Creole Economics: Caribbean Cunning under the French Flag,* Austin, Texas, University of Texas Press.
Bryan, D. and M. Rafferty (2007). "Financial Derivatives and the Theory of Money." *Economy and Society* 36: 134–58.
Bryan, D. and M. Rafferty (2013). "Fundamental Value: A Category in Transformation." *Economy and Society* 42 (1): 130–53.
Buchan, J. (1997). *Frozen Desire: An Inquiry into the Meaning of Money,* London, Picador.
Buchanan, I. and N. Thoburn (2008). *Deleuze and Politics,* Edinburgh, Scotland, Edinburgh University Press.
Buckley, R. P. (1999). *Emerging Markets Debt: An Analysis of the Secondary Market,* The Hague, Kluwer Law International.

Bukharin, N. (2003). *Imperialism and World Economy*, London, Bookmarks Publications.
Cable, V. (2009). *The Storm: The World Economic Crisis and What It Means*, London, Atlantic Books.
Caffentizis, C. G. (1989). *Clipped Coins, Abused Words and Civil Government: John Locke's Philosophy of Money*, New York, Autonomedia.
Cahn, E. S. (1999). "Time Dollars, Work and Community: From 'Why?' to 'Why Not?.'" *Futures* 31 (5): 499–509.
Callinicos, A. (2009). *Imperialism and Global Political Economy*, Cambridge, U.K., Polity Press.
Callinicos, A. (2010). *Bonfire of Illusions: The Twin Crises of the Liberal World*, Cambridge, U.K., Polity.
Callon, M. (1986). "The Sociology of an Actor-Network: The Case of the Electric Vehicle." *Mapping the Dynamics of Science and Technology: Sociology of Science in the Real World*, M. Callon, J. Law, and A. Rip, Eds. London, Macmillan: 19–34.
Canto-Mila, N. (2005). *A Sociological Theory of Value: Georg Simmel's Sociological Relationism*, Bielefeld, Germany, Transcript-Verlag.
Carruthers, B. G. (2010). "Knowledge and Liquidity: Institutional and Cognitive Foundations of the Subprime Crisis." *Research in the Sociology of Organizations* 30: 157–82.
Carruthers, B. G. and S. Babb (1996). "The Color of Money: Greenbacks and Gold in Postbellum America." *American Journal of Sociology* 101 (6): 1556–1591.
Casarino, C. (2002). *Modernity at Sea: Melville, Marx, Conrad in Crisis*, Minneapolis, University of Minnesota Press.
Castells, M. (1999). "Grassrooting the Space of Flows." *Urban Geography* 20 (4): 294–302.
Chaum, D. (1983). "Blind Signatures for Untraceable Payments." *Advances in Cryptology: Proceedings of Crypto 82*. D. Chaum, R. L. Rivest, and A. T. Sherman, Eds. New York, Plenum Publishing Corporation.
Chernomas, R. (1984). "Keynes on Post-Scarcity Society." *Journal of Economic Issues* XVIII (4): 1007–26.
Chick, V. and S. C. Dow (2013). "Financial Institutions and the State: A Re-examination." *Monetary Economies of Production: Banking and Financial Circuits and the Role of the State*, L.-P. Rochon and M. Seccareccia, Eds.. Cheltenham, U.K., Edward Elgar Publishing: 99–111.
Choonara, J. (2009). *Unravelling Capitalism: A Guide to Marxist Political Economy*, London, Bookmarks Publications.
Chown, J. (2003). *A History of Monetary Unions*, London, Routledge.
Cicero, M. T. (2009). *Philippic Orations, I, II, III, V, VII*, Charleston, SC, Bibliolife, LLC.
Clark, G. (1994). *Onions Are My Husband: Survival and Accumulation by West African Market Women*, Chicago, University of Chicago Press.
Clark, N. (2010). "Volatile Worlds, Vulnerable Bodies: Confronting Abrupt Climate Change." *Theory, Culture & Society* 27 (2–3): 31–53.
Codere, H. (1968). "Money-Exchange Systems and a Theory of Money." *Man* 3: 557–77.
Coggan, P. (2011). *Paper Promises: Money, Debt and the New World Order*, London, Allen Lane.
Cohen, B. J. (1998). *The Geography of Money*, Ithaca, Cornell University Press.
Cohen, B. J. (2004). *The Future of Money*, Princeton, NJ, Princeton University Press.
Cohen, B. J. (2011). *The Future of Global Currency: The Euro Versus the Dollar*, Abingdon, U.K., Routledge.
Collins, D., J. Morduch, et al. (2010). *Portfolios of the Poor: How the World's Poor Live on $2 a Day*, Princeton, NJ, Princeton University Press.
Collins, R. (2000). "Situational Stratification: A Micro–Macro Theory of Inequality." *Sociological Theory* 18: 17–43.
Collom, E. (2007). "The Motivations, Engagement, Satisfaction, Outcomes, and Demographics of Time Bank Participants: Survey Findings from a U.S. System." *International Journal of Community Currency Research* 11: 36–83.

Comte, A. (1896). *The Positive Philosophy*, London, George Bell & Sons.
Conefrey, T. and J. Fitzgerald (2010). "Managing Housing Bubbles in Regional Economies under EMU: Ireland and Spain." *National Institute Economic Review* 211 (1): 91–108.
Cooley, J. K. (2008). *Currency Wars: How Forged Money Is the New Weapon of Mass Destruction*, New York, Skyhorse Publishing.
Coriat, I. H. (1924). "A Note on the Anal Character Traits of the Capitalist Instinct." *Psychoanalytic Review* 11: 435–37.
Crouch, C. (2009). "Privatised Keynesianism: An Unacknowledged Policy Regime." *British Journal of Politics and International Relations* 11: 382–99.
Crump, T. (1981). *The Phenomenon of Money*, London, Routledge.
Crump, T. (1992). *The Anthropology of Numbers*, Cambridge, U.K., Cambridge University Press.
Dai, W. (1998). "B-Money." http://www.weidai.com/bmoney.txt, accessed November 2, 2012.
Dalton, G. (1965). "Primitive Money." *American Anthropologist* 67: 44–65.
Dalton, G. (1969). "Theoretical Issues in Economic Anthropology." *Current Anthropology* 10 (1): 63–102.
Dana, C. A. (1927). "Proudhon and His Bank of the People." *Proudhon's Solution to the Social Problem*, H. Cohen, Ed. New York, Vanguard Press.
Davies, G. (1994). *A History of Money: From Ancient Times to the Present Day*, Cardiff, University of Wales Press.
Davis, G. F. (2009). *Managed by the Markets: How Finance Re-Shaped America*, Oxford, U.K., Oxford University Press.
de Brunhoff, S. (1971). *L'Offre de Monnaie*, Paris, F. Maspero.
de Brunhoff, S. (1973). *Marx on Money*, New York, Urizen Books.
de Goede, M. (2005). *Virtue, Fortune, and Faith: A Genealogy of Finance*, Minneapolis, University of Minnesota Press.
de Goede, M. (2012). *Speculative Security: The Politics of Pursuing Terrorist Monies*, Minneapolis, University of Minnesota Press.
de Grauwe, P. (2010). "How to Embed the Eurozone in a Political Union." *Completing the Eurozone Rescue: What More Needs to Be Done?* R. Baldwin, D. Gros, and L. Laeven, Eds. London, Centre for Economic Policy Research: 29–32.
de Grauwe, P. (2012). *Economics of Monetary Union*, Oxford, U.K., Oxford University Press.
de Grauwe, P. and W. Mosen (2009). "Gains for All: A Proposal for a Common Euro Bond." *Intereconomics* May–June: 132–35.
de Saussure, F. (1915). *Course in General Linguistics*, Toronto, McGraw-Hill.
Del Mar, A. (1885). *The Science of Money*, London, George Bell & Sons.
Del Mar, A. (1895). *History of Monetary Systems*, London, Effingham Wilson.
Deleuze, G. (1995). *Negotiations*, New York, Columbia University Press.
Deleuze, G. (2004). *Difference and Repetition*, London/New York: Continuum.
Deleuze, G. and F. Guattari (1987). *A Thousand Plateaus: Capitalism and Schizophrenia*, London/New York: Continuum.
Deleuze, G. and F. Guattari (2004). *Anti-Oedipus: Capitalism and Schizophrenia*, London and New York, Continuum.
Derrida, J. (1994). *Given Time: I, Counterfeit Money*, Chicago, University of Chicago Press.
Derrida, J. (2001). *On Cosmopolitanism and Forgiveness*, London, Routledge.
Derrida, J. (2004). "Countersignature." *Paragraph* 27 (2): 7–42.
Derrida, J. (2005). *Rogues: Two Essays on Reason*, Stanford, CA, Stanford University Press.
Derrida, J. (2006). *Specters of Marx: The State of the Debt, the Work of Mourning and the New International*, London, Routledge.
Desmonde, W. H. (1962). *Magic, Myth, and Money*, New York, Free Press of Glencoe.
Desmonde, W. H. (1976). "On the Anal Origin of Money." *The Psychoanalysis of Money*, E. Borneman, Ed. New York, Urizen Books: 107–11.

Desnos, R. (2008). *Essential Poems and Writings of Robert Desnos*, M. A. Caws, Ed. Victoria, BC, Canada, Commonwealth Books/Black Widow Press.
Doctorow, C. (2003). *Down and Out in the Magic Kingdom*, New York, Tor Books.
Dodd, N. (1994). *The Sociology of Money*, Cambridge, U.K., Polity Press.
Dodd, N. (2001). "What is 'Sociological' about the Euro?" *European Societies* 3 (1): 23–39.
Dodd, N. (2005a). "Laundering 'Money': On the Need for Conceptual Clarity within the Sociology of Money." *European Journal of Sociology* 46 (3): 387–411.
Dodd, N. (2005b). "Reinventing Monies in Europe." *Economy and Society* 34 (4): 558–83.
Dodd, N. (2007). "On Simmel's Pure Concept of Money: A Response to Ingham." *European Journal of Sociology* 48 (2): 273–94.
Dodd, N. (2008). "Goethe in Palermo: Urphanomen and Analogical Reasoning in Simmel and Benjamin." *Journal of Classical Sociology* 8: 411–45.
Dodd, N. (2011). "'Strange Money': Risk, Finance and Socialized Debt." *The British Journal of Sociology* 62 (1): 175–94.
Dodd, N. (2012). "Simmel's Perfect Money: Fiction, Socialism and Utopia in the Philosophy of Money." *Theory, Culture & Society* 29 (7/8): 146–76.
Douglas, C. H. (1918). "The Delusion of Super-Production." *The English Review* December 1918.
Douglas, C. H. (1974). *Economic Democracy*, Sudbury, Suffolk, U.K., Bloomfield Books.
Douglas, C. H. (1979). *Social Credit*, Sun City, Az, Institute of Economic Democracy.
Douglas, M. (1967). "Primitive Rationing." *Themes in Economic Anthropology*, R. Firth, Ed. London, Tavistock: 119–45.
Douglass, F. (1852). "What to the Slave Is the Fourth of July?" *Frederick Douglass: Selected Speeches and Writings*, P. S. Foner, Ed. Chicago, Lawrence Hill: 188–206.
Douthwaite, R. (2006). *The Ecology of Money*, Cloughjordan, Ireland, Feasta. http://www.feasta.org/documents/moneyecology/contents.htm.
Dumas, G. (2010). *Globalization Fractures*, London, Profile Books.
Dumouchel, P. and J.-P. Dupuy (1978). *L'Enfer des Choses René Girard et la Logique de l'Economie*, Paris, Seuil.
Durkheim, E. (1899). "De la définition des phénomènes religieux." *Année sociologique* 2: 1–28.
Durkheim, E. (1997). *The Division of Labor in Society*, New York, Free Press.
Durkheim, E. (2001). *The Elementary Forms of Religious Life*, Oxford, U.K., Oxford University Press.
Eagleton, T. (2012). *Why Marx Was Right*, New Haven, CT/London, Yale University Press.
Earley, J. S. (1994). "Joseph Schumpeter: A Frustrated 'Creditist.'" *New Perspectives in Monetary Macroeconomics*, G. Dymski and R. Pollin Eds. Ann Arbor, University of Michigan Press: 337–51.
Economou, M., M. Madianos, et al. (2011). "Increased Suicidality amid Economic Crisis in Greece." *Lancet* 378: 1459.
Eggertsson, G. B. and P. Krugman (2012). "Debt, Deleveraging and the Liquidity Trap: A Fisher-Minsky-Koo Approach." *The Quarterly Journal of Economics* 127 (3): 1469–513.
Eichengreen, B. (2007). "The Breakup of the Euro Area." NBER Working Paper No. 13393, Cambridge, MA, National Bureau of Economic Research, http://www.nber.org/papers/w13393.
Eichengreen, B. (2008). *Globalizing Capital: A History of the International Monetary System*, Princeton, NJ, Princeton University Press.
Einzig, P. (1948). "New Light on the Origin of Money." *Nature* December 25: 983–85.
Einzig, P. (1966). *Primitive Money in Its Ethnological, Historical, and Economic Aspects*, London, Eyre and Spottiswoode.
Ekman, M. (2012). "Understanding Accumulation: The Relevance of Marx's Theory of Primitive Accumulation in Media and Communication Studies." *Triple C* 10 (2): 156–70.
Elias, N. (1994). *The Civilizing Process*, 2 vols. Oxford, U.K., Blackwell.

Engels, F. (2010). *Socialism: Utopian and Scientific*, Washington, DC, Pathfinder Press.
Esparza, L. E. and P. Lapegna (2007). "The Limits of Connected Lives Theory." *Sociological Forum* 22: 606–11.
Estrella, A. (2002). "Securitization and the Efficacy of Monetary Policy," *Economic Policy Review* May: 243–55.
European Central Bank (ECB) (2008). "The Role of Banks in the Monetary Policy Transmission Mechanism." *Monthly Bulletin* August: 85–98. www.ecb.europa.eu/pub/pdf/other/pp85–98mb200808en.pdf.
European Central Bank (ECB) (2010). "Monetary Policy Transmission in the Euro Area, a Decade after the Introduction of the Euro." *Monthly Bulletin*, May: 85–98. www.ecb.europa.eu/pub/pdf/other/mb201005en_pp85–98en.pdf.
European Central Bank (ECB) (2013). *The Eurosystem Household Finance and Consumption Survey*, Frankfurt am Main, Germany, European Central Bank, December 17. https://www.ecb.europa.eu/pub/pdf/other/ecbsp2en.pdf.
Evans, M. S. (2009). "Zelizer's Theory of Money and the Case of Local Currencies." *Environment and Planning A* 41 (5): 1026–41.
Evans Pritchard, A. (2012). "Greek Agony Drags on as Asphyxiation Bloc Wins." *The Daily Telegraph* (London). June 18.
Faraizi, A., T. Rahman, et al. (2010). *Microcredit and Women's Empowerment: A Case Study of Bangladesh*, Abingdon, U.K., Routledge.
Fenichel, O. (1938). "The Drive to Amass Wealth." *Psychoanalytical Quarterly* 7: 69–95.
Ferenczi, S. (1916). "The Ontogenesis of the Interest in Money." *Contributions to Psychoanalysis*, E. T. Jones, Ed. Toronto, Richard G. Badger.
Fine, B. and C. Lapavitsas (2000). "Markets and Money in Social Theory: What Role for Economics?" *Economy and Society* 29 (3): 357–82.
Finley, M. (1982). *Economy and Society in Ancient Greece*, London, Chatto and Windus.
Fisher, I. (1933). "The Debt-Deflation Theory of Great Depressions." *Econometrica* 1 (4): 337–57.
Fisher, I., H. R. Cohrssen, et al. (1933). *Stamp Scrip*, New York, Adelphi Company.
Fisher, M. (2009). *Capitalist Realism: Is There No Alternative?* London, Zero Books.
Foster, W. and W. Catchings (1926). *The Dilemma of Thrift*, Newton, MA, Pollak Foundation for Economic Research.
Foucault, M. (2005). *The Order of Things*, London, Routledge.
Foucault, M. (2008a). *The Birth of Biopolitics: Lectures at the Collège de France, 1978–1979*, Basingstoke, U.K.: Palgrave Macmillan.
Foucault, M. (2008b). *Introduction to Kant's Anthropology*, Los Angeles, Semiotext(e).
Foucault, M. (2013). *Lectures on the Will to Know: Lectures at the College de France 1970–1971 with Oedipal Knowledge*, Basingstoke, U.K., Palgrave-Macmillan.
Fountoulakis, K., I. Grammatikopoulos, et al. (2012). "Health and the Financial Crisis in Greece." *Lancet* 379: 1001–1002.
Fourcade, M. (2013). "The Economy as a Morality Play, and the Implications for the Eurozone Crisis." *Moral Categories in the Financial Crisis*, M. Fourcade, P. Steiner, W. Streeck and C. Woll, Eds. Paris, Max Planck Sciences Po Centre on Coping with Instability in Market Societies: 21–27.
Fournier, M. (1989). *Marcel Mauss: An Intellectual Biography*, Princeton, NJ, Princeton University Press.
Frank, T. (2001). *One Market under God: Extreme Capitalism, Market Populism, and the End of Economic Democracy*, New York, First Anchor Books.
Fratzscher, M. and A. Mehl (2011). "China's Dominance Hypothesis and the Emergence of a Tri-Polar Global Currency System." ECB Working Paper No. 1392, September 30.
Freixas, X. and J.-C. Rochet (2008). *Microeconomics of Banking*, Cambridge, MA, MIT Press.
Freud, S. (1908). "Character and Anal Erotism." *The Standard Edition of the Complete Psychological Works of Sigmund Freud, Vol. 9*, London, Hogarth Press: 169–75.

Freud, S. (2005). *Civilization and Its Discontents,* New York, Norton.
Friedman, M. (1969). *The Optimum Quantity of Money and Other Essays,* Piscataway, NJ, Aldine Transaction.
Frisby, D. (1985). *Fragments of Modernity: Theories of Modernity in the Work of Simmel, Kracauer and Benjamin,* Cambridge, U.K., Polity Press.
Frisby, D. (1992). *Simmel and Since,* London, Routledge.
Frisby, D. (2002). *Georg Simmel,* London, Routledge.
Fromm, E. (1947). *Man for Himself:* An Inquiry into the Psychology of Ethics, Abingdon, Oxon., Routledge.
Fromm, E. (1963). *The Dogma of Christ and Other Essays on Religion, Psychology and Culture,* London, Routledge.
Fromm, E. (1966). *You Shall Be as Gods: A Radical Interpretation of the Old Testament and its Tradition,* Greenwich, CT, Fawcett.
Fromm, E. (1976). *To Have or To Be,* New York, Harper and Row.
Fromm, E. (1994). *Escape from Freedom,* New York, Henry Holt & Company Inc.
Fromm, E. (2002). *The Sane Society,* London, Routledge.
Fukuyama, F. (1995). *Trust:* The Social Virtues and the Creation of Prosperity, New York: Free Press Paperbacks.
Galbraith, J. K. (1975). *Money: Whence It Came, Where It Went,* Boston, Mass, Houghton Mifflin.
Gell, A. (1992). *The Anthropology of Time: Cultural Constructions of Temporal Maps and Images,* Oxford, U.K., Berg.
Gelleri, C. (2009). "Chiemgauer Regiomoney: Theory and Practice of a Local Currency." *International Journal of Community Currency Research* 13: 61–75.
Gesell, S. (1892). *The Natonalization of Money,* Buenos Aires, Argentina, typescript.
Gesell, S. (1951). *Currency Reform as a Bridge to the Social State,* trans. P. Pye, typescript.
Gesell, S. (2007). *The Natural Economic Order,* Frankston, TX, TGS Publishers.
Geyer, M. H. (2001). "One Language for the World: The Metric System, International Coinage, Gold Standard, and the Rise of Internationalism, 1850–1900." *The Mechanics of Internationalism: Culture, Society and Politics from the 1840s to the First World War,* M. H. Geyer and J. Paulmann, Eds. Oxford, U.K., Oxford University Press: 55–92.
Gide, A. (1990). *The Counterfeiters,* Harmondsworth, U.K., Penguin.
Giddens, A. (1985). *The Nation-State and Violence,* Cambridge, U.K., Polity Press.
Gilbert, E. (1998). "'Ornamenting the Facade of Hell': Iconographies of Nineteenth-Century Canadian Paper Money." *Environment and Planning D: Society and Space* 16 (1): 57–80.
Gilbert, E. (2005). "Common Cents: Situating Money in Time and Place." *Economy and Society* 34 (3): 357–88.
Gilroy, P. (1993). *The Black Atlantic: Modernity and Double Consciousness,* London/New York, Verso.
Girard, R. (1972). *Violence and the Sacred,* Baltimore, Johns Hopkins University Press.
Glassman, J. (2006). "Primitive Accumulation, Accumulation by Dispossession, Accumulation by 'Extra-Economic' Means." *Progress in Human Geography* 30 (5): 608–25.
Glendinning, S. (2011). *Derrida: A Very Short Introduction,* Oxford, U.K., Oxford University Press.
Godelier, M. (1972). "The Object and Method of Economic Anthropology." *Rationality and Irrationality in Economics,* M. Godelier, Ed. New York, Monthly Review Press: 243–319.
Godelier, M. (1988). *The Mental and the Material,* London/New York, Verso.
Godelier, M. (1999). *The Enigma of the Gift,* Cambridge, U.K., Polity Press.
Godschalk, H. (2012). "Does Demurrage Matter for Complementary Currencies?" *International Journal of Community Currency Research* 16: 58–69.
Goffman, A. (2009). "On the Run: Wanted Men in a Philadelphia Ghetto." *American Sociological Review* 74: 339–57.

González, J. J. (2005). *Essential Theological Terms*, Louisville, KY: Westminster John Knox Press.
Goodhart, C. A. E. (1997). "One Government, One Money." *Prospect* March: 1–3.
Goodhart, C. A. E. (1998). "The Two Concepts of Money: Implications for the Analysis of Optimal Currency Areas." *European Journal of Political Economy* 14 (3): 407–32.
Goodhart, C. A. E. (2005a). "Book Review: *Credit and State Theories of Money: The Contributions of A. Mitchell Innes.*" *History of Political Economy* 37: 759–61.
Goodhart, C. A. E. (2005b). "What Is the Essence of Money?" *Cambridge Journal of Economics* 29 (5): 817–25.
Goodhart, C. A. E. (2008). "The Continuing Muddle of Monetary Theory: A Steadfast Refusal to Face Facts." *Lionel Robbins's Essay on the Nature and Significance of Economic Science*, F. Cowell and A. Witzum, Eds. London, STICERD, London School of Economics: 292–305.
Gordon, B. J. (1961). "Aristotle, Schumpeter, and the Metallist Tradition." *Quarterly Journal of Economics* 75 (4): 608–14.
Gordon, B. J. (1964). "Aristotle and the Development of Value Theory." *Quarterly Journal of Economics* 78 (1): 116–28.
Goux, J.-J. (1990). *Symbolic Economies after Freud and Marx*, Ithaca, NY, Cornell University Press.
Goux, J.-J. (1994). *The Coiners of Language*, Norman, OK, University of Oklahoma Press.
Goux, J.-J. (1999). Cash, Check or Charge? *The New Economic Criticism: Studies at the Intersection of Literature and Economics*, M. Woodmansee and M. Osteen, Eds. New York, Routledge: 114–27.
Grabill, S. J., Ed. (2007). *Sourcebook in Late-Scholastic Monetary Theory: The Contributions of Martín de Azpilcueta, Luis De Molina, and Juan de Mariana*, Idaho Falls, ID, Lexington Books.
Graeber, D. (2001). *Toward an Anthropological Theory of Value: The False Coin of Our Own Dreams*, Basingstoke, U.K., Palgrave Macmillan.
Graeber, D. (2011). *Debt: The First 5,000 Years*, Brooklyn, NY/London, Melville House Publishing.
Graeber, D. (2013). *The Democracy Project: A History. A Crisis. A Movement*, London, Penguin.
Grahl, J. (2000). "Money as Sovereignty: The Economics of Michel Aglietta." *New Political Economy* 5 (2): 291–316.
Granovetter, M. (1985). "Economic Action and Social Structure: The Problem of Embeddedness." *American Journal of Sociology* 91 (3): 481–510.
Graziani, A. (2009). *The Monetary Theory of Production*, Cambridge, U.K., Cambridge University Press.
Greco, T. H. (2009). *The End of Money and the Future of Civilization*, White River Junction, VT, Chelsea Green Publishing Company.
Green, S. F. (2005). *Notes from the Balkans: Locating Marginality and Ambiguity on the Greek-Albanian Border*, Princeton, NJ, Princeton University Press.
Green, S. F. (2008). "Eating Money and Clogging Things Up: Paradoxes of Elite Mediation in Epirus, North-Western Greece." *The Sociological Review* 56 (S1): 260–82.
Greenham, D. (2001). "Norman O. Brown, Herbert Marcuse and the romantic tradition." Ph.D. thesis, University of Nottingham, U.K.
Gregory, C. A. (1997). *Savage Money*, Amsterdam, Taylor & Francis.
Gregory, C. A. (2012). "On Money Debt and Morality: Some Reflections on the Contribution of Economic Anthropology." *Social Anthropology* 20 (4): 380–96.
Grierson, P. (1978). "The Origins of Money." *Research in Economic Anthropology* 1: 1–35.
Grignon, P. (2006). *Money as Debt* (film), Moonfire Studio, Canada. https://www.youtube.com/watch?v=CB5M5nuTD9w.
Grignon, P. (2009). *Money as Debt II* (film), Moonfire Studio, Canada. https://www.youtube.com/watch?v=6_lB3AJSMRg.
Grossman, R. S. (2010). *Unsettled Account: The Evolution of Banking in the Industrialized World since 1800*, Princeton, NJ, Princeton University Press.

Guttmann, R. (2003). "La Monnaie entre Violence et Confiance." *L'Annee de la Regulation* 7: 207–17.
Guyer, J. (2004). *Marginal Gains: Monetary Transactions in Atlantic Africa,* Chicago, University of Chicago Press.
Habermas, J. (1986). *Knowledge and Human Interests,* Cambridge, U.K., Polity Press.
Habermas, J. (1987). *The Theory of Communicative Action,* Cambridge, U.K., Polity Press.
Habermas, J. (1996). "Georg Simmel on Philosophy and Culture: Postscript to a Collection of Essays." *Critical Inquiry* 22 (3): 403–14.
Habermas, J. (2012). *The Crisis of the European Union: A Response,* Cambridge, U.K., Polity Press.
Haldane, A. (2010). "The $100 Billion Question." Speech, Institute of Regulation & Risk, Hong Kong, March 30, Basel, Switzerland, Bank for International Settlements. www.bis.org/review/r100406d.pdf.
Haldane, A. (2011). "Control Rights (and Wrongs)." Wincott Annual Memorial Lecture, October 24. *Economic Affairs* 32 (2): 47–58.
Haldane, A. (2012). "On Being the Right Size." Speech to the Institute of Economic Affairs 22nd Annual Series, The 2012 Beesley Lectures, October 25.
Hall, R. B. and T. J. Biersteker (2002). *The Emergence of Private Authority in Global Governance,* Cambridge, U.K., Cambridge University Press.
Hallsmith, G. and B. Lietaer (2011). *Creating Wealth: Growing Local Economies with Local Currencies,* Gabriola Island, BC, Canada, New Society Publishers.
Hamacher, W. (2002). "Guilt History: Benjamin's Sketch 'Capitalism as Religion.'" *Diacritics* 32: 81–106.
Hann, C. and K. Hart (2009). *Market and Society: The Great Transformation Today,* Cambridge, U.K., Cambridge University Press.
Hann, C. and K. Hart (2011). *Economic Anthropology: History, Ethnography, Critique,* Cambridge, U.K., Polity Press.
Hardt, M. and A. Negri (2001). *Empire,* Cambridge, Mass., Harvard University Press.
Hardt, M. and A. Negri (2005). *Multitude: War and Democracy in the Age of Empire,* Penguin.
Hardt, M. and A. Negri (2009). *Commonwealth,* Cambridge, Mass., Harvard University Press.
Harman, C. (2009). *Zombie Capitalism: Global Crisis and the Relevance of Marx,* London, Haymarket Books.
Harnik, J. (1919). "Some Data from Cultural History Relating to the Subject of the Money Complex and Anal Eroticism." *The Psychoanalysis of Money,* E. Borneman, Ed. New York, Urizen Books: 105–106.
Hart, K. (1986). "Heads or Tails? Two Sides of the Coin." *Man* 21: 637–56.
Hart, K. (2001). *Money in an Unequal World,* New York/London, Texere.
Hart, K. (2005a). "Money: One Anthropologist's View." *A Handbook of Economic Anthropology,* J. G. Carrier, Ed. Cheltenham, U.K., Edward Elgar Publishing: 160–75.
Hart, K. (2005b). "Notes Towards an Anthropology of Money." *Kritikos.* 2 (June). http://intertheory.org/hart.htm.
Hart, K. (2007). "Marcel Mauss: In Pursuit of the Whole. A Review Essay." *Comparative Studies in Society and History* 49: 1–13.
Hart, K., J.-L. Laville, et al., Eds. (2010). *The Human Economy,* Cambridge, U.K., Polity Press.
Harvey, D. (1991). *The Condition of Postmodernity: An Enquiry into the Origins of Cultural Change,* Oxford, U.K., Wiley-Blackwell.
Harvey, D. (1996). *Justice, Nature and the Geography of Difference,* Oxford, U.K., Blackwell.
Harvey, D. (2000). *Spaces of Hope,* Edinburgh, Scotland, Edinburgh University Press.
Harvey, D. (2005a). *A Brief History of Neoliberalism,* Oxford, U.K., Oxford University Press.
Harvey, D. (2005b). *The New Imperialism,* Oxford, U.K., Oxford University Press.
Harvey, D. (2006). *The Limits to Capital,* London/New York, Verso.
Harvey, D. (2010a). *A Companion to Marx's Capital,* London/New York, Verso.

Harvey, D. (2010b). *The Enigma of Capital and the Crises of Capitalism*, London, Profile Books.
Harvey, D. (2012). *Rebel Cities: From the Right to the City to the Urban Revolution*, London, Verso.
Hayek, F. A. (1976). *Denationalisation of Money, The Argument Refined*, London, Institute of Economic Affairs.
Hegel, G. W. F. (1991). *Elements of the Philosophy of Right*, Cambridge, U.K., Cambridge University Press.
Helleiner, E. (2001). "One Money, One People? Political Identity and the Euro." Trent International Political Economy Centre Working Paper 01/6.
Helleiner, E. (2003). *The Making of National Money: Territorial Currencies in Historical Perspective*, Ithaca, NY, Cornell University Press.
Henderson, W. (1999). *John Ruskin's Political Economy*, London, Routledge.
Herndon, T., M. Ash, et al. (2013). "Does High Public Debt Consistently Stifle Economic Growth? A Critique of Reinhart and Rogoff." Political Economy Research Institute Working Paper Series No. 322.
Hilferding, R. (2007). *Finance Capital: A Study in the Latest Phase of Capitalist Development*, London, Routledge.
Hirsch, F. (1978). *Social Limits to Growth*, Cambridge, MA, Harvard University Press.
Hirsch, F. and J. Goldthorpe, Eds. (1978). *The Political Economy of Inflation*, Cambridge, MA, Harvard University Press.
Hobson, J. A. (1902). *Imperialism: A Study*, Nottingham, U.K., Spokesman Books.
Holland, E. W. (1999). *Deleuze and Guattari's Anti-Oedipus: Introduction to Schizoanalysis*, London, Routledge.
Hollier, D. (1988). "Foreword: Collage." *The College of Sociology 1937–39*, D. Hollier, Ed. Minneapolis, University of Minnesota Press: viii–xxix.
Hollier, D. (1989). *Against Architecture: The Wrtings of Georges Bataille*, Cambridge, MA, MIT Press.
Hollier, D. (1995). "The Use Value of the Impossible." *Bataille: Writing the Sacred*, C. B. Gill, Ed. London/New York, Routledge: 133–53.
Hollingdale, R. J. (1999). *Nietzsche: The Man and His Philosophy*, Cambridge, U.K., Cambridge University Press.
Holloway, J. (2010). *Crack Capitalism*, London, Pluto Press.
Hörisch, J. (2000). *Heads or Tails: The Poetics of Money*, Detroit, Wayne State University Press.
Hubert, H. and M. Mauss (1981). *Sacrifice: Its Nature and Functions*, Chicago, University of Chicago Presss, ix, 165.
Hudson, M. (2004). "The Archaeology of Money: Debt Versus Barter Theories of Money's Origins." *Credit and State Theories of Money: The Contributions of A. Mitchell Innes*, L. R. Wray, Ed. Cheltenham, U.K., Edward Elgar Publishing: 99–127.
Hudson, M. (2011). "Debt Slavery: Why It Destroyed Rome, Why It Will Destroy Us Unless It's Stopped." *Counterpunch*, December 2, http://www.counterpunch.org/2011/12/02/debt-slavery-%E2%80%93-why-it-destroyed-rome-why-it-will-destroy-us-unless-it%E2%80%99s-stopped/.
Hudson, M. (2012). *The Bubble and Beyond: Ficitious Capital, Debt Deflation and Global Crisis*, New York, Institute for the Study of Long-term Economic Trends.
Humphrey, C. (1985). "Barter and Economic Disintegration." *Man* 20: 48–72.
Hutchinson, S. (1992). "The Cattle of Money and the Cattle of Girls among the Nuer, 1930–83." *American Ethnologist* 19 (2): 294–316.
Hutchinson, S. (1996). *Nuer Dilemmas: Coping with Money, War, and the State*, Berkeley and Los Angeles, University of California Press.
Hutnyk, J. (2003). "Bataille's Wars: Surrealism, Marxism, Fascism." *Critique of Anthropology* 23: 264–88.
Ingham, G. (1998). "On the Underdevelopment of the 'Sociology of Money.'" *Acta Sociologica* 41: 3–18.

Ingham, G. (2001). "Fundamentals of a Theory of Money: Untangling Fine, Lapavitsas and Zelizer." *Economy and Society* 30 (3): 304–23.

Ingham, G. (2003). "Schumpeter and Weber on the Institutions of Capitalism: Solving Swedberg's 'Puzzle.'" *Journal of Classical Sociology* 3 (3): 297–309.

Ingham, G. (2004a). "The Emergence of Capitalist Credit Money." *Credit and State Theories of Money: The Contributions of A. Mitchell Innes*, L. R. Wray, Ed. Cheltenham, U.K., Edward Elgar Publishing: 173–222.

Ingham, G. (2004b). *The Nature of Money*, Cambridge, U.K., Polity Press.

International Monetary Fund (IMF) (2006). "Global Financial Stability Report: Market Developments and Issues." Washington, DC, International Monetary Fund.

International Monetary Fund (IMF) (2008). *Sovereign Wealth Funds—A Work Agenda*, IMF Monetary and Capital Markets and Policy Development Review Departments, Washington, DC, International Monetary Fund.

Isaac, B. (1993). "Retrospective on the Formalist–Substantivist Debate." *Research in Economic Anthropology*, B. Isaac, Ed. Greenwich, CT, JAI Press: 213–33.

Issing, O. (2008). *The Birth of the Euro*, Cambridge, U.K., Cambridge University Press.

Jameson, F. (2007). *Archaeologies of the Future: The Desire Called Utopia and Other Science Fictions*, London/New York, Verso.

Jarry, A. (1977). *The Ubu Plays*, London, Nick Hern Books.

Kaelberer, M. (2004). "The Euro and European Identity: Symbols, Power and the Politics of European Monetary Union." *Review of International Studies* 30 (2): 161–78.

Kaldor, N. (1970) "The New Monetarism." *Lloyds Bank Review* 17: 1–17.

Kaldor, N. (1982) *The Scourge of Monetarism*, Oxford, U.K.: Oxford University Press.

Kant, I. (1887). *The Philosophy of Law*, Clark, NJ, The Lawbook Exchange, Ltd.

Karatani, K. (2003). *Transcritique: On Kant and Marx*, Cambridge, MA, MIT Press.

Karim, L. (2008). "Demystifying Micro-Credit: The Grameen Bank, NGOs, and Neoliberalism in Bangladesh." *Cultural Dynamics* 20 (1): 5–29.

Kaufman, E. (2001). *The Delirium of Praise: Bataille, Blanchot, Deleuze, Foucault, Klossowski*, Baltimore, Johns Hopkins University Press.

Kaufmann, W. A. (1975). *Nietzsche: Philosopher, Psychologist, Antichrist*, Princeton, NJ, Princeton University Press.

Kay, J. (2009). *Narrow Banking: The Reform of Banking Regulation*, London, Centre for the Study of Financial Innovation.

Kay, J. (2010). "Should We Have 'Narrow Banking'?" London, London School of Economics and Political Science, www.johnkay.com/2011/06/02/should-we-have-'narrow-banking', accessed 28 March 2014.

Kellermann, P. (2008). "Soziologie des Geldes." *Handbuch der Wirtschaftssoziologie*, A. Maurer, Ed. Wiesbaden, Germany, VS Verlag für Sozialwissenschaften: 320–40.

Kelly, K. (1995). *Out of Control: The New Biology of Machines, Social Systems, and the Economic World*, New York, Basic Books.

Kennedy, E. (2004). *Constitutional Failure: Carl Schmitt in Weimar*, Durham, NC, and London, Duke University Press.

Keynes, J. M. (1933). "National Self-Sufficiency." *The Yale Review* 22: 755–69.

Keynes, J. M. (1937). "The General Theory of Employment." *The Quarterly Journal of Economics* XIV: 109–23.

Keynes, J. M. (1972). *Essays in Persuasion*, London, W.W. Norton & Company.

Keynes, J. M. (1973). *The Collected Writings of John Maynard Keynes, Vol. XIV*, Cambridge, U.K., Cambridge University Press.

Keynes, J. M. (1976). *A Treatise on Money*, New York, Harcourt Brace Jovanovich.

Keynes, J. M. (2008). *The General Theory of Employment, Interest and Money*, New Delhi, India, Atlantic Publishers.

Keynes, J. M. (2008). *The General Theory of Employment, Interest and Money*, http://www.bnpublishing.com.
Kiyotaki, N. and J. Moore (2002). "Evil Is the Root of All Money." *The American Economic Review* 92: 62–66.
Klossowski, P. (1997). *La Monnaie Vivante*, Paris, Rivages Poche.
Knapp, G. F. (1924). *The State Theory of Money*, London, Macmillan.
Knorr Cetina, K. and U. Bruegger (2002). "Global Microstructures: The Virtual Societies of Financial Markets." *American Journal of Sociology* 107 (4): 905–50.
Knorr Cetina, K. and A. Preda (2007). "The Temporalization of Financial Markets: From Network to Flow." *Theory, Culture & Society* 24 (7–8): 116–38.
Kocherlakota, N. R. (1998). "Money Is Memory." *Journal of Economic Theory* 81: 232–51.
Krippner, G. R. (2001). "The Elusive Market: Embeddedness and the Paradigm of Economic Sociology." *Theory and Society* 30 (6): 775–810.
Krippner, G. R. (2005). "The Financialization of the American Economy." *Socio-Economic Review* 3 (2): 173–208.
Krippner, G. R. (2011). *Capitalizing on Crisis: The Political Origins of the Rise of Finance*, Cambridge, Mass, Harvard University Press.
Krippner, G. R. and A. S. Alvarez (2007). "Embeddedness and the Intellectual Projects of Economic Sociology." *Annual Review of Sociology* 33: 219–40.
Krueger, D. W. (1986). "Money, Success, and Success Phobia." *The Last Taboo: Money as Symbol and Reality in Psychotherapy and Psychoanalysis*, D. W. Krueger, Ed. New York, Brunner and Mazel: 3–16.
Krugman, P. (2002). "Crises: The Next Generation." *Economic Policy in the International Economy: Essays in Honor of Assaf Razin*, A. Razin, E. Helpmann and E. Sadka, Eds. Cambridge, U.K., Cambridge University Press.
Krugman, P. (2012). *End This Depression Now!* New York/London, W. W. Norton and Company.
Lagi, M., K. Z. Bertrand, et al. (2011). "The Food Crises and Political Instability in North Africa and the Middle East." New England Complex Systems Institute Working Paper.
LaGuerre, M. (1982). *Upper Belair Infrastructure. Urban Life in the Caribbean: A Case Study of Haiti*, Cambridge, U.K., Schenkman Publishing.
Lapavitsas, C. (2003). *Social Foundations of Markets, Money and Credit*, London, Routledge.
Lapavitsas, C. (2009). "Financialisation, or the Search for Profits in the Sphere of Circulation." Research on Money and Finance Discussion Paper No. 14, London, School of African and Oriental Studies, University of London. www.soas.ac.uk/rmf/papers/file51263.pdf.
Lapavitsas, C. (2012). "It Is in Greece's Interest to Leave the Euro." *The Financial Times* (London), May 23.
Latour, B. (2005). *Reassembling the Social: An Introduction to Actor-Network-Theory*, Oxford, U.K., and New York: Oxford University Press.
Laum, B. (2006). *Heiliges Geld: Eine Historische Untersuchung über den Sakralen Ursprung des Geldes*, Berlin, Semele Verlag.
Law Reform Commission of Ireland (2010). *Personal Debt Management and Debt Enforcement*, Dublin, Ireland, Law Reform Commission, www.lawreform.ie/_fileupload/Reports/r100 Debt.pdf.
Lazzarato, M. (2011). *The Making of Indebted Man*, Los Angeles, Semiotext(e).
LeClair, E. and H. Schneider, Eds. (1968). *Economic Anthropology*, New York, Holt, Rinehart and Winston.
Leigh, W. A. and D. Huff (2007). *African Americans and Homeownership: The Subprime Lending Experience, 1995 to 2007*, Washington DC, Joint Center for Political and Economic Studies.
Leiris, M. (1963). "De Bataille l'impossible 'Documents.'" *Critique* 195–96: 685–93.
Lenin, V. (1999). *Imperialism: The Highest Stage of Capitalism*, Sydney, Australia, Resistance Books.

Lerner, A. (1947). "Money as a Creature of the State." *American Economic Review* 37: 312–17.
Levav, J. and P. McGraw (2009). "Emotional Accounting: How Feelings about Money Influence Consumer Choice." *Journal of Marketing Research* 46: 66–80.
Lietaer, B. (2002). *The Future of Money: Creating New Wealth, Work and a Wiser World*, London, Century.
Lietaer, B. and S. Belgin (2011). *New Money for a New World*, Boulder, CO, Qiterra Press.
LiPuma, E. (1999). *The Meaning of Money in the Age of Modernity*, Pittsburgh, University of Pittsburgh Press.
LiPuma, E. and B. Lee (2004). *Financial Derivatives and the Globalization of Risk*, Durham, NC, and London, Duke University Press.
Locke, J. (1695). *Further Considerations Concerning Raising the Value of Money, Wherein Mr Lowndes's Arguments for It in His Late Report Concerning an Essay for the Amendment of the Silver Coins, Are Particularly Examined*, London, A. and J. Churchill.
Locke, J. (1696). *Some Considerations of the Consequences of the Lowering of Interest, and Raising the Value of Money*, London, A. and J. Churchill.
Lotringer, S. and S. Cohen (2001). *French Theory in America*, London, Routledge.
Lotringer, S. and C. Marazzi, Eds. (2008). *Autonomia: Post-Political Politics*, Cambridge, Mass, MIT Press.
Lukács, G. (1971). *History and Class Consciousness*, London, Merlin Press.
Luxemburg, R. (2003). *The Accumulation of Capital*, London, Routledge.
Lyotard, J.-F. (1993). *Political Writings*, London, UCL Press.
Macdonald, J. (2003). *A Free Nation Deep in Debt: The Financial Roots of Democracy*, Princeton, NJ, Princeton University Press.
MacKenzie, D. (2008). *An Engine, Not a Camera: How Financial Models Shape Markets (Inside Technology Series)*, Cambridge, Mass, MIT Press.
MacKenzie, D. (2011). "The Credit Crisis as a Problem in the Sociology of Knowledge." *American Journal of Sociology* 116 (6): 1778–841.
Magee, B. (1979). *Men of Ideas*, New York, Viking.
Malinowski, B. (1921). "The Primitive Economics of the Trobriand Islanders." *Economic Journal*. 31: 1–16.
Malinowski, B. (1922). *Argonauts of the Western Pacific*, London, Routledge.
Mandarini, M. (2006). "Marx and Deleuze: Money, Time, and Crisis." *Polygraph* 18: 73–97.
Mandeville, B. (1989). *The Fable of the Bees*, London, Penguin.
Manning, R. D. (2000). *Credit Card Nation: The Consequences of America's Addiction to Credit*, New York, Basic Books.
Marazzi, C. (1995). "Money in the World Crisis: The New Basis of Capitalist Power." *Global Capital, National State, and the Politics of Money*, W. Bonefeld and J. Holloway, Eds. Basingstoke, U.K., Macmillan: 69–91.
Marazzi, C. (2008). *Capital and Language: From the New Economy to the War Economy*, Los Angeles, Semiotext(e).
Marazzi, C. (2010). *The Violence of Financial Capitalism*, Los Angeles, Semiotext(e).
Marcel, J.-C. (2003). "Bataille and Mauss: Dialogue of the Deaf?" *Economy and Society* 32 (1): 141–52.
Marcuse, H. (1955). *Eros and Civilization: A Philosophical Inquiry into Freud*, Boston, Beacon Press.
Marcuse, H. (1997). "Some Social Implications of Modern Technology." *The Essential Frankfurt School Reader*, A. Arato and E. Gebhardt, Eds. New York, Continuum.
Markowits, D. (2004). "Contract and Collaboration." *Yale Law Journal* 113: 1417–518.
Martin-Nelson, J. (2007). "An Engineer's View of an Ideal Society: The Economic Reforms of C. H. Douglas, 1916–1920." *Spontaneous Generations* 1 (1).
Marx, K. (1894). *Capital, Vol. III*, Harmondsworth, U.K., Penguin/NLR.
Marx, K. (1978). *Capital, Vol. II*, Harmondsworth, U.K., Penguin.

Marx, K. (1982). *Capital, Vol. I*, Harmondsworth, U.K., Penguin.
Marx, K. (1987). *The Poverty of Philosophy*, London, Lawrence & Wishart.
Marx, K. (1996) "Critique of the Gotha Programme." *Marx: Later Political Writings*, T. Carver, Ed. Cambridge: Cambridge University Press: 208–26.
Marx, K. (2000a). "Economic and Philosophical Manuscripts." *Marx: Selected Writings*, D. McLellan, Ed. Oxford: Oxford University Press: 83–120.
Marx, K. (2000b). "On James Mill." *Marx: Selected Writings*, D. McLellan, Ed. Oxford: Oxford University Press: 124–33.
Marx, K. (2005a). *Grundrisse: Foundations of the Critique of Political Economy*, Harmondsworth, U.K., Penguin.
Marx, K. (2005b). *The Poverty of Philosophy*, New Delhi, Global Vision Publishing House.
Marx, K. (2009). *A Contribution to the Critique of Political Economy*, Charleston, BiblioLife, LLC.
Marx, K. (2012). *On the Jewish Question*, Chicago, Aristeus Books.
Marx, K. and F. Engels (2004). *The Communist Manifesto*, Harmondsworth, U.K., Penguin.
Maurer, B. (2002). "Repressed Futures: Financial Derivatives' Theological Unconscious." *Economy and Society* 31 (1): 15–36.
Maurer, B. (2005). *Mutual Life, Limited: Islamic Banking, Alternative Currencies, Lateral Reason*, Princeton, NJ, Princeton University Press.
Maurer, B. (2006). "The Anthropology of Money." *Annual Review of Anthropology* 35: 15–36.
Maurer, B. (2007). "Incalculable Payments: Money, Scale, and the South Afircan Offshore Grey Money Amnesty." *African Studies Review* 50 (2): 125–38.
Maurer, B. (2011). "Money Nutters." *Economic Sociology: The European Electronic Newsletter* 12 (3): 5–12.
Mauss, M. (1969). "Les Origines de la Notion de Monnaie." *Texte Reproduit in Marcel Mauss, Oeuvres. 2. Représentations Collectives et Diversité des Civilisations*, M. Mauss, Ed. Paris, Les Éditions de Minuit: 106–12.
Mauss, M. (1990). *The Gift: The Form and Reason for Exchange in Archaic Societies*, NewYork/London, W. W. Norton & Co.
May, T. C. (1992). "The Crypto Anarchist Manifesto." http://www.activism.net/cypherpunk/crypto-anarchy.html, accessed November 2, 2012.
McCloskey, D. N. (1998). *The Rhetoric of Economics*, Madison, University of Wisconsin Press.
McCulley, P. (2001a). "Capitalism's Beast of Burden." *Fed Focus*, Newport Beach, CA, PIMCO.
McCulley, P. (2001b). "Look, Honey, I Caught A Liverwurst!" *Fed Focus*, Newport Beach, CA, PIMCO.
McKinnon, R. (2000). "Mundell, the Euro, and Optimum Currency Areas." Department of Economics Working Paper 009, University of Stanford.
McLeay, M., A. Radia, and R. Thomas (2014). "Money Creation in the Modern Economy." *Bank of England Quarterly Bulletin* Q1: 14–27.
McNally, D. (2009). "From Financial Crisis to World-Slump: Accumulation, Financialisation, and the Global Slowdown." *Historical Materialism* 17: 35–83.
Mead, G. H. (1994). "Review of *Philosophie des Geldes*." *Georg Simmel: Critical Assessments*, D. Frisby, Ed. London, Routledge: 144–46.
Meltzer, F. (2011). *Seeing Double: Baudelaire's Modernity*, Chicago, University of Chiacgo Press.
Menger, K. (1892). "On the Origin of Money." *The Economic Journal* 2: 239–477.
Messori, M. (1997). "The Trials and Misadventures of Schumpeter's Treatise on Money." *History of Political Economy* 29: 639–73.
Minsky, H. P. (1975). *John Maynard Keynes*, New York, Columbia University Press.
Minsky, H. P. (1986). *Stabilizing an Unstable Economy*, New Haven, CT, Yale University Press.
Minsky, H. P. (1992). "The Financial Instability Hypothesis." Jerome Levy Economics Institute, Working Paper No. 74, Annandale-on-Hudson, NY, Levy Economics Institute of Bard College. www.levyinstitute.org/pubs/wp74.pdf.

Minsky, H. P. (1993a). "Finance and Stability: The Limits of Capitalism." Jerome Levy Economics Institute, Working Paper No. 93, Annandale-on-Hudson, NY, Levy Economics Institute of Bard College. www.levyinstitute.org/pubs/wp93.pdf.
Minsky, H. P. (1993b). "Schumpeter and Finance." *Market and Institutions in Economic Development: Essays in Honor of Paolo Sylos Labini*, S. Biasco, A. Roncaglia and M. Salavati, Eds. London, Macmillan: 103–115.
Minsky, H. P. (2008). "Securitization." *The Levy Economics Institute of Bard College Policy Note* 2008 (2).
Mintz, S. W. (1961). "Standards of Value and Units of Measurement in the Fond-des-Nègres Market Place, Haiti." *The Journal of the Royal Anthropological Institute* 91 (1): 23–38.
Mintz, S. W. (1967). "Pratik: Haitian Personal Economic Relationships." *Peasant Society: A Reader*, J. M. Potter, M. N. Diaz, and G. M. Foster, Eds. Boston, Little, Brown and Company.
Mintz, S. W. (2012). *Three Ancient Colonies: Caribbean Themes and Variations*, Cambridge, MA, Harvard University Press.
Miró, J. (1992). *Joan Miró: Selected Writings and Interviews*, M. Rowell, Ed. Boston, Da Capo Press.
Mitchell, D. (2004). *Cloud Atlas*, New York, Random House.
Mitchell-Innes, A. M. (1913). "What Is Money?" *Credit and State Theories of Money: The Contributions of A. Mitchell Innes*, L. R. Wray, Ed. Cheltenham, U.K., Edward Elgar Publishing: 14–49.
Mitchell-Innes, A. M. (1914). "The Credit Theory of Money." *Credit and State Theories of Money: The Contributions of A. Mitchell Innes*, L. R. Wray, Ed. Cheltenham, U.K., Edward Elgar Publishing: 50–78.
Miyazaki, H. (2005). "The Materiality of Finance Theory." *Materiality*: 165–81.
More, S. T. (2004). *Utopia*, Harmondsworth, U.K., Penguin.
Morrill, C. (1995). *The Executive Way*, Chicago, University of Chicago Press.
Mundell, R. (1961). "A Theory of Optimum Currency Areas." *American Economic Review* 51 (4): 657–65.
Mundell, R. (2004). "Comment on Academic Exclusion: The Case of Alexander Del Mar." *European Journal of Political Economy* 20 (1): 69–71.
Mundell, R. (2012). "The Case for a World Currency." *Journal of Policy Modeling* 34 (4): 568–78.
Munn, N. D. (1992). *The Fame of Gawa: A Symbolic Study of Value Transformation in a Massim (Papua New Guinea) Society*, Durham, NC, and London, Duke University Press.
Musto, M., Ed. (2012). *Marx for Today*, London, Routledge.
Nakamoto, S. (2008). "Bitcoin: A Peer-to-Peer Electronic Cash System." bitcoin.org/bitcoin.pdf, accessed March 29, 2014.
Naqvi, M. and J. Southgate (2013). "Banknotes, Local Currencies and Central Bank Objectives." *Bank of England Quarterly Bulletin* 53 (4): 317–25.
Negri, A. (2004). *Time for Revolution*, New York, Continuum.
Negri, A. (2009). "Communism: Some Thoughts on the Concept and Practice." *Generation Online*. http://www.generation-online.org/p/fp_negri21.htm.
Nelson, A. and F. Timmerman, Eds. (2011). *Life Without Money: Building Fair and Sustainable Economies*, London, Pluto Press.
Nettlau, M. (1996). *A Short History of Anarchism*, London, Freedom Press.
Neu, J. (2005). *In Memoriam Norman O. Brown*, Santa Cruz, CA, New Pacific Press.
Neuwirth, R. (2011). *Stealth of Nations: The Global Rise of the Informal Economy*, New York, Pantheon Books.
Newton, T. (2003). "Credit and Civilization." *British Journal of Sociology* 54 (3): 347–71.
Nietzsche, F. (1973). *The Will to Power: In Science, Nature, Society and Art*, New York, Random House.
Nietzsche, F. (1979). *Ecce Homo: How One Becomes What One Is*, Harmondsworth, U.K., Penguin.
Nietzsche, F. (1980). *On the Advantage and Disadvantage of History for Life: Thoughts Out of Season, Pt. 2*, Cambridge, MA, Hackett Publishing Company.

Nietzsche, F. (1996a). *Human, All Too Human: A Book for Free Spirits,* Cambridge, U.K., Cambridge University Press.
Nietzsche, F. (1996b). *On the Genealogy of Morals,* Oxford, U.K., Oxford University Press.
Nietzsche, F. (1996c). *Philosophy in the Tragic Age of the Greeks,* Washington, DC, Regnery Publishing Inc.
Nietzsche, F. (1997a). *Daybreak: Thoughts on the Prejudices of Morality,* Cambridge, U.K., Cambridge University Press.
Nietzsche, F. (1997b). *Untimely Meditations,* Cambridge, U.K., Cambridge University Press.
Nietzsche, F. (1999). *The Birth of Tragedy and Other Writings,* Cambridge, U.K., Cambridge University Press.
Nietzsche, F. (2001). *The Gay Science: With a Prelude in German Rhymes and an Appendix of Songs,* Cambridge, U.K., Cambridge University Press.
Nietzsche, F. (2003a). *Beyond Good and Evil,* Harmondsworth, U.K., Penguin.
Nietzsche, F. (2003b). *Thus Spoke Zarathustra,* Harmondsworth, U.K., Penguin.
Nietzsche, F. (2003c). *Writings from the Late Notebooks,* Cambridge, U.K., Cambridge University Press.
Nishibe, M. (2001). "Ethics in Exchange and Reciprocity." *Competition, Trust, and Cooperation: A Comparative Study,* Y. Shionoya and K. Yagi, Eds. Berlin and Tokyo, Springer-Verlag: 77–95.
Nishibe, M. (2006). "The Theory of Labour Money: Implications of Marx's Critique for the Local Exchange Trading System (LETS)." *Marx for the 21st Century,* H. Uchida, Ed. Abingdon, U.K., Routledge: 89–103.
North, P. (1999). "Explorations in Heterotopia: Local Exchange Trading Schemes (LETS) and the Micropolitics of Money and Livelihood." *Environment and Planning D: Society and Space* 17 (1): 69–86.
North, P. (2005). "Scaling Alternative Economic Practices? Some Lessons from Alternative Currencies." *Transactions of the Institute of British Geographers* 30 (NS): 221–33.
North, P. (2007). *Money and Liberation: The Micropolitics of Alternative Currency Movements,* Minneapolis, University of Minnesota Press.
Noys, B. (2000). *Georges Bataille: A Critical Introduction,* London, Pluto Press.
Nsouli, S. M. (2006). "Petrodollar Recycling and Global Imbalances." Speech, CESifo International Spring Conference, Berlin, March 23–24 .
O'Brien, R. (1992). *Global Financial Regulation: The End of Geography,* New York, Council on Foreign Relations.
O'Rourke, K. (2011). "A Summit to the Death." *Project Syndicate,* December 9. http://www.project-syndicate.org/commentary/a-summit-to-the-death, accessed March 29, 2014.
Ohmae, K. (1990). *The Borderless World,* New York, Harper Collins.
Orhangazi, Ö. (2008). *Financialization and the US Economy,* Cheltenham, U.K., Edward Elgar Publishing.
Orléan, A. (2013). "Money: Instrument of Exchange or Social Institution of Value?" *Financial Crises and the Nature of Money: Mutual Developments from the Work of Geoffrey Ingham,* J. Pixley and G. Harcourt, Eds. Basingstoke, U.K., Palgrave Macmillan: 46–69.
Owladi, J. (2010). "Statistical Reporting of Securitisations." *Monetary and Financial Statistics: February 2010,* London, Bank of England.
Pamuk, S. (2000). *A monetary history of the Ottoman Empire,* Cambridge, U.K., Cambridge University Press.
Park, R. (1931). "Soziologische Vorlesungen von Georg Simmel: Gehalten an der Universität Berlin im Wintersemester 1899." *Chicago Society for Social Research Series 1* 1 (50).
Parsons, T. (1968). "On the Concept of Value-Commitments." *Sociological Inquiry* 38 (2): 135–60.
Parsons, T. (1991). *The Social System,* London, Routledge.
Parsons, T. and N. Smelser (2010). *Economy and Society: A Study in the Integration of Economic and Social Theory,* London, Routledge.

Patton, P. and J. Protevi (2003). "Introduction." *Between Deleuze and Derrida*, P. Patton and J. Protevi, Eds. New York, Continuum: 1–14.

Peacock, M. S. (2011). "The Political Economy of Homeric Society and the Origins of Money." *Contributions to Political Economy* 30 (1): 47–65.

Pearce, F. (2003). "Introduction: The Collège de Sociologie and French Social Thought." *Economy and Society* 32 (1): 1–6.

Peebles, G. (2012). *The Euro and Its Rivals: Currency and the Construction of a Transnational City*, Bloomington, Indiana University Press.

Perelman, M. (2000). *The Invention of Capitalism: Classical Political Economy and the Secret History of Primitive Accumulation*, Durham, NC, and London, Duke University Press.

Perroux, F. (1948). *Le Plan Marshall: Ou l'Europe Nécessaire au Monde*, Paris, Librairie de Médicis.

Piaget, J. (1971). *Structuralism*, London, Routledge.

Pixley, J. (2012a). *Emotions in Finance: Booms, Busts and Uncertainty*, Cambridge, U.K., Cambridge University Press.

Pixley, J. (2012b). "Introduction." *New Perspectives on Emotions in Finance:* The Sociology of Confidence, Fear and Betrayal, J. Pixley, Ed. Abingdon, U.K., Routledge: 1–22.

Plato. (2000). *The Republic*, Cambridge, U.K., Cambridge University Press.

Plender, J. (2012). "Capitalism in crisis: The code that forms a bar to harmony." *Financial Times* (London). January 8.

Poe, E. A. (1991). *The Gold Bug and Other Stories*, New York, Dover Publications.

Polanyi, K. (1957a). "The Economy as Instituted Process." *Trade and Market in the Early Empires: Economies in History and Theory*, K. Polanyi, C. Arensberg, and H. Pearson, Eds. Glencoe, IL, Free Press: 243–69.

Polanyi, K. (1957b). *The Great Transformation*, Boston, Beacon Press.

Polanyi, K. (1968). "The Semantics of Money-Uses." *Primitive, Archaic and Modern Economies: Essays of Karl Polanyi*, G. Dalton, Ed. Boston, Beacon Press.

Polillo, S. (2011). "Money, Moral Authority, and the Politics of Creditworthiness." *American Sociological Review* 76 (3): 437–64.

Polillo, S. (2013). *Conservatives Versus Wildcats: A Sociology of Financial Conflict*, Stanford, CA, Stanford University Press.

Poling, C. (2008). *André Masson and the Surrealist Self*, New Haven, CT, Yale University Press.

Ponsot, J.-F. and S. Rossi, Eds. (2009). *The Political Economy of Monetary Circuits: Tradition and Change in Post-Keynesian Economics*, Basingstoke, U.K., Palgrave-Macmillan.

Poovey, M. (2001). "The Twenty-First-Century University and the Market: What Price Economic Viability?" *Differences* 12: 1–16.

Pozsar, Z., T. Adrian, et al. (2012). "Shadow Banking." Federal Reserve Bank of New York Staff Report No. 458.

Prattis, I. J. (1973). "The State of the Arts in Economic Anthropology: Reflections on a Theme." *Canadian Review of Sociology and Anthropology* Special issue, 10 (3): 193–98.

Preda, A. (2009). *Framing Finance: The Boundaries of Markets and Modern Capitalism*, Chicago, University of Chicago Press.

Prelec, D. and G. Loewenstein (1998). "The Red and the Black: Mental Accounting of Savings and Debt." *Marketing Science* 17 (1): 4–28.

Proudhon, J.-F. (1927). *Proudhon's Solution of the Social Problem*, New York, Vanguard Press.

Pryor, F. L. (1977). *The Origins of the Economy: Comparative Study of Distribution in Primitive and Peasant Economies*, New York, Academic Press.

Pyyhtinen, O. (2010). *Simmel and "The Social,"* Basingstoke, U.K., Palgrave Macmillan.

Quiggin, A. H. (1949). *A Survey of Primitive Money: The Beginnings of Currency*, London, Methuen.

Rajan, R. G. (2005). "Remarks on Global Current Account Imbalances and Financial Sector Reform with Examples from China." Speech at Cato Institute, Washington, DC, November 3.

Rajan, R. G. (2011). *Fault Lines: How Hidden Fractures Still Threaten the World Economy*, Princeton, NJ, Princeton University Press.
Rand, A. (2007). *Atlas Shrugged*, London, Penguin.
Rankin, K. N. (2001). "Governing Development: Neoliberalism, Microcredit, and Rational Economic Woman." *Economy and Society* 30 (1): 18–37.
Rasmus, J. (2010). *Epic Recession: Prelude to Global Depression*, London, Pluto Press.
Rawls, J. (2001). *The Law of Peoples*, Cambridge, MA, Harvard University Press.
Reinhart, C. M. and K. S. Rogoff (2009). *This Time Is Different: Eight Centuries of Financial Folly*, Princeton, NJ, Princeton University Press.
Ricardo, D. (1821). *On The Principles of Political Economy and Taxation*, London, John Murray.
Richardson, J. (2002). *Nietzsche's System*, Oxford, U.K., Oxford University Press.
Rickards, J. (2011). *Currency Wars: The Making of the Next Global Crisis*, New York, Portfolio/Penguin.
Riegel, E. C. (1944). *Private Enterprise Money: A Non-Political Money System*, New York, Harbinger House.
Riegel, E. C. (1976). *The New Approach to Freedom*, Los Angeles, Heather Foundation.
Riegel, E. C. (1978). *Flight from Inflation: The Monetary Alternative*, Los Angeles, The Heather Foundation.
Risse, T. (2003). "The Euro between National and European Identity." *Journal of European Public Policy* 10 (4): 487–505.
Risse, T., D. Engelmann-Martin, et al. (1999). "To Euro or Not to Euro? The EMU and Identity Politics in the European Union." *European Journal of International Relations* 5 (2): 147–87.
Robertson, J. (2012). *Future Money: Breakdown or Breakthrough?* Cambridge, U.K., Green Books.
Robertson, J. M. (1892). *The Fallacy of Saving: A Study in Economics*, London/New York, S. Sonnenschein/Scribner's.
Roitman, J. (2003). "Unsanctioned Wealth; or, The Productivity of Debt in Northern Cameroon." *Public Culture* 15: 211–37.
Rorty, R. (1989). *Contingency, Irony and Solidarity*, Cambridge, U.K., Cambridge University Press.
Rotman, B. (1993). *Signifying Nothing: The Semiotics of Zero*, Stanford, CA, Stanford University Press.
Roubini, N. (2010). "Medicine for Europe's Sinking South." *Financial Times* (London). February 2.
Rousseau, J.-J. (1991). *Emile; or On Education*, Harmondsworth, U.K., Penguin Classics.
Rousseau, J.-J. (2004). *The Social Contract or Principles of Political Right*, Whitefish, MT, Kessinger Publishing.
Rousseau, J.-J. and J. G. Herder (1966). *On the Origin of Language: Two Essays*, Chicago, University of Chicago Press.
Rowbotham, M. (1998). *The Grip of Death: A Study of Modern Money, Debt Slavery and Destructive Economics*, Charlbury, U.K., Jon Carpenter Publishing.
Roxburgh, C., S. Lund, et al. (2010). *Debt and Deleveraging: The Global Credit Bubble and Its Economic Consequences*, San Francisco and Shanghai, McKinsey Global Institute.
Ruskin, J. (1928). *Time and Tide and Munera Pulveris*, London, Macmillan.
Ruskin, J. (1997). *Unto This Last and Other Writings*, Harmondsworth, U.K., Penguin.
Russell, E. F. (1993). *The Great Explosion*, New York, Carroll and Graf.
Rutledge, E. J. (2009). *Monetary Union in the Gulf: Prospects for a Single Currency in the Arabian Peninsula*, London, Routledge.
Ryan-Collins, J., T. Greenham, et al. (2012). *Where Does Money Come From?* London, New Economics Foundation.
Sahlins, M. D. (1972). *Stone Age Economics*, New York: Aldine de Gruyter.
Sandel, M. (2012). *What Money Can't Buy: The Moral Limits of Markets*, London, Allen Lane.

Sarthou-Lajus, N. (1997). *L'Ethique de la Dette,* Paris, Presses Universitaires de France.
Sassen, S. (1991). *Global City: New York, London, Tokyo,* Princeton, NJ, Princeton University Press.
Sassen, S. (1999). "Whose City Is It? Globalization and the Formation of New Claims." *Sustainable Cities in the 21st Century,* A. F. Foo and B. K. P. Yuen, Eds. Singapore, Singapore University Press: 145–62.
Sassen, S. (2009). "Cities in Today's Global Age." *SAIS Review* XXIX (1): 3–32.
Saussure, see de Saussure.
Say, J.-B. (2001). *A Treatise on Political Economy,* Piscataway, NJ, Transaction Publishers.
Schäuble, W. (2010). "Why Europe's Monetary Union Faces Its Biggest Crisis." *Financial Times* (London), March 11.
Schmitt, C. (1991). *Theodor Däubler's "Nordlicht": Drei Studien über die Elemente, den Geist und die Aktualität des Werkes,* Berlin, Duncker u. Humblot GmbH.
Schmitt, C. (1994). *Die Diktatur,* Berlin, Duncker u. Humblot.
Schmitt, C. (2003). *The Nomos of the Earth: In the International Law of the Jus Publicum Europaeum,* Candor, NY, Telos Press.
Schmitt, C. (2004). *Der Wert des Staates und die Bedeutung des Einzelnen,* Berlin, Duncker & Humblot GmbH.
Schmitt, C. (2006). *Political Theology: Four Chapters on the Concept of Sovereignty,* Chicago, University of Chicago Press.
Schmitt, C. (2007). *The Concept of the Political,* Chicago, University of Chicago Press.
Schmitt, C. (2014) *Dictatorship,* Cambridge, U.K., Polity Press.
Scholem, G. (1971). *The Messianic Idea in Judaism,* New York, Schocken Books.
Schopenhauer, A. (1966). *The World as Will and Representation, Vol. 2,* New York, Dover Publications.
Schumpeter, J. A. (1986). *History of Economic Analysis,* London, Routledge.
Schumpeter, J. A. (1991). "Money and Currency." *Social Research*: 504–43.
Schumpeter, J. A. (2003). *Capitalism, Socialism and Democracy,* London, Routledge.
Schumpeter, J. A. (2008). *The Theory of Economic Development,* New Brunswick, NJ, Transaction Publishers.
Scott, B. (2014). "Crypto-Patriarchy: The Problem of Bitcoin's Male Domination." *The Heretic's Guide to Global Finance: Hacking the Future of Money,* January 12, http://suitpossum.blogspot.co.uk/2014/01/crypto-patriarchy-problem-of-bitcoins.html.
Scott, C. (1966). "The Obsolete 'Anti-Market' Mentality: A Critique of the Substantive Approach to Economic Anthropology." *American Anthropologist* 68: 323–45.
Scott, C. (1969). "The Anti-Market Mentality Re-Examined: A Further Critique of the Substantive Approach to Economic Anthropology." *Southwestern Journal of Anthropology* 25: 378–406.
Scott, C. (1973). Economic Anthropology: Problems in Theory, Method, and Analysis. *Handbook of Social and Cultural Anthropology,* J. J. Honigmann, Ed. Chicago, Rand McNally.
Seaford, R. (2004). *Money and the Early Greek Mind,* Cambridge, U.K., Cambridge University Press.
Semenova, A. (2011). "Would You Barter with God? Why Holy Debts and Not Profane Markets Created Money." *American Journal of Economics and Sociology* 70 (2): 376–400.
Seyfang, G. (2001). "Community currencies: small change for a green economy." *Environment and Planning A* 33 (6): 975–96.
Seyfang, G. (2002). "Tackling Social Exclusion with Community Currencies: Learning from LETS to Time Banks." *International Journal of Community Currency Research* 6 (3): 1–11, http://ijccr.net/2012/05/23/tackling-social-exclusion-with-community-currencies-learning-from-lets-to-time-banks/.
Seyfang, G. (2004a). "Time Banks: Rewarding Community Self-Help in the Inner City?" *Community Development Journal* 39 (1): 62–71.

Seyfang, G. (2004b). "Working Outside the Box: Community Currencies, Time Banks and Social Inclusion." *Journal of Social Policy* 33 (1): 49–71.
Shell, M. (1978). *The Economy of Literature*, Baltimore, Johns Hopkins University Press.
Shiller, R. J. (2008). *The Subprime Solution*, Princeton, NJ, Princeton University Press.
Shipton, P. (1991). "Time and Money in the Western Sahel: A Clash of Cultures in Gambian Local Rural Finance." *Markets in Developing Countries: Parallel, Fragmented and Black*, M. Roemer and C. Jones, Eds. Washington, DC/San Francisco, ICS Press: 113–39.
Shipton, P. (1995). "How Gambians Save: Culture and Economic Strategy at an Ethnic Crossroads." *Money Matters: Instability, Values and Social Payments in the Modern History of West African Communities*, J. Guyer, Ed. Portsmouth, NH, Heinemann: 245–76.
Simiand, F. (1934). "La Monnaie, Réalité Sociale." *Les Annales Sociologiques* 1: 1–58.
Simmel, G. (1902). "Tendencies in German Life and Thought Since 1870." *Englischsprachige Veröffentlichungen 1893–1910*, D. Frisby, Ed. Berlin, Suhrkamp: 167–202.
Simmel, G. (1968). "Sociological Aesthetics." *Georg Simmel: The Conflict in Modern Culture and Other Essays*, P. K. Etzkorn, Ed. New York, Teachers College Press: 68–80.
Simmel, G. (1991a). "Money in Modern Culture." *Theory, Culture & Society* 8: 17–31.
Simmel, G. (1991b). *Schopenhauer and Nietzsche*, Champaign, University of Illinois Press.
Simmel, G. (1997). *Simmel on Culture: Selected Writings*, London, Sage.
Simmel, G. (2002). "The Metropolis and Mental Life." *The Blackwell City Reader*, G. Bridge and S. Watson, Eds. Oxford, U.K., and Malden, MA, Wiley-Blackwell: 11–19.
Simmel, G. (2004). *The Philosophy of Money: Third Enlarged Edition*, London, Routledge.
Simmel, G. (2009). *Sociology: Inquiries into the Construction of Social Forms*, Leiden, Germany, Brill.
Simons, H. C. (1948). *Economic Policy for a Free Society*, Chicago, University of Chicago Press.
Sinn, H.-W. and T. Wollmershäuser (2011). "Target Loans, Current Account Balances and Capital Flows: The ECB's Rescue Facility." *International Tax and Public Finance* 19 (4), 468–508.
Sitton, J. F., Ed. (2010). *Marx Today: Selected Works and Recent Debates*, New York, Palgrave Macmillan.
Skidelsky, R. and E. Skidelsky (2012). *How Much Is Enough? The Love of Money, and the Case for the Good Life*, London, Allen Lane.
Smith, A. (2007). *The Theory of Moral Sentiments*, New York, Cosimo Classics.
Smith, A. (2008). *An Inquiry into the Nature and Causes of the Wealth of Nations*, Oxford, U.K., Oxford University Press.
Smith, D. W. (2003). "Deleuze and Derrida, Immanence and Transcendence: Two Directions in Recent French Thought." *Between Deleuze and Derrida*, P. Patton and J. Protevi, Eds. London, Continuum: 46–66.
Smith, D. W. (2012). *Essays on Deleuze*, Edinburgh, Scotland, Edinburgh University Press.
Smith, T. R., Ed. (1919). *Baudelaire: His Prose and Poetry*, New York, The Modern Library.
Smithin, J. (2008). "The Rate of Interest, Monetary Policy, and the Concept of 'Thrift.'" *International Journal of Political Economy* 37 (2): 26–48.
Sontag, S. (2009). *Illness as a Metaphor and AIDS and Its Metaphors*, London, Penguin.
Soros, G. (2009). "The Eurozone Needs a Government Bond Market." *Financial Times* (London). February 18.
Spannos, C. (2008). *Real Utopia: Participatory Society for the 21st Century*, Oakland, CA, AK Press.
Sperber, J. (2013). *Karl Marx: A Nineteenth-Century Life*, New York/London, W. W. Norton and Co.
Spiegel, H. W., Ed. (1991). *The Growth of Economic Thought*, 3rd ed., Durham, NC, Duke University Press.
Spinoza, B. (1996). *Ethics*. London, Penguin.
Staudt, K. (1998). *Free Trade? Informal Economies at the U.S.–Mexico Border*, Philadelphia, Temple University Press.

Steiner, P. (2008). "Who Is Right about the Modern Economy: Polanyi, Zelizer, or Both?" *Theory and Society* 38 (1): 97–110.
Stephens, H. M. (1915). "Nationality and History." Annual address of the president of the American Historical Association, Washington, DC, December 28, *American Historical Review* 21 (2): 225–36.
Stephenson, N. (1994). *The Diamond Age*, London, Penguin.
Stephenson, N. (1999). *Cryptonomicon*, London, Random House.
Stigum, M. and A. Crescenzi (2007). *Stigum's Money Market*, 4th ed., Toronto, McGraw-Hill.
Stoekl, A. (2007). *Bataille's Peak: Energy, Religion, and Postsustainability*, Minneapolis, University of Minnesota Press.
Strange, S. (1986). *Casino Capitalism*, Manchester, U.K., Manchester University Press.
Strange, S. (1994a). "From Bretton Woods to the Casino Economy." *Money, Power and Space*, S. Corbridge, R. Martin, and N. Thrift, Eds. Oxford, U.K., Blackwell: 49–62.
Strange, S. (1994b). *States and Markets*, London and New York, Continuum.
Strange, S. (1998a). *Mad Money*, Manchester, U.K., Manchester University Press.
Strange, S. (1998b). "What Theory? The Theory in *Mad Money*." Centre for the Study of Globalisation and Regionalisation Working Paper No. 18/98, Coventry, U.K., University of Warwick.
Strange, S. (1999). "The Westfailure System." *Review of International Studies* 25 (3): 345–54.
Strathern, M. (1992). "Qualified Value: The Perspective of Gift Exchange." *Barter, Exchange and Value: An Anthropological Approach*, C. Humphrey and S. Hugh-Jones, Eds. Cambridge, U.K., Cambridge University Press: 169–91.
Streeck, W. (2011). "The Crises of Democratic Capitalism." *New Left Review* 71: 5–29.
Streeck, W. (2013). "The Construction of a Moral Duty for the Greek People to Repay Their National Debt." *Moral Categories in the Financial Crisis*, M. Fourcade, P. Steiner, W. Streeck, and C. Woll, Eds. Paris, Max Planck Sciences Po Center on Coping with Instability in Market Societies: 14–20.
Stuckler, D. and S. Basu (2013). *The Body Economic: Why Austerity Kills*, New York, Basic Books.
Stuckler, D., S. Basu, et al. (2011). "Effects of the 2008 Financial Crisis on Health: A First Look at European Data." *Lancet* 378: 124–25.
Swedberg, R. (1991). *Joseph A. Schumpeter: His Life and Work*, Cambridge, U.K., Polity Press.
Swedberg, R. (2000). *Max Weber and the Idea of Economic Sociology*, Princeton, NJ, Princeton University Press.
Swedberg, R. (2003). "Answer to Geoffrey Ingham." *Journal of Classical Sociology* 3 (3): 311–14.
Szabo, N. (2008). "Bit Gold." http://unenumerated.blogspot.co.uk/2005/12/bit-gold.html, accessed November 2, 2012.
Taibbi, M. (2010). *Griftopia: Bubble Machines, Vampire Squids, and the Long Con That Is Breaking America*, New York, Spiegel and Grau.
Thaler, R. (1999). "Mental Accounting Matters." *Journal of Behavioral Decision Making* 12 (3): 183–206.
Thiemann, C., F. Theis, et al. (2010). "The Structure of Borders in a Small World." *PLoS ONE* 5 (11): e15422. doi:15410.11371/journal.pone.0015422.
Thilenius, G. (1921). "Primitives Geld." *Archiv für Anthropologie* 18: 1–34.
Thompson, E. P. (1971). "The Moral Economy of the English Crowd in the 18th Century." *Past and Present* 50 (1): 76–136.
Thoreau, H. D. (1995). *Walden: Or, Life in the Woods*, New York, Dover Publications Inc.
Titmuss, R. (1971). *The Gift Relationship*, New York, Vintage Press.
Tognato, C. (2012). *Central Bank Independence: Cultural Codes and Symbolic Performance*, New York, Palgrave Macmillan.
Toscano, A. (2010) "Axiomatic." *The Deleuze Dictionary Revised Edition*, A. Parr, Ed. Edinburgh, Edinburgh University Press: 21–23.

Trachtman, R. (1999). "The Money Taboo: Its Effects in Everyday Life and in the Practice of Psychotherapy." *Clinical Social Work Journal* 27 (3): 275–88.
Truman, E. M. (2010). *Sovereign Wealth Funds: Threat or Salvation?* Washington DC, Peterson Institute for International Economics.
Tsoukalis, L. (2012). "Greece in the Euro Area: Odd Man Out, or Precursor of Things to Come?" *Resolving the European Debt Crisis*, W. R. Cline and G. B. Wolff, Eds. Brussels, Belgium, Peter G. Peterson Institute for International Economics: 19–35.
Turgot, A.-R.-J. (1999). *The Formation and Distribution of Wealth: Reflections on Capitalism*, London, Othila Press.
Turkel, R. A. (1988). "Money as a Mirror of Marriage." *Journal of the American Academy of Psychoanalysis* 16: 525–35.
Turner, J. A. (2009). *The Turner Review: A Regulatory Response to the Global Banking Crisis*, London, Financial Services Authority.
Twain, M. (1957). *The Complete Short Stories of Mark Twain*, C. Neider, Ed. New York, Bantam Dell.
Varul, M. Z. (2006). "Waste, Industry and Romantic Leisure: Veblen's Theory of Recognition." *European Journal of Social Theory* 9 (1): 103–17.
Veblen, T. (2009). *The Theory of the Leisure Class: An Economic Study of Institutions*, Oxford, U.K., Oxford University Press.
Velthuis, O. (2005). *Talking Prices: Symbolic Meanings of Prices on the Market for Contemporary Art*, Princeton, NJ, Princeton University Press.
Vercellone, C. (2010). "The Crisis of Value and the Becoming-Rent of Profit." *Crisis in the Global Economy: Financial Markets, Social Struggles, and New Political Scenarios*, A. Fumagalli and S. Mezzadra, Eds. Los Angeles, Semiotext(e): 85–118.
Vilar, P. (2011). *A History of Gold and Money: 1450–1920*, London, Verso.
Virno, P. (2004). *A Grammar of the Multitude*, Los Angeles, Semiotext(e).
von Chamisso, A. (2008). *Peter Schlemihl*, Richmond, U.K., Oneworld Classics.
von Mises, L. (1998). *Human Action: A Treatise on Economics*, Auburn, AL, Ludwig von Mises Institute.
Wade, R. (2009). "Iceland as Icarus." *Challenge* May–June, 52 (3): 5–33.
Warburton, P. (1999). *Debt and Delusion: Central Bank Follies That Threaten Economic Disaster*, London, Allen Lane.
Weber, F. (2001). "Settings, Interactions and Things: A Plea for a Multi-integrative Ethnography." *Ethnography* 2 (4): 475–99.
Weber, M. (1958). "Religious Rejections of the World and Their Directions." *From Max Weber: Essays in Sociology*, H. H. Gerth and C. Wright Mills, Eds. New York: Oxford University Press: 323–61.
Weber, M. (1978). *Economy and Society*, Berkeley and Los Angeles, University of California Press.
Weber, M. (2001). *The Protestant Ethic and the Spirit of Capitalism*, London, Routledge.
Wendt, A. (1992). "Anarchy is what states make of it: The social construction of power politics." *International Organization* 46 (2): 391–425.
Wherry, F. F. (2008). "The Social Characterizations of Price: The Fool, the Faithful, the Frivolous, and the Frugal." *Sociological Theory* 26 (4): 363–79.
Wichterich, C. (2012). "The Other Financial Crisis: Growth and Crash of the Microfinance Sector in India." *Development* 55 (3): 406–12.
Wilson, K. and M. Levin (2010). *Savings and Chance: Learning from the Lottery to Improve Financial Services in Haiti*, Medford, MA, Feinstein International Center, July 20.
Winner, L. (1985). "Do Artifacts Have Politics?" *The Social Shaping of Technology*, D. Mackenzie and J. Wajcman, Eds. Buckingham, U.K., Open University Press: 28–40.
Wittgenstein, L. (2007). *Zettel*, Berkeley and Los Angeles, University of California Press.
Wolf, M. (2010). *Fixing Global Finance*, New Haven, CT/London, Yale University Press.

Wolff, K. H., Ed. (1950). *The Sociology of Georg Simmel,* New York, The Free Press.
Wolman, D. (2012). *The End of Money: Counterfeiters, Preachers, Techies, Dreamers—and the Coming Cashless Society,* Philadelphia, Da Capo Press.
Wray, L. R. (1998). "Modern Money." Jerome Levy Economics Institute, Working Paper No. 74, Annandale-on-Hudson, NY, Levy Economics Institute of Bard College. www.levyinstitute.org/pubs/wp252.pdf.
Wray, L. R. (2004a). "Conclusion: The Credit Money and State Money Approaches." *Credit and State Theories of Money: The Contributions of A. Mitchell Innes,* Cheltenham, U.K., Edward Elgar Publishing: 223–62.
Wray, L. R., Ed. (2004b). *Credit and State Theories of Money: The Contributions of A. Mitchell Innes,* Cheltenham, U.K., Edward Elgar Publishing.
Wray, L. R. (2006). *Understanding Modern Money,* Cheltenham, U.K., Edward Elgar Publishing.
Wray, L. R. (2010). "A Minskian Explanation of the Causes of the Currrent Crisis." *Multiplier Effect: The Levy Economics Institute Blog,* Bard College, Annandale-on-Hudson, NY, http://multiplier-effect.org/?cat=25.
Wray, L. R. (2012). *Modern Money Theory: A Primer on Macroeconomics for Sovereign Monetary Systems,* Basingstoke, U.K., and New York: Macmillan.
Wright, E. O.(2010). *Envisioning Real Utopias,* London, Verso.
Wuthnow, R. (1996). *Poor Richard's Principle: Recovering the American Dream through the Moral Dimension of Work, Business, and Money,* Princeton, NJ, Princeton University Press.
Yaron, R. (1988). *The Laws of Eshnunna,* Leiden, Germany, Brill.
Yarrow, A. L. (2008). *Forgive Us Our Debts: The Intergenerational Dangers of Fiscal Irresponsibility,* New Haven, CT/London, Yale University Press.
Young, J. (2010). *Friedrich Nietzsche: A Philosophical Biography,* Cambridge, U.K., Cambridge University Press.
Zaloom, C. (2003). "Ambiguous Numbers: Trading Technologies and Interpretation in Financial Markets." *American Ethnologist* 30 (2): 258–72.
Zarlenga, S. A. (2002). *The Lost Science of Money,* Valatie, NY, American Monetary Institute Charitable Trust.
Zazzaro, A. (2002). "How Heterodox Is the Heterodoxy of the Monetary Circuit Theory? The Nature of Money and the Microeconomy of the Circuit." Università Politecnica delle Marche (I), Dipartimento di Scienze Economiche e Sociali, working paper, Ancona, Italy.
Zbaracki, M. J. and M. Bergen (2008). "Pricing Structure and Structuring Price." Alfred P. Sloan Foundation Industry Studies Annual Conference 2008, Boston, web.mit.edu/is08/pdf/Zbaracki.pdf.
Zelizer, V. A. (1978). "Human Values and the Market: The Case of Life Insurance and Death in Nineteenth-Century America." *American Journal of Sociology* 84 (3): 591–610.
Zelizer, V. A. (1981). "The Price and Value of Children: The Case of Children's Insurance." *American Journal of Sociology* 86 (5): 1036–56.
Zelizer, V. A. (1985). *Pricing the Priceless Child: The Changing Social Value of Children,* New York, Basic Books.
Zelizer, V. A. (1997). *The Social Meaning of Money: Pin Money, Paychecks, Poor Relief, and Other Currencies,* Princeton, NJ, Princeton University Press.
Zelizer, V. A. (2004). "Circuits of Commerce." *Self, Social Structure and Beliefs: Explorations in Sociology,* J. C. Alexander, G. T. Marx, and C. Williams, Eds. Berkeley, University of California Press: 122–44.
Zelizer, V. A. (2005a). "Circuits within Capitalism." *The Economic Sociology of Capitalism,* V. Nee and R. Swedberg, Eds. Princeton, NJ, Princeton University Press: 289–322.
Zelizer, V. A. (2005b). *The Purchase of Intimacy,* Princeton, NJ, Princeton University Press.
Zelizer, V. A. (2006a). "Circuits in Economic Life." *European Economic Sociology Newsletter* 8 (1): 30–35.

Zelizer, V. A. (2006b). "Do Markets Poison Intimacy?" *Contexts* 5 (2): 33–38.
Zelizer, V. A. (2011). *Economic Lives: How Culture Shapes the Economy*, Princeton, NJ, Princeton University Press.
Zelizer, V. A. (2012). "How I Became a Relational Economic Sociologist and What Does That Mean?" *Politics and Society* 40 (2): 145–74.
Žižek, S. (2004). "The Parallax View." *New Left Review* 25 (January–February): 219–35.
Žižek, S. (2009). *First as Tragedy, Then as Farce*, London, Verso.
Zuckoff, M. (2006). *Ponzi's Scheme: The True Story of a Financial Legend*, New York, Random House.

INDEX

Aberhart, William, 357
Abeille, 350
abundance, age of, 155; and God, 176; monetary, 372; versus scarcity, 176
accumulation by dispossession, 63, 66, 68, 243. *See also* primitive accumulation
accursed share (*part maudite*), 164, 202, 203, 204; defined, 176
actor network theory, 296
Adorno, Theodor, 7, 172n, 326
Agamben, Giorgio, 7, 42, 260, 266–67, 388; on bare life (*la nuda vita*), 266; on the camp, 267n; on crisis, 260, 266; on the exception, 267; *Means Without End*, 266
Aglietta, Michel, 43–46, 250, 389
Akin, David, 292
alchemy, 56n, 154
Alexander, Jeffrey, 16
allegory, 35n26, 143, 153, 161, 165, 184, 186, 187
Allen, John, 233, 277–78
Althusser, Louis, *Reading Capital*, 229
Ambrosino, Georges, 172n
American Civil War, 212
American Express, 377
Americanization, 299
American Monetary Institute, 113
Amis, Martin, 171
Amsterdam Council, 254
anarchism, 100, 313; and *Autonomia Operaia*, 72; and Bitcoin, 369n; and capitalism, 61, 68; in financial markets, 199; and the free market, 298, 299; in Hardt and Negri, 239; and Proudhon, 357; and utopia, 313, 331, 357, 381. *See also* crypto-anarchy
Anaximander, 145
Andersen, Gavin, 369–70
animal spirits, 45
anthropology, 7, 39, 164, 269, 390; cultural, 297; of money, 279, 285, 294, 295

Apollo, 136, 154, 155
Aquinas, Thomas, 314, 325, 327, 337
Aqoba, 365
Arab Spring, 2–3
arbitrage, 301, 303
Arendt, Hannah, 151
Argentina, alternative monies, 316; insolvency crisis, 69, 148, 392
Aristotle, 17, 27n17, 39n35, 223, 337; *The Nicomachean Ethics*, 93
Arrighi, Giovanni, 61n22
Arrow-Debreu general equilibrium model, 111n
art, 17, 202
art auction, 202
art market, 201
assemblage, 238
asset relief program, 116
association, in Karatani, 84; in Simmel, 84n42
Atkins, Ralph, 206n39
Auster, Paul, 35
austerity, 90, 126–32, 133, 134; and debt, 388; and the destruction of capital, 88; and economic recovery, 21; economic and monetary policies in support of, 3, 5, 22, 88; effects of, 382; and financial repression, 69; forced, 75–76, 77; government programs in pursuit of, 2, 70, 78, 90, 388; and guilt, 256; and neurosis, 153, 159; the politics of, 92, 153; and restricted economy, 208
'Austrian' theory of money, 5, 17, 362, 368
authority, market, 220
Autonomia Operaia, 72–73, 240–41, 246
Autonomism. *See Autonomia Operaia*
Ayer, Alfred Jules, 36n

Babb, Sarah, 211–12
Babylonia, 23–24
Bailey, Samuel, 84

421

INDEX

bailout, banking, 100, 116, 127, 128, 130, 131, 254, 256; of Continental Illinois, 119; and debt jubilee, 202
Baja Beach Club, 377
Bakunin, Mikhail, 357
Balibar, Étienne, on Europe, 261–62, 262–63; *Reading Capital*, 229; on sovereignty, 262; *We, The People of Europe?*, 261
Banco Bilbao Vizcaya Argentaria (BBVA), 257
Banco Centro do Brasil, 15, 20n
Bank of America, 380n
Bank of England, 2, 66n27, 107, 109, 113, 115, 122, 130, 314n2, 373
Bank of France, 352
Bank of Japan, 2, 131n57
Bank of the People, 352, 354, 360, 361
banking, 12, 68, 105, 111–12; bailout, 100, 116, 127, 128, 130, 131, 254, 256; concentration, 114; crises, 111; in Deleuze and Guattari, 234–5; and GDP, 114; in Hilferding, 60; investment, 116, 123, 124, 133n; in Marx, 55, 56; merchant, 116; in microeconomic theory, 111; and money creation, 87, 95, 112–13, 374; narrow, 133; and the New York fiscal crisis, 75; and religion, 156; and speculation, 118; and the state, 102, 106, 236, 382; universal, 116; and utopia, 316. *See also* disintermediation; intermediation; shadow banking
banknotes, 35n27, 36, 373, 387; fake, 200; in Benjamin, 42, 143; in Keynes, 178; in Marx, 55; in Proudhon, 352–54; in Twain, 185
bankocracy, 64, 66
bankruptcy. *See* insolvency
Baptiste, Espelencia, 303
Barclays, 221
bare life, 249–50, 266
barter, 17, 230, 326, 342; and the double coincidence of wants, 17–18, 19, 21, 314n2; ethnographic evidence of, 19; and the evolution of money, 18–20, 21, 22, 26, 96, 359; inefficiency of, 19–20; and LETS, 85, 86; in Marx, 53; versus monetary exchange, 19–20, 42–43; and sacrifice, 25
Barthes, Roland, 34
Bashō, Matsuo, 331
Bataille, Georges, 13, 151, 166–79, 196, 200, 202, 205, 209; on the accursed share, 164, 176; *The Accursed Share*, 166, 176, 195; on antiutilitarianism, 167, 168; on base materialism, 164, 167, 169–70, 172; *Documents*, 169; on energy, 173, 177, 183, 192; on gambling, 175; on gift exchange, 176, 195–6; on heterogeneous matter, 164, 167, 169–70, 172, 209; on heterology, 169, 170; on life, 174–75; on the Marshall Plan, 207–8; and Mauss, 165; on money, 170, 173–75; *On Nietzsche*, 175; "The Notion of Expenditure," 171; on potlatch, 172; "The Psychological Structure of Fascism," 173–74; on religion, 175–76; on the sacred, 165, 167, 168, 172–73, 175, 176; on sacrifice 167, 168; on social homogeneity, 174; "The Sorcerer's Apprentice," 173, 174; *The Trial of Gilles de Rais*, 165; on unproductive expenditure, 167, 170, 171–72, 177–78, 179, 183; "The Use Value of D. A. F. de Sade," 163, 170. *See also* general economy; restricted economy
Baudelaire, Charles, 35, 141; on debt, 184; "The Double Room," 184–5; "La Fausse Monnaie" ("Counterfeit Money"), 182–84, 209; *Fusées*, 209–10; "Get Drunk," 185n; *Intimate Journals*, 182; on money, 182, 184–85; *The Painter of Modern Life*, 184; on prostitution and gambling, 165; *Le Spleen de Paris*, 182, 184; on time, 184–85
Baudrillard, Jean, 13, 189–204, 386; and Bataille, 165; on the clone, 165; on cool money, 193–94, 391; on debt, 201–2; on de Saussure, 190–91; end of political economy, 191; on fetish money, 195; on floating money, 191, 244; *For a Critique of the Political Economy of the Sign*, 202; on the fractal stage of value, 189, 193; "Global Debt and Parallel Universe," 201; on hyperreality, 193; "Hypotheses on Terrorism," 197; on impossible exchange, 198, 203; on inflation, 192–93, 209; on the law of value, 189, 190; on Marx, 190–91, 192, 195; on Mauss, 165; on money, 194–95, 199–200, 202–3; on money and language, 190; on overaccumulation, 192; on the political economy of signs, 35; on the reality principle, 190, 191–92, 202, 209; *Seduction*, 202; on seduction, 194; on sign value, 191; on

simulation, 195; on symbolic exchange, 192, 195–96; *Symbolic Exchange and Death*, 191
Beckert, Jens, 16, 280
becoming rent of the profit, 243
Benda, Julien, 172n
Benjamin, Walter, 5, 12, 34–35, 142–49, 153, 155, 156, 165, 172n, 195, 201, 247, 274; on allegory, 35n26, 143; on the angel of history, 148n; *The Arcades Project*, 143; on banknotes, 42, 143; on Baudelaire, 141; "Capitalism as Religion," 136, 143–49, 342; on conventional history, 144–5; "Critique of Violence," 266; on cult versus theology, 143–44; on debt, 143, 231; on debt and guilt, 91, 144–45, 159; on eternal recurrence, 141, 144; "Fate and Character," 144, 266; on guilt history, 144–45, 147, 156; on the guilty God, 146, 147, 148, 158, 168n; "The Meaning of Time in the Moral Universe," 144–45; on mere life (*das bloße Leben*), 266; on Messianic time; 335; on money and fate, 143; on money and time, 145; on Nietzsche, 143, 390; "One-Way Street," 142, 224; *The Origin of German Tragic Drama*, 146; on the religious structure of capitalism, 143–44, 159; on *Schuld*, 144, 146; on the temporal structure of capitalism, 144; on *Übermensch*, 148–49, 391–92; on the Weimar inflation, 142–43
"Beowulf," 385, 386
Berardi, Franco, 72
Bergen, Mark, 17
Bhagwati, Jagdish, 206
Bibliothèque Nationale, 165
Biersteker, Thomas J, 220
bill of exchange, 105, 108, 217; in Simmel, 125
Binswanger, Hans Christoph, 56n
biology, 228
biopolitics, 238, 248
biopower, 239–40, 249
Birch, David, 314n2
bit gold, 363
Bitcoin, 9, 14, 43n, 47, 213, 214, 292, 315, 316, 362–72, 380; anonymity of, 310; burning of, 204–5; and China, 368n34; and deflation, 362, 368; and democracy, 369, 370; demography of, 369n; energy costs of, 367; and gold, 362, 368; and hoarding, 370; and horizontalism, 379–80; and libertarianism, 105; and Ponzi finance, 368; and price crashes, 21–22; price of, 21–22; as a rival to state currency, 9, 227, 369; and scarcity, 21; success as money, 22; and trust, 362, 364, 369, 371
Bitcoin Foundation, 369
Blackstone Group, 221n11
Blanc, Jérôme, 292–93
Bloch, Ernst, 315
Block, Fred, 279
B-money, 363
BNP Paribas, 257
Böcklin, Arnold, 140
Bodin, Jean, 223–24; *Response to the Paradoxes of Malestroit*, 318 *Six Books of the Commonwealth*, 261; on sovereignty, 261–62
Bohannan, Paul, 283–84, 285, 292, 302
bonds, 108, 118n, 122, 126, 127; Bowie, 194; city, 75; Eurozone, 257, 258n38; government, 58, 69, 91, 107, 110, 129n52, 130, 133n, 206n39, 257, 267; in Marx, 64; and money, 392; treasury, 74
Borges, Jorge Louis, 10, 200, 385, 393, 394
Bourdieu, Pierre, 46, 91n, 292
Boyd, Stowe, 227
Braudel, Fernand, 61n22
Breton, André, 169, 331; *Second Manifesto of Surrealism*, 169, 313, 314
Bretton Woods, 45, 70, 71, 72, 74–76, 78, 79, 88, 98–99, 122, 192, 194, 207, 220, 236, 245, 298–99
BRICS economies, 89, 214
Brixton Pound, 380
Brown, Norman, 12, 136, 142, 149–58, 196; on Bataille, 205; on culture, 150; on history and neurosis, 149, 336, 342; on immortality, 153; *Life Against Death*, 149, 154; on money and bodily waste, 151–52; on money, capitalism, and guilt, 150–51, 153, 156, 159; on the money complex, 150, 154, 156, 158, 229, 351; on Nietzsche, 152, 154–55, 156; on sacred money, 155–56, 389
Bruegger, Urs, 230, 293
Bruno, Giordano, 169
Bryan, Dick, 62, 198
Bukharin, Nikolai, 60–61
Burckhardt, Jacob, 247
business cycle, 76, 111, 117

Cable, Vince, 50
Caffentizis, George, 219
Cahn, Edgar, 342
Caillois, Roger, 172n
calculation, 125; of gifts, 187–88; of money, 17, 34, 217, 287, 295–98, 301, 302, 303, 305; and restricted economy, 207; in Simmel, 324; and socialism, 329; and symbolic exchange, 198
Caldwell, Mike, 369
Callon, Michel, 292
Cameroon, 301
Campanella, Tommaso, 321–22
Canadian Social Credit Movement, 357
capital, 80, as an axiomatic, 232; fixed, 67; illusory, 69; interest-bearing, 56, 154; and money, 64, 67, 70; in Proudhon, 352–53; self-expanding, 55, 57n18, 58, 82, 83, 154; surplus, 68; synthesis of, 81; and time, 234
capital controls, 207
capital reserve requirements, 121
capitalism, 2, 10, 12, 14, 100; in Baudrillard, 191–92; casino, 122, 132; catastrophic stage of, 195; cognitive, 75–76, 241, 249; and colonialism, 60; in crisis, 67, 81; and debt, 5, 12; debt history of, 145, 146; in Deleuze and Guattari, 230; disorganized, 298; and eternal recurrence, 141; financial, 41, 51, 64, 68, 166, 392; and the financial crisis, 50, 135; and financial instability, 117; and the financial system, 3; global, 197; and guilt, 145, 156, 159; history of, 96; and imperialism, 60; instability of, 57; and language 39; in Marx, 59–60; mature stage of, 64; merchant versus industrial, 80; militarization of, 60–61; in Minsky, 117; monopoly stage of, 191, 197, 209; planned laissez-faire, 280; pre-history of, 63–64; production-centered, 62; rational, 217; and reality, 193; and redemption, 145–46, 159; in Schumpeter, 113–15; and taxation, 217; and war, 60. *See also* financial system; Wall Street system
capitalist credit money, 108, 109
Carruthers, Bruce, 211–12
Carlyle, Thomas, 138
Casarino, Cesare, 222
Casascius coins, 364

cash, 1, 30n22, 36n, 38, 43, 117, 214, 286, 308; and anonymity, 227, 363, 366; as bullion, 97; versus credit, 62, 104; declining use of, 213n6; in Derrida, 183; and freedom, 227, 379; and hoarding, 128; in Keynes, 347; in Marx, 52, 54, 57, 58–59, 62, 66; in Minsky, 117–19; as the monetary base, 73; morality of, 96; and the quantity of money, 122n; as a safe haven, 88; and security, 227; as utopian, 96
cash nexus, 135
cash pools, 116
casino capitalism, 122, 132
Castells, Manuel, 221n12
castration complex, 150
Catchings, Waddill, 347
central banking, 13, 22, 44–46, 76–77, 116, 117, 213n7, 299; and bit gold, 353; and Bitcoin, 364, 371; and Bretton Woods, 70, 99, 245; and colonialism, 64; and confidence in money, 45; and the credit-debtor conflict, 109–10; and demand stimulus, 70; in the Eurozone, 107n, 129, 252, 254, 255, 261, 263, 265, 270; and financial crisis, 1–2, 4, 76–77, 127, 388; independence of, 20; and inflation, 132; in modern monetary theory, 107; and monetarism versus Keynesianism, 192; and monetary disturbances, 54n11, 70; and monetary governance, 69–70, 115, 246; and monetary policy, 121–22; in Proudhon, 352; and public debt, 217–18; and the sacred character of money, 46; and the state, 66n27, 96, 219, 378; and the treasury, 109; and war, 96. *See also* quantitative easing
chartalism, 26, 47, 103–4, 359. *See also* neochartalism
Chaucer, Geoffrey, 343
Chaum, David, 363
Chavy, Jacques, 172n
Chick, Victoria, 106n19, 213n4
Chiemgauer, 350
China Investment Corporation (CIC), 221n11
cho-shutsu, 83n, 84
Christianity, 142, 160, 167, 186n15; in Brown, 150, 158; concept of God, 339; and debt, 26, 231; forgiveness, 187; in

Fromm, 340–41; guilt economy of, 143, 147; in Nietzsche, 135, 141, 181, 389; and punishment, 144; view of society, 320
Cicero, 225
circuits of commerce, 292–94, 351
Citibank, 392
CitiGroup, 221
city, and monetary relations, 30; and property, 177; sacrifice, 171–72
class. *See* social class
code, 35–36, 39, 41; in Deleuze and Guattari, 229–30; genetic, 230
Codere, Helen, 36, 297
cognitive capitalism, 75–76, 249
cognitive labor, 76
Cohen, Benjamin J, 212n3
Cohrssen, Hans, 349
coinage, 15, 16, 25, 36, 42n40, 95, 97, 261; clipping, 219; versus debt, 95, 104–5; and *nomisma*, 223; and violence, 96–97. *See also* specie
CoinLab, 369
Coinye West, 370n40
Coleman, James, 287n
collateralized debt obligations (CDOs), 123, 214
Collège de Sociologie (College of Sociology), 165, 172–73, 203
Collins, Daryl, 289–90
Collins, Randall, 292
colonialism, 60, 64, 230, 240, 243
Commerzbank, 258n38
commodity fetishism, 72, 195, 215, 273, 299, 340
commodity money, 23, 53, 83
commodity theory of money, 236, 359
commons, 249, 268, 380
communism, 49, 84, 250, 361
complementary currency, 5, 14, 214, 237, 315, 360
compound interest, 146–47, 153, 156, 159
Comte, Auguste, 316
conceptual utopia, 317, 328, 330
confidence, 16, 31n24, 45, 124, 353, 362, 374n, 383, 387; and Ponzi finance, 58, 117–18; in society, 137
consumerism, 171, 197, 341; militant, 338
consumers, 65, 307, 310, 355; and debt, 91, 110, 128; and deflation, 72; in Hardt and Negri, 247, 249; and inflation, 72; and just pricing, 356; and local currencies, 374n; versus producers, 109, 375; and unequal pricing, 326, 327, 328–29; wasteful, 164n; as workers, 81, 86, 356
contactless, payment, 377
contagion, financial, 2, 43n, 77; and violence, 44
cool money, 193–94, 391
Cooley, Charles, 276
cooperatives, 84, 86, 345
Copernican revolution, 169
counterfeit money, in Baudelaire, 182, 185; in Derrida, 165, 182, 185, 186, 188, 198, 209; and finance, 199; in Nietzsche, 137; as simulacra, 200; and sovereignty, 224, 226; and war, 43
countergift, 25
cowrie shells, 21, 300
credit, 6, 11; versus cash, 104; and colonialism, 64; debt free, 356; in Harvey, 67–68; versus money, 73; mutual, 316, 353; old-style versus interest-bearing, 94; and social peace, 96–97. *See also* credit creation; free credit
Crédit Agricole, 258
credit contraction, 57, 61, 79, 118–19, 134. *See also* credit crisis; credit crunch
credit creation, 74, 374
credit crisis, 52, 56, 57, 61, 70–71, 73, 76, 79, 88; and social inequality, 79. *See also* credit contraction; credit crunch
credit crunch, 50, 58. *See also* credit contraction; credit crisis
credit inflation, in Marx, 56–57, 58, 61; in Minsky, 117
credit money, 12, 52, 65, 80, 81, 344, 376; accumulation of, 55, 69, 73; in Baudrillard, 194; versus commodity money, 51, 62, 73, 78, 96, 100; as debt, 58–59; defined, 55; in Deleuze and Guattari, 234–35; and the financial system, 56, 108, 218; and gold, 73–74; and hoarding, 54, 58; Marx's theory of, 55–59; and the monetary base, 78–79; in Minsky, 121; private forms of, 121; and regular money, 55, 87; versus token money, 54–55, 58; and trust, 97, 98
credit money regime, 98–99
Crédit Mutuel, 365
credit rating agencies, 132

credit ratings, 43n, 124
credit theory of money, 93, 104–5, 236, 359
creditworthiness, 91, 106; institutionalization of, 218–19
creolization, 302
Crouch, Colin, 76
cryptoanarchism, 363
cryptography, 42; and Bitcoin, 362
cultural labor, 76
cultural sociology, of prices, 62n24
cultural turn, 81
culture, 13; and money, 13–14
cumal (slave-girls), 97
currency, 73; versus money, 5. *See also* pure territorial money
currency wars, 2, 43, 71, 214
Cypriot banking crisis, 9

Dai, Wei, 363
d'Astorg, Bertrand, 172n
Däubler, Theodor, 224
Davidson, Paul, 106n19
Davis, Gerald, 10
de Azpilcueta, Martin, 314
de Brunhoff, Suzanne, 51n, 61n21; *L'Offre de Monnaie* ("The Money Supply"), 235
de Goede, Marieke, 41n, 43
De Grauwe, Paul, 257
de Lacouperie, Albert Terrien, 283
de Rougement, Denis, 172n
de Sade, Marquis, 155, 169
de Saussure, Ferdinand, 37, 38–39, 40, 47, 180, 189n, 190–91, 232
de Sismondi, Simonde, 65
death instinct, 150
death of God, 135, 140–41, 148, 158, 160, 181, 273, 340, 389, 391
debt, 12, 13, 67; amnesty, 26, 92; and austerity, 134; aversion to, 91; Babylonian, 26, 92, 95; in Baudrillard, 201–2; and capital, 57; collectivized, 92, 93; cosmic, 26; and credit money, 58–59; criminalization of, 96, 98, 100; in Deleuze and Guattari, 231; in Derrida, 187–88; and evil, 92, 96, 188; and everyday life, 89; excessive, 90–91; financial, 89, 95, 100, 156, 159, 393; forgiveness, 95, 100 134; freedom from, 90, 91, 104, 383; in gift exchange, 32; and God, 146; government, 90n4; and guilt, 136, 146, 156, 159; household, 89n3, 255, 392–93; jubilee, 26, 100; litigation, 96; Maussian, 144; and money, 12, 25, 92–93, 100, 105–6, 113, 121, 126, 148, 217–18, 248; moral economy of, 12, 89, 90–92, 136, 144, 158, 185, 205; national, 98; Nietzschean, 144; peonage, 95–96, 243, 393; and power, 91, 101, 136, 144, 146, 147, 157; primordial, 24–25, 101, 231; public, 64, 65, 89–90, 126, 385, 388; and redemption, 145–46; and religion, 24–25, 26, 47, 135; and risk, 123; and slavery, 94–95, 97–98; and social welfare, 79; socialized, 125; and society, 25, 94; and sovereignty, 2, 58, 66n27, 91, 110–11, 127, 129, 131, 219, 242, 253, 257–58, 265, 388; and suicide, 92; suspension of, 157; and time, 201, 298; transferable, 106; of the United States, 99; and violence, 91n, 100, 101; and *Wergild*, 24–25. *See also* credit money; debt relation
debt ceiling, 90
Debt Management Office, 107, 218
debt relation, 92, 102, 105, 106, 123, 125, 132, 147
debt widows, 92
debt-free money, 92, 94, 158–59
deflation, 12, 72, 75, 88, 127, 131, 133, 134, 318, 361, 391; and Bitcoin, 362, 368; of credit, 117, 118, 119, 120n; in Deleuze and Guattari, 237; and epic recession, 128; and hoarding, 347; Japanese, 2; versus inflation, 131
Del Mar, Alexander, 103n14
Deleuze, Gilles, 13, 227–37, 241; on alliance and filiation, 232, 234; *Anti-Oedipus*, 228; on axiomatics, 232; on banking, 234–35; on capital and time, 234; on coding and decoding, 229–30, 231, 233–34; on debt, 231; on deflation, 237; on desire, 227, 228–30, 235, 237, 348; on desiring machines, 229; on deterritorialization, 228, 230, 241; on flow, 229, 233–34, 260, 348; on Marxist economics, 234–35; on molarity and molecularity, 230; on money, 231–32; on the monetary mass, 235–37; on payment money versus finance money, 234–37, 244, 248, 251, 256–57, 267; on schizoanalysis, 229; on sexuality, 228; on the socius, 251; on space, 232–33; *A Thousand Plateaus*, 228, 229n23

demand management, 68, 75, 125, 178; in the Eurozone, 208
dematerialization, 39, 41
democracy, 130, 315n; and Bitcoin, 369, 370; and debt, 132, 134; in Derrida, 209–10; economic, 338, 355, 338–39; in the Eurozone, 128–29, 256; and global capital, 245; in Hardt and Negri, 239–40, 244n, 245–46; and money, 212n2, 361; in Polanyi, 282; in Proudhon, 355; and public debt, 126, 130; in Schmitt, 224
demurrage, 85n45, 349–51; and Freicoin, 371
deposit insurance, 116, 213n4, 369
deregulation, 121
derivatives, 35, 62, 66, 87, 113, 121, 122, 194, 213, 251, 277
Derrida, Jacques, 13, 42, 179–89, 198, 209; on counterfeit money, 182, 188; on debt, 187–88; and Deleuze and Guattari, 227; on democracy, 180, 209–10; *différance*, 180; on forgiveness, 165, 187; on gift exchange, 182–83, 188; *Given Time*, 165; on hospitality, 165; on justice, 180, 187, 209; on law, 180, 187, 209; on *logos*, 181; on Marx, 181, 186; and Mauss, 165, 187; on meaning and time, 180–81; on money, 180, 181–82; philosophy of language, 179–81; *Rogues*, 209; on sovereignty, 165, 209; *Specters of Marx*, 181; on money and spectralization, 181–82, 183, 186, 189
desire, 138, 175, 313; in Deleuze and Guattari, 227, 228–30, 235, 237, 348; in Freud, 152, 228n; globalization, 241; in Goux, 40n; in Hardt and Negri, 240–41; for immortality, 153, 157; for money, 45, 52, 125, 151, 274, 330, 340; and mimesis, 44; and value, 27–29; and waste, 151
Desmonde, William, 296
Desnos, Robert, 169
despotism, 197, 232, 233, 321, 322
deterritorialization, 13, 228, 230, 241, 251. *See also* reterritorialization
devaluation, 78, 126, 267; and Bretton Woods, 70; competitive, 2; crisis, 68–69, 70–71, 75, 225, 265; and inflation, 70. *See also* currency wars; internal devaluation
difference, in Deleuze and Guattari, 227–28; in Derrida, 227
digital money, 36, 41–43, 47, 214, 307

Dionysus, 136, 154, 155, 205, 251, 351; and money, 142, 175
direct monetary financing, 131
Discover, 377
disintermediation, 352, 363, 370, 379
division of labor, 63, 150, 151, 234, 324
Doctorow, Cory, 381
Dogecoin, 370n40
dollar, United States, 99, 299, 302
dollarization, 214
Douglas, Clifford Hugh, 355–57, 372, 382
Douglas, Mary, 283
Douglas Credit Party, 357
Douglass, Frederick, 222
Douthwaite, Richard, 374–76
Dow, Sheila, 106n19, 213n4
Dubief, Henri, 172n
Dumas, Charles, 207–8
Durkheim, Émile, 46, 170, 173; on prices, 16; on religion, 15, 101, 308; on sacrifice, 167–68; on the social basis of contract, 31; on society, 8, 268; on sociology, 168
Dumézil, Georges, 172n
Duthuit, George, 172n
dystopia, 223, 383; and the market, 281

ecological money, 374–76
economic anthropology, 279, 285
Economic Cooperation Administration (ECA), 207
economic growth, 67, 374
economic liberalism, 322, 323–24, 325, 326, 329, 372n, 382; versus socialism, 323–25, 329, 383
economics, 3, 7, 20, 38, 53, 99, 119, 170, 196, 205–6, 251, 282, 283, 308, 318, 390; of austerity, 159; 'Austrian', 362; behavioral, 91, 290–91; of desire, 236; and guilt, 150–51; heterodox, 7; and intimacy, 289; Keynesian, 7, 178–79; Marxist, 234; neoclassical, 29; primitive, 155; and religion, 231; restricted, 178–79, 186, 207
economy of credit, 94
economy of interest, 94
Eckhart, Meister, 332, 334
Eichengreen, Barry, 245, 255–56
Einzig, Paul, 19, 282
Elias, Norbert, 276–77
Elizabeth I, 108
embeddedness, 279, 280–81, 285, 289
emotional labor, 241

empire, 77; in Hardt and Negri, 238–41; versus imperialism, 243–44
encryption, 36
endogenous money, 105, 108n23
energy, and base materialism, 169, 172; in Bataille, 173, 177, 183, 192; cost, 132; in de Sade, 169; in Deleuze and Guattari, 169; in Freud, 336; and money, 355, 375–76
Engels, Friedrich, 68, 391
epic recession, 128. *See also* Great Depression
eternal recurrence. *See* eternal return
eternal return, 12, 140–41, 142, 144, 145, 149, 152, 157, 391
ethics, 228, 380; *faux* Christian, 389; in Fromm, 337; in Kant, 84; and microcredit, 358; in Simmel, 317, 319–20, 326
ethnography, 295–96
euro, 9, 20, 46, 78–79, 129, 133, 206, 213, 214, 251–66, 268, 270, 286, 304–5, 350; multiplicity of, 252, 258, 286
European Central Bank (ECB), 2, 20n, 122, 206n39, 254, 261, 263, 265, 270
European Commission, 256n35, 261
European Community Treaty, 253
European Financial Stability Fund, 255
European monetary integration, 15n2, 20–21
European Payments Union (EPU), 207
Eurozone, 1, 251–66, 304; apartheid in, 263; austerity within, 22, 90, 92, 130, 134, 256; bailouts within, 256; banking union for, 253, 258; break-up of, 253; and culture, 270; and Cyprus, 259, 265, 369; debt crisis of, 2, 50, 77–79, 88, 216, 251–52; democracy within, 128–29; and Europe, 263–64; and Germany, 208, 255, 260; government debt in, 90, 133, 134; and Greece, 1, 91–92, 129n52, 148, 208, 254, 257, 264, 265; and identity, 256; internal devaluation within, 78, 388; and Ireland, 254–55, 257; and Italy, 208; and Malta, 259n39, monetary policy within, 79; 253–54, 270; payment imbalances within, 78, 206, 255; periphery of, 2, 46, 78, 90, 134, 242, 256n34, 259, 263–64; and Portugal, 259; public support for, 253, 256; shared borrowing within, 257; and Slovakia, 257, 259n39; and Slovenia, 257, 259n39; sovereignty within, 46, 127, 129, 252, 253, 255, 261, 264–66, 267; and Spain, 254–55, 259, 265; Stability and Growth Pact, 254; as a transfer union, 206; *Troika*, 261, 265; unemployment within, 129. *See also* European Central Bank, Maastricht Treaty
evil, 92, 96, 188, 209
exchange, 101, versus production, in Marx, 81; in Simmel, 27–28
exchange notes, 352–53
exchange rates, 78, 122, 214, 245; and the Eurozone, 255, 260, 265; fixed, 207, 253, 255; flexible, 78; floating, 45n, 71, 72, 74, 75, 122
"exorbitant privilege," 99
expenditure, 13; unproductive, 164, 167, 170, 171–72 177–78, 179, 183, 205

Facebook credits, 292
faith, and Calvin, 176; and counterfeit money, 183, 184; and gold, 280–81; and Luther, 175, 228n20; in markets, 383; and money, 31n24, 125, 183, 184, 219, 274, 386, 389; and the national debt, 147; and religion, 262, 331; and society, 137
falling rate of profit, 59, 65, 67
Fannie Mae, 123
fascism, 174, 361
fashion, 141
Faust, 56n, 158, 314
Federal Bureau of Investigation (FBI), 366
Federal Reserve, 1, 107, 119n39, 131
Federal Reserve Bank of Minneapolis, 20n
Federal Reserve Bank of New York, 20n
Ferenczi, Sándor, 151, 154
fetishization, 35n26, 62, 72, 82, 83, 86, 154, 195, 215, 271, 273, 299, 334, 340
feudalism, 40, 64, 65, 100, 115, 277
fiat money. *See* state fiat money
fiction, and economic expectations, 16; and language, 36; and the free market, 338; and money, 6, 235, 317; and monetary policy, 110; in Simmel, 317; and truth, 36
fictitious capital, 55, 56, 58, 62, 65, 68–69, 70, 83, 194, 243; Marx's definition of, 57n16; in Ricardo, 59n
finance, etymology, 201; versus money, 61–62, 66, 125; social study of, 295
finance capital, 60, 64, 68, 74, 232, 249
financial engineering, 124

financial expropriation, 79
financial innovation, 121
financial instability hypothesis, 117, 124
financial repression, 69
financial system, 3; and crisis formation, 69; expansion of, 114; relationship to GDP, 114. *See also* capitalism; Wall Street system
financialization, 10, 36, 61n22, 66–67, 391; and banking, 114; and the Eurozone crisis, 79; of money, 245, 298; as privatized Keynesianism, 76
First World War, 50, 59, 103, 225, 245, 256, 356, 362
fiscal cliff, 90, 386
fiscus, 261–62
Fisher, Irving, 120n41, 314; on the paradox of thrift, 347; on stamp scrip, 314, 349
Fisher, Mark, 193
floating money, 191, 244
flow, 227, 232, 233–34, 244; and financial markets, 233n
Fond-des-Nègres marketplace, 302
Foster, William, 347
Foucault, Michel, 25, 238, 239, 391; death of "man," 389–90; desire, 229; on *homo economicus*, 390; on Nietzsche, 389–90, 391; *The Order of Things*, 228
Fourcade, Marion, 91
Fourier, Charles, 324
fractional reserve lending, 95, 111, 113, 116, 199n26
Frank, Thomas, 315
Frankfurt School, 322, 326–27
Franklin, Benjamin, 176
fraud, 113, 117n, 120, 132, 137, 199, 313, 368
Freddie Mac, 123
free credit, 352
free labor, 98
free market money, 360, 362
free money, 348
free trade 281
Freicoin, 348n, 349n, 370–71
French Revolution, 84, 355
Freud, Sigmund, 150, 228, 332, 334; *Civilization and Its Discontents*, 152; on money and saving, 151, 336
Friedman, Milton, 131, 330–31
Frisby, David, on Nietzsche, 136–37, 141–42; on Simmel, 137

Fromm, Erich, 14, 85n45, 345, 356, 372, 382; on economic democracy, 338–39; *Escape from Freedom*, 331; on having versus being, 315, 331–38; on hoarding, 336, 340–41, 350–51; on the humanistic utopia, 315, 333–34, 338–39, 374; on language, 332; *Man for Himself*, 331, 341; on Marx, 339; "Medicine and the Ethical Problem of Modern Man," 340; on Messianic time, 335, 338; on money, 334, 339–40, 341, 346; on the Shabbat, 334–35, 338; on spiritual poverty, 334; *To Have or To Be?*, 330; on time, 334–35, 338, 341; on utopia, 315; *You Shall Be as Gods*, 332, 333
Fukuyama, Francis, 125n49
fundamental value, 198

Galbraith, John Kenneth, 7, 11, 17, 111, 116, 133, 387
gambling, 164, 175, 202–3
Gapper, John, 366
G8, 239
Gemeinschaft (community), 155, 378
General Agreement on Tariffs and Trade (GATT), 241
general economy, 13, 164, 196, 198, 205; defined, 176; in Klossowski, 203; and the Marshall Plan, 207–8; and money, 172
general equilibrium theory, 38n, 111n
general equivalent, 42, 82, 85, 194, 202, 234–36, 245
general intellect, 77, 248
geography, 7, 18n6, 66, 67, 221, 237, 238; of money, 242
Gesell, Silvio, 85n45, 348–51, 371, 376, 381, 382; on free money, 348
Gesellschaft (society), 155, 351, 381
Gide, André, 185
Giddens, Anthony, 287
gift exchange, 25, 30–34, 157, 195–96; in Bataille, 176; in Derrida, 165, 182–83, 188; in Mauss, 31–33, 183, 188; in modern society, 33; versus monetary exchange, 30–31; as self-sacrifice, 150–51; and symbolic exchange, 196. *See also* impossible gift; true gift
Girard, René, 43–44
Giscard d'Estaing, Valéry, 99
global bank, 69
global city, 241, 242–43

globalization, 66, 122, 215, 251, 279, 302; in Baudrillard, 197; and empire, 238–41; of finance, 120; in Hardt and Negri, 237–38, 241; in Harvey, 243; of money, 216, 242–43; in Sassen, 242–43
Godelier, Maurice, 390
Godschalk, Hugo, 350
Goethe, Johann, 92, 138, 211, 267, 314, 328, 331; on the primal plant, 332; on the *Urphänomen*, 328
Goffman, Alice, 293
gold, 42, 52, 55, 66, 96, 188, 299, 375; artificial, 56n; and banknotes, 36n; as a 'barbarous relic', 22; and Bitcoin, 362, 368; and capital, 69; and credit money, 73–74; decoupled from dollar, 45–46, 99, 298; demonetization of, 74, 88; discovery of, 63; and fiat money, 62; in the First World War, 225–26; in Marx, 53, 58–59, 62–63; and the monetary base, 69; New World, 223; and paper money, 185; price of, 22; and primitive accumulation, 63, 66; and religion, 45–46; reserves of, 74; and Peter Schlemihl, 186; and the sea, 222; and slavery, 43
gold bug, 26, 185
gold standard, 22, 36n, 46, 55, 62, 73, 192, 348, 349; compared with the euro, 79; and imperialism, 73n31; in Polanyi, 280–81
golden calf, 271, 333, 340
Goldman Sachs, 114
Goldscheid, Rudolf, 321n
Goldthorpe, John, 73n30
Goodhart, Charles, 15n2, 20–21
Google Wallet, 377, 378, 381
Gordon, Barry J, 93n11
gourde, 302
Goux, Jean-Joseph, 39–43, 182, 185, 191
Graeber, David, 94–102; on adornment as money, 205, 282; on bullion versus credit money, 96–97, 225n16; on the human versus commercial economy, 97; on money and violence, 96–97; on primitive accumulation, 98; on society, 101
Grameen America, 358
Grameen Bank, 357–58
grammatology, 41. *See also* writing
Granovetter, Mark, 280
Great Depression, 22, 349, 350. *See also* epic recession

Greco, Thomas H, 360n
greed, 50, 56, 198, 315n, 332, 341, 348
Green, Sarah, 303–4
Gregory, Chris, 298–300, 306, 308; on microcredit, 358n18, 358n20
Gresham, Thomas, 108
Grierson, Philip, 24
Grignon, Paul, 113
Guastella, René, 172n
Guattari, Félix, 13, 227–37, 241; on alliance and filiation, 232, 234; *Anti-Oedipus*, 228; on axiomatics, 232; on banking, 234–35; on capital and time, 234; on coding and decoding, 229–30, 231, 233–34; on debt, 231; on deflation, 237; on desire, 227, 228–30, 235, 237, 348; on desiring machines, 229; on deterritorialization, 228, 230, 241; on flow, 229, 233–34, 260, 348; on Marxist economics, 234–35; on molarity and molecularity, 230; on money, 231–32; on the monetary mass, 235–37; on payment money versus finance money, 234–37, 244, 248, 251, 256–57, 267; on schizoanalysis, 229; on sexuality, 228; on the socius, 251; on space, 232–33; *A Thousand Plateaus*, 228, 229n23
guilt, 12; and capitalism, 145, 156; and debt, 136, 144; in Derrida, 187; and God, 146; and history, 144–46; and money, 157, 159; moral economy of, 144; and neurosis, 150–51; in Nietzsche, 136. *See also Schuld*
Gulf War, 197
Guyer, Jane, 14, 298, 300–303

Habermas, Jürgen, 152, 274–75, 287n, 327
Haiti, 302–3
Hall, Rodney Bruce, 220
Hamacher, Werner, 145
Hann, Chris, 285
Hardt, Michael, 13, 77, 237–51, 293; on bare life, 249–50; on biopower, 239–40; on the commons, 249, 380; *Commonwealth*, 237, 245, 250; on desire, 241; *Empire*, 237, 250; on empire, 238–41, 260, 263; on finance, 249–50; on globalization, 237–38; on imperialism, 237–38; on money, 241–42, 244, 245–46, 250–51; *Multitude*, 237; on the multitude, 238, 239, 246, 247–49, 351; on reterritorialization, 241; on the

society of control, 239–40; on sovereignty, 238, 239, 244, 245, 247
Hart, Keith, 8, 14, 19n7, 31n23, 284, 285, 306–10, 351, 394; on the memory bank, 308–9
Harvey, David, 11, 51, 54n12, 66–71, 76, 192, 374, 390; on credit crisis, 70–71, 73, 88; *The Enigma of Capital and the Crises of Capitalism*, 166; on financialization, 61n22; on globalization and money, 215–16, 243; *Justice, Nature and the Geography of Difference*, 215; on the monetary base, 69; on overaccumulation, 166; on potlatch, 166; on primitive accumulation, 63, 65; on the spatial fix, 66, 68, 192, 238, 243; on the temporal fix, 68, 192, 243
hau. See *mana*
Hayek, Friedrich, 105, 360
hedge finance, 117, 118
hedge funds, 66, 114, 116, 124, 166, 202, 216, 392
Hegel, Georg Wilhelm Friedrich, 51, 140, 327, 333
Heidegger, Martin, 247
helicopter money, 131
Helleiner, Eric, 217
Heraclitus, 333
heterology, 169, 170
hierarchy, and classification, 170; and debt, 91, 101–2; and language, 39; and religion, 25; and the organization of money, 69, 71, 72, 232, 283–84, 379; and politics, 306; and Ponzi finance, 58; and society, 12, 241, 294–95, 311, 352; and the Tiv, 283–84
high-powered money, 108, 110, 121, 213n8
Hilferding, Rudolf, 51, 61, 62, 65, 68, 74n33; *Finance Capital*, 60
Hirsch, Fred, 73n30, 287
historical materialism, 169
Hitler, Adolf, 155
hoard, versus reserve, 54n11
hoarding, 33, 85n45, 305; and Bitcoin, 370; and capitalism, 166; of cash, 128; and deflation, 347; and demurrage, 349, 350; and Freicoin, 371; in Fromm, 336, 340–41; in Marx, 52, 53–54, 58, 61, 67, 181, 274, 348. *See also* miser
Hobbes, Thomas, 223, 246
Hobson, John, 60
Hollingdale, Reginald John, 389
Holloway, John, 10
homo economicus, 44, 390
homo mimeticus, 44
honor price, 97
Hörisch, Jochen, 314
horizontalism, 379–80
Horkheimer, Max, 172n
Horst, Heather, 303
household budget, compared to government finances, 131, 267, 388
Hubert, Henri, 167; *Sacrifice: Its Nature and Function* (with Mauss), 167
Hudson, Michael, 23–24, 26, 129–32, 153, 243
human economy, 34, 47, 97–98, 272, 308
Humphrey, Caroline, 19
Husserl, Edmund, 227
Hutchinson, Sharon, 284, 303
hyperinflation, 130
hyperreality, 193

Icelandic crisis, 127
iconography, 42
immanence, in Deleuze and Guattari, 227; in Derrida, 227; in Hardt and Negri, 241, 244
imperialism, 60, 68; versus empire, 243–44; in Hardt and Negri, 237–38
impossible gift, 186
impressionism, 140
Indecent Proposal, 203
indigenization, 299
inequality. *See* social inequality
inflation, 13, 44, 69, 70, 72, 74n32, 103, 122, 132, 318, 360, 372, 374; in Baudrillard, 192–93; and the creditor-debtor conflict, 109; versus deflation, 131; and the destruction of capital, 88; and LETS, 86; in Minsky, 118–19; the political economy of, 73n30; and war, 226
informal economy, 214
information, 36
infrastructure, of capitalism, 67; of money, 14, 379, 380; of society, 392; of the state, 212, 217
ING Bank, 258n38
Ingham, Geoffrey, 8, 19, 24, 95, 108–11, 127, 218, 374; on the English monetary system, 219; on Marx, 59n; on money as sovereignty, 110; and Wray, 110–11

432 INDEX

insolvency, 156, 158, 304, 305, 327; of Argentina, 148, 392; of banks, 49; of California, 77; and the destruction of money, 148; as 'discipline', 71; in the Eurozone, 264; fiscal, 75; of Lehman Brothers, 49, 50, 114, 220; of New York, 77; of society, 1, 11, 90, 148, 392; sovereign, 90, 260–61, 267; universal, 201
insolvency crisis, versus liquidity crisis, 52
insurance, 16, 288–89
intellectual labor, 76
intellectualism, 29–30
interest rates, 2, 70, 76, 91, 107, 109, 115, 118, 121, 123, 128, 131–32, 325, 358, 371; in the Eurozone, 254–55, 257–58; negative, 350
intermediation, 121, 124. *See also* disintermediation
internal devaluation, 78, 388
International Monetary Fund (IMF), 71, 74n31, 90n4, 99, 119, 214n, 221, 239, 241, 261, 375; austerity doctrine of, 130, 134
international trade, 65, 99, 222
Internet, 5, 21, 49, 50n4, 247, 292, 307, 310
Intesa SanPaolo, 258n38
Iranian crisis, 90n6
Irving, Washington, 92
Islamic finance, 149
Issing, Otmar, 46
iZettle, 377

James, William, 36n
Jameson, Frederick, 313
Jarry, Alfred, 35, 201
Jesus, 334
Joan of Arc, 165
Juárez, Geraldine, 204
jus publicum Europaeum, 222
just price theory, 16, 325, 326, 356. *See also* true prices
just wage, 343

Kant, Immanuel, 27, 34, 81, 83, 86, 227; and the transcendental apperception X, 82
Karatani, Kojin, 8, 12, 80–87, 245; on association, 84; on the base and superstructure, 84; on capital, state and nation, 84; on Kant, 81; on LETS, 84–87, 345; on the parallax view, 80–81, 205; on *phenomenon* versus *noumenon*, 82; and Simmel, 27–8, 320; *Transcritique*, 80; on

the transcendental apperception X, 82; on the transcendental illusion, 82
Kaufmann, Walter, 140
Kay, John, 366, 369
Keynes, John Maynard, 8, 12, 20n, 22, 45, 50, 66, 108n24, 178–79, 296; "*Auri Sacra Fames*," 155; on austerity, 130; on compound interest, 153; on convention, 119, 120; on deflation, 318; on demand management, 68, 75, 178; "Economic Possibilities for Our Grandchildren," 153, 155; *The General Theory of Employment, Interest and Money*, 178, 229; on Gesell, 349; on inflation, 318; on Knapp, 103, 104; on the liquidity premium, 125, 347, 349; on Marx, 59; in Minsky, 117, 119; on money, 125; on money of account, 8, 109–10, 297; on the paradox of thrift, 347; "Social Consequences of Changes in the Value of Money," 318; *A Treatise on Money*, 104, 112
Keynesianism, 74–75, 117, 125, 192, 208, 265; privatized, 76
Kierkegaard, Søren, 228n20
Kiva, 316, 358, 380
Kiyotaki, Nobuhiro, 92n
Klossowski, Pierre, 172n; on living coin (*la monnaie vivante*), 194, 203–4, 388
Knapp, Georg Friedrich, 12, 20n, 102–4, 105–6, 108, 121, 255; definition of money, 103
Knorr Cetina, Karin, 230, 233n, 293
Kocherlakota, Narayana, R, 309n
Kojève, Alexandre, 172n
Krämer, Jörg, 206
Krippner, Greta, 10–11, 280, 285, 289
Krugman, Paul, 127, 129, 198–99, 347; on Bitcoin, 367; on Minsky, 119–20
Kula ring, 31

La Rochelle, Drieu, 172n
labor, 74, 78, 98, 129, 139, 144. 176, 192, 195, 228, 229, 239, 240, 298, 353; abstract, 248; and capital, 70, 71, 72, 232, 238, 337; and consumption, 85; crises of, 67; depersonalization of, 340; exploitation of, 67; as a fictitious commodity, 57n16, 280, 311; and money, 56, 245, 343; ownership of, 63; productivity of, 70, and value, 69, 156, 189, 191, 328, 344; vitality of, 343. *See also* cultural labor; emotional labor;

intellectual labor; labor market; precarious labor
labor market, 242
labor money, 80, 84–85, 314, 316, 325–26, 327n, 342–46, 375. *See also* time banks; time dollars
labor movement, 75
labor theory of value, 344
Lacan, Jacques, 40–41, 172n
LaGuerre, Michel, 303
Landsberg, Paul-Louis, 172n
language, economy of, 36; in Fromm, 332; and god, 35; as metaphor; 35–36; and money, 35–36, 37–38, 40, 47, 180, 185, 190; and referentiality, 77; and the social bond, 39
Lapavitsas, Costas, 78n
Latour, Bruno, 292
Laum, Bernhard, 20n8, 25, 45, 112
law, 4, 17
Lazzarato, Maurizio, 160n8, 231n25
Lee, Benjamin, 62
Lehman Brothers, 1, 49, 50, 114, 116, 220
Leiris, Michel, 168, 172n
leisure, 155
leisure class, 151
Lenin, Vladimir, 11, 51, 60, 66, 68; on Hilferding, 61; on money versus finance, 61
Leontief, Wassily, 117
leverage, 114, 116, 119–20
Lévi-Strauss, Claude, 172n
Lewitzky, Anatole, 172n
libertarianism, 21, 26, 72n, 105, 199, 293, 315n, 331, 360, 369n, 381, 382
LIBOR affair, 120
Lichtenberg, Georg Christoph, 145
Linden dollars, 292
Linton, Michael, 85
Linux Foundation, 369
LiPuma, Edward, 62, 296
liquidity, 4, 52n8, 116, 131n57, 264n, 287
liquidity crisis, 52n8
liquidity guarantee program, 127–28
liquidity premium, 125, 347, 348, 349
liquidity risk, 124
Lisbon Treaty, 265
Litecoin, 370n40
living currency, 203–4, 233, 342
local currency, 14, 105, 214, 286, 292, 293, 294, 315, 325, 360, 373; limited purpose nature of, 373

local exchange trading scheme (LETS), 84–87, 293, 316, 344, 345, 350, 360, 376, 381; and barter, 85, 86; defined, 84–85; origins of, 84
local trade, 325
Locke, John, 151, 219
logical positivism, 36n
"Lord Keynes," 368
Lotringer, Sylvère, 227
Louis XIV, 321
Lukács, György, 275n
Luxemburg, Rosa, 11, 51, 64–65, 66, 67; on accumulation, 65, 68
luxury, 13
Lyotard, Jean-François, 39

Maastricht Treaty, 206n37, 253, 255, 263; convergence criteria, 253–54, 263–64
Mabile, Pierre, 172n
Machiavelli, Niccolò, 246
MacKenzie, Donald, 200
Madoff, Bernard, 198
Magee, Bryan, 36n
Malinowski, Bronislaw, 31, 32, 33
Malthus, Thomas, 65
mana, 31, 195; relationship to currency, 33
Mandeville, Bernard, *Fable of the Bees*, 347
Mann, Thomas, 247
Marazzi, Christian, 11, 72–78, 240–41, 246, 249; on bare life, 249–50, 266–67; on cognitive capitalism, 76; on finance, 249–50; on monetary terrorism, 75
Marcuse, Herbert, 149
marginal utility, 29
markets, 16; authority of, 220; as an axiomatic, 232; in Baudrillard, 196; and colonialism, 60; in food, 3; in Hardt and Negri, 241, 243–34; internal versus external, 65; and monetary governance, 21; and the origins of money, 18–19, 23, 24, 44, 95; in Polanyi, 279–81; and scarcity, 196; versus states, 247, 306–7; and symbolic exchange, 196
Marlowe, Christopher, 92
Marshall, Alfred, 276
Marshall, George, 206
Marshall Plan, 166, 206–7
Marx, Karl, 13, 66, 211, 213, 232, 238, 240, 271, 275, 276, 291, 295, 311, 332, 334, 351; on alienation, 273–74, 341; on banks, 50, 55, 56; on banknotes, 55; on barter, 53;

Marx, Karl (*continued*)
   Capital, 39, 49, 51, 56, 62, 63, 67, 80, 83, 147n, 236, 295, 361, 391; on capitalism, 59–60; on cash, 52, 54, 57, 58–59, 62, 66; *The Communist Manifesto,* 181; on compound interest, 147n; on the contradictions of capitalism, 72, 83; on the contradictions of money, 50, 51–55, 57, 61, 63, 71, 75, 80, 87, 273, 344, 347–48, 390; and credit crisis, 88, 133; on credit inflation, 56–57, 58, 61; on credit money versus the monetary base, 78–79; "The Critique of the Gotha Programme," 84; on dead labor, 337; definition of money, 8, 11–12, 51n; on the destruction of capitalism, 146; *The Economic and Philosophic Manuscripts of 1844,* 56n, 181n8, 295, 334; on fictitious capital, 57n16; and the financial crisis, 49–51; on the functions of money, 51–52; on gold, 53, 58–59, 62–63, 79, 151; *Grundrisse,* 39n36, 51, 64, 80, 250, 273, 274, 344, 351; on hoarding, 52, 53–54, 58, 61, 67, 181, 274, 348; on labor money, 344–45; on the law of value, 61; and LETS, 85, 87; on money of account, 51n, 54; on money as fetish, 62; on the money form, 39, 51n, 52; on money and language, 34, 39n36; "On James Mill," 273; *On the Jewish Question,* 274; on the origins of money, 52–53; *The Poverty of Philosophy,* 51, 53; on primitive accumulation, 63–66, 67, 98, 148, 222; on Proudhon, 53, 72, 84; on public debt, 147–48, 154; on religion, 340; on Ricardo, 59; and Simmel, 137; on Smith, 63
Masson, André, 169
MasterCard, 377, 380n
mature money economy, 27, 137, 322, 330
Maurer, Bill, 8, 35, 296, 297, 378n50
Mauss, Marcel, 164, 198, 200, 267; and Bataille, 165; and Derrida, 165; *The Gift,* 31, 32, 167, 168, 195; on gift exchange, 31–34, 183, 188; on money, 32, 170; on the origins of money, 32–33; on religion, 167; on sacrifice, 167; *Sacrifice: Its Nature and Function* (with Hubert), 167; on sociology, 168
May, Timothy, 363
Mayer, Hans, 172n
McCloskey, Deirdre, 38n34

McCulley, Paul, 119n39
McLuhan, Marshall, 194, 195
Mead, George Herbert, 319
measurement, 18, 24, 25, 28–29, 37, 39, 103n14, 112, 174, 194, 259, 274, 297, 302–3, 325, 343, 344, 345, 390; of culture, 138; of honor, 97; of humans, 97; of labor, 70; of money and time, 145; of moral worth, 91; of the quantity of money, 122n, 213; of value, 51, 52n8, 70, 71; of wealth, 71
Meltzer, Françoise, 184
memory bank, 308–9
Mencken, Henry Louis, 343n13
Menger, Carl, 17–23, 25, 26, 45, 47, 105n17, 236, 359, 362; definition of money, 18n5; and Simmel, 137
mental accounting, 290–91
Mephistopheles, 92
mercantilism, 66
Merrill Lynch, 114, 221
Mesopotamia, 95
Messianic time, 335, 338
metallism, 102, 383
Methodenstreit, 285
metropolis, 250
microcredit, 357–58
Midas, 153
migrant workers, 293
migration, 226, 240, 263, 293, 305
mimesis, 43–45; and financial panic, 77
minimum wage, 325, 382
Minsky, Hyman, 50, 58, 66, 108, 117–21, 124; on securitization, 120–21. *See also* financial instability hypothesis
Minsky moment, 119, 120. *See also* Ponzi stage
MintTheCoin, 385–86, 387, 393
Mintz, Sydney, 302–3
Miró, Jean, 169
miser, 49, 54, 152, 208, 346–47. *See also* hoarding
Mississippi bubble, 126
Mitchell, David, 350
Mitchell, Wesley C., 276
Mitchell-Innes, Alfred, 12, 102–3, 104–6, 108, 111, 121, 248, 353–54, 359
mobile money, 14, 315, 377–79; versus the state, 379
mobility, 226, 240, 333
models, 21, 227

modern monetary theory, 106
monetarism, 73n30, 120, 121, 192, 330
monetary base, 58, 69, 70, 73, 78–79, 131n59, 213
monetary circuit theory, 105n18, 106n19, 108n23
monetary circuits, 272
monetary crisis, 59, 61, 70, 386, 391
Money Freedom Declaration, 360
monetary governance, 71, 72, 74, 76, 212, 246, 347; and the Asian crisis, 76–77
monetary pluralism, 379, 383, 387
monetary policy, 20, 45n, 57, 76, 388; and demand stimulus, 125, 178, 208; in an epic recession, 128; in the Eurozone, 79; 253–54, 270; as fiction, 110; and the financial crisis, 2; and financial markets, 246; in Fromm, 337; in Ingham, 109–10; in Knapp. 103; in Marx, 57; according to modern monetary theory, 107; in Polanyi, 281; and the quantity of money, 122n; and securitization, 121–22, 123; and sovereignty, 262
monetary production economy, 108
monetary realism, 198, 386–88
monetary reform, 9, 14, 80
monetary space, 13, 109, 218, 221, 227, 242–43, 252–53; and the Eurozone, 256–57, 258, 261; sovereign nature of, 237
monetary union, 214, 252, 264n
money, abolition of, 14, 57; as adornment, 205, 282; and alienation, 33; in anthropology, 279, 285, 294, 295; versus barter, 19–20, 42–43; and capital, 64, 67, 70, 75, 86; as charta (ticket), 103n14; as a claim upon society, 4, 7, 8, 13, 14, 26, 92, 93, 94, 102, 103, 124, 125, 133, 226, 238, 267, 268, 310, 351, 389, 394; as code, 35–36; as colorless, 30–31, 32, 33; and commodities, 80–81; competing definitions of, 5n, 6; creation of, 70, 87, 109, 111, 112–13, 127, 130, 131, 374; as a creature of law, 93, 103n15, 104; versus credit, 73; and culture, 13–14, 269–70, 283; versus currency, 5; as debt, 12, 92–93, 94, 100, 102, 105–6, 113, 121, 126, 148, 217–18; dematerialization of, 39, 41; denationalization of, 105; diversity of, 47–48; early forms of, 25, 32–33, 37, 40, 230–31; as Esperanto, 34–35; evolution of, 18–20,
21, 23, 42; as the exception, 261, 265, 393; and excrement, 152, 334, 351; as a fetishized social relation, 62, 82n, 83, 86, 195, 271, 334; as a fiction, 6, 186, 235, 317; as a fictitious commodity, 279, 280; versus finance, 60–61, 66, 125; as flow, 227, 232, 233–34; and freedom, 227, 360, 372, 379, 383; as the general equivalent, 42, 82, 85, 194, 202, 234–36, 245; and geopolitical space, 213–14; as a god, 273–74; and guilt, 157, 159; iconography of, 42; as an idea, 6, 48, 277, 394; and identity, 272; as an infrastructural technology, 217; invention of, 21, 37; and language, 35–36, 37–38, 40, 47, 180, 185, 190; and measurement, 18, 24, 25, 28–29, 37, 39, 103n14, 112, 145, 174, 194, 259, 274, 297, 302–3, 325, 343, 344, 345, 390; and memory, 308–9; as MO-M4, 121–22, 213n8, 350; and military power, 43, 66n27, 95, 96, 98, 99, 226, 276, 298; multiplicity of, 271, 288, 373, 382, 387; and the multitude, 246; as neurosis, 150; origins of, 11, 15–16, 21, 44, 52–53, 389; as a pacifier, 24n12, 44; as a process, 6, 8, 88, 271, 272, 294, 359, 372, 376, 386, 387, 389, 392, 393; as a promise, 100–101, 105, 110; psychoanalytic theory of, 152; and public debt, 130, 147, 217–18; and religion, 4, 24, 25, 273–74, 275; and semiotics, 38, 41, 179, 297; as a simulacrum, 35n28, 188–89, 193; as a social bond, 45, 79; as social currency, 97; social foundations of, 124; as a social leveler, 138–39, 274, 275, 295, 322, 325; the social life of, 4, 5, 8–10, 12, 62, 72, 74, 110, 159, 174, 186, 226, 268, 351, 361, 362, 371–72, 386, 388, 391–92, 393, 394; and social power, 51; and social rank, 171, 177, 283–84, 285, 292, 294–95, 302; and social reproduction, 283; and social ties, 289–90; and socialism, 14, 80; as socialized debt, 125, 267; as sociological numismatics, 34; special versus general purpose, 279, 282–83; spectral, 181; and speech, 37, 42; subalternate versus superalternate, 299, 301; and sublimation, 152; as a symbol, 35, 203; as a thing, 6, 72, 74, 75, 82, 270; 271, 272, 294, 361, 362, 371–72, 386, 387, 389, 393; as a total social fact, 31n24, 33; as TWINTOPT, 106n20; as the unit of

money (*continued*)
    account, 234; as the universal equivalent, 58, 62, 63, 194, 245, 274, 344; and utopia, 10; as *valuta*, 103, 104, 108; as waste, 12–13; and *Wergild*, 24; and writing, 36, 37, 41n, 42. *See also* complementary currency; cool money; counterfeit money; credit money; debt-free money; digital money; ecological money; endogenous money; floating money; helicopter money; high-powered money; LETS; local currency; perfect money; postnational money; private money; sacred money; savage money; state fiat money; stateless money; territorial money
money of account, 8, 51, 54, 104, 109–10, 219n, 292, 297; in the Eurozone, 258–59
money manager capitalism, 120
money supply, 121, 122n, 211, 318, 319–20, 349n
Monnerot, Jules, 172n
monopoly, 59, 60
monopoly capitalism, 191, 197, 209
Montandon, George, 283
Moore, Basil, 106n19
Moore, Demi, 203
Moore, Heidi, 386
Moore, John H, 92n
M-Pesa, 377–78
More, Thomas, 14, 313, 339
Morgan Stanley, 114, 221
Morrill, Calvin, 292
Morris, William, 327n
Mosaic law, 26
Moses, 332–33
Mt. Gox, 366, 367, 369
multitude, and money, 77, 268; and finance, 248; in Hardt and Negri, 238, 239, 246, 247–49, 351; versus society, 293; in Spinoza, 77
Mundell, Robert, 253
Munn, Nancy, 215
mutualism, 353, 354, 357, 360, 363, 372, 382
mutuality, 101
myth, 16–17, 47

Nakamoto, Satoshi, 364, 381, 382
Namecoin, 370n40
Nantes, 165
narrow banking, 133
nationalism, 240

nation-state, 8
natural money, 361
nature, 155, 185, 188, 189, 232, 311, 328; in Bashō, 331; in Bataille, 196; in Baudrillard, 196; in Benjamin, 331; versus civilization, 283; in Fromm, 334–35, 337; in Goethe, 331; immortality of, 141; irrationality of, 77n; in Marx, 58; in Nietzsche, 141, 154; in Polanyi, 280, 311; in Proudhon, 354; and sacrifice, 168; state of, 223; in Tennyson, 331
negative equity, 132
Negri, Antonio, 13, 77, 237–51, 293; on bare life, 249–50; on biopower, 239–40; on the commons, 249, 380; *Commonwealth*, 237, 245, 250; on desire, 241; *Empire*, 237, 250; on empire, 238–41, 260, 263; on finance, 249–50; on globalization, 237–38; on imperialism, 237–38; on money, 241–42, 244, 245–46, 250–1; on money and community, 250; *Multitude*, 237; on the multitude, 238, 239, 246, 247–49, 351; on reterritorialization, 241; on the society of control, 239–40; on sovereignty, 238, 239, 244, 245, 247; *Time for Revolution*, 266; on time, 251
neochartalism, 103, 106–11, 1, 12n, 254, 359. *See also* chartalism
neoliberalism, 68, 130, 192, 193, 197–98, 270, 291, 331, 383; and utopia, 304–5, 315n, 383
neurosis, 12
neutral money, 9, 271, 273, 283, 285, 297, 318–19, 329n
New Deal, 70, 72
new economic sociology, 279
New Economics Foundation (NEF), 374
new economy, 76, 77
New World, 13, 222, 223
New York fiscal crisis, 75, 77; parallels with Eurozone crisis, 79
Newton, Isaac, 109
Nicolayon, Sismondito, 65
Nietzsche, Friedrich, 12, 13, 36n, 136–42, 178, 181, 247, 271, 275, 291, 295, 318, 340; on bankers, 137; *Beyond Good and Evil*, 136, 141; *The Birth of Tragedy*, 154; on calculation and thought, 147, 295; on culture, 138; *Daybreak*, 135, 137, 148–49; on debt, 89, 135, 231; on desire, 229; *Ecce Homo*, 142; on ethics, 228; *The Gay*

Science, 160; *On the Genealogy of Morals*, 135–36, 147, 152; on guilt, 136; *Human, All Too Human*, 139–40; on inheritance, 153; on modernity, 137; on money, 135–36, 137, 138–39, 273, 274, 389; on nobility, 138, 139, 323; on nobility of mind, 138; *Philosophy in the Tragic Age of the Greeks*, 145; on prices, 139–40, 147; on promising and memory, 152, 157; *ressentiment*, 160; on the sea, 222; and socialism, 139; on society, 138; on superman, 148; *Thus Spoke Zarathustra*, 135, 141, 142, 351; on the transvaluation of all values (*Umwertung aller Werte*), 141, 205, 274; *Untimely Meditations*, 135, 161; *Writings from the Late Notebooks*, 137. *See also* death of God; eternal return; *Übermensch*
Nigeria, 301
ninety-nine percent, 3, 129–30, 370–71
nihilism, 141, 142
Nishibe, Makoto, 345
Nixon, Richard, 45, 98–99, 244
Nixon shock, 45n
Nobel Prize, 330
nomos, 262, of the Earth, 222, 223
nongovernmental organizations (NGOs), 239
nonpecuniary values, 287, 294
North, Peter, 373
North Atlantic Treaty Organization (NATO), 239
Nostradamus, 49
Nuer, 284
numismatics, 165; sociological, 34
nummus, 223, 262

occultism, 7, 11; and capital, 56, 154
Occupy movement, 1, 3, 50, 130n55, 201, 267, 370
Oedipus complex, 149, 150, 230
Oesterreichische Nationalbank, 20n
Old Glory Mint, 361
one trillion dollar platinum coin, 385, 386, 387, 392
optimal currency area (OCA), 20, 253
order of worth, 200
Organisation for Economic Co-operation and Development (OECD)
Orléan, André, 19, 43–46, 250; on Mauss, 32
Ortega y Gasset, José, 247

overaccumulation, in Bataille, 176; in Baudrillard, 192; and financialization, 61n22; in Harvey, 68, 166, 243; Marxian concept of, 65, 88, 205
overbanking, 122, 124
overproduction, 57, 73
Owen, Robert, 342

Pan, 77, 246
panic, etymology, 77n; financial, 77
paradox of thrift, 208, 347, 348
parallax view, 80–81, 205
Park, Robert, 319
Parsons, Talcott, 8, 34, 230, 276n
patriarchy, 336
Patton, Paul, 227
Paulhan, Jean, 172n
payday loans, 325
PayPal, 378, 380n
Peace of Westphalia, 216
Pecunix, 42, 316
Peebles, Gustav, 304–5
peer-to-peer (P2P) currencies, 105, 365, 370
peer-to-peer (P2P) lending, 247, 316
peer-to-peer (P2P) payment networks, 365
pension fund socialism, 77
pension funds, 59, 68, 75, 110, 129n52, 132, 221, 243
pensioners, 2, 22, 72, 77, 88, 126
perfect money, 14, 30, 197, 315, 316, 317–22, 326, 328–30, 339, 341, 356–57, 375, 382
perfect society, 30, 315, 316, 320–21, 322, 326, 329–30, 351
Perroux, François, 207
philanthropy, 166
Pixley, Jocelyn, 315n
Plato, 200, 313
Platonism, 322, 326
Plender, John, 50
Poe, Edgar Allen, 185
poetry, 313, 314, 331
Polanyi, Karl, 13, 36, 57n16, 271, 279–86, 291, 292, 294, 299, 306; on the double movement, 128, 280, 311; on embeddedness, 279, 280–81, 285; on fictitious commodities, 279–80; on formal versus substantive approaches to the economy, 285; *The Great Transformation*, 279, 282, 284, 286; on limited and general purpose money, 279, 282–83, 285, 286, 325, 373; on the market, 372, 279–81; on money

Polanyi, Karl (*continued*)
  and language, 297; on planned laissez-faire capitalism, 280
Polillo, Simone, 218–19
Polybius, *Histories*, 239
Ponzi, Charles, 117n
Ponzi finance, 58, 117n, 118, 199; and Bitcoin, 368
Ponzi stage, 120. *See also* Minsky moment
Poovey, Mary, 296
Pope Francis, 270–71
Posner, Eric, 368
postcapitalism, 83, 251
post-Fordism, 72, 75–76, 77, 238, 240–41, 248, 249, 341
postindustrialism, 39
post-Keynesianism, 76; monetary theory, 112n, 106n19; and neochartalism, 106
postmodernism., 238, 239
postnational money, 238
poststructuralism, 238
potlatch, 33, 155, 166, 172
power, 172, 222, 272, 389; in Agamben, 266; and banking, 115; in Baudrillard, 196, 197–98; and capital, 61n22, 64, 69, 81, 129, 234, 245, 340; and debt, 91, 101, 136, 144, 146, 147, 157; in Deleuze and Guattari, 230–31, 233, 250–51; and divinity, 274; and economics, 221, 310; in the Eurozone, 261, 265, 266; and the exception, 261, 266, 393; of finance, 121, 129; in Foucault, 25n13; in Fromm, 332, 335, 337; of the gift, 31, 33, 195; in Hardt and Negri, 238–39, 240, 241, 244, 245–46, 248; and markets, 109, 121, 129, 286; and the military, 99; of monetary institutions, 4, 69, 134, 316, 380n, 385; and money, 10, 33, 34, 42, 44, 51, 152, 154, 181–82, 246, 248, 274, 283, 284, 285, 295, 298–99, 300, 306, 307, 308, 342–43, 346, 351; in Nietzsche, 135, 141, 144, 161, 389; and *nomos*, 223, 262; in Proudhon, 352; in Schmitt, 223, 224, 261, 266n; and sovereignty, 26, 223, 262; of the state via money, 4, 9, 71, 73–74, 75, 96, 103, 110, 113, 212, 214, 261, 298–99, 309, 360; of states, 107n, 129; versus society, 102; supranational, 236–37, 238–39, 242; and symbolic exchange, 196, 198; and violence, 44; and wealth, 166, 343. *See also* social power; symbolic power

PPCoin, 370n40
Praet, Peter, 20n
precarious labor, 248
precious metal, 18n6, 21, 36, 151
Preda, Alex, 233n
predestination, 146
Prévost, Pierre, 172n
price regulation, 325
pricing, 16–17
primitive accumulation, 63–66, 67, 98, 222; defined, 63; in Harvey, 63, 68; and money, 148; and the state, 64
private enterprise money, 359–61, 372
Private Enterprise Money Committee, 360
private money, 223
private property, 19n7, 51; in Fromm, 336
privatization by credit, 130
Protevi, John, 227
Proudhon, Pierre-Joseph, 351–55, 357, 361, 372, 381, 382; on association, 84, 86; Bank of Exchange, 352; Bank of the People, 352, 354–55, 360, 361; *Les Confessions d'un Révolutionnaire*, 357; *The Creation of Order in Humanity*, 343n12; on general bankruptcy, 1, 6, 11; in Marx, 53; on monetary reform, 72, 313–14, 315; *Solution of the Social Problem*, 352; on the state, 353, 357; on utopia, 352
Pryke, Michael, 233, 277–78
Pryor, Frederick, 292
pseudoindividualism, 326
psychoanalysis, 12, 39, 40, 149, 157–58, 171; and guilt, 150; and Marxism, 228–29; and money, 152; and waste, 171–72; of work and play, 155
public debt, 64, 65, 89–90, 126, 127, 130, 149, 154, 217–18
public finance, 126
pure gift, 186, 187, 189
pure territorial money, 212n3. *See also* currency; territorial money
pyramids, 151

quality theory of money, 299–300
quantification, 27–30, 47, 109n25, 296–97
quantitative easing, 2, 15n2, 22, 88, 130
quantity theory of money, 59n, 300, 318
Quesnay, François, 37
Quiggin, Alison Hingston, 283

INDEX 439

Rabelais, François, 322
Rafferty, Michael, 62, 198
Rand, Ayn, 315n
Rasmus, Jack, 128
Rawls, John, 373
real economy, 366; versus monetary-financial economy, 75, 76, 88, 98, 114, 132
realism, 185, 193, 198, 200. *See also* monetary realism
realistic utopia, 373
reality principle, 150, 190, 191–92, 209
Redford, Robert, 203
Regiogeld, 350
reification, 82, 271
relational work, 289–90
relationism, defined, 29; and value, 318, 326
religion, 4; in Bataille, 175–76; and credit money, 57, 58; and debt, 24–25, 26, 47, 135; in Deleuze and Guattari, 228; and derivatives, 35; and gift exchange, 33; and gold, 45–46; in Mauss, 167; as a metaphor for finance, 10; as a metaphor for money, 274, 275; and the obligatory nature of money, 25–26; as opiate, 340; origins of, 15; and the origins of money, 24–25; and social control, 44; and society, 44; and usury, 95
remittances, 293
renminbi, 214
rent, as theft, 353
rent-seeking, 66–67, 132, 393. *See also* becoming rent of the profit
rentier system, 132
rentiers, 74, 110n, 127, 130; in Keynes, 127, 130, 133
restricted economy, 166, 175, 178–79, 186, 198, 205, 206, 207; defined, 176; in Klossowski, 203
resurrection, 158
reterritorialization, 241
Ricardo, David, 59, 84, 228
Rickards, James, 22–23
Riegel, Edwin, 359–61, 372, 381, 382
Ripple, 316
risk, aversion, 122, 124; and banking, 116, 121; and casino capitalism, 122; flight from, 58; and monetary substitutes, 61; securitization, 123, 124; socialization, via money, 88; and society, 124; and sovereign debt, 127
risk-free borrowing, 99, 125

Robbins, Joel, 292
Robertson, John, 347
Roitman, Janet, 91, 144
Rolling Jubilee, 201–2
Rorty, Richard, 11
Rotman, Brian, 35
Roubini, Nouriel, 22
Rousseau, Jean-Jacques, 37–38, 39, 320
Royal Bank of Scotland, 258n38
Rowbotham, Michael, 199n26
Royal Mint, 109
Ruskin, John, 89, 93, 159, 315, 327n, 381; on labor money, 314, 342–43, 345–46
Russell, Eric Frank, 381

Sachs, Hans, 275
sacred, in Bataille, 163, 165, 167, 168, 172–73, 175, 176; and capitalism, 144; and children, 289; and industrialism, 340; in Mauss, 170; and money, 16, 46, 47, 136, 150, 153, 155–56, 158, 283, 287, 296, 389, 394; and society, 173; and violence, 173
sacred money, 16, 46, 47, 136, 150, 153, 155–56, 158, 283, 287, 296, 389, 394
sacrifice, 17, 24, 25, 165; and barter, 25; in Bataille, 168; in Durkheim, 168; and the gift, 168; in Hubert and Mauss, 168; and the obligatory nature of money, 25–26; in Simmel, 28–29; and transgression, 168; and violence, 43–44
Sahlins, Marshall, 196
Sandel, Michael, 270
Sarthou-Lajus, Nathalie, 144
Sartre, Jean-Paul, 172n
Sassen, Saskia, 220, 242–43
Satan, 334
Saussure. *See* de Saussure
savage money, 298
savings and loans associations, 120
Say, Jean-Baptiste, 53n10
Say's Law, 53, 58, 80
scarcity, 12–13, 22, 155, 166, 178, 193, 196; and abundance, 176; of information, 193; and the market, 196; and restricted economy, 176; of time, 196
Schäuble, Wolfgang, 264
Schlemihl, Peter, 55, 186, 201
Schmitt, Carl, 13, 222–25, 247, 260–61; "The Age of Neutralizations and Depoliticizations," 225; *Die Diktatur*, 224; on the exception, 261, 265; on money, 224–25;

Schmitt, Carl (*continued*)
  Political Theology, 224; *Der Wert des Staates und die Bedeutung des Einzelnen*, 224. See also *nomos*; state of exception
Schopenhauer, Arthur, 36n, 140, 157, 327; territorial space, 261
Schuld, 136, 144, 146
Schumpeter, Joseph, 12, 16, 27n17, 50, 111–16, 117, 118, 270, 276n; on Aristotle, 93n11; on banking, 112–13; *Capitalism, Socialism and Democracy*, 115; on culture, 269, 310; on entrepreneurship, 115, 116; *History of Economic Analysis*, 112; on Knapp, 103–4; on Marx, 59; on the sociology of money, 112; *The Theory of Economic Development*, 112–13
science, 7, 170; in Fromm, 341; linguistics, 38; monetary, 269, 310; sociology of, 371; of writing, 41
science and technology studies (STS), 371
scientific management, 355
Seaford, Richard, 25, 223
Second World War, 99, 363
Secure American Gold Exchange, 361
securitization, 120–21, 122, 123–24, 198
security, 36
seigniorage, 378, 380
semiotics, 38, 41, 179, 297
shadow banking, 116, 123, 124
Shakespeare, William, *King Lear*, 224; *The Merchant of Venice*, 186; *Timon of Athens*, 181
Shell, Marc, 35n29
Shiller, Robert, 314
sign, 35, 36, 39n35
signatures, theory of, 42
Silk Road, 366
Simiand, François, 32n
Simmel, Georg, 27–30, 271, 276n, 291, 294, 295, 311, 316–30, 333, 382; on absolute and relative equality, 320, 321–22, 346, 356, 375; on adornment and money, 205; on aesthetics, 321–22; on alienation, 33, 273, 274–75, 324; on calculation, 295, 324; on colorless money, 30–31, 32; on culture, 138, 273; on the dyad, 28; on fictions, 317, 320, 329; on historical materialism, 276; "How is society possible?," 27, 84n42, 320; in intellectualism, 29–30, 316; and Kant, 27–28, 320; on measurement, 28–29, 390; on money as a claim upon society, 4, 7, 8, 13, 14, 26, 92, 93, 110, 124, 125, 137, 226, 238, 267, 268, 310, 351, 389; on money as an idea, 6, 48, 277; on labor money, 344; on Marx, 278; "The Metropolis and Mental Life," 139; on the metropolis, 250; on the miser and the spendthrift, 346–47; on money and culture, 276–77; on money and the individual, 158; on money as language, 34; "Money in Modern Culture," 275; on the monetary association, 323–24; on money and religion, 275; on Nietzsche, 137, 138, 318, 322, 323, 391–92; on nobility of mind, 138, 142, 323; on the objectification of culture, 275–76, 281; on perfect money, 14, 30, 315, 316, 317–22, 326, 328–30, 339, 341, 356–57, 375, 382; on the perfect society, 30, 315, 316, 320–21, 322, 326, 329–30, 351; *The Philosophy of Money*, 6–7, 27, 136, 137, 138, 140, 197, 275, 276, 277, 281, 315, 319, 321, 330; on relationism, 29, 318, 326; on sacrifice, 28–29; *Schopenhauer and Nietzsche*, 138, 139, 140; "On the Significance of Numbers for Social Life," 324n; on socialism, 14, 139, 140, 197, 314n3, 316, 322–25, 329, 344, 355, 382–83; on sociation (*Vergesellschaftung*), 28; on society, 27, 28, 268, 325, 327, 351; "Sociological Aesthetics," 321; *Soziologie*, 27, 315, 320, 324, 351; on squandering, 170–71; on stable money, 317–18; on symmetry and asymmetry, 197, 321–22; on the theory of value, 27–29, 137, 325–26; on the tragedy of culture, 276, 322, 330; on *Übermensch*, 142; on unequal pricing, 316, 326, 327–29; on utopianism, 328, 344, 346, 383; on valuation, 28–29, 325, 326; on *Wergild*, 24; "The Women's Congress and Social Democracy," 138
simulacrum, in Baudrillard, 35n28, 193, 197, 199–200; in Derrida, 181, 184, 188–89
simulation, 195
Skidelsky, Edward, 270
Skidelsky, Robert, 270
slavery, 43, 63, 94–95, 97–98, 148, 301
Smith, Adam, 63; on debt, 91, 96; on the division of labor, 151, 228; on the paradox of thrift, 347
Smith, Daniel, 227, 231

social class, and money, 75; and subprime lending, 76n
social credit. *See* mutualism
Social Credit Political League, 357
social economy, 354
social facts, 167n. *See also* total social fact
social inequality, 79, 339; and debt, 91, 102; and money, 389
social lending, 14
social, power 32, 51, 72, 392
social welfare, 79
socialism, 14, 115, 146, 160, 240, 244, 313, 315, 337, 357; and bank bailouts, 116; in Benjamin, 146; ethical, 320; versus liberalism, 323–25, 329, 382, 383; and money, 315, 316–17, 321, 322; in Simmel, 14, 139, 140, 197, 314n3, 316, 322–25, 329, 344, 355, 382–83
Société Générale, 258
society, 8, 13, 14, 71, 101; as community, 8, 93, 309, 351; of control, 239–40; and debt, 25, 94; and faith, 137; and fictitious commodities, 280; and finance, 122; and the financial crisis, 79, 102; and God, 148, 158; hierarchical concept of, 352; and the individual, 125; and money, 4, 7, 8, 13, 14, 26, 92, 93, 94, 102, 103, 124, 125, 133, 226, 238, 267, 268, 281; and the multitude, 293; as nation, 8, 309; as nation-state, 8, 309; in Nietzsche, 138; and power, 102; in Rousseau, 37–38; and the sacred, 173; and self-repression, 150; as state, 8, 26, 106, 211, 226; and territory, 226; and trust, 137. See also *Gemeinschaft*, *Gesellschaft*; perfect society
socius, 251
Sontag, Susan, 190
South Sea bubble, 126
South Sea Company, 126
sovereign debt, 2, 58, 66n17, 71, 91, 110, 127, 129, 131, 219, 242, 253, 257–58, 265, 388
sovereign wealth funds, 66, 220–21
sovereignty, 216, 245, 250, in Agamben, 266n; and banks, 116, 237; in Balibar, 261–62; in Bodin, 223–24, 261–62; in Derrida, 165, 185, 209; in the Eurozone, 46, 127, 129, 252, 253, 255, 261, 264–66, 267; and the *fiscus*, 261–62; in Hardt and Negri, 238, 239, 244, 245, 247; of the individual, 185, 360; and insolvency, 260–61; in Karatani, 86–87; and law, 224; in Marx, 53; and monetary governance, 45, 246, 307–8; and money, 20, 43, 44, 77, 110, 217, 237, 246–47, 249, 251; and the multitude, 247; in Proudhon, 53; in Schmitt, 223–24, 266, 267; and the state, 106; and territory, 226. *See also* sovereign debt
spatial fix, 66, 68, 192, 238
special drawing rights (SDRs), 214
special investment vehicles (SIVs), 116, 123
specie, 15. *See also* coinage
speculation, 3n, 18n4, 22, 44, 61n20, 201; and fictitious capital, 68–69; financial, 70, 75–76; in Marx, 56–58, 64; in Minsky, 117, 118; in property, 113; as violence, 44
speculative finance, 118
speech, and money, 37, 42; versus writing, 180–81
speed, of circulation, 201n29, 390; of debt contraction, 119; of electronic trade, 307; of mobile payments, 378, 379; and the transmission of information, 36
Spengler, Oswald, 247
Sperber, Jonathan, 50n5
spheres of exchange, 283–84
Spinoza, Baruch, 247, 251, 332, 337, 338; on desire, 229; ethics, 228; *Ethics*, 335; multitude, 77, 238, 239, 246, 268, 293
spiritual poverty, 334
Square Wallet, 378, 379
stagflation, 68, 192
stamp scrip, 314, 349
state, 5, 6, 13, 14, 26, 299–300; and accumulation by dispossession, 68; and banking, 102, 106, 236, 382; as a borrower, 71; and capitalism, 68; and civil society, 220; and colonialism, 60; and the conflict between creditors and debtors, 109–10; and cooperatives, 84; and credit money, 57; and empire, 77; and finance, 51, 59–60, 66, 111; and free market money, 360; as the guarantor of money, 46, 79, 111, 235; and imperialism, 60, 300; infrastructural power of, 212, 217; and insolvency, 267; lender of last resort, 74, 246; versus market, 247, 306–7; and money of account, 104, 109–10, 297; and the monetary base, 79; and monetary governance, 4, 21, 26, 71, 74, 379; and monopoly capitalism, 60–61; naming rights over of money, 104, 105, 109–10,

state (*continued*)
111; and the origins of money, 18–19; and primitive accumulation, 64, 66, 68; in Proudhon, 353, 357; in Rousseau, 38; in Schmitt, 224; and seigniorage, 378; and society, 8, 26, 106, 211, 226; taxation, 103; violence. 96. *See also* deterritorialization; territory

state fiat money, 8, 20n, 55, 58, 62, 69, 88, 102, 107–8, 223, 231, 286, 307, 359, 364, 366, 368, 382–83, 387; versus Bitcoin, 388; versus LETS, 86; and the legalization of interest, 96

state of exception (*Ausnahmezustand*), 224
state of nature, 223
state theory of money, 103–4, 359
stateless money, 236
Statistical Service of Greece, 254
Steiner, Phillipe, 291, 293
Stephenson, Neal, *Cryptonomicon*, 42, 363n; *The Diamond Age*, 376–77
Stoekl, Allan, 169
Stop of the Exchequer (1672 default), 219
Stop the War, 49
Strange, Susan, 121–26, 132–33, 134n, 194, 237, 245, 247, 298; death of money, 122, 133, 392; and Keynes, 125; on globalization, 216; overbanking, 122, 124; on Simmel, 124; on 'Westfailure', 220
Streeck, Wolfgang, 91–92, 128–29
Stroud Pound, 350
structuralism, 39
Struve, Peter, 65
sublimation, 152, 155, 169, 228
subprime crisis, 2, 3n, 50, 69, 76, 100, 120, 234, 358
subprime lending, 123, 249–50, 358
subprime mortgage market, 2, 234
suicide, 92, 133, 198
surplus, 13, 151
surplus value, 74, 80, 81, 85, 236–37
surveillance, 310
symbol, monetary, 35, 36; in Goux, 39–40
symbolic exchange, 179, 192, 196–97, 198, 204; versus monetary exchange, 196, 198
symbolic forms, 82
symbolic power, 36
symbology, 40
Szabo, Nick, 363

tally, 105
Taylor, Erin, 303
taxes, 24, 25–26, 374, 378, 379, 383; as debt, 105–6, 231; and the definition of money, 95, 103, 106, 217, 231, 283, 300, 359–60; and deflation, 133; in Deleuze and Guattari, 231; and demurrage, 349, 371; in the Eurozone, 252, 254, 255, 257; evasion of, 329; and the financial crisis, 127; and modern capitalism, 217; in modern monetary theory, 106–7, 110; and the poor, 327; and public debt, 64, 126, 127; and sacrifice, 25–26; and sovereignty, 219, 261–62; and the state theory of money, 103–4; and territory, 226, 264; and tribute, 25–26; in Weber, 217
technical utopia, 315, 338n
techno-utopia, 362, 371–72
Tennyson, Alfred, 331, 332
terra nullius, 223
territorial money, 216, 217, 219, 246, 294 298. *See also* currency; pure territorial money
territory, 13, 60; sea, 222–23
terrorism, 197, 198
Thaler, Richard, 290
theory, actor network, 296; critical, 327, 331; European, 301; as experimentation, 227
Thilenius, Georg, 283
Third Reich, 224
Thompson, Edward Palmer, 325
Thoreau, Henry David, 151
Tietmeyer, Hans, 46n43
time, in Baudelaire, 184–85; and calculation, 298; and capital, 234; and capitalism, 144, 145; and circulation, 87; and compound interest, 147, 151, 153, 159; and debt, 201; in Derrida, 210; and financial markets, 233n; and guilt, 145; and labor money, 342–46; and language, 180–81; as money, 86, 176; in Negri, 251; and Peter Schlemihl, 186; scarcity of, 196; and the Shabbat, 334–35, 338, 341; and utopia, 335, 342; and the Zahir, 385, 394. *See also* Messianic time
time banks, 344
time dollars, 214, 293, 345–46, 375, 376. *See also* labor money; time banks

Titmuss, Richard, 286–87
Tiv, 283–84
tobacco, 185, 189, 209
Tognato, Carlo, 46
too big to fail, 119
Tor, 366
total social fact, 31, 33, 170, 195
trade, 18, 21, 68, 94, 96, 97, 108, 112, 122, 161, 218, 233, 252, 294, 302, 325; and borders, 307; and colonialism, 222; and the development of money, 23, 26, 31n23, 219, 222, 359, 360; and gold, 299; and LETS, 84; liberalization, 207; traders, 284; Wall Street, 200, 293, 299. *See also* barter; free trade; international trade; local trade
tragedy, 145
transcendental apperception X, defined, 82
transcritique, defined, 83
treasury, 106, 109, 115, 178; and central banking, 109; and the Eurozone, 107, 255; in modern monetary theory, 107. *See also fiscus*; United States Treasury
Treasury bill standard, 99
treasury bills, 124
tribute, 16. 17, 23–24, 53, 353
true prices, 356–57. *See also* just price theory
Truman Plan, 166, 206
trust, 4, 19, 97, 98, 124, 125, 303, 306, 309, 360, 387; and Bitcoin, 363, 364, 371
Turgot, Anne-Robert-Jacques, 37
Turing, Alan, 363n
Twain, Mark, "The Million Pound Bank Note," 185
Twitter, 22, 385

Übermensch, 12, 136, 140, 142, 143, 148–49, 150, 157, 158, 160, 391, 392
Ubu Roi, 35, 201
uncertainty, 319; in Baudrillard, 194, 196; in the economy, 16, 122–23, 347; in Keynes, 125–26; in linguistics, 180, 191n; and mimesis, 44; and paper money, 225
unequal pricing, 316, 326, 327–29
UniCredit, 258n38
unilateral gift, 198
Union Bank of Switzerland (UBS), 221
universal guaranteed income, 339, 356
United Nations (UN), 99, 239
United States Treasury, 99, 107, 385, 386

universal equivalent, 58, 62, 63, 194, 245, 274, 344
Urphänomen, 328
use value, 190
usury, 64, 94, 95, 96, 147, 307, 313, 353, 358n20, 378n50, 380
Utah Gold and Silver Depository, 361
Utah Monetary Summit, 361
utility, 151, 191; versus waste, 164
utopia, 10, 14, 100n, 251, 280; and anarchism, 381; and cash, 96; finance, 315; humanistic, 315, 333–34, 338–39, 374; and libertarianism, 381; and the market, 315, 372n; and money, 304, 315, 326–27, 341–42, 355, 375, 376, 382–83, 386–87; and neoliberalism, 304–5, 315n; in Proudhon, 352; and socialism, 322; and time, 335, 342; and unequal pricing, 327–8. *See also* conceptual utopia; realistic utopia; technical utopia; techno-utopia

valorization, 73, 231n25, 242
valuation, 28–29, 40, 160, 215, 272, 295, 305, 302, 325, 326; and morality, 292; in Nietzsche, 137
value, 36; in Baudrillard, 189; in linguistics, 38–39; of money, 37, 41, 48; in Nietzsche, 137; versus price, 29; in Simmel, 27–29, 318, 325–26. *See also* nonpecuniary values
valuns, 360
Vatican, 166
Veblen, Thorsten, 151; *The Theory of the Leisure Class*, 164
Veblen good, 164
Vedove Bianche (White Widows), 92
Velthius, Olav, 16–17, 293
Ven, 316
Vercellone, Carlo, 243
Vietnam War, 99, 298
violence, 47, 68; and debt, 91n, 100, 101; in de Sade, 169; and economics, 64; in the Eurozone, 261; and the financial crisis, 77n; generalized forms of, 225n16; and honor, 97; and mimesis, 43–45; and money, 43–46, 96, 250; and the sacred, 173; and the state, 96. *See also* war
Virno, Paolo, 72, 77, 246, 248
Visa, 377, 379, 380n

von Chamisso, Adelbert, *Peter Schlemihls wundersame Geschichte (Peter Schlemihl's Miraculous Story)*, 55n14, 186, 201n31
von Mises, Ludwig, 318
Vorontsov, Vasily, 65

Wade, Robert, 127
wages, 70, 73, 74–75, 78, 96, 139, 234, 242, 244, 249, 260, 289, 343, 345, 356, 361, 370n42; of sin, 231. *See also* minimum wage
Wahl, Jean, 172n
Waldberg, Patrick, 172n
Waldviertler regional currency, 350
Wall Street System, 3. *See also* capitalism; financial system
Wallace, Henry, 149
war, 31n23, 121n, 126, 133, 266, 338, 360; in Bataille, 171, 174, 176; and capitalism, 60; in Cicero, 225; and empire, 238, 239; and gold, 225; its impact on money, 95–96, 97, 100, 225–26; and monopoly capitalism, 60; and Schmitt, 261. *See also* First World War; Second World War; Vietnam War; violence
war against terror, 43
Warburton, Peter, 199
Warren, Josiah, 342
Warwick, University of, 73n30
waste, 12–13, 151; and the gift, 186; and money, 175, 184, 204; versus utility, 164
Wave and Pay, 377
Weber, Florence, 292
Weber, Max, 109, 247, 276n, 292, 302, 317; on capitalism and religion, 143, 155, 175; on charisma, 247; on Knapp, 103; on money and the modern state, 217; on prices, 109n25; *The Protestant Ethic and the Spirit of Capitalism*, 156, 175; on taxation, 217
Weimar inflation, 131n57, 142, 224, 387
welfare. *See* social welfare
Wendt, Alexander, 220
Wergild, 24, 302
Western Union, 380n

Westphalia. *See* Peace of Westphalia
Westphalian system, 216–27, 238
Where's George?, 226
Wherry, Frederick, 164n
Whuffie, 214, 316, 381
WikiLeaks, 380n
Wittgenstein, Ludwig, 390
workers, 59, 72, 73, 74, 75–76, 77, 81, 242, 244, 345, 352; and cooperatives, 84; and consumers, 81, 86, 356; in Proudhon, 353–54; in the public sector, 77, 88, 126. *See also* migrant workers; workers' associations; workers' movement
workers' associations, 323–24
workers' movement, 81n
World Bank, 241
world money, 70, 298
World Trade Center (WTC), 197–98
World Trade Organization (WTO), 99, 239, 241
Wray, Randall, 103, 300, 359–60, 374; on the Eurozone, 107n, 255; and Ingham, 110–11; on Knapp, 104, 359; and neo-chartalism, 106–8
Wriston, Walter, 392, 393
writing, 36, 37, 41n, 42, 297; versus speech, 180–81. *See also* grammatology

xenomoney, 35

Yunus, Muhammad, 357

Zbaracki, Mark, 17
Zelizer, Viviana, 8, 14, 16, 48, 286–94, 308; on classical social thought, 273; on circuits of commerce, 292–94, 351; on culture, 272; on earmarking, 286, 290–92; on intimacy, 289; on money and homogenization, 287–88; on multiple monies, 288, 292, 373; *Pricing the Priceless Child*, 288; on relational money, 289; on relational work, 289, 292, 294; on relational (versus mental) accounting, 291; on remittances, 293; on Simmel, 287
Žižek, Slavoj, 199